THE ROUTLEDGE HANDBOOK OF EAST EUROPEAN POLITICS

The Routledge Handbook of East European Politics is an authoritative overview that will help a wide readership develop an understanding of the region in all its political, economic, and social complexity. Including Central Europe, the Baltic republics, South Eastern Europe, and the Western Balkans, as well as all the countries of the former Soviet Union, it is unrivalled in breadth and depth, affording a comprehensive overview of Eastern European politics provided by leading experts in the fields of comparative politics, international relations, and public administration. Through a series of cutting-edge articles, it seeks to explain and understand patterns of Eastern European politics today.

The Routledge Handbook of East European Politics will be a key reference point both for advanced-level students developing knowledge about the subject, researchers producing new material in the area, and those interested and working in the fields of East European Politics, Russian Politics, EU Politics, and more broadly in European Politics, Comparative Politics, Democratization Studies, and International Relations.

Adam Fagan is Professor of European Politics and Head of the School of Politics and International Relations at Queen Mary University of London, UK. His previous works include *Europeanization of the Western Balkans* (2015) and *Europe's Balkan Dilemma* (2010). He is also the co-editor of the journal *East European Politics*.

Petr Kopecký is Professor of Political Science and Director of Central and East European Studies Center at Leiden University, the Netherlands. His research has published in, among others, the *European Journal of Political Research*, *European Union Politics*, *Party Politics*, *Political Studies*, and *West European Politics*. He is also the co-editor of the journal *East European Politics*.

'The Handbook brings together a group of leading European and American experts who comprehensively address almost all important aspects of post-communist politics in Eastern Europe. It will be indispensable in the classroom and as a resource for other researchers.'

– *Michael Bernhard, University of Florida, US*

'*The Routledge Handbook of East European Politics* highlights the diversity and relevance of the region. Both are extremely timely messages in academic and policy circles. The Handbook is bound to become a standard reference point in the discussion about the first twenty-five years of post-communism. It brings together a stellar group of scholars who take stock, survey the empirical and conceptual contributions of social science research on the region, and map avenues for future research. The relationship between international and domestic processes of change, the role of historical legacies, and the discrepancy between formal rules and institutions on the one hand and actual practices on the other hand, are key themes highlighted throughout the Handbook.'

– *Gwendolyn Sasse, University of Oxford, UK*

THE ROUTLEDGE HANDBOOK OF EAST EUROPEAN POLITICS

Edited by
Adam Fagan and Petr Kopecký

LONDON AND NEW YORK

First published 2018
by Routledge

2 Park Square, Milton Park, Abingdon, Oxfordshire OX14 4RN
52 Vanderbilt Avenue, New York, NY 10017

Routledge is an imprint of the Taylor & Francis Group, an informa business

First issued in paperback 2020

British Library Cataloguing-in-Publication Data
A catalogue record for this book is available from the British Library

Library of Congress Cataloging-in-Publication Data
A catalog record for this book has been requested

ISBN: 978-1-138-91975-4 (hbk)
ISBN: 978-0-367-50009-2 (pbk)

Typeset in Bembo
by Apex CoVantage, LLC

CONTENTS

List of figures   *viii*

List of tables   *ix*

List of contributors   *x*

Introduction   1
Adam Fagan and Petr Kopecký

PART I
The state of democracy   **7**

1   Democracy and democratisation in post-communist Europe   9
    Andrew Roberts

2   Belated transitions in South Eastern Europe   27
    Florian Bieber

3   Explaining Ukraine   39
    Andrew Wilson

PART II
Political institutions   **53**

4   Core executives in Central Europe   55
    Martin Brusis

5   Eastern Europe's semi-presidential regimes   67
    Thomas Sedelius and Jenny Åberg

6   Institutionalising parliaments in Central and Eastern Europe   82
    Josephine T. Andrews

7   Political parties and party organisations   100
    Allan Sikk

8   The rule of law   113
    Martin Mendelski

9   Bureaucracies in Central and Eastern Europe and the Western Balkans   126
    Jan-Hinrik Meyer-Sahling

10 Federalism in Eastern Europe during and after communism   139
    James Hughes

PART III
Elections and political participation   **155**

11 Elections and electoral participation   157
    Sarah Birch

12 Voters and parties in Eastern Europe   169
    Zsolt Enyedi and Kevin Deegan-Krause

13 Social movements after communism   184
    Ondřej Císař

14 The study of protest politics in Eastern Europe in the search of theory   197
    Grzegorz Ekiert and Jan Kubik

PART IV
Minorities and identity politics   **211**

15 Understanding ethnic minorities in Eastern Europe   213
    Sherrill Stroschein

16 The plight of Eastern Europe's Roma   225
    Peter Vermeersch

17 The representation of women   237
    Frank C. Thames

18 The struggle for LGBT rights   245
    Conor O'Dwyer

19 Politics at the fringes?: Eastern Europe's populists, racists, and extremists   254
    Cas Mudde

PART V
Policy issues and policy choices   **265**

20 Varieties of capitalism in Eastern Europe   267
    Dorothee Bohle

21 Dealing with the past: post-communist transitional justice   281
    Vello Pettai and Eva-Clarita Pettai

22 "The West, the East and the rest": the foreign policy orientations of
    Central Eastern European countries   295
    Elsa Tulmets

23 Combatting corruption   307
    Tatiana Kostadinova and Maria Spirova

24 East European exceptionalism: foreign domination in finance   319
    Rachel A. Epstein

PART VI
International relations and actors   **331**

25 Enlargement and Europeanisation in Central and Eastern Europe:
    accession and beyond   333
    Antoaneta L. Dimitrova

26 NATO enlargement and the post-communist states   346
    Mark Webber

27 Russia in the region   358
    Richard Sakwa

Index   *369*

FIGURES

1.1	Freedom House scores	10
1.2	Polity scores	11
4.1	A map of executive capacity	63
6.1	Worldwide Governance Indicator 'Control of Corruption' for CEE 1996–2014	93
7.1	Seat shares of genuinely new parties by elections	104
7.2	Trends of genuinely new party success	105
7.3	Party identification and party membership	108
7.4	Feeling of closeness to a political party	108
8.1	Varieties of the rule of law in Central and Eastern Europe	114
8.2	Rule of law development in CEE	115
12.1	Effective number of parliamentary parties in Eastern and Central Europe over time	171
12.2	Positions of political parties on economic and cultural questions in Eastern and Western Europe according to expert surveys, 2006	173
12.3	Dassonneville and Hooghe findings regarding Pedersen Index in parliamentary elections in Western, Southern, and Eastern Europe adapted to a single horizontal and vertical scale	175
12.4	Examples of Eastern and Central European political divides according to degree of symmetry and closure	179

TABLES

5.1	Constitutional type and presidential power scores in Eastern Europe and the post-Soviet countries	70
5.2	Regions covered in studies on semi-presidentialism, percentages	72
5.3	Top seven countries covered in studies on semi-presidentialism, percentages	73
6.1	Partisan features of CEE parliaments	88
7.1	Genuinely new parties	103
11.1	Electoral systems in Eastern Europe	158
11.2	Turnout in Eastern Europe	162
13.1	Varieties of activism	187
15.1	Ethnic minority groups in East European countries	217
19.1	Electoral results of main far-right parties in Eastern Europe in percentage of national vote, 1989–2015	256
19.2	Participation in government by far-right parties, 1989–2015	256
20.1	Typologies of East European varieties of capitalism	272
20.2	Explaining East European varieties of capitalism	275
21.1	An integrated conceptual framework for examining transitional justice	285
24.1	Eastern Europe, new member states of the EU: foreign bank ownership	320

CONTRIBUTORS

Jenny Åberg is a PhD student in Political Science at Dalarna University, Sweden.

Josephine T. Andrews is Associate Professor at the Department of Political Science, University of California at Davis, USA.

Florian Bieber is Professor of Southeast European Studies and Director of the Centre for Southeast European Studies at the University of Graz, Austria.

Sarah Birch is Professor of Political Science and Director of Research at the Department of Political Economy, King's College London, UK.

Dorothee Bohle is Professor of Political Science at the Department of Political and Social Sciences, European University Institute, Italy.

Martin Brusis is Member and Principal Investigator of the Graduate School for East and Southeast European Studies at the Ludwig-Maximilian University of Munich, Germany.

Ondřej Císař is Associate Professor at the Department of Sociology, Charles University, Czech Republic.

Kevin Deegan-Krause is Associate Professor of Political Science at the Department of Political Science, Wayne State University, USA.

Antoaneta L. Dimitrova is Associate Professor at the Institute of Public Administration, Leiden University, the Netherlands.

Grzegorz Ekiert is Lawrence A. Tisch Professor of Government and Director of the Center for European Studies at Harvard University, USA.

Zsolt Enyedi is Professor at the Department of Political Science, Central European University, Hungary.

Contributors

Rachel A. Epstein is Professor at the Josef Korbel School of International Studies and Academic Co-director of the Colorado European Union Center of Excellence, University of Denver, USA.

Adam Fagan is Professor of European Politics and Head of the School of Politics and International Relations, Queen Mary University of London, UK.

James Hughes is Professor of Comparative Politics at the Department of Government, London School of Economics and Political Science, UK.

Petr Kopecký is Professor of Political Science and Director of Central and East European Studies Center, Leiden University, the Netherlands.

Tatiana Kostadinova is Professor of Political Science at the Department of Politics and International Relations, Florida International University, USA.

Jan Kubik is Professor of Slavonic and East European Studies and Director of the School of Slavonic and East European Studies, University College London, UK.

Martin Mendelski is Postdoctoral Researcher at Max Planck Institute for the Study of Societies, Germany.

Jan-Hinrik Meyer-Sahling is Professor of Political Science at the School of Politics and International Relations, University of Nottingham, UK.

Cas Mudde is Associate Professor at the Department of International Affairs, University of Georgia, USA.

Conor O'Dwyer is Associate Professor at the Department of Political Science and the Center for European Studies, University of Florida, USA.

Eva-Clarita Pettai is Senior Researcher at the Institute of Government and Politics, University of Tartu, Estonia.

Vello Pettai is Professor of Comparative Politics at the Johan Skytte Institute of Political Studies, University of Tartu, Estonia.

Andrew Roberts is Associate Professor at the Department of Political Science, Northwestern University, USA.

Richard Sakwa is Professor of Russian and European Politics at the School of Politics and International Relations, University of Kent, UK.

Thomas Sedelius is Associate Professor in Political Science at Dalarna University, Sweden.

Allan Sikk is Senior Lecturer in Comparative Politics at the School of Slavonic and East European Studies, University College London, UK.

Maria Spirova is Associate Professor of Comparative Politics and International Relations at the Institute of Political Science, Leiden University, the Netherlands.

Sherrill Stroschein is Senior Lecturer in Politics at the Department of Political Science, University College London, UK.

Frank C. Thames is Associate Professor at the Department of Political Science, Texas Tech University, USA.

Elsa Tulmets is Marie Curie Fellow at the Center for International Studies, Sciences Po Paris, France.

Peter Vermeersch is Professor of Political Science at the Centre for Research on Peace and Development, University of Leuven, Belgium.

Mark Webber is Professor of International Politics and Head of the School of Government and Society, University of Birmingham, UK.

Andrew Wilson is Professor of Ukrainian Studies at the School of Slavonic and East European Studies, University College London, UK.

INTRODUCTION

Adam Fagan and Petr Kopecký

It is now just over a quarter of a century since the 'revolutionary changes' swept the region of Eastern Europe and led to the transition from communist regimes to democracy. Twenty-five years is a considerable vantage point to consider not only the events that have occurred in the region, but also the scholarship on this region. Academic perceptions of the particularism and specificity of the post-communist, ex-Soviet states have undoubtedly changed. In the years immediately after the revolutions of 1989 and the dissolution of the USSR, the prospect of a handbook on "East European Politics" being required all these years later would have seemed unimaginable to many. For many scholars in the 1990s, these countries were viewed as being on a rapid transit towards westernisation. Their new leaders had shown little enthusiasm for experimentation, preferring instead to copy practices from their established liberal democratic neighbours. If Soviet-style communism had imprinted its legacies on the politics of these countries, the impact would be short term and quickly annihilated by the forces of new-liberal capitalism and liberal democracy. Foreign direct investment was not just a high pressure hose for the economy; it would also sort out communist-era bureaucracies and state institutions that stood in the way of the free movement of people, labour, and capital. We would, it was assumed, study these countries from the perspective of comparative politics; acknowledge for sure the regional variation that came from their rapid and recent consolidation of new institutions, but this could be undertaken as part of a broader study of 'European Politics' that already accommodated and acknowledged 'Southern Europe' and post-authoritarian states. Differences between 'new' and 'old' Europe, such that they persisted, would be little more than variation in how, for example, legislatures or party systems functioned.

These were of course heady days of optimism: the 'return to Europe' of the 'capitals of the ancient states of Central and Eastern Europe' was taking place, and a new reinvigorated Europe was in the making. The old divisions had gone and Europeanisation would ensure rapid reform. As always in the social sciences, however, there were dissenting voices. Rather than seeing the legacies of communism as a short-term phenomenon, there was a group of scholars that viewed the inheritance of planned economies and one-party rule as a potential impediment, if not an insurmountable obstacle, on the road towards markets and liberal democracy. One of the most prominent among those voices was Klaus Offe (1991), describing the momentous changes in early 1990s as a 'triple transition', for simultaneously involving transition from autocracy to democracy, centrally planned to a market economy, and the unresolved issues of nation- and state-building. The regime changes in the region assumed a unique character in the history of political transformations. Never before was the magnitude of political and economic change so large, and the secessionist threats and potential for national disunity so real, as in Eastern Europe in 1989. Precisely because of this unique character of post-communist transitions, and the depth of the decay and stagnation of the communist regimes in the period that preceded it, the prospects for democracy in the region were viewed with considerable scepticism: instead of functioning liberal democracy and market economy, many observers expected an 'authoritarian turn', civilian stride, intra-regional conflicts, and states that are perpetually involved in economic crisis, poverty, and large-scale social dislocations.

As we rapidly approach a point at which the Central and East European states have been 'post-communist' for as long as they were 'communist', is there really any merit in, or necessity to, study their distinctiveness beyond their having endured Soviet-style communism many years ago? Why are we still studying these countries as a group? Why are we still comparing them to each other, and framing our analysis in terms of their communist past? What has gone wrong, or failed to transpire?

The simple answer, as illustrated throughout the chapters of this Handbook, is that we perhaps failed to appreciate the profound and deeply entrenched variation between these states that existed prior to the transition to democracy. Consequently, we are now confronted with a region that displays a huge diversity of outcomes, both in terms of the regime types, as well as institutional arrangements within the countries' political, economic, and social systems, and even policy outcomes. Such diversity among a group of states that have followed not dissimilar political and economic trajectories needs explaining. Indeed, as Roberts notes in his overview, the regime outcomes are arguably the most diverse of any (democratising) region in the world. There are obvious success stories: the transitions in Central Europe, in Slovenia, and in the three Baltic states led quickly to the establishment of democracies in which major political and social actors accepted the established constitutional order. However, Bulgaria and Romania went through a more complex path of political reform and, as Bieber explains (see also Hughes), transitions in most of the Balkan region were severely impacted and temporarily halted by the ethno-national conflicts and authoritarian agendas of leaders such as Slobodan Milosevic in Serbia and Franjo Tudjman in Croatia. Even today, Bosnia-Herzegovina, Macedonia, Kosovo, Montenegro, and Albania all remain locked in an uncertain cycle of political and economic crisis. And, as Wilson notes (also Sakwa), an even bleaker picture emerges when we zoom into the (part of) post-Soviet Eastern Europe, a sub-region characterised by autocracies and hybrid regimes (see also Levitsky and Way 2010; Hale 2015).

To complicate things further, several countries that were considered the most stable, consolidated and prosperous of post-communist democracies have recently experienced a rise in populist politics and authoritarian tendencies of leaders like Viktor Órban in Hungary and Jaroslav Kaczynski in Poland, a phenomenon now commonly denoted under the term of 'democratic backsliding' and 'illiberal consolidation' (see e.g. Dawson and Hanley 2016). Indeed, what is recorded in several of the contributions to this Handbook, and not simply those dealing with Russia, the Ukraine, and the Balkans, is lingering and resurgent authoritarianism. Although the electoral success of the far right in the region is far from impressive (Mudde), the liberal revolution is incomplete, disrupted, and in retreat if one looks at it from the perspective of LGBT rights (O'Dwyer), minority protection (Stroschein, Vermeersch), or civil society and social movements in general (Císař, Ekiert and Kubik), or the setback in the fight against the political corruption (Kostadinova and Spirova). As Císař concludes, the 'thin liberal façade that national political cultures in countries such as Bulgaria, Hungary, Poland, Slovakia, and the Czech Republic erected in the EU accession process [have] withered away in the years since accession'. There is no consensus as to whether this democratic malaise amounts to a regime category of its own, or whether it should be analysed as a question of (varying degree of) democratic quality. However, it seems to be clear that classifying the regime outcomes in the region as if they were a two-horse race between (consolidated) democracies on the one hand, and autocracies on the other hand, would be an oversimplification.

A diversity similar to that of regime outcomes is observed in the richness of institutional configurations within the region, and also the policy choices of the various post-communist governments. The chapters assembled in the Handbook record and explore this variation: on the macro level, as Bohle shows, the regions' states have adopted different forms of capitalist economies; on a meso-level, readers are invited to appreciate the region's different forms of bureaucracies (Meyer-Sahling), core executives (Brusis) and executive-legislative relations (Andrews, Sedelius and Åberg), judiciary (Mendelski), electoral systems (Birch), and parties and party systems (Sikk, Enyedi and Deegan-Krause). The questions of how to deal with the communist past (Pettai and Pettai) or geopolitical orientation of foreign policies (Tulmets) have also been addressed differently by the countries in the region. However, while the diversity of regimes has led to some scholarly ambiguity as to how to classify and evaluate it, the emergence of different institutional structures and policy choice has encouraged comparative explorations whose findings and theoretical implications often transcend the boundaries of the region. Indeed, nearly each and every chapter in this Handbook highlights one or more studies that have become, or are fast becoming, major reference sources within the general literature. In that sense at least, the region has certainly become a social science laboratory for probing the explanatory power of different theoretical approaches, and exploring the causes and effects of institutions and policies, in both qualitative and quantitative fashion.

It is not our intention in this short introduction to summarise all the contributions in the volume. Rather, we wish to briefly highlight what we perceive to be two key themes that we want to emphasise as a precursor to the readings of the individual chapters. The first of these is the role of the international environment in shaping the trajectories of political change in the region in general, and the transformative power of Europe in particular. Several of the contributions highlight the extent to which the impact of external forces in shaping regime change and political developments is simultaneously under- and overestimated. On one hand, there is a tendency, especially apparent within the early transition literature inspired by the scholarship on Latin America and Southern Europe (e.g. Przeworski 1991; Linz and Stepan 1996; Munck and Skalnik-Leff 1997; but also Bunce 1995), to focus almost exclusively on the agency of domestic actors and constraints with regard to institutional development. This is in many respects a legacy of the rational choice–inspired transitions approach to regime change, but is also consistent with the historical sociology approach to understanding political developments in the region. Yet, as almost all of the contributions illustrate, external steerage of the economy, society, and political processes has been significant. The main manifestation of this external influence has come from the EU as part of the Europeanisation via enlargement agenda, and to a much lesser extent from NATO, other international actors and agencies have played a no less obsequious role as donors, capacity-builders, consultants, and investors. On the other hand, there is a distinct tendency, as noted by Dimitrova, to assume all progressive change comes from the EU and from external pressure. In other words, there is a discernible tendency in the literature to underplay 'bottom-up' or domestic pressures for change, or ignore domestic sources of institutional origins. Moreover, it is by now very clear that external influence has not always favoured progressive and democratic change. As Bieber argues in his chapter, the distinct shift towards semi-authoritarianism in South Eastern Europe has actually been nurtured rather than threatened by Europeanisation.

The second key theme that we want to emphasise is the role of communist legacies in our analysis of transition and consolidation. Reading the chapters in the Handbook, it becomes clear that even twenty-five years after 'the transition' we are forced to recognise that for all of the countries of the region – including those that joined the EU in 2004 and 2007, but also those successor states of the former USSR that have long departed from liberal and democratic paths – the legacies of communism and their particular exit from it have shaped and continue to shape political processes, both formal and informal. However, it is also clear that explanations emphasising legacies of the past are often weak on the exact causal mechanisms by which some legacy matters, and thus tend to underestimate explanatory power of factors that have little to do with the past. For example, is the widespread popular distrust towards political parties (see Sikk; Enyedi and Deegan-Krause) a legacy of the past communist regime, or is it driven by the performance and functioning of the current parties? As we move away from communism in time, the factors that are not related to it should in theory increase in importance. Therefore, and as many chapters in the Handbook emphasise, any serious analysis that aims to show whether history or its particular legacy matters must now be underpinned by a careful conceptualisation of a 'legacy', and tied to a systematic elimination of rival explanations.

This leads us to perhaps the most fundamental theme explored and alluded to by all the contributors: the tension between formal processes and laws on one hand, and actual practices and lived realities on the other. This binary undoubtedly frames analysis of the transformative power of Europe and the EU (Dimitrova). But it seems to run much deeper. Regardless of enlargement and the pace of Europeanisation, there is from every perspective a tension between the persistence and tenacity of communist-era legacies, and the new institutions and processes. This is arguably what characterises and constitutes 'post-communism'. In certain cases this becomes manifest as a transmutation of new institutions and procedures. For example, much of the current discussion on 'illiberalism', 'patronal politics' or 'democratic backsliding' is framed in terms of subversion of formal democratic process by authoritarian tendencies rooted in informal rules and institutions. Interestingly, none of the contributions in the Handbook goes as far as to suggest that the post-communist institutions are empty shells; rather, the Western semblance invariably disguises a complexity that is characteristic of these countries' historic path through modernity, or is actually typical of practice globally. In other words, the apparent 'distinctiveness' of the post-communist institutions or processes is perhaps better understood as these countries departing from the particularism of Western models, or adapting such models to work in complex situations. Moreover, the capacity of post-communist states to avoid the gloomy predictions of the cynics is sometimes due, it appears, precisely to this hybridity. Rachel Epstein, in her chapter on banking and financial reform, highlights how unusually high levels of foreign bank ownership in Eastern Europe did not lead to economic Armageddon as many had predicted in the 1990s and 2000s, but in fact enabled some degree of stability by weakening state-bank ties. From this perspective, as Epstein concludes, the post-communist states could actually be trailblazing a model of financial regulation and economic organisation to be followed by all European states in the wake of the global crisis. This is indeed a reversal of the standard interpretation of the East European states as laggards of the West, locked into an endless quest to 'catch up'.

Our intention as editors has been to compile a Handbook that would provide a comprehensive overview of Eastern European politics authored by leading experts in various fields of study. We have chosen a primarily geographically based definition of *Eastern Europe* for this Handbook including Central Europe, the Baltic republics, South Eastern Europe, and the Western Balkans, as well as the countries of the former Soviet Union that are generally considered to be part of Europe (i.e. Russia, Ukraine, Belarus, and Moldova). Throughout each section and the individual chapters the term 'Eastern Europe' will be used as a common label for all these sub-regions and their countries. However, the book does not cover the post-Soviet Central Asia and the Caucasus.

The book is structured into six sections. The first section reflects on the state of democracy in the region, providing a macro-perspective on the region and its parts which is essential for understanding the specific political developments and issues that are treated in the sections that follow. The key political institutions are the subject of analysis in Part II. Part III ventures into the realm of political participation, both conventional and non-conventional. The region's multi-cultural and multi-ethnic make-up is reflected in the chapters of Part IV. Part V covers some of the most important policy issues, including economic reforms, transitional justice, foreign policy choices and efforts to combat corruption. The Handbook concludes with Part VI on Eastern Europe's relations with the outside world, and the impact of the region on international community. Although we were not able to cover all important themes and topics, and also lost some contributions along the way, we believe that the Handbook's comprehensiveness is unsurpassed. Importantly, each chapter represents a cutting-edge article aiming to provide state of the art over-view in a relevant sub-field. We asked our authors to address historical and intellectual develop-ment in their topic; outline the work of key contributors and critically evaluate the major claims, existing approaches, and developments within their topic; and explain why their area or sub-field is still important and what future developments and research agendas might be anticipated. Inev-itably for an academic enterprise of this sort, not all contributions follow this structure perfectly, nor stick rigidly to the particular thematic or geographic remit. But we were very lucky to work with a group of outstanding scholars, each of whom understood the endeavour and deliv-ered excellent chapters. It is to them that this book is dedicated. We also wish to acknowledge our gratitude as editors for the support and inspiration offered by Andrew Taylor and Sophie Iddamalgoda from Routledge. Our editorial assistant, Indraneel Sircar, did a tremendous job. Any errors, intellectual or editorial, are our fault.

References

Bunce, Valerie. 1995. "Should Transitologists Be Grounded?" *Slavic Review* 54(1): 111–127.

Dawson, James and Sean Hanley. 2016. "The Fading Mirage of the 'Liberal Consensus'." *Journal of Democracy* 27(1): 21–33.

Hale, Henry. 2015. *Patronal Politics: Eurasian Regime Dynamics in Comparative Perspective*. New York: Cambridge University Press.

Levitsky, Steven and Lucan Way. 2010. *Competitive Authoritarianism: Hybrid Regimes After the Cold War*. New York: Cambridge University Press.

Linz, Juan and Alfred Stepan. 1996. *Problems of Democratic Transition and Consolidation: Southern Europe, South America and Post-Communist Europe*. Baltimore, MD: Johns Hopkins University Press.

Munck, Gerardo L. and Carol Skalnik-Leff. 1997. "Modes of Transition and Democratization: South America and Eastern Europe in Comparative Perspective." *Comparative Politics* 29(3): 343–362.

Offe, Claus. 1991. "Capitalism by Democratic Design? Democratic Theory Facing the Triple Transition in East Central Europe." *Social Research* 58(4): 865–892.

Przeworski, Adam. 1991. *Democracy and the Market*. Cambridge: Cambridge University Press.

PART I

The state of democracy

1

DEMOCRACY AND DEMOCRATISATION IN POST-COMMUNIST EUROPE[1]

Andrew Roberts

Few areas of post-communist politics have been studied as intensively as the fate of democracy and in few areas has the conventional wisdom shifted as radically – from initial joy at the fall of communism, to pessimism about the legacies of the past, to optimism again with entry into the European Union, and finally to more qualified assessments today. As Kitschelt (2003) points out, no other region in the world has as diverse and I would add shifting regime outcomes. Whenever things seem to stabilise, new events inevitably shake up received understandings.

Given the diversity of outcomes and the amount of research on the region, this review will inevitably be partial.[2] Nevertheless, I will attempt to cover what I consider the seminal and most influential theories of the collapse of communism, regime outcomes, and the consolidation and quality of democracy.

I will start with a brief description of the key facts about democracy which include the dramatic and unpredicted shift in politics in 1989 and the subsequent "return to diversity". I then turn to explanations for the fall of communism where I discuss both the standard account which emphasises a loss of legitimacy and the power of civil society as well as more complete theories that outline the micro-mechanisms of collapse and put weight on tipping points and organisational bank runs. I briefly digress to address allegations that scholarship on the region failed for not being able to predict the collapse.

The heart of the chapter discusses theories of regime outcomes – why some countries became democratic and others authoritarian. Many of the early responses to the changes emphasised proximate factors related to the course of the transition such as elite bargaining, the outcomes of initial elections, and external influence. However, recently a consensus has started to emerge that these factors have deeper roots in communist and pre-communist legacies including socio-economic modernisation, education, religion, and ethnic divisions.

I consider separately recent shifts in regime outcomes – particularly the colour revolutions as well as democratic backsliding – and whether their causes are different from the causes of the initial transitions. I also discuss the appearance of hybrid regimes that have found an equilibrium in between democracy and autocracy.

After considering these regime outcomes across the region, I turn more specifically to the countries of East Central Europe. Here I assess the multiple dimensions of democratic consolidation and the finding that democratic endurance coexists with weak civic engagement and institutional shortcomings. Finally, I turn to the various conceptions of democratic quality and the contrast between the surprisingly positive evaluations that have emerged from scholars and the negative perceptions of most citizens. The chapter concludes with research frontiers.

Simple facts

To set the stage for the following sections, I begin with a few simple facts about democracy in the post-communist region. Figures 1.1 and 1.2 present these facts graphically. They show the Freedom House and Polity ratings of democracy in the region from the late 1980s to 2014. For new countries, their scores are linked to the scores of the countries from which they declared their independence. Three facts stand out.

First, countries in the communist bloc were among the most undemocratic in the world up to nearly the moment of transition. They shared more or less the same political system led by a communist party that held all power in politics and the economy. Human rights existed in name only and elections were always a charade. Despite retreating from the brutality of the Stalin era, few had truly liberalised. Poland, Hungary, and Yugoslavia were the states that stood out as somewhat more permissive in their treatment of civil society and independent economic initiatives, but even they still outlawed genuine opposition and fell short on standard measures of democracy.

Second, there was a swift, radical, and unpredicted shift in the politics of the satellite states in 1989 as the individual communist parties surrendered their monopoly on power. Poland was the

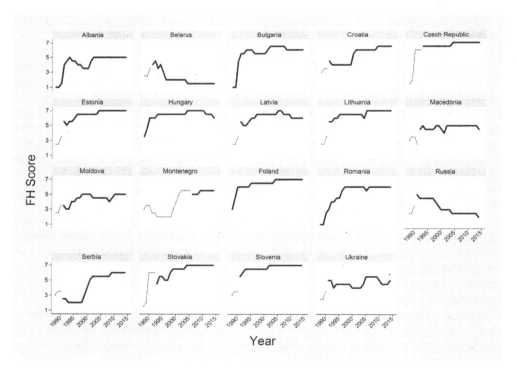

Figure 1.1 Freedom House scores

Note: These scores represent the average of Freedom House's political rights and civil liberties scores. I have reversed the direction of the scores so that 7 represents most free and 1 least free. Thin lines indicate scores for the predecessor country and thick lines the successor country.

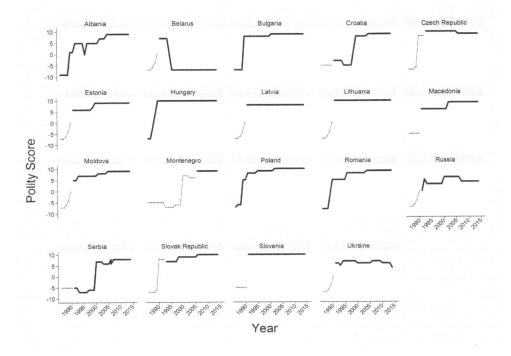

Figure 1.2 Polity scores

Note: Polity scores range from +10 (most democratic) to −10 (most autocratic). Thin lines indicate scores for the predecessor country and thick lines the successor country.

leader, holding semi-free elections in June 1989. Their example was quickly followed by the end of communist hegemony in Hungary, East Germany, Czechoslovakia, Bulgaria, and Romania, with Yugoslavia and Albania joining along the way. Communist rule gave way soon afterward in the Soviet Union, which broke apart in 1991. Given the dismal status quo in the region, these changes almost always led to substantial democratisation with the exception of the new Central Asian states, which are not covered here.

Third, after this rapid change, the outcomes of these transitions were widely divergent. Indeed, the regime outcomes are arguably the most diverse of any region in the world. A number of states in the region very quickly became almost complete democracies, meaning that they received nearly the highest possible assessments from organisations like Freedom House and Polity. These states were largely on the western border of the region and include Bulgaria, the Czech Republic, Estonia, Hungary, Latvia, Lithuania, Poland, and Slovenia. Another group, largely on the eastern side of the region, barely budged from their undemocratic heritage; this group includes just about all of Central Asia (with the exception of Kyrgyzstan). Meanwhile, a number of countries had bumpier paths. Some experienced substantial problems but ultimately joined the first group, a pattern that describes Slovakia, Croatia, Serbia, and Romania. A few of these − Albania, Macedonia, Moldova, and Ukraine − settled at a lower level of democracy or as hybrid regimes. Another group meanwhile looked to be democratising early in the transition but then fell back into a resolutely non-democratic equilibrium. This path applies to Belarus, Russia, and the Caucasus. In short, democracy has evolved in different ways across the region.

The fall of communism

Why did communism fall?[3] The conventional wisdom about mechanisms goes something like this (see, for example, Chirot 1990–91; Dallin 1992): economic decay in the 1970s and 1980s undermined the legitimacy of the regimes which was premised on providing better living conditions. This in turn prompted leaders, particularly Gorbachev, to engage in reforms like *glasnost* and *perestroika* (Brown 1996; Almond 1999). These reforms failed because they did not address the fundamental problems of the economy (Kornai 1992). Their failure undermined the confidence of the regime and encouraged civil society. It was at this point that people power brought down the regime (Tismaneanu 1992). Interestingly, very few scholars mention the explanation most common among the lay public: Reagan's military build-up.

But as Kalyvas (1999) points out, there is a large difference between decay – which can last for a long time – and breakdown. More specifically, dissatisfaction by itself could not overthrow the regime; genuine civil society as opposed to mass demonstrations played a small role in the actual revolutions (Solidarity in Poland would be the exception), and reformers like Gorbachev believed in communism to the very end. Indeed, while external observers were acutely aware of stagnation, most saw more important sources of stability.

A number of scholars have thus tried to propose stronger mechanisms for the collapse. Most prominent has been Bunce (1999). Her argument is that communist institutions were subversive – they at once created a unified public and divided elites. The institutions of communism homogenised citizens by giving them similar socio-economic positions and thus similar interests. For Bunce, it is no surprise that communism gave birth to a movement calling itself Solidarity. This explanation, however, only goes halfway because it does not account for the timing of the collapse. Bunce thus turns to a second process – borrowed from social movement theory – changes in the political opportunity structure. During the 1980s, a number of events combined to give the public the space to overthrow the regime. Specifically, leadership succession crises, the introduction of "great reforms" like *perestroika*, and the opening up of the international system gave citizens the opportunity to make 1989 an *annus mirabilis*.

A number of scholars have gone even deeper into the micro-mechanisms of these dynamics. On the elite side, a key work is Solnick's (1999) *Stealing the State*. He argues that Gorbachev's reforms exacerbated the weakness of bureaucratic control in the Soviet Union. As central direction declined, bureaucrats began to appropriate organisational assets for their own purposes, and this theft hollowed out the regime. Feedback effects accelerated the process as insiders grabbed what they could, lest they be left with nothing. Solnick calls this an "organisational bank run", and it undid the power of the communist regime over the economy and the country. Roeder's (1993) *Red Sunset* shows further how the form of the Communist Party made adaptation difficult. Reforms forced the party into competition, but it did not know how to compete. Members were so used to obeying orders from above that they had difficulty responding to criticisms from new actors.

But the elite side does not provide a full explanation. Even a weakened communist party overawed the small and disorganised dissident groups that existed; the dissidents more than anyone were aware of this power differential. Somehow a push from the public at large would be needed.

It is hard to ignore the role of nationalism in providing this push. Most of the transitions in the region involved some form of national liberation – whether it was escaping from the yoke of external domination in the case of the satellite states, or breaking free from a perceived dominating nationality in the case of the non-central republics of the Soviet Union and Yugoslavia.

Beissinger (2002) focuses on the process of collective mobilisation in the Soviet Union that led to declarations of sovereignty. He argues that structural features mattered – nationalities with better institutions, more resources, and larger grievances were more likely to mobilise – but, after studying some 6,000 events, he finds that these events created their own momentum. There were tides of protest and early movers influenced later ones, so that by the end even the least well-situated groups were carried along on the wave.

These theories still have trouble explaining the individual-level calculations leading to the collapse because active protest carried significant risks and coordination was difficult. The main solution here is to invoke tipping point dynamics. Kuran (1991) argues that in deeply repressive regimes like the Soviet bloc, citizens are fearful of expressing their true opinions; they engage in preference falsification. While dissatisfaction with the regime may have been widespread, citizens never knew what their neighbours were thinking, and the regime exacerbated the problem by forcing citizens to publicly express their support for communism and exerting strict control over the media. Kuran argued that such situations are likely to lead to cascades and tipping points – when enough people gathered on the streets, others would follow (see also Lohmann 1994). So what was necessary was for enough people to go out without being arrested or shot. This happened with the loosening of controls and one-off focal events like the attack on a regime-sponsored parade in Czechoslovakia.

These effects played out equally at the international level. Once the opposition in Poland was able to secure relatively free elections without a crackdown or Soviet intervention, this emboldened the Hungarians, whose success in turn inspired the East Germans and so on. Garton Ash (1990: 78) memorably described these demonstration effects or snowballing in a remark to Václav Havel: "In Poland it took ten years, in Hungary ten months, in East Germany ten weeks: perhaps in Czechoslovakia it will take ten days!" His prediction was more or less correct, and Bulgaria and Romania completed the process about as quickly.

The unpredicted and unpredictable collapses

Were these revolutions inevitable and thus predictable? Few scholars saw the fall of communism coming and of those who arguably did, none thought it would come as early as 1989. Despite widespread acknowledgment of stagnation and decay in the 1970s and 1980s, the dominant emphasis in the literature, even as Gorbachev introduced *glasnost* and *perestroika*, was on the stability of these regimes.

The failure of the scholarly community to foresee the revolution has been used to criticise political scientific approaches to the region and to politics in general. Some argued merely that it reflected a widespread inability of experts to predict (Tetlock 2006), while others saw it as an indictment of the methods of normal social science (Gaddis 1992/93; Hopf 1993).

However, while the pre-revolution study of the region surely had its problems, the failure to predict these revolutions is not necessarily a symptom of the failures of social science or area studies. The reasons are both theoretical and practical.

Theoretically, although prediction is an important goal of social science and theories should ultimately be judged by their predictive accuracy, social science should not be held to the standard of making predictions of the form: event X will happen at time Y. Social scientists are not soothsayers. Popper pointed out that even physics makes very few predictions of this type (the exceptions are events like solar eclipses). Instead, social science theories will typically make conditional predictions of the form: if X occurs, then Y is likely to follow.

The second reason is that we have good explanations for why the regime collapse came so suddenly and unpredictably. These are the "tipping point" and "bank run" explanations described in the previous section. Kuran (1991) thus argues that the timing of such revolutions are almost inherently unpredictable.

This is not to say that scholars were blameless. Hanson (2003) and Almond (1999) have argued that Sovietologists were too much in thrall to either totalitarian or revisionist theories which blinded them to the importance of ideology and left them unable to understand a reformer like Gorbachev who could both believe in and undermine communist ideology, the essential glue holding the system together. Nevertheless, these arguments are less about the failures of social science than the specifics of pre-1989 debates in the field.

Explanations of regime outcomes

Though the communist regimes fell throughout the region, the outcomes of the collapse were extremely varied. King (2000), quoting Rothschild, calls it a "return to diversity" and Kitschelt (2003) adds that no other region in the world features as much diversity of regime types. The obvious question then is why some countries became democratic and others did not, and why there were subsequent exits and entrances to the democratic and authoritarian categories. Explanations for this diversity focus alternatively on events and decisions that took place in the wake of communism's fall and those that emphasise the influence of communism and even the pre-communist era (Kitschelt 2003). I will consider each of these approaches in turn.

Proximate factors

Proximate explanations emphasise the break that took place in 1989 and 1991. While few argue that these events created a tabula rasa, many do point to the openness of this period. Thus, Bunce and Csanádi (1993) highlight the high degree of uncertainty as both interests and institutions were in a great deal of flux. Elster et al. (1998) use the metaphor of rebuilding a boat at sea. Offe (1991) meanwhile describes the simultaneity of tasks confronting politicians – the triple transition of creating democratic institutions, a market economy, and a new state – which put large burdens on their capabilities.

Other scholars took as their jumping-off point the transitology approach which emphasised the importance and agency of elite actors. These arguments saw transitions as proceeding from negotiations between the regime and opposition, as had arguably happened in Latin America and Southern Europe (for contrasting perspectives on these comparisons, see Schmitter and Karl [1994] and Bunce [1995]).

The most influential version of this approach was Przeworski (1991), who argued that democratisation began with splits in the regime but then required moderates in the regime to unite with moderates in the opposition to isolate regime hardliners and radicals in the opposition. Together they could agree on compromises or pacts which would not provoke hardliners to repress. In this spirit, Roeder (1994) claimed that a balance of power between the regime and opposition was key for democratisation in the post-Soviet states since it induced both sides to compromise (see also Bova 1991). The presence of successful roundtable talks in many countries seemed to confirm this theory (Elster 1996).

Most scholars of the region, however, ultimately came to reject this approach. They maintain instead that compromise was the wrong strategy and that real progress came through mass mobilisation and uncompromising demands (Bunce 2003; King 2000). Fish (1998a, 1998b) found that the best predictor of democracy and reform was the outcome of the first relatively free elections – if the opposition won, then democracy was highly likely, while a victory for the former communists meant continued authoritarianism.

McFaul (2002) echoes and expands on this argument. He argues that the best path is for the opposition to dominate and dictate a democratic outcome along with radical economic reforms.

Conversely, balanced transitions typically lead to "partial democracy or protracted and oftentimes violent confrontations" (his main examples are Moldova, Russia, and Ukraine), while imbalances in favour of the regime lead to autocracies (McFaul 2002: 223). Anomalies to these patterns can be explained by controversies over borders which propelled nationalist leaders to power and set back democracy in Armenia, Bosnia and Herzegovina, Georgia, and Croatia, and proximity to the West which helped Bulgaria and Romania.

Other studies have made claims for the effect of the type or mode of transition.[4] Munck and Leff (1997) thus contend that whether the fall of the regime took place through negotiation, extrication, or rupture affected the transition and the consolidation of democracy (for another account see Huntington [1991]). It is not clear, however, that the expectations of these theories have been borne out or that these factors can be separated from others. Linz and Stepan (1992) meanwhile argue that in ethnically diverse societies the correct sequencing of regional and national elections was paramount in order to develop national identities before regional and ethnic ones.

An important implication of many proximate approaches is that democracy can be crafted by elites provided they make the correct choices (Di Palma 1990). Besides willingness to compromise or press demands, a key place where democracy could be crafted is in the choice of new institutions. Many scholars have noticed that countries that chose parliamentary regimes were more democratic than those who chose presidential or even super-presidential regimes (Commander and Frye 1999; Ishiyama and Velten 1998; Lijphart and Waisman 1996).[5] Parliamentarism, particularly when combined with proportional representation, gave representation to more groups, encouraged coalition-making, and limited the power of executives to act unilaterally.

Others put weight on the decision to engage in market reforms. Early accounts, drawing on the Latin American experience, predicted that reforms would undermine democracy because of their unpopularity (Przeworski 1991). After the fact, it became apparent that reform actually supported democratisation and vice versa in the post-communist region at least in part because of the economic failures of the *ancien régime* (Bunce 2001).

A number of scholars have emphasised international factors. Indeed, in many statistical analyses proximity to a Western capital is the strongest predictor of democracy. Kopstein and Reilly (2000) have provided the most sophisticated version of these explanations. They distinguish between stocks (a country's neighbours) and flows (the movement of resources and people between countries). They find that both good neighbours and interaction with the West have a positive effect on democracy. Shleifer and Treisman (2014) concur in emphasising how countries have converged to the non-communist countries closest to their borders: Central Europe towards Germany, the Baltics towards Finland, and the Caucasus towards Turkey.

An additional mechanism for these effects is the efforts of external actors, particularly the EU, to promote democracy. Vachudova (2005), for example, distinguishes between the passive leverage described earlier and the active leverage of conditionality (also Grabbe 2006). Schimmelfennig and Scholtz (2008) provide statistical support for the idea that the political conditionality of EU membership has strong and positive effects on democracy even controlling for transnational exchanges and development. Kelley (2004) shows how external efforts were often effective in improving minority rights. Jacoby (2006) adds that these external influences almost always require some level of domestic support and so coalitions between external and domestic actors are more likely to bear fruit than either non-engaged inspiration or external fiat. The best conditions for external influence are thus divided governments in countries that are plausible candidates for membership in international organisations. Because of the importance of conditionality, some predicted backsliding once EU accession was achieved, but Levitz and Pop-Eleches (2010) argue that this did not occur, at least in the early stages.

These proximate explanations have been criticised in a number of ways. Kitschelt (2003) believes that they tell us too little. The key independent variables are too close to the outcomes. How much are we learning if we say that democracy emerged because democratic actors were more powerful? We want to understand why those actors were stronger, which leads us deeper into the past. Further, the results of the transition seem to be too ordered for them to be purely the result of choice. There must be structural forces at work for the democratic gradient to be as strong as it is with democracies on the Western side of the region and autocracies further east. Proximate factors may not be as associated with agency as one might expect.

Historical factors

These criticisms led many scholars to look for deeper roots of democracy. Some of the earliest reactions to the fall of communism took this view and were characterised by a sense of gloom. Thus, Jowitt (1992: 304, 293) pointed to a Leninist legacy characterised by "fragmented, mutually suspicious societies with little religio-cultural support for tolerant and individually self-reliant behavior" which would favour "an authoritarian, not a liberal democratic capitalist, way of life." Sztompka (1993) referred to "civilisational incompetence" in the region, and Janos (1991: 111) saw military societies leading to democracy as "a dream, or mere façade".

Contrary to these cultural approaches, those focusing on social and economic factors were more optimistic. Countries in the region were among the richest and most educated in the world which had not yet democratised, and modernisation theory predicts that countries with higher incomes, more educated citizens, and greater urbanisation are more likely to become or remain democratic (Przeworski et al. 2000; Boix and Stokes 2003). This explanation also appears to fit the democratic gradient across the post-communist region: richer countries have performed better (if one accounts for oil wealth as a hindrance to democracy, the fit is even better). Kurtz and Barnes (2002) find evidence of a more class-based version of modernisation theory: a large agricultural sector appears to hinder democratisation.

Pop-Eleches (2014) challenges this explanation. He notes first of all that post-communist countries democratically underperformed relative to their high incomes. Moreover, in his statistical analysis, GDP per capita and education have little effect on democratisation in the post-communist region. He attributes this to the distortions in centrally planned industrialisation. As a consequence, not only did post-communist countries suffer a deficit in civil involvement and political participation, but the deficits had a unique class bias. The middle classes, who are the strongest democrats, tend not to participate in politics, while the lower classes, who are less enthusiastic democrats, are more likely to participate.

While there is still debate over the influence of modernisation, many scholars have turned to other historical legacies that explain democratic outcomes. Some look back to the pre-communist era and isolate religious and cultural factors. The most successful cases of democratisation have Protestant and Catholic traditions which arguably lead to more individualism, tolerance, and separation of Church and State – all factors that encourage peaceful competition and alternations of power. Conversely, a number of scholars have noted the negative impact of Islam, which according to Fish (2002) is due not just to the absence of the aforementioned factors, but to subordination of women.

Ethnic diversity is another demographic factor that appeared to impede democracy, not just in countries wracked by civil war like Yugoslavia or the Caucasus, but also in Bulgaria, Romania, and Slovakia where it gave impetus to nationalist parties. The Baltics faced a more distinct problem in dealing with a Russian minority and they sometimes pursued illiberal policies in a generally democratic framework (Roeder 2004). Fish and Kroenig (2006), however, challenge this conclusion and argue that diversity per se does not impede democracy although conflict does.

Kitschelt and his collaborators (Kitschelt et al. 1999; Kitschelt 2003) emphasise the bureaucratic legacies of these countries. He argues that the early adoption of a formal-rational bureaucracy was a key precondition for later democratisation. Others emphasise stateness issues, in particular the problems that brand-new countries faced in having to create institutions from scratch (Linz and Stepan 1996; Ganev 2005). Fortin (2012) in fact names state strength as close to a necessary condition for democracy in the region.

Darden and Grzymała-Busse (2006) put forward one of the more rigorous accounts of pre-communist legacies. They focus on the amount and content of pre-communist schooling. Countries where most of the population was literate before communism and where education was imbued with nationalist content were much less hospitable to communism and more supportive of the anti-communist opposition in 1989. This sort of schooling gave citizens values and ideas of legitimacy at odds with communism and made communism appear as a step backward, an alien and anti-modern imposition. Horowitz (2003) takes a similar tack in arguing that countries with "frustrated national ideals", that is those with high levels of pre-communist economic development and political independence, are more likely to embrace democracy.

Pop-Eleches (2007) provides one of the most systematic tests of these varied theories (though to be fair almost all of these works do include multivariate statistical tests). He uses time-series cross-national models to compare the effects of cultural/religious heritage, social conditions/modernisation, and economic legacies with more proximate explanations like initial elections, institutional choices, and external influence. His findings, however, are nuanced. Legacies as a whole have a considerable effect (much greater than the effect of proximate variables which are typically favoured in tournament of variables set-ups) and this effect actually becomes stronger over time, but no one legacy has universal effects.

Instead, he claims that different legacies have effects on different aspects of democracy. Thus, the adoption of democratic institutions (measured by Polity scores) is related to urbanisation, a non-Muslim heritage, longer statehood, and less distorted economies. By contrast, the move from formal institutions to actual civil and political rights (proxied by Freedom House scores) is related to Western Christianity, ethnic divisions, interwar statehood, and urbanisation. Finally, democratic deepening (which includes vibrant intermediate institutions and a responsive bureaucratic apparatus and is represented by the Nations in Transit scores) is related again to Western Christianity and ethnic diversity.

These deeper accounts are typically criticised for lacking mechanisms or for not adequately testing their mechanisms (Kitschelt 2003), though some suffer from this problem more than others. It is also difficult to separate individual legacies, many of which are highly collinear. The statistical methods used to make these claims, moreover, rely more on association than any stronger inferential tools like instrumental variables or natural experiments, a problem which applies equally to proximate explanations (Frye 2012). Nevertheless, something like a consensus has emerged on the importance of legacies, though questions remain about exactly which legacies and how they function.

The colour revolutions, hybrid regimes, and backsliding

By the late 1990s, many scholars believed that there were two types of transitions (Vachudova and Snyder 1996) leading to two sorts of outcomes (Kitschelt 2003) – the consolidated democracies and the autocracies. The middle category seemed to be emptying out as countries gravitated to one equilibrium or another. The strongest support for this thesis came from places like Russia,

Belarus, Ukraine, and Kyrgyzstan, which looked liberal and democratic early in the transition, but then evolved in an authoritarian direction. Yet, events along with theoretical innovations have called this view into doubt.

In the first case, a number of countries that had seemed to have settled into the authoritarian category moved out of it. Slovakia, admittedly a softer form of authoritarianism, was the pioneer in 1998, but it was followed by similar transitions in Croatia and Serbia, and then later by Ukraine, Georgia, and Kyrgyzstan. These so-called colour revolutions have provoked a considerable amount of theorising.[6]

Bunce and Wolchik (2011) describe a new form of transition which they call the electoral model. They argue that where opposition groups are able to unify, run an ambitious campaign, conduct voter registration and turnout drives, collaborate with civil society, and oversee parallel vote tabulations, they can force out authoritarian leaders at election time. This model is modular and has been transferred from one country to another (for another modular model see Beissinger 2007). The question is whether these electoral revolutions have been real transformations. Arguably they have in Slovakia, Croatia, and Serbia; the cases of Ukraine, Georgia, and Kyrgyzstan are less clear (Kalandadze and Orenstein 2009; Pop-Eleches and Robertson 2014).

A more sceptical view has been put forward by Hale (2015), who describes a general patronal politics syndrome in many post-Soviet states. These states are characterised by presidents with significant formal powers as well as informal powers based on patronage. He argues that such states are prone to regime cycles. Most of the time it behoves elites to unite behind the president, but at certain moments – a leader's death, planned successions, or elections – a lame-duck syndrome induces contestation among elites. When this contestation is resolved – typically in accord with the incumbent's popularity – the winner then consolidates their rule with the considerable resources at their disposal. We thus see cycles of consolidation and contestation within a generally authoritarian setting.

While Hale focuses on the collective action incentives among elites – whether to line up behind the incumbent or defect – Tucker (2012) emphasises collective action among the public. He argues that electoral fraud lowers the cost of participating and raises the likelihood of success by providing a focal point for action. This approach emphasises the fragility of these regimes, but it is cautious about expecting democracy to follow once a new regime is put in place.

Other scholars have challenged the twofold division of democracy and autocracy by developing a third regime type, which has alternatively been called a hybrid regime or competitive or electoral authoritarianism. Levitsky and Way (2010: 5) define competitive authoritarian regimes as those where "democratic institutions exist and are widely viewed as the primary means of gaining power, but in which incumbents' abuse of the state places them at a significant advantage vis-à-vis their opponents." The problems are less electoral fraud than unfair distribution of state resources, biased media coverage, and harassment of the opposition. Bribery, co-optation, and subtle forms of persecution are more common than out-and-out prohibitions of the opposition. There are tensions within this regime type because democratic rules remain in place and can serve as a focal point for protest, leading to the revolutions or cycles described earlier. The strength of links with the West along with the organisational power of the government are other key factors determining the trajectory of these regimes.

A final issue here is the explanation for countries once counted clearly in the democratic camp who appear to have regressed. Part of this issue – whether even the acknowledged democracies are functioning well – will be considered in the next sections. Here the challenge is to explain the undemocratic and illiberal practices which have taken root in Hungary after Orbán's election in 2010 (Bánkuti et al. 2012), but have also recently been seen in Poland and Slovakia. They include attacks on constitutional courts and the rule of law, violations of civil rights, restrictions on the independence of the media, and policies designed to weaken opposition parties and strengthen the executive. These problems have been linked with the economic crisis, European integration, and migration and are arguably emerging in Western Europe as well. This regression may well be the key issue for the future of democracy in the region, but it has not yet received the sustained scholarly attention that it deserves.

Democratic consolidation in East Central Europe

In the following sections, I focus on the more democratic countries of East Central Europe – the Czech Republic, Hungary, Poland, Slovakia, and Slovenia, which are widely seen as the democratic leaders of the region. Given the relative success of these countries, scholars have focused their attention on the questions of consolidation and quality. Are these democracies consolidated and are they of high quality?

The basic idea of consolidation is that a democracy is consolidated when it becomes the only game in town. This could be interpreted most simply in terms of the survival or duration of democracy, famously in the two-turnover test – a democracy is consolidated when power is transferred from government to opposition twice. The countries considered here have easily passed this test. Indeed, some argue that they pass it too easily – elections are close to a lottery (Innes 2002) and incumbents almost always lose (Roberts 2008).[7]

Most scholars, however, have focused on lower-level indicators of consolidation such as attitudes (citizens believe in democracy and hold democratic attitudes), behaviour (citizens act democratically by participating in politics and forgoing violence), and institutions (countries have a functioning economy and state apparatus) (Schedler 2001; Linz and Stepan 1996).

Rose and collaborators (Rose et al. 1998) have been the most prolific writers on the attitudinal dimensions of consolidation thanks to their New Democracies Barometer series of surveys in the region. Rose argues in favour of the Churchill hypothesis, that what is important is support for democracy relative to authoritarian rule (following Churchill's claim that democracy is the worst form of government except for all the others). He finds that there is little endorsement of non-democratic alternatives, whether a return to communism or rule by the army, a strong leader, or a monarch. Citizens further typically do not expect democracy to be overthrown or parliament to be suspended anytime soon.[8]

Recent and comprehensive work by Pop-Eleches and Tucker (2014), however, reveals that support for democracy is significantly weaker in the post-communist region than elsewhere and that this weakness is connected with communist legacies. Even Rose et al. (1998) find that citizens throughout the region are very dissatisfied with the functioning of democracy and have little trust in institutions, producing a phenomenon that they call "broke-backed democracy".

Others focus on behavioural measures of consolidation, which include such phenomena as violence, rejection of elections, and transgressions of authority. Overt political violence and intimidation are relatively rare in East Central Europe. The same applies to opposition parties rejecting elections, though little research has explored these indicators. Anti-system parties do exist in these countries, but the communist successor party in the Czech Republic is one of the few that has consistently polled well enough to affect politics and it does so mainly by complicating coalition formation. This problem, however, may be becoming more widespread, considering parties like Jobbik in Hungary or Kotleba – People's Party Our Slovakia in Slovakia.

More attention has been paid to civil society which Putnam et al. (1993) have linked with the functioning of democracy. Howard (2003) has demonstrated the weakness of civil society in the region – citizens join voluntary associations to a much lower extent than other regions of the world. Bernhard and Kaya (2012), however, reject this blanket characterisation and argue that the picture is more diverse, particularly if one considers actual protests instead of survey responses. Conversely, Kopecký and Mudde (2003) find something worse – manifestations of uncivil society which includes skinheads in Hungary and the Self-Defence party in Poland.

The region also scores poorly on other more directly political aspects of participation. Voter turnout has declined substantially from high levels after the transition, but Pacek et al. (2009) and Kostadinova (2003) argue that voters are aware of the importance of different elections and act accordingly. Other forms of direct participation like signing petitions or participating in boycotts are also low (Bernhard and Karakoç 2007). Pop-Eleches (2014) finds further that well-situated individuals are less likely to participate, which is worrisome given that social status correlates with support for democracy.

A third aspect of consolidation is institutional or structural. Schedler (2001) sees levels of development and poverty as important because citizens need a minimal level of well-being to participate effectively. Though countries in the region suffered extremely severe transitional recessions, most have recovered since then and improvements in standards of living are often obscured by measured data (Schleifer and Treisman 2014). Nevertheless, poverty and inequality have increased dramatically since 1989 and suffered another blow with the recent economic crisis. Linz and Stepan (1996) emphasise rule of law, a functioning state apparatus, and economic society. All three areas have received extensive attention from scholars with most criticism highlighting corruption and weak rule of law.

Stepping away from standard indicators, a number of authors have pointed to illiberal trends in the region. Krastev (2007) delivered an early warning about political polarisation, rejection of consensual politics, and organised intolerance across the region. He saw these trends as a reaction to democracy without choices where liberal reforms were introduced without public support. Dawson and Hanley (2016) similarly argue that liberalism rests on a narrow base and observe that leaders are bending democratic rules in addition to acting in illiberal ways.

Given these problems, however, it is an open question why these countries are as democratic and stable as they are. Schneider (2009) argues that not only has the region reached high levels of consolidation, it has done so far more quickly than any other recently transitioning region. Perhaps values trump behaviour and institutions. International institutions like the EU and NATO have likely played a consolidating role through conditionality, aid, and advice (Vachudova 2005; Whitehead 2001). Economic growth has arguably helped, as has the absence of alternative ideologies.

While consolidation was a fashionable topic at the turn of the millennium, it has since lost much of its appeal. One of the problems is the absence of a standard definition of consolidation and an accompanying set of indicators. Many of the elements of consolidation described earlier have received considerable attention, but there are few larger comparative studies of consolidation that have identified the relative degree or even the causes of consolidation (for an exception see Schneider 2009). Scholars instead have turned to either explanations of the persistence of democracy or to the quality of democracy.

The quality of democracy

Even for countries that fit well into the democratic category, scholars and citizens have expressed doubts about how well democracy is functioning. In a textbook treatment, Sakwa (1999: 116–117) argued that the "gulf between formal and substantive democracy is in most places the defining feature of post-communist democratization". These doubts have recently been summed up in the concept of democratic quality. Nevertheless, scholars have not come to an agreement either on the right way of defining democratic quality or on their assessments of the quality of democracy in post-communist Europe.

In some ways these studies overlap with work on democratisation and democratic consolidation. Thus, it is common to use Freedom House or Polity scores as a measure of democratic quality. There are two concerns with this practice. First, quality of democracy should arguably be different from democracy itself. Second, some post-communist countries have received perfect scores on these measures, while they clearly do not have perfect democracies. Several elements of democratic consolidation like support for democracy and participation are also frequently included in studies of democratic quality, blurring the distinction there as well.

A number of scholars have attempted to develop comprehensive assessments of democratic quality. The Democracy Barometer considers three elements of democracy – freedom, control, and equality – which are formed out of a large number of lower-level indicators (Bühlmann et al. 2011). According to these measures, the post-communist region has shown the most improvement of any region between 1990 and 2007 and receives higher ratings than Latin America and Asia, but less than the established democracies (Bühlmann 2011). The largest improvements are in transparency, while the region performs poorly in rule of law and participation.

The Bertelsmann Transformation Index (Bertelsmann Stiftung 2014) considers a broader set of categories – stateness, political participation, rule of law, stability of democratic institutions, and political and social integration – using 18 different indicators. They similarly find that the post-communist region performs relatively well, with all the countries in East Central Europe except Hungary receiving their highest ranking of "democracies in consolidation", and the Czech Republic, Poland, Slovenia, and Slovakia figuring in their top 10 of 129 countries. Berg-Schlosser (2004) also finds relatively high quality among the countries of East Central Europe, using off-the-shelf measures of governance quality, spending priorities, socio-economic performance, social inequalities, and political unrest.

The Nations in Transit index is Freedom House's attempt to go beyond their standard political rights and civil liberties scores by considering the seven areas of national democratic governance, electoral process, civil society, independent media, local democratic governance, judicial framework and independence, and corruption (Freedom House 2016). Although these assessments do not allow comparisons outside the post-communist region, they do deliver the disturbing news of a substantial decline in democratic quality in East Central Europe since its peak in 2006, with much of the decline driven by Hungary. Specific worries about the region include illiberal leaders and rising xenophobia.

While most assessments of quality are based on multiple criteria, Roberts (2009) has developed a concept that focuses entirely on citizen rule. He argues that the purpose of democratic institutions is to give citizens power, but it is often unclear if they actually do so. He finds that citizens in these countries do have a reasonable level of control – they hold politicians accountable for poor performance at elections and governments mostly respond to public opinion – but parties often present ambiguous programs and do not follow through on their promises.

Surprisingly, the main attempts to produce comprehensive assessments of democratic quality in the region deliver relatively positive results. This contrasts with domestic perceptions which are almost entirely negative. These differences might be explained by comparison effects – countries in East Central Europe are doing better than most other new democracies, but citizens compare their countries to Western Europe – or by the different criteria used by scholars and citizens. The gap may also be due to a number of negative phenomena considered later in this volume such as weak parties (Sikk in this volume), populism (Mudde in this volume), corruption (Kostadinova and Spirova in this volume), and inequality, which are not always included in assessments of democratic quality. More disturbingly, there is growing evidence that quality is declining in the region and so these positive assessments may be out of date.

Research frontiers

Discussions of regime type have been the dominant form of writing on the post-communist region, but they have arguably run their course.[9] Few scholars are still writing about the reasons communism fell and the causes of initial regime outcomes. In fact, it is hard to see where new hypotheses, methods, or data would come from. This is a well-tilled field and arguably new insights are more likely to come from historians excavating the details of the transition (for an example, see Krapfl 2013) than from multivariate methods where the cause is overdetermined and leverage for separating legacies and choices is hard to come by.

Work will continue on current regime trajectories. One mystery is the seeming backsliding of countries like Hungary and Poland that appeared to have achieved democratic consolidation. Is it simply a perfect storm of economic problems, government party scandals, and EU ineffectiveness that have produced these problems, which are in any case fleeting? Or are there deeper causes and more long-lasting effects? (Krastev 2007; Dawson and Hanley 2016). In short, how worried should we be about democracy in East Central Europe?

Conversely, is there any light at the end of the tunnel in autocratic regimes like Russia, Belarus, and the Caucasus? Celebrations about the colour revolutions in this part of the region appear to be premature, but some like Motyl (2016) see cracks in the edifice of Russian authoritarianism. What would have to happen for these regimes to move in a democratic direction? Are Russia's attempts to destabilise its neighbours a sign of strength or a last gasp to divert attention in the face of a declining economy?

More positively, there is much work to be done on how these regimes function. There is considerable divergence here between scholars studying the democratic and authoritarian parts of the region. For more authoritarian states or hybrid regimes, the frontier is on the multiple ways that leaders keep themselves in power (Hale 2015). How do they deploy resources through political organisations, the state apparatus, and the media in order to keep opposition weak and divided while fighting off external influence?

For the more democratic countries, the frontier is representation – who governs and with what results. Much of this work can be put under the heading of democratic quality with the caveat that undemocratic practices like corruption (Kostadinova and Spirova in this volume), discrimination against minorities (Stroschein in this volume), politicisation of the bureaucracy Meyer-Sahling in this volume), and inequality threaten this quality. In this sense, understanding politics is converging with research traditions on the established democracies.

This raises a final question of whether there are actually two Europes (Western and Eastern or EU and non-EU) or even three (Western, good Eastern, and bad Eastern). Donald Rumsfeld saw the new NATO members from the East as bringing a new and better perspective on democracy and democratisation. The recent immigration crisis, however, has shown a different and less tolerant face to post-communist democracy. Hanley (2014) claims interestingly that it is now Western Europe which is converging with the practices of Eastern Europe rather than the other way around. Developments starting in 1989 would have thus come full circle.

Notes

1 This work was supported by the Grant Agency of the Czech Republic under the auspices of the project "The Quality of Democracy: The Czech Republic in Comparative Perspective" (GA 15–2274S). The author wishes to thank Jordan Gans-Morse and Grigore Pop-Eleches for helpful comments.
2 Gans-Morse (2004) found 131 articles on post-communist transitions in only ten journals over the years 1991–2003.
3 An excellent summary of theories can be found in Holmes (1997).

4 For details on the transition process in individual countries, see Dawisha and Parrot (1997a, 1997b, 1997c).

5 See Zielonka (2001) for a series of excellent country studies on the adoption of new institutions. Given the strong tendency of former Soviet countries (except for the Baltics) to adopt presidential and semi-presidential systems and the satellite countries to adopt parliamentarism, this choice might be viewed more as a structural force than a choice. See Frye (1997) for more on the origins of presidential institutions.

6 The term "colour" comes from the fact that the events in Ukraine were called the Orange Revolution, those in Georgia the Rose Revolution, and those in Kyrgyzstan the Tulip Revolution.

7 A caveat is that recent events in Hungary have caused some observers to downgrade its democratic status.

8 Miller et al. (1998) confirm these conclusions in a separate survey where they find that support for liberal and democratic values the region (as opposed to nationalist ones) was almost indistinguishable from the UK.

9 In an early review of literature on the region, Kubicek (2000) finds that about 15 per cent of articles focused on the democratic transition.

Bibliography

Almond, Mark. 1999. "1989 Without Gorbachev: What If Communism Had Not Collapsed?" In Niall Ferguson, ed. *Virtual History: Alternatives and Counterfactuals*. New York: Basic Books: 392–415.

Bánkuti, Miklós, Gábor Halmai, and Kim Lane Scheppele. 2012. "Disabling the Constitution." *Journal of Democracy* 23(3): 138–146.

Beissinger, Mark. 2002. *Nationalist Mobilization and the Collapse of the Soviet State*. New York: Cambridge University Press.

Beissinger, Mark. 2007. "Structure and Example in Modular Political Phenomena: The Diffusion of the Bulldozer/Rose/Orange/Tulip Revolutions." *Perspectives on Politics* 5(2): 259–276.

Berg-Schlosser, Dirk. 2004. "The Quality of Democracies in Europe as Measured by Current Indicators of Democratization and Good Governance." *Journal of Communist Studies and Transition Politics* 20(1): 28–55.

Bernhard, Michael and Ekrem Karakoç. 2007. "Civil Society and the Legacies of Dictatorship." *World Politics* 59(4): 539–567.

Bernhard, Michael and Ruchan Kaya. 2012. "Civil Society and Regime Type in European Post-Communist Countries." *Taiwan Journal of Democracy* 8(2): 1–13.

Bertelsmann Stiftung, ed. 2014. *Transformation Index BTI: Political Management in International Comparison*. Gutersloh: Verlag Bertelsmann Stiftung.

Boix, Carles and Susan Stokes. 2003. "Endogenous Democratization." *World Politics* 55(4): 517–549.

Bova, Russell. 1991. "Political Dynamics of the Post-Communist Transition: A Comparative Perspective." *World Politics* 44(1): 113–138.

Brown, Archie. 1996. *The Gorbachev Factor*. Oxford: Oxford University Press.

Bühlmann, Marc. 2011. "The Quality of Democracy: Crises and Success Stories." Paper presented at the IPSA-ECPR joint conference in Sao Paolo.

Bühlmann, Marc, Wolfgang Merkel, Lisa Muller, and Bernhard Wessels. 2011. "The Democracy Barometer: A New Instrument to Measure the Quality of Democracy and Its Potential for Comparative Research." *European Political Science* 11(1): 519–536.

Bunce, Valerie. 1995. "Should Transitologists Be Grounded?" *Slavic Review* 54(1): 111–127.

Bunce, Valerie. 1999. *Subversive Institutions: The Design and Destruction of Socialism and the State*. New York: Cambridge University Press.

Bunce, Valerie. 2001. "Democratization and Economic Reform." *Annual Review of Political Science* 4: 43–65.

Bunce, Valerie. 2003. "Rethinking Recent Democratization: Lessons From the Postcommunist Experience." *World Politics* 55(2): 167–192.

Bunce, Valerie and Maria Csanádi. 1993. "Uncertainty in Transition: Postcommunism in Hungary." *East European Politics and Societies* 7(2): 240–276.

Bunce, Valerie and Sharon Wolchik. 2011. *Defeating Authoritarian Leaders in Postcommunist Countries*. New York: Cambridge University Press.

Chirot, Daniel. 1990–1991. "What Happened in Eastern Europe in 1989?" *Praxis International* 10(3/4): 278–305.

Commander, Simon and Timothy Frye. 1999. "The Politics of Postcommunist Economic Reform." In *Transition Report 1999*. London: EBRD.

Dallin, Alexander. 1992. "The Causes of the Collapse of the Soviet Union." *Post-Soviet Affairs* 8(2): 279–302.

Darden, Keith and Anna Grzymała-Busse. 2006. "The Great Divide: Precommunist Schooling and Post-communist Trajectories." *World Politics* 59(1): 83–115.

Dawisha, Karen and Bruce Parrott, eds. 1997a. *The Consolidation of Democracy in East-Central Europe.* Cambridge: Cambridge University Press.

Dawisha, Karen and Bruce Parrott, eds. 1997b. *Politics, Power, and the Struggle for Democracy in South-East Europe.* Cambridge: Cambridge University Press.

Dawisha, Karen and Bruce Parrott, eds. 1997c. *Democratic Changes and Authoritarian Reactions in Russia, Ukraine, Belarus, and Moldova.* Cambridge: Cambridge University Press.

Dawson, James and Sean Hanley. 2016. "The Fading Mirage of the 'Liberal Consensus'." *Journal of Democracy* 27(1): 21–33.

Di Palma, Giuseppe. 1990. *To Craft Democracies: An Essay on Democratic Transitions.* Berkeley: University of California Press.

Elster, Jon, ed. 1996. *The Roundtable Talks and the Breakdown of Communism.* Chicago: University of Chicago Press.

Elster, Jon, Claus Offe, and Ulrich K. Preuss. 1998. *Institutional Design in Post-communist Societies: Rebuilding the Ship at Sea.* New York: Cambridge University Press.

Fish, M. Steven. 1998a. "Democratization's Requisites: The Postcommunist Experience." *Post-Soviet Affairs* 14(3): 212–247.

Fish, M. Steven. 1998b. "The Determinants of Economic Reform in the Post-communist World." *East European Politics and Societies* 12(1): 31–78.

Fish, M. Steven. 2002. "Islam and Authoritarianism." *World Politics* 55(1): 4–37.

Fish, M. Steven and Matthew Kroenig. 2006. "Diversity, Conflict, and Democracy: Some Evidence From Eurasia and East Europe." *Democratization* 13(5): 828–842.

Fortin, Jessica. 2012. "Is There a Necessary Condition for Democratization? The Role of State Capacity in Postcommunist Countries." *Comparative Political Studies* 45(7): 903–930.

Freedom House. 2016. *Nations in Transit 2016.* New York: Rowman & Littlefield.

Frye, Timothy. 1997. "A Politics of Institutional Choice: Post-Communist Presidencies." *Comparative Political Studies* 30(5): 523–552.

Frye, Timothy. 2012. "In From the Cold: Institutions and Causal Inference in Postcommunist Studies." *Annual Review of Political Science* 15: 245–263.

Gaddis, John Lewis. 1992/93. "International Relations Theory and the End of the Cold War." *International Security* 17(3): 5–58.

Ganev, Venelin. 2005. "Postcommunism as an Episode of State-Building: A Reversed Tillyan Perspective." *Communist and Post-Communist Studies* 38(4): 425–445.

Gans-Morse, Jordan. 2004. "Searching for Transitologists: Contemporary Theories of Post-Communist Transitions and the Myth of a Dominant Paradigm." *Post-Soviet Affairs* 20(4): 320–349.

Garton Ash, Timothy. 1990. *The Magic Lantern: The Revolution of '89 Witnessed in Warsaw, Budapest, Berlin, and Prague.* New York: Vintage.

Grabbe, Heather. 2006. *The EU's Transformative Power: Europeanization Through Conditionality in Central and Eastern Europe.* Basingstoke: Palgrave Macmillan.

Hale, Henry. 2015. *Patronal Politics: Eurasian Regime Dynamics in Comparative Perspective.* New York: Cambridge University Press.

Hanley, Sean. 2014. "Two Cheers for Czech Democracy." *Czech Journal of Political Science* 3: 161–176.

Hanson, Stephen E. 2003. "Sovietology, Post-Sovietology, and the Study of Postcommunist Democratization." *Demokratizatsiya* 11(1): 142–149.

Holmes, Leslie. 1997. *Postcommunism: An Introduction.* Cambridge: Polity Press.

Hopf, Ted. 1993. "Getting the End of the Cold War Wrong." *International Security* 18(2): 202–208.

Horowitz, Shale. 2003. "Sources of Post-communist Democratization: Economic Structure, Political Culture, War, and Political Institutions." *Nationalities Articles* 31(2): 119–137.

Howard, Marc Morjé. 2003. *The Weakness of Civil Society in Post-Communist Europe.* New York: Cambridge University Press.

Huntington, Samuel. 1991. *The Third Wave: Democratization in the Late Twentieth Century.* Norman: University of Oklahoma Press.

Innes, Abby. 2002. "Party Competition in Postcommunist Europe: The Great Electoral Lottery." *Comparative Politics* 35(1): 85–104.

Ishiyama, John and Matthew Velten. 1998. "Presidential Power and Democratic Development in Post-Communist Politics." *Communist and Post-communist Studies* 31(3): 217–234.

Jacoby, Wade. 2006. "Inspiration, Coalition, and Substitution: External Influences on Postcommunist Transition." *World Politics* 58: 623–651.

Janos, Andrew. 1991. "Social Science, Communism, and the Dynamics of Political Change." *World Politics* 44(1): 81–112.

Jowitt, Ken. 1992. *New World Disorder: The Leninist Extinction.* Berkeley: University of California Press.

Kalandadze, Katya and Mitchell A. Orenstein. 2009. "Electoral Protests and Democratization: Beyond the Color Revolutions." *Comparative Political Studies* 42(11): 1403–1425.

Kalyvas, Stathis. 1999. "The Decay and Breakdown of Communist One-Party Systems." *Annual Review of Political Science* 2: 323–343.

Kelley, Judith. 2004. *Ethnic Politics in Europe: The Power of Norms and Incentives.* Princeton, NJ: Princeton University Press.

King, Charles. 2000. "Post-Post-Communism: Transition, Comparison, and the End of 'Eastern Europe'." *World Politics* 53(1): 143–172.

Kitschelt, Herbert. 2003. "Accounting for Postcommunist Regime Diversity." In Grzegorz Ekiert and Stephen Hanson, eds. *Capitalism and Democracy in Central and Eastern Europe.* New York: Cambridge University Press.

Kitschelt, Herbert, Zdenka Mansfeldová, Radoslaw Markowski, and Gabor Toka. 1999. *Post-Communist Party Systems: Competition, Representation, and Inter-Party Cooperation.* Cambridge: Cambridge University Press.

Kopecký, Petr and Cas Mudde, eds. 2003. *Uncivil Society? Contentious Politics in Postcommunist Europe.* London: Routledge.

Kopstein, Jeffrey and David Reilly. 2000. "Geographic Diffusion and the Transformation of the Postcommunist World." *World Politics* 53(1): 1–37.

Kornai, János. 1992. *The Socialist System: The Political Economy of Communism.* Princeton, NJ: Princeton University Press.

Kostadinova, Tatiana. 2003. "Voter Turnout Dynamics in Post-Communist Europe." *European Journal of Political Research* 42(6): 741–759.

Krapfl, James. 2013. *Revolution With a Human Face: Politics, Culture, and Community in Czechoslovakia, 1989–1992.* Ithaca, NY: Cornell University Press.

Krastev, Ivan. 2007. "The Strange Death of the Liberal Consensus." *Journal of Democracy* 18: 56–63.

Kubicek, Paul. 2000. "Post-Communist Political Studies: Ten Years Later, Twenty Years Behind." *Communist and Post-Communist Studies* 33(3): 295–309.

Kuran, Timur. 1991. "Now Out of Never: The Element of Surprise in the East European Revolution of 1989." *World Politics* 44(1): 7–48.

Kurtz, Marcus J. and Andrew Barnes. 2002. "The Political Foundations of Post-communist Regimes: Marketization, Agrarian Legacies, or International Influences." *Comparative Political Studies* 35(5): 524–553.

Levitsky, Steven and Lucan Way. 2010. *Competitive Authoritarianism: Hybrid Regimes After the Cold War.* New York: Cambridge University Press.

Levitz, Philip and Grigore Pop-Eleches. 2010. "Why No Backsliding? The EU's Impact on Democracy and Governance Before and After Accession." *Comparative Political Studies* 43: 457–485.

Lijphart, Arend and Carlos H. Waisman, eds. 1996. *Institutional Design in New Democracies: Eastern Europe and Latin America.* Boulder: Westview.

Linz, Juan and Alfred Stepan. 1992. "Political Identities and Electoral Sequencing: Spain, the Soviet Union, and Yugoslavia." *Daedalus* 121: 123–139.

Linz, Juan and Alfred Stepan. 1996. *Problems of Democratic Transition and Consolidation: Southern Europe, South America and Post-Communist Europe.* Baltimore, MD: Johns Hopkins University Press.

Lohmann, Susanne. 1994. "The Dynamics of Informational Cascades: The Monday Demonstrations in Leipzig, East Germany, 1989–1991." *World Politics* 47(1): 42–101.

McFaul, Michael. 2002. "The Fourth Wave of Democracy and Dictatorship: Noncooperative Transitions in the Postcommunist World." *World Politics* 54(2): 212–244.

Miller, Warren L., Stephen White, and Paul Heywood. 1998. *Values and Political Change in Postcommunist Europe.* Basingstoke, Hampshire: Macmillan.

Motyl, Alexander. 2016. "Lights Out for the Putin Regime: The Coming Russian Collapse." *Foreign Affairs*, January 27.

Munck, Gerardo L. and Carol Skalnik Leff. 1997. "Modes of Transition and Democratization: South America and Eastern Europe in Comparative Perspective." *Comparative Politics* 29(3): 343–362.

Offe, Claus. 1991. "Capitalism by Democratic Design? Democratic Theory Facing the Triple Transition in East Central Europe." *Social Research* 58(4): 865–892.

Pacek, Alexander C., Grigore Pop-Eleches, and Joshua A. Tucker. 2009. "Disenchanted or Discerning? Turnout in Post-Communist Elections, 1990–2004." *The Journal of Politics* 71(2): 473–491.

Pop-Eleches, Grigore. 2007. "Historical Legacies and Post-Communist Regime Change." *The Journal of Politics* 69(4): 908–926.

Pop-Eleches, Grigore. 2014. "Communist Development and the Post-Communist Democratic Deficit." In Mark Beissinger and Stephen Kotkin, eds. *Historical Legacies of Communism in Russia and Eastern Europe*. New York: Cambridge University Press: 28–51.

Pop-Eleches, Grigore and Graeme Robertson. 2014. "After the Revolution: Long-term Effects of Electoral Revolutions." *Problems of Post-Communism* 61(4): 3–22.

Pop-Eleches, Grigore and Joshua Tucker. 2014. "Communist Socialization and Post-Communist Economic and Political Attitudes." *Electoral Studies* 33: 77–89.

Przeworski, Adam. 1991. *Democracy and the Market*. Cambridge: Cambridge University Press.

Przeworski, Adam, Michael E. Alvarez, Jose Antonio Cheibub, and Fernando Limongi. 2000. *Democracy and Development: Political Institutions and Well-Being in the World, 1950–1990*. New York: Cambridge University Press.

Putnam, Robert D., Robert Leonardi, and Raffaella Nanetti. 1993. *Making Democracy Work: Civic Traditions in Modern Italy*. Princeton, NJ: Princeton University Press.

Roberts, Andrew. 2008. "Hyperaccountability: Economic Voting in Eastern Europe." *Electoral Studies* 27(3): 533–546.

Roberts, Andrew. 2009. *The Quality of Democracy in Eastern Europe: Public Preferences and Policy Reforms*. New York: Cambridge University Press.

Roeder, Philip G. 1993. *Red Sunset: The Failure of Soviet Politics*. Princeton, NJ: Princeton University Press.

Roeder, Philip G. 1994. "Varieties of Post-Soviet Authoritarian Regimes." *Post-Soviet Affairs* 10(1): 61–101.

Roeder, Philip. G. 2004. "National Self-Determination and Postcommunist Popular Sovereignty." In Alina Mungiu-Pippidi and Ivan Krastev, eds. *Nationalism After Communism*. Budapest, Hungary: Central European University Press: 199–230.

Rose, Richard, William Mishler, and Christian Haerpfer. 1998. *Democracy and Its Alternatives: Understanding Post-Communist Societies*. Baltimore, MD: Johns Hopkins University Press.

Sakwa, Richard. 1999. *Postcommunism*. Buckingham: Open University Press.

Schedler, Andreas. 2001. "Measuring Democratic Consolidation." *Studies in Comparative International Development* 36(1): 66–92.

Schimmelfennig, Frank and Hanno Scholtz. 2008. "EU Democracy Promotion in the European Neighbourhood: Political Conditionality, Economic Development and Transnational Exchange." *European Union Politics* 9(2): 187–215.

Schmitter, Philippe and Terry Lynn Karl. 1994. "The Conceptual Travels of Transitologists and Consolidologists: How Far to the East Should They Attempt to Go." *Slavic Review* 54(1): 173–185.

Schneider, Carsten Q. 2009. *The Consolidation of Democracy: Comparing Europe and Latin America*. London: Routledge.

Shleifer, Andrei and Daniel Treisman. 2014. "Normal Countries: The East 25 Years After Communism." *Foreign Affairs*, November–December.

Solnick, Steven. 1999. *Stealing the State: Control and Collapse in Soviet Institutions*. Cambridge, MA: Harvard University Press.

Sztompka, Piotr. 1993. "Civilizational Incompetence: The Trap of Postcommunist Societies." *Zeitschrift fur Soziologie* 22(2): 85–95.

Tetlock, Philip E. 2006. *Expert Political Judgment: How Good Is It? How Can We Know?* Princeton, NJ: Princeton University Press.

Tismaneanu, Vladimir. 1992. *Reinventing Politics: Eastern Europe From Stalin to Havel*. New York: Free Press.

Tucker, Joshua. 2012. "Enough! Electoral Fraud, Collective Action Problems, and Post-Communist Colored Revolutions." *Perspectives on Politics* 5(3): 535–551.

Vachudova, Milada Anna. 2005. *Europe Undivided: Democracy, Leverage, and Integration After Communism*. Oxford: Oxford University Press.

Vachudova, Milada Anna and Tim Snyder. 1996. "Are Transitions Transitory? Two Types of Political Change in Eastern Europe Since 1989." *East European Politics and Societies* 11(1): 1–35.

Whitehead, Laurence. 2001. "Democracy and Decolonization: East-Central Europe." In Laurence Whitehead, ed. *The International Dimensions of Democratization: Europe and the Americas*. New York: Oxford University Press.

Zielonka, Jan, ed. 2001. *Democratic Consolidation in Eastern Europe*. Oxford: Oxford University Press.

2

BELATED TRANSITIONS IN SOUTH EASTERN EUROPE

Florian Bieber

Introduction

When communist regimes began falling in the autumn of 1989 in Central and Eastern Europe, this wave also included Bulgaria, Romania, Yugoslavia, and Albania, the latter two of which were outside the Soviet sphere of influence. However, strikingly, the countries of the region were late-comers in comparison to Central Europe and the process was protracted and difficult. Bulgaria and Romania overthrew long-ruling dictators in November and December 1989, just a few weeks after East Germany and Czechoslovakia. However, in Yugoslavia, there were no mass pro-tests against communist rule, with the partial exception of Slovenia, and the ruling party fractured along republican lines, organising multi-party elections throughout 1990, without surrendering power in some republics until much later (especially Serbia and Montenegro). In Albania, the mass protests began only in 1990, and it would take nearly two years for free and fair elections that would see a defeat of the incumbent socialist Party of Labour.

Even after the first multi-party elections in South Eastern Europe, semi-authoritarian rule persisted for most of the 1990s to a greater extent than in Central Europe. Some of these semi-authoritarian rulers were part of the communist nomenclature which had managed to transition into the post-communist period, such as Ion Iliescu in Romania or Slobodan Milošević in Serbia, whereas in other countries the new "democratic" leaders (usually also belonging to the commu-nist nomenclature at some point) displayed authoritarian tendencies, such as Franjo Tudjman in Croatia or Sali Berisha in Albania. In the context of the Yugoslav disintegration, these authori-tarian systems were closely intertwined with the wars beginning in 1991 and the instrumental use of nationalism.

A second wave of democratic transitions took place between 1996 and 2000 in Romania, Serbia, and Croatia, which brought opposition candidates to power who pursued a clear policy of democratic reforms and European Union (EU) integration. This delay in comparison to Central Europe has translated into a delayed accession process to the EU. Slovenia was able to join with the big bang enlargement of 2004, whereas Romania and Bulgaria joined only in 2007, followed by Croatia in 2013. The other countries of the so-called Western Balkans (Bosnia and Herzegovina, Serbia, Montenegro, Albania, Macedonia, and Kosovo) remain at varying stages of the integration process.

Since the mid-2000s, there has been a wave of democratic reversals, as a new generation of semi-authoritarian rulers has come to power, from Nikola Gruevski in Macedonia in 2006 to Milorad Dodik in Republika Srpska (the predominately Serb entity within Bosnia and Herzegovina). Thus, the process of democratisation appears reversible and all indicators suggest that most countries in South Eastern Europe remain examples of unconsolidated democracies.

This chapter will explore the nature of this difficult transition and examine key explanations offered in the literature. An important preliminary observation is that the different trajectory of communism in Yugoslavia and Albania (compared to the other countries of Central and Eastern Europe), plus the delayed and partially violent nature of the transitions, has resulted in the countries of the so-called Western Balkans (a term first used to describe former Yugoslavia, minus Slovenia, plus Albania)[1] being analysed and studied separately from other post-communist countries, including Romania and Bulgaria. Furthermore, the different paths to EU accession have entrenched this particular configuration of the region, and this has resulted in a paucity of cross-regional comparison. Thus, there is less of a unified literature on South Eastern Europe, but often a focus on the post-Yugoslav countries, including Albania. For instance, neither the two post-communist countries of the region (Bulgaria and Romania) nor the two non-communist South Eastern European countries (Turkey and Greece) tend to be included in comparative studies. Slovenia's relatively peaceful path towards independence, devoid of authoritarian episodes, has also meant that the country is often considered together with the Central European states that entered the EU in 2004, and not with its former fellow Yugoslav republics.

This chapter focuses on the post-Yugoslav republics, but also considers the wider post-communist South Eastern European context and thus seeks to identify not just post-Yugoslav particularities of transition, but also highlights commonalities with other countries. In order to capture the particular nature of the transition in South Eastern Europe, this chapter will address three questions:

1   What explains the later end of communist rule in South Eastern Europe as opposed to Central Europe?
2   What caused the persistence of semi-authoritarian rule during most of the 1990s?
3   What explains the structural and long-term difficulties in the consolidation of democracy in South Eastern Europe?

In answering these questions, the main approaches in the scholarly debate will be considered. The chapter will conclude by identifying directions for future research.

Explaining the late end of communist rule

It is hard to identify a single unifying explanation for the delayed collapse of communist rule in South Eastern Europe, as the four communist regimes of the regions displayed a large degree of variety. Albania and Romania constituted probably the most repressive types of communist rule in Europe, whereas Yugoslavia had been, with a few exceptions, the most liberal communist system. On the other hand, both Yugoslavia and Albania were not under Soviet control, thus Soviet policies of glasnost, perestroika and the renouncement of the Brezhnev Doctrine by Gorbachev in 1989 had little direct impact on the two countries.

The delay in the fall of communism in Albania and Yugoslavia thus could be explained in part by the lack of dependency on the Soviet Union. However, the communist regimes struggled with similar challenges as elsewhere, such as decreasing economic productivity, grievances among the population (as far as they could be visible in a country such as Albania), a growing legitimacy deficit, the death of dominant long-time rulers (Tito in 1980, Hoxha in 1985), and persistent economic crisis, expressed in shortages and a decline in citizens' quality of life. The survival of the regimes in Albania and Yugoslavia, however, did not rest on an external power for military and economic support. Protests and opposition could similarly not direct their grievances towards an external actor, which had closely linked anti-communist protest and anti-Soviet and anti-Russian sentiment elsewhere and facilitated a powerful combination of nationalist and democratic grievances.

Indeed, late communist rulers in both Yugoslavia and Albania could brush aside the Soviet reform movement as irrelevant for their countries. However, by early 1990, Yugoslavia and Albania were the only countries of Central and Eastern Europe which had not committed themselves to multi-party elections. As such, the system of government appeared increasingly anachronistic. In the case of Yugoslavia, the pressure for political liberalisation came from Slovenia, which had been a more liberal republic within Yugoslavia, with a well-developed civil society and critical public by the late 1980s. Here, critical media (*Mladina*), artists (*Neue Slowenische Kunst*), and intellectuals lobbied for a political opening and a reform of the Yugoslav system (Silber and Little 1996).

A unifying feature of all four South Eastern European countries under communist rule was the relative weakness of dissident groups. In Albania and Romania, this was largely due to the particularly repressive nature of the regime. In Bulgaria, the regime was less oppressive, but opposition to communist rule was nonetheless marginal and had fewer prominent members than in countries of Central Europe, such as Hungary, Czechoslovakia, or Poland. In Yugoslavia, the relatively liberal nature of the regime provided a 'safety valve', thus criticism of the government was possible and widespread, yet organised dissent was curtailed. However, by the late 1980s, there had been rising dissident movements in Slovenia and Serbia, although the different priorities prevented the emergence of a unified Yugoslav dissident movement. Thus, critics of communist rule in Serbia focused on criticising the decentralisation of the country and disadvantages Serbs were perceived to experience, whereas in Slovenia, the authoritarian nature of the Yugoslav system was the main rallying point of opposition.

Persistence of semi-authoritarian rule

Questions of stateness and the status of minorities facilitated new or old governments to mobilise nationalism and retain authoritarian practices. This pattern was particularly pertinent in the post-Yugoslav space, but also identifiable in other cases, such as Romania and Slovakia (Fisher 2006, Stroschein 2014).

In Romania, as in Slovakia, the Hungarian minority was instrumentalised by authoritarian leaders as a threat that helped justify authoritarian rule. The Iliescu government in Romania also drew on the communist nomenclature. In Serbia and Croatia, the state of war between 1991 and 1995, and for Serbia in 1998–1999, allowed not only for more repressive policies towards the opposition; it also resulted in the public space being dominated by war, atrocities (real and invented), and nationalist propaganda that benefited the incumbents.

In Romania, the defeat of the Iliescu government in 1996 was based on a broad democratic coalition challenging the incumbent and the decreasing salience of the perceived threat from the Hungarian minority (Gallagher 2005). A similar transition occurred in Slovakia in 1998, and in Croatia and Serbia in 2000. In Croatia, the death of the dominant figure of the 1990s, Franjo Tudjman, deprived the ruling Croatian Democratic Community (HDZ) of their leader, and the end of the wars and the peaceful reintegration of the last Croatian territory by 1998 robbed the government of the ability to mobilise along nationalist lines as had been the case at earlier elections. Instead, corruption and mismanagement prevailed in the electoral campaign (Gagnon 2004). Serbia followed suit the same year. Following the lost war in Kosovo in 1999, economic hardship, and increasing authoritarianism, Slobodan Milošević was overthrown in mass protests following contested elections with considerable Western support for the opposition (Spoerri 2014, Bunce and Wolchik 2011).

Authoritarian patterns were not limited to countries with significant majority-minority contestation, as Albania highlights. Here, the authoritarian rule of the first Berisha government (1992–1997) emerged despite the absence of any significant minorities or nationalism as an important political force. Weak state institutions and the high level of polarisation between the dominant Democratic Party and the Socialist Party (the former Communist Party of Labour) enabled authoritarian rule to go largely unchallenged. The mass exodus of Albanians to Italy and Greece and the near anarchical conditions of the mass protests highlighted the consequences of the paranoid and isolationist communist rule and the shallow roots of statehood – Albania existed barely two decades as an independent country prior to communist rule (Abrahams 2015).

The second wave of democratic revolutions included elements of popular protest or even uprisings (as in Albania) via the ballot box to trigger protests or confirm the loss of power of incumbents. They often relied on unified opposition coalitions (as in Romania, Croatia, or Serbia) and outside support. The relative isolation of these semi-authoritarian regimes vis-à-vis other Central and South Eastern European countries also mattered as EU integration gathered pace in the late 1990s and they became laggards in that process (Boduszyński 2010).

The rise of new semi-authoritarian regimes

The early 2000s witnessed a considerable improvement of democratic governments in South Eastern Europe, and all governments at least nominally shared the goals of EU integration and democratic rule. However, institutions had often been considerably weakened during the 1990s, and the state capture of the 1990s was not easily undone as former elites often retained formidable forces, or alternatively sought new patrons in political systems that had become patrimonial (Cohen and Lampe 2011). In some cases, semi-authoritarian rulers of the 1990s returned to office, such as Ion Iliescu in Romania in 2000 and Sali Berisha in Albania in 2005. However, here, the structural changes and the EU integration process prevented a relapse into the semi-authoritarian patterns of the previous decade. Instead, a new generation of semi-authoritarian rulers came to power, based on the promise of EU integration and reform, while relying on patronage and populism.

In 2006, the conservative International Macedonian Revolutionary Organization-Democratic Party for Macedonian National Unity (VMRO-DPMNE) took office and under Prime Minister Nikola Gruevski instituted a nationalist semi-authoritarian regime which systematically undermined independent institutions and built a robust patronage network. Similar patterns could be found in Republika Srpska, where Milorad Dodik and his Alliance of Independent Social Democrats (SNSD) has been dominant since 2006, and in Serbia, where the populist Serbian Progressive Party (SNS) of Aleksandar Vučić, a former extreme nationalist, has dominated since 2012. In Montenegro, there has been no transfer of power through elections since 1990 with the Democratic Party of Socialists (DPS) as successors to the Communist Party retaining power uninterrupted. By 1997, the party had shifted under the leadership of Milo Djukanović from a Serb nationalist policy that supported Milošević to a pro-independence party committed to EU integration and reform. These new semi-authoritarian governments combine formal commitment to EU integration and reforms with informal mechanisms of control and patronage, thus resorting to undemocratic strategies to retain power. Populist parties with an authoritarian penchant have been similarly successful in Bulgaria, with Citizens for European Development of Bulgaria (GERB) led by Boyko Borisov, and in Romania with Victor Ponta of the Social Democratic Party (PSD). An overarching feature is the support for EU integration, while resorting to populist messages, including nationalism, and securing political control through the use of informality and patronage.[2] Unlike comparable tendencies in Hungary since the election of Viktor Orbán as prime minister in 2010, these regimes have not fundamentally altered the legal and constitutional structure. They have exercised control largely through the informal party and personal control. Thus, they are characterised by a democratic façade and gradual adaptation of the EU's *acquis communautaire*, while ensuring that rule of law and institutional safeguards can be bypassed (Pula 2016). Thus the illegal recordings of the Gruevski government, revealed by the opposition in 2015, suggest that the inner circle used the police and the judiciary to punish political opponents, direct control over both public and private media, and use ethnic Macedonians from Albania in voting fraud, among others. Relentless campaigning, the use of state resources to dominate the public agenda, frequent early elections, and a weak and fragmented opposition characterise the pattern of rule in Macedonia, Serbia, and Montenegro. Unlike Vladimir Putin, they inherited imperfect, yet largely democratic institutions and a multi-party system. Furthermore, the goal of EU integration is widely held among citizens and not disputed by the semi-authoritarian rulers. Unlike Recep Tayyip Erdoğan of Turkey or Viktor Orbán, they lack a strong ideological commitment or basis, even if some, like the VRMO-DPMNE in Macedonia, do draw on nationalism.

These regimes are characteristic of countries that have experienced 'stateness' issues, that is, challenges to the nature and structure of the state and delayed and weak democratisation in the early 2000s (Džihić and Segert 2012). The delay of the 1990s meant that institutions functioned under democratic governments for a shorter period of time and these often maintained and used the authoritarian patterns and structures they inherited. For example, the Serbian president Boris Tadić (2004–2012) remained president of the ruling Democratic Party, even though this arguably contravened the Serbian constitution and thus transformed a constitutionally weak president into a factually strong presidency.

The pattern of democratisation in South Eastern Europe since 1990 highlights the non-linear nature of process. It is marked by a delay in comparison to other countries in Central Europe, a longer period of semi-authoritarian rule in the 1990s and a number of important reversals since the mid-2000s. However, considering comparable semi-authoritarian experiences in Slovakia and setbacks since 2010 in Hungary and Poland, it would be too simplistic to overemphasise a pattern of successful democratic consolidation in Central Europe and one of failed and late democratisation in South Eastern Europe.

Explaining the delayed transition

Next, we will examine different debates and explanatory approaches to explain one or several of the features of the delayed democratic transition in South Eastern Europe, including historical legacies, the particularities of the nature of the transition, the role of nationalism and conflict, state weakness, and the particular type of economic transformation.

Historical institutionalism

The argument of historical legacies draws on the particularities of the past in South Eastern Europe as an explanatory factor for the nature of transition in the region. This perspective was reflected in often crude Balkanist stereotyping that viewed the region as backward, tribal, and violent (Todorova 1997).

However, more sophisticated scholarship of South Eastern Europe does note the specificities of the region. Sundhaussen (1999), for example, has noted particular historical characteristics that mark South Eastern Europe, including a high level of ethnic diversity, a Byzantine-Orthodox and Islamic-Ottoman heritage, a developmental delay in the modern era, and a strong role of great powers, among others. Alina Mungiu-Pippidi (2005) has argued that South Eastern Europe is characterised by a high level of particularism, that is, low levels of trust in the state and abstract institutions and instead reliance on informal networks. However, such arguments easily fall into a deterministic trap and often fail to explain the origins of such patterns. In particular, the Ottoman origins, often claimed, are hard to map over such long periods of time.

A different strand of the historical institutionalist approach focuses less on the pre-Socialist legacies, such as the Ottoman heritage or late and incomplete state-building, but rather on the institutional structures of socialism. Jović (2008) argues that late socialist Yugoslavia was ideo-logically committed to the gradual erosion of state structures, the "withering away of the state" wherein most decisions are taken by local units of self-management (both in the economic and administrative sense) or the republics, with the Yugoslav state acting only as the final arbiter. Thus, the disintegration of the state was not so much an unintended consequence, but part of the ideological vision of Yugoslav communists, even if they did not plan or desire the violent breakup of the country. While not explicitly examining the delay in democratisation, the text speaks to the importance of socialist legacies. The variety of communist regimes in South Eastern Europe, as noted earlier, however, cannot explain regional patterns, but rather only country-specific pathways.

The nature of transition

As discussed earlier, the nature, timing, and trajectory of the transformation process or "transition" differed between South Eastern and Central Europe. In addition to occurring later than in most Central European countries, the transition in South Eastern Europe also featured fewer mass protests against the communist regimes with the notable exception of Slovenia and Romania. In addition, there was considerably more violence during the transition in South Eastern Europe, in particular in Yugoslavia and Romania. However, as noted earlier, there was considerable variation in both the regimes and their downfall in South Eastern Europe, so much so that one cannot speak in terms of a distinctly South Eastern European path. Nev-ertheless, most are characterised by the persistence of communist incumbents after the first round of multi-party elections. The success of renamed communist parties occurred when the opposition was weak and the regime could pre-empt a strengthening opposition through early election, as has been the case in Romania and Serbia. Alternatively, in some cases, the parties replacing them emulated authoritarian policies and often drew heavily on the communist nomenclature, as in Croatia, Albania, or Bosnia and Herzegovina. Here, opposition and dissi-dent groups had been weak, and nationalism provided a convenient ground for political mobi-lisation. Some scholars have focused on the nature of communism in South Eastern Europe to explain the transition: the greater level of personalised authoritarianism and clientelist control resulted in a more serious institutional crisis and weaker challengers than in Central Europe (Gallagher 2003, 11–12).

On the other hand, Koinova (2013) and Bieber (2008) locate the key moment in terms of his-torical institutionalist legacies as being in the early phase of transition. They suggest that the pat-tern of majority-minority interaction established then shaped the relationship and thus the nature of transition in the subsequent period. Thus, the new institutional set-up of the country shapes the subsequent transformation, whether this pertains to interethnic relations or the structures of democracy. Thus, the sequencing of the transition process matters and often occurred to the disadvantage of establishing democratic structures in South Eastern Europe (Džihić and Segert 2012). In Serbia, for example, the new constitution was drafted and ratified by referendum prior to the first multi-party elections. The constitution had strong authoritarian features and favoured the Milošević regime.

The next crucial moment during the transition process is the holding of the first multi-party elections and whether there are strong parties advocating reform and democratisation or whether the main parties focus on issues such as nationalism. Vachudova (2005, 35–48) argues that it was in regimes without a strong anti-communist opposition that allowed either incumbents to retain power (Romania and Bulgaria) or for new parties to use nationalism to build patronage networks (Slovakia). This argument could be extended to most post-Yugoslav states, with the partial exception of Slovenia.

Furthermore, the presence of mass protests at the beginning of transition matters, as this signals popular support for change. For Bunce (2003, 171), this sets apart the most successful from the delayed transitions. While Albania and Romania witnessed large anti-communist protests in South Eastern Europe, Serbia saw protests, but they were not anti-systemic; rather they focused on improving living conditions of workers and later turned nationalist, but not inherently anti-communist. The victory of illiberal nationalists at the first elections either through use of communist regimes (Serbia) or by the opposition (Croatia) (Bunce 2011) subsequently sets the stage for delayed democratisation, as these regimes are reluctant to reform and more likely to seek confrontation with minorities.

Altogether, this line of argument suggests that the particular nature of the transition, popular or pre-empted by incumbent elites and the associated parties and structures, determines the nature of the transition and the likelihood of democratic consolidation.

The instrumental use of conflict and nationalism

Looking beyond the transition itself, it is important to consider the impact of war and nationalism in delaying democratic transition. One of the weaknesses in the literature on democratisation during the 1990s and early 2000s has been the relative neglect of the post-Yugoslav space. The wars and crisis made them anomalies rather than exemplifiers of failed or delayed transition (Vladisavljević 2014).

One important argument made to explain the delay of transition in the post-Yugoslav space is the disintegration of the country and the ensuing wars. Thus, violence and nationalism created a context in which democratisation would be suspended or reduced to majoritarianism. Here, we find two strands of argument. The dominant argument has been that nationalism is a strong mobilising tool and easily available in times of political transition (Oberschall 2000). Thus, Snyder has argued that young democracies are particularly vulnerable to a takeover by nationalists. His argument and that of others is that in the time of democratic transition, the political system needs to be renegotiated which increases fears of minorities of exclusion and desires of majorities to reassert their dominance. In addition, weak institutions and suddenly open public debate without limitations can give an audience to nationalist arguments and provide little structural and symbolic restraints (Snyder and Ballentine 1996, Snyder 2000).

This argument has been challenged in the Yugoslav context, with Caspersen showing that radicalisation took place as part of a post-election intra-party competition and not in order to maximise voter support (Caspersen 2010). Instead, both Gordy and Gagnon have made the argument that the use of war and nationalism served incumbent elites to preserve and secure power (Gordy 1999, Gagnon 2004).

A third approach draws on the 'prisoners' dilemma' argument to explain the situation in Bosnia and Herzegovina, as well as other cases. This explanation seeks to explain why voters support nationalist parties when survey data indicates their support for moderate or cross-national options instead. The argument here is that voters make a reluctant choice for their 'own' nationalists for fear that others would vote for theirs and they would be left without protection (Mujkić and Hulsey 2010, Stojanović 2014). Thus, democratic competition becomes a security dilemma where nationalism offers protection and at the same time escalated fear of the other.[3] Consequently, democratic processes are undermined and either fail or lead to delayed transition.

Finally, Bunce argues that the effect of nationalism is modified by the timing, suggesting that early nationalist mobilisation is more likely to lead to an escalation between titular majorities and minorities that can lead to conflict and delayed transition, whereas late nationalist mobilisation allows for mobilisation around liberal democratic goals. She notes that the Baltics and Slovenia fit the latter pattern, while Serbia, Armenia, Croatia, and Slovakia better fit the former (Bunce 2003, 177–178). However, this argument difficult to uphold, as there was not much nationalist mobilisation in Croatia for nearly two decades prior to the first elections, and in the case of Bosnia and Herzegovina, we similarly do not find an important nationalist mobilisation prior to 1989. Thus, it is not clear how timing explains variation between Slovenia – where nationalism appeared before Bosnia or Croatia on the political agenda of the 1980s – and Serbia.

What appears important is the direction of nationalism and salience of it for domestic political contestation. Thus, while in Slovenia the 'erased' were a group of residents who were eliminated from the official registers in country after not applying for citizenship within a narrow time window, there was no systematic mobilisation against minorities and the main target of nationalism as directed at the outside, that is, Serbia and Yugoslavia. In Croatia, Serbia, or Bosnia and Herzegovina, on the other hand, a key actor against which nationalist mobilisation took place was within the republican boundaries, allowing for nationalist polarisation within the republics, rather than just between republics. Once nationalist mobilisation is not just used against an 'outsider', but also within a polity, as the republics of Yugoslavia were, this led to polarisation and subsequently enabled the use of force.

While these approaches differ in the assessment of the mechanisms through which nationalism and war delay democratisation, they clearly identify a similar causal link.

State weakness and capture

One common argument is that the incomplete process of nation state construction delayed transition. Thus, more heterogeneous and contested states could not focus on democratisation, but were instead distracted by questions of how to define polity, citizenship, access to institutions, and so forth. However, as Bunce points out, this does not help explain why some very homogenous countries like Albania struggled, while diverse countries such as Estonia or new countries like Slovenia managed to establish fairly robust democracies (2011).

A striking and consistent feature of most Balkan states, however, has been weak state capacity, especially when it comes to the equal and consistent enforcement of norms, and the strong role of patronage and other aspects of informality (Bojicic-Dzelilovic 2013). This control of resources and institutions through informal structures often benefits a small elite, based on a close nexus of political and economic influence, often empowered through structures emerging in the early 1990s during the first phase of transformation and the wars (Džihić and Segert 2012). These have been aspects accentuated by the Yugoslav wars in most of the successor states, but are also shared to varying degrees in Albania, Romania, and Bulgaria. Ethnonationalism is thus a tool of state control, but necessarily a cause. Instead, these mechanisms operate on the basis of party loyalty, kinship, and personal ties, not on the grounds of ethnicity or such markers of identity (Koutkova 2015).

Balkan neoliberalism

In recent years, there has been a rise in neo-Marxist analysis of the transition process in South Eastern Europe. The rise of this approach is closely linked to the persistent economic crisis in Europe since 2008 and a broader increase of studies critical of the hegemony of neoliberal economic thought since 1989. Štiks and Horvat (2015) argue that the economic liberalisation and privatisation empowered predatory elites and led to widespread impoverishment and persistence of nationalist and undemocratic governments. This is part of a wider debate, more developed in ethnographic studies of post-socialism which outline the insecurities, impoverishment, and vulnerability of many citizens in the post-Socialist period (Humphrey and Mandel 2002, Kideckel 2008, Bajić-Hajduković 2014).

The general model of neoliberal capitalism, however, cannot explain the delay of democratic transition in South Eastern Europe, as this model was broadly implemented from the Baltics to South Eastern Europe. However, as Bohle and Greskovits (2012) have argued, the types of capitalism vary greatly in Central and Eastern Europe. They argue that in three of the four Balkan cases examined – Croatia, Bulgaria, and Romania – weak states and patronage structures that partly originate in Socialism stood in the way of managing relations between labour and new capitalists, resulting in a particular predatory type of capitalism (Bohle and Greskovits 2012, 194). However, their argument suggests that it is not the particular variant of capitalism that led to a delay in democratisation, but rather the other way around. A particular feature of the transformation during the 1990s was the limited degree of economic liberalisation. They included less liberalisation and privatisation than in Central Europe during the 1990s, especially in the first half of the decade, closely coinciding with the persistence of late communist nomenclature in office (Åslund 1996). Others have pointed out that the economic trajectory of the 1990s, in particular the wars, positioned South Eastern Europe in a European "super-periphery" with weak states, high unemployment, and large disparities (Bartlett 2009). Again, these are not causes, but rather consequences of persistent semi-authoritarianism of the 1990s, and might have been contributing factors – compounded by the global economic crisis after 2008 – to the rise of new forms of semi-authoritarianism.

Assessment and further research

The study of democratic transition in South Eastern Europe has long been overshadowed by research on war and nationalism, which in itself has been isolated from other research in post-communist Europe (Gagnon 2014). There has been sporadic comparative research that has bridged the divide between post-Yugoslav and other post-communist countries (Koinova 2013, Fisher 2006, Dawson 2014), highlighting that it is fruitful to cross this invisible divide.

The focus on Central Europe and the 'successful' cases of democratic transformation has resulted in a research bias that often results in looking at South Eastern Europe as merely the case of failure or incomplete democratisation, often shaped by Balkanizing perspectives on the region. The debates on the particular democratisation path in South Eastern Europe highlight that there is no singular cause for the variation to Central Europe and within the region itself. The research has highlighted the importance of legacies, while avoiding historical determinism, the particularity of the transition itself, and the debilitating influence of nationalism and weak state structures to the process.

There are two large themes in the literature that have just begun to be explored and merit further attention: the role of informality and the return to semi-authoritarian forms of government. While informality has been subject to research in recent years, its dynamics and in particular its interrelationship with democratisation processes remains ill-understood. Some research on the subject is beginning to emerge from political scientists (Dolenec 2013) and anthropologists (Kutkova 2015). Closely connected is a fairly limited understanding of political parties, as the understanding of parties remains shaped by Western European perspectives. While they have been discussed somewhat in the literature (see Lewis 2000, Stojarová and Emerson 2009), the dynamics of patronage and their symbiotic relationship with state institutions remains only partially understood (Bértoa and Taleski 2016). This is in large part due to the difficulty of measuring informality and illicit activities and misconceptions about the role of parties based on research in Central and Western Europe.

The link between the different 'crisis of democratisation' in the 1990s and since 2006 also remains under-researched, to identify both continuities and differences. Closely linked is the question of the causes of informality. Whereas they are often attributed to the 1990s and the particularities of the delayed transition, there are origins in the Socialist period. However, the informal practices and politics of patronage of late Socialism remain a subject meriting further research. Finally, the categorisation of the post-Yugoslav space (or the Western Balkans) as distinct from other countries already in the EU, such as Bulgaria and Romania or for that matter Greece, persists with the danger of inbuilt bias, assuming that EU integration creates a distinct form of democratisation and transformation. Instead, understanding similarities might be more fruitful and challenge these biases (Dawson 2014, Bieber and Ristić 2012). Similarly, the understanding of democratisation processes still remains often steeped in assumptions about the progression from illiberal to liberal democracy, rather than either a back and forth or a stagnation and relatively stable form of unconsolidated democracy, as widely used measures of democracy, such as Nations in Transit of Freedom House[4] or the Bertelsmann Transformation Index suggest.[5]

Notes

1 With Croatian EU accession in 2013, the country is no longer included in political structures associated with the Western Balkans, but usually remains included in academic discussions.
2 There is no overarching study of this phenomena.
3 This argument has been made not in the case of elections, but for minority-majority violence in Croatia and Romania (Roe 2005).
4 https://freedomhouse.org/report/nations-transit/nations-transit-2016.
5 www.bti-project.org/en/home/.

Bibliography

Abrahams, Fred C. 2015. *Modern Albania: From Dictatorship to Democracy in Europe.* New York: New York University Press.

Åslund, Anders. 1996. "Introduction: The Balkan Transformation in a Comparative Perspective." Ian Jeffries (ed.), *Problems of Economic and Political Transformation in the Balkans.* London and New York: Pinter, 1–12.

Bajić-Hajduković, Ivana. 2014. "Introduction: Balkan Precariat." *Contemporary Southeastern Europe* 1(2), 1–6, available at: www.suedosteuropa.uni-graz.at/cse/en/introduction_balkan_precariat

Bartlett, Will. 2009. "Economic Development in the European Super-Periphery: Evidence From the Western Balkans." *Economic Annals* 54(181): 21–44.

Bértoa, Fernando Casal and Dane Taleski. 2016. "Regulating Party Politics in the Western Balkans: The Legal Sources of Party System Development in Macedonia." *Democratization* 23(3): 545–567.

Bieber, Florian. 2008. "Regulating Minority Parties in Central and South-Eastern Europe." Benjamin Reilly and Per Nordlund (eds.), *Political Parties in Conflict-Prone Societies: Regulation, Engineering and Democratic Development.* Tokyo, New York and Paris: UNU Press, 95–125.

Bieber, Florian and Irena Ristić. 2012. "Constrained Democracy: The Consolidation of Democracy in Yugoslav Successor States." *Southeastern Europe* 36(3): 373–397.

Boduszyński, Mieczyslaw. 2010. *Regime Change in the Yugoslav Successor States: Divergent Paths Toward a New Europe.* Baltimore, MD: Johns Hopkins University Press.

Bohle, Dorothee and Béla Greskovits. 2012. *Capitalist Diversity on Europe's Periphery.* Ithaca, NY: Cornell University Press.

Bojicic-Dzelilovic, Vesna. 2013. "Informality, Inequality and Social Reintegration in Post-War Transition." *Studies in Social Justice* 7(2): 211–228.

Bunce, Valerie. 2003. "Rethinking Recent Democratization: Lessons From the Postcommunist Experience." *World Politics* 55(2): 167–192.

Bunce, Valerie. 2011. "The Political Transition." Sharon L. Wolchik and Jane L. Curry (eds.), *Central and East European Politics: From Communism to Democracy.* Lanham, MD: Rowman and Littlefield, 31–52.

Bunce, Valerie and Sharon Wolchik. 2011. *Defeating Authoritarian Leaders in Postcommunist Countries.* Cambridge: Cambridge University Press.

Caspersen, Nina. 2010. *Contested Nationalism: Serb Elite Rivalry in Croatia and Bosnia in the 1990s.* Oxford: Berghahn Books.

Cohen, Lenard and John R. Lampe. 2011. *Embracing Democracy in the Western Balkans: From Postconflict Struggles Toward European Integration.* Washington, DC: Woodrow Wilson Centre Press.

Dawson, James. 2014. *Cultures of Democracy in Serbia and Bulgaria: How Ideas Shape Publics.* Farnham and Burlington, VT: Ashgate.

Dolenec, Danijela. 2013. *Democratic Institutions and Authoritarian Rule in Southeast Europe.* Colchester: ECPR Press.

Džihić, Vedran and Dieter Segert. 2012. "Lessons From 'Post-Yugoslav' Democratization Functional Problems of Stateness and the Limits of Democracy." *East European Politics and Societies,* 26(2), 239–253.

Fisher, Sharon. 2006. *Political Change in Post-Communist Slovakia and Croatia: From Nationalist to Europeanist.* New York: Palgrave.

Gagnon, V. P., Jr. 2004. *The Myth of Ethnic War: Serbia and Croatia in the 1990s.* Ithaca, NY: Cornell University Press.

Gagnon, V. P., Jr. 2014. "Political Science and the Yugoslav Dissolution: The Evolution of a Discipline." Florian Bieber, Armina Galijaš and Rory Archer (eds.), *Debating the End of Yugoslavia.* Farnham and Burlington, VT: Ashgate, 56–66.

Gallagher, Tom. 2003. *The Balkans After the Cold War: From Tyranny to Tragedy.* London and New York: Routledge.

Gallagher, Tom. 2005. *Modern Romania: The End of Communism, the Failure of Democratic Reform, and the Theft of a Nation.* New York: New York University Press.

Gordy, Eric. 1999. *The Culture of Power in Serbia. Nationalism and the Destruction of Alternatives.* University Park: Pennsylvania State University Press.

Humphrey, Caroline and Ruth Mandel. 2002. "The Markets of Everyday Life: Ethnographies of Postsocialism." Caroline Humphrey and Ruth Mandel (eds.), *Markets and Moralities: Ethnographies of Postsocialism.* Oxford and New York: Berg, 1–16.

Jović, Dejan. 2008. *Yugoslavia: A State That Withered Away.* West Lafayette, IN: Purdue University Press.

Kideckel, David A. 2008. *Getting By in Postsocialist Romania: Labor, the Body, and Working-Class Culture.* Bloomington: Indiana University Press.

Koinova, Maria. 2013. *Ethnonationalist Conflict in Postcommunist States: Varieties of Governance in Bulgaria, Macedonia, and Kosovo.* Philadelphia: University of Pennsylvania Press.

Kutkova, Karla. 2015. "The Importance of Having Štela: Reproduction of Informality in the Democratization Sector in Bosnia." Jeremy Morris and Abel Polese (eds.), *Informal Economies in Post-Socialist Spaces Practices, Institutions and Networks.* Basingstoke and New York: Palgrave Macmillan, 139–153.

Lewis, Paul G. 2000. *Political Parties in Post-Communist Eastern Europe.* London and New York: Routledge.

Mujkić, Asim and John Hulsey. 2010. "Explaining the Success of Nationalist Parties in Bosnia and Herzegovina." *Politička Misao: Croatian Political Science Review* 47(2): 143–158.

Mungiu-Pippidi, Alina. 2005. "Deconstructing Balkan Particularism: the Ambiguous Social Capital of Southeastern Europe." *Southeast European and Black Sea Studies* 5(1): 49–68.

Oberschall, Anthony. 2000. "The Manipulation of Ethnicity: From Ethnic Cooperation to Violence and War in Yugoslavia." *Ethnic and Racial Studies* 23(6): 982–1001.

Pula, Besnik. 2016. "The Budding Autocrats of the Balkans." *Foreign Policy,* 15 April, available at: http://foreignpolicy.com/2016/04/15/the-budding-autocrats-of-the-balkans-serbia-macedonia-montenegro/.

Roe, Paul. 2005. *Ethnic Violence and the Societal Security Dilemma*. Milton Park: Routledge.

Silber, Laura and Allan Little. 1996. *The Death of Yugoslavia*. London: Penguin.

Snyder, Jack. 2000. *From Voting to Violence: Democratization and Nationalist Conflict*. New York: W. W. Norton.

Snyder, Jack and Karen Ballentine. 1996. "Nationalism and the Marketplace of Ideas." *International Security* 21(2): 5–40.

Spoerri, Marlene. 2014. *Engineering Revolution: The Paradox of Democracy Promotion in Serbia*. Philadelphia: University of Pennsylvania Press.

Štiks, Igor and Srećko Horvat. 2015. "Introduction: Radical Politics in the Desert of Transition." Igor Štiks and Srećko Horvat (eds.), *Welcome to the Desert of Post-Socialism*. London: Verso, 1–17.

Stojanović, Nenad. 2014. "When Non-nationalist Voters Support Ethno-nationalist Parties: The 1990 Elections in Bosnia and Herzegovina as a Prisoner's Dilemma Game." *Southeast European and Black Sea Studies* 14(4): 607–625.

Stojarová, Vera and Peter Emerson (eds.). 2009. *Party Politics in the Western Balkans*. London: Routledge.

Stroschein, Sherrill. 2014. *Ethnic Struggle, Coexistence, and Democratization in Eastern Europe*. Cambridge: Cambridge University Press.

Sundhaussen, Holm. 1999. "Europa Balcanica: Der Balkan Als Historischer Raum Europas." *Geschichte und Gesellschaft: Zeitschrift für historische Sozialwissenschaft* 25: 626–653.

Todorova, Maria. 1997. *Imagining the Balkans*. Oxford and New York: Oxford University Press.

Vachudova, Milada Anna. 2005. *Europe Undivided: Democracy, Leverage & Integration After Communism*. Oxford: Oxford University Press.

Vladisavljević, Nebojša. 2014. "Does Scholarly Literature on the Breakup of Yugoslavia Travel Well?" Florian Bieber, Armina Galijaš and Rory Archer (eds.), *Debating the End of Yugoslavia*. Farnham and Burlington, VT: Ashgate, 67–79.

3

EXPLAINING UKRAINE

Andrew Wilson

The 'Ukraine Crisis' that exploded in 2014 was in fact many crises, and not all of them of Ukraine's making (Wilson, 2014b). Much academic debate ensued as to whether the main problems were internal or external, pre-existing or artificial (Portnov, 2015). This chapter cannot cover everything that has been written on these and other subjects in the last twenty-five years, even before the recent upsurge of scholarly attention. The chapter hence serves as a selection of some of the best work both before and after 2014, concentrating almost exclusively on Western sources available in English.

The crisis came just shy of a quarter century since the end of the Soviet Union in 1991. Paradoxically, Ukraine both played a considerable and even decisive part in the Soviet endgame (Plokhy, 2014) and was unprepared for the independence that followed. Modern Ukraine is a kaleidoscope of different regions with different histories, many of which have taken their turn to be at the forefront of previous eras of independence; but the period since 1991 is the first time all have co-existed together in an independent state (Plokhy, 2015). Modern Ukraine was established more by Soviet power than by Ukrainian nationalism, both in terms of its borders and the institutional and cultural legacies that have shaped the era since 1991. Ukrainians themselves often talked of 'project Ukraine' after 1991 – a new state and in many ways a new nation, unsure whether its many internal differences were a strength or a weakness.

This chapter is in four main parts. First is an introduction, which segues with an examination of underlying regional and linguistic distinctions within Ukraine. Special attention is paid to the position of the Crimea and the Donbas region before war broke out in 2014. Second is an examination of the political system, including both formal arrangements of the constitution and the 'informal politics' that lies beneath. The third section describes the tension between a corrupt and predatory state and a civil society that has grown in strength since 1991, resulting in the 'Orange Revolution' in 2004 and the 'Revolution of Dignity' in 2014. The fourth section looks at Russia's subsequent annexation of Crimea and the causes and consequences of the war in the east.

Introduction

Most analyses that came out after independence in 1991 placed Ukraine within a conventional transition paradigm. Although Motyl (1993, 1997) stressed how difficult transforming totalitarianism would be, and how building an effective state would have to come first, as the pre-existing

Ukrainian Soviet Socialist Republic was more of a cartographical than an administrative reality. Others talked of Ukraine's exceptional problems facing three, or even four, simultaneous transitions: building a new state, a democracy, a functioning economy, and a new sense of national identity (Kuzio, 2001).

It also became commonplace to argue that Ukraine had achieved independence without a revolution. The opposition movement to communist rule in Ukraine during the Gorbachev era was not strong enough to win power on its own or to push for radical change. The main group, Rukh, could only win a quarter of the vote in the areas of west Ukraine that had once been under Habsburg rule and in areas with large concentrations of Ukrainian-speaking elites, including the capital Kyiv. Moreover, the movement was split on whether or not to cooperate with former communists so long as they backed independence. Those in favour accepted a 'Grand Bargain' in 1991 – former communist elites were in charge of the transition, and shaped it to their benefit (D'Anieri, 2007b, chapter four). There was no formal 'round table' process to encourage proper compromise.

By the late 1990s the idea of Ukraine's 'transition' was exposed as a teleological fallacy. Hale (2015) argued that post-Soviet states like Ukraine were characterised by rigidity more than by change, and were stuck in cycles of 'patronal politics'. Patronal networks were so deeply embedded that local regimes remained stuck in hybridity, 'alternately moving toward or away from democracy and autocracy while never quite seeming to make a decisive leap to one or the other' (Hale, 2015, p. 5). Revolution or democratic breakthrough is therefore not what it seems. 'The moving parts of highly patronalistic politics . . . arrange and rearrange themselves in regular, even predictable ways that might on the surface look like a regime "change" but that in reality reflect a stable core of informal institutions and operating principles' (Hale, 2015, p. 15).

Another model was Way's (2004) idea of 'pluralism by default', rather than by successful transition. D'Anieri (2007a, 2011) argued in a similar fashion that Ukraine's structural constraints made a profound shift in *either* direction unlikely, either a democratic breakthrough or an authoritarian consolidation – at least until Viktor Yanukovych was president from 2010 to 2014.

The regional question

Regional divisions were a key part of this 'pluralism by default' picture, promoting both balance and gridlock (Barrington and Herron, 2004; Sasse, 2010). Birch (2000, p. 1017) and others have argued that regional differences are a factor in themselves, more salient than other constituent factors like language: 'careful analyses of individual-level data reveal that even when socio-demographic attributes are controlled for, region still exerts an independent influence'. Moreover, Birch argued, the difference between regions is not purely economic, but is mainly an accumulated political culture effect, due to the differing historical experiences of the different regions.

A second key issue is the depth and severity of regional divides, especially when the very existence of the current Ukrainian state came under threat in 2014. However, it has always been misleading to depict Ukraine as sharply and evenly polarised, and therefore split down the middle, as many were tempted to argue in 2014. Part of the legacy effect of so many different regional histories was that identities and politics in particular regions were hybrid and/or fluid (Pirie, 1996). This was especially true of the regions between the 'poles' of Lviv and Donetsk (Rodgers, 2008; Zhurzhenko, 2010). If Rukh represented a quarter of the population in 1990–1991, then the other three quarters were not solidly against Rukh's nationalist and pro-Ukrainian policies, but were made up of a mixture of neo-Soviet, Russian-speaking, and dual-identity populations, both Russian-Ukrainian and Ukrainian-regional (Wilson, 2002).

Both high politics and identity politics remained fractured in the 1990s. The 2000s saw some consolidation of national identity and the rise of a new post-Rukh reform movement after the Gongadze scandal. In eastern and southern Ukraine, however, the pragmatic patronalism of President Kuchma (1994–2005) was replaced by the more ideological Party of Regions. Both sides deliberately polarised elections around identity issues from 2004 to 2012, as neither really wanted to fight on issues of corruption and state capture. Mutual distrust and negative stereotyping between the regions, and between the regions and Kyiv, would perhaps have been better contained by formal power-sharing mechanisms, rather than the uncertain informal rules of balance in Ukrainian politics, which were always perceived to be at risk when power threatened to change hands in Kyiv. Internal identity politics was also interconnected with foreign policy preferences, and was in part defined by them (Gentile, 2015). Regional polarisation within Ukraine was exacerbated by foreign policy battles, rather than the other way around.

On the other hand, public opinion remained fairly stable in 2013 and has shown extensive support for statehood, despite these internal divisions. Interestingly, the main factors shifting sentiment were not internal identity issues, but rather were either economic or external. Support for independence decreased during times of economic crisis, particularly in the early 1990s and in 1998–1999, but rose when Russia (not Ukraine) was in conflict with its neighbours, most notably in 1994 (the beginning of the first Chechen war) and 2008 (the war in Georgia). Overall, apart from the dip in the early 1990s, support for Ukrainian independence remained remarkably stable at around three quarters of the population (Khmel'ko, 2011; 'Issledovanie', 2011).

Two surveys by Kulyk (2015), in 2012 and 2014, go further and show a gradual shift towards a more solid national identity. Those identifying primarily with the nation rose from 51 per cent to 61 per cent, the number identifying primarily with their region remained steady at 9 per cent, while parochial (village or city) identities declined from 28 per cent to 21 per cent.

The language question

Ukraine has had constant disputes about language, even before independence in 1991; the first attempt to solve the problem was a 'Law on Languages' passed in the Communist era in 1989. The Ukrainosphere is still small (Olszański, 2012), given that Ukrainian is the state language. The share of Ukrainian in mass media and popular culture is much less than the percentage of ethnic Ukrainians at the last census in 2001, which was 77.8 per cent, or those who gave Ukrainian as their 'mother tongue', which was 67.5 per cent. In terms of day-to-day use, many more ethnic Ukrainians are de facto Russophone or use the hybrid known as *surzhyk*; the share of regular users of Russian and Ukrainian is more or less even, but the use of Russian is slanted towards urban areas and groups with more education.

When Russian speakers have complained about 'Ukrainisation', it has been about threats to exclusively Russian mono-lingualism in urban areas of the east and south. This dates from the requirement in the 1996 constitution, strengthened by a 2000 Constitutional Court ruling, requiring the use of Ukrainian 'in all spheres of social life [*suspil'noho zhyttia* – interpreted to mean official state communications] on all the territory of Ukraine'. There has also been a gradual administrative increase in the number of schoolchildren with Ukrainian as 'their primary language of instruction . . . to 82 percent by 2011' (Arel, 2014). The 2012 law 'On the Principles of State Language Policy' adopted under Yanukovych was controversial, not because Russian needed protection to survive or thrive, but rather because it threatened to allow Russian speakers to get around the bureaucratic push towards supporting Ukrainian.

Language has been politicised, both directly and as a proxy for broader identity politics, in all elections since 1994. However, the language issue always faded in importance between elections, because politicians ignored their promises and civic activism did not really sustain the issue. Since 2014, Ukraine is no longer divided into two camps, both eager to exploit the issue; eastern and southern Ukraine first shrank with the loss of Crimea and half the Donbas and then was transformed by the war. The annexation of Crimea and the war with Russian-backed forces has increased the salience of the political culture divide between all Ukrainians and Putin's Kremlin, rather than ethnic or linguistic divides. In a 2011 Pew survey, 84 per cent of Ukrainians held a favourable view of Russia; that dropped to 35 per cent in 2014 following the Crimean events – and to only 21 per cent by May 2015 (Toal and O'Loughlin, 2015; 'Ukraine: Russian Influence Unwelcome', 2014)

Crimea and the Donbas before 2014

Academic debate had long looked at the special problems of Crimea and the Donbas before the eruption of protests and military conflict in 2014. In the early years of independence, the Donbas was regarded as having both the most 'Soviet' identity of any region in Ukraine and strong social identities (by class and age). This Soviet identity was then gradually replaced, not by overt Russian nationalism, but by a strong regional identity, which was compatible with broader Ukrainian or Russian identities, so long as the Donbas had autonomy (Kuromiya, 2008, 2015). The number citing a regional identity in the Donbas was 69.5 per cent in 2004 (Hrytsak, 2007, p. 50).

Crimea remained a special case, although even here there was some effort to promote a regional identity of the 'Crimean people'. According to the local academic Mal'gin (2000),

> irredentism was never the dominant mentality of the Russian-speaking majority in the peninsula . . . the idea of recreating the Crimean autonomy was based primarily on the need to distance itself from Moscow and establish local control over the use of resources of the Crimea and its environment . . . In this respect, Crimean autonomism was very reminiscent of regionalism in Siberia and the Urals, with their views on the value of a small regional homeland.

This idea of Crimea as a local 'small homeland', however, was also founded on multiple supposed external threats, an amalgam of opposition to 'Ukrainianism as a myth', 'Euro-Atlanticism as a geopolitical construct', 'the myth of Crimean Tatar indigenousness', and Crimeans' own apathy (Filatov, 2011), as well as hostility to Moscow, Kyiv, and eventually the Donbas (see below) as external rulers.

Patronal or clan politics cut both ways in both Crimea and the Donbas: it reconciled local populations to Ukraine so long as 'our guys' were in charge, but it made local politics very volatile whenever a change of power looked possible at a national level. Opinion on the question of 'separation' from Ukraine was thus often volatile. 'Autonomy' was valued as much as 'union' (with Russia), so the exact wording of opinion polls could yield different responses. In 2012, 40 per cent in Crimea preferred 'autonomy within Ukraine' whereas 38 per cent backed 'autonomy within Russia' ('Vse men'she Krymchan khotiat videt' poluostrov v sostave Rossii', 2012).

Formal politics

Ukraine was the last post-Soviet state to adopt a new constitution, in 1996. Before then arrangements were confusing and ad hoc. After 1996, the new system was technically 'semi-presidential', with a dual executive headed by both a president and a prime minister, but the prime minister was largely dependent on the president. Parliament could only ratify the president's choice of prime minister, and the president's decrees had similar authority to normal legislation, although the president had only limited dissolution powers (Protsyk, 2003). The separation of powers between the three branches of state was imperfect: the president appointed the all-powerful chief prosecutor, a hangover from the 'people's justice' of the Soviet era; the highest court, the Constitutional Court, was not independent but subject to 'balanced control', which in fact meant gridlock – a third of its eighteen members were appointed by parliament, a third by the president, and a third by a Congress of Judges (which gave the president an additional avenue of influence). The state was unitary, with the exception of Crimea's federal status. However, the power of Crimea's government was again checked by veto powers held by the president in Kyiv.

Informal power also clustered around the president (see below). The system was therefore de facto presidential (D'Anieri, 2007b). It almost tipped towards super-presidentialism in 2000, when second president Leonid Kuchma organised a controversial referendum to aggrandise presidential power. His attempts were derailed by the Gongadze scandal.

One of the few achievements of the Orange Revolution in 2004 was that a coalition of forces agreed to change the constitution to give parliament more power – but their different aims meant a largely botched reform process. 'Orange' forces wanted a 'more European' system. The old guard and the oligarchs (see below) thought they were well-entrenched in parliament and this would protect them against radical change.

The new constitution first sought to strengthen the party system. All 450 MPs would now be elected by proportional representation (PR) on national lists. An 'imperative mandate' was introduced to stop 'political tourism': MPs had to stay in the parties that they were elected to represent or be expelled. A formal 'majority' would be created from party groups in any new parliament, and the prime minister would only be answerable to that majority. Parliament would sit for five years.

The new system began with two 'false starts'. The changes came into force in 2006, by which time the original 'Orange' government had collapsed. The 2006 elections then produced deadlock and eventual power-sharing with Yushchenko's 2004 opponent, Viktor Yanukovych, as prime minister, which ended in further confrontation and new elections in 2007. This time the system worked better, and Yuliya Tymoshenko was made prime minister until 2012.

But this more balanced version of the constitution never worked as well as its supporters had hoped – partly because the changes were prepared in haste, and partly because they institutionalised competition and overlapping competences between the president and prime minister. Yushchenko, Tymoshenko, and Yanukovych were constantly at odds, or plotting against each other in turn, from 2004 to 2010.

There was therefore less resistance to Yanukovych's centralisation of power after he won the 2010 election, with the presidency taking over the other branches of government. Tymoshenko was still prime minister under the terms of the 2004 constitution, but was removed after accusations of bribery and pressure on MPs' business interests, and replaced by a Party of Regions' loyalist, Mykola Azarov. Next was a legal reform in the summer of 2010 to establish complete executive control over the judiciary. Two new courts were created, the Higher Civil Court and High Criminal Court, to bypass those that still had some semblance of independence. Other courts were purged. The High Council of Justice and High Qualifying Commission were given vast new powers over judicial appointments, salaries, promotions, and dismissals – all under the executive branch.

The weakened Constitutional Court restored the 1996 constitution in October 2010, but this only capped the process of centralising control. But Yanukovych did much more than restore the status quo that had existed before the Orange Revolution. Kuchma had used informal politics to manipulate Ukrainian democracy, while Yanukovych progressively dismantled it. Kuchma balanced the oligarchy (see below); Yanukovych tried to lead it and was much more corrupt (Wilson, 2014a). The Yanukovych era was also exceptional for having such a strong, even hegemonic and authoritarian, ruling party in the Party of Regions (Kuzio, 2015), used to channel control over all the branches of state authority. The newly supine courts were used for a string of 'political prosecutions' against opponents in 2011, including Tymoshenko, who was sentenced to seven years in jail and fined $188 million. Changes made for the 2012 legislative elections gave Yanukovych even more control: the 'imperative mandate' was ignored, and half of MPs were now elected from territorial constituencies where vote-buying and voter intimidation was easier.

The old 'Orange' constitution was restored after Yanukovych's flight in February 2014, but was still not amended properly. Once again, changes were made in haste, and constitutional reform was no longer a priority after the annexation of Crimea and the outbreak of war in east Ukraine. Early elections for both president and parliament in May and October 2014, with Crimea and half of the Donbas unable to vote and public opinion radicalised, led to self-declared 'reformists' controlling the presidency, parliament, and government, but conflicts continued beneath the surface. The 2004 constitution still seemed to institutionalise conflict, with the government appointed in December 2014 collapsing in February 2016.

Informal politics

Another reason why constitutional engineering never had the desired effect was that broader problems were channelled through the political and constitutional system. 'Informal politics' trumped formal politics. Moreover, the practices that maintain what locals call '*sistema*' (Ledeneva, 2013) – patronal networks, and the exchange of money and favour across nominal barriers of politics, media, and business – have acquired the ability to reproduce themselves.

One such practice was described by Wilson (2005) as 'virtual politics': public politics in Ukraine, and other post-Soviet states, had become corrupted by what locals called 'political technology'. In such a world, constitutions and public policy statements did not really matter (Hale, 2011). Many parties were entirely fake; most established parties were to some degree fronts for business interests. A whole universe of dirty tricks existed around them, from the abuse of 'administrative resources' to fix elections on the ground to the use of agents and agents provocateurs to manipulate other political parties. 'Political technology' was therefore the key to what Levitsky and Way (2010) called 'competitive authoritarian' regimes, and their need to slant apparently open competition for power in incumbents' favour.

Neither the Orange Revolution nor the Euromaidan led to the disappearance of 'political technology'. The key problem was that patronal networks and oligarchs continued to control mainstream television, from which most Ukrainian citizens took their political cues, and sold their proxies and 'project' parties and politicians on these channels. In March 2016 the main oligarch-controlled television channels had a market share of 75 per cent ('Top channels', 2016).

Ukraine is also one of the most oligarchic post-Soviet states – as of 2013 the richest fifty individuals controlled almost half of GDP (Wilson, 2013). Ukrainian politics was first exposed as a naked fight between equally corrupt clans when President Kuchma clashed with his former Prime Minister Pavlo Lazarenko in 1998–1999 (Lazarenko was accused of embezzling $200 million and received a nine-year prison sentence after fleeing to the US in 2006). This was quickly followed by the Gongadze scandal in 2000–2001 (Darden, 2001), the death of the editor of Ukraine's first investigative internet site 'Ukrainian Truth' (*Ukraïns'ka pravda*), and President Kuchma's apparent complicity in the scandal revealed by recordings covertly made in his office in 1999–2000.

The Ukrainian oligarchy has proven extremely adept at maintaining its influence, despite Ukraine having had five presidents since 1991 to potentially disrupt their power (Matuszak, 2012). The state is weaker than in Russia, and there has never been any local equivalent of the imprisonment of Russia's richest man Mikhail Khodorkovskii in 2003, to rein in oligarchic influence. Façade politics and 'political technology' gives the Ukrainian oligarchs perfect methods for exercising influence behind the scenes. Oligarchic rent-seeking remains the main factor behind Ukraine's corrupt politics and economic underperformance (Wilson, 2013).

The Orange Revolution

Oligarchy, corruption, and informal practice do not always go unchallenged. Ukraine has had at least two would-be 'revolutions', in 2004 and 2014. The first, the 'Orange Revolution' in 2004, was sparked by protests against a fraudulent election, as Yanukovych manoeuvred to succeed Kuchma as president. Hundreds of thousands occupied the Maidan (the main square) in central Kyiv for seventeen days (Wilson, 2005; McFaul and Åslund, 2006). The protests were framed against the Kuchma era and the hope for a more democratic future; but Beissinger has cited survey evidence to depict the Orange protestors as just as partisan as their opponents: they 'were highly diverse in their preferences on most of the major issues of the day, and most were weakly committed to the values of the revolution's democratic master narratives' (2013, p. 16). The protests were ultimately also focused on elite outcomes; the crowds wanted to see Viktor Yushchenko elected president, and then they went home.

Bunce and Wolchik (2011) attributed the success of the protests to their innovative tactics, especially the carnivalesque use of telegenic images, and 'strategic non-violence' tactics taken from Gene Sharp (Wilson, 2008) to exploit the weak spots of 'competitive authoritarian' regimes (Mitchell, 2012). D'Anieri (2006) and Levitsky and Way (2006), on the other hand, stressed elite weaknesses, namely the quick disappearance of elite unity behind Yanukovych and in the security forces and the reluctance to use repression. The growth of civil society was a largely premature factor in 2004 (Lutsevych, 2013); non-governmental organisations (NGOs) and independent media really came into their own during and after the Euromaidan (Way, 2014).

Five years of 'Orange' government produced many important changes, including a new constitution, freer and fairer elections, a more pluralistic media free from state censorship (though not from oligarchs' control), and a change in attitudes on the key historical issue of the Holodomor (the famine of the 1930s). But there was no reprise of the campaign to clean up the economy when Yushchenko was prime minister in 1999–2001; the 'oligarchy' remained untouched, and there was huge disappointment relative to expectations. Continuing corruption led to the phenomena of 'Ukraine fatigue' abroad and 'Orange fatigue' at home. Yanukovych was able to exploit both to consolidate power in 2010–2013 – the most damning evidence of the limited gains of the 'Orange' years (O'Brien, 2010).

Foreign policy: between informal Russia and the bureaucratic West

Russia reacted to the Orange Revolution by building up its 'soft power' abroad (Popescu and Wilson, 2009; Horvath, 2012; Lutsevych, 2016). New NGO networks and media projects in states like Ukraine added to existing informal business networks to bind together Russian and Ukrainian patronalism. Although Yushchenko briefly attempted to exclude the GRU from Crimea, he did little to combat the build-up of these networks. When Yanukovych signed an agreement with Russia on extending the lease of the Black Sea Fleet in April 2010, secret protocols gave a green light to Russian infiltration of all the Ukrainian 'force' ministries – defence, interior, and security services (Kuzio, 2012).

Russia began working hard at exporting 'alternative identities' to Ukraine (Zhurzhenko, 2014), aiding the rise of separatist sentiments in both Crimea and the Donbas (Katchanovski, 2014), but these were still minority sentiments. According to opinion polls in early 2014, only 41 per cent backed union with Russia in Crimea ('How relations between Ukraine and Russia should look', 2014), and only 27.5 per cent in Donetsk and 30.3 per cent in Luhansk (with only 11.9 per cent and 13.2 per cent 'definitely' preferring union) ('Mneniia i vzgliady', 2014).

Russia concentrated on exploiting Ukraine's informal politics. This meant it was playing on familiar turf. However, it was the nature of informal politics that local clients were not always reliable, as they had their own networks. European Union (EU) involvement, on the other hand, was based on Ukraine adopting EU norms, rules and policy instruments, without too much analysis of the realities of patronal and informal politics; and the US version of conditionality put more emphasis up front on democracy and human rights (McFaul, 2007). Some critics have accused both Washington and Brussels of pushing the idea of 'broader Europe' at the expense of a 'greater Europe' including Russia, and using Ukraine as a geopolitical wedge to push back Russia (Sakwa, 2015b). Russia was supposedly moved to intervene by its perceived sense of threat from the West in general and NATO in particular (Mearsheimer, 2014; Sakwa, 2015a), though some of the same authors have also minimised the level of Russian involvement. The particular threat to the Russian Black Sea base in Crimea is perhaps a more plausible explanation for intervention (Treisman, 2016).

The EU missed an opportunity to upgrade relations to a more strategic level just after the 2004 Orange Revolution. Ukraine was offered a series of technocratic policies, including bilateral negotiations on an Association Agreement with a Deep and Comprehensive Free Trade Agreement (DCFTA) begun in 2007 and finished in 2012, and the Eastern Neighbourhood Policy launched in 2009 (Wolczuk and Dragneva-Lewers, 2015). However, by 2012 the deterioration of democracy under Yanukovych, symbolised by the imprisonment of Tymoshenko, meant the Association Agreement was put on hold, even before Yanukovych dramatically halted negotiations to unfreeze it in November 2013.

Russia, on the other hand, began to ramp up plans for its rival Eurasian Economic Union (EEU) after Putin was re-elected as Russian president in 2012. The conflict between the EU and EEU was often presented as mainly a dispute between rival trade blocs, but it was also about informal politics, with the Yanukovych elite trying to preserve local corrupt practices.

The conflict was also about rival sovereignty projects. The key weakness of the EU's Eastern Partnership policy was that it did not offer the pooled sovereignty security benefits enjoyed by EU member states, while exposing Ukraine to Russian hostility; not because of much-heralded yet often minimal direct trade impacts, but because of the potential losses to informal Russian business in Ukraine. The key weakness of the EEU, on the other hand, was that it was dominated by Russia and by Russia's informal politics. It could not be a version of the EU, because without any local rule of law, it implied a massive loss of sovereignty to any joiners.

The key weakness of the Yanukovych government was that it tried to do two things at once: it was linked to Russian interests by informal politics, but it also continued the long Ukrainian tradition of using foreign policy as a balancing strategy to build up weak sovereignty (Gnedina, 2015). The final contradiction was that Yanukovych's opponents looked on the EU Agreement instrumentally, as a way of pushing back against Yanukovych's domestic project. The political crisis that erupted in 2013 combined all these tensions, and it was all the more powerful because it was not just about trade.

The Revolution of Dignity

Few predicted, however, the protests that became known as the 'Revolution of Dignity' in 2013–2014 (for an exception, see Motyl, 2013), although several commentators had identified underlying stresses that threatened the regime of President Yanukovych in the long run (Riabchuk, 2012).

The protests were sparked by Yanukovych rejecting the deal with the EU and were in the same (core) place as the 2004 'Maidan'; but they lasted for three months and went through many different phases. At their outset, many interpreters and protest leaders still talked and thought within the old paradigm of non-violent and self-limiting 'revolution' (Ackerman et al., 2014); but by the time of the dénouement in February 2014, they had clearly evolved into something else, even if it was not clear what this was, even two years later. Applebaum (2014) claimed in January 2014 that 'the "color revolution" model is dead': what were 'competitive authoritarian' regimes in the 2000s were now more firmly entrenched and defended, and would take different tactics to dislodge.

The nature of the protests also changed radically over three months – ironically because they initially seemed unlikely to succeed against the regime, and there was no obvious or agreed exit strategy. Onuch and Sasse (2016) stress 'the fluid and contingent nature of cleavages commonly portrayed as fixed and politically salient'. 'Neither the regime nor the party-based political opposition and activists were able to fully comprehend or manage this inherent diversity. Their misjudgements, in turn, created opportunities for the rise of radical voices and violent repertoires'.

The role of Ukrainian nationalists in the protests and eventual uprising has been much discussed, and that of the far right in particular (Shekhovtsov, 2015). In February 2014 the Euromaidan Self-Defence forces had thirty-nine *sotnia* (literally 'hundreds', approximately translated to a 'military company') of variable size, which meant a maximum of about 12,000 individuals in total. The main far-right group Right Sector was the twenty-third *sotnia*, with around 300 estimated members in January. The Freedom Party (*Svoboda*) was the second *sotnia*, with about 150 members (Likachev, 2014). Three hundred or even 450 activists can make a difference, but Right Sector was neither a Leninist vanguard party leading an assault on power, nor a Trotskyist group using entryism to leverage influence over larger organisations. In fact, it was the other way around. Criminal groups muscled their way in, and oligarchs bought influence.

There are distasteful and dangerous nationalists in Ukraine, like everywhere else; but most are of a new vintage (Olszański, 2015). Ukraine's old nationalists were part of the old politics; mainly for show, often as a cover for business interests, and nearly always infiltrated, controlled, and neutered by the local security services. Their poor performance in the 2014 elections was widely noticed, but the trauma of war has produced some increase in support since then – which is the opposite causation to Russia claiming Ukrainian fascism as *casus belli*.

Events in Crimea and the East

Russia's annexation of Crimea in spring 2014 was a surprise to most, because it was designed to succeed by surprise; but Crimea had long been seen as a flashpoint, particularly after the war in Georgia in 2008 (Popescu and Wilson, 2009). The annexation itself could hardly be described as anything other than a coup (Berezovets, 2015; Temirgaliev, 2016). Although there was clearly some support for the pro-Russian position (see above), the key mechanics of the takeover were armed force and disregard for constitutional principle, rather than popular mobilisation. There were big crowds in Sevastopol in the days before the coup, many of whom were connected to the Russian fleet, but in the local capital Simferopol pro-Russian and anti-Maidan forces were always outnumbered by the Crimean Tatars, plus a smattering of pro-Maidan forces including local football 'ultras' (Temirgaliev, 2016). The cover story of Sevastopol troops and Russian special forces being local 'self-defence forces' did not last long ('Putin's narrative on Crimea takes an evolutionary leap', 2015). All of the key decisions were taken at gunpoint, by a possibly inquorate local assembly (Berezovets, 2015).

The causes of the conflict in the Donbas are, however, still disputed, particularly the question of whether the events had mainly internal or external causes (for an overview see Wilson, 2016b). Analysts such as Kudelia (2014) and Giuliano (2015) have focused primarily on internal Ukrainian factors, namely alienation from Kyiv and the politics of the Maidan. Zhukov (2016) argues for the predominance of economic motives, arguing that anti-Kyiv resistance was strongest in areas dominated by the industries (machine-building) most at risk from any disruption of trade with Russia – and from Russian sanctions. Arel and Driscoll (2015) emphasise 'regime collapse' in Kyiv.

However, Wilson (2016b) argued that although a baseline of discontent clearly existed, the key triggers towards conflict escalation were all external, that is Russian. Anti-Kyiv protests were not surprising in 2014, but Ukrainian political life since 1991 had been shaken but not fundamentally altered by the Euromaidan. Without Russian involvement, a civil conflict would not have escalated into a full-blown war (Mitrokhin, 2015; Sutyagin, 2015).

Russia's measures included covert GRU support for initial activists and demonstrations, the 'bussing in' of extra numbers to reinforce those demonstrations from across the border, the stationing of Russian troops on the border to destabilise the situation, the supply of men and materials, and increasingly direct military involvement in the summer of 2014, *before* the decisive battle at Ilovaisk in August ('Russia's Path to War', 2015).

Regional elites also made a massive difference. In Kharkiv, Kyiv did a deal with corrupt local leaders, allowing them to stay in power so long as they did not engage with separatists. Dnipropetrovsk elites reinvented themselves as guardians of the new Ukraine. But in the Donbas both the former Yanukovych elite and key remaining local oligarchs either actively facilitated the protests or played both sides (Portnov, 2016). That said, further research is very much needed in all of these areas.

After 2014

The Euromaidan, the fall of Yanukovych, the annexation of Crimea, and the war in the east have finally provided stimuli to invigorate Ukraine's hitherto sclerotic political system. Ukraine has become both more nationalist (Olszański, 2015) and more relaxed about internal pluralism (Hrytsak, 2015). Ukraine may finally have the key civic ideas (protest, martyrs, and a successful defensive war) that a civic identity needs; and previously blurred identities in the east and south may be consolidating (Zhurzhenko, 2014; Fomina, 2014; Riabchuk, 2015).

On the other hand, as after the Orange Revolution, it has proven extremely difficult to reform Ukraine's dysfunctional institutions and corrupt informal culture (Wilson, 2016a). Important reforms were made under duress in 2014, including fiscal retrenchment, some military reform, and steps towards energy independence. It was hoped that the relative ceasefire achieved in the east in September 2015 would allow renewed focus on domestic reform, but it did the opposite. Political stasis and corruption returned at the highest levels. Presidential and parliamentary elections in 2014, and local elections in 2015, failed to 'reboot' the political system, which remained rife with informal politics, political technology, and the interpenetration of money and media.

Conclusions

A quarter of a century after the fall of communism in East Central Europe in 1989 and the Soviet Union in 1991, the Ukrainian example showed that transforming 'post-communist' states and societies was even harder than the original attempt to move away from communism. The academic paradigms that dominated Ukrainian studies in the years immediately after 1991, particularly the focus on transition, were therefore long out of date. Work that was based on too much Russian mythology exaggerated problems of stasis by endorsing the idea of a fatally divided or even non-existent Ukraine. Studies that looked at Ukraine through the lens of the EU's European Neighbourhood Policy shared many of the same faults of that policy, namely a Brussels-centred teleology of voluntary approximation to EU norms and practices and an over-focus on elites. There were, however, many encouraging signs of democratisation from below, with the impressive growth of civil society.

The most promising areas for future academic study might therefore be the self-replicating nature of post-communism and the strength of the challenge from below. Analysts will also keep returning to the dramatic events of 2014, because so much was compressed into such a short time, and the seismic consequences are yet to fully unfold.

Bibliography

Ackerman, P., Bartkowski, M. and Duvall, J. (2014), 'Ukraine: A Non-Violent Victory', *Open Democracy*, 3 March, www.opendemocracy.net/civilresistance/peter-ackerman-maciej-bartkowski-jack-duvall/ukraine-nonviolent-victory

Applebaum, A. (2014), 'Ukraine Shows the "Color Revolution" Model Is Dead', *The Washington Post*, 25 January, www.washingtonpost.com/opinions/anne-applebaum-ukraine-shows-the-color-revolution-model-is-dead/2014/01/24/c77d3ab0-8524-11e3-8099-9181471f7aaf_story.html

Arel, D. (2014), 'Double Talk: Why Ukrainians Fight Over Language', *Foreign Affairs*, 18 March, www.foreignaffairs.com/articles/russian-federation/2014-03-18/double-talk

Arel, D. and Driscoll, J. (2015), 'The Civil War in Ukraine', draft paper in preparation; see the authors' presentation at, www.youtube.com/watch?v=BfQ9IgTNu-M

Barrington, L. and Herron, E. (2004), 'One Ukraine or Many? Regionalism in Ukraine and Its Political Consequences', *Nationalities Papers*, 32(1), pp. 53–86.

Beissinger, M. R. (2013), 'The Semblance of Democratic Revolution: Coalitions in Ukraine's Orange Revolution', *American Political Science Review*, 107(3), pp. 574–92.

Berezovets, T. (2015), *Anektsiya: ostriv Krim. Khroniky "hibrydnoï viiny"* [*Annexation: Island Crimea. Chronicle of "Hybrid War"*] (Kyiv: Bright Star).

Birch, S. (2000), 'Explaining the Regional Effect in Ukrainian Politics', *Europe-Asia Studies*, 52(6), pp. 1017–41.

Bunce, V. and Wolchik, S. (2011), *Defeating Authoritarian Leaders in Postcommunist Countries* (Cambridge: Cambridge University Press).

D'Anieri, P. (2006), 'Explaining the Success and Failure of Post-Communist Revolutions', *Communist and Post-Communist Studies*, 39(3), pp. 331–50.

D'Anieri, P. (2007a), 'Ethnic Tensions and State Strategies: Understanding the Survival of the Ukrainian State', *Journal of Communist Studies and Transition Politics*, 23(1), pp. 4–29.

D'Anieri, P. (2007b), *Understanding Ukrainian Politics: Power, Politics, and Institutional Design* (Armonk: M. E. Sharpe).

D'Anieri, P. (2011), 'Structural Constraints in Ukrainian Politics', *East European Politics and Societies*, 25(1), pp. 28–46.

Darden, K. (2001), 'Blackmail as a Tool of State Domination: Ukraine Under Kuchma', *East European Constitutional Review*, 10(2–3), pp. 67–71.

Filatov, A. (2011), 'Russkii Krym: vneshnie ugrozy i vnutrennie vyzovy. Krym poka izbegaet ukraintsva' [Russian Crimea: External Threats and Internal Challenges. Crimea Avoids Ukrainianism Until Now], *Russkie.org*, 18 November, www.russkie.org/index.php?module=fullitem&id=24007

Fomina, J. (2014), 'Language, Identity, Politics – The Myth of Two Ukraines', *Institute of Public Affairs/ Bertelsmann*, April, www.isp.org.pl/uploads/pdf/594958479.pdf

Gentile, M. (2015), 'West Oriented in the East-oriented Donbas: A Political Stratigraphy of Geopolitical Identity in Luhansk, Ukraine', *Post-Soviet Affairs*, 31(3), pp. 201–23.

Giuliano, E. (2015), 'The Social Bases of Support for Self-determination in East Ukraine', *Ethnopolitics*, 14(5), pp. 513–22.

Gnedina, E. (2015), 'Multi-Vector' Foreign Policies in Europe: Balancing, Bandwagoning or Bargaining?', *Europe-Asia Studies*, 67(7), pp. 1007–29.

Hale, H. E. (2011), 'Formal Constitutions in Informal Politics: Institutions and Democratization in Post-Soviet Eurasia', *World Politics*, 63(4), pp. 581–617.

Hale, H. E. (2015), *Patronal Politics: Eurasian Regime Dynamics in Comparative Perspective* (Cambridge: Cambridge University Press).

Horvath, R. (2012), *Putin's Preventive Counter-Revolution: Post-Soviet Authoritarianism and the Spectre of Velvet Revolution* (London: Routledge).

'How Relations Between Ukraine and Russia Should Look Like? Public Opinion Polls' Results' (2014), *KIIS*, 4 March, http://kiis.com.ua/?lang=eng&cat=reports&id=236&page=1

Hrytsak, Y. (2007), 'Istoriia dvokh mist: L'viv i Donets'k u porivnial'nii perspektyvi' [A History of Two Cities: L'viv and Donetsk in Comparative Perspective], in Hrytsak, Y., Portnov, A., and Susak, V. (eds.), 'L'viv-Donets'k: sotsial'ni identychnosti v suchasnii Ukraïni' [L'viv-Donets'k: Social Identities in Modern Ukraine], special issue of *Ukraïna Moderna*, 12(2), pp. 27–60.

Hrytsak, Y. (2015), 'Rethinking Ukraine', in Wilson, A. (ed.), *What Does Ukraine Think?* (London: ECFR); www.ecfr.eu/publications/summary/what_does_ukraine_think3026, pp. 34–44.

'Issledovanie: Chuvstvo zavisimosti v Ukraintsakh probuzhdayut Tuzla, Chechnya i Gruziya' [Research: A Sense of Independence in Ukrainians Is Awakened by Tuzla, Chechnya and Georgia] (2011), *Korrespondent*, 17 July, http://korrespondent.net/ukraine/politics/1240292-issledovanie-chuvstvo-nezavisimosti-v-ukraincah-probuzhdayut-tuzla-chechnya-i-gruziya

Katchanovski, I. (2014), 'East or West? Regional Political Divisions in Ukraine Since the "Orange Revolution" and the "Euromaidan"', Paper prepared for presentation at the Annual Meeting of the American Political Science Association, Washington, DC, 28–31 August 2014, http://papers.ssrn.com/sol3/Papers.cfm?abstract_id=2454203

Khmel'ko, V. E. (2011), 'Suverenitet yak zahal'no natsional'na tsinnist': sotsiolohichnyi aspekt' [Sovereignty as a General National Value: Sociological Aspect]; http://old.kiis.com.ua/pub/2011/sverenitet.pdf

Kudelia, S. (2014), 'Domestic Sources of the Donbas Insurgency', *PONARS Eurasia Policy Memo*, no. 351, September, www.ponarseurasia.org/memo/domestic-sources-donbas-insurgency

Kulyk, V. (2015), 'One Nation, Two Languages? National Identity and Language Policy in Post-Euromaidan Ukraine', *Ponars Eurasia Policy Memo*, no. 389, September, www.ponarseurasia.org/memo/one-nation-two-languages-national-identity-and-language-policy-post-euromaidan-ukraine

Kuromiya, H. (2008), 'The Donbas – The Last Frontier of Europe?', in Schmidtke, O. and Yekelchyk, S. (eds.), *Europe's Last Frontier? Belarus, Moldova, and Ukraine Between Russia and the European Union* (New York: Palgrave Macmillan), pp. 97–114.

Kuromiya, H. (2015), *Zrozumity Donbas* [*Understanding the Donbas*] (Kyiv: Dukh i Litera).

Kuzio, T. (2001), 'Transition in Post-Communist States: Triple or Quadruple?', *Politics*, 21(3), pp. 168–77.

Kuzio, T. (2012), 'Russianization of Ukrainian National Security Policy Under Viktor Yanukovych', *Journal of Slavic Military Studies*, 245(4), pp. 558–81.

Kuzio, T. (2015), 'Rise and Fall of the Party of Regions Political Machine', *Problems of Post-Communism*, 62(3), pp. 174–86.

Ledeneva, A. (2013), *Can Russia Modernise? Sistema, Power Networks and Informal Governance* (Cambridge: Cambridge University Press).

Levitsky, S. and Way, L. (2006), 'The Dynamics of Autocratic Coercion After the Cold War', *Communist and Post-Communist Studies*, 39(3), pp. 387–410.

Levitsky, S. and Way, L. (2010), *Competitive Authoritarianism: Hybrid Regimes After the Cold War* (Cambridge: Cambridge University Press).

Likachev, V. (2014), '"Pravyi sector" i drugie: natsional-radikaly i ukrainskii politicheskii krizis kontsa 2013 – nachala 2014 goda' ["Right Sector" and Others: National-Radicals in the Ukrainian Political Crisis of the End of 2013 – The Start of 2014], *Polit.ru*, 6 September, http://polit.ru/article/2014/09/06/radical_nationalism

Lutsevych, O. (2013), 'How to Finish a Revolution: Civil Society and Democracy in Georgia, Moldova and Ukraine', *RIIA Briefing Paper*, January, www.chathamhouse.org/publications/papers/view/188407

Lutsevych, O. (2016), 'Agents of the Russian World: Proxy Groups in the Contested Neighbourhood', *Chatham Hose Paper*, April, www.chathamhouse.org/publication/agents-russian-world-proxy-groups-contested-neighbourhood

Mal'gin, A. (2000), 'Novoe v samosoznanii etnicheskikh grupp Kryma' [New in the Self-knowledge of Ethnic Groups of Crimea], www.archipelag.ru/authors/malgin/?library=1172; first published in *Ostrov Krym*, no. 3.

Matuszak, S. (2012), 'The Oligarchic Democracy: The Influence of Business Groups on Ukrainian Politics', *OSW Studies*, no. 42, www.osw.waw.pl/sites/default/files/Prace_42_EN.pdf

McFaul, M. (2007), 'Ukraine Imports Democracy: External Influences on the Orange Revolution', *International Security*, 32(2), pp. 45–83.

McFaul, M. and Åslund, A. (eds.). (2006), *Revolution in Orange: The Origins of Ukraine's Democratic Breakthrough* (Washington, DC: Carnegie Endowment).

Mearsheimer, J. J. (2014), 'Why the Ukraine Crisis Is the West's Fault: The Liberal Delusions That Provoked Putin', *Foreign Affairs*, September–October, www.foreignaffairs.com/articles/russia-fsu/2014-08-18/why-ukraine-crisis-west-s-fault

Mitchell, L. A. (2012), *The Color Revolutions* (Philadelphia: University of Pennsylvania Press).

Mitrokhin, N. (2015), 'Infiltration, Instruction, Invasion: Russia's War in the Donbass', *Journal of Soviet and Post-Soviet Politics and Society*, 1(1), pp. 219–50.

'Mneniia i vzgliady zhitelei yugo-vostoka Ukrainy: aprel' 2014' [The Views and Opinions of Residents of the South-east of Ukraine: April 2014] (2014), *Zn.ua* (Dzerkalo tyzhnia) website, 18 April, http://zn.ua/UKRAINE/mneniya-i-vzglyady-zhiteley-yugo-vostoka-ukrainy-aprel-2014-143598_.html

Motyl, A. J. (1993), *Dilemmas of Independence: Ukraine After Totalitarianism* (New York: Council of Foreign Relations Press).

Motyl, A. J. (1997), 'Structural Constraints and Starting Points: The Logic of Systemic Change in Ukraine and Russia', *Comparative Politics*, 29(4), pp. 437–47.

Motyl, A. J. (2013), 'The Yanukovych Ruin and Its Aftermath', Parts 1 and 2, *World Affairs Journal Blog*, January, starting at www.worldaffairsjournal.org/blog/alexander-j-motyl/yanukovych-ruin-and-its-aftermath-part-1

O'Brien, T. (2010), 'Problems of Political Transition in Ukraine: Leadership Failure and Democratic Consolidation', *Contemporary Politics*, 16(4), pp. 335–67.

Olszański, T. A. (2012), 'The Language Issue in Ukraine: An Attempt at a New Perspective', *OSW Studies*, no. 40, Centre for Eastern Studies, www.osw.waw.pl/sites/default/files/prace_40_en.pdf

Olszański, T. A. (2015), 'Ukraine's Wartime Nationalism', *Centre for Eastern Studies*, Commentary no. 179, 28 August, www.osw.waw.pl/en/publikacje/osw-commentary/2015-08-19/ukraines-wartime-nationalism

Onuch, O. and Sasse, G. (2016), 'The Maidan in Movement: Diversity and the Cycles of Protest', *Europe-Asia Studies*, 68(3), pp. 556–87.

Pirie, P. (1996), 'National Identity and Politics in Southern and Eastern Ukraine', *Europe-Asia Studies*, 48(7), pp. 1079–104.

Plokhy, S. (2014), *The Last Empire: The Final Days of the Soviet Union* (New York: Basic Books).

Plokhy, S. (2015), *The Gates of Europe: A History of Ukraine* (London: Allen Lane).

Popescu, N. and Wilson, A. (2009), *The Limits of Enlargement-Lite: European and Russian Power in the Troubled Neighbourhood* (London: European Council on Foreign Relations), http://ecfr.eu/content/entry/ecfr_eastern_neighbourhood_wilson_popescu

Portnov, A. (2015), 'Post-Maidan Europe and the New Ukrainian Studies', *Slavic Review*, 74(4), pp. 723–31.

Portnov, A. (2016), 'How "Eastern Ukraine" Was Lost', *Open Democracy*, 14 January, www.opendemocracy.net/od-russia/andrii-portnov/how-eastern-ukraine-was-lost

Protsyk, I. (2003), 'Troubled Semi-presidentialism: Stability of the Constitutional System and Cabinet in Ukraine', *Europe-Asia Studies*, 55(7), pp. 1077–95.

'Putin's Narrative on Crimea Takes an Evolutionary Leap' (2015), *Kyiv Post*, 11 March, www.kyivpost.com/article/content/kyiv-post-plus/putins-narrative-on-crimea-annexation-takes-an-evolutionary-leap-383183.html

Riabchuk, M. (2012), *Gleichschaltung: Authoritarian Consolidation in Ukraine 2010–2012* (Kiev: KIS).

Riabchuk, M. (2015), 'The "Two Ukraines" Reconsidered: The End of Ukrainian Ambivalence?', *Studies in Ethnicity and Nationalism*, 15(1), pp. 138–56.

Rodgers, P. (2008), *Nation, Region and History in Post-Communist Transitions: Identity Politics in Ukraine, 1991–2006* (Stuttgart: Ibidem-Verlag).

'Russia's Path to War' (2015), *Bellingcat*, 21 September, www.bellingcat.com/wp-content/uploads/2015/09/russia_s_path_s__to_war.pdf

Sakwa, R. (2015a), *Frontline Ukraine: Crisis in the Borderlands* (London: I. B. Tauris).

Sakwa, R. (2015b), 'The Death of Europe? Continental Fates After Ukraine', *International Affairs*, 91(3), pp. 553–79.

Sasse, G. (2010), 'The Role of Regionalism', *Journal of Democracy*, 21(3), pp. 99–106.

Shekhovtsov, A. (2015), 'The Spectre of Ukrainian "Fascism": Information Wars, Political Manipulation, and Reality', in Wilson, A. (ed.), *What Does Ukraine Think?* (London: ECFR); www.ecfr.eu/publications/summary/what_does_ukraine_think3026, pp. 80–88.

Sutyagin, I. (2015), 'Russian Troops in Ukraine', *Royal United Services Institute Briefing Paper*, March, https://rusi.org/sites/default/files/201503_bp_russian_forces_in_ukraine.pdf

Temirgaliev, R. (2016), Interviewed by Petr Kozlov, 'Rustam Temirgaliev o razvitii sobytii, privedshikh k referendumu v Krymu' [Rustam Temirgaliev on the Development of Events Leading to the Referendum in Crimea], *Vedomosti*, 16 March, www.vedomosti.ru/politics/characters/2015/03/16/esli-eto-imelo-opredelennuyu-rezhissuru-rezhisseru-nuzhno-postavit-pyat-s-plyusom

Toal, G. and O'Loughlin, J. (2015), 'How Popular Are Putin and Obama in Crimea and Eastern Ukraine?', *Washington Post, Monkey Cage*, 22 January, www.washingtonpost.com/blogs/monkey-cage/wp/2015/01/22/how-popular-are-putin-and-obama-in-crimea-and-eastern-ukraine/

'Top channels' (2016), http://tampanel.com.ua/en/rubrics/canals/

Treisman, D. (2016), 'Why Putin Took Crimea: The Gambler in the Kremlin', *Foreign Affairs*, May–June.

'Ukraine: Russian Influence Unwelcome' (2014), *Pew*, 8 May, www.pewglobal.org/2014/05/08/chapter-2-ukraine-russian-influence-unwelcome/

'Vse men'she Krymchan khotiat videt' poluostrov v sostave Rossii' [Fewer Crimeans Want to See the Peninsula as Part of Russia] (2012), *Dzerkalotyzhnia*, 12 September, http://zn.ua/POLITICS/vse_menshe_krymchan_hotyat_videt_poluostrov_v_sostave_rossii.html

Way, L. (2004), 'The Sources and Dynamics of Competitive Authoritarianism in Ukraine', *Journal of Communist Studies and Transition Politics*, 20(1), pp. 143–61.

Way, L. (2014), 'Civil Society and Democratization', in 'The Maidan and Beyond', *Journal of Democracy*, 25(3), pp. 35–44.

Wilson, A. (2002), 'Elements of a Theory of Ukrainian Ethno-national Identities', *Nations and Nationalism*, 8(1), pp. 31–54.

Wilson, A. (2005), *Virtual Politics: Faking Democracy in the Post-Soviet World* (London and New Haven: Yale University Press).

Wilson, A. (2008), 'Ukraine's "Orange Revolution" of 2004: The Paradoxes of Negotiation', in Timothy Garton Ash and Andrew Roberts (eds.), *Civil Resistance and Power Politics: The Experience of Non-Violent Action From Gandhi to the Present* (Oxford: Oxford University Press), pp. 335–353.

Wilson, A. (2013), 'Ukraine', in Isobel Coleman, I. and Lawson-Remer, T. (eds.), *Pathways to Freedom: Political and Economic Lessons From Democratic Transitions* (New York: Council on Foreign Relations), pp. 181–200.

Wilson, A. (2014a) 'Ukraine: The New Sick Country of Europe', in Mungiu-Pippidi, A. (ed.), *The Anticorruption Frontline: The Anticorruption Report vol. 2* (Germany: Barbara Budrich), pp. 16–24.

Wilson, A. (2014b), *Ukraine Crisis: What It Means for the West* (London and New Haven: Yale University Press).

Wilson, A. (2016a), 'Survival of the Richest: How Oligarchs Block Reform in Ukraine', *ECFR*, 14 April, www.ecfr.eu/publications/summary/survival_of_the_richest_how_oligarchs_block_reform_in_ukraine6091

Wilson, A. (2016b), 'The Donbas in 2014: Explaining Civil Conflict Perhaps, But Not Civil War', *Europe-Asia Studies*, 68(4), pp. 631–52.

Wolczuk, K. and Dragneva-Lewers, R. (2015), *Ukraine Between the EU and Russia: The Integration Challenge* (London: Palgrave Pivot).

Zhukov, Y. M. (2016), 'Trading Hard Hats for Combat Helmets: The Economics of Rebellion in Eastern Ukraine', *Journal of Comparative Economics*, 44(1), pp. 1–15.

Zhurzhenko, T. (2010), *Borderlands Into Bordered Lands: Geopolitics of Identity in Post-Soviet Ukraine* (Stuttgart: Ibidem-Verlag).

Zhurzhenko, T. (2014), 'A Divided Nation? Reconsidering the Role of Identity Politics in the Ukraine Crisis', *Die Friedens Warte*, no. 1–2, www.friedens-warte.de/en/heftarchiv/2014/heft-1-2/195-1-2-2014-content.html

PART II

Political institutions

4

CORE EXECUTIVES IN CENTRAL EUROPE

Martin Brusis

Introduction

Core executives have become increasingly important political actors and arenas due to several interlinked developments affecting both states and societies. Modernisation has weakened the ties between political parties and voters, making parties more dependent on state resources and, in particular, access to government. Since the political process has become more dominated by media communication, political controversy tends to be framed between chief executives and rival political leaders. Global economic integration has narrowed the policy discretion of nation states and fostered the spread of non-majoritarian institutions entrusted with regulatory functions. These trends have been associated with the growing weight of policy output as a source of legitimacy, in contrast to 'input legitimacy' derived from democratic elections. Among the three branches of state power, executives control most of the tools available to influence policy outputs and the interventions of both domestic and international regulatory agencies. The crisis and politicisation of European integration have further enhanced the salience of national (chief) executives compared to national legislatures and supranational institutions. As a result, many of the choices characterising politics and policymaking are now made or shaped at the centres of executives.

This chapter discusses the 'core executive' both as an empirical field of actors, institutions, and behavioural practices at the centres of Central European governments and as a theoretical concept formulated to study this field. The term 'core executive' was initially proposed by Dunleavy and Rhodes (1990) to describe the centre of the British government from a functional perspective. The core executive comprises 'all those organizations and procedures which coordinate central government policies, and act as final arbiters of conflict between different parts of the government machine' (Rhodes, 1995, 12, Dunleavy and Rhodes, 1990). In the UK, these functions are performed by 'the complex web of institutions, networks and practices surrounding the prime minister, cabinet, cabinet committees and their official counterparts, less formalised ministerial "clubs" or meetings, bilateral negotiations and interdepartmental committees', including the coordinating departments at the centre of government (Rhodes, 1995, 12). The notion of a core executive represents a conceptual innovation insofar as it

1 Focuses on neutral functions rather than specific institutions like the prime minister or cabinet which may convey normative connotations and cultural bias;

2   Goes beyond a formal institutional analysis to investigate the empirical practice and resources of policy coordination, including both its political and administrative dimensions;

3   Reflects the fragmented network of institutions that emerged from neoliberal reforms of government and substituted the traditional framework of cabinet government.

Replacing hierarchic, Weberian models of central government by market mechanisms, negotiations, and networks as modes of governance, these reforms are viewed as part of a broader 'hollowing-out of the state', a process that has also been driven by growing international interdependencies, the privatisation of public services and devolution (Rhodes, 1994). As a consequence, the spatial metaphor 'core' seems more appropriate than 'top', and heads or centres of government now appear to be more aptly characterised by their coordination and arbitration functions than by 'instructing' or 'ordering'. The notion of political power underlying the concept of the core executive is relational and contingent (Rhodes and Tiernan, 2015, Elgie, 2011): in order to achieve their goals, prime ministers and core political actors depend on other actors and must exchange resources such as authority, expertise, or money with them (Rhodes, 1997, 203).

Apart from these assumptions, the concept of the core executive initially did not bear any implications for the likely or desirable distribution of power, the prevalent modes of governance, or the roles of political actors in central government. This indeterminacy has facilitated its diffusion from the original British context to other Westminster systems as well as to continental European and even to presidential systems of government (Helms, 2005, Weller et al., 1997). However,

> [the] essential malleability of the term 'core executive' is [also] the reason why its use has become *de rigueur*. It is a wonderfully convenient term. The result, though, is that the universe of 'core executive studies' includes a great deal of work that could, quite happily, use a different term and have no less analytical purchase.
>
> *(Elgie, 2011, 72)*

The remainder of this chapter distinguishes two paradigms that have shaped core executive studies focusing on Central Europe and that reflect the recent history of the region: transition and Europeanisation. A third paradigm of 'executive governance' is suggested as a perspective for future work. The main argument of the chapter is that the trend towards centralised executive authority in several Central European countries suggests complementing the analysis of institutional arrangements with a broader analysis of governance. Such an approach would relate institutions to policies and their outcomes, highlighting possible drawbacks of centralisation and trade-offs between different functions or policy objectives.

Emergence and studies of post-socialist core executives

Scholars have used the core executive concept in various ways and have sought to fill it with different meanings. One tendency has been to associate the concept with the centralisation of power around the chief executive (Peters et al., 2000, 7, Poguntke and Webb, 2005, 5). Scholars studying Central Europe have adopted this idea and argued that post-socialist central governments lack an 'effective core executive' that would be able to exercise political leadership and perform the coordination and arbitration functions associated with the generic concept of the core executive (Goetz and Margetts, 1999, 426, Dimitrov et al., 2006, Goetz and Wollmann, 2001). This argument assumes, first, that the collapse of the state socialist systems of government has led to an institutional fragmentation in central government, engendering 'a vacuum of policy leadership' within the executive (Dimitrov et al., 2006, 8).

Second, the argument interprets the evolution of post-socialist core executives as a 'governmentalisation' (Goetz and Wollmann, 2001), that is, as the transformation of a subordinated and fragmented administration into a cohesive government that is able to demonstrate political leadership (Dimitrov et al., 2006, 206–207). This perspective views the formation of a core executive centred on the prime minister as a functionally necessary process of transforming executives into governments adopting the roles played by governments in liberal democracies. 'State institutions had to be shaped in a way that allowed them to be effectively directed by political parties in government' (Dimitrov et al., 2006, 8).

Dimitrov and his co-authors do not hesitate to emphasise the contingency of a convergence with Western government systems. However, their approach continues to be rooted in a 'transition paradigm' (Carothers, 2002) since it frames Central European core executives in comparison to Western points of reference and assumes that post-socialist political actors develop an interest in building a leadership-type core executive. Their empirical study documents the difficulties of this catch-up project by observing that the new democratic political elites by the early 2000s had institutionalised 'effective core executives' only in Hungary and partially in Poland (after 2001), but not in Bulgaria and the Czech Republic (Dimitrov et al., 2006, 230–231). Political actors in the latter two countries returned to decentralised core executives after episodes of personalised prime ministerial dominance under Prime Ministers Kostov (1997–2001) and Klaus (1992–1997), respectively.

The literature on executives in Eastern Europe broadly agrees that systems of government were structured similarly during the state socialist regimes since these regimes shared the main ideological basis of political rule, Marxism-Leninism, and its idea about the leading role of the Socialist or Communist Party (cf., for example, Baylis, 1989). The body heading the executive, the Council of Ministers, was subordinated to the Central Committee of the Communist (or Socialist) Party and its Politburo. While the two party institutions formed the centre of political power, the Council of Ministers was confined to implementing political decisions. The Council was formally a collective and collegiate body headed by a chairperson; in practice, the Council and the wider executive were segmented into numerous different ministries closely involved in administering the state, economy, and society.

The subordination of the executive under the party leadership de facto fused the party and the executive, transforming the state socialist party into a part of the state. Reform initiatives in several state socialist countries sought to enhance the professional-legal rationality and autonomy of government, but did not challenge (or were hindered from questioning) the leadership claim of the ruling Communist parties. It was the breakdown of the state socialist regimes that disrupted the formal link between the party and the state. Those executive institutions that prevailed were exposed to a fundamentally transformed political and institutional constellation. Given the inherited segmentation of ministerial administration, the available organisational resources were most conducive to models of ministerial or bureaucratic government where individual ministers or senior civil servants have significant decision-making powers (Dunleavy and Rhodes, 1990, Elgie, 1997).

Most studies on the emerging post-socialist executives in Eastern Europe have focused on how the role of a president was institutionalised in this constellation (see for example Protsyk, 2011; Sedelius and Åberg in this volume). This scholarly interest reflected major political debates and struggles in all countries of the region during the political transition, the revision of constitutions, and the consolidation of new, democratic, or authoritarian political regimes. Moreover, researchers also examined the powers of the president vis-à-vis the executive and the legislature because the design of these relationships defines a system of government as parliamentary, presidential, or hybrid (for example, semi-presidential) in political science. This literature rarely uses the concept of a core executive and rather discusses its associated coordination and arbitration functions under broad terms such as 'leadership' or 'governance' (Holmes, 2014, Taras, 2013).

After more than two decades of post-socialism, there is a clear and strong correlation between the emergence and consolidation of democracy and the institutional choice for constraining presidential powers over the executive (Holmes, 2014, 648). All new European Union (EU) member states in Central Europe and the six South Eastern European accession candidate states (as of 2015) either had parliamentary government or premier-presidential government with a popularly elected president exercising limited powers (Sedelius and Åberg in this volume).[1]

Blondel and his co-authors have claimed that the decision for a parliamentary democracy in Eastern Europe implied a 'cabinet system of government' (Blondel, 2001, Blondel, 2007). Since parliamentary democracy is defined by the parliamentary accountability of government, Blondel et al. infer that this accountability refers to a collective body, the cabinet, which represents the government as a whole and formally takes its decisions collectively. A cabinet consists of the prime minister, other ministers, and possibly also other leading executive officials. To differ from presidential government, the cabinet, according to Blondel et al.,

> has to be, at least to some extent, 'collective' or at least 'collegial': decisions are taken 'together'. This requirement of 'togetherness' is regarded as central to the cabinet system because such a mode of operation is felt to be a more liberal, more democratic and therefore superior form of decision-making.
>
> *(Blondel et al., 2007, 5)*

Cabinet government is seen as preferable compared to a system where ministers depend on the head of government, a practice 'which smack[s] of authoritarianism' (Blondel et al., 2007, 6).

While Blondel et al. also study centres of government in post-socialist Eastern Europe and share the 'transition paradigm' with Dimitrov et al. (2006, Blondel and Müller-Rommel 2001, Blondel et al. 2007), their approach differs in several respects. First, they are less interested in the trajectories of institutional development and rather seek to map the procedures and institutional environment of cabinet decision-making synchronically by covering fifteen and seven East Central and South Eastern European countries, respectively (Blondel and Müller-Rommel, 2001, Blondel et al., 2007).[2]

Second, Dimitrov et al. view institutional change as the result of institutional legacies, critical junctures, and actors' choices, drawing on the theoretical tools of historical institutionalism (Thelen, 1999). In contrast, the work of Blondel et al. is grounded in the empirical institutionalist tradition of comparative politics (cf., for example, Lijphart, 1999). They start by identifying a general problem of cabinet systems: the trade-off between representativeness and efficiency (Blondel et al., 2007, 4ff.). Institutional change is then conceived as the result of political actors' efforts to 'streamline' cabinet systems, aimed at reducing the inefficiencies of collective decision-making. For example, governments established procedural arrangements to reduce the workload of cabinets (particularly through cabinet committees and cabinet secretariats). These streamlining efforts are likely to be less effective than in Western European executives because, among other reasons, prime ministers have lacked political authority and party systems have been unstable in several countries (Blondel et al., 2007, 17–18).

To examine their hypotheses about streamlining efforts and obstacles, Blondel et al. conducted a survey of 230 former ministers who held office during the period from 1990 to 2003 in ten East European countries. They observed that the ministers not only indicated a general satisfaction with the functioning of 'their' cabinets and a general willingness to approximate the operational standards of Western European cabinets, but also that ministers' factual statements about cabinet meetings, secretariats, and cabinet committees broadly resembled Western European practice. These findings led the authors to conclude that the surveyed East European countries 'have successfully adopted the parliamentary-cabinet system of government in the early 1990s' and have 'a governmental system which compares well with the governmental systems of Western Europe' (Blondel and Andreev, 2001, 193).

Third, both studies disagree about the empirical relevance and conceptual status of cabinets for understanding core executives in Central Europe. Blondel et al. do not use the concept of the core executive and rather retain the notion of the cabinet as a necessary and normatively desirable corollary of parliamentary democracy and as a functioning institution of inter-ministerial cooperation. Of the ministers surveyed, 36 per cent stated that the prevailing negotiation style of 'their' prime minister was to build consensus, while only 16 per cent noted that their prime minister tended to force solutions (Blondel et al., 2007, 183).

In contrast, Dimitrov et al. distinguish between 'a cabinet type of government' and a cabinet 'type of core executive' (2006, 35–36). Whereas the core executive refers to the empirical practice and internal structures of coordination/arbitration (centralised vs. decentralised), the 'type of government' refers to the formal-legal constitution of government. Cabinet 'government' exists if the cabinet as a whole is elected by and accountable to parliament. In contrast with Bulgaria and the Czech Republic, Hungary and Poland do not strictly fulfil these definitional criteria, because Hungary's parliament elects the prime minister (upon the president's proposal) but does not approve the composition of the cabinet. Poland's constitution enables the Sejm to take a vote of non-confidence against individual ministers (in addition to the option of a non-confidence vote against the whole Council of Ministers).

The idea behind this conceptual distinction between types of core executive and government is to mark the distinctness of the core executive concept as opposed to cabinet/prime ministerial government and to capture cross-national and cross-temporal empirical variation in more detail. Dimitrov et al. observe a cabinet-type core executive only for the brief 1989–1991 period in Poland, noting the difficulties of sustaining a cabinet model of decision-making in practice: 'Centralization around the prime minister offered a relatively straightforward answer to coordination requirements compared to more contingent coordination patterns that prioritize collegiality, collectivity, and inclusiveness' (Dimitrov et al., 2006, 11). Thus, whereas Blondel et al. find empirical evidence of cabinet-type collective and collegial decision-making practices, this contradicts the prevalence of segmented ministerial or centralised prime-ministerial core executives noticed by Dimitrov et al.

Europeanising core executives

The enlargement of the EU and the membership aspiration of East European states have facilitated institutional reforms of core executives and provided a new paradigm for core executive studies in Eastern Europe. The EU does not have formal rules about how the executives of its member states are to be organised or how decisions should be taken in national cabinets. However, it is possible to identify requirements and expectations with regard to governmental organisation that had (and have) to be met by East European states in the process of EU accession and during membership.

The EU has considered the rule of law a key condition for accession. Executive government is expected to act through legal regulations and within the limits set by law. Although there are no EU rules on how to organise intra-executive coordination, the functional requirements of EU policymaking have induced governments to intensify policy coordination across sectors and among leading civil servants. The European Commission has encouraged more effective core executives by stressing the need for strategic planning capacity, a unified civil service (see Meyer-Sahling in this volume), horizontal coordination, and mainstreaming of policies. Lacking a formal legal basis to impose these objectives as conditions, the Commission created the Support for Improvement in Governance and Management (SIGMA) programme jointly with the Organisation for Economic Co-operation and Development (OECD). SIGMA and World Bank experts with a background in the 'Anglo-governance school' (Marinetto, 2003) promoted stronger government offices endowed with comprehensive coordination functions (cf., for example, James and Ben-Gera, 2004, Ben-Gera, 2004, Manning et al., 1999). Negotiation and transposition requirements further increased the power of core executives in relation to line ministries and specialised agencies (Grabbe, 2001, 1018, Lippert and Umbach, 2005). Participation in the Council formations and in the EU's comitology caused governments to create the roles of central coordinators and an 'inner core' of ministries primarily involved in managing EU issues (Laffan, 2008, 133).

The enlargement rounds of 2004/2007/2013 and the dynamics of European integration between the early 1990s and the early 2000s generated a wave of 'Europeanisation' research that mainly examines the impact of the EU and European integration for domestic polities, politics, and public policies. Within the Europeanisation paradigm, scholars typically ask how the EU influences domestic institutional and political changes or how such changes can be explained by the interaction of the EU and other possible causes.

In his comparative study of core executives and Europeanisation in the Czech Republic, Hungary, and Poland, Zubek argues that EU pressures to step up the transposition of EU legislation encouraged domestic policy entrepreneurs to push for core executive reinforcement (2008, 2011). However, the success of such reinforcement was contingent on domestic 'coalition politics, prime ministerial preferences, and institutional legacies' (Zubek, 2008, 157).

Zubek's work is notable in two respects. First, he draws on rational choice institutionalism to conceive the relations between ministers and the prime minister (Ostrom, 1990). In his view, the reinforcement of a core executive constitutes a strategy to address 'ministerial non-responsiveness' or departmentalism. 'The core executive represents a unique institutional response to collective dilemmas in the production of the legal rules that bring diffuse benefits to many voters and require interministerial cooperation' (Zubek, 2008, 5). This interpretation enables Zubek to operationalise the core executive concept by specifying position, authority, and information rules that facilitate the monitoring and supervision of line ministries. The presence of these rules, which may be sustained by prime ministerial or cabinet government, indicates a 'strong "European" core executive' (Zubek, 2008, 156).

Second, Zubek conceptualises the core executive (changes) both as a response variable and as an explanatory variable. Placing this variable within an extended cause-effect chain allows to understand the drivers of core executive changes and to assess the policy impact of these changes. Zubek and other scholars influenced by the Europeanisation paradigm tend to agree that domestic political actors decisively influenced the institutional arrangements of EU policy coordination and executive governance in East European countries (Brusis, 2004, Dimitrova and Toshkov, 2007, Fink-Hafner, 2014). Political parties as well as political leaders and their interests are found to matter more than institutional legacies or EU incentives (for a dissenting position, cf. Meyer-Sahling and Veen, 2012, Meyer-Sahling and van Stolk, 2015).

Both 'Europeanisation' and 'transition' studies of core executives have identified the strength and structure of domestic political competition as important dimensions explaining cross-national variation (Baylis, 2007, Dimitrov et al., 2006, Müller-Rommel, 2001, 199), thereby confirming insights from the broader literature on comparative government (Blondel and Müller-Rommel, 1993, Lijphart, 1999). In Hungary, for example, polarised political competition has generated prime ministerial government backed by elaborate devices of administrative coordination. In contrast, a more multipolar constellation of parties in the Czech Republic has rendered the prime minister a consensus-seeker among powerful ministers and extra-governmental actors, shifting the onus of executive coordination towards the political level (Brusis, 2004).

Several other studies have treated the configuration of the core executive as an explanatory variable, claiming that it makes a difference for empirical policy outcomes. Centralised, cohesive core executives, for example, are likely to have ensured a quicker transposition of EU legislation, lower budget deficits and a better quality of regulatory impact assessment (Hallerberg, 2010, Staroňová, 2010, Zubek, 2011).

Towards executive governance studies?

Thus, to make more sense of the core executive concept, students of Central Europe have identified varieties of core executives (prime ministerial – cabinet – ministerial, political vs. administrative coordination, formal-informal, etc.) and embedded them in cause-effect sequences. Those studies that adhere more closely to the generic concept and/or originate from the sub-discipline of comparative public administration have tended to evaluate stronger and more centralised coordination positively (Dimitrov et al., 2006). However, there has also been a strand of the literature, usually from the sub-field of comparative government/politics, that has emphasised the benefits of power dispersion, more accountable officeholders and constraints on executive authority (cf., for example, Orenstein, 2001). A key argument in this literature is that a robust political competition can cause 'governing parties to moderate their rent seeking, anticipate an exit from office by building formal constraints, and co-opt the opposition through power-sharing measures that limit (. . .) any one party's ability to gain private benefits from the state' (Grzymała-Busse, 2007, 10, see also O'Dwyer, 2006, Kopecký, 2008).

The importance of executive accountability is reinforced by broader empirical trends in East European democracies that have increased the dominance of executives and governing parties and eroded accountability institutions such as parliaments, opposition parties, constitutional courts, the judiciary, civil society organisations, and independent media (cf., for example, Rupnik and Zielonka, 2013). These changes can be seen as a reaction to the growth of non-majoritarian institutions and external, transnational constraints that have widened the gap between responsible and responsive government (Mair, 2013). Responsibly governing parties that adjust their policies to the expectations of international financial markets and EU institutions enable anti-establishment parties to present themselves as 'truly' responsive to voters' concerns. Having entered government, the latter parties seek to combine responsive, populist policies with measures to constrain public scrutiny and political competition, aimed at silencing criticism from abroad or home.

While a centralised core executive, the normative ideal of many core executive studies, does not necessarily contradict executive accountability, the trend towards more powerful executives and 'dominant-power politics' (Carothers, 2002) suggests a more cautious and context-sensitive evaluation of institutional arrangements and change in East European core executives. One conceptual strategy to achieve this is to elaborate a paradigm of 'executive governance' that embeds the institutional analysis of core executives and provides a 'missing link' between institutions and policies and their outcomes. Put differently, there is a need to review the early association of the core executive concept with centralisation and to complement centralisation with other dimensions or qualities of executive governance.

An example of how a new paradigm could be developed will now be suggested. The example distinguishes two dimensions of core executive activities, drawing on the 'Sustainable Governance Indicators' (SGI), a dataset that has been created by the Bertelsmann Foundation, a think tank based in Germany (Brusis, 2009). The data is collected by annual expert surveys covering forty-one EU and OECD member states.[3] Country experts assess and rate questions on the practices and procedures of planning, consultation, coordination, communication, decision-making, and policy implementation in executives.

A Principal Component Analysis of the expert ratings for twenty-four questions from the 2015 edition reveals two components (dimensions) that may be labelled 'Implementation Capacity' and 'Information-Processing Capacity'.[4] These two dimensions correspond to the broader concept of 'governance capacity' proposed by Pierre and Peters (2005):

> The capacity of the state to make and enforce binding decisions on the society and to do so without significant involvement of, or competition from, societal actors (. . .) [In addition,] states must be open to a wide range of information, including much that is uncomfortable and dissonant, if it is to be successful in governing. (. . .) the state must be in close contact with the society and utilize social information openly and accurately when governing.
>
> *(Pierre and Peters, 2005, 46)*

This combination of enforcement capacity and societal openness is very similar to the two constituent dimensions of 'authority' and 'inclusion' in Gerring and Thacker's 'centripetal theory of democratic governance' (Gerring and Thacker, 2008, 17).

The 'Implementation Capacity' dimension is best represented by SGI items that evaluate the extent to which government offices have sectoral policy expertise, determine the agenda of cabinet meetings, coordinate among line ministries, support ministerial compliance, and monitor policy implementation. 'Information-Processing Capacity' mainly consists of items that assess the extent to which core executive actors use regulatory impact assessments and consult with strategic planning units, non-governmental experts, and societal actors in order to deliberate and prepare decisions.

Figure 4.1 plots the standardised scores of countries based on these two dimensions, with higher scores indicating higher capacities. As the figure shows, the Baltic states and Poland in early 2015 formed a cluster of executives with similar, relatively developed implementation and information-processing capacities. In contrast, Bulgaria, Croatia, Romania, and Slovenia constitute a distinct cluster situated among the executives with relatively low capacities. Whereas Hungary's executive appears to be an outlier in its combination of centralised enforcement authority with insulation from society, the Czech Republic combines relatively well-developed consultation procedures with a lack of centralised coordination and monitoring. The positioning of Hungary's executive indicates that its model of a leader-type core executive centred on Prime Minister Orbán suffers from weak practices of information-gathering, consultation, and foresight.

The country reports prepared for the 2015 SGI edition show that government offices in Hungary, Poland, Latvia, and Lithuania have the most developed capacities to evaluate policies substantively, whereas these capacities are more limited or lacking in Bulgaria, Croatia, the Czech Republic, Estonia, and Slovakia. In the latter countries, government offices are also confined to formal-technical checks of documents envisaged for cabinet meetings. Their policy coordination functions are (partially) performed by cabinet-level bodies or leading ministry officials below the ministers. Among the government offices with stronger policy evaluation capacities, some

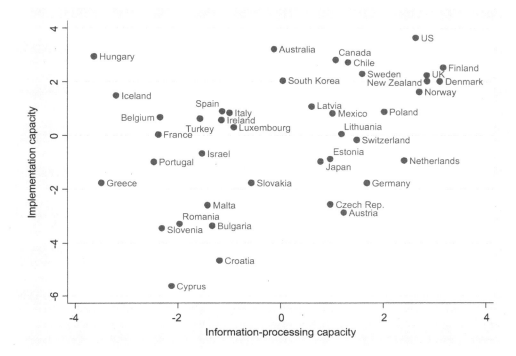

Figure 4.1 A map of executive capacity

may also return such documents on policy grounds and are involved by line ministries in the preparation of policy proposals (Hungary and Poland, and to some extent also in Croatia, Latvia, Lithuania, and Romania).

In countries with weaker government offices, senior civil servants or cabinet committees and committees involving both ministers and other officials or experts tend to play a more significant role in inter-ministerial coordination. Bureaucracy-led coordination appears to be most prevalent in the Baltic states, while departmentalist practices are more pronounced, for example, in Bulgaria and Slovakia. Slovenia's government relies on an elaborate system of cabinet committees to prepare cabinet decisions, whereas Estonia has instead established a practice of weekly consultative cabinet meetings to discuss pending issues. Informal coordination among political leaders has crucial importance in all Central European countries, necessitated by the need for, and tradition of, governing coalitions.

Conclusion

Cross-nationally comparative expert surveys constitute an important method for studying executive governance because they allow us to relate culturally ingrained interpretations – and the interpretations of interpretations favoured by the latest version of the Anglo-governance school (Bevir and Rhodes, 2010) – to interpretations in other national contexts. Such surveys provide one important agenda of future research. Expert surveys can and should be complemented by (1) studies and theory-building on the micro-mechanisms of executive governance (cf., for example, Rasch et al., 2015) and (2) holistic, contextualising perspectives on core executives as networks of contingent and contested, culturally bound 'practices with fuzzy boundaries' and meanings in action (Bevir, 2007, 163).

The SGI survey and comparativists such as Blondel or Müller-Rommel have integrated Central European core executives as additional cases into broader European or global research designs, indicating that 'Central Europe' or 'post-socialist' may persist as regional or historical identifiers, but no longer constitute substantively defining attributes of these country cases. The principal-agent approach to core executives elaborated in rational choice institutionalism lagged behind in absorbing Central Europe,[5] but is likely to reach out to the Central European cases soon. By 2015, core executives in the non-EU countries of South Eastern and Eastern Europe continued to be underexplored or even terra incognita. This is due both to the lack of resources in the local social sciences and the diminishing returns of including more peripheral countries into large cross-national comparativist projects. Contextualised case studies that reconstruct the institutional dynamics of these executives from a reflected nativist perspective are another promising avenue of research.

The lack of such studies is particularly regrettable since the under-institutionalised core executives of this world would provide rich empirical evidence of 'court politics', advocated as one of the promising new directions of core executive research (Rhodes and Tiernan, 2015). This notion captures the 'shift from formal decision-making processes in cabinet (. . .) to informal processes involving (. . .) the prime minister and a small group of carefully selected courtiers' (Savoie, 2008, 16–17). These aspects of 'court politics' have for a long time been a focus of interest for researchers studying Russia (cf., for example, Kryshtanovskaya and White, 2005), but they have also been scrutinised in Central European countries with stronger autochthonous social science traditions. The British and West European scholarship on core executives could benefit from tapping such local knowledge accumulated in its periphery.

Notes

1 Premier-presidential systems differ from president-parliamentary systems of government insofar as the latter systems enable the president to dismiss the prime minister and cabinet without the legislature's approval (Shugart and Carey, 1992). The term super-presidentialism denotes a governmental system, for example in Russia, where the president and his/her administration *de facto* suspend the separation of powers and supervise or guide the activities of the legislature and the judiciary (Taras, 2013).

2 The 2007 volume analyses Bulgaria, the Czech Republic, Hungary, Poland, Romania, Slovakia, Slovenia, and the Baltic States; the 2001 volume also includes Albania, Bosnia-Herzegovina, Croatia, Macedonia, Moldova, and Serbia/Yugoslavia.

3 Cf. http://sgi-network.org for a detailed description of the methodology and the dataset.

4 The two components together explain 71 per cent of the variance in the data.

5 Despite Zubek's bridge-building, major works remained confined to the usual West European cases (cf., for example, Strøm et al., 2003).

References

Baylis, T. A. (1989) *Governing by Committee: Collegial Leadership in Advanced Societies.* Albany: State University of New York Press.

Baylis, T. A. (2007) 'Embattled Executives: Prime Ministerial Weakness in East Central Europe', *Communist and Post-Communist Studies*, 40(2), pp. 81–106.

Ben-Gera, M. (2004) *Co-Ordination at the Centre of Government: The Functions and Organisation of the Government Office* [SIGMA Paper]. Paris: OECD, p. 35.

Bevir, M. (2007) 'Core Executive', in Bevir, M. (ed.) *Encyclopedia of Governance.* Thousand Oaks, CA: SAGE, pp. 162–163.

Bevir, M. and R. A. W. Rhodes (2010) *The State as Cultural Practice.* Oxford: Oxford University Press.

Blondel, J. (2001) 'Cabinets in Post-Communist East-Central Europe and in the Balkans', in Blondel, J. and F. Müller-Rommel (eds.) *Cabinets in Eastern Europe*. Houndmills, Basingstoke: Palgrave, pp. 1–14.

Blondel, J. (2007) 'The Cabinet as the New Form of Government in Post-Communist Democracies', in Blondel, J., F. Müller-Rommel and D. Malová (eds.) *Governing New European Democracies*. Houndmills, Basingstoke: Palgrave Macmillan, pp. 3–20.

Blondel, J. and S. A. Andreev (2001) 'Bulgaria', in Blondel, J. and F. Müller-Rommel (eds.) *Cabinets in Eastern Europe*. Basingstoke: Palgrave, pp. 131–141.

Blondel, J. and F. Müller-Rommel (eds.) (1993) *Governing Together: The Extent and Limits of Joint Decision-Making in Western European Cabinets*. London: Macmillan.

Blondel, J. and F. Müller-Rommel (eds.) (2001) *Cabinets in Eastern Europe*. Basingstoke: Palgrave.

Blondel, J., F. Müller-Rommel and D. Malová (eds.) (2007) *Governing New European Democracies*. Houndmills, Basingstoke: Palgrave Macmillan.

Brusis, M. (2004) 'Europeanization, Party Government or Legacies? Explaining Executive Governance in Bulgaria, the Czech Republic and Hungary', *Comparative European Politics*, 2(2), pp. 163–184.

Brusis, M. (2009) 'Designing Sustainable Governance Indicators: Criteria and Methodology', in Stiftung, B. (ed.) *Sustainable Governance Indicators*. Gütersloh: Verlag Bertelsmann Stiftung, pp. 71–100.

Carothers, T. (2002) 'The End of the Transition Paradigm', *Journal of Democracy*, 13(1), pp. 5–21.

Dimitrov, V., K. H. Goetz and H. Wollmann (2006) *Governing After Communism: Institutions and Policymaking*. Lanham: Rowman & Littlefield.

Dimitrova, A. and D. Toshkov (2007) 'The Dynamics of Domestic Coordination of EU Policy in the New Member States: Impossible to Lock In?', *West European Politics*, 30(5), pp. 961–986.

Dunleavy, P. and R.A.W. Rhodes (1990) 'Core Executive Studies in Britain', *Public Administration*, 68(1), pp. 3–28.

Elgie, R. (1997) 'Models of Executive Politics: A Framework for the Study of Executive Power Relations in Parliamentary and Semi-Presidential Regimes', *Political Studies*, 45, pp. 217–231.

Elgie, R. (2011) 'Core Executive Studies Two Decades On', *Public Administration*, 89(1), pp. 64–77.

Fink-Hafner, D. (2014) 'Post-Accession Politicization of National EU Policy Coordination: The Case of Slovenia', *Public Administration*, 92(1), pp. 39–54.

Gerring, J. and S. C. Thacker (2008) *A Centripetal Theory of Democratic Governance*. Cambridge: Cambridge University Press.

Goetz, K. H. and H. Z. Margetts (1999) 'The "Solitary Center": The Core Executive in Central and Eastern Europe', *Governance*, 12(4), pp. 425–453.

Goetz, K. H. and H. Wollmann (2001) 'Governmentalizing Central Executives in Post-Communist Europe: A Four-Country Comparison', *Journal of European Public Policy*, 8(6), pp. 864–887.

Grabbe, H. (2001) 'How Does Europeanization Affect CEE Governance? Conditionality, Diffusion and Diversity', *Journal of European Public Policy*, 8(6), pp. 1013–1031.

Grzymała-Busse, A. (2007) *Rebuilding Leviathan: Party Competition and State Exploitation in Post-Communist Democracies*. Cambridge: Cambridge University Press.

Hallerberg, M. (2010) 'Political Power, Fiscal Institutions and Budgetary Outcomes in Central and Eastern Europe', *Journal of Public Policy*, 30(1), pp. 45–62.

Helms, L. (2005) *Presidents, Prime Minister and Chancellors: Executive Leadership in Western Democracies*. Houndmills, Basingstoke: Palgrave Macmillan.

Holmes, L. (2014) 'Post-Communist Leadership', in Rhodes, R.A.W. and P. T'Hart (eds.) *The Oxford Handbook of Political Leadership*. Baden-Baden: Nomos, pp. 642–658.

James, S. and M. Ben-Gera (2004) *A Comparative Analysis of Government Offices in OECD Countries*. Paris: OECD (GOV/PGC/MPM/RD(2004)).

Kopecký, P. (2008) 'Political Parties and the State in Post-Communist Europe: The Nature of Symbiosis', in Kopecký, P. (ed.) *Political Parties and the State in Post-Communist Europe*. London, New York: Routledge, pp. 1–23.

Kryshtanovskaya, O. and S. White (2005) 'Inside the Putin Court: A Research Note', *Europe-Asia Studies*, 57(7), pp. 1065–1075.

Laffan, B. (2008) 'Core Executives', in Graziano, P. and M. P. Vink (eds.) *Europeanization: New Research Agendas*. Houndmills, Basingstoke: Palgrave Macmillan, pp. 128–140.

Lijphart, A. (1999) *Patterns of Democracy: Government Forms and Performance in Thirty-Six Countries*. New Haven, CT, London: Yale University Press.

Lippert, B. and G. Umbach (2005) *The Pressure of Europeanisation: From Post-Communist State Administrations to Normal Players in the EU System*. Baden-Baden: Nomos.

Mair, P. (2013) *Ruling the Void: The Hollowing Out of Western Democracy*. London: Verso.

Manning, N., N. Barma, J. Blondel, E. Pilichowski and V. Wright (1999) *Strategic Decisionmaking in Cabinet Government: Institutional Underpinnings and Obstacles* [World Bank Sector Studies Series]. Washington: World Bank.

Marinetto, M. (2003) 'Governing Beyond the Centre: A Critique of the Anglo-Governance School', *Political Studies*, 51(3), pp. 592–608.

Meyer-Sahling, J.-H. and C. van Stolk (2015) 'A Case of Partial Convergence: The Europeanization of Central Government in Central and Eastern Europe', *Public Administration*, 93(1), pp. 230–247.

Meyer-Sahling, J.-H. and T. Veen (2012) 'Governing the Post-Communist State: Government Alternation and Senior Civil Service Politicisation in Central and Eastern Europe', *East European Politics*, 28(1), pp. 1–19.

Müller-Rommel, F. (2001) 'Cabinets in Post-Communist East-Central Europe and the Balkans: Empirical Findings and Research Agenda', in Blondel, J. and F. Müller-Rommel (eds.) *Cabinets in Eastern Europe*. Houndmills, Basingstoke: Palgrave, pp. 193–201.

O'Dwyer, C. (2006) *Runaway State-Building: Patronage Politics and Democratic Development*. Baltimore, MD: Johns Hopkins University Press.

Orenstein, M. (2001) *Out of the Red: Building Capitalism and Democracy in Postcommunist Europe*. Ann Arbor: University of Michigan Press.

Ostrom, E. (1990) *Governing the Commons: The Evolution of Institutions for Collective Action*. Cambridge: Cambridge University Press.

Peters, B. G., R. A. Rhodes and V. Wright (eds.) (2000) *Administering the Summit: Administration of the Core Executive in Developed Countries*. London: Macmillan Press.

Pierre, J. and B.G. Peters (2005) *Governing Complex Societies: Trajectories and Scenarios*. New York: Palgrave Macmillan.

Poguntke, T. and P. Webb (2005) 'The Presidentialization of Politics in Democratic Societies: A Framework for Analysis', in Poguntke, T. and P. Webb (eds.) *The Presidentialization of Politics: A Comparative Study of Modern Democracies*. Oxford: Oxford University Press, pp. 1–25.

Protsyk, O. (2011) 'Semi-Presidentialism Under Post-Communism', in Elgie, R., S. Moestrup and Y.-S. Wu (eds.) *Semi-Presidentialism and Democracy*. Houndmills, Basingstoke: Palgrave Macmillan, pp. 98–116.

Rasch, B. E., M. Shane and J. A. Cheibub (eds.) (2015) *Parliaments and Government Formation: Unpacking Investiture Rules*. Oxford: Oxford University Press.

Rhodes, R. A. (1994) 'The Hollowing Out of the State: The Changing Nature of the Public Service in Britain', *The Political Quarterly*, 65(2), pp. 138–151.

Rhodes, R. A. (1995) 'From Prime Ministerial Power to Core Executive', in Rhodes, R. A. and P. Dunleavy (eds.) *Prime Minister, Cabinet and Core Executive*. London: Macmillan, pp. 11–37.

Rhodes, R. A. (1997) '"Shackling the Leader?": Coherence, Capacity and the Hollow Crown', in Weller, P., H. Bakvis and R. A. Rhodes (eds.) *The Hollow Crown: Countervailing Trends in Core Executives Transforming Government*. Houndmills, Basingstoke: Macmillan, pp. 198–223.

Rhodes, R. A. and A. Tiernan (2015) 'Executive Governance and Its Puzzles', in Massey, A. and K. Miller (eds.) *International Handbook of Public Administration and Governance*. Chelmsford: Edward Elgar, pp. 81–103.

Rupnik, J. and J. Zielonka (2013) 'Introduction: The State of Democracy 20 Years on: Domestic and External Factors', *East European Politics and Societies*, 27(1), pp. 3–25.

Savoie, D. J. (2008) *Court Government and the Collapse of Accountability in Canada and the United Kingdom*. Toronto: University of Toronto Press.

Shugart, M. S. and J. M. Carey (1992) *Presidents and Assemblies: Constitutional Design and Electoral Dynamics*. Cambridge: Cambridge University Press.

Staroňová, K. (2010) 'Regulatory Impact Assessment: Formal Institutionalization and Practice', *Journal of Public Policy*, 30(1), pp. 117–136.

Strøm, K., W. C. Müller and T. Bergman (eds.) (2003) *Delegation and Accountability in Parliamentary Democracies*. Oxford: Oxford University Press.

Taras, R. (2013) 'Executive Leadership', in White, S. (ed.) *Developments in Central and East European Politics 5*. Basingstoke: Palgrave Macmillan, pp. 139–155.

Thelen, K. (1999) 'Historical Institutionalism in Comparative Politics', *Annual Review of Political Science*, 2, pp. 369–404.

Weller, P., H. Bakvis and R. A. Rhodes (eds.) (1997) *The Hollow Crown: Countervailing Trends in Core Executives*. Houndmills, Basingstoke: Macmillan.

Zubek, R. (2008) *Core Executive and Europeanization in Central Europe*. Houndmills: Palgrave Macmillan.

Zubek, R. (2011) 'Core Executives and Coordination of EU Law Transposition: Evidence From the New Member States', *Public Administration*, 89(2), pp. 433–450.

5

EASTERN EUROPE'S SEMI-PRESIDENTIAL REGIMES*

Thomas Sedelius and Jenny Åberg

How power is distributed between the executive and legislative branches significantly influences the capacity of a new constitutional order to guard against autocracy. The list of East European presidents that have strived for constitutional reforms, which would considerably increase their own spheres of power, is quite extensive. Even with the exception of outright authoritarian leaders like Lukashenko in Belarus and his counterparts in Central Asia, there are many examples. For instance, Iliescu in Romania, Kuchma and Yanukovych in Ukraine, Lucinschi and Snegur in Moldova, Wałęsa in Poland, and Yeltsin in Russia did all at some point during their incumbency challenge the constitutional order in their countries.

Semi-presidentialism is a system of government whereby a directly elected president shares executive power with a prime minister and government that enjoys the support of an elected legislature. This has become a very popular form of government worldwide and has emerged as the most common regime type in Eastern Europe, totalling twenty countries as of 2016 (Elgie 2015). Since the fall of communism, it has been debated whether presidential systems are less conducive to democracy than parliamentarism. Linz (1990) claimed that presidentialism carries a number of built-in perils that undermine the fostering of democracy, for example, the president's fixed term in office, the winner-take-all logic of presidential elections, and the risk of presidential omnipresence and authoritarian rule. As a category in between, semi-presidentialism has been seen by some scholars as carrying similar perils as presidentialism (Linz 1994) while others have considered it as a flexible and power-sharing system with the potential of combining some of the advantages of both parliamentarism and presidentialism (Sartori 1996). In one way or the other, the majority of studies on semi-presidentialism have related to the overarching question of whether semi-presidentialism as such is good or bad for democratisation and political stability.

The aim of this chapter is to provide a review on the sub-field of semi-presidentialism, emphasising its relevance to Eastern Europe. By reviewing 327 relevant publications covering the period 1970–2015, we will map out the main trends and important findings in the field of semi-presidentialism, and indicate some research gaps for the benefit of future research.

We start by defining the distinct features of semi-presidentialism and its sub-types in relation to presidentialism and parliamentarism. Challenges of definitions and classifications are at the core of the research field's development, and some of the key arguments will be addressed in this regard. We will then move on to a general classification of the constitutional regimes in Eastern Europe and the post-communist countries in the Caucasus and Central Asia, where the variations in regime types and presidential power are reported. The subsequent sections are devoted to a review of some of the core themes of semi-presidential research on Eastern Europe, where we report on dominant approaches and the main findings in the literature. Finally, we identify and suggest some relevant avenues for future research on semi-presidentialism in Eastern Europe and beyond.

Defining parliamentarism, presidentialism, and semi-presidentialism

Adopting a distinction between parliamentarism and presidentialism is quite straightforward. *Parliamentarism* has an authority structure based on mutual dependence. The chief executive (the prime minister and his cabinet) is dependent on the consent of the parliament, and parliament in turn is dependent on the executive, which is entitled to dissolve parliament and call new elections. The head of state (the president or monarch) upholds mainly ceremonial powers and is not directly elected. *Presidentialism*, on the other hand, is defined by (1) a popularly elected chief executive (president) who names and directs the composition of government, and in which (2) the terms of the president and parliament are fixed, and are not contingent on mutual confidence (Shugart and Carey 1992: 19).

Although many analysts would disagree that there is a single and generally accepted definition of parliamentarism and presidentialism, defining semi-presidentialism has proved an even more complicated task. Duverger (1980) is a major landmark. He provided a definition of semi-presidentialism including three criteria: (1) the president is elected by universal suffrage; (2) the president possesses quite considerable powers; and (3) there is also a prime minister and other ministers who possesses executive and governmental power and can stay in office only with the consent of the parliament (1980: 4). Duverger's definition remained dominant until the late 1990s, although the second and non-institutional criterion that "the president possesses quite considerable powers" was a source of debate and already caused confusion early on. Different scholars approached this vague criterion differently, and the list of semi-presidential countries varied extensively from one study (Stepan and Skach 1993) to another (Lijphart 1999). Shugart and Carey (1992) proposed an alternative by providing a distinction between two sub-types of semi-presidentialism: (1) *president-parliamentary* systems, where (a) the president is elected by a popular vote for a fixed term in office, (b) the president appoints and dismisses the prime minister and other cabinet ministers, and (c) the prime minister and cabinet ministers are subjected to parliamentary as well as presidential confidence; and (2) *premier-presidentialism* systems, where (a) the president is elected by a popular vote for a fixed term in office, (b) the president selects the prime minister who heads the cabinet, but (c) authority to dismiss the cabinet rests exclusively with the parliament (Shugart and Carey 1992: 23–24; Shugart 2005: 333). Elgie went even further and removed any references to the powers of the president and proposed that semi-presidentialism is "where a constitution makes provision for both a directly elected fixed-term president and a prime minister and cabinet who are collectively responsible to the legislature" (1999: 13).

Since the early 2000s, Elgie's strictly constitutional definition of semi-presidentialism and Shugart and Carey's two sub-types – premier-presidentialism and president-parliamentarism – have become widely used in the literature. Quite strong critique has remained, however, and it has predominantly concerned the variation in presidential powers between different semi-presidential regimes, even within the same sub-category. Siaroff (2003) and Cheibub, Elkins, and Ginsburg (2014) go as far as to argue that the whole category of semi-presidentialism is inadequate. Instead they suggest that scholars should stick to the distinction between presidentialism and parliamentarism, combining this with measures of presidential powers. This kind of critique is neither new nor irrelevant, but it ignores a basic fundament, namely that semi-presidentialism is unique in terms of origin and survival of the government. In principal-agent terms, the government is at the mercy of two separate agents of the electorate, that is, the president and the parliament (Schleiter and Morgan-Jones 2010).

In line with other scholars (Elgie 2011), we suggest that the most fruitful way of approaching semi-presidentialism is to use the distinction between premier-presidentialism and president-parliamentarism in combination with measures of presidential powers. In the subsequent section, we will categorise the East European countries accordingly.

Parliamentary and semi-presidential regimes in Eastern Europe

Table 5.1 provides an overview of the constitutional arrangements in twenty-eight post-communist countries. Adopting the definitions of premier-presidentialism and president-parliamentarism, we note that semi-presidentialism is by far the most common constitutional arrangement in Eastern Europe. In fact, there are only eight cases of parliamentarism and four case of pure presidentialism. Parliamentary and premier-presidential constitutions are dominant in Central Europe, while president-parliamentarism is spread among the post-Soviet constitutions, and pure presidentialism is found only among the dictatorships in Central Asia. Among the seven countries that adopted president-parliamentarism in the 1990s, only three of them are left with this kind of semi-presidential arrangement in 2016 (Azerbaijan, Belarus, and Russia).

We also report on a measure of presidential power developed by Doyle and Elgie (2016). A considerable number of presidential power indexes are available in the literature (e.g. Siaroff 2003; Roper 2002) and the main advantage of this one is that it is based on twenty-eight of such already existing measures. In addition, Doyle and Elgie have generated their dataset on a larger number of countries with longer time series than other existing ones. The scores are in the range from 0 to 1 in separate time periods following constitutional changes of a country's presidential powers.

The average presidential power scores confirms an expected continuum where the parliamentary countries score lowest at 0.170, followed by the premier-presidential countries at 0.243, the president-parliamentary countries at 0.482, and the presidential countries at 0.617. Over the course of the post-communist period, several countries have amended or revised their post-communist constitutions in such a comprehensive way that they have shifted from one constitutional category to another. The constitutional revisions in Croatia 2001 and Georgia 2013 represent shifts from president-parliamentarism to premier-presidentialism, by stating in their revised constitutions that the government should only be subordinated to parliamentary confidence for its survival and not, as was the case prior to these changes, to both the president and the parliament. Moldova, in 2000, changed the method of presidential elections from a popular vote to indirect elections, that is, a shift from premier-presidentialism to parliamentarism. Ukraine is the most volatile case in terms of constitutional changes and has moved back and forth along a continuum between democracy and authoritarianism throughout the post-Soviet era marked by periods of constitutional and political instability. The 1996 president-parliamentary constitution was revised through amendments into a premier-presidential system in the wake of the Orange Revolution, 2006–2010. In both cases, demands for constitutional reform – particularly to combat presidential autocracy – were central to political mobilisation. The result was constitutional change that responded to these demands, by shifting from president-parliamentarism to premier-presidentialism. These constitutional amendments were quickly reversed by the Yanukovych regime in October 2010, bringing back the president-parliamentary system again between 2010 and 2014. The Euromaidan protests once again led to the return to a premier-presidential system in early 2014.

Table 5.1 Constitutional type and presidential power scores in Eastern Europe and the post-Soviet countries

Constitutional type	Country	Presidential power Doyle and Elgie (2016), Prespow1 Normalized score (Standard error) Year interval
Parliamentarism	Albania 1998–	0.141 (0.027) 1998–
	Czech Republic 1993–2012	0.142 (0.036) 1993–2000, 0.257 (0.103) 2001–2011
	Estonia 1992–	0.184 (0.032) 1992–
	Hungary 1990–	0.275 (0.045) 1991–2011
	Latvia 1993–	0.133 (0.025) 1992–1997 0.010 (–) 1998–
	Macedonia 1991–	0.116 (0.031) 1992–
	Moldova 2000–	0.272 (0.069) 2001–
	Slovakia 1992–1999	0.173 (0.033) 1993–1998
Average Prespow1 score		0.170
Premier-presidentialism	Armenia 2005–	0.650 (–) 2006
	Bulgaria 1992–	0.183 (0.044) 1992–
	Croatia 2001–	0.291 (0.074) 2001–
	Czech Republic 2012–	–
	Georgia 2013–	–
	Lithuania 1992–	0.282 (0.044) 1993–
	Kyrgyzstan 2007–	–
	Moldova 1991–2000	0.288 (0.091) 1991–1994 0.240 (0.059) 1995–2000
	Montenegro 2007–	–
	Poland 1997–	0.241 (0.044) 1997–
	Romania 1991–	0.250 (0.033) 1992–
	Serbia 2006–	–
	Slovakia 1999–	0.043 (0.032) 1999–2001 0.189 (0.139) 2002–
	Slovenia 1991–	0.118 (0.019) 1992–
	Ukraine 2006–2010, 2014–	0.329 (0.206) 2005–2010
Average Prespow1 score		0.243
President-parliamentarism	Armenia 1995–2005	0.403 (0.060) 1995–2005
	Azerbaijan 1995–	0.699 (0.070) 1996–2002
	Belarus 1994–	0.545 (0.067) 1994–1996 0.615 (0.094) 1997–
	Croatia 1990–2001	0.335 (0.050) 1991–2000
	Georgia 1995–2013	0.166 (–) 1990–1995 0.588 (0.071) 1996–2003 0.557 (–) 2004–
	Kyrgyzstan 1993–2007	0.459 (0.089) 1993–1995
	Russia 1993–	0.269 (0.073) 1992–1993 0.561 (0.056) 1994–
	Ukraine 1996–2006, 2010–2014	0.440 (0.061) 1996–2004 0.464 (0.065) 2011–

Constitutional type	Country	Presidential power *Doyle and Elgie (2016), Prespow1* *Normalized score (Standard error) Year interval*
Average Prespow1 score		0.482
Presidentialism	Kazakhstan 1995–	0.661 (0.008) 1996–
	Tajikistan 1994–	0.498 (0.051) 1995–
	Turkmenistan 1995–	0.662 (0.070) 1996–2002
	Uzbekistan 1992–	0.645 (0.056) 1995–
Average Prespow1 score		0.617

Note: Doyle and Elgie (2016) have developed two sets of scores, Prespower1 and Prespower2, and there are some differences in statistical specifications behind the two. In terms of standard errors for the European countries, however, there are similar and acceptable ranges, and we have thus decided to report only the Prespower1 scores here.

Sources: Doyle and Elgie (2016) and Elgie (2015).

Croatia (2001 onwards), Georgia (2013 onwards), Moldova (2000 onwards), and Ukraine (2006–2010 and 2014 onwards) represent cases with constitutional changes from a president-dominated system towards government models in which the cabinet becomes explicitly anchored in the parliament. In several post-Soviet countries, the trend has been the reverse. Belarus and several of the Central Asian countries – Kyrgyzstan, Tajikistan, and Uzbekistan – have been headed by authoritarian presidents, and constitutional amendments have been adopted in order to strengthen already strong presidencies. Generally, the post-communist countries with the strongest presidential powers are also the ones with the worst records of democracy. Proponents of parliamentarism have argued that presidential systems are less conducive to democracy and therefore that parliamentary systems should be the constitutional option for transitional regimes (Linz 1990, 1994), and we will return to these arguments later. The pattern of democracy and autocracy in Eastern Europe and the post-Soviet countries indeed lends support to arguments linking parliamentarism with democracy. However, strong presidencies have been adopted where obstacles unrelated to the constitution are at play. Thus, we have reasons to be cautious about positing causal relations between constitutional regime type and level of democracy. Still, there is no need to exaggerate this caution: the political development in several of the post-Soviet states is troublesome for any advocate of presidential solutions in transitional regimes. In countries like Belarus and Russia, the strong presidential component, introduced from the outset of independence, has contributed to legitimise and reinforce already authoritarian tendencies. The strong presidency has provided a constitutionally sanctioned tool for accumulating power in the hands of presidents that have been less than interested in promoting democratic reforms.

Semi-presidentialism: a growing research field with Eastern Europe at its core

As part of a research project on semi-presidentialism, we have recently conducted a structured literature review on semi-presidential research (Åberg and Sedelius 2016). We will report on some of our findings from this project, which are of relevance to Eastern Europe. The first part of the review,[1] including 327 publications, was a mapping and coding exercise with the purpose of identifying main research themes and gaps. The second part had an in-depth approach and consisted of a limited number of publications (sixty-five), where we reviewed the main theoretical and empirical directions more closely.

It is only from the late 1990s that we can observe a considerable increase in semi-presidential studies, which logically follows the transitions in Eastern Europe and the gradually developing coherence around definitions and classifications of semi-presidentialism. A series of edited volumes by Elgie and his colleagues plays a key role in the sharp rise of studies since the turn of the new millennium (Elgie 1999; Elgie et al. 2007; Elgie and Moestrup 2008; Elgie et al. 2011). By offering a common conceptual framework and a comparative orientation towards analysing political stability and democratisation in nascent and established democracies with semi-presidential constitutions, especially among the post-communist countries, these volumes sparked a new wave of scholarly interest on semi-presidentialism.

When we categorise the identified publications according to covered region, as in Table 5.2, post-communist countries make up for almost 30 per cent of all studies on semi-presidentialism. Eastern Europe is at the empirical core of the sub-field, followed by Western democracies. There are still considerably fewer publications on semi-presidentialism from other regions.

Russia, Poland, Romania, and Ukraine are among the top seven countries most frequently analysed in the literature (Table 5.3). In various ways, those countries can be considered laboratory cases for studying key aspects of the pros and cons of semi-presidentialism in a transitional context, not least on substantial questions regarding constitutional effects and regime direction (Metelska-Szaniawska 2009), variation in presidential powers, and intra-executive relations (Fortin 2013; Protsyk 2006), shifts in party system structures and executive-legislative relations, and cohabitation (Clark 2010; Elgie and McMenamin 2011; also Andrews in this volume). In addition, Russia and Ukraine (1996–2006, 2010–2014) represent two less than democratic cases of president-parliamentarism, whereas Poland and Romania are recent European Union (EU) members with premier-presidential constitutions. The French Fifth Republic – as an established democracy with a nearly sixty-year record of premier-presidentialism – continues to be the standard reference point for theoretical and empirical analysis. From our review data we also find that single case studies have been the predominant research design whenever post-communist countries are included. About 60 per cent of all studies including Eastern European cases focus on one single country.

Table 5.2 Regions covered in studies on semi-presidentialism, percentages

Region	Per cent (no. of cases)
Post-communist countries	29 (80)
Western democracies	24 (68)
Mix of regions	22 (62)
Europe	9 (24)
Asia	8 (21)
Middle East including Turkey	4 (11)
Africa	3 (8)
South and Latin America and the Caribbean	1 (2)
Total	100 (276)

Table 5.3 Top seven countries covered in studies on semi-presidentialism, percentages

Country	Per cent (no. of cases)
France	31 (46)
Russia	14 (21)
Poland	13 (19)
Taiwan	13 (19)
Finland	11 (17)
Romania	10 (15)
Ukraine	8 (12)
Total	100 (149)

Core research themes

Democratisation and the assumed perils of (semi-)presidentialism

Linz's arguments from the early 1990s have established much of the basic elements of the regime type debate as well as the research on semi-presidentialism. Based on observations mainly in Latin America, Linz (1990, 1994) raised the argument that presidentialism is less conducive to democracy than parliamentarism. He argued that there are structural characteristics of presidential systems that make it more likely that they will encounter difficulties, which might contribute to the breakdown of democracy. He associated those difficulties to four factors: (1) the president's fixed term in office; (2) dual legitimacy, that is, both the president and the parliament rely on a popular mandate; (3) the winner-take-all character of presidential elections; and (4) the risk of personalisation of power. Linz claimed that semi-presidentialism shares these features of presidentialism and, moreover, that the responsibility in a semi-presidential system is diffuse and that conflicts therefore are possible and even likely (Linz 1994: 52). His warning that semi-presidentialism (and presidentialism) becomes dependent on the personality and abilities of the president is certainly relevant to East European countries where different presidents, in different ways, have set their imprints on the whole shaping of the political systems.

We should recall the difference between the two sub-types of semi-presidentialism, however. Under premier-presidentialism the government is subjected to parliamentary support only for its survival. President-parliamentarism, by contrast, provides both the parliament and the president with powers over cabinet termination. So, in addition to the risk of authoritarian dominance by the president (e.g. Russia), the dependent and uncertain political position of the government in-between the president and the parliament (e.g. Ukraine 1996–2006) is an additional factor in president-parliamentary regimes. The dual loyalty of the government is thus likely to produce conflict and political stalemate. Sokolowski (2001) showed how the budget process in Russia under Yeltsin was severely hampered by president-parliamentarism. The government, caught between the demands of the president and the parliament, repeatedly adopted unrealistic budgets and upheld economic policies without fiscal discipline. While distancing himself from the responsibility of the economic policies, Yeltsin intervened and directed the course of the budget priorities. The cabinet was very much left on its own, and the budgets, consequently, became products designed to satisfy all kinds of demands. Furthermore, president-parliamentarism usually gives the president the power to dissolve the parliament, which in addition to the powers over both government formation and termination, places the president in a very strong position.

Considering that the president-parliamentary countries in Eastern Europe also provided considerable legislative and appointive powers to their presidents during the 1990s (Table 5.1), presidential dictatorship was to be expected in several cases.

Premier-presidentialism, on the contrary, provides the possibility of combining an often perceived need of presidential leadership with a government firmly anchored in parliament. A visible president with abilities of channelling hope and unity under turbulent periods could work for political stability and democratisation. The popular mandate upheld by the premier-presidential president adds a dimension of increased legitimacy and status. A popularly elected president is capable of functioning as an agent of the electorate, rather than of the parties. In addition, the relatively larger share of formal powers vested in the premier-presidential presidency as compared to its counterpart in parliamentary systems might work to the benefit of the president as an arbiter of the constitution, and of national stability. There is also a major pitfall, however, illustrated by several of the countries in Eastern Europe. Rather than serving as a safeguard of the constitution, a number of post-communist presidents have instead worked to undermine the constitutional order by proposing extensive demands for increased power, also under premier-presidentialism. During their incumbency, Iliescu, Lucinschi, Snegur, Wałęsa, and Yushchenko did all at some point challenge the premier-presidential order in their respective country. Not vastly different from their authoritarian counterparts in Belarus and Central Asia, they campaigned for a larger share of power to be invested in the presidency and for constitutional changes towards stronger presidential rule. Imposing constitutional changes is a high-risk strategy in terms of democratisation and political stability. For example, the repeated attempts by Lucinschi (1997–2000) in Moldova to alter the means of power in favour of the presidency resulted in increased polarisation between the executive and legislative branches, widespread popular cynicism, and legislative blocking of Lucinschi's proposals even in policy areas not directly related to the constitution. In addition, challenging the constitution demands considerable political resources and attention. Other policy issues tend to be secondary in relation to the overarching goal of settling the constitutional disputes. The recurring constitutional clashes in Ukraine – under both forms of semi-presidentialism – have hindered effective policy work by demanding immense political attention, while at the same time reinforcing widespread cynicism among the citizens (Sedelius 2015). In such contexts, the institutional arrangement of semi-presidentialism in both its forms may contribute to undermining the legitimacy of the constitution and ultimately the prospects for democratic governance.

Intra-executive conflict and cohabitation

As showed by the constitutional pattern earlier, the democratic record of president-parliamentarism in Eastern Europe is considerably weaker than for premier-presidentialism. A key factor favouring premier-presidentialism over president-parliamentarism is that the former provides the possibility of combining presidential leadership with a government anchored in parliament, which is positive for fostering more institutionalised political party structures. On the other hand, premier-presidential countries show higher levels of intra-executive conflicts, that is conflicts between the president and prime minister, which have been a core issue of semi-presidential research.

In premier-presidential systems, executive-legislative divides between the president and parliament are likely to appear as intra-executive conflict between the president and the cabinet. Because the legislature has the exclusive power to dismiss the prime minister, the cabinet is dependent on parliamentary support for claiming authority to control the executive branch, and its political orientation is likely to be in the parliament's favour rather than in the president's.

Intra-executive conflicts are thus to be expected, and especially during cohabitation, that is, "where the president and prime minister are from opposing parties and where the president's party is not represented in cabinet" (Elgie 2011: 12).

Cohabitation has been labelled the Achilles heel of semi-presidentialism (Elgie and McMenamin 2011) as it increases the risk of intra-executive tension between the president and the prime minister (Strøm 2000). Although the French Fifth Republic showed abilities to overcome the challenges of cohabitation early on, Suleiman (1994) warned that it might not work smoothly in other circumstances. In a transitional context, the conflict potential is exacerbated by ambiguous and fluid distribution of authority and by low levels of institutionalisation (Skach 2005). Cohabitation is a potential peril as it carries the risk of conflict and stalemate. For instance, Romania's periods of cohabitation between President Băsescu and Prime Minister Popescu-Tăriceanu in 2007–2008, and between President Băsescu and Prime Minister Ponta in 2012–2014, were marked by intense conflict and government crises, which escalated into attempts of impeachment against President Băsescu (Gherghina and Miscoiu 2013). Cohabitation is, however, not only portrayed as a risk, but as a built-in flexibility of semi-presidentialism. In fact it is difficult to identify cases of regime collapse as a consequence of cohabitation (Elgie 2010, 2011) and it has often proven to be quite well-managed (Elgie and McMenamin 2011).

Intra-executive conflict, however, does not occur only under cohabitation, and different studies have reported on the frequency of intra-executive conflict in Eastern Europe (Protsyk 2006). Sedelius and Mashtaler (2013) showed that intra-executive conflict occurred in about one third of all the president-cabinet relations analysed in eight post-communist countries during the period 1991–2011. Some instances of these conflicts – for example, between President Wałęsa and several prime ministers in Poland in 1991–1995, between President Yushchenko and Prime Minister Yanukovych in Ukraine in 2006–2007, and between President Băsescu and Prime Minister Ponta in Romania in 2012 – resulted in political instability and impasse. Sedelius and Ekman (2010) find a statistically significant effect between intra-executive conflict and pre-term resignation of governments under both premier-presidential and president-parliamentary systems in Eastern Europe. They argue that the president's constitutionally weaker position vis-à-vis the prime minister is outweighed by the president's stronger prestige and popularity. Survey data in Eastern Europe report that trust in the president is consistently higher than for any other political institution including the prime minister (see e.g. Ekman et al. 2014; New Europe Barometer 1991–2005; New Russia Barometer 1992–2012). By publicly criticising the government through media and official speeches the president can make it difficult for the prime minister to stay in office. Particularly in the 1990s, this was effectively used by presidents to force certain prime ministers to step down as a consequence, for example, President Wałęsa against the Pawlak cabinet in Poland in 1995; President Zhelev against the Videnov cabinet in Bulgaria in 1997; and President Adamkus against the Vagnorious cabinet in Lithuania in 1999 (Sedelius 2006).

The greater popularity of presidents as compared to the prime ministers is related to the limits placed on their governmental powers. Presidents in premier-presidential regimes are not closely associated with unpopular economic measures or with the day-to-day squabbling in parliament. They have projected themselves to be above party politics, being somewhat elevated from the usual political quarrels. A telling example is Wałęsa, who often claimed to speak for the unrepresented part of the public and exploited his earned popularity as the determined political dissident during the early transition. Some of the prevailing trust in the presidency can be viewed in light of the early popularity of characters such as Havel, Wałęsa, and Zhelev, who earned much of their reputation as political dissidents in the late communist era, which propelled them to positions of prominence in the early post-communist period. Post-communist prime ministers, by contrast, have in many cases been more anonymous figures. This is obviously a source of conflict within the executive. In a nutshell, this relates to the dual legitimacy structure built into the premier-presidential system. Both the president and the prime minister can claim legitimacy on popular elections, but the former leans on a direct electoral mandate while the latter is indirectly elected through parliamentary elections.

Conflict over appointments, dismissals, policy reforms, and constitutional prerogatives are logical expressions of the institutional competition embedded into the dual executive structure of semi-presidentialism. But they also reflect some of the specific and contextual challenges that the post-communist countries have faced in the process of institutionalisation and transition. Still, we find no clear evidence for arguing that intra-executive conflict by itself has been behind any regime breakdowns in Eastern Europe, although it has clearly been an involved factor in severe constitutional struggles, for example, in Romania and Ukraine.

Presidentialisation and party system factors

In accordance with Linz's arguments for parliamentarism over presidentialism, scholars have stressed the importance of a strong and coherent parliamentary arena as well as a consolidated party system in order for semi-presidential democracies to avoid the risk of presidential dictatorship (Kitschelt 1999; Protsyk 2006).

A common feature of the premier-presidential constitutions is that the latter is required to be above partisan politics. The Lithuanian constitution, for example, requires that the president must suspend his activities in political parties until a new presidential election campaign, and the Polish constitution prohibits the president from holding other offices and other public functions. These provisions, primarily aimed at keeping the president politically independent and as serving the whole nation, may complicate the efforts of the presidents to mobilise support for their initiatives, thereby weakening the links between the president and the parliament. In practice, however, there are differences with respect to the strength of the links between the presidents and their affiliated parties despite the constitutional requirements to relinquish all such links. The Lithuanian and Polish cases show that presidents who have no clear party identification prior to their term in office, for example, Adamkus and Wałęsa, tend to resort to the appeals of popular support and legitimacy more often than their counterparts – for example, Brazauskas and Kwaśniewski, who had identifiable, although informal, party links (Pugaciauskas 2000).

Semi-presidentialism includes aspects of presidentialisation of political parties (Passarelli 2015). Samuels and Shugart (2010) have as one of their main claims that in particular president-parliamentarism, just like presidentialism, will tend to have "presidentialised parties". By party presidentialisation they mean that parties – in organising to win presidential elections – delegate considerable discretion to their leaders-as-executives to shape their electoral and governing strategies, and thereby lose the ability to hold their agents to account (2010: 37).

The presidential effects on the party system are also related to the electoral system. Whereas most of the premier-presidential countries in Eastern Europe have employed proportional representation (PR) electoral systems, providing a stronger role to the parties in the parliament, president-parliamentary countries in the post-Soviet region have mainly opted for mixed or majoritarian electoral formulas, producing more non-affiliated candidates and weaker party systems (Protsyk 2006; also Birch in this volume). For instance, Ukraine has tried out three different electoral systems for parliamentary elections: a single member district (SMD) system in 1994–1998, a parallel mixed system in 1998–2002, a closed List PR system in 2006–2007, and a return to the mixed electoral system in 2012. Party system development in Ukraine, as in many other post-Soviet countries, has been characterised less by ideology and programmatic appeals than by patronage and clientelistic linkages (Protsyk and Wilson 2003). The electoral systems have indeed encouraged personalised campaign strategies, and aspiring politicians have prioritised local clientelistic networks over collective efforts of party-building. President-parliamentarism in combination with a strong majority component in the electoral system tends to discourage efforts of party-building while supporting single individual leaders and more personalised politics. As such, the weak system of checks and balances and strong presidential dominance under the president-parliamentary systems in the post-Soviet countries has largely allowed the presidents to be intentional in creating barriers for party development (Chaisty, Cheeseman, and Power 2012).

Underexplored issues on semi-presidentialism in Eastern Europe and elsewhere

During the course of our literature review, we identified a number of research issues that have received surprisingly little attention. We will mention three of them briefly with some general comments: (1) the prime minister's relative power and position; (2) the role of the bureaucracy and public administration; and (3) implications of the EU on the dual executive structure.

The prime minister's relative power and position

The influence of Linz's arguments on the perils of presidentialism has steered scholarly attention towards the president as the natural starting point for semi-presidential research. As mentioned earlier, there are many variants of presidential power indexes existing in the literature – a considerable number of studies analysing intra-executive relations, divided government, and cohabitation – and we seem to know a great deal on the president's position vis-à-vis the party system. As such, it is rather surprising to see how few studies that actually address the prime minister's power position. In our review of abstracts, we identified only 1 out of 327 publications where the main focus was on the side of the prime minister. In the full-text analysis the picture became somewhat more nuanced, but we found only four out of sixty-five publications examining this issue. The prime minister is thus treated as a second-order issue in the research, and we believe that there are good reasons to counter this imbalance.

The ambitions of the prime minister are known to affect the level of intra-executive conflict (Lazardeux 2014), and certain powers on appointment and foreign policy, for example, are often shared between the prime minister and the president (Elgie and Griggs 2013). We seem to lack a proper structure for describing the various features and powers separating one prime minister from the other, which obstructs the ability to properly compare changes in real use of such powers, for example, under cohabitation and non-cohabitation.

The role of the bureaucracy and public administration

The link between the dual executive and the bureaucratic apparatus has received little attention in semi-presidential studies. In our sample, only 7 out of 327 semi-presidential publications have bureaucracy issues as a main focus, and countries in Eastern Europe are present in only 3 of them. The bureaucracy is a central part of the democratic chain of representation and accountability (Schleiter and Morgan-Jones 2010; Strøm 2000) and in theories on veto players, the bureaucratic actors are identified as crucial in the policy process and its outcomes (Tsebelis 2000). Semi-presidential studies have a clear focus on presidential powers but most often without including bureaucratic resources as part of presidential powers and abilities. When creating an index of the strength of the legislatures in a number of post-communist countries, Fish (2006) includes administrative resources as part of the legislature's overall capacity and finds, for example, that the Russian Duma is not only weak in its constitutional and party basis, but also in terms of relative administrative resources. To the extent that many East European countries are institutionalising their political system, the bureaucracy as such is often far behind (Zubek and Goetz 2010; also Meyer-Sahling in this volume). We believe that research on semi-presidentialism would benefit from more studies on the bureaucratic state apparatus in order to better grasp the variation of intra-executive politics and policy co-ordination in different semi-presidential regimes.

The EU and semi-presidentialism

The extent to which the EU is important to intra-executive and executive-legislative politics in semi-presidential countries is another aspect that deserves more research attention. Only 7 out of 327 publications in our review treat EU-related issues as a main focus. For example, we have very little research on the role and division of power between the president and the prime minister in relation to the EU institutions. In terms of intra-executive relations between the president and prime minister, EU membership and representation challenge the division of labour between the two actors, as foreign policy cannot be easily separated from domestic issues at the EU level. In some cases representation and coordination of EU policy have surfaced into open conflict, such as in Poland between President Kaczyński and Prime Minister Tusk in 2008, and in Romania between President Băsescu and Prime Minister Ponta in 2012 (Jasiewicz and Jasiewicz-Betkiewicz 2009; Raunio 2012). Raunio (2012) finds that EU membership tends to strengthen the prime minister's relative powers vis-à-vis the president by means of representation in EU as well as by increased importance of the prime minister's office – at the expense of the foreign policy department and the presidency. How the East European EU-member states operate EU-policy and representation is of relevance for understanding the real world of semi-presidential decision making. Future studies on rules, organisational arrangements, and conventions that structure the coordination between the president and the prime minister in this regard would also need to go beyond both nation state borders and formal constitutional rules to identify institutional solutions that facilitate successful policymaking.

Conclusions

Variants of semi-presidentialism are the most common constitutional choice in Eastern Europe. Following the post-communist transitions, parliamentarism and premier-presidentialism prevailed in Central Europe, whereas president-parliamentarism was installed among the majority of the post-Soviet countries. More recently, the trend has been to limit presidential powers even among the post-Soviet countries and also to abandon president-parliamentarism (Armenia, Georgia, and Ukraine). As of 2016, only the authoritarian regimes of Azerbaijan, Belarus, and Russia are left with president-parliamentary constitutions. The pattern of democratisation in Eastern Europe indeed lends support to the warnings once raised by Linz and his followers. The post-communist countries with the strongest power vested in their presidencies are also the ones with the worst records of democratisation, and president-parliamentarism as such finds no evident support in the academic literature.

Our literature review shows that comparative studies of post-communist semi-presidentialism, including many single-case analyses, have been essential to the advancement of theory testing and new research questions. Although Linz's arguments on the perils of presidentialism (and semi-presidentialism) are still highly influential, the sub-field has largely left the strategy of using semi-presidentialism as a single independent variable in itself. Instead more recent studies are occupied with issues such as the variation and logics behind intra-executive and executive-legislative relations, and the president's powers and relation to the political parties.

We finally identified some research issues that we think have received too little attention in the literature on semi-presidentialism. We mentioned the lack of studies on the position and powers of the prime minister, the role and importance of the bureaucratic apparatus, and the potential effects of EU membership on executive-legislative politics in semi-presidential regimes. We believe that more studies on these and related aspects would take the semi-presidential research further – and the semi-presidential countries in Eastern Europe are indeed critical cases in these regards.

Notes

* We are grateful to the Swedish Research Council, Project No. 2014–1260, for financial support of this research.
1 We searched mainly in two databases, Web of Science and the International Bibliography of the Social Sciences, where we limited our search by a set of semantic varieties on the term "semi-presidentialism". We also added the most relevant items including books and articles found in the list of publications from the website *The Semi-Presidential One* by Robert Elgie (2007–2015), and from searches on Google Scholar.

References

Åberg, J., and Sedelius, T. (2016). *A structured review of semi-presidential studies: Assumptions, debates and deviating foundations.* Paper presented on the 24th International Political Science Association (IPSA) Conference. Poznań, Poland, July 2016.

Chaisty, P., Cheeseman, N., and Power, T. (2012). Rethinking the 'presidentialism debate': Conceptualizing coalitional politics in cross-regional perspective. *Democratization*, 21(1), 72–94.

Cheibub, J., Elkins, Z., and Ginsburg, T. (2014). Beyond presidentialism and parliamentarism. *British Journal of Political Science*, 44(3), 515–544.

Clark, W. (2010). Boxing Russia: Executive-legislative powers and the categorization of Russia's regime type. *Demokratizatsiya*, 19(1), 5–22.

Doyle, D., and Elgie, R. (2016). Maximizing the reliability of cross-national measures of presidential power. *British Journal of Political Science*, 46(4), 731–741.

Duverger, M. (1980). A new political system model: Semi-presidential government. *European Journal of Political Research*, 8(2), 165–187.

Ekman, J., Berglund, S., and Duvold, K. (2014). *Baltic Barometer 2014.* [Datafile]. Stockholm: Södertörn University.

Elgie, R. (Ed.) (1999). *Semi-Presidentialism in Europe.* Oxford: Oxford University Press.

Elgie, R. (2007–2015). The Semi-presidential One [blog]. www.semipresidentialism.com

Elgie, R. (2010). Semi-presidentialism, cohabitation and the collapse of electoral democracies, 1990–2008. *Government and Opposition*, 45(1), 29–49.

Elgie, R. (2011). *Semi-presidentialism: Sub-types and democratic performance.* Oxford: Oxford University Press,

Elgie, R. (2015). Three waves of semi-presidential studies. *Democratization*, 22(7), 1–22.

Elgie, R., and Griggs, S. (2013). *French politics: Debates and controversies.* London: Routledge.

Elgie, R., and McMenamin, I. (2011). Explaining the onset of cohabitation under semi-presidentialism. *Political Studies*, 59(3), 616–635.

Elgie, R., and Moestrup, S. (Eds.) (2007). *Semi-presidentialism outside Europe: A comparative study.* New York: Routledge.

Elgie, R., and Moestrup, S. (Eds.) (2008). *Semi-presidentialism in Central and Eastern Europe.* Manchester: Manchester University Press.

Elgie, R., Moestrup, S., and Wu, Y.-S. (Eds.) (2011). Semi-presidentialism and democracy. New York: Palgrave Macmillan.

Fish, M.S. (2006). Stronger legislatures, stronger democracies. *Journal of Democracy*, 17(1), 5–20.

Fortin, J. (2013). Measuring presidential powers: Some pitfalls of aggregate measurement. *International Political Science Review*, 34(1), 91–112.

Gherghina, S., and Miscoiu, S. (2013). The failure of cohabitation: Explaining the 2007 and 2012 institutional crises in Romania. *East European Politics & Societies and Cultures*, 27(4), 668–684.

Jasiewicz, K., and Jasiewicz-Betkiewicz, A. (2009). Poland. In *European Journal of Political Research*. The Political Data Yearbook, 48(7–8): 1073–1079.

Kitschelt, H. (1999). *Post-communist party systems: Competition, representation, and inter-party cooperation.* Cambridge: Cambridge University Press.

Lazardeux, S. (2014). *Cohabitation and conflicting politics in French policymaking.* New York: Palgrave.

Lijphart, A. (1999). *Patterns of democracy: Government forms and performance in thirty-six countries.* New Haven, CT: Yale University Press.

Linz, J. J. (1990). The perils of presidentialism. *Journal of Democracy*, 1(1), 51–69.

Linz, J. J. (1994). Presidential or parliamentary democracy: Does it make a difference? In J. J. Linz and A. Valenzuela, eds. *The failure of presidential democracy.* Volume 1. Baltimore, MD: Johns Hopkins University Press, 3–87.

Metelska-Szaniawska, K. (2009). Constitutions and economic reforms in transition: An empirical study. *Constitutional Political Economy*, 20(1), 1–41.

New Baltic Barometer 1993–2004, CSPP School of Government & Public Policy. University of Strathclyde, Glasgow.

New Europe Barometer 1991–2005, CSPP School of Government & Public Policy. University of Strathclyde, Glasgow.

New Russia Barometer 1992–2012, CSPP School of Government & Public Policy. University of Strathclyde, Glasgow.

Passarelli, G. (Ed.) (2015). *The presidentialization of political parties: Organizations, institutions and leaders.* New York: Palgrave Macmillan.

Protsyk, O. (2006). Intra-executive competition between president and prime minister: Patterns of institutional conflict and cooperation under semi-presidentialism. *Political Studies*, 54(2), 219–244.

Protsyk, O., and Wilson, A. (2003). Centre politics in Russia and Ukraine: Patronage, power and virtuality. *Party Politics*, 9(6), 703–727.

Pugaciauskas, V. (2000). Semi-presidential institutional models and democratic stability: Comparative analysis of Lithuania and Poland. In *Lithuanian Political Science Yearbook 1999*. Vilnius: Vilnius University, 1–26.

Raunio, T. (2012). Semi-presidentialism and European integration: Lessons from Finland for constitutional design. *Journal of European Public Policy*, 19(4), 567–584.

Roper, S. D. (2002). Are all semipresidential regimes the same? A comparison of premier-presidential regimes. *Comparative Politics*, 34(3), 253–272.

Samuels, D., and Shugart, M. S. (2010). *Presidents, parties, and prime ministers: How the separation of powers affects party organization and behavior.* Cambridge: Cambridge University Press.

Sartori, G. (1996). *Comparative constitutional engineering: An inquiry into structures, incentives and outcomes.* Basingstoke: Macmillan.

Schleiter, P., and Morgan-Jones, E. (2010). Who's in charge? Presidents, assemblies, and the political control of semipresidential systems. *Comparative Political Studies*, 43(11), 1415–1441.

Sedelius, T. (2006). *The tug-of-war between presidents and prime ministers: Semi-Presidentialism in Central and Eastern Europe.* Dissertation. Örebro: Örebro Studies.

Sedelius, T. (2015). Party presidentialization in Ukraine. In G. Passarelli, ed. *The presidentialization of political parties: Organizations, institutions and leaders.* New York: Palgrave Macmillan.

Sedelius, T., and Ekman, J. (2010). Intra-executive conflict and cabinet instability: Effects of semi-presidentialism in Central and Eastern Europe. *Government and Opposition*, 45(4), 505–530.

Sedelius, T., and Mashtaler, O. (2013). Two decades of semi-presidentialism: Issues of intra-executive conflict in Central and Eastern Europe 1991–2011. *East European Politics*, 29(2), 109–134.

Shugart, M. S. (2005). Semi-presidential systems: Dual executive and mixed authority patterns. *French politics*, 3(3), 323–351.

Shugart, M. S., and Carey, J. M. (1992). *Presidents and assemblies: Constitutional design and electoral dynamics.* New York: Cambridge University Press.

Siaroff, A. (2003). Comparative presidencies: The inadequacy of the presidential, semi-presidential and parliamentary distinction. *European Journal of Political Research*, 42(3), 287–312.

Skach, C. (2005). Constitutional origins of dictatorship and democracy. *Constitutional Political Economy*, 16(4), 347–368.

Sokolowski, A. (2001). Bankrupt government: Intra-executive relations and the politics of budgetary irresponsibility in El'tsin's Russia. *Europe-Asia Studies*, 53(4), 541–572.

Suleiman, E. N. (1994). Presidentialism and political stability in France. In J. J. Linz and A. Valenzuela, eds. *The failure of presidential democracy.* Volume 1. Baltimore, MD: Johns Hopkins University Press, 137–162.

Stepan, A., and Skach, C. (1993). Constitutional frameworks and democratic consolidation: Parliamentarism versus presidentialism. *World Politics*, 46(1), 1–22.

Strøm, K. (2000). Delegation and accountability in parliamentary democracies. *European Journal of Political Research*, 37(3), 261–289.

Tsebelis, G. (2000). Veto players and institutional analysis. *Governance*, 13(4), 441–474.

Zubek, R., and Goetz, K. H. (2010). Performing to type? How state institutions matter in East Central Europe. *Journal of Public Policy*, 30(1), 1–22.

6

INSTITUTIONALISING PARLIAMENTS IN CENTRAL AND EASTERN EUROPE

Josephine T. Andrews

Introduction

The literature on legislatures in Central and Eastern Europe (hereafter CEE) is part of a broader inquiry into the adoption and implementation of democratic institutions in the aftermath of the collapse of communist political and economic systems between 1989 and the end of 1991. Beginning with a focus on the design of basic constitutional structures (Lijphart 1992, Geddes 1996, Elster et al. 1998), that is, the parliamentary and semi-presidential systems characteristic of new democracies in CEE (Shugart 2005), inquiry quickly expanded to include the development of other institutions essential to parliamentary democracy, especially political parties and party systems (Bielasiak 2002, Tavits 2005), cabinets (Blondel and Müller-Rommel 2001), and implications of the dual executive (Protsyk 2005). Once it became clear that post-communist countries in Europe would have the opportunity to join the European Union (EU) assuming they could meet the Copenhagen Conditions, it was necessary to understand the impact of the EU's accession process on both institutional design and development, and this inspired a substantial and growing literature in and of itself (Grabbe 2002, Malová and Haughton 2002). Initially, most of this work focused directly or indirectly on the relationship between institutional design and the success of democratisation; even work on the impact of the EU on institutional development was centrally concerned with the success of EU conditionality on democratisation (Schimmelfennig and Scholtz 2008).

Beginning in the second decade of democratic transition, scholars increasingly focused on the degree to which the new parliaments had become sufficiently autonomous, internally complex, and stable to support effective policymaking, a process generally referred to as 'legislative institutionalisation' (Mansfeldová 2011). Recognition of the importance of legislative institutionalisation was partly the result of scholarship demonstrating significant variation in acceding countries' ability to do more than superficially comply with EU conditionality (Dimitrova 2010). Only recently have scholars begun to address the reasons for variation in parliamentary performance across CEE (Jahn and Müller-Rommel 2010).

For the purposes of this chapter, I focus predominantly on analyses of the fifteen post-communist countries which at the time of this writing had experienced at least fifteen years of sustained democratic transition and which are widely considered to be democracies. This set of cases includes five former republics of the Soviet Union (Lithuania, Latvia, Estonia, Ukraine, and

Moldova), six former satellites (Poland, Czech Republic, Slovakia, Hungary, Bulgaria, and Romania), three former republics of Yugoslavia (Slovenia, Croatia, and Macedonia) and one additional Balkan country, Albania.[1]

The chapter is divided into three sections, each corresponding to a major phase in the chronological progression of study of legislatures in CEE. The first section focuses on institutional design, the second on legislative institutionalisation, and the third on legislative performance. In the first section, I discuss the early literature on constitutional design and succeeding work on development of related institutions including party systems, the dual executive, and cabinets. In the second section, I discuss literature on legislative institutionalisation, especially as it concerns professionalisation of members of parliament, development of internal structures such as party councils and committees, and the impact of EU conditionality. In the third section, I present a puzzle – given the relative similarity in institutional design of countries in CEE (all are parliamentary or semi-presidential), why is there such significant variation in legislative performance?

Institutional design of parliament

Constitutional design

Taking advantage of the accessibility and transparency of constitutional negotiations in CEE, whether occurring in parliaments, specially elected constitutional assemblies, or in extra-parliamentary round tables, scholars contributed to an influential literature on institutional design. One body of work analysed the negotiations themselves, describing a process in which two or more strategic actors, all of whom interested in ensuring themselves a role in the new democratic system, bargained over specific institutional features such as the presence or absence of a directly elected president (Lijphart 1992, Geddes 1996, Elster et al. 1998), presence of an upper parliamentary chamber (Osiatynski 1996), and structure of the state as unitary or federal in nature (Calda 1996). According to the logic of this rational-choice perspective, bargaining by multiple actors in which all are uncertain about their future electoral chances will result in rules that both maximise the chance for each to gain seats in the new legislature (Shvetsova 2003, Andrews and Jackman 2005) and the opportunity for those that do gain seats to participate in policymaking (Geddes 1996). Following this logic, we would expect countries in CEE to adopt proportional electoral rules and parliamentary systems of government. In those cases where one party was popular enough to believe that its leader could win a national presidential contest, we might expect adoption of a semi-presidential system (Geddes 1996, Sajó 1996).

Scholars also focused on a second factor, the influence of Europe's parliamentary tradition, in some cases embodied in past constitutional experience (e.g. Poland, Estonia, Latvia, Lithuania, and Czechoslovakia), and for others in the influence of West European templates (Malová and Haughton 2002). The two most relevant constitutional templates were those of the French Fifth Republic, with its innovative semi-presidential design, and post-war Germany, which introduced the electoral threshold as a means to limit the access of small parties to national politics (Elster 1991, Olson and Norton 1996). Hence, among the fifteen CEE countries listed in the introduction, all adopted either parliamentary or semi-presidential systems (also Sedelius and Åberg in this volume). Further, all of the CEE countries imposed electoral thresholds on their proportional electoral tiers (also Birch in this volume). For countries that began the transition later, such as the former republics of Yugoslavia, the goal of joining the EU ensured that they would adopt constitutional designs in line with West European norms (Schimmelfennig and Scholtz 2008, Renner and Trauner 2009, Bieber 2011).

In the case of two of the CEE countries, Moldova and Ukraine, Crowther has noted that a significant delay between collapse of the communist systems and design and adoption of new constitutions meant that neither of these two countries was able to make a radical break with its Soviet past. Instead, these two countries adopted new constitutions under the oversight of parliaments elected during the Soviet period, and in Ukraine also under a powerful president elected during the Soviet period (Crowther 2011, p. 148). Furthermore, dominance of Soviet-era elites led to poorly designed constitutions that failed to demarcate between the powers of executive and legislature (Wolczuk 2001).

In summary, constitutions throughout CEE were the result of negotiation, whether through vigorous and productive debate as in Poland or through tepid and drawn-out discussion as in Ukraine. Case studies of negotiations highlight the paramount role of strategic elites who were more intent on the short-term goal of political survival than on ensuring successful democratisation (Elster 1996). It may be, however, that the process of negotiation, which contributed to adoption of parliamentary forms of government, is itself of paramount importance in ensuring democratic success. This conclusion is supported both by comparison of the quality of democracy across countries in which robust, multi-party negotiations occurred versus those in which negotiations were flawed (e.g. Romania and Bulgaria) or delayed (e.g. Moldova and Ukraine) and by Wright's systematic analysis (2008). In addition, all of the countries in CEE, including Ukraine and Moldova, were influenced by proximity to Europe and by Europe's long tradition of parliamentary government, a tradition embodied in the pseudo-democratic structure of these countries' prior communist systems (Ludwikowski 1996). It is not surprising, therefore, that all adopted some form of parliamentarism.

Among the fifteen post-communist democracies considered in this study, initially six were parliamentary (Albania, Czech Republic, Estonia, Hungary, Latvia, and Slovakia) and nine were semi-presidential (Bulgaria, Croatia, Lithuania, Macedonia, Moldova, Poland, Romania, Slovenia, and Ukraine). All fifteen parliaments were ascribed considerable powers. Except in the case of Poland and Ukraine, heads of state, whether indirectly elected by parliament or directly elected by the population, were given few legislative or non-legislative powers (Metcalf 2000). Further, since the early 1990s, five of the countries have made major changes to the structure of executive legislative relations, which have served either to strengthen or leave undiminished the powers of parliament.[2] In fact, a comparison of the institutional powers of parliaments in CEE with those of Western Europe, as captured by Fish and Kroenig's Parliamentary Powers Index (2009), shows that parliaments in CEE are as strong as or stronger than parliaments in Western Europe (Andrews 2014).

Characteristics of party systems in CEE and implications for parliament

Since the onset of the transition, scholars have noted the strikingly high number of parties competing and winning seats in parliamentary elections across the region (Rose and Munro 2003; also Sikk in this volume). Although this was especially true of early elections (Bielasiak 2002, Reich 2004), parliaments in CEE continue to include relatively high effective numbers of political parties (see Table 6.1). Given that in every country in the region, proportional representation or a mixed electoral system involving a proportional tier of substantial size was adopted, a multi-party system was to be expected (Birch 2001, Moser and Scheiner 2012). Nevertheless, stable party systems have been slow to develop (Tavits 2005, Lewis 2007). Many CEE parliaments continue to experience significant changes in the composition of parties competing and gaining seats in parliament, a phenomenon captured by the volatility in parliamentary membership from election to election (Toka 1995, Mair 1997, Sikk 2005, Tavits 2008, Andrews and Bairett 2014). Thus, high party fragmentation and low party system institutionalisation characterise parliaments in the new democracies of CEE.

Executive-legislative relations and intra-executive conflict

After the adoption of basic constitutional rules in the early 1990s, institutional arrangements including those delineating the powers of legislature and executive took time to stabilise (Kopecký 2004). Given that in most of these countries constitutions could be changed by supermajorities in parliament, significant constitutional changes have continued to occur through the present.

Initially, because the focus of both constitutional design and change lay with newly elected parliaments across the region, parliaments were at the centre of new democratic politics (Ágh 1995). As yet untested constitutional divisions of power between parliament, cabinet, and president, whether elected by parliament or the people, meant that in the early years executives appeared weak relative to legislatures. Party fragmentation and lack of loyalty among party members hampered newly installed governments in their efforts to ensure that their programmes were passed by parliament (Malová and Haughton 2002, Kopecký 2004). However, as countries confronted the daunting task of rebuilding economic and political institutions in line with strict International Monetary Fund (IMF) and EU standards, the role of legislative agenda-setter moved from parliaments to governments (Mansfeldová 2011, Fink-Hafner 2011, Kopecký 2004). Indeed, in the final phase of EU accession, the parliamentary agenda was dominated by passage of EU law, a process directed by the governments of the acceding countries. Thus, the relative power of parliament and executive has shifted since the transition began, with governments becoming increasingly important and powerful actors (Olson and Norton 2007).

With the increase in governmental power has come increased conflict within the executive branch itself in countries with both a prime minister and an elected president. Because much of our prior understanding of the relationship between president and prime minister in semi-presidential systems was based on analysis of France, a country with stable majority government, the creation of many new semi-presidential systems that rely primarily on coalition government provided the opportunity for greater understanding of the dynamics of this increasingly common governmental type. Among the fifteen countries on which this chapter focuses, and taking into account recent constitutional changes, ten are semi-presidential. If we consider also Serbia and Montenegro, that number reaches twelve. Thus, most of the new democracies in CEE have adopted parliamentary systems with a directly elected president. Although it is not inconceivable that conflict could emerge between a prime minister and president, each of which is elected by parliament (Tavits 2009), it is much less likely than when the prime minister and president are answerable to different constituencies.

Conflict between presidents and prime ministers in CEE is not uncommon and was an object of study soon after democratic transition began (Baylis 1996). Reasons for such conflict include ambiguity in the constitutional responsibilities of president and prime minister, differences in the constituencies to which each executive is responsible, incongruence of electoral cycles, and the legitimacy conferred on the president by direct election (Elgie 2011).

Protsyk analyses how the composition of cabinet, whether single or multi-party, majority, minority or technocratic, and the relative party affiliation of president and prime minister, impact the potential for conflict (2005, 2006). Building a dataset of intra-executive conflict based on reports in the *East European Constitutional Review*, Protsyk finds that conflict is least likely when the prime minister heads a majority coalition and when the president and prime minister are from the same party. Conflict is most likely when the prime minister and president are from different parties, even if the prime minister heads a majority government. Thus, cohabitation is a major contributor to intra-executive conflict. Even so, Protsyk finds that in CEE, "presidents challenge prime ministers, who are backed by a solid parliamentary majority, more often than the French experience of cohabitation would suggest" (2005, p. 151). There is some evidence that presidents are more likely to challenge prime ministers when the prime minister heads a minority or technocratic cabinet. According to Protsyk, parliamentary fragmentation contributes to intra-executive conflict, because it is strongly related to occurrence of minority and technocratic governments (2005, pp. 152–153).

Using an expanded set of sources, Sedelius and Mashtaler (2013) generate a dataset of seventy-six instances of intra-executive conflict between 1991 and 2011. They are primarily interested in the frequency as well as the subject of conflict over the time period. They categorise conflict as being 'low' or 'high', and they report few differences in their own assessment of the degree of conflict with that of Protsyk (2005), thus confirming the validity of their coding. They too find that cohabitation is associated with heightened conflict, as is minority government. In addition, Sedelius and Mashtaler find that the rate of intra-executive conflict has remained constant from the early to later periods. Most interestingly, they find that throughout the twenty-year period, struggles between president and prime minister erupt most often when presidents attempt to expand their powers by broadening the interpretation of the their constitutional prerogatives against the resistance of prime ministers who view this as encroachment into the proper domain of prime minister and cabinet (2013, p. 118). Conflict over policy is almost as frequent (2013, table 6.4). Finally, they find no difference between the two sub-types of semi-presidential systems, premier-presidential and president-parliamentary (Shugart and Carey 1992) in rate and type of conflict. Although most studies of intra-executive conflict examine the causes of conflict, Sedelius and Ekman (2010) find that such conflict is itself a significant predictor of cabinet instability, the subject of the next sub-section.

In summary, studies of intra-executive conflict in CEE have provided a framework in which to understand the nature and causes of intra-executive conflict, which has greatly expanded our understanding of executive dynamics in semi-presidential systems. However, debate continues as to the implications of intra-executive conflict for democratic performance (Elgie 2011).

Government stability

Few would disagree with the statement that party governments in CEE have been relatively unstable (Blondel and Müller-Rommel 2001, Nikolenyi 2004, Grotz and Weber 2012). Data collected by Müller-Rommel et al. (2004) on twelve CEE countries demonstrates that government turnover is generally quite high (Grotz and Weber 2012, table 6.1). For example, the proportion of governments that survived until the end of their terms ranges from a low of 21 per cent in Latvia to a high of 63 per cent in Hungary. On average, only 38 per cent of all governments in these twelve countries survived until the end of their terms. Somer-Topcu and Williams show that among the CEE countries that joined the EU in the fourth enlargement, the average cabinet duration was about fifty days shorter than the average duration in Western Europe (2008, table 6.1).

If caretaker governments are included in the calculation of government duration, as Conrad and Golder argue they should be, the duration of cabinets in CEE is shortened (2010, p. 126). Conrad and Golder modify the Müller-Rommel et al. data by including duration of caretaker cabinets as well as those installed following an election.[3] According to Conrad and Golder, in an environment such as CEE in which there is a high level of government turnover, it is important to differentiate the duration of electorally installed governments from caretaker governments that under these circumstances may occupy cabinet for substantial periods of time (2010, p. 132).

Efforts to clarify the impact of party system fragmentation on cabinet duration find that while the effective number of parties in parliament has no direct effect on cabinet, the number of parties in government significantly shortens the expected duration (Somer-Topcu and Williams 2008), and this finding holds when studies include duration of caretaker governments (Tzelgov 2011, Grotz and Weber 2012). Further, Tzelgov finds that inclusion of former communist parties in the cabinet increases cabinet survival, a finding confirmed by Grotz and Weber. These authors suggest that in CEE, cabinet duration is affected by the complexity of the transitional environment – a part of which consists of the unique role of former communist parties, which must be incorporated via interactions with standard predictors of cabinet stability (Grotz and Weber 2012).

What are the consequences of cabinet instability? Are these consequences deleterious to democratisation and parliamentary performance? Initially, scholars believed that cabinet instability would hinder the ability of newly independent post-communist countries to adopt a coherent program of economic policy reform (Alesina et al. 1996). Conrad and Golder assert that extensive experience of caretaker governments (which will occur in countries with high government turnover) may impede a country's ability to implement economic reform (2010, p. 132). Meyer-Sahling and Veen find that in those countries where government change is frequent and involves change in ideological composition of the cabinet, incoming ministers seek to politicise the senior ranks of civil service (2012). However, Hellman finds that "postcommunist countries with a greater dispersion of political power and a larger number of veto points in the policymaking process have stabilized faster and more effectively than countries in which political power is more concentrated" (1998, fig. 6.8). Mirroring Hellman's findings, Jahn and Müller-Rommel find that the number of parties in government had no impact on economic policy output, but it increased numbers of institutional veto players and so improved economic policymaking (2010).

While cabinet instability is especially high in CEE, we do not yet know if this is a neutral result of competitive multi-party democracy in a region with very little prior democratic experience and only weakly institutionalised political parties (with the notable exception of former communist parties) or a sign of institutional dysfunction (see also Enyedi and Deegan-Krause in this volume). It is worth noting that there appears to be no relationship between cabinet stability and success of democratisation. In Table 6.1, I present data on average number of parties in the cabinets of fifteen CEE countries (which include the twelve analysed by Grotz and Weber 2012), and demonstrate that not only are multi-party cabinets the norm in CEE, but cabinets range in size from one or two members to as many as five, six, or seven. In addition, Table 6.1 presents the high level of prime ministerial turnover across the region. Countries with highly unstable cabinets include almost equal numbers of those struggling to consolidate democracy (e.g. Ukraine, Moldova, and Albania) and those widely deemed to be consolidated (e.g. Poland, Latvia, Lithuania, and the Czech Republic).

In summary, CEE is characterised by strong parliamentary government, fairly high levels of intra-executive conflict in those countries that adopted semi-presidential systems, fragmented party systems, and high government turnover. While some scholars are concerned that intra-executive conflict and cabinet instability may prove deleterious to democracy, it is also possible that we are witnessing a 'new normal' given historical circumstances unique to the region and the institutional combinations installed in the wake of communism's collapse.

Table 6.1 Partisan features of CEE parliaments[4]

Country	Years constitutional democracy	ENPP First election and Most recent election prior to 2013	Number of parties in cabinet, lowest to highest	Average number of parties in cabinet, start of transition to 2012	Number of prime ministers, beginning of transition to present	Prime ministers per year	Average checks: DPI[5] measure of veto players	Polity 2015
Poland	1990 to present	10.86 to 2.82	2 to 7	2.6	17	.65	4.25	10
Czech Republic	1992 to present	4.8 to 4.51	1 to 3	2.2	10	.43	5.5	8
Slovakia	1992 to present	3.19 to 4	1 to 4	3.4	7	.3	4.25	10
Hungary	1990 to present	3.79 to 2	1 to 3	2.2	9	.36	3.5	10
Bulgaria	1991 to present	2.41 to 3.34	1 to 3	1.6	11	.44	2.75	9
Romania	1993 to present	4.78 to 3.61	2 to 5	3.15	14	.56	6.25	9
Estonia	1993 to present	5.9 to 3.84	1 to 3	2.5	9	.36	3.75	9
Latvia	1993 to present	5 to 3.93	3 to 7	4.5	15	.65	5	8
Lithuania	1993 to present	3 to 5.79	1 to 4	2.5	13	.57	3	10
Ukraine	1994 to present	10 to 3.3	1 to 3	1.7	14	.61	4.5	6
Moldova	1994 to present	2.62 to 3.23	1 to 4	1.6	13	.57	2.25	8
Slovenia	1990 to present	6.61 to 4.43	2 to 6	3.9	10	.48	4.75	10
Macedonia	1994 to present	3.65 to 2.9	3 to 5	3.2	7	.28	2.25	9
Croatia	2000 to present	2.92 to 2.99	1 to 6	3.6	10	.48	2.75	9
Albania	1991 to present	1.88 to 2.21	2 to 7	4.6	12	.5	2.25	9

Legislative institutionalisation

The second major body of work on legislatures in CEE concerns the degree to which parliaments have developed the capacity for consistent and effective policymaking, a process generally known as institutionalisation. The concept was first introduced by Polsby (1968), and although his original definition has been continually debated and revised (Copeland and Patterson 1994), legislative institutionalisation is generally operationalised in terms of stability and professionalisation of membership and staff, and development of internal rules and structures to facilitate lawmaking and ensure autonomy from other institutions especially the executive (Olson and Norton 1996). Scholarship has focused on three main aspects of institutionalisation: stability and professionalisation of members of parliament, development of committees, and the influence of the EU and the accession process. I discuss each in turn.

Parliamentary membership

Although the literature on parliamentary membership in CEE does not yet include a systematic analysis of predictors of professionalisation, multi-country case studies provide sufficient information to compare levels of professionalisation across parliaments. I summarise findings across a number of these studies and draw several general conclusions.

It is necessary to recognise the impact of low party system institutionalisation on instability of parliamentary membership. Electoral volatility in CEE is comparatively high; in fact, levels of volatility were initially historically the highest recorded in any of the world's regions (Bielasiak 2002) and, unlike post-democratisation levels of volatility in Latin America, continue to be unusually high today (Andrews and Bairett 2014; also Enyedi and Deegan- Krause in this volume). By definition, high levels of electoral volatility, such as the 20 per cent to 60 per cent common in CEE over the first six democratic elections (Andrews and Bairett 2014, fig. 6.1), lead to high levels of turnover from parliament to parliament. Thus, low levels of party system institutionalisation in CEE have impeded the development of a stable core of experienced representatives in many if not most of these countries.

A number of scholars have confirmed that professionalisation of parliamentary representatives, especially in terms of parliamentary experience, is quite low across CEE (Ilonszki and Edinger 2007), although there is important variation across cases (Chiva 2007, Protsyk and Matichescu 2011, Crowther 2011, Khmelko 2011).

Ilonszki and Edinger (2007) present a multi-country study comparing professionalisation and parliamentary service of MPs across Croatia, Czech Republic, Estonia, Hungary, Latvia, Lithuania, Poland, Romania, Russia, and Slovakia.[6] In general, they find that although the professionalisation of deputies prior to entering parliament has increased considerably since founding elections, stability of parliamentary membership remains low. Relating to experience, they find that across all nine CEE parliaments over the first five terms, the proportion of MPs with prior experience in at least one political office had risen considerably in all parliaments since the founding election (Ilonszki and Edinger 2007, p. 155 discussion, table 6.4), with the exception of Poland where the proportion was very high in the first parliament (86 per cent) and remained high. Relating to stability of membership, they find considerable instability across all parliaments. Turnover in parliamentary membership ranges from 31 per cent in Hungary's fourth term to 60 percent in Estonia's fifth term, although since the founding elections it has declined in all of the CEE countries except Estonia (2007, table 6.5). Mansfeldová reports similar trends (2011, table 6.1), as do Shabad and Slomczynski for Poland and the Czech Republic (2002, tables 6.4 and 6.5). Ilonszki and Edinger express a concern shared by other scholars:

High turnover rates in most of the post-communist parliaments more than a decade after regime change limit professionalization of the representative elites. Thus, the masses of newcomers regularly entering the parliament after each and every election have become a major concern.

(2007, p. 157)

In a study of MPs in Hungary and Romania, Chiva argues that MPs in Romania have been active in their parties for long periods of time; therefore, professionalisation in Romania is increasing despite high levels of parliamentary turnover (2007). Unfortunately, an alternative interpretation is possible. Protsyk and Matichescu describe political parties in Romania as clientelistic, fostering close connections with the business community (2011). They report that political corruption involving the relationship between political parties and business is a recurring topic in the Romania media (Protsyk and Matichescu 2011, p. 211). Furthermore, they suggest that business experience is not an indicator of increased professionalisation of parliamentary membership but of the corruption of the relationship between business and the political system (2011, pp. 211–213). "Unlike parties in consolidated Western European democracies, the Romanian parties rely heavily in their candidate selection practices on very small and highly elitist groups of business managers" (2011, p. 220). They argue that it is important to retain concept validity when defining professionalisation of parliamentary membership; experience within the party may not offer the same kind of 'professionalisation' as parliamentary experience.

In a similar vein, Crowther demonstrates that stability of parliamentary membership is not a sufficient measure of professionalisation. Over several articles, Crowther has argued that legislatures in Moldova and Ukraine are poorly institutionalized, even though statistics on turnover in parliamentary membership for Moldova (Crowther 2014, table 10.4) and Ukraine (Semenova 2014, table 12.2) show a similar downward trend to that of other CEE countries. Crowther explains poor legislative institutionalisation in Moldova and Ukraine not in terms of MPs experience in the post-communist period, but in terms of their connections to the communist-era elite and Communist Party (2011, 2014). Khmelko echoes Crowther in asserting that in post-Soviet countries (e.g. Ukraine and Moldova) the new elites are actually just the old elites in new clothes, and they have perpetuated patronage systems based on the same regional and industrial groupings that they represented in the Soviet era (2011, pp. 194–195). According to this line of reasoning, an important characteristic of highly institutionalised legislatures is not only stability of membership but a complete or near-complete break in membership with old communist-era institutions.

In conclusion, although turnover in parliamentary membership is decreasing across CEE, it is still high overall. Furthermore, variation in rates of turnover is significant, implying an increasing gap between those countries in which a professional core of deputies is evolving and those countries where this has yet to happen. Significantly, countries with the lowest level of professionalisation appear to be those that had the closest ties to the Soviet Union and hence the deepest experience of the Soviet model of patrimonial communism (Kitschelt et al. 1999).

Institutional complexity: party factions and committees

Party factions and committees exist in both semi-presidential and parliamentary systems, but their relative importance to policymaking depends on the institutional and partisan characteristics of the system (Olson 1980, Shaw 1990). According to Norton and Olson, scholars have found an 'interrelationship' between institutional and partisan features, "with the most important variable being that of party" (2007, p. 7). In situations of single-party dominance, committees are weak and dominated by the majority party. However, in many of the countries in CEE, multi-party coalitions are the rule, and in these cases the interrelationship between parties and committees is more complex. Where parties are particularly weak, as in Ukraine, committees may emerge as the focal point of legislative activity; however, the quality of policymaking is low (Olson and Crowther 2002, Whitmore 2006). Committees are most effective when parties are strong and exercise control over their membership and agendas. Thus, the effectiveness of committees depends, in part, on the organisation of party factions.

In a study of seven parliaments from the Czech Republic, Hungary, Moldova, Poland, Russia, Slovenia, and Ukraine, Khmelko reports that by the end of the second decade all seven had formed a "collegial parliamentary leadership council responsible for agenda setting, prioritizing and scheduling legislative activities" (2011, p. 201). The names of these councils differ, but all are the result of efforts by parliament to improve its effectiveness and enhance the role of political parties vis-à-vis other parliamentary elites such as the speaker (2011). Strengthening of the parliamentary party groups (or factions) has also been a priority of parties across the seven countries in Khmelko's study. To the extent that the party factions remain coherent and avoid excessive party switching, they are able to play a significant role in the assignment of committee leadership positions.

Changes in committee membership are common due to significant changes in composition of legislative membership from election to election. In addition, although committees tend to reflect specific government ministries, there has been considerable adjustment in the number and jurisdiction of committees in almost all countries during the time period (Zajc 2007, Nalewajko and Wedołowski 2007, Ilonszki 2007). Thus the role of committees varies considerably across CEE. In general, however, the internal organisation of parliaments throughout CEE has increased substantially over the past two decades (Mansfeldová 2011).

EU conditionality

No discussion of legislative institutionalisation in CEE is complete without review of the impact of EU conditionality on institutional change and development, a process that is ongoing in countries even after accession. Of course, the prospect of EU membership – which required newly independent post-communist countries to embrace both democratic institutions and a market economy, two of the three conditions for accession (Grabbe 2002) – had a profound impact on the adoption of parliamentary government, embracing of press freedom, and implementation of market reform across CEE (Malová and Haughton 2002). However, it was the accession process itself, which requires a country to adopt and implement the entire body of EU law, that has had the most impact on legislative institutionalisation (Grabbe 2002, pp. 254–256). This undertaking requires massive legislative activity and output, and it requires the creation and augmentation of many other institutions including the judiciary and state bureaucracy.

However, as a number of scholars have noted, while the process of EU accession clearly prompted successful democratic transition (Schimmelfennig 2007, Schimmelfennig and Scholtz 2008), which is especially evident in problematic cases such as Slovakia and Romania (Pridham 2002), the process has been less uniformly successful in ensuring widespread and deep institutional change (Dimitrova 2010). As Pridham noted, "Accession countries respond formally by making necessary institutional changes and passing relevant legislation such as on minority rights. But their full satisfaction, including their implementation in practice, is not always easy to achieve" (2002, p. 959).

After the accession of eleven post-communist countries to the EU, the most relevant question is whether formal rule adoption will lead to continued institutional and long-term policy change (Dimitrova 2010, p. 138). As Dimitrova describes, EU conditions and the adoption of the *acquis communautaire* required the creation of an "institutional framework supporting the functioning of EU politics," but it did not and could not determine future interpretation of these rules or future changes to them. Furthermore, post-accession, domestic political actors are on their own in terms of continued institutionalisation (2010, pp. 139–140). Scholars have already noted significant problems for certain countries in complying with EU rules with regard to democracy (e.g. Hungary and Romania; Sedelmeier 2014) and corruption control (e.g. Bulgaria; Vachudova 2009). Thus, we should expect, and indeed find, significant variation with regard to continued institutionalisation of both *acquis* and non-*acquis* rules (Dimitrova 2010, p. 145).

Explaining variation in institutional performance: agenda for future research

Despite the fact that the institutional power of parliaments in CEE, both in the countries that have so far joined the EU as well as those hoping to join, is as high as that found in Western Europe, widespread variation exists in how well these parliamentary democracies are running their countries. We see emerging a group of relatively high-performing parliaments in the former Soviet satellites of Poland, Hungary, the Czech Republic, and Slovakia; in the former Baltic Republics of Estonia, Latvia, and Lithuania; in two exceptionally low-performing parliaments in Moldova and Ukraine; with the rest ranging in between.

The concept of 'governance' is now widely used to capture variation in the quality of government performance in such areas as corruption control, rule of law, spending on education and healthcare, and economic reform. Work on the impact of constitutional design on governance finds that parliamentary systems promote higher quality governance than do presidential systems. Several studies find that parliamentary systems are associated with lower corruption than presidential systems (Gerring and Thacker 2004, Lederman et al. 2005, Kunicova and Rose-Ackerman 2005). Persson and Tabellini (2004) find that parliamentary systems spend more consistently on public goods such as education and healthcare, which leads to more robust human development. In a study of multiple indicators of government performance, Gerring, Thacker, and Moreno find that parliamentary systems are associated with significantly higher rule of law and bureaucratic quality, slightly lower corruption, and significantly stronger economic and human development than presidential systems (2009).

In the parliamentary context of CEE, insofar as governments are constituted by and responsible to parliament,[7] the quality of governance reflects the effectiveness of both the parliamentary majority in its ability to articulate a coherent policy programme for its government to implement and of the opposition in holding the government accountable. Thus, the quality of governance is an appropriate measure of legislative performance. As already discussed, legislatures in CEE are institutionally strong; thus, we might expect consistently strong performance on governance indicators across the region. Instead, we find that the quality of governance in these new democracies is generally much lower than that in Western Europe, and there is considerable variation across CEE. Furthermore, and most problematic, the quality of governance has improved little since the beginning of transition.

The Worldwide Governance Indicators are a widely used source for cross-country data on governance.[8] Among the six indicators, 'Control of Corruption' captures one of the most politically salient problems affecting countries throughout the region (Hellman 1998, Hellman et. al. 2000, Kostadinova 2012, Bagashka 2014). Across CEE the general lack of progress on controlling corruption is remarkable (Figure 6.1; also Kostadinova and Spirova in this volume). Even CEE countries in which economic growth has been consistently strong have not been immune to serious corruption.

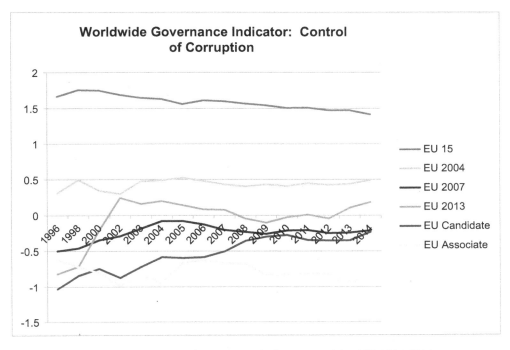

Figure 6.1   Worldwide Governance Indicator 'Control of Corruption' for CEE 1996–2014

Countries included in EU 2004 are Czech Republic, Estonia, Hungary, Latvia, Lithuania, Poland, Slovakia, Slovenia; in EU 2007 are Bulgaria and Romania; in EU 2013 Croatia; in EU Candidate Albania and Macedonia; and in EU Associate Moldova and Ukraine.

The evidence presented in Figure 6.1 strongly suggests that in the area of corruption control, those countries that were the worst performers initially tend to be the worst performers today.[9] The eight CEE countries that joined the EU in 2004 entered the Union substantially below the EU average for corruption control but above the average for Romania and Bulgaria, both of whom joined in 2007. Corruption control in Croatia, which joined the EU in 2013, has remained somewhere between the average for those that joined in 2004 and those that joined in 2007, despite substantial improvement in the years prior to 2002. Corruption control in the two CEE countries not yet on a path to membership, Moldova and Ukraine, remains abysmal. The increase in corruption control in Romania and Bulgaria in the years prior to signing the Accession Treaty, and the steady increase in the two candidate countries Albania and Macedonia as they progress towards signing an Accession Treaty, underscore the powerful impact of the accession process (Renner and Trauner 2009). Just as dramatically, the lack of continued improvement across all of the countries after accession underscores the EU's inability to force new members to continue the political, economic, and social reforms that were conditions of their entrance. It is now generally accepted that EU criteria should require more progress on administrative reform prior to accession than was the case for those CEE countries that have already joined, especially Romania and Bulgaria (Vachudova 2009). As Batory discusses, the process of EU accession changes the formal institutional framework within an acceding country, but implementation of EU law post-accession has so far fallen outside the EU's control (2012).

Although it may be possible to explain the lack of continued progress on corruption control on the shortcomings inherent in the process of EU accession, an important puzzle remains: why have countries' quality of governance changed so little relative to each other over the course of the past twenty years? Countries in the Southern Balkans have continued to perform worse than those in the Central and Northern regions of Eastern Europe, and Moldova and Ukraine have remained profoundly corrupt.

It is tempting to attribute these patterns to each country's Soviet-era legacy of communism. Differences in post-Soviet performance across countries deeply integrated into the Soviet system, such as Ukraine and Bulgaria, to those more economically and politically independent, such as Poland and Hungary, call attention to the possible explanatory importance of recent history. In their investigation of predictors of economic policy reform, Jahn and Müller-Rommel (2010) find that the strongest predictor of policy reform was communist legacy. That is, a country's starting point after the collapse of communism was the best predictor of its parliament's ability to pass a comprehensive program of economic reform. Spendzharova and Vachudova make a similar argument in explaining the failure of EU accession to reduce corruption in Bulgaria and Romania (2012).

However, an explanation of legislative performance that rests on a country's communist legacy is theoretically unsatisfactory. Consider the cases of Estonia, Latvia, and Lithuania, which were Soviet Republics like Moldova and Ukraine, yet are far less corrupt. The former republics of Yugoslavia were more integrated into the European Common Market than any of the other post-communist countries, and yet they are among the worst performers today. Poland emerged from communism as one of the poorest countries in Eastern Europe, yet it has improved its quality of governance more than any of the other CEE countries. And, as already mentioned, constitutional variation across all of the cases is minimal. Thus, explaining variation in legislative performance remains an enticing question for future research.

To date, there are very few multi-country empirical investigations into the predictors of corruption control and other types of government effectiveness across CEE; thus, it is premature to attempt an explanation of variation in parliamentary effectiveness. However, those studies that do exist underscore the importance of a multivariate, multi-country approach. In their three-country study of party patronage, Kopecký and Spirova analyse expert survey data covering the Czech Republic, Hungary, and Bulgaria and an additional twelve West European countries. Comparing an index of patronage (constructed from survey responses) across all fifteen country cases, the authors find that patronage levels in the three CEE countries fall within the range of index values for Western Europe. Furthermore, the authors find complex variation across the three CEE countries in levels of patronage within institutional type and policy areas. Thus, although Kopecký and Spirova do not rule out the importance of CEE countries' communist-era legacy, they conclude that expectations based strictly on communist-era legacy cannot explain variation they observe, especially the lack of clear differences between Hungary and Bulgaria (2011).

In their ten-country analysis of policy performance, using an alternative measure of legislative effectiveness, Jahn and Müller-Rommel find that government strength (related to parliamentary strength) does not increase policy performance, but rather the number of extra-parliamentary institutional veto players does. An index constructed of three components including communist-system type (following Kitschelt et al. 1999), prior democratic experience, and type of regime breakdown has a strong and significant impact on policy performance. Finally, they find that foreign direct investment (FDI) and economic openness increase policy performance. Thus, the predictors of good governance are complex. Certainly a country's communist past matters, but so do other historical factors, and the impact of history on governance depends on other country characteristics such as diversity of extra-parliamentary institutions and investment climate.

Mirroring Kopecký and Spirova's findings, Jahn and Müller-Rommel show that importance of predictors varies across policy areas.

Although the literature on legislative performance is in its infancy, early studies show conclusively that no single factor can explain variation across CEE. To begin to understand variation in legislative and democratic performance across CEE, scholars must carry out multi-country studies and incorporate multivariate research methods. It is especially important to unpack the influence of history. Studies of political networks like that carried out by Kopecký and Spirova seem especially promising.

Concluding remarks

Taken in its entirety, scholarship on the new parliaments in CEE has greatly expanded our understanding of how strong and effective legislatures are created, from initial institutional design through evolution of internal parliamentary structures. The importance of early multi-party constitutional negotiations cannot be overstated. In those CEE countries in which a balanced institutional design emerged early in the transition, elections have remained competitive, and the internal institutions of effective legislatures, especially committee systems organised by parties, have developed accordingly. The two least institutionalised legislatures in CEE are in Moldova and Ukraine, neither of which managed to establish a stable, balanced constitution at the beginning of its transition. Despite the fact that all of the parliaments in CEE, with the exception of Moldova and Ukraine, have managed to pass an economic reform programme sufficiently effective to promote growth, and all have either joined the EU or are on track to join, most continue to experience a high level of government instability as well as turnover in parliamentary membership. Traditionally, political scientists have considered such instability to be deleterious to effective governance. Without further study, we can only speculate about the contribution of internal instability in CEE parliaments to the low quality of governance in CEE today. Given the richness of institutional and organisation detail covered by the extant literature, it is up to the next generation of scholarship to identify those features of parliamentary systems that most promote good governance and in so doing address a question central to comparative politics.

Notes

1 Although Belarus, Serbia, Montenegro, Bosnia and Herzegovina, and Kosovo are geographically located in CEE, I mostly exclude them from my analysis because they lack sufficient democratic experience and/ or have not yet established clear sovereignty. After a single election, the post-communist government in Belarus reverted to strong authoritarianism, and the legislature has never functioned as a representative deliberative body. Serbia and Montenegro did not establish independence until 2006, and neither Bosnia and Herzegovina nor Kosovo has yet emerged as a clearly sovereign entity. Likewise I exclude Russia, which spans two continents and vies with both the EU and China for respective regional dominance. Furthermore, Russia is not a democracy.

2 For example, Moldova's 1994 constitution included a directly elected president with considerable powers; however, in 2000 the election of the president became the responsibility of parliament. Although both Slovakia and the Czech Republic added a directly elected president to their parliamentary systems (Slovakia in 1999 and the Czech Republic in 2012), neither altered the powers of the parliament. Ukraine, which adopted a semi-presidential system with the most powerful president in Eastern Europe, altered its constitution in 2006 to reduce the power of the president and augment the power of parliament, although the power of the president was temporarily restored from 2010 to 2014. Hungary introduced a new constitution in 2012 that increased the power of parliament.

3 In Conrad and Golder's data, a government begins on the date it is installed (the date of investiture) and it ends on the date that new elections are held (and the mandate of the prior government ends). The cabinet that remains in office between the date of the most recent election and the date that the new cabinet takes office is a caretaker cabinet, regardless of whether or not it includes the incumbent parties.

4 Except for data on DPI variable 'Checks' and values from Polity, all data were collected by the author.
5 World Bank Database of Political Institutions, http://econ.worldbank.org/WBSITE/EXTERNAL/ EXTDEC/EXTRESEARCH/0,,contentMDK:20649465~pagePK:64214825~piPK:64214943~ theSitePK:469382,00.html.
6 I do not include Ilonszki and Edinger's (2007) results for Russia in my discussion.
7 Because only parliament has the right to dismiss the government in all of the semi-presidential systems in CEE, these systems fall into Shugart and Carey's category of premier-presidential (1992). The only exceptions occurred in Ukraine between 1996 and 2006 and between 2010 and 2014.
8 The Worldwide Governance Indicators are created by aggregation of over thirty data sources, especially surveys of enterprises, citizens, and experts created by independent institutes, think tanks, nongovernmental organisations, and private firms. Although susceptible to criticism as indirect measures of government, the Worldwide Governance Indicators are generally considered superior to single-source measures. For a description of the methodology and interpretation of indicator values as well as access to the data see the following web site: http://info.worldbank.org/governance/wgi/index. aspx#home.
9 Data on World Governance Indicators 'Rule of Law' and 'Government Effectiveness' show similar trends.

References

Ágh, A. 1995. The Experiences of the First Democratic Parliaments in East Central Europe. *Communist and Post-Communist Studies*, 28(2): 203–214.

Alesina, Alberto, Sule Ozler, Nouriel Roubini, and Phillip Swagel. 1996. Political Instability and Economic Growth. *Journal of Economic Growth*, 1(2): 189–211.

Andrews, Josephine. 2014. Legislatures in Central and Eastern Europe. Chapter 31 in Shane Martin, Thomas Saalfeld, and Kaare W. Strøm (eds.) *Oxford Handbook of Legislative Studies*. New York: Oxford University Press, pp. 647–675.

Andrews, Josephine and Richard L. Bairett Jr. 2014. Institutions and the Stabilization of Party Systems in the New Democracies of Central and Eastern Europe. *Electoral Studies*, 33: 307–321.

Andrews, Josephine T. and Robert W. Jackman. 2005. Strategic Fools: Electoral Rule Choice Under Extreme Uncertainty. *Electoral Studies*, 24(1): 65–84.

Bagashka, Tanya. 2014. Unpacking Corruption: The Effect of Veto Players on State Capture and Bureaucratic Corruption. *Political Research Quarterly*, 67(1): 165–180.

Batory, Agnes. 2012. Why Do Anti-Corruption Laws Fail in Central and Eastern Europe? A Target Compliance Perspective. *Regulation & Governance*, 6(1): 66–82.

Baylis, Thomas A. 1996. Presidents Versus Prime Ministers: Shaping Executive Authority in Eastern Europe. *World Politics*, 48(3): 297–323.

Bieber, Florian. 2011. Building Impossible States? State-Building Strategies and EU Membership in the Western Balkans. *Europe-Asia Studies*, 63(10): 1783–1802.

Bielasiak, Jack. 2002. The Institutionalization of Electoral and Party Systems in Postcommunist States. *Comparative Politics*, 34(2): 189–210.

Birch, Sarah. 2001. Electoral Systems and Party Systems in Europe East and West. *Perspectives on European Politics and Society*, 2(3): 355–377.

Blondel, Jean and Ferdinand Müller-Rommel. 2001. *Cabinets in Eastern Europe*. New York: Palgrave.

Calda, Miloš. 1996. The Roundtable Talks in Czechoslovakia. In Jon Elster (ed.) *The Roundtable Talks and the Breakdown of Communism*. Chicago: University of Chicago Press, pp. 135–177.

Chiva, Cristina. 2007. The Institutionalisation of Post-Communist Parliaments: Hungary and Romania in Comparative Perspective. *Parliamentary Affairs*, 60(2): 187–211.

Conrad, Courtenay Ryals and Sona N. Golder. 2010. Measuring Government Duration and Stability in Central Eastern European Democracies. *European Journal of Political Research*, 49(1): 119–150.

Copeland, G. W. and S. C. Patterson. 1994. *Parliaments in the Modern World*. Ann Arbor: University of Michigan Press.

Crowther, William E. 2011. Second Decade, Second Chance? Parliament, Politics and Democratic Aspirations in Russia, Ukraine and Moldova. *Journal of Legislative Studies*, 17(2): 147–171.

Crowther, William E. 2014. Legislative Elite Formation in Moldova: Continuity and Change. In Elena Semenova, Michael Edinger, and Heinrich Best (eds.) *Parliamentary Elites in Central and Eastern Europe: Recruitment and Representation*. New York: Routledge, pp. 219–240.

Dimitrova, Antoaneta L. 2010. The New Member States of the EU in the Aftermath of Enlargement: Do New European Rules Remain Empty Shells? *Journal of European Public Policy*, 17(1): 137–148.

Elgie, Robert. 2011. *Semi-Presidentialism: Sub-Types and Democratic Performance.* New York: Oxford University Press.

Elster, Jon. 1991. Constitutionalism in Eastern Europe: An Introduction. *University of Chicago Law Review*, 58: 447–482.

Elster, Jon (ed.). 1996. *The Roundtable Talks and the Breakdown of Communism.* Chicago: University of Chicago Press.

Elster, J., C. Offe, and U. K. Preuss. 1998. *Institutional Design in Post-communist Societies: Rebuilding the Ship at Sea.* New York: Cambridge University Press.

Fink-Hafner, D. 2011. Interest Representation and Post-Communist Parliaments Over Two Decades. *Journal of Legislative Studies*, 17(2): 215–233.

Fish, S. and M. Kroenig. 2009. *The Handbook of National Legislatures: A Global Survey.* New York: Cambridge University Press.

Geddes, B. 1996. Initiation of new democratic institutions in Eastern Europe and Latin America. In A. Lijphart and C. H. Waisman (eds.) *Institutional Design in New Democracies: Eastern Europe and Latin America.* Boulder: Westview Press, pp. 15–41.

Gerring, John and Strom C. Thacker. 2004. Political Institutions and Corruption: The Role of Unitarism and Parliamentarism. *British Journal of Political Science*, 34(2): 295–330.

Gerring, John, Strom C. Thacker and Carola Moreno. 2009. Are Parliamentary Systems Better? *Comparative Political Studies*, 42(3): 327–359.

Grabbe, Heather. 2002. European Union Conditionality and the 'Acquis Communautaire'. *International Political Science Review*, 23(3): 249–268.

Grotz, Florian and Till Weber. 2012. Party Systems and Government Stability in Central and Eastern Europe. *World Politics*, 64(4): 699–740.

Hellman, Joel. 1998. Winners Take All: The Politics of Partial Reform in Postcommunist Transitions. *World Politics*, 50(2): 203–234.

Hellman, Joel, Geraint Jones and Daniel Kaufmann. September 2000. *Seize the State, Seize the Day: State Capture, Corruption and Influence in Transition.* World Bank Policy Research Working Paper No. 2444. Available at SSRN: http://ssrn.com/abstract=240555.

Ilonszki, Gabriella. 2007. From Minimal to Subordinate: A Final Verdict? The Hungarian Parliament, 1990–2002. *Journal of Legislative Studies*, 13(1): 38–58.

Ilonszki, Gabriella and Michael Edinger. 2007. MPs in Post-Communist and Post-Soviet Nations: A Parliamentary Elite in the Making. *Journal of Legislative Studies*, 13(1): 142–163.

Jahn, Detlef and Ferdinand Müller-Rommel. 2010. Political Institutions and Policy Performance: A Comparative Analysis of Central and Eastern Europe. *Journal of Public Policy*, 30(special issue 1): 23–44.

Khmelko, Irina. 2011. Internal Organisation of Post-Communist Parliaments Over Two Decades: Leadership, Parties, and Committees. *Journal of Legislative Studies*, 17(2): 193–214.

Kitschelt, Herbert, Zdenka Mansfeldová, Radoslaw Markowski, and Gabor Toka. 1999. *Post-communist Party Systems.* Cambridge: Cambridge University Press.

Kopecký, Petr. 2004. Power to the Executive! The Changing Executive-Legislative Relations in Eastern Europe. *Journal of Legislative Studies*, 10(2–3): 142–153.

Kopecký, Petr and Maria Spirova. 2011. 'Jobs for the Boys'? Patterns of Party Patronage in Post-Communist Europe. *West European Politics*, 34(5): 897–921.

Kostadinova, Tatiana. 2012. *Political Corruption in Eastern Europe: Politics After Communism.* Boulder, CO: Lynne Rienner.

Kunicova, Jana and Susan Rose-Ackerman. 2005. Electoral Rules and Constitutional Structures as Constraints on Corruption. *British Journal of Political Science*, 35(4): 573–606.

Lederman, Daniel, Norman V. Loayza, and Rodrigo R. Soares. 2005. Accountability and Corruption: Political Institutions Matter. *Economics and Politics*, 17(1): 1–35.

Lewis, Paul G. 2007. Party Systems in Post-communist Central Europe: Patterns of Stability and Consolidation. *Democratization*, 13(4): 562–583.

Lijphart, A. 1992. Democratization and Constitutional Choices in Czecho-Slovakia, Hungary and Poland, 1989–1991. *Journal of Theoretical Politics*, 4(2): 207–223.

Ludwikowski, R. R. 1996. *Constitution-Making in the Region of Former Soviet Dominance.* Durham, NC: Duke University Press.

Mair, Peter. 1997. *Party System Change: Approaches and Interpretations.* Oxford: Clarendon Press.

Malová, Darina and Tim Haughton. 2002. Making Institutions in Central and Eastern Europe, and the Impact of Europe. *West European Politics*, 25(2): 101–120.

Mansfeldová, Zdenka. 2011. Central European Parliaments Over Two Decades – Diminishing Stability? Parliaments in Czech Republic, Hungary, Poland, and Slovenia. *Journal of Legislative Studies*, 17(2): 128–146.

Metcalf, L. K. 2000. Measuring Presidential Power. *Comparative Political Studies*, 33(5): 660–685.

Meyer-Sahling, Jan-Hinrik and Tim Veen. 2012. Governing the Post-Communist State: Government Alternation and Senior Civil Service Politicisation in Central and Eastern Europe. *East European Politics*, 28(1): 4–22.

Moser, Robert G. and Ethan Scheiner. 2012. *Electoral Systems and Political Context: How the Effects of Rules Vary Across New and Established Democracies*. New York: Cambridge University Press.

Müller-Rommel, Ferdinand, Katja Fettelschoss, and Philipp Harfst. 2004. Party Government in Central Eastern European Democracies: A Data Collection (1990–2003). *European Journal of Political Research*, 43(6): 869–893.

Nalewajko, Ewa and Włodzimierz Wedołowski. 2007. Five Terms of the Polish Parliament, 1989–2005. *Journal of Legislative Studies*, 13(1): 59–82.

Nikolenyi, Csaba. 2004. Cabinet Stability in Post-Communist Central Europe. *Party Politics*, 10(2): 123–150.

Norton, Philip and David M. Olson. 2007. Post-Communist and Post-Soviet Legislatures: Beyond Transition. *Journal of Legislative Studies*, 13(1): 1–11.

Olson, David M. 1980. *The Legislative Approach*. New York: Harper & Row.

Olson, David M. and William Crowther. 2002. *Committees in Post-Communist Democratic Parliaments: Comparative Institutionalization*. Columbus: Ohio State University Press.

Olson, David M. and Philip Norton. 1996. *The New Parliaments of Central and Eastern Europe*. London: Frank Cass.

Olson, David M. and Philip Norton. 2007. Post-Communist and Post-Soviet Parliaments: Divergent Paths From Transition. *Journal of Legislative Studies*, 13(1): 164–196.

Osiatynski, Wiktor. 1996. The Roundtable Talks in Poland. In Jon Elster (ed.) *The Roundtable Talks and the Breakdown of Communism*. Chicago: University of Chicago Press, pp. 21–68.

Persson, Torsten and Guido Tabellini. 2004. Constitutional Rules and Fiscal Policy Outcomes. *American Economic Review*, 94(1): 25–45.

Polsby, Nelson. 1968. The Institutionalization of the US House of Representatives. *American Political Science Review*, 62(1): 144–168.

Pridham, Geoffrey. 2002. EU Enlargement and Consolidating Democracy in Post-Communist State – Formality and Reality. *Journal of Common Market Studies*, 40(5): 953–973.

Protsyk, Oleh. 2005. Politics of Intraexecutive Conflict in Semipresidential Regimes in Eastern Europe. *East European Politics and Societies*, 19(2): 135–160.

Protsyk, Oleh. 2006. Intra-Executive Competition Between President and Prime Minister: Patterns of Institutional Conflict and Cooperation Under Semi-Presidentialism. *Political Studies*, 54(2): 219–244.

Protsyk, Oleh and Marius Lupsa Matichescu. 2011. Clientelism and Political Recruitment in Democratic Transition: Evidence From Romania. *Comparative Politics*, 43(2): 207–224.

Reich, Gary. 2004. The Evolution of New Party Systems: Are Early Elections Exceptional? *Electoral Studies*, 23(2): 235–250.

Renner, Stephan and Florian Trauner. 2009. Creeping EU Membership in Southeast Europe: The Dynamics of EU Rule Transfer to the Western Balkans. *Journal of European Integration*, 31(4): 449–465.

Rose, Richard and Neil Munro. 2003. *Elections and Parties in New European Democracies*. Washington, DC: Congressional Quarterly Press.

Sajó, András. 1996. The Roundtable Talks in Hungary. In Jon Elster (ed.) *The Roundtable Talks and the Breakdown of Communism*. Chicago: University of Chicago Press, pp. 69–98.

Schimmelfennig, Frank. 2007. European Regional Organizations, Political Conditionality, and Democratic Transformation in Eastern Europe. *East European Politics and Societies*, 21(1): 126–141.

Schimmelfennig, Frank and Hanno Scholtz. 2008. EU Democratic Promotion in the European Neighbourhood; Political Conditionality, Economic Development and Transnational Exchange. *European Union Politics*, 9(2): 187–215.

Sedelius, Thomas and Joakim Ekman. 2010. Intra-executive Conflict and Cabinet Instability: Effects of Semi-presidentialism in Central and Eastern Europe. *Government and Opposition*, 45(4): 505–530.

Sedelius, Thomas and Olga Mashtaler. 2013. Two Decades of Semi-presidentialism: Issues of Intra-executive Conflict in Central and Eastern Europe 1991–2011. *East European Politics*, 29(2): 109–134.

Sedelmeier, Ulrich. 2014. Anchoring Democracy From Above? The European Union and Democratic Backsliding in Hungary and Romania After Accession. *Journal of Common Market Studies*, 52(1): 105–121.

Semenova, Elena. 2014. Parliamentary Representation in Post-communist Ukraine: Change and Stability. In Elena Semenova, Michael Edinger, and Heinrich Best (eds.) *Parliamentary Elites in Central and Eastern Europe: Recruitment and Representation*. New York: Routledge, pp. 261–283.

Shabad, Goldie and Kazimierz M. Slomczynski. 2002. The Emergence of Career Politicians in Post-Communist Democracies: Poland and the Czech Republic. *Legislative Studies Quarterly*, 27(3): 333–359.

Shaw, M. 1990. Committees in Legislature. In P. Norton (ed.) *Legislatures*. New York: Oxford University Press, pp. 237–271.

Shugart, Matthew S. 2005. Semi-Presidential Systems: Dual Executive and Mixed Authority Patterns. *French Politics*, 3(3): 323–351.

Shugart, Matthew S. and John M. Carey. 1992. *Presidents and Assemblies: Constitutional Design and Electoral Dynamics*. New York: Cambridge University Press.

Shvetsova, Olga. 2003. Endogenous Selection of Institutions and Their Exogenous Effects. *Constitutional Political Economy*, 14(3): 191–212.

Sikk, Allan. 2005. How Unstable? Volatility and the Genuinely New Parties in Eastern Europe. *European Journal of Political Research*, 44(3): 391–412.

Somer-Topcu, Zeynep and Laron K. Williams. 2008. Survival of the Fittest? Cabinet Duration in Postcommunist Europe. *Comparative Politics*, 40(3): 313–329.

Spendzharova, Aneta B. and Milada Anna Vachudova. 2012. Catching Up? Consolidating Liberal Democracy in Bulgaria and Romania After EU Accession. *West European Politics*, 35(1): 39–58.

Tavits, Margit. 2005. The Development of Stable Party Support: Electoral Dynamics in Post-Communist Europe. *American Journal of Political Science*, 49(2): 283–298.

Tavits, Margit. 2008. On the Linkage Between Electoral Volatility and Party System Instability in Central and Eastern Europe. *European Journal of Political Research*, 47(5): 537–555.

Tavits, Margit. 2009. *Presidents With Prime Ministers: Do Direct Elections Matter?* New York: Oxford University Press.

Toka, Gabor. 1995. Parties and Electoral Choices in East – Central Europe. In Geoffrey Pridham and Paul G. Lewis (eds.) *Stabilising Fragile Democracies: Comparing New Party Systems in Southern and Eastern Europe*. New York: Routledge, pp. 100–125.

Tzelgov, Eitan. 2011. Communist Successor Parties and Government Survival in Central Eastern Europe. *European Journal of Political Research*, 50(4): 530–558.

Vachudova, Milada Anna. 2009. Corruption and Compliance in the EU's Post-Communist Members and Candidates. *Journal of Common Market Studies*, 47(s1): 43–62.

Whitmore, Sarah. 2006. Challenges and Constraints for Post-Soviet Committees: Exploring the Impact of Parties on Committees in Ukraine. *Journal of Legislative Studies*, 12(1): 32–53.

Wolczuk, Kataryna. 2001. Ukraine: Tormented Constitution-Making. In J. Zielonka (ed.) *Democratic Consolidation in Eastern Europe*. Oxford: Oxford University Press.

Wright, Joseph. 2008. Political Competition and Democratic Stability in New Democracies. *British Journal of Political Science*, 38(2): 221–245.

Zajc, Drago. 2007. Slovenia's National Assembly, 1990–2004. *Journal of Legislative Studies*, 13(1): 83–98.

7

POLITICAL PARTIES AND PARTY ORGANISATIONS

Allan Sikk

Stable parties that successfully perform their representative function and connect to citizens are essential for democratic consolidation (Innes, 2002; Kreuzer and Pettai, 2004; Roberts, 2010; Tavits, 2013). Whether such parties will form in new European democracies has been questioned previously (see Mair, 1997), but some degree of democratic stability has been achieved in the new East European EU member states – particularly if we contrast them to most of the former Soviet Union or Western Balkans. This chapter focuses on the development of political parties in countries that joined the EU in the first wave of Eastern enlargement in 2004 and 2007; trends elsewhere in other post-communist countries differ considerably because of much lower levels of political stability or political freedoms.

This chapter first looks at types of parties found in the region using a combination of two common approaches: party families and party development. The second section focuses in on the remarkably successful genuinely political parties without clear roots in the transition period and the related phenomenon of major parties suddenly becoming defunct. We then look at the internal life of parties through the analytical lens of party resources: symbiosis with the state, party organisations, and membership. The conclusion summarises important trends since the early 1990s and critically discusses the relationship between party development and democratic quality.

Party types

Eastern Europe has been rich in the number and variety of its political parties; to understand and analyse them, several approaches to party classification have been used. *Party families* is a classic and generally insightful approach that identifies similar parties across countries (Beyme, 1985; Hloušek and Kopeček, 2010). However, some parties defy easy classification, some families are internally diverse, and parties can even change families. Also, it is not obvious why West European party families should provide a good guide to understanding parties elsewhere. First, even if patterns of party competition in Eastern Europe have come to resemble Western Europe, a unique division – the communist legacy – remains important in the former (Rohrschneider and Whitefield, 2013, p. 84). Second, many East European parties have traits that are at odds with their reference "families" in the West (for a discussion on the centre-right, see Hanley, 2004); others are programmatically vague or flexible – note the transformation of Fidesz in Hungary from a liberal to a conservative party (Kiss, 2002).

A related approach to classification is based on parties' membership in European party organisations. Yet, sometimes foes in national politics sit together, and close allies are in different party groups in the European Parliament. For example, as of 2016, the Czech, Estonian, Lithuanian, and Slovak delegations to European People's Party or the Alliance of Liberals and Democrats included parties both from national government and opposition benches.

Three broad groups of parties can be distinguished using a *developmental approach*: (1) former communists; (2) parties rooted in anti-communist movements; and (3) new parties, usually set up by charismatic leaders. The simple threefold classification covers most but not all important parties. For example, a small number of parties trace their history back to the pre-communist period – significant examples currently include the Czech Social Democratic Party (ČSSD), the Latvian Farmers' Union (LZS), and the Lithuanian Social Democratic Party (LSDP, now merged with the ex-communist Democratic Labour Party, LDDP).

The 1990s saw the astounding reinvention of *former communist parties* as reformed social democrats. They joined respective party internationals and became central actors in national politics – particularly in Hungary (MSZP), Poland (Democratic Left Alliance, SLD) and Lithuania (LDDP) (Grzymała-Busse, 2002; Ishiyama, 1997). Former communists are also strong in Bulgaria and Romania (BSP and PSD, respectively), where they did not undergo as dramatic a metamorphosis because of the different mode of transition (Grzymała-Busse, 2002; Spirova, 2005).

Initial scholarly interest in ex-communist parties has waned somewhat as predictions about the long-term prospects of SLD and MSZP (Ishiyama, 1997) turned out to be premature. SLD became marginalised after the 2006 elections and was left out of the Sejm in 2015. MSZP weakened after mass protests in 2006 following the leaking of an audio recording of its leader's speech during a closed-door session; MSZP has remained in the parliament, but in the shadow of Fidesz and its former self. At the time of writing, BSP and PSD, as well as the more orthodox Communist Party of Bohemia and Moravia (KSČM), look more stable than successful reformers, with the exception of LDDP.

Some communist-era *satellite parties* have also adapted to democratic party competition, such as the Czech Christian and Democratic Union–Czechoslovak People's Party (KDU–ČSL) and Polish People's Party (PSL). Finally, even where ex-communist parties have all but vanished, some centrist parties have been dominated by former economic or political nomenklatura. Some of them were highly successful in the 1990s, such as the Estonian Coalition Party (K), its rural sister party People's Union (ERL), and Latvia's Way (LC). The Liberal Democracy of Slovenia (LDS), the dominant party in the country in 1990s, had roots in the former Communist Youth Organisation (Krašovec and Haughton, 2011, p. 200).

The weakening of ex-communist parties in Hungary and Poland coincided with the rise of economically left-leaning but socially conservative parties – Fidesz and Law and Justice (PiS), respectively. Both can be linked to *former anti-communist movements*. Still, most parties with roots in anti-communist movements belong to the centre-right mainstream, such as the Czech Civic Democratic Party (ODS), Homeland Union–Lithuanian Christian Democrats (TS-LKD), Slovenian Democratic Party (SDS), and Estonian Pro Patria Union (IL). In Poland, both PiS and the more liberal Citizens' Platform (PO) have roots in the Solidarity alliance that became a victim of its descendants' success in 2001 and has since reverted to a trade union.

Successful *ethno-nationalist radical right parties*, largely overlapping with the "populist radical right" (Mudde, 2007; also Mudde in· this volume), have been a concern for the prospects of liberal democracy and have received ample scholarly attention. Some of these parties have roots in anti-communist movements, for example, the League of Polish Families (LPR) and the Latvian National Alliance (NA); while others have tenuous links, for example, Jobbik (Hungary), Ataka (Bulgaria), Greater Romania Party (PRM), Dawn (Czech Republic), the Slovak

National Party (SNS), People's Party–Our Slovakia (ĽSNS), and the Estonian Conservative People's Party (EKRE).

Ethno-nationalist radicals have won modest representation in the parliament: in 2016, they held 10–20 per cent of seats only in Slovakia, Latvia, and Hungary, and few of such parties have been popular over several years, entered national government, or influenced them directly (Minkenberg, 2007, p. 36). However, they have, worryingly, encouraged radical rhetoric among mainstream parties, particularly in Hungary and Slovakia (Pirro, 2015). The ethno-nationalist right has often been strong in countries with prominent ethnic minorities (Bulgaria, Slovakia, and Latvia), but also in relatively ethnically homogenous Hungary and Poland. On the other hand, the ethno-nationalist right was absent from the Estonian parliament during 1999–2015 despite a sizeable Russian-speaking minority in the country.

The radical right can benefit from the presence of strong *ethnic minority parties*, particularly if they enter the government (Bustikova-Siroky, 2014). Various incarnations have been in strong in Latvia, where the Harmony Centre (SC) became the largest party in 2011. Minority parties have also been strong in Romania (the Democratic Union of Hungarians, UDMR), Bulgaria (Movement for Rights and Freedom, DPS), and Lithuania (the Electoral Action of Poles). The latter two have at times also been included in national governments. No ethnic minority party has been represented in the Estonian Parliament since 1999, as the predominantly ethnic Estonian Centre Party (KE), with roots in the moderate wing of the independence movement, has achieved a near-monopoly of ethnic Russian representation. In contrast, in Slovakia, the mostly ethnic Hungarian Most–Híd has recruited Slovak candidates and driven the more traditional Party of the Hungarian Community out of parliament in 2010.

Parties: new and old

East European parties, except for pre-communist and communist successor parties, are new compared to nearly all parties in Western democracies. However, a crucial distinction can be made between those with roots in late communist or early post-communist years and those lacking such connections, for example at the level of senior personnel. The continued success of the former has generally contributed to the institutionalisation of the party system established in early 1990s, while the latter – some of which were already discussed at the end of the previous section – have often disrupted the fragile equilibrium.

Tracing the development of parties poses problems. In the first parliaments, broad movements split up as issues other than communist/anti-communist dimensions took precedence – largely a natural development reflecting changes in political and social conditions. This disintegration was often followed by some consolidation in the form of mergers (for example, the setting up of Solidarity Electoral Action, AWS in Poland) and disappearance of minor parties, but also by further splits and other forms of reorganisation. The transformations have often been complex, involving several parties or alliances exchanging political personnel in various directions.

Distinguishing between old and new parties is complicated, as: (1) there have been considerably more electoral coalitions – that can obscure their constituent parties – than in Western Europe (Ibenskas, 2015; Marinova, 2015), and (2) many seemingly new formations have been strongly related to previously existing ones.

Coalitions were common in early post-communist elections, but have remained prominent in Latvia, Lithuania, Poland, and Romania. In 2010 Latvian parliamentary elections, all six "electons" – to use a common name for parties and coalitions (Sikk, 2013) – winning seats were electoral coalitions. Some countries have discouraged coalitions by setting them higher electoral thresholds (Lithuania and Poland) or prohibiting them in parliamentary elections (Estonia).

Such measures were introduced to prevent (temporary) coalitions that can slow down party system consolidation by helping parties to enter parliament without ensuring cooperation later. However, some coalitions have endured over a number of elections and developed permanent organisational links, for example, Fidesz and the Christian Democratic People's Party (KDNP) in Hungary (since 2006) and the Union of Greens and Farmers in Latvia (ZZS, since 2002). Some electoral coalitions have transformed into proper parties, for example, Unity (*Vienotiba*) after winning 2010 elections in Latvia. Yet other coalitions have been pragmatic and short-lived, particularly those in Romania or involving the Lithuanian LSDP.

Coalitions, splits, and mergers make it difficult to identify new political parties. An important distinction regards parties set up by leading figures of established parties and those with weak or no links to existing party politics. Such *genuinely new parties* (Sikk, 2005) have often been remarkably successful (see Table 7.1) – six of their leaders became prime ministers after their first election (LS, JL, NDSV, PMC, RP, and GERB). To these we can add (1) parties that won the biggest number of votes but did not form a government (PS and DP); (2) Smer (Slovakia), which became truly successful only in its second election; and (3) the Latvian People's Party (TP), created by a former independent prime minister who occupied the office soon again. Some genuinely new parties have been radical-right populists (Jobbik, PRM) or more vaguely populist (Polish Self-Defence, Lithuanian TPP and DP). Others have been post-materialist with an East European flavour (the Greens in the Czech Republic and Estonia), anti-political promoting electoral reform (Kukiz in Poland), or single-issue parties (the Lithuanian Way of Courage promised to tackle a supposed paedophile ring).

Table 7.1 Genuinely new parties (more than 15 per cent of votes)

Party	Country	First election	Votes %	Leader	Political office after election
National Movement Simeon II (NDSV)	Bulgaria	2001	42.7	Simeon Borisov	PM
Citizens for European Development (GERB)	Bulgaria	2009	39.7	Boyko Borisov	PM
Party of Miro Cerar (PMC)	Slovenia	2014	34.6	Miro Cerar	PM
Positive Slovenia (PS)	Slovenia	2011	28.5	Zoran Janković	–
Labour Party (DP)	Lithuania	2004	28.4	Viktor Uspaskich	–
Res Publica (RP)	Estonia	2003	24.6	Juhan Parts	PM
New Era (JL)	Latvia	2002	24.0	Einars Repše	PM
Zatlers' Reform Party (ZRP)	Latvia	2011	20.8	Valdis Zatlers	–
New Union (Social Liberals) (NS-SL)	Lithuania	2000	19.6	Artūras Paulauskas	Speaker
ANO2011	Czech Republic	2013	18.7	Andrej Babiš	Minister of Finance
Liberal Union (LLS)[a]	Lithuania	2000	17.3	Rolandas Paksas	PM
Jobbik	Hungary	2010	16.7	Dávid Kovács	–
TOP 09	Czech Republic	2010	16.7	Karel Schwarzenberg	Minister of Foreign Affairs
National Resurrection Party (TPP)	Lithuania	2008	15.1	Arūnas Valinskas	Speaker of Seimas

Note: [a] LLS had a single MP before 2000, but transformed entirely in 1999.

All genuinely new parties have used some "populist" anti-establishment rhetoric, easily explained by their outsider status. However, the most successful ones (nearly all in Table 7.1) have had a centrist or liberal outlook and have been dubbed "centrist populists" or "unorthodox parties" (Učeň, 2007; Pop-Eleches, 2010). They have often fought on the ideological territory of established parties, mostly distinguishing themselves by "newness" (Sikk, 2011) – a combination of charisma, projected integrity, and competence, sometimes combined with calls for democratic reforms (Hanley and Sikk, 2014). A mainstream, catch-all appeal has been a crucial factor behind their success, even if extremist parties in general outperform centrists (see Ezrow et al., 2014 whose data includes only one party from Table 7.1). Such *anti-establishment reform parties* have been successful both in economic good and bad times, but benefit from rising levels of perceived corruption in relatively less corrupt countries (Hanley and Sikk, 2014). Notably, mainstream genuinely new parties have been conspicuous by their absence in Romania where, until recently, corruption has been highest among the countries covered in this chapter.

Figure 7.1 shows the distribution of seats won by genuinely new parties in elections by countries. Their average success has been lowest in Hungary and Romania and highest in Bulgaria, Slovenia, and Lithuania. There is significant within-country variation – nearly all countries have had elections where genuinely new parties won no seats and elections where they have been highly successful, reaching near-majority twice in Bulgaria. Figure 7.2 shows no overall trend over time, but genuinely new parties have become more successful in two periods: (1) between 2000 and 2005, shortly before or after the countries joined the EU; and (2) since 2010, the Czech Republic and Slovenia – with previously stable party systems – experienced two consecutive elections with high levels of genuinely new party success.

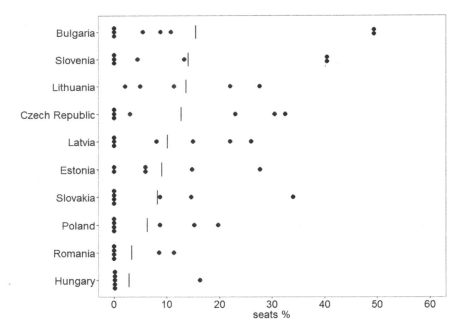

Figure 7.1 Seat shares of genuinely new parties by elections

Note: Dots indicate elections, horizontal lines average seat shares by countries.

Source: Author's calculations. Data: allansikk.eu/HBEEP.

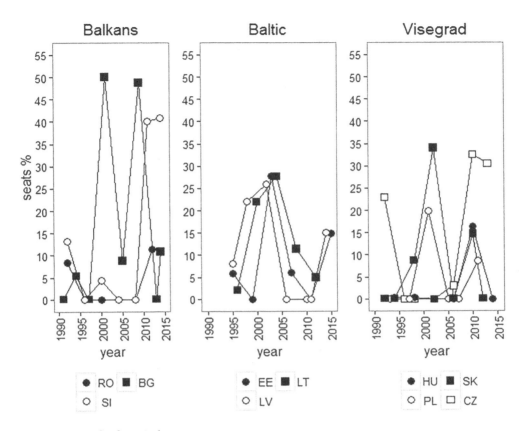

Figure 7.2 Trends of genuinely new party success
Source: Author's calculations. Data: allansikk.eu/HBEEP.

Most of the successful new parties have burned out quickly. NDSV, PS, ZRP, NS-SL, and TPP saw their popularity plummet almost immediately after their initial success. LLS, RP, and JL lost independent existence following mergers with older parties, but many of their leaders continue in national politics. Of the parties listed in Table 7.1, only DP managed to survive more than a decade in its original form, albeit obtaining a new legal identity to avoid charges of fraudulent funding. By 2016, some newer parties (GERB, ANO2011, and TOP09) had retained considerable support or increased it (Jobbik).

In parallel with the breakthroughs of genuinely new parties, several parties that dominated political systems in the 1990s have disappeared without leaving easily identifiable descendants. Eight parties leading governments for years were no longer in the parliament or in existence by 2016: AWS and SLD (Poland); K (Estonia), LC and TP (Latvia); People's Party–Movement for a Democratic Slovakia (HZDS) and Slovak Democratic and Christian Union–Democratic Party (SDKÚ-DS); and LDS (Slovenia). Other key parties from 1990s and 2000s have been severely weakened, for example, ODS in the Czech Republic and MSZP in Hungary. However, such "party deaths" may not be as tragic as the term implies. A party may have simply achieved its core aims – for example, parties whose raison d'être was defeating communism were redundant once it was achieved. Parties can also liquidate if the objectives of their leaders or patrons have been achieved, for example favourable laws passed or personal fortunes amassed. Either way, leaders of defunct parties may still continue in politics or enjoy political retirement as wealthy businesspeople. Obviously, for some parties, disappearance may be tragic, and it is empirically difficult to test the "achievement of aims" hypothesis, even though parties often decay following scandals and many former leaders of defunct parties did become wealthy following their spell in government. This could mean that some parties or leaders may be motivated less by the prospect of re-election but try to achieve as much as possible while in power, regardless of political costs (Sikk, 2006, pp. 154–156). If so, such "disposable" parties undermine a core principle of electoral (retrospective) accountability, particularly as they set examples for other political entrepreneurs. Finally, persistence and change can also go together – despite the instability of the Lithuanian party system, the two parties (TS-LKD and LSDP) that dominated almost all governments in the twenty-five years after the fall of communism remained the largest parliamentary parties in 2016.

Party organisation

In order to perform their essential functions properly, parties need at least some form of organisation. They need to coordinate activities between different fora, such as the government, the parliament, regional and local politics, members, candidates and voters, and reach different voters and regions in a country. East European parties have been diverse in terms of their organisation and eager to innovate around classical models of party organisation. In particular, they have been skilfully substituting traditional partisan resources of membership and organisational structure by others such as money, visible leaders, or easily digestible campaign messages.

Parties' organisational features can partly be linked to their developmental paths. For example, despite limited electoral appeal, the Czech communist successor party KSČM has retained one of the biggest membership organisations in the region (Linek and Pecháček, 2007). Recent studies have shown that party organisation and membership base can be beneficial for parties' electoral success (Tavits, 2013; Ibenskas, 2014), still offering limited protection against subsequent failures (Hanley, 2015).

Even if membership organisations have benefited some parties, the parties in the region are very diverse. In contrast, genuinely new parties have often been set up by political entrepreneurs with easy access to money for marketing to compensate for a lack of a proper organisation (at least initially). Parties broadly emulating the "business firm" model of Silvio Berlusconi's *Forza Italia* (Hopkin and Paolucci, 1999) have been common in Central and Eastern Europe – for example, the Czech ANO2011 and Lithuanian DP with a degree of fusion between party organisation and its leader's business (Tomšič and Prijon, 2013; Olteanu and Nève, 2014).

Other resources that have compensated for rudimentary organisation are easy-to-digest "populist" messages and charismatic and prominent leadership. Many new parties have very weak organisations simply because they have often been created very shortly before elections – as little as six (SMC) or eleven (NDSV) weeks prior to the election. Brand-new parties with only a handful of members can have advantages – competitors and the media have less time to discover or invent scandals and leaders face little internal pressures from members. For such parties (also in Western Europe), membership and organisation matter relatively little, certainly in terms of initial success. Still, organisational weakness has been a key reason why most of the genuinely new parties have fizzled out fast. Those more successful over time – for example, Smer, JL (later transformed into Unity), DP, and GERB – have usually gone on to develop more intricate organisations.

Another important development has been the growing symbiosis of political parties and the state (Kopecký, 2006). All countries in the region have introduced *direct public funding* to political parties, the last being Latvia in 2010 (Biezen and Kopecký, 2014). Established "resource-poor and power-hungry" parties, in particular, have benefited from increased public funding in addition to resources provided by party patronage when in power (Kopecký and Spirova, 2011, p. 897; Kopecký et al., 2012). Financial dependence on public funding is notably higher among East European parties compared to most of their West European counterparts. The availability of public funding for political parties has lowered incentives for parties to seek resources (financial and otherwise) elsewhere by developing strong membership organisation and links with the rest of the society (Biezen and Kopecky 2014, p. 171). Public subsidies have also helped benefiting parties to survive even following electoral backlashes (for example, in Poland, see Casal Bértoa and Walecki, 2014). Still, genuinely new party successes show that cartelisation at the level party system has been limited. The combination of a privileged status and policy space constrained by Europeanisation/globalisation space (Blyth and Katz, 2005) has made established parties complacent, blaming forces beyond their control for unpopular or ineffective policies. Ironically, that has partly helped to prepare ground for electoral earthquakes by anti-establishment reform parties.

Levels of *party membership* have been falling in Eastern Europe, in line with the trends in the West, albeit from a lower starting point. Biezen et al. (2012) report that party membership remains below the European average except in Bulgaria, Estonia, and Romania. In the decade until the late 2000s, it dropped everywhere by 25 per cent or more, except in Estonia and Poland (Biezen et al., 2012, p. 32). Some countries have established rather stringent membership requirements – particularly Romania and Slovakia, where 25,000 and 10,000 founding members are required for registration, respectively. In contrast, fewer than fifty founding members are required in Bulgaria, Hungary, and Poland (Cabada et al., 2014, pp. 108–109). Such requirements are not necessarily reflected in overall party membership levels; for example, it remains low in Slovakia. While required membership is medium in Estonia (1,000, 500 from 2014), the membership lists are public. To protect themselves against defections, parties usually maintain a healthy surplus of members as only officially registered parties can contest parliamentary elections.

Figure 7.3 shows trends in party membership and *identification* based on the European Social Survey until 2010 (when a question on party membership was last included). It shows notable decreases in membership almost everywhere. Countries with higher levels of membership have also seen a notable drop in party identification between 2008 and 2010, particularly pronounced in Slovenia and the Czech Republic where the party system ruptured during that period.

Figure 7.4 shows that voters' attachment to parties is generally very weak (also Enyedi and Deegan-Krause in this volume). Strong identification is strikingly low in Estonia and Slovenia despite relatively high membership levels – many members do not feel "very close" to their parties. On the other hand, closeness is substantially stronger than party membership in countries with low membership levels, particularly in Hungary. Only Bulgaria has both high levels of identification and membership. Hence, one should be careful with interpreting survey-based membership figures (although perhaps more reliable than figures reported by parties) as an indicator of strength between parties and the society at large. Links can be relatively strong where membership is relatively low and vice versa.

Also, stronger party identification does not necessarily bode well for democracy – Hungary and Bulgaria have recently experienced democratic setbacks. Strong identification might not be conducive for liberal democracy if it is the effect of parties that are over-institutionalised, personalistic, or heavily involved in patronage or cultivating clientelist linkages. Such linkages may promote electoral stability (Gherghina, 2014), but could in the long run be even more dangerous for the quality of democracy than political fragmentation or party system dynamism (Enyedi, 2016; Gurov and Zankina, 2013; Schedler, 1995). Finally, large membership and forms of active

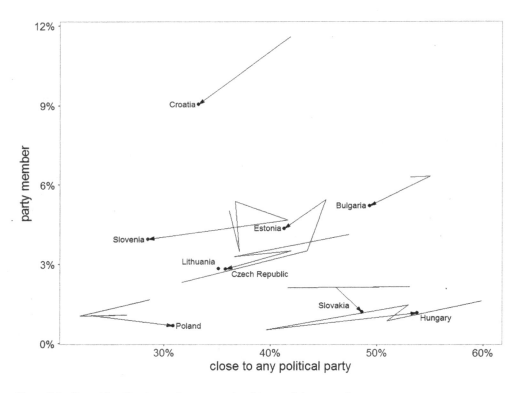

Figure 7.3 Party identification and party membership, trends by countries

Source: European Social Survey ending in Round 5 (2010), author's calculation (weights applied). Data: allansikk.eu/HBEEP.

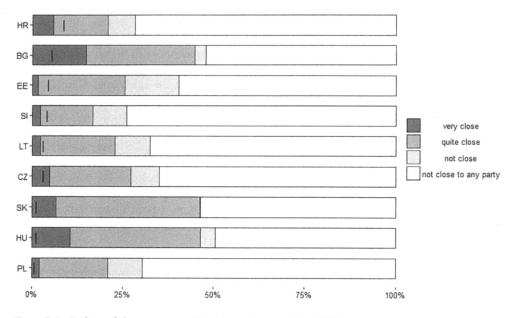

Figure 7.4 Feeling of closeness to a political party (by countries, 2010)

Note: Horizontal lines show the overall level of party membership. Those in the first three categories reported some closeness to a political party ("not close at all" combined with "not close").

Source: European Social Survey, Round 5, author's calculations (weighted). Data: allansikk.eu/HBEEP.

engagement (for example, internal ballots) that link leadership directly to individual members may in fact be a form of elite control. Genuine intra-party democracy entails development of mid-level structures to promote deliberation and act as an incubator for alternative leadership (Enyedi, 2014). For that, large membership may not necessarily be required given the pan-European tendency away from amateur politicians and politics becoming a profession rather than a vocation (Biezen and Poguntke, 2014).

Our understanding of how political parties work and how they are linked to party system stability, electoral volatility, and democratic quality has until recently been constrained by limitations of comparative data. Recently, more data spanning space and time has been collated. One major new direction in party studies is the extant research on *party regulation*. The region has been characterised by restrictions on party registration (deposits, membership requirements, and ideological limitations), yet limited regulations on internal party affairs; considerable state subsidies, yet light oversight of party finances (Casal Bértoa and van Biezen, 2014). However, the effects and determinants of party regulation need further research. Another extant stream of literature focuses on *electoral candidates* that can be seen as a link between parties as membership and electoral organisations. Thanks to greater availability of data, new insights have been gained about campaigns and district-level spending (Trumm, 2015, based on the Comparative Candidates Survey), the role of parties in inhibiting female representation (Allik, 2015) as well as general patterns of candidate change as a key aspect of party change (Sikk and Köker, 2015).

Conclusion

Representative democracy needs institutionalised parties and party systems, but there are only limited signs of either in Eastern Europe. Excessive change and fragmentation makes it more difficult for voters to understand the available electoral options and for parties to coordinate legislative and executive activities. Nearly all countries discussed in this chapter have seen breakthroughs by often vaguely defined but extremely popular new parties with no roots in previously existing political parties. It is likely that political parties and party systems here (but also in Western Europe, for example, Spain, Greece, Italy, Austria, Germany, and the Netherlands) are converging towards a new equilibrium of party politics where new parties are frequent and innovative (not necessarily in a positive sense) in their ideological profiles and organisational features (for example, on "memberless parties", see Mazzoleni and Voerman, 2016).

Many argue that stable parties are necessary – but not sufficient – for the quality of democracy (Mainwaring, 1999; Casal Bértoa, 2014); yet even stability itself cannot be the sole aim. Some stability in parties is necessary for accountability, responsiveness, and quality of representation, but democratic party systems need to be open so that new parties can reflect social changes and "underperforming" parties could be replaced by prophets and purifiers, respectively (Lucardie, 2000).

Perhaps the most striking observation when comparing earlier literature on party consolidation with more recent developments is how premature many of the predictions were regarding institutionalisation. Electoral ruptures have occurred in the face of seeming stability that might have been stagnation in disguise – for example, the recent events in the Czech Republic and Slovenia or the downfall of former communist parties in Hungary and Poland. Yet, there is little evidence that instability poses the worst problem for democracy – if anything, the recent political dominance of conservative forces in Poland and Hungary seems to be more problematic, echoing Grzymała-Busse's (2007) arguments about the importance of healthy party competition for preventing excessive state capture. It is worth keeping in mind that institutionalized parties and party systems may or may not be consolidated democracies (Hicken and Martinez Kuhonta, 2011).

From a normative point of view, one may nostalgically lament that the "golden age" of Western European party politics (that probably never was; see Webb, 2002, p. 11) has not reached Eastern Europe. The odds were always against it as the region democratised in an era of "postmodern" politics (Kitschelt et al., 1999), where the context of party formation led them to resemble contemporary parties in the older democracies (Biezen, 2005) or even leap-frog them. Can democracy survive or thrive in the new era of party politics? It could be difficult, but civil society, domestic interests, and international actors must strive to make the unstable kind of party politics serve the quality of democracy as best as it can. Alternatives – such as stable mass-membership parties with clear ideological profiles based on "frozen" conflict dimensions, backed up by voters with strong partisan attachments – may no longer be possible in Central and Eastern Europe or elsewhere, since Western Europe is also experiencing de-institutionalisation (Chiaramonte and Emanuele, 2015).

Bibliography

Allik, M. (2015) Who stands in the way of women? Open vs. closed lists and candidate gender in Estonia. *East European Politics*, 31 (4), pp. 429–451.

Beyme, K. von (1985) *Political Parties in Western Democracies*. Aldershot, Gower.

Biezen, I. van (2005) On the theory and practice of party formation and adaptation in new democracies. *European Journal of Political Research*, 44 (1), pp. 147–174.

Biezen, I. van and Kopecký, P. (2014) The cartel party and the state: Party-state linkages in European democracies. *Party Politics*, 20 (2), pp. 170–182.

Biezen, I. van, Mair, P. and Poguntke, T. (2012) Going, going . . . gone ? The decline of party membership in contemporary Europe. *European Journal of Political Research*, 51 (1), pp. 24–56.

Biezen, I. van and Poguntke, T. (2014) The decline of membership-based politics. *Party Politics*, 20 (2), pp. 205–216.

Blyth, M. and Katz, R. (2005) From catch-all politics to cartelisation: The political economy of the cartel party. *West European Politics*, 28 (1), pp. 33–60.

Bustikova-Siroky, L. (2014) Revenge of the radical right. *Comparative Political Studies*, 47 (12), pp. 1738–1765.

Cabada, L., Hloušek, V. and Jurek, P. (2014) *Party Systems in East Central Europe*. Lanham, MD, Lexington Books.

Casal Bértoa, F. (2014) Party systems and cleavage structures revisited: A sociological explanation of party system institutionalization in East Central Europe. *Party Politics*, 20 (1), pp. 16–36.

Casal Bértoa, F. and van Biezen, I. (2014) Party regulation and party politics in post-communist Europe. *East European Politics*, 30 (3), pp. 295–314.

Casal Bértoa, F. and Walecki, M. (2014) Regulating Polish politics: 'Cartel' parties in a non-collusive party system. *East European Politics*, 30 (3), pp. 330–350.

Chiaramonte, A. and Emanuele, V. (2015) Party system volatility, regeneration and de-institutionalization in Western Europe (1945–2015). *Party Politics* (Published online before print 25 August 2015).

Enyedi, Z. (2014) The discreet charm of political parties. *Party Politics*, 20 (2), pp. 194–204.

Enyedi, Z. (2016) Populist polarization and party system institutionalization: The role of party politics in de-democratization. *Problems of Post-Communism*, 63 (4), pp. 210–220.

Ezrow, L., Homola, J. and Tavits, M. (2014) When extremism pays: Policy positions, voter certainty, and party support in postcommunist Europe. *Journal of Politics*, 76 (2), pp. 1–13.

Gherghina, S. (2014) *Party Organization and Electoral Volatility in Central and Eastern Europe: Enhancing Voter Loyalty*. Oxford, Routledge.

Grzymała-Busse, A. M. (2002) *Redeeming the Communist Past: The Regeneration of Communist Parties in East Central Europe*. Cambridge, Cambridge University Press.

Grzymała-Busse, A. M. (2007) *Rebuilding Leviathan: Party Competition and State Exploitation in Post-communist Democracies*. Cambridge, Cambridge University Press.

Gurov, B. and Zankina, E. (2013) Populism and the construction of political charisma post-transition politics in Bulgaria. *Problems of Post-Communism*, 60 (1), pp. 3–17.

Hanley, S. (2004) Getting the right right: Redefining the centre-right in post-communist Europe. *Journal of Communist Studies and Transition Politics*, 20 (3), pp. 9–27.

Hanley, S. (2015) All fall down? The prospects for established parties in Europe and beyond. *Government and Opposition*, 50 (2), pp. 1–24.

Hanley, S. and Sikk, A. (2014) Economy, corruption or floating voters? Explaining the breakthroughs of anti-establishment reform parties in eastern Europe. *Party Politics*, 22 (4), pp. 522–533.

Hicken, A. and Martinez Kuhonta, E. (2011) Shadows from the past: Party system institutionalization in Asia. *Comparative Political Studies*, 44 (5), pp. 572–597.

Hloušek, V. and Kopeček, L. (2010) *Origin, Ideology and Transformation of Political Parties*. Farnham, Ashgate.

Hopkin, J. and Paolucci, C. (1999) The business firm model of party organisation: Cases from Spain and Italy. *European Journal of Political Research*, 35 (3), pp. 307–339.

Ibenskas, R. (2014) Activists or money? Explaining the electoral success and persistence of political parties in Lithuania. *Party Politics*, 20 (6), pp. 879–889.

Ibenskas, R. (2015) Understanding pre-electoral coalitions in central and Eastern Europe. *British Journal of Political Science* (Published online before print on 23 February 2015), pp. 1–19.

Innes, A. (2002) Party competition in postcommunist Europe: The great electoral lottery. *Comparative Politics*, 35 (1), pp. 85–104.

Ishiyama, J. T. (1997) The sickle or the rose?: Previous regime types and the evolution of the ex-communist parties in post-communist politics. *Comparative Political Studies*, 30 (3), pp. 299–330.

Kiss, C. (2002) From liberalism to conservatism: The federation of young democrats in post-communist Hungary. *East European Politics & Societies*, 16 (3), pp. 739–763.

Kitschelt, H., Mansfeldová, Z., Markowski, R. and Toka, G. (1999) *Post-Communist Party Systems: Competition, Representation, and Inter-Party Cooperation*. Cambridge, Cambridge University Press.

Kopecký, P. (2006) Political parties and the state in post-communist Europe: The nature of symbiosis. *Journal of Communist Studies and Transition Politics*, 22 (3), pp. 251–273.

Kopecký, P., Mair, P. and Spirova, M. (2012) *Party Patronage and Party Government: Public Appointments and Political Control in European Democracies*. Oxford, Oxford University Press.

Kopecký, P. and Spirova, M. (2011) 'Jobs for the boys'? Patterns of party patronage in post-communist Europe. *West European Politics*, 34 (5), pp. 897–921.

Krašovec, A. and Haughton, T. (2011) Money, organization and the state: The partial cartelization of party politics in Slovenia. *Communist and Post-Communist Studies*, 44 (3), pp. 199–209.

Kreuzer, M. and Pettai, V. (2004) Political parties and the study of political employment: New insights from the postcommunist democracies. *World Politics*, 56 (4), pp. 608–633.

Linek, L. and Pecháček, Š. (2007) Low membership in Czech political parties: Party strategy or structural determinants? *Journal of Communist Studies and Transition Politics*, 23 (2), pp. 259–275.

Lucardie, P. (2000) Prophets, purifiers and prolocutors: Towards a theory on the emergence of new parties. *Party Politics*, 6 (2), pp. 175–185.

Mainwaring, S. (1999) *Rethinking Party Systems in the Third Wave of Democratization: The Case of Brazil*. Stanford, CA, Stanford University Press.

Mair, P. (1997) *Party System: Approaches and Interpretations*. Oxford, Oxford University Press.

Marinova, D. M. (2015) A new approach to estimating electoral instability in Parties. *Political Science Research and Methods*, 3 (2), pp. 265–280.

Mazzoleni, O. and Voerman, G. (2016) Memberless parties: Beyond the business-firm party model? *Party Politics* (published online before print on 25 January 2016).

Minkenberg, M. (2007) *Transforming the Transformation?: The East European Radical Right in the Political Process*. Oxford, Routledge.

Mudde, C. (2007) *Populist Radical Right Parties in Europe*. Cambridge, Cambridge University Press.

Olteanu, T. and Nève, D. de (2014) Business firm or rather business men parties? *IPSA/AISP 23rd World Congress of Political Science, Montréal*.

Pirro, A. (2015) *The Populist Radical Right in Central and Eastern Europe: Ideology, Impact, and Electoral Performance*. Oxford, Routledge.

Pop-Eleches, G. (2010) Throwing out the bums: Protest voting and unorthodox parties after communism. *World Politics*, 62 (2), pp. 221–260.

Roberts, A. (2010) *The Quality of Democracy in Eastern Europe: Public Preferences and Policy Reforms*. Cambridge, Cambridge University Press.

Rohrschneider, R. and Whitefield, S. (2013) *The Strain of Representation: How Parties Represent Diverse Voters in Western and Eastern Europe*. Oxford, Oxford University Press.

Schedler, A. (1995) *Under and Overinstitutionalization: Some Ideal Typical Propositions Concerning New and Old Party Systems*. Kellogg Institute Working Paper #213, March 2015. Available online: https://www3.nd.edu/~kellogg/publications/workingpapers/WPS/213.pdf.

Sikk, A. (2005) How unstable? Volatility and the genuinely new parties in Eastern Europe. *European Journal of Political Research*, 44 (3), pp. 391–412.

Sikk, A. (2006) *Highways to Power: New Party Success in Three Young Democracies*. Tartu, Tartu University Press.

Sikk, A. (2011) Newness as a winning formula for new political Parties. *Party Politics*, 18 (4), pp. 465–486.

Sikk, A. (2013) Electoral congruence and novelty: Accounting for partially new parties. Paper presented at the *ECPR Joint Sessions of Workshops*, Mainz, 11–16 March.

Sikk, A. and Köker, P. (2015) Candidate turnover and party system change in central and Eastern Europe. Paper presented at the *ECPR General Conference*. Montreal, 26–29 August.

Spirova, M. (2005) Political parties in Bulgaria – Organizational trends in comparative perspective. *Party Politics*, 11 (5), pp. 601–622.

Tavits, M. (2013) *Post-Communist Democracies and Party Organization*. Cambridge, Cambridge University Press.

Tomšič, M. and Prijon, L. (2013) Person-based politics in Italy and Slovenia: Comparing cases of leadership's individualisation. *International Social Science Journal*, 64 (213–214), pp. 237–248.

Trumm, S. (2015) What does it take to get elected in a post-communist democracy?: Explaining the success and failure of parliamentary candidates in Estonia. *East European Politics & Societies*, 30 (1), pp. 169–188.

Učeň, P. (2007) Parties, populism, and anti-establishment politics in East Central Europe. *SAIS Review*, 17 (1), pp. 49–62.

Webb, P. (2002) Introduction: Political parties in advanced industrial democracies. In P. Webb, D. Farrell and I. Holliday (eds), *Political Parties in Advanced Industrial Democracies*. Oxford, Oxford University Press, pp. 1–15.

8

THE RULE OF LAW

Martin Mendelski

Introduction

Establishing the rule of law has been one of the key challenges (next to building capitalism and democracy) for post-communist countries.[1] However, not all post-communist countries have overcome this challenge and transitioned to the rule of law. How can the rule of law be established? Practitioners have responded to this question by stressing different means (laws, judiciaries and enforcement bodies) and objectives (legality, equality before the law, law and order, predictability) of rule of law reform. Judges have argued that the rule of law requires above all judicial independence and the institutional and material safeguards to maintain it. Businessmen and economists have emphasised the importance of judicial efficiency to reduce the length of proceedings, the respect of property rights, and the enforcement of contracts. Politicians have used the rule of law as a buzzword with changing meanings, calling for judicial accountability, judicial independence, or the fight against corruption. Legal experts have advised building judicial capacity and adopting best practices (including "best" legal frameworks, international standards, anti-corruption agencies, judicial academies, etc.) to improve the rule of law. International donors, with their different priorities and agendas, have emphasised a plethora of issues to establish the rule of law, such as judicial capacity building (EU, USAID, and World Bank), respect for human rights and a fair trial (ECtHR), fight of corruption, improved judicial review, judicial independence, impartiality and training (Council of Europe and EU), law and order and minority rights (OSCE), and in general the adaptation to European and international legal standards through processes of institutional transplantation and approximation. What becomes obvious is the heterogeneity of means, goals, opinions, agendas, and priorities of diverse stakeholders, which makes rule of law reform a complex, expensive, and challenging issue.

After more than two decades of legal and judicial reform, there is evidence that post-communist countries from Central Europe and the Baltic states (CEB) have tackled the challenge of rule of law reform better than countries from South Eastern Europe (SEE) and the Commonwealth of Independent States (CIS) (see Figures 8.1 and 8.2). Empirical evidence points to persisting differences in the rule of law, exhibiting an advanced group (CEB) and two laggard groups (SEE and CIS). Despite several reform waves and despite the millions of dollars and euros spent on rule of law promotion from abroad, most of the countries from SEE and CIS seem not to have established the rule of law. Considering the different levels of the rule of law in post-communist

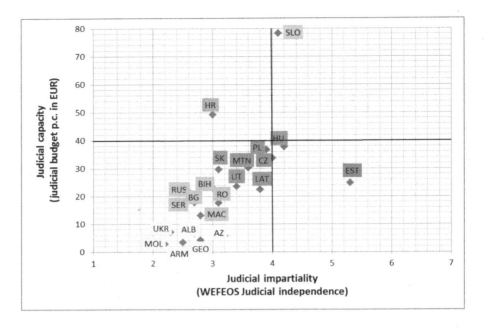

Cluster	Rule of law variety	Countries
1	Very weak rule of law	Georgia (GEO), Moldova (MOL), Armenia (ARM), Azerbaijan (AZ), (Ukraine) UKR, Albania (ALB),
2	Weak rule of law	Bulgaria (BG), Romania (RO), Serbia (SER), Macedonia (MAC), Bosnia and Herzegovina (BIH), Russia (RUS)
3	Moderate rule of law	Poland (PL), Czech Republic (CZ), Hungary (HU), Latvia (LAT), Lithuania (LIT), Montenegro (MTN), Slovakia (SK)
4	Strong rule of law (type A)	Estonia (EST)
5	Strong rule of law (type B)	Slovenia (SLO)

Figure 8.1   Varieties of the rule of law in Central and Eastern Europe

Source: Own elaboration based on judicial budget data from the European Commission for the Efficiency of Justice (CEPEJ) and the judicial independence indicator from the World Economic Forum Executive Survey (WEFEOS).

Note: Judicial independence is measured on a scale from 1 (worst) to 7 (best). Data reflects the average values between 2001/2002 and 2012/2014.

countries (despite similar and continuous external pressure for legal and judicial reform), it can be stated that this region has experienced a transition towards a "varieties of the rule of law" (see Figure 8.1), which consists in systematic differences in the level of judicial capacity, impartiality as well in other aspects, such as judicial review, separation of powers, quality of laws, and so forth (see Mendelski 2014).

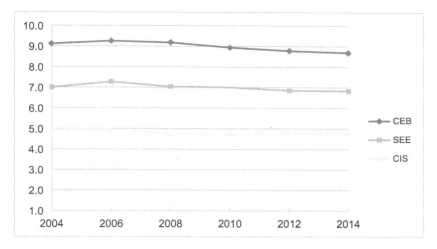

Figure 8.2 Rule of law development in CEE

Source: Bertelsmann Transformation Index 2016, www.bti-project.org/de/index/.

Notes: CEB (Central Europe and the Baltics) includes the Czech Republic, Estonia, Hungary, Latvia, Lithuania, Poland, Slovakia, and Slovenia; SEE (South Eastern Europe) includes Albania, Bosnia and Herzegovina, Bulgaria, Croatia, Kosovo, Macedonia, Montenegro, Romania, and Serbia; CIS (Commonwealth of Independent States) includes Armenia, Azerbaijan, Belarus, Georgia, Moldova, Russia, and Ukraine.

How has the rule of law developed in Central and Eastern Europe (CEE) since the collapse of communism? What explains the dissimilar development of the rule of law among European post-communist countries? These fundamental questions have been addressed by legal and political science scholars dealing with the rule of law in CEE (e.g. Schwartz 2000; Sadurski et al. 2006; Coman and De Waele 2007; Magen and Morlino 2009; Piana 2010; Dallara 2014; Mendelski 2014, 2015, 2016). The answers to these questions have been manifold. They reflect diverse methodologies to measure (e.g. qualitative case studies vs. quantitative, indicator-based analysis) and different explanatory factors to account for rule of law development (e.g. domestic and external, structural, actor-related and process-related variables). This chapter reviews the existing literature on the rule of law in CEE and focuses on the literature which has tried to account for uneven rule of law development across post-communist countries. It proceeds as follows. First, it identifies major trends and explanations of rule of law development in CEE. Second, it identifies the gaps in the existing literature and in particular the methodological and conceptual challenges for rule of law scholars. Third, it presents an integrated causal explanation for rule of law development and proposes a research agenda for the future.

The rule of law: trends and explanations

Trends in rule of law development

How has the rule of law developed in CEE since the collapse of communism? This question is difficult to answer empirically, at least for the first decade of post-communist transition, for which valid and reliable rule of law indicators are not available (see Oman and Arndt 2010). Since the late 1990s and early 2000s, two commonly used rule of law indicators exhibit lack of progress and even decline. The Freedom House judicial framework and independence index decreased between 1997 and 2014, from 3.4 to 3.0 for CEE on an inverted scale where 1 = worst and 7 = best. The Bertelsmann Stiftung's Transformation Index (BTI) rule of law index decreased slightly between 2004 and 2014, from 7.1 to 6.9 on a scale of 1 to 10, where 1 = worst and 10 = best. These stagnating and even declining trends, despite the millions of euros spent on judicial reform and rule of law promotion, are puzzling and suggest that the rule of law is a sticky or path-dependent phenomenon (see Prado and Trebilcock 2009), and also that externally promoted reforms are not able to change the dominant logic of governance. The BTI rule of law indicator from Figure 8.2 reflects this almost unchanged but persisting trend in the rule of law across three groups of post-communist countries. The indicator also shows that some countries (CEB) are better evaluated than others (from SEE, CIS) and that there is hardly a catching-up of the laggard groups. When we look behind the aggregated scores we can find only three countries which either considerable improved (for example, Moldova +1.8) or decreased (for example, Hungary − 2.5, Azerbaijan − 1.3) with regard to this indicator. All other countries from the region remained at a similar level, suggesting little impact of donor-driven rule of law reforms.

The persisting post-communist diversity in the rule of law is also identified in scholarly work. First, authors recognise several "success cases" from the advanced group (CEB), for example, Hungary, Poland, the Czech Republic, and Estonia, which managed relatively early to attain high levels of judicial independence and constitutional review (Schwartz 2000; Seibert-Fohr 2012; Coman 2014), judicial capacity (Anderson et al. 2005), judicial accountability (Piana 2010), and judicial impartiality (Mendelski 2014). Also Slovenia, Latvia, and Slovakia (after 2000) were assessed as relatively successful cases with regard to judicial reform (Pridham 2008; Dallara 2014). Second, authors have identified "intermediate cases" from SEE, such as Romania, Bulgaria, Slovakia, or Serbia. These countries have progressed across some elements of the rule of law, such as judicial independence or judicial capacity, but did not improve or even regressed across others elements of the rule of law, such as judicial impartiality, accountability, and integrity (see Magen and Morlino 2009; Mendelski 2012, 2013b; Schönfelder 2005; Bobek and Kosar 2014; Hipper 2015). Third, authors who dealt with countries from the CIS and partly from SEE, identified predominantly "cases of failure", that is, country cases where judicial and legal reforms did not lead to the rule of law. The absence of the rule of law in the Western Balkans and post-Soviet countries is reflected in politicised judicial systems, defective constitutional review, weak separation of powers, weak or ineffective horizontal accountability institutions, insufficient judicial capacity, presence of (judicial) corruption, and a low quality of legislation (see Schwartz 2000; Trochev 2008; Popova 2012; Magen and Morlino 2009; Morlino and Sadurski 2010; Mendelski 2012, 2013a, 2013b, 2015; Natorski 2013; Dallara 2014; Radin 2014; Peshkopia 2014; Capussela 2015). In short, persistent diversity can be identified among post-communist countries.

When we analyse trends in the rule of law, we need to bear in mind that the rule of law as a contested concept can mean different things to different scholars and can therefore be measured through different methods, which might result in different evaluations of the rule of law in a particular country. This explains partly why one country is sometimes evaluated as a success case and other times as a case of failure (e.g. Romania and Serbia). In this regard, three methodological pitfalls of rule of law assessment in CEE can be observed.

First, most of the literature has relied on qualitative methodology (case studies, comparisons of few cases) thus offering only restrictive, non-generalisable insights about rule of law development in the region. Second, several scholars have resorted to questionable indicators of the rule of law (for example, from the World Bank and Freedom House) which have been criticised for lack of objectivity, transparency, reliability, and replicability (see Oman and Arndt 2010; Giannone 2010; Høyland et al. 2012; Steiner 2014; Cooley and Snyder 2015). Third, assessment of the rule of law has been relatively narrow and unsystematic, focusing on the quality of the judiciary and constitutional courts, and above all on their degree of independence and power to exert review. Scholars as well as providers of rule of law indicators have barely measured the inherent quality of law (inner morality of law, see Fuller 1969), that is, the stability, coherence, generality, and enforcement characteristics of laws. Only recently was this lacuna filled by the World Justice Project, which provides indicators to assess the quality of laws. One problem with such a narrow and non-systematic assessment is that the notion of the rule of law is reduced to the empowerment of the judiciary (judicialisation of politics), a misguided best-standards recipe, which has resulted in several countries in independent but unaccountable judiciaries, judicial councils, constitutional courts, and a worrying trend towards "juristocracy" (Hirschl 2009; Mendelski 2016).

Explanations of differences in the rule of law

Judicial reform literature: structure and agency matter

Differences in rule of law development in CEE have been explained by a plethora of selective factors, such as historical institutional legacies, informal judicial culture, EU conditionality, reformist actors, and reform processes (see Coman and De Waele 2007). To explain rule of law variation, several authors have stressed the importance of *structural preconditions* and in particular of communist and pre-communist institutional legacies (e.g. institutional legacy of the Habsburg and Ottoman Empires), which might have survived in some areas and impacted on the modes of judicial and administrative governance (Mendelski 2009, 2014; Mendelski and Libman 2014; Kühn 2011; Beers 2010; Dallara 2014). These legacy explanations were not meant as predetermined historical, institutional and cultural trajectories from which countries could not escape, but rather stressed the path-dependent nature of the rule of law (see Prado and Trebilcock 2009) alongside more recent explanatory variables (e.g. impact of international organisations, formal institutional reforms). Besides structural preconditions, scholars emphasised the relevance of *domestic agency*. It was argued that (domestic political and judicial) actors and in particular their interests, strategic and short-term calculations, and the balance of powers between them matter for the success of judicial reform as well as effective constitutional judicial review (Magalhaes 1999; Schwartz 2000; Trochev 2008; Piana 2010).

The rule of law promotion literature: a defective reform process

Another explanation for differences in the rule of law was attributed to the quality of the *reform process*. In particular, the rule of law promotion literature (Jensen and Heller 2003; Channell 2006; Carothers 2006; Kleinfeld 2012; Mendelski 2014) has explained rule of law and reform failure by criticising the badly designed reform strategies of international donors (for example, the World Bank, EU, and USAID) as well as their insufficient or defective implementation. Scholars and practitioners from this literature have identified a plethora of motives for reform failure such as "problems of knowledge" (Carothers 2006), wrong assumptions and incentives (Channell 2006), a focus on the formal and institutional means rather than the ends (Kleinfeld 2012; Jensen and Heller 2003), lack of capacity (Kleinfeld 2012; Anderson et al. 2005), a top-down elitist approach to reform (Mendelski 2012), donor heterogeneity which translates into legal and incoherent judicial systems (Mendelski 2013b), and too much focus on quantitative than on qualitative assessment of the rule of law (Mendelski 2016). Although the rule of law promotion literature has dealt only partly with CEE countries (see Mendelski 2014), its insights are relevant for understanding the defective reform approach of external donors (USAID, ABA/CEELI, World Bank, and EU).

The EU's rule of law promotion literature: conditionality, capacity and empowered change agents

More recently, a growing number of scholars have analysed the role of the European Union (namely, EU conditionality) in the development of the rule of law (Sadurski et al. 2006; Magen and Morlino 2009; Morlino and Sadurski 2010; Bozhilova 2007; Mendelski 2012, 2013a, 2013b, 2014, 2015, 2016; Coman 2014; Pridham 2007a, 2007b, 2008; Piana 2010; Kochenov 2008; Natorski 2013; Dallara 2014; Parau 2015; Hipper 2015). Two main insights can be drawn from this literature.

First, scholars find a weak, limited or mixed (differentiated) impact of the EU on the rule of law (Bozhilova 2007; Dallara 2014; Pridham 2007a, 2007b, 2008; Piana 2010; Magen and Morlino 2009; Morlino and Sadurski 2010; Mendelski 2012). For instance, most authors in the edited volume by Sadurski et al. (2006) discover an ambiguous impact of the EU. The reason is that while the goals of the EU's rule of law promotion are honourable ("spreading democracy and the rule of law"), often the means and processes of this promotion and transplantation (which tend to be elitist, technocratic, instrumentalised, and non-democratic) are highly problematic. Another edited volume by Magen and Morlino (2009), which analyses the EU's impact on the rule of law in hybrid regimes (Ukraine, Romania, Serbia, and Turkey), discovers that while EU conditionality works for rule adoption, rule implementation and internalisation are incomplete (Magen and Morlino 2009). Several single-country case studies on Romania (Mendelski 2012; Parau 2015; Hipper 2015), Ukraine (Natorski 2013), Bulgaria (Bozhilova 2007), Latvia, and Slovakia (Pridham 2008) find that the EU is often able to push judicial, legal, and anti-corruption reforms but is not really effective in promoting the rule of law or only some selective aspects of it, such as judicial capacity, the establishment of formal judicial structures and formal rules. In short, this literature shows that the EU's impact seems to be differential and highly context-dependent, that is, it varies across countries, country clusters, and dimensions of the rule of law.

Second, scholars claim that this differential impact of the EU in CEE (and the divergent development in the rule of law) can be explained by three main factors. First, some authors attribute differences in EU conditionality effectiveness to diverse *domestic conditions*, including adverse and favourable structural conditions (historical legacies, political stability, high institutional and administrative capacity) and beneficial informal institutions which facilitate EU-driven reforms (Pridham 2005; Sadurski et al. 2006; Magen and Morlino 2009; Mendelski 2009, 2014; Dallara 2014); Second, the differential impact of the EU is attributed to *agency-related* explanations which focus on the costs and benefits for self-interested reformers and on power struggles between reformist change agents and reform-resisting veto players (Pridham 2005; Magen and Morlino 2009; Mendelski 2011, 2014; Bozhilova 2007; Dallara 2014). In particular, several authors have highlighted positively the role of reformist "change agents" to push reforms and to bring about the rule of law, for instance in "semi-liberal countries" such as Romania, Slovakia and Serbia (Magen and Morlino 2009; Pridham 2005, 2008; see Kleinfeld 2012). Mendelski (2014, 2015, 2016) has in contrast argued and shown that liberal "change agents" often apply similar questionable reform methods as "illiberal" reform opponents. The reason is that both types of actors are (or become) embedded in the same particularist social order and therefore either assimilate or exit without meaningful results. Third, some researchers argue that the reform *process* (reflected in the EU's approach to rule of law promotion and evaluation) matters (Sadurski et al. 2006; Mendelski 2014, 2015). In this regard, scholars argue that the consistency of external donor conditionality is important (Sadurski 2006; Dallara 2014) and that the EU (embodied by the European Commission) lacks a sufficiently well-elaborated methodology to allow a consistent and objective evaluation of the rule of law (Kochenov 2008; Dimitrov et al. 2014; Toneva-Metodieva 2014;

Mendelski 2015, 2016). On the domestic side, authors critically stress that the newly created judicial structures are often politicised, instrumentalised, or captured by change agents or veto players and thus undermine judicial independence and the rule of law (Mendelski 2013b, 2015, 2016; see Bozhilova 2007; Natorski 2013; Bobek and Kosar 2014; Radin 2014; Beširević 2014; Kuzmova 2014; Capussela 2015; Parau 2015).

In conclusion, after years of research we still do not know whether and under which conditions rule of law promotion and judicial reform (as advanced by the EU and international donors) establishes or rather undermines the rule of law. Reasons for this inconclusive finding can be explained by three main factors which will be addressed in the next section.

Critique of the literature

There are currently three key problems which reduce the explanatory power of the literatures with regard to rule of law promotion and development in CEE. First, the main literatures propose a few selective explanatory variables to explain rule of law development, which are reflected in a variety of selective structural, agency, and process-related factors (e.g. historical legacies, judicial culture, lack of domestic capacity, the nature of EU conditionality, power balance between domestic veto players and change agents, the reform strategy of donors). While some authors explained rule of law development through external-domestic and agency-structure nexuses (e.g. Pridham 2005), we still have only little knowledge about how these diverse variables are causally connected (for instance through causal mechanisms) and whether the relationship between the interdependent variables vary across time and space. So far only few scholars (for example, Mendelski 2014) have provided a more integrated, causal explanation of how the deeper structural and the shallower agency-related explanations (Kitschelt 2003), as well as process-related factors, are causally linked to each other.

Second, the methodology of most of the literature dealing with the rule of law in CEE can be criticised with regard to the research design. Most relevant studies are qualitative in nature, applying process tracing in few selected case studies or addressing few cases in geographically restricted regions (either CEB, SEE, or CIS). There is only one cross-regional mixed-method study (combining qualitative and quantitative methodology) which analyses rule of law development across all European post-communist countries (see Mendelski 2014). In order to overcome the restricted findings of single-cases and regional-specific studies, broader and more systematic comparative studies with a larger number of cases are needed which would help to discover why some countries manage to establish the rule of law and others not.

Third, most of the extant literature assumes that rule of law reforms as advanced by pro-EU, reformist change agents lead to progress and implicitly that obstruction of reforms by reform-opposing veto players undermines the rule of law (e.g. Magen and Morlino 2009; Pridham 2005). Authors suggest therefore to identify veto players and to reduce their number or their power (Magen and Morlino 2009; Kleinfeld 2012). While at first glance this argument makes sense, upon further investigation this assumption proves to be highly problematic as it does not consider that also change agents (mis)use the "rule of law as a political weapon" (Maravall 2003), for instance by politicising and instrumentalising the transplanted laws and newly created judicial and anti-corruption structures. Thus, under the conditions of an already weak rule of law, externally empowered and unconstrained reformist change agents may undermine the rule of law. This proposition makes sense if one moves beyond the assumption of a purely positive impact of external EU conditionality and domestic change agents. The implication is straightforward: rule of law reforms can result in different outcomes. They can improve and maintain but also undermine the rule of law. More reforms do not mean automatically more progress in the rule of law. What often makes the difference is the way reforms are conducted, and this depends on the social order in which reformers are embedded (Mendelski 2014).

In sum, most of the discussed literature on the rule of law in CEE proposes arguments and findings which remain restrictive and incomplete. What is needed is therefore a more comprehensive and integrated explanation which combines different methodologies, approaches, and literatures, and by so doing broadens the theoretical and methodological lens through which external rule of law promotion and reform can be analysed. The next section will briefly present such an integrated causal theory to explain rule of law development in CEE and the EU's impact on it.

Healthy and pathological reform cycles: towards an integrated causal theory

Mendelski (2014, 2015, 2016) has empirically analysed the EU's impact on the rule of law in post-communist countries (CEB, SEE, and CIS) and provided a more integrated, mechanism-based and context-sensitive explanation to account for rule of law diversity. His work shows that EU-driven rule of law reforms often result in a considerable increase of judicial capacity and substantive legality (that is, the approximation to Western standards) but have a negatively reinforcing impact on judicial impartiality and formal legality, that is, the "inner morality of law" (Fuller 1969), for instance by producing more unstable, incoherent, and less enforced laws.

Mendelski (2014) argues that the EU's impact on the rule of law depends on the social order in which reformers and reform processes are located. Thus, whereas reforms consolidate the rule of law in already advanced rule of law countries (CEB), they undermine the rule of law in weak rule of law countries (SEE and CIS). This uneven development is reflected, for instance, in the degree of "legal pathologies" (e.g. legal instability, incoherence, lack of enforcement, and politicisation) which tend to be reinforced negatively by EU-driven reforms in closed-access social orders (in SEE and CIS). These pathological effects of Europeanisation occur when empowered but unchecked reformers instrumentalise judicial and anti-corruption reforms (including newly created anti-corruption agencies, judicial structures, and laws), as occurred for instance in Moldova and Romania. In contrast, the "pathological power" of the EU (see Mendelski 2015) is less harmful in consolidated, open-access social orders (e.g. Poland and Estonia) where it is constrained by reform-resisting and independent horizontal accountability institutions (e.g. constitutional courts, ombudsmen, and judicial councils). In short, reforms can both consolidate *and* undermine the rule of law. What makes the difference is the quality of the reform process, which depends on the underlying conditions in a country in which domestic actors (reformers) are embedded.

To explain differences in the rule of law more systematically, Mendelski (2014) proposes an integrated causal theory of *healthy (virtuous) and pathological (vicious) reform cycles*, which combines structure, agency, and process-related variables and which links these different explanatory variables in a causally and cumulative way (see Myrdal 1957). The main implication of his "reform cycle theory" is that reforms in general (and EU conditionality in particular) are not transformative but reinforcing; that is, reformers tend to reproduce the respective social order in which they are embedded and thus cement the post-communist divergence in the rule of law.

The uneven effects of EU-driven reform can be elucidated on the examples of judicial self-organisation and horizontal accountability institutions, such as judicial councils, constitutional courts, and anti-corruption agencies. These newly created or empowered institutions have been established in this region as a general panacea to improve the rule of law. However, their functioning differed across countries. Whereas judicial councils, anti-corruption agencies and constitutional courts have worked relatively well (that is, in an impartial way) in established democracies from most Visegrád and Baltic states, they became unaccountable, politicised, and polarised in less advanced countries in SEE and CIS. Rather than being guarantors of judicial independence and the rule of law, most judicial councils, constitutional courts, and anti-corruption agencies in the region evolved into politicised, polarised, unaccountable, and non-transparent bodies that tended to undermine the rule of law (Schwartz 2000; Seibert-Fohr 2012; Börzel and Pamuk 2012; Coman 2014; Bobek and Kosar 2014; Capussela 2015; Beširević 2014; Mendelski 2015, 2016). It could be argued that these transplanted judicial structures, rather than improving judicial independence, oversight, and constraints on the executive, simply opened up different channels of political influence and misuse. In contrast, in more advanced countries from CEB, such pathological reform effects were mitigated by reform-resisting interinstitutional institutions, which experienced a more healthy reform process (which was more gradual, less politicised, more coherent, and accountable) and resulted in the consolidation of the rule of law (Mendelski 2014).

Conclusion: challenges for future research

The rule of law, as a contested theoretical concept, is difficult to measure empirically and difficult to create in the short term. After decades of research and judicial reform, we still do not know how to transition to the rule of law, especially when reforms are being pushed from abroad. This rather pessimistic claim is reflected in the sobering findings in the academic literature and the empirical rule of law indicators, for example, from BTI or Freedom House indicators, which remain at a similar level despite considerable reform efforts in CEE. What can be concluded from the literature and the empirical data is that the post-communist division in terms of the rule of law has persisted. The rule of law has experienced a path-dependent development and there was hardly any long-lasting, transformative catch-up of laggard countries from SEE and the former Soviet Union. A second conclusion is that there are plenty of explanatory factors which may account for uneven trends and levels in the rule of law, suggesting that there may be multiple paths and combinations how to get to the rule of law (that is, equifinality).

There are three main possibilities for future research to tackle existing lacunae in the study of the rule of law in CEE. The first challenge is to better integrate different explanatory variables in a causal theory that allows distinguishing between the different positive and negative as well as short-term and long-term effects of external rule of law promotion. This requires from scholars first of all devising an integrated concept of the rule of law (and its underlying dynamics) which pays attention to the interaction of its different dimensions and its components (see Mendelski 2014 for such an attempt). It equally requires taking into account the diverse interrelationships between explanatory variables (such as structural preconditions, external conditionality, reform strategy, and domestic reformist actors), and the effects these variables have under different domestic conditions. In short, we need a more integrated, systemic, and context-dependent analysis of the rule of law in CEE.

A second challenge is to improve the research design and implicitly the measurement of the rule of law. First, the rule of law is a complex and emergent phenomenon which needs to be assessed from a comprehensive and systematic perspective that considers the interplay and balance between different rule of law elements/dimensions (e.g. between judicial independence and judicial accountability). Scholars and practitioners should abstain from assessing the rule of law through a "more is better" mindset which focuses on the selective performance of atomised rule of law aspects, such as constitutional review, judicial independence, and judicial capacity. It is the complementary combination of elements which leads to the rule of law, not their additive, atomised improvement (Mendelski 2016). Second, systematic assessment of the rule of law requires first of all a shift from small-*n* case-studies towards a large-*N* research design, ideally combining qualitative and quantitative methodology in a mixed-method research design. Only by measuring the broad patterns and trends in the rule of law and discovering the causal processes and mechanisms behind them will we gain more systematic insights into how to transition to the rule of law. The methodological challenge for quantitative scholars is then to measure rule of law development with the help of objective data and subjective indicators in a reliable, valid, and replicable way. Assessing the rule of law depends on the indicators one chooses (Skaaning 2010). Therefore, scholars should choose wisely or preferably employ better data to measure the rule of law and in particular the "inner morality of law" (i.e. the stability, coherence, generality, and enforcement of rules), a key element which has been often disregarded.

A third challenge is to provide sound policy recommendations based on conceptually and empirically grounded findings, which take into account the diverse domestic preconditions of CEE countries. This challenge implies several things. First, it requires refraining from transplanting first-best standards or solutions from abroad which do not work on the ground and more than often become "legal irritants" (Teubner 1998). Second, it requires reconsidering the mistaken assumption of the beneficial consequences of external rule of law promotion (and of reform) under difficult domestic conditions. In other words, reforms can under certain conditions undermine the rule of law and make things worse. Third, it requires assessing rule of law development in an impartial way (in order to avoid bias and double standards) and to pay attention to procedural quality of reform and lawmaking (in order to avoid pathological effects) (see Mendelski 2016).

Finally, there is considerable research potential to uncover the negative consequences (pathologies) of the EU's rule of law promotion and assessment, as recently undertaken by several scholars (see Mendelski 2015, 2016; Slapin 2015; Pech 2016; Bobek and Kosar 2014; Dimitrov et al. 2014; Toneva-Metodieva 2014). In particular, it would be interesting to discover which combinations of domestic conditions and external (EU) conditionality result in unintended and pathological effects, such as lower quality of laws, political instability, more systemic incoherence, increased levels of politicisation and conflict, and so forth. Discovering reform pathologies and unintended consequences and analysing the "dark side of Europeanisation" (Börzel and Pamuk 2012) may help to improve the EU's currently naive approach to rule of law promotion/assessment and its dwindling legitimacy in CEE.

Note

1 I conceive of the rule of law as a socially, politically, and historically embedded mode of governance which includes two main components: (1) *quality of laws*, that is, clear, general, stable, coherent, and enforced laws; and (2) *quality of the judicial system*, that is, a capable, independent, accountable, and impartial judicial system. Human rights are not included and not analysed in this chapter.

References

Anderson, J. H., Bernstein, D. S., and Gray, C. W. (2005). *Judicial Systems in Transition Economies: Assessing the Past, Looking to the Future.* Washington: World Bank.

Beers, D. J. (2010). A Tale of Two Transitions: Exploring the Origins of Post-Communist Judicial Culture in Romania and the Czech Republic. *Demokratizatsiya, 18*(1): 28–55.

Beširević, V. (2014). "Governing Without Judges": The Politics of the Constitutional Court in Serbia. *International Journal of Constitutional Law, 12*(4): 954–979.

Bobek, M., and Kosar, D. (2014). Global Solutions, Local Damages: A Critical Study in Judicial Councils in Central and Eastern Europe. *German Law Journal, 15*(2): 1257–1292.

Börzel, T. A., and Pamuk, Y. (2012). Pathologies of Europeanisation: Fighting Corruption in the Southern Caucasus. *West European Politics*, *35*(1): 79–97.

Bozhilova, D. (2007). Measuring Successes and Failures of EU-Europeanization in the Eastern Enlargement: Judicial Reform in Bulgaria. *European Journal of Law Reform*, *9*(2): 285–319.

Capussela, A. L. (2015). *State-Building in Kosovo: Democracy, Corruption and the EU in the Balkans*. London: IB Tauris.

Carothers, T. (2006). *Promoting the Rule of Law Abroad: In Search of Knowledge*. Washington, DC: Carnegie Endowment for International Peace.

Channell, W. (2006). Lessons Not Learned: Problems With Western Aid for Law Reform in Post-Communist Countries. *Journal of Comparative Law*, *1*(2): 321–337.

Coman, R. (2014). Quo Vadis Judicial Reforms? The Quest for Judicial Independence in Central and Eastern Europe. *Europe-Asia Studies*, *66*(6): 892–924.

Coman, R., and De Waele, J. M. (2007). *Judicial Reforms in Central and Eastern European Countries*. Bruges: Vanden Broele.

Cooley, A., and Snyder, J. (Eds.). (2015). *Ranking the World*. Cambridge: Cambridge University Press.

Dallara, C. (2014). *Democracy and Judicial Reforms in South-East Europe: Between the EU and the Legacies of the Past*. Heidelberg: Springer.

Dimitrov, G., Haralampiev, K., Stoychev, S., and Toneva-Metodieva, L. (2014). *The Cooperation and Verification Mechanism: Shared Political Irresponsibility Between the European Commission and the Bulgarian Governments*. Sofia: St. Kliment Ohridski University Press.

Fuller, L. L. (1969). *The Morality of Law*. New Haven, London: Yale University Press.

Giannone, D. (2010). Political and Ideological Aspects in the Measurement of Democracy: The Freedom House Case. *Democratization*, *17*(1): 68–97.

Hipper, A. M. (2015). *Beyond the Rhetorics of Compliance: Judicial Reform in Romania*. Wiesbaden: Springer.

Hirschl, R. (2009). *Towards juristocracy: The origins and consequences of the new constitutionalism*. Cambridge, MA: Harvard University Press.

Høyland, B., Moene, K., and Willumsen, F. (2012). The Tyranny of International Index Rankings. *Journal of Development Economics*, *97*(1): 1–14.

Jensen, E. G., and Heller, T. C. (2003). *Beyond Common Knowledge. Empirical Approaches to the Rule of Law*. Stanford, CA: Stanford University Press.

Kitschelt, H. (2003). Accounting for outcomes of postcommunist regime diversity: What counts as a good cause? in: G. Ekiert and S. Hanson (Eds.), *Capitalism and Democracy in Central and Eastern Europe*. New York: Cambridge University Press, pp. 49–88.

Kleinfeld, R. (2012). *Advancing the Rule of Law Abroad: Next Generation Reform*. Washington, DC: Carnegie Endowment for International Peace.

Kochenov, D. (2008). *EU Enlargement and the Failure of Conditionality: Pre-accession Conditionality in the Fields of Democracy and the Rule of Law*. Alphen aan den Rijn: Wolters Kluwer.

Kühn, Z. (2011). *The Judiciary in Central and Eastern Europe: Mechanical Jurisprudence in Transformation?* Leiden: Brill.

Kuzmova, Y. (2014). Bulgarian Specialized Criminal Court After One Year: A Misplaced Transplant, an Instrument of Justice, or a Tool of Executive Power. *Boston University International Law Journal*, *32*(1): 227–262.

Magalhaes, P. C. (1999). The Politics of Judicial Reform in Eastern Europe. *Comparative Politics*, *32*(1): 43–62.

Magen, A., and Morlino, L. (2009). *International Actors, Democratization and the Rule of Law. Anchoring Democracy?* New York: Routledge.

Maravall, J. M. (2003). The rule of law as a political weapon, in: A. Przeworski and J. M. Maravall (Eds.), *Democracy and the Rule of Law* (Vol. 5). Cambridge: Cambridge University Press, pp. 261–301.

Mendelski, M. (2009). The Impact of the European Union on Governance Reforms in Post-Communist Europe: A Comparison Between First and Second-Wave Candidates. *Romanian Journal of Political Science*, *9*(2): 42–64.

Mendelski, M. (2011). Rule of Law Reforms in the Shadow of Clientelism: The Limits of the EU's Transformative Power in Romania. *Polish Sociological Review*, *2*(174): 235–253.

Mendelski, M. (2012). EU-Driven Judicial Reforms in Romania: A Success Story? *East European Politics*, *28*(1): 23–42.

Mendelski, M. (2013a). Where does the European Union make a difference? Rule of law development in the Western Balkans and beyond, in: A. Elbasani (Ed.), *European Integration and the Western Balkans: Europeanization or Business as Usual?* London: Routledge, pp. 101–118.

Mendelski, M. (2013b). They Have Failed Again! Donor-driven Promotion of the Rule of Law in Serbia. *Südost-Europa: Zeitschrift für Politik und Gesellschaft, 61*(1): 79–113.

Mendelski, M. (2014). *The Limits of the European Union's Transformative Power: Pathologies of Europeanization and Rule of Law Reform in Central and Eastern Europe,* doctoral dissertation: University of Luxembourg.

Mendelski, M. (2015). The EU's Pathological Power: The Failure of External Rule of Law Promotion in South Eastern Europe. *Southeastern Europe, 39*(3): 318–346.

Mendelski, M. (2016). Europeanization and the Rule of Law: Towards a Pathological Turn. *Southeastern Europe, 40*(3): 346–384.

Mendelski, M., and Libman, A. (2014). Demand for Litigation in the Absence of Traditions of Rule of Law: An Example of Ottoman and Habsburg Legacies in Romania. *Constitutional Political Economy, 25*(2): 177–206.

Morlino, L., and Sadurski, W. (Eds.). (2010). *Democratization and the European Union: Comparing Central and Eastern European Post-communist Countries.* New York: Routledge.

Myrdal, G. (1957). *Economic Theory and Under-developed Regions.* London: Gerald Druckworth.

Natorski, M. (2013). Reforms in the Judiciary of Ukraine: Domestic Practices and the EU's Policy Instruments. *East European Politics, 29*(3): 358–375.

Oman, C. P., and Arndt, C. (2010). *Measuring Governance.* OECD Policy Brief No. 39, OECD.

Parau, C. E. (2015). Explaining Governance of the Judiciary in Central and Eastern Europe: External Incentives, Transnational Elites and Parliamentary Inaction. *Europe-Asia Studies, 67*(3): 409–442.

Pech, L. (2016). The EU as a Global Rule of Law Promoter: The Consistency and Effectiveness Challenges. *Asia Europe Journal, 14*(1): 7–24.

Peshkopia, R. (2014). *Conditioning Democratization: Institutional Reforms and EU Membership Conditionality in Albania and Macedonia.* London: Anthem Press.

Piana, D. (2010). *Judicial Accountabilities in New Europe: From Rule of Law to Quality of Justice.* Farnham, Surrey, Burlington, VT: Ashgate Pub.

Popova, M. (2012). *Politicized Justice in Emerging Democracies: A Study of Courts in Russia and Ukraine.* Cambridge: Cambridge University Press.

Prado, M., and Trebilcock, M. (2009). Path Dependence, Development, and the Dynamics of Institutional Reform. *University of Toronto Law Journal, 59*(3): 341–380.

Pridham, G. (2005). *Designing Democracy: E.U. Enlargement and Regime Change in Post-Communist Europe.* New York: Palgrave.

Pridham, G. (2007a). The Effects of the European Union's Democratic Conditionality: The Case of Romania During Accession. *Journal of Communist Studies and Transition Politics, 23*(2): 233–258.

Pridham, G. (2007b). The Scope and Limitations of Political Conditionality: Romania's Accession to the European Union. *Comparative European Politics, 5*(4): 347–376.

Pridham, G. (2008). The EU's Political Conditionality and Post-Accession Tendencies: Comparisons From Slovakia and Latvia. *JCMS: Journal of Common Market Studies, 46*(2): 365–387.

Radin, A. (2014). Analysis of Current Events: Towards the Rule of Law in Kosovo: EULEX Should Go. *Nationalities Papers, 42*(2): 181–194.

Sadurski, W., Czarnota, A. W., and Krygier, M. (2006). *Spreading Democracy and the Rule of Law? The Impact of EU Enlargement on the Rule of Law, Democracy and Constitutionalism in Post-communist Legal Orders.* Dordrecht: Springer.

Schönfelder, B. (2005). Judicial Independence in Bulgaria: A Tale of Splendour and Misery. *Europe-Asia Studies, 57*(1): 61–92.

Schwartz, H. (2000). *The Struggle for Constitutional Justice in Post-communist Europe.* Chicago: University of Chicago Press.

Seibert-Fohr, A. (Ed.). (2012). *Judicial Independence in Transition* (Vol. 233). Heidelberg: Springer Science & Business Media.

Skaaning, S.-E. (2010). Measuring the Rule of Law. *Political Research Quarterly, 63*(2): 449–460.

Slapin, J. (2015). How Membership in the European Union Can Undermine the Rule of Law in Emerging Democracies. *West European Politics, 38*(3): 627–648.

Steiner, N. D. (2014). Comparing Freedom House Democracy Scores to Alternative Indices and Testing for Political Bias: Are US Allies Rated as More Democratic by Freedom House? *Journal of Comparative Policy Analysis: Research and Practice, 18*(4): 329–349.

Teubner, G. (1998). Legal Irritants: Good Faith in British Law or How Unifying Law Ends Up in New Divergencies. *The Modern Law Review, 61*(1): 11–32.

Toneva-Metodieva, L. (2014). Beyond the Carrots and Sticks Paradigm: Rethinking the Cooperation and Verification Mechanism Experience of Bulgaria and Romania. *Perspectives on European Politics and Society*, *15*(4): 534–551.

Trochev, A. (2008). *Judging Russia: The role of the constitutional court in Russian politics 1990–2006*. Cambridge: Cambridge University Press.

9

BUREAUCRACIES IN CENTRAL AND EASTERN EUROPE AND THE WESTERN BALKANS

Jan-Hinrik Meyer-Sahling

Introduction

The establishment of modern, professional bureaucracies has been a major objective of post-communist transformation. Indeed, administrative transformation and reform have been instrumental for the success of the political and economic transformation and the integration of Central and Eastern Europe and the Western Balkans into the European political, economic, and security structures.[1] Linz and Stepan (1996), for instance, list a 'usable state bureaucracy' as one of six arenas of consolidated democracy. The quality of a country's bureaucracy is also widely recognised to affect the prospects of economic development (Evans and Rauch 1999), the management of EU accession (Hille and Knill 2006, Zubek 2008) and the implementation of EU policies (Falkner and Treib 2008).

The debate on the reform of public bureaucracies[2] in post-communist Europe has centred on three major themes: (1) the trajectories and outcomes of reform; (2) the drivers and obstacles of reform; and (3) the consequences of emerging administrative structures and practices for political, economic, and social outcomes.

For the most part, debate has focused on reform pathways and the type of public administration that has emerged in the region, in particular, whether the communist legacy of public administration has been overcome, the extent to which public administration has come to share features of the main Western models of bureaucracy, or whether a new, distinctly post-communist type of public administration has emerged in the region.

Today, the question 'which model' in and for post-communist Europe remains as topical as ever. Vigorous debate continues over the suitability of the Weberian, new public management (NPM), or mixed models such as the Neo-Weberian State model for the post-communist context (Dan and Pollitt 2015, Drechsler and Kattel 2008, Randma-Liiv 2009). In empirical terms, attempts to classify public administration in the region have been largely futile. There is by now a general agreement that public administration in the region is characterised by diversity and the absence of a singular model of post-communist public administration. Yet public administration also retains a number of region-specific features such as persisting institutional instability, informality and the personalisation of institutions, a discrepancy between formal rules and administrative practices, and widespread politicisation of personnel policy and administrative decision-making.

The second major theme has been concerned with the determinants of public administration reform and practices in the region. Explanatory accounts have favoured middle-range theories that focus on identifying the causal effect of particular variables or the explanation of specific features of post-communist administration such as institutional instability or the politicisation of the civil service. The most prominent explanations have focused on the role of historical legacies, political parties, Europeanisation, and more recently, the global financial and economic crisis.

Third, more recently, the debate has shifted towards the performance of post-communist public administration and hence the study of public administration as an independent variable. Studies of corruption, the transposition and implementation of EU policies and fiscal performance represent the starting point for this line of research. However, many of the big questions regarding the performance of bureaucracies remain unanswered, in particular, the relation between bureaucracy and democratic and economic developments in the region.

Trajectories of public administration reform in post-communist Europe

The field of comparative public administration in Western established democracies is, by and large, thematically organised. Comprehensive overviews that cover several components of reform such as Pollitt and Bouckaert's (2011) study of public management reform in Western democracies are rare for Central and Eastern Europe (Bouckaert et al. 2011, Nemec 2010) and have not yet been conducted for the Western Balkans. This section therefore begins with the debate surrounding the transformation of public administration after the end of communism. It then discusses in more detail the areas of civil service reform and politicisation followed by prominent public management reforms such as the establishment of independent agencies, performance management, and public financial management. The section concludes with an attempt to characterise the outcomes of administrative reform in post-communist Europe.

Administrative transformation after the change of regime

Initially, research on public administration in post-communist Europe focused on the task of administrative transformation. It defined the main features of the 'real-existing socialist administration' (König 1992) to identify what it takes to make public administration compatible with constitutional democracy and a liberal market economy. Accordingly, the focus was on the need for eliminating the leading role of the communist party in favour of multi-party democracy and to bring public administration under the rule of law; to abandon the principle of democratic centralism for far-reaching decentralisation and the introduction of local self-government; to overcome the unity of politics and the economy by engaging in large-scale privatisation and liberalisation, and by reorganising government ministries and agencies to account for the radically altered role of the state in managing the economy; and to replace the over-politicised cadre administration and nomenclature system with a professional civil service that is formalised by law and independent from political interference.

Despite the enormous task, studies were initially positive in relation to the process of transformation, as they expected a gradual westernisation of public administration. For instance, Hesse (1998: 170–171) suggested that public administration in post-communist Europe would gradually move through stages of transformation, consolidation, modernisation, and 'adaptation towards the state of the art of public sector performance as observed in Western environments, as well as towards the pressures brought about by the preparation for EU membership'.

By contrast, studies of administrative transformation that appeared in the late 1990s and early 2000s were more sceptical. Taking stock, these studies emphasised delays in many areas of reform, incomplete and contradictory legal frameworks, implementation gaps, a major discrepancy between formal rules and administrative practice, and widespread political interference with personnel policy (Nunberg 1999, Verheijen 1999, 2001). The reform record raised questions with regard to the type of public administration that would be emerging in post-communist Europe. Goetz and Wollmann (2001), for instance, asked whether we are witnessing the emergence of 'defective administrations' in the region or a new, specifically post-communist type of administration that differs from types of administration that prevail in the West.

Research on post-communist public administration since the early 2000s has qualified the sceptical evaluations. It is characterised by a growing differentiation along prominent themes in the field of comparative public administration such as the institutionalisation of core executives (Dimitrov et al. 2006), the agencification of public administration (Koprić et al. 2012, Randma-Liiv et al. 2011, Van Thiel 2011), civil service reform and politicisation (Meyer-Sahling 2009, 2012, Randma-Liiv and Järvalt 2011), performance management (Peters 2008, Verheijen and Dobrolyubova 2007), and the co-ordination of EU policies (Dimitrova and Toshkov 2007, Lippert et al. 2001, Zubek 2008). The next section focuses on civil service developments in order to illustrate the trajectories and outcomes of reform across the region in more detail.

Civil service reform and politicisation

Studies of civil service reform and politicisation cover a wide range of civil service management functions in most Central and Eastern European countries and, more recently, the Western Balkans (Meyer-Sahling 2009, Randma-Liiv and Järvalt 2011). Moreover, they compare institutional frameworks, the quality of their implementation and the support of civil servants for different models of bureaucracy.

The research shows that institutional reform pathways have varied considerably across countries. Focusing on the initial adoption of civil service laws as the key step towards the professionalisation of the civil service, Hungary was the first among the Central and Eastern European cases to adopt a civil service law in 1992. Latvia and Lithuania followed in 1994 and 1995, respectively. However, in both cases the implementation was incomplete, leading to the adoption of new laws in Lithuania in 1999 and in Latvia in 2000. Estonia passed the first civil service law in 1995, to come into force in 1996. Poland adopted a law in 1996. However, the implementation was suspended after the 1997 election when it had become evident that the outgoing government had used the law to freeze political appointees into permanent civil service positions. The civil service law was revised and a new law was passed in 1998.

Romania (1999), Bulgaria (1999), Slovakia (2001), and Slovenia (2002) adopted civil service laws in the context of preparing for EU accession. The Czech Republic also passed a civil service law for the first time in 2002 but, apart from a very small number of provisions, it was not implemented. It took the Czech Republic until 2014 to pass a new law that is by now also applied in practice. All the other countries have significantly amended their first laws and indeed most have replaced them at least once over the last twenty-plus years. In other words, diverse pathways of reform have gone hand in hand with institutional instability and problems of implementation, albeit to different degrees.

Looking at the level of professionalisation across the region, the evidence suggests that the Baltic states have progressed further than the other Central and Eastern European countries, in particular, Romania, Bulgaria, and Croatia. The differences are best captured by studies of senior civil service politicisation (Meyer-Sahling and Veen 2012, Kopecký and Spirova 2011).

They show low levels of politicisation for Estonia, Latvia and, with qualifications, Lithuania. By contrast, Poland and Slovakia come out with the highest levels of politicisation, while Hungary, the Czech Republic, and Slovenia are in an intermediate position yet closer to Poland and Slovakia. The evidence for Romania and Bulgaria is not fully comparable but suggests high levels of politicisation similar to Poland and Slovakia (Volintiru 2015, Spirova 2012).[3]

Civil service reform and politicisation in the Western Balkans shares many features of the development in the new member states (Meyer-Sahling 2012). Civil service laws have been adopted in all countries, but compared to the Central and Eastern European cases reforms were delayed due to the wars of Yugoslav succession. Most of the story of reform therefore begins after the end of the wars and the beginning of the Stabilisation and Association Process with the EU. Albania and Macedonia were the first countries to adopt civil service laws in 1999 and 2000, respectively.[4] At the state level of Bosnia and Herzegovina, a civil service law was passed in 2002 following the imposition of the law by the Office of the High Representative. Montenegro and Serbia passed their first civil service laws in 2004 and 2005, respectively, and hence still during the life of the State Union of both states. Kosovo was the last country that adopted a law in 2010, that is, two years after declaring independence in 2008. Like in Central and Eastern Europe, laws have been amended and even replaced in several countries, suggesting again that trajectories of reform differ but stability has not yet been achieved.

Civil service developments in the Western Balkans are further characterised by a major discrepancy between formal rules and actual practices of personnel management. Most puzzlingly, despite the presence and enforcement of professional civil service rules such as merit standards and procedures, there is a widespread perception that non-merit selection criteria such as political loyalty, family and clan relations, and ethnic belonging are more important than professional qualifications (Doli et al. 2012, Elbasani 2013, Meyer-Sahling et al. 2015).

There is so far no study of politicisation that is directly comparable to Central and Eastern Europe. However, preliminary evidence suggests that politicisation reaches deeply into the administration – in particular in Macedonia, where it can reach four to five levels down the hierarchy, and hence deeper than shown for Poland and Slovakia in the mid- and late 2000s. In addition, it appears that the quality of politicisation differs from Central and Eastern Europe. Old-style patronage based on clientelist exchanges of jobs for votes and services are entrenched in many countries, especially Kosovo and Macedonia.

The question remains as to whether reform outcomes in post-communist Europe differ from patterns that prevail in Western democracies, particularly Western Europe. There is an emerging body of literature that explicitly compares reform developments in East and West. These pan-European studies suggest that the Baltic states align more closely with the cluster of low politicisation cases in North West Europe, while Hungary is more similar to the Central European neighbours such as Germany and Austria (Bach et al. 2015). The proximity of the Czech Republic and Hungary to Germany and Austria also emerged from studies of party patronage (Kopecký et al. 2012).

Inevitably, the comparison of politicisation in East and West sheds doubt on the 'differentness' of public administration in Central and Eastern Europe and the Western Balkans. In terms of theoretical and methodological approaches, the emerging body of research indicates a normalisation of public administration insofar as the East is increasingly integrated into broader debates in comparative public administration. Substantively, the findings point towards the emergence of new 'families of administrations' in Europe (cf. Castles 1993) as a result of transformation and Europeanisation over the last twenty-five years. However, many of the core attributes of post-communist public administrations such as institutional instability are usually not adequately captured by the East-West comparisons that have been conducted so far. Moreover, the question remains whether the conclusions for civil service reform and politicisation hold for other areas of public administration reform.

Agency reform, performance management, and public financial management after the crisis

Research on other areas of public management reform tend to by and large support the findings for civil service reform and politicisation. First, research on the establishment of executive agencies finds considerable variation in the number, type, and tasks delegated to agencies across the region. Comparing to Western Europe, agencification in the 1990s and early 2000s is characterised by a 'larger scope' and 'higher speed' (Van Thiel 2011).

Starting in the mid-2000s and, in particular, after the beginning of the global and financial crisis, Central and Eastern Europe embarked on a U-turn that started a process of de-agencification (Randma-Liiv et al. 2011). In addition to evidence for instability resulting from continuous agency reform, there has been frequent reference to the politicisation of formally independent agencies (Beblavý et al. 2012, Randma-Liiv et al. 2011). Moreover, evidence for the Western Balkans, including Croatia here, indicates problems of management that stem from inadequate legal frameworks and a lack of capacity in terms of both resources and the expertise of agency personnel (Koprić et al. 2012).

Second, performance management is a core component of NPM reforms, which have been viewed sceptically by academic observers for post-communist Europe (Drechsler 2005, Verheijen and Coombes 1998). Yet the evidence suggests that performance management tools have been taken up widely in Central and Eastern Europe, in particular, in the Baltic states (Verheijen and Dobrolyubova 2007, Hammerschmid and Löffler 2015, Peters 2008). In practice, it has been more difficult to make performance management systems work. The validity of performance indicators and the quality of performance information are frequently questioned. In particular, performance information is often not used even when it is produced (Nõmm and Randma-Liiv 2012).

Third, it is important to draw attention to the growing literature on fiscal crisis management in Central and Eastern Europe. This work has addressed the impact of the crisis on public administration reform (Kickert et al. 2015) and on decision-making inside government (Savi and Randma-Liiv 2015). It shows that certain cutback measures such as hiring and pay freezes were most frequently applied across Europe.

However, the scale and style of fiscal consolidation varied, primarily, depending on the severity of the crisis. The Baltic states, for instance, applied deeper cuts and did so across public administration rather than in a targeted manner. By contrast, Slovenia took a more moderate approach, as it could benefit from the quicker recovery of the German and Austrian economies. In other words, the fiscal consolidation experience supports the argument that new families of administrations have been emerging in Europe (see also Epstein in this volume).

Which model of public administration for post-communist Europe?

What overall picture emerges and how does it relate to the models of public administration that have dominated the debate in post-communist Europe? Overview assessments argue that public administration in the Baltic states, particularly in Estonia, embodies a large number of NPM features, while 'mixed models' that combine Weberian and NPM features have emerged in the other Central and Eastern European and the South Eastern European member states of the EU (Nemec 2010, Bouckaert et al. 2011). It is a matter of debate whether the mixed models amount to the emergence of Neo-Weberian States in the region (Drechsler and Kattel 2008, Randma-Liiv 2009).

No assessments of this kind have so far been conducted for the Western Balkan states. The evidence suggests that they also approximate a mixed model, even though Weberian elements remain stronger for the time being, while NPM reforms have only recently become more prominent in administrative reform programmes (Meyer-Sahling 2012).

The classification of reform trajectories and outcomes along the dominant Western models of bureaucracy allows for broad comparisons between East and West and integrates the study of post-communist public administrations into wider academic debates. Yet features such as institutional instability, informality, and the personalisation of institutions figure prominently in analyses across components of reform in the region but classic models of bureaucracy do not adequately account for them.

The role of politicisation in post-communist public administration also remains puzzling. Weberian reforms in much of Central and Eastern Europe, South Eastern European member states, and the Western Balkans have gone along with (the persistence of) widespread political interference with personnel policy and administrative decision-making. NPM reformers in the Baltic states have experienced less politicisation but are surely not immune to politicisation pressures (Nakrošis 2015). What we observe in Central and Eastern Europe and the Western Balkans does therefore point towards the emergence of 'bureaucracies with adjectives' rather than plain Weberian, NPM, Neo-Weberian, or mixed models of bureaucracy.

Explaining administrative reform and practices in post-communist Europe

Studies of the professionalisation of bureaucracies point to a large number of political, economic, social, and international explanatory factors (for a comprehensive overview, see Schuster 2015). In the context of Central and Eastern Europe and the Western Balkans, the focus has been on the role of historical legacies, the EU, political parties, and political competition. So far there have been virtually no attempts to integrate explanatory approaches nor to build a general theory of post-communist public administration.

First, approaches that stress the impact of the communist-type administration build on legacy explanations of democratisation and administration traditions on public management reform (Kitschelt et al. 1999, Painter and Peters 2010). They stress the stickiness and persistence of institutions, administrative practices, and mentalities from the past. Accordingly, the communist tradition of public administration has often been invoked to explain the politicisation of the civil service and the weakness of formal institutions (Verheijen 2001). Yet there are only few studies that invoke historical legacies to explain variation in administrative reform outcomes. The work by Kopecký and Spirova (2011) on party patronage is an exception. They rely on the distinction of bureaucratic, national-accommodative, and patrimonial communism in Kitschelt et al. (1999) to explain differences in politicisation in the Czech Republic, Hungary, and Bulgaria.

Second, political parties figure prominently in explanations of administrative reform and practices. In the post-communist context, parties had a strong incentive to 'exploit' the state rather than to invest in state professionalisation (Grzymała-Busse 2007, O'Dwyer 2006). Parties were new and lacked organisational resources. Providing state resources including jobs in exchange for votes offered a promising strategy of party-building and consolidation. Moreover, the state was seen as weak, as it was associated with the failure of communism and, in particular, it was subject to major structural and personnel change after transition.

Grzymała-Busse (2007) shows that 'robust competition' mitigated the incentive of governing parties to exploit the state and, instead, to invest in state professionalisation. Robust competition presupposes a critical opposition that is both unified and credible to replace the government.

Under these conditions, the opposition has the capacity to monitor government, which in turn has an incentive to build institutions as signals for transparent, non-corrupt behaviour. Looking across a range of administrative reform areas, Grzymała-Busse (2007) argues that robust competition explains why Hungary embarked much earlier on reform than, for instance, the Czech Republic and Slovakia.

The main challenge for arguments that focus on institutional reform trajectories stems from the weakness of formal institutions in post-communist Europe and hence the difficulty of making an inference from the presence of formal rules to actual behaviour (Dimitrov et al. 2006). One alternative approach focuses on the explanation of politicisation practices (Meyer-Sahling and Veen 2012). It assumes that parties make appointments for the sake of political control, especially at the top of the civil service. The incentive to make appointments is greatest when politicians have the perception that they cannot control – or trust – the bureaucrats they are meant to collaborate with during policymaking and implementation.

Meyer-Sahling and Veen (2012) argue that the perceived problems of control are greatest when government changes are characterised by wholesale alternations between parties from competing blocs of parties. The evidence suggests that the regular alternations between competing blocs in countries such as Poland, Slovakia, and Hungary create problems of control, which create incentives for political appointments and, over time, lead to creeping politicisation down the administrative hierarchies. By contrast, the long-term dominance in government of centre-right parties in Estonia and Latvia accompanied by partial changes of government provided conditions for the gradual de-politicisation of the senior civil service, growing stabilisation, and competence levels at the top.

The argument travels beyond the first wave of accession countries to South Eastern Europe and the Balkans (Meyer-Sahling 2012). For most countries, two blocs that regularly alternate in power can be identified (Enyedi and Casal Bértoa 2011). However, the Balkans also indicate that explanations of politicisation practices require attention to more factors than government alternations. The organisation of parties and their modes of mobilisation, ethnic fragmentation, and economic underdevelopment complicate the situation and provide additional incentives for politicisation.

The third prominent explanation of administrative reform and practice has focused on the role of the European Union. Initially, this work emphasised the impact of conditionality before and after EU accession. EU conditionality has been especially associated with civil service reform and studies of agencification. In the case of the latter, Van Thiel (2011) and Randma-Liiv et al. (2011) emphasise the need to reorganise public administration and to build agencies in the context of adopting the *acquis communautaire*. Accordingly, the spectacular rise in the number of agencies has been traced to EU demand for change, mostly specified in annual EU progress reports.

Dimitrova (2005) and Camyar (2010) have developed the conditionality argument further by taking into account the effect of domestic mediating factors. Focusing on civil service reform, Dimitrova (2005) found that 'all' candidate countries established or amended civil service laws and developed training programmes in order to meet EU demand for change. However, the effectiveness of conditionality hinged on the degree of misfit between EU demand and the state of reform at the time when negotiations were opened and the presence of domestic veto players. Accordingly, Estonia and Hungary faced fewer pressures for change than the other countries. Furthermore, the failure of the Czech government to implement the civil service law before accession is traced to the long-standing opposition of Czech parties to reform the civil service in accordance with EU recommendations.

The reference to the Czech case also points to one of the main weaknesses of conditionality: the focus on formal rule adoption but limited attention to the quality of implementation and cultural change in public administration. Dimitrova (2010), for instance, argued that EU conditionality-driven changes led to the establishment of formal rules as 'empty shells'.

The argument surrounding the ambiguity of conditionality gained further momentum after EU accession. Because the European Commission has no particular instruments available to sanction non-compliance in non-*acquis* areas after accession, concerns were raised that governments in Central and Eastern Europe would have an incentive to reverse reforms they had passed before accession under the pressure of conditionality. Yet analysis of post-accession developments revealed diverse pathways in the area of civil service reform (Meyer-Sahling 2011). The Baltic states continued pre-accession reforms by and large until the fiscal crisis required a new course of action. By contrast, the other Central and Eastern Europe countries were more prone to reversing pre-accession reforms. Poland and Slovakia stood out insofar as they abolished central coordinating civil service offices that had been established before accession.

So far, there are only a few studies of the Europeanisation of public administration that focus on other, non-conditionality-based mechanisms. For the pre-accession period, Papadimitriou and Phinnemore (2004) explored the impact of the EU twinning programme on institutional change and social learning among public servants. More recently, Meyer-Sahling et al. (2016) applied theories of international socialisation to show how contact of public servants to EU rules and procedures in the context of their day-to-day work promotes their professional socialisation. The professionalisation of the civil service is hence found to occur as a by-product of the integration of Central and Eastern European executives into the European Administrative Space rather than the direct, top-down effect of EU policies.

While most approaches have focused on historical legacies, political parties and the EU, this is not to say that other factors play no role in explanations of public administration reform in the region. For instance, the debate has recently shifted towards the impact of the global financial and economic crisis. The crisis accounts for both general trends and cross-country variation in crisis management (Kickert et al. 2015). Yet there is still no comprehensive explanation of public administration reform and practices that integrates explanatory accounts comparable to the explanations of capitalist diversity in the region.

Performance of post-communist public administration

There is still much less research on the impact of bureaucratic structures and practices on policy outcomes, as well as political, social, and economic development. To some extent this reflects the trajectory of reform in the region. As Bunce (1997: 162) explains, as long as institutions are in the process of formation and hence unsettled, 'institutions are best understood as dependent, not independent, variables'. While correct, this does not diminish the importance of the question. To the contrary, it raises additional challenges on how to theorise the effect of precarious institutions and how to design research to assess the performance of institutions in an uncertain, dynamic context.

The relation between civil service reform and corruption has received relatively more attention when looking across the emerging literature on the performance of post-communist bureaucracy. Neshkova and Kostadinova (2012), for instance, show that corruption levels, as measured by the Transparency International Corruption Perception Index, decreased after civil service laws were adopted in South Eastern Europe. Meyer-Sahling and Mikkelsen (2016) qualify this finding. Based on a survey of civil servants in five countries from Central and Eastern Europe and the Western Balkans, they show that the effectiveness of civil service laws depends on the quality of their implementation. Moreover, they find that merit recruitment reduces corruption in the ministerial bureaucracy, while the politicisation of appointments is associated with higher levels of corruption (see also Heywood and Meyer-Sahling 2013, Kostadinova and Spirova in this volume).

Second, in relation to the Europeanisation of public administration, Hille and Knill (2006) and Toshkov (2008) show that the quality of a country's bureaucracy is associated with progress of accession as measured by EU progress reports and the transposition of the EU *acquis*. Zubek (2008) focuses on Poland, the Czech Republic, and Hungary to show how the centralisation of the core executive explains transposition records during the pre-accession period. There is also evidence that the quality of bureaucracy has an impact on the quality of implementation as opposed to transposition records. Extending the research on the implementation of EU policies to old member states, Falkner and Treib (2008) show that the lack of administrative capacity explains why Central and Eastern Europe is conceptualised as a 'world of dead letters'.

Third, the organisation of the core executive has been examined in relation to the fiscal performance of Central and Eastern Europe. Brusis and Dimitrov (2001) and Dimitrov et al. (2006) examine the impact of the position of prime ministers and finance ministers during the first decade after transition. Importantly, they show that core executive reforms tended to be ineffective in the initial period after their adoption. However, as new executive configurations started to settle, their performance in tackling the fiscal crisis of the late 1990s improved significantly (see Brusis in this volume). Hallerberg and Yläoutinen (2010) extend this argument to show how fiscal governance rules suitable for different political constellations do indeed affect the fiscal performance of Central and Eastern European states.

Fourth, most recently there has been an emerging debate on the impact of NPM reforms. Dan and Pollitt (2015) argue that the NPM 'can work' in Central and Eastern Europe, thereby challenging the arguments that the NPM is not suitable for the post-communist context. They primarily point to positive evaluations in the areas of performance management and benchmarking (e.g. Verheijen and Dobrolyubova 2007). However, Drechsler and Randma-Liiv (2015) argue that there is still little systematic evidence on the impact of NPM designs and practices to allow for a conclusion as fundamental as this. The emerging debate clearly sets an agenda for empirical research that employs effective designs to assess these kinds of questions in the future.

Conclusion and future research

This chapter examined the development of public administration in Central and Eastern Europe and the Western Balkans. Over time, the field of public administration has matured in that it has covered a wide range of areas of public administration reform. Moreover, recent pan-European studies that integrate cases from East and West point to a normalisation insofar as research on public administration in Central and Eastern Europe and, still to a lesser extent, the Western Balkans are concerned.

However, there is no consensus on how best to describe public administration in post-communist Europe, even after twenty-five years of reform. The evidence suggests that public administration in the region has come to incorporate a mix of Weberian and NPM models of bureaucracy. Questions remain whether the mixed models that have emerged amount to variants of Neo-Weberian States.

Despite the importance of Western models of bureaucracy, the chapter has also shown that post-communist public administration continues to be characterised by region-specific features such as persisting institutional instability, informality and the personalisation of institutions, problems of implementation including a far-reaching mismatch between formal rule and administrative practices, and the widespread politicisation of personnel policy and administrative decision-making. Yet the relevance of these features varies across regions.

Future research will have to provide comprehensive empirical evaluations of public administration reform in post-communist Europe comparable to Pollitt and Bouckaert's (2011) analysis of Western democracies. Moreover, conceptual efforts will be needed to better capture the idiosyncrasies of post-communist public administration in relation to the main Western models of administration.

The communist legacy of public administration has conventionally been the prime candidate to explain the differentness of post-communist public administration. The specifically post-communist nature of party formation, political competition, and EU accession have added to the particularities of reform pathways and outcomes in the region. We might expect that the effect of the communist legacy and the EU accession process diminish over time, creating conditions for the normalisation of the context of public administration in Central and Eastern Europe (but arguably not yet in the Western Balkans).

Domestic political and bureaucratic incentives as well as general pressures of Europeanisation that apply similarly in old and new member states are therefore becoming relatively more important, but it will have to be subject to future study whether they have the capacity to overcome the region-specific features of public administration. Moreover, efforts are needed to explore the role of factors that have so far received little attention in studies of public administration reform. In particular, the impact of ethnic diversity in many parts of Central and Eastern Europe and the Western Balkans calls for closer scrutiny.

The chapter also explored questions of the performance of post-communist public administration. Research on corruption, Europeanisation, and fiscal performance indicate that the quality of bureaucracy does indeed matter for outcomes in the region. However, the performance of post-communist administration remains much less understood. It arguably represents a major area for future research. For instance, there still remains little engagement with the big questions of bureaucratic performance, notably the relation between bureaucracy and democracy and between bureaucracy and economic development. In particular, the role of bureaucracy in promoting and, more importantly in light of recent developments, in preventing 'democratic backsliding' (Bermeo 2016) remains unexplored and an exciting agenda for future research.

Notes

1 In this chapter, I refer to Central and Eastern Europe as the countries that joined the EU between 2004 and 2013. The Western Balkans include the six remaining candidate and potential candidate states from South Eastern Europe. When speaking about post-communist Europe, I refer to both Central and Eastern Europe and the Western Balkans. The chapter excludes the Eastern neighbourhood of the EU.
2 In this chapter, the term bureaucracy refers to the non-elected part of the executive. The focus will be on the central state administration. The terms public bureaucracy and public administration will be used synonymously.
3 For recent studies of senior civil service politicisation that seek to capture developments over time, see Staroňová and Gajduschek (2013), Nakrošis (2015), and Hajnal and Csengödi (2014).
4 Albania had already passed a civil service law in 1994 but did not implement it in the context of the political and economic crisis of the mid- and late 1990s.

References

Bach, T., G. Hammerschmid, and L. Löffler (2015) *More Delegation, More Political Control? Politicization of Senior Level Appointments in 18 European Countries.* Paper presented at European Group on Public Administration Annual Conference, Toulouse, France, August 2015.

Beblavý, M., E. Sic?áková-Beblavá, and D. Ondrusova (2012) He Who Appoints the Piper: Understanding Reasons and Implications of Agency Management "Politicisation" in Slovakia. *NISPACee Journal of Public Administration and Policy* 5(2): 121–139.

Bermeo, N. (2016) On Democratic Backsliding. *Journal of Democracy* 27(1): 5–19.

Bouckaert, G., V. Nakrošis, and J. Nemec (2011) Public Administration and Management Reforms in CEE: Main Trajectories and Results. *NISPACee Journal of Public Administration and Policy* 4(1): 9–29.

Brusis, M. and V. Dimitrov (2001) Executive Configuration and Fiscal Performance in Post-Communist Central and Eastern Europe. *Journal of European Public Policy* 8(6): 888–910.

Bunce, V. (1997) Presidents and the Transition in Eastern Europe. In K. von Mettenheim (Ed.), *Presidential Institutions and Democratic Politics: Comparing Regional and National Contexts.* Baltimore, MD: Johns Hopkins University Press, pp. 161–176.

Camyar, I. (2010) Europeanization, Domestic Legacies and Administrative Reforms in Central and Eastern Europe: A Comparative Analysis of Hungary and the Czech Republic. *Journal of European Integration* 32(2): 137–155.

Castles, F. G. (Ed.) (1993) *Family of Nations: Patterns of Public Policy in Western Democracies.* Aldershot: Dartmouth.

Dan, S. and C. Pollitt (2015) NPM Can Work: An Optimistic Review of the Impact of New Public Management Reforms in Central and Eastern Europe. *Public Management Review* 17(9): 1305–1332.

Dimitrov, V., K. H. Goetz, and H. Wollmann (2006) *Governing After Communism.* Boulder, CO: Rowman and Littlefield.

Dimitrova, A. (2005) Europeanization and Civil Service Reform in Central and Eastern Europe. In F. Schimmelfennig and U. Sedelmeier (Eds.), *The Europeanization of Central and Eastern Europe.* Ithaca, NY: Cornell University Press, pp. 71–90.

Dimitrova, A. (2010) The New Member States of the EU in the Aftermath of Enlargement: Do New European Rules Remain Empty Shells? *Journal of European Public Policy* 17(1): 137–148.

Dimitrova, A. and D. Toshkov (2007) The Dynamics of Domestic Coordination of EU Policy in the New Member States: Impossible to Lock In? *West European Politics* 30(5): 961–986.

Doli, D., F. Korenica, and A. Rogova (2012) The Post-Independence Civil Service in Kosovo: A Message of Politicization. *International Review of Administrative Sciences* 78(4): 665–691.

Drechsler, W. (2005) The Re-Emergence of 'Weberian' Public Administration After the Fall of New Public Management: The Central and Eastern European Perspective. *Halduskultuur – Administrative Culture* 6: 94–108.

Drechsler, W. and T. Randma-Liiv (2016) In Some Central and Eastern European Countries, Some NPM Tools May Sometimes Work: A Reply to Dan and Pollitt's 'NPM can work'. *Public Management Review* 18(10): 1559–1565.

Drechsler, W. and R. Kattel (2008) Towards the Neo-Weberian State? Perhaps, But Certainly Adieu NPM!. *NISPAcee Journal of Public Administration and Policy* 1(2): 95–99.

Elbasani, A. (2013) EU Administrative Conditionality and Domestic Obstacles: Slow, Hesitant and Partial Reform in Post-Communist Albania. In A. Elbasani (Ed.), *European Integration and Transformation in the Western Balkans: Europeanization or Business as Usual?* London: Routledge, pp. 85–100.

Enyedi, Z. and F. Casal Bértoa (2011) Patterns of Party Competition (1990–2009). In P. Lewis and R. Markowski (Eds.), *Europeanising Party Politics? Comparative Perspectives on Central and Eastern Europe.* Manchester: Manchester University Press, pp 116–142.

Evans, P. and J. E. Rauch (1999) Bureaucracy and Growth: A Cross-National Analysis of the Effects of Weberian State Structures on Economic Growth. *American Sociological Review* 64(5): 748–765.

Falkner, G. and O. Treib (2008) Three Worlds of Compliance or Four? The EU15 Compared to the New Member States. *Journal of Common Market Studies* 46(3): 293–313.

Goetz, K. H. and H. Wollmann (2001) Governmentalizing Central Executives in Post-Communist Europe: A Four-Country Comparison. *Journal of European Public Policy* 8(6): 864–887.

Grzymała-Busse, A. (2007) *Rebuilding Leviathan: Party Competition and State Exploitation in Post-Communist Democracies.* Cambridge: Cambridge University Press.

Hajnal, G. and S. Csengödi (2014) When Crisis Hits Superman: Change and Stability of Political Control and Politicization in Hungary. *Halduskultuur – Administrative Culture* 15(1): 39–57.

Hallerberg, M. and S. Yläoutinen (2010) Political Power, Fiscal Institutions and Budgetary Outcomes in Central and Eastern Europe. *Journal of Public Policy* 30(1): 45–62.

Hammerschmid, G. and L. Löffler (2015) The Implementation of Performance Management in European Central Governments: More a North-South Than an East-West Divide. *NISPACee Journal of Public Administration and Policy* 8(2): 1–15.

Hesse, J. J. (1998) Rebuilding the State: Administrative Reform in Central and Eastern Europe. In SIGMA (Ed.), *Preparing Public Administration for the European Administrative Space*. Paris: SIGMA, Papers No. 23, pp. 168–179.

Heywood, P. and J.-H. Meyer-Sahling (2013) Danger Zones of Corruption: How Management of the Ministerial Bureaucracy Affects Corruption Risks in Poland. *Public Administration and Development* 33(3): 191–204.

Hille, P., and C. Knill (2006) It's the Bureaucracy, Stupid'. The Implementation of the Acquis Communautaire in EU Candidate Countries, 1999–2003. *European Union Politics* 7(4): 531–552.

Kickert, W., T. Randma-Liiv, and R. Savi (2015) Politics of Fiscal Consolidation in Europe: A Comparative Analysis. *International Review of Administrative Sciences* 81(3): 562–584.

Kitschelt, H., Z. Mansfeldová, R. Markowski, and G. Tóka (1999) *Post-Communist Party Systems: Competition, Representation, and Inter-Party Cooperation*. Cambridge: Cambridge University Press.

König, K. (1992) The Transformation of a 'Real Socialist' Administrative System Into a Conventional West European System. *International Review of Administrative Sciences* 58: 147–161.

Kopecký, P., P. Mair, and M. Spirova (Eds.) (2012) *Party Patronage and Party Government in European Democracies*. Oxford: Oxford University Press.

Kopecký, P. and M. Spirova (2011) Jobs for the Boys? Patterns of Patronage in Post-Communist Europe. *West European Politics* 34(5): 897–921.

Koprić, I., P. Kovač, and A. Musa (2012) Agencies in Three South Eastern European Countries: Politics, Expertise and Law. *NISPAcee Journal of Public Administration and Policy* 5(2): 17–44.

Linz, J. and A. Stepan (1996) *Problems of Democratic Transition and Consolidation: Southern Europe, South America and Post-Communist Europe*. Baltimore, MD: Johns Hopkins University Press.

Lippert, B., G. Umbach and W. Wessels (2001) Europeanisation of CEE Executives: EU Membership Negotiations as a Shaping Power. *Journal of European Public Policy* 8(6): 980–1012.

Meyer-Sahling, J.-H. (2009) *The Sustainability of Civil Service Reform in Central and Eastern Europe Five Years After Accession*. SIGMA Paper No. 44. Paris: OECD.

Meyer-Sahling, J.-H. (2011) The Durability of EU Civil Service Policy in Central and Eastern Europe After Accession. *Governance* 24(2): 231–260.

Meyer-Sahling, J.-H. (2012) *Civil Service Professionalisation in the Western Balkans*. SIGMA Paper Nr. 48. Paris: OECD.

Meyer-Sahling, J.-H., W. Lowe, and C. van Stolk (2016) Silent Professionalisation: EU Exposure and the Professional Socialisation of Public Officials in Central and Eastern Europe. *European Union Politics* 17(1): 162–183.

Meyer-Sahling, J.-H., K.S. Mikkelsen (2016) Civil Service Laws, Merit, Politicization, and Corruption: The Perspective of Public Officials From Five East European Countries. *Public Administration* 94(4): 1105–1123.

Meyer-Sahling, J.-H., K. S. Mikkelsen, D. Ahmetovic, M. Ivanova, H. Qeriqi, R. Radevic, A. Shundi, and V. Vlajkovic (2015) *Improving the Implementation of Merit Recruitment Procedures in the Western Balkans: Analysis and Recommendations*. Danilovgrad: ReSPA.

Meyer-Sahling, J.-H. and T. Veen (2012) Governing the Post-Communist State: Government Alternation and Senior Civil Service Politicisation in Central and Eastern Europe. *East European Politics* 28(1): 1–19.

Nakrošis, V. (2015) The Turnover and Politicisation of Lithuanian Public Sector Managers. *World Political Science Review* 11(1): 1–22.

Nemec, J. (2010) New Public Management and Its Implementation in CEE: What Do We Know and Where Do We Go? *NISPAcee Journal of Public Administration and Policy* 3(1): 31–52.

Neshkova, M. and T. Kostadinova (2012) The Effectiveness of Administrative Reform in New Democracies. *Public Administration Review* 72(3): 324–333.

Nõmm, K. and T. Randma-Liiv (2012) Performance Measurement and Performance Information in New Democracies: A Study of the Estonian Central Government. *Public Management Review* 14(7): 859–879.

Nunberg, B. (Ed.) (1999) *The State After Communism: Administrative Transitions in Central and Eastern Europe*. Washington, DC: World Bank.

O'Dwyer, C. (2006) *Runaway State-Building: Patronage Politics and Democratic Development*. Baltimore, MD: Johns Hopkins University Press.

Painter, M., and B. G. Peters (Eds.) (2010) *Administrative Traditions: Inheritances and Transplants in Comparative Perspective*. Basingstoke: Palgrave.

Papadimitriou, D. and D. Phinnemore (2004) Europeanization, Conditionality and Domestic Change: The Twinning Exercise and Administrative Reform in Romania. *Journal of Common Market Studies* 42(3): 619–639.

Peters, B. G. (Ed.) (2008) *Mixes, Matches and Mistakes: New Public Management in Russia and the Former Soviet Republics*. Budapest: Open Society Institute.

Pollitt, C. and G. Bouckaert (2011) *Public Management Reform: A Comparative Analysis: New Public Management, Governance and the Neo-Weberian State*. 3rd ed. Oxford: OUP.

Randma-Liiv, T. (2009) New Public Management Versus Neo-Weberian State in Central and Eastern Europe. In C. Pollitt, G. Bouckaert, T. Randma-Liiv, and W. Drechsler (Eds.), *A Distinctive European Model? The Neo-Weberian State*. Bratislava: NISPAcee Press, pp. 69–81.

Randma-Liiv, T. and J. Järvalt (2011) Public Personnel Policies and Problems in the New Democracies of Central and Eastern Europe. *Journal of Comparative Policy Analysis* 13(1): 35–49.

Randma-Liiv, T., V. Nakrošis, and G. Hajnal (2011) Public Sector Organization in Central and Eastern Europe: From Agencification to De-Agencification. *Transylvanian Review of Administrative Sciences* Special Issue: 160–175.

Savi, R. and T. Randma-Liiv (2015) Decision-Making in Times of Crisis: Cutback Management in Estonia. *International Review of Administrative Sciences* 81(3): 479–497.

Schuster, C. (2015) *When the Victor Cannot Claim the Spoils: Institutional Incentives for Professionalizing Patronage States*. PhD Thesis, London School of Economics and Political Science.

Spirova, M. (2012) A Tradition We Don't Mess With: Party Patronage in Bulgaria. In P. Kopecký, P. Mair, and M. Spirova (Eds.), *Party Patronage and Party Government in European Democracies*. Oxford: Oxford University Press, pp. 54–73.

Staroňová, K. and G. Gajduschek (2013) Civil Service Reform in Slovakia and Hungary: The Road to Professionalisation? In C. Neuhold and S. Vanhoonacker (Eds.), *Civil Servants and Politics: A Delicate Balance*. Basingstoke: Palgrave Macmillan, pp. 123–151.

Toshkov, D. (2008) Embracing European Law: Compliance With EU Directives in Central and Eastern Europe. *European Union Politics* 9(3): 379–402.

Van Thiel, S. (2011) Comparing Agencification in Central Eastern European and Western European Countries: Fundamentally Alike in Unimportant Respects? *Transylvanian Review of Administrative Sciences* Special Issue: 15–32.

Verheijen, T. (Ed.) (1999) *Civil Service Systems in Central and Eastern Europe*. Cheltenham: Edward Elgar.

Verheijen, T. (Ed.) (2001) *Politico-Administrative Relations: Who Rules?* Bratislava: NISPAcee.

Verheijen, T. and D. Coombes (Eds.) (1998) *Innovations in Public Management: Perspectives From East and West Europe*. Cheltenham: Edward Elgar.

Verheijen, T. and Y. Dobrolyubova (2007) Performance Management in the Baltic States and Russia: Success Against the Odds? *International Review of Administrative Sciences* 73(2): 205–215.

Volintiru, C. (2015) The Exploitative Function of Party Patronage: Does It Serve the Party's Interest? *East European Politics* 31(1): 39–55.

Zubek, R. (2008) *Core Executive and Europeanization in Central Europe*. Basingstoke: Palgrave.

10

FEDERALISM IN EASTERN EUROPE DURING AND AFTER COMMUNISM

James Hughes

One of the earliest political visionaries of federalism in Eastern Europe, interwar Polish leader Józef Piłsudski, famously remarked to former socialist comrades that "we both took a ride on the same red tram, but while I got off at the stop marked Polish independence, you wish to travel to the station Socialism" (Macmillan, 2002: 208). Piłsudski's modernising vision of an intermarum (międzymorze) federation of republics under Polish hegemony from the Baltic to the Black Sea, acting as a bulwark against Russia, failed to overcome the power of nationalist particularism (Snyder, 2003). Among the many paradoxes of communism in Eastern Europe is that many socialist and communist internationalists were transformed over time into nationalists. In certain countries with multinational societies, especially the Soviet Union, great efforts were made by the ruling communist parties to recognise the political importance of national and ethnic cleavages, in the process compromising the internationalist tenets of communist ideology and its paramount attention to class-based cleavages. Although many of the nine states that made up communist Eastern Europe prior to 1991 were significantly multinational in character, six were unitary states and only three were federal. One of the six unitary states – the German Democratic Republic (GDR) – was absorbed by a mutually agreed treaty into a unified federal Germany in 1990 (though without the referendum required by the German constitution of 1949). In countries such as the Soviet Union (USSR), Yugoslavia, and Czechoslovakia, communist parties engaged in sophisticated federal institutional engineering to recognise and embed certain national and ethnic cleavages in the organisation of state power. The three communist federal states have been generally discussed more within debates about the reasons for their systemic collapse rather than their stability over many decades, with communist federations being widely seen as being "façade" forms of federalism and otherwise unviable states because of their institutionalisation of nationalism and ethnicity. What, then, if any, is the relationship between ethnofederalism and the break-up of communist federations? The puzzle is what explains the resilience of communist federations over many decades, their breakdown in the late 1980s and early 1990s in three cases, the post-communist survival and durability of federalism in Russia, and the continuing attraction of the concept as a conflict management device in the wider region (e.g. in Russia and Bosnia and Herzegovina).

Federalism under communism

Riker's theory of federalism assumed that a rational "federal bargain" underlay its establishment, driven by geopolitical concerns with either an external threat or to engage in expansionist ambitions (Riker, 1964). Piłsudski's idea of an intermarum federation fits within the theory as regards the external threat. Communist federations, however, were not easily accommodated within the Rikerian theory because they were constructed on the basis of ideological motivations. The several communist federations that were established during the twentieth century followed the Russian model on the basis of a Stalinist paradox which attempted to reconcile Marxism and nationalism. Stalin had spoken in 1934 of a Marxist formula with regard to cultures: that they should be "socialist in content and national in form" with the ultimate aim of building a common culture and language, but the thinking applied equally to the notion of the state. In Stalin (1913), he proposed that there should be only a small number of multicultural "regional autonomies" for the most important "crystallised units" of the Tsarist Empire. The Leninist 1918 Russian and 1924 Soviet constitutions organised the communist state on a more generous territorialised national principle, with all sub-units having a "titular" nationality, and smaller ethnic groups often having autonomous areas. This system of "institutionalised multinationality" (Brubaker, 1996) provided a framework within which national identities, territories, and borders were constructed, often ahistorically and artificially (most obviously in the Central Asian republics of the USSR). This invention of ethnicity was developed by policies to promote language and culture, and a careful crafting of historical mythologies, literary nationalism, folk traditions, ethnic symbols, and so on. Stalin was the main source for this communist policy in the 1920s and 1930s. One of the core policy elements of the "Stalin Revolution" was the institutional engineering of Soviet federalism in ways which promoted a multiplicity of territorialised national cultures and integrated national elites into the Soviet project. In the first instance, this usually involved terror, exterminating old elites and extending membership of the Communist Party of the Soviet Union and its associated privileges to new national and ethnic elites (Armstrong, 1982). The policies led Martin (2001) to characterise Stalin's USSR as an "affirmative action empire". These policies were accompanied by a high degree of centralisation of state power through the communist party.

There were important differences of size, geostrategic position, ethnic homogeneity and variation, and temporal factors in the construction of communist federations. Soviet and Russian ethnofederalism was constructed in the 1920s, Yugoslavia's under Tito in the 1940s and 1970s, and Czechoslovakia's in the aftermath of the Soviet-led invasion and failure of the "Prague Spring" of 1968. By the late 1970s the USSR had developed into the most complex of the ethnofederations with a constitutional patchwork of fifteen Union Republics, twenty autonomous republics, eight autonomous *oblasti* (regions), ten autonomous *okrugi* (areas) (sub-units that were mostly within the Russian Soviet Federative Socialist Republic [RSFSR]), and with around 130 recognised cultural linguistic groups. By the time of collapse in 1989–1991, the federations differed radically in their size and complexity, measured by the extent to which they were nationally or ethnically heterogeneous or homogenous. The constituent parts of Czechoslovakia were highly homogenous (94 per cent Czech including Moravians, and 86 per cent Slovak respectively). In Yugoslavia only Slovenia and Kosovo (about 90 per cent each) were significantly homogenous, and all other republics were an ethno-religious mosaic; Bosnia and Herzegovina in particular was characterised by ethnic diversity. In the USSR there were few ethnically homogenous Union Republics (Armenia and Turkmenistan being the most homogenous). Many national sub-units in the USSR had significant Slav, mainly Russian, settler populations. Within the RSFSR three national sub-units had significant ethnic mixes (Tatarstan, Bashkortostan, and Dagestan) and only one of the nationally defined sub-units was significantly ethnically homogenous (Chechnya, about 75 per cent Chechen). In the USSR and Yugoslavia there was an ideologically impelled policy to create a new supra-national identity 'Soviet' and 'Yugoslav', whereas there was never a 'Czechoslovakian' identity, nor an attempt to create one.

Both Yugoslavia's constitution of 1974 and the USSR constitution of 1977 claimed that the federations were "voluntary" unions (USSR, 1977; Yugoslavia, 1974). While the constitutions mentioned the 'right of secession', no clear mechanism was specified by which they could implement this right, and there was a broad requirement of mutual agreement for border revisions. The break between Tito and Stalin in 1948 had intensified the definition of Yugoslavia as a national communist federal state, and the Serbs' perception was that the new state was created at their expense. The 1974 constitution only strengthened this perception as nationality became the defining feature of the state structure. The constitution marked a drift towards a more confederal relationship, with Yugoslavia defined as a "state community". Six socialist republics and two autonomous regions, both within Serbia (Vojvodina and Kosovo), were declared to be "constituent" units and "sovereign". In contrast, large Serb minorities were included within other socialist republics without any special autonomy arrangement, for example in Krajina in Croatia and in parts of Bosnia and Herzegovina. This decentralising tendency was compounded by the transformation of party leaderships in the republics into semi-independent fiefdoms.

Explaining the collapse of communist federations

The three communist era state federations disintegrated into twenty-four internationally recognised independent nation states and several other unrecognised nation state–like entities. The disintegration process was peaceful and by mutual consent in Czechoslovakia, but was often contested and extremely violent in Yugoslavia and the USSR. The collapse of these federations gave rise to a new genre of political science literature which identified the similarities in the state structure of these communist states as being decisive in their collapse. The argument is not only that ethnofederalism is inherently destabilising for states but that there was a *causative* relationship between communist forms of ethnofederal state-building and the collapse of these states in 1989–1991.

An institutionalist theory of the collapse of communist federations is most directly addressed in the work of Roeder (1991, 1993), Brubaker (1996), Bunce (1999a, 1999b), and Skalnik-Leff (1999) among others. Roeder (1991) was among the first political scientists to propose that ethnofederalism was, in fact, a major source of political instability in communist systems. Unlike democracies, where political organisation was largely grounded in class cleavages that usually crosscut national and ethnic ones, communist states were engineered around making the national and elite cleavages salient and, consequently, provided institutional resources for national and ethnic elites. Roeder argues that a legitimacy crisis of tensions and contradictions accumulated over a thirty-five-year period in the USSR, peaking in 1989, which created an institutional deadlock on transformation (Roeder, 1993). The relative winners in Soviet development were, he suggests, the most nationalistic entrepreneurs – the Baltic Republics. Ethnofederalism gave nationalists in these republics institutional power and resources to challenge federal redistribution policies, with their secessions being driven by such economic calculations. Apart from downplaying the history of Baltic nationalism, this thirty-five-year legitimacy crisis story stresses structural institutional factors over other contingent factors at work in producing the crisis in the late 1980s.

More precise explanations for the timing of collapse are offered by Linz and Stepan (1992) and Bunce (1999b), who suggest that the contingency of democratic transition in the late 1980s and early 1990s made communist federations "subversive institutions". Empowered by democratising reforms and electoral politics, this institutional architecture became a platform for the mobilisation of nationalist and ethnic politics, and thus generated centrifugal forces that tore the federal states apart. Linz and Stepan termed this an "electoral sequencing" problem: if the first major free elections are conducted not at the national or federal level but at the regional or federal constituent level, then democracy tends to empower national and ethnic secessionist movements (Linz and Stepan, 1992). The basic premise of the "institutional" explanation is that elites in the constituent units of the communist federations had in their institutions a "basic strategic advantage, an advantage unavailable to minority groups in unitary multinational states" (Skalnik-Leff, 1999: 231).

Bunce (1999a) further contrasts the "peaceful" dismemberments of Czechoslovakia and the USSR, compared with the "violent" dismemberment of Yugoslavia. The explanation she advances for this categorisation is that while Yugoslavia had a much longer tradition of horizontality and "decentralisation", which rendered it more gridlock-prone after Tito, its federal institutions – in particular the military – were Serb-dominated and prepared to intervene directly to preserve the federation. Her argument does not hold, however, for the USSR, where there was sporadic violence and the federal institutions such as the armed forces, police and state security agency (KGB) were Russian-dominated; and a certain degree of force was employed at key junctures in certain places (Georgia 1989, Azerbaijan 1990, Estonia and Lithuania 1991, and Moscow 1991); but these agencies proved unwilling or incapable of acting decisively to preserve the USSR by force, while usually taking active part in conflicts which did occur after the dissolution. A great deal of violence also occurred in the ex-USSR after the collapse in 1991, including wars in Chechnya and Tajikistan which were among the bloodiest conflicts in Eastern Europe. These and other post-Soviet conflicts emerged from the politics of the collapse and cannot be logically separated from the process of collapse itself. Indeed, Bunce overlooks one of the key aspects of horizontality in both Yugoslavia and the USSR which increased the potential for armed conflict, namely, the decentralisation of weapons stocks throughout the state.

In sum, the institutionalist critique of ethnofederalism seeks a "magic bullet" explanation as to why communist ethnofederal states collapsed when they did. The explanations advanced in support of the theory, however, tend to rely on certain contingent factors of elite choices and calculations, rather than systemic "institutional" ones. They do not account for the resilience of ethnofederalism over many decades, and especially in the era after Stalinism, when the authoritarian coercion of communist states was significantly reduced. This suggests that ethnofederalism itself had legitimacy and is not the key destabilising factor. Nor do these works account for the sustainability of ethnofederations comparatively in other regions (McGarry and O'Leary, 2009). They also suffer from a problem of misattribution of historical causation in the rise of nationalism and national and ethnic conflicts in Eastern Europe during the Gorbachev reform era. Arguably, it was not simply a question of institutional resources for nationalist mobilization, but what nationalists did with their power. Nationalist political efforts to deinstitutionalise ethnofederalism and centralise power to the leaderships of dominant ethnic groups caused conflict in several cases, for example in Georgia and Moldova (Hughes and Sasse, 2001), and this argument applies equally as well to Kosovo.

Indeed, three critical factors in the collapse of ethnofederations are largely overlooked in the institutionalist critiques: the roles of political agency/leadership; spillover effects within the region; and external intervention. It is implausible to suggest that ethnofederalism would have collapsed without the presence of Gorbachev as USSR leader, the absence of Tito in Yugoslavia, or the spillover effect of Gorbachev's policies on the Klaus and Mečiar rivalry that precipitated the break-up of Czechoslovakia. Gorbachev's reforms assumed an immensity of scope that was difficult for any political leadership to control. In particular, Gorbachev adopted three policies – perestroika (economic reform), glasnost (openness), and democratisation (in practice more akin to liberalisation) – that eroded the authority of the communist system and led to its eventual collapse (Hough, 1997). Gorbachev miscalculated the differential impact of his reforms since the timescales for potential returns on economic reforms were much longer compared with the immediately destabilising results of democratisation and social reform (Ellman and Kontorovich, 1992). In the case of the USSR's collapse, the debates pivot between the "essentialist" advocates, who point to the inherent illegitimacy of communist rule, those who criticise Gorbachev's leadership skills and policy choices (Dallin, 1992), and those who are more sympathetic to Gorbachev and persuaded by the role of contingency in the reform period of 1985–1991 (Brown, 2004). Communist systems had muddled through sporadic crises across the region since the 1950s; however, by 1989 the multiple crises caused by the reforms had discredited communism across most of Eastern Europe and the USSR. Gorbachev's refusal to rely on coercion to sustain his own authority, let alone maintain Soviet power over the Warsaw Pact states, opened space for counter-communist political alternatives and led to the empowerment of nationalist movements.

The emergence of nationalist crises in the USSR is less directly related, in fact, to the two-decade-long era of economic stagnation from the 1970s, or to redistribution policies, but is linked more to central government policies aimed at reform, such as targeting corruption by changing the ethnofederal equilibrium in leadership (producing the riots in Kazakhstan in 1986) or in the way that glasnost reawakened historically rooted nationalist grievances (Nagorno-Karabakh in 1987–1988, the Baltic states and Georgia in 1988–1989; Suny, 1993). Gorbachev's moves to liberalise and introduce democratisation permitted national and ethnic political mobilisation from below, and also incentivised hitherto compliant national and ethnic elites into using their institutional resources to seek and articulate new forms of legitimacy rooted in national and ethnic grievances, historical and contemporary, and subsequently to challenge the communist one-party system of rule. Cultural intelligentsias were at the forefront of the new nationalism, notably in Armenia, Georgia, the Baltic states, Russia, and Yugoslavia. The fragmentation of ruling elites at all levels fuelled an increasing articulation of ethnic demands and inter-ethnic competition, leading to a surge in inter-ethnic tensions. Beissinger (2002) uses sophisticated process-tracing methods to prove how the bulk of mass protests during the period of collapse in the USSR were driven by nationalist and ethnic grievances rather than pro-democracy sentiments. Communist states experienced similar pressures for liberalisation and trends of nationalist mobilisation, and this affected states whether they were ethnofederal or not.

The link between institutions and contingency can be illustrated well by examining the ambiguities in communist federal constitutional frameworks. Under communist monism, constitutional ambiguities were meaningless, but they became imbued with political power under conditions of liberalisation. For example, these constitutions embodied vague formulations about "peoples" and the "sovereignty" of "constituent units". There was an intricate formal institutional structure of consensual decision-making and mutual vetoes as protective devices against ethnic domination, while real decisional power lay in party bodies. In the USSR, Yugoslavia, and Czechoslovakia, liberalisation and transition produced an elite fragmentation and weakening of party structures, which led to constitutional gridlock and exacerbated national and ethnic tensions. In 1989–1991 there was a "contagion" effect in the Soviet Union of *matreskha* (nested) nationalism leading to the so-called parade of sovereignties or the war of laws – a multiplicity of constitutional claims and counterclaims that made for administrative and political disorder. Gorbachev's attempts to refederalize the USSR into a more confederal-type structure were hindered by Yeltsin's rise to power on the back of a mobilization of latent Russian nationalism and antagonism at the costs of supporting the Soviet bloc and the other parts of the USSR. Yeltsin cleverly thwarted Gorbachev and undermined his authority by manipulating the Soviet constitution. Even when Gorbachev successfully negotiated a new confederal Novo-Ogarevo Treaty, the so-called 9-plus-1 agreement (nine existing Union Republics plus the USSR government) of May 1991, it was fatally undermined by the failed coup of communist hardliners in August 1991 and Yeltsin's instincts to dissolve the USSR in the aftermath of the coup (Hough, 1997).

The 1974 Yugoslav constitution, for example, prevented any decision being adopted in the federal parliament if it was opposed by any one federal unit, including the autonomous provinces. In fact, the federal parliament was inquorate if a delegation from a constituent unit was not present. The constitution required a unanimous vote, and any one delegation could paralyse the federal parliament. This device was precisely what led to the institutional collapse of the Yugoslav system in the summer of 1991 over Slovenia's secession. Similarly, a federal presidency was created – principally for Tito (he was president for life) – but in the absence of Tito this was to be a collective presidency, which rotated among all Socialist Republics and autonomous provinces and required unanimity. These kinds of constitutional power-sharing and veto devices were designed to enforce consensus and impose stability in the federal system by protecting against hegemony by any single ethnic group, but they also created conditions for constitutional impasse.

Similarly, the Czechoslovakian Law on the Federation of October 1968 established a minority veto in the federal parliament (Czechoslovakia, 1968). Designed to prevent Czech majority domination of Slovaks, the law held that constitutional and other important law reforms had to be approved by a special majority. Just 38 of the 300 parliamentarians in the lower house could block legislation and 31 parliamentarians from either republic could stop constitutional reform outright. As the powers of the federal government were increased, the question of economic policy and investment distribution between the two constituent parts of the federation became the main undercurrent of Czechoslovak politics. Gorbachev's perestroika widened the political and economic divisions between the Czech and Slovak elites over how to respond to the need for reform. The divisions were reinforced by the differential territorial impact of the transition reforms after 1989. They had a more detrimental impact on Slovakia because of its greater concentration of obsolete military-industrial production and raw material extraction industries, leading to outmigration and low skills levels, and poor attractiveness for foreign investment. The result was widespread unemployment and greater relative impoverishment in Slovakia. These historical and structural differences framed the different politics of the two lands during the transition, with new ideological cleavages also being a prominent aspect of the confrontation, as Czech Prime Minister Václav Klaus pushed for radical neoliberalism and the Slovaks adopted a more gradual approach under the national communist Prime Minister Mečiar (Kraus and Stanger, 2000). The federal veto power was the principal cause of the frustration of Klaus's economic liberals in 1992 by the Slovak representatives under Mečiar. This was a key factor in impelling Klaus and Mečiar's rush for the "velvet divorce". The Slovaks argued that "sovereignty" for Slovakia was compatible with a common state, whereas the Czech political elite around Klaus argued that it was not (Wolchik, 1994; Innes, 2001).

Czechoslovakia and Yugoslavia offer much evidence that economic factors were critically important for the collapse of the federations. Bookman (1993) suggests that when constituent units "re-evaluate" the benefits of membership of a federation, the main consideration is the relative perception of economic injustice based on budgetary and investment allocations, revenue sharing (whether a region is a donor or recipient of subsidies), central sectoral biases in investment and pricing, shares of foreign exchange, and external funding. The units at the extremes, the wealthiest and poorest, are most at risk of secessionism. This may account for why secessionism was strongest in Slovenia, the Baltic states, and Czech lands, and indeed we see similar trends elsewhere in Europe (e.g. in Catalonia in Spain, Flanders in Belgium, Lombardy in Italy, and Scotland in the UK). Belonging to a federation, Bookman argues, becomes a cost-benefit calculation that may be mobilised by ethnic entrepreneurs along ethno-regional-religious fissures. Slovenia, for example, accounted for just 8.4 per cent of the population of Yugoslavia but generated 16.8 per cent of its gross domestic product (GDP) in the late 1980s. Along with Croatia, Slovenia wanted to decrease its contributions to the federal budget fund but was institutionally blocked.

In addition to the within-region spillover effects of Gorbachev's reforms there were also powerful international influences that shaped the collapse of communist federations. The geographical proximity of Central and Eastern Europe, and the history of the Cold War, made the states of this region a primary geostrategic concern for the Western Alliance. The collapse of communism occurred contemporaneously with a historical trend for deeper integration within the European Community (EC), later the European Union (EU), which developed into an even more ambitious strategy of capturing states in the region for the Western orbit by a policy of eastwards enlargement of the EU and expansion of NATO (despite assurances to the contrary given to Gorbachev during the negotiations over German unification). Initially, the US under the Bush presidency and European great powers took a cautious position on the dissolution of communist federations and the recognition of new states, anticipating and fearing the violent destabilisation of the region. President Bush even equated independence movements with "local despotism" and "suicidal nationalism" in an infamous speech in August 1991 in Kiev, where he urged support for Novo-Ogarevo. This caution changed into active promotion from late 1991, partly in response to the de facto dissolution of the USSR and Yugoslavia, and partly due to the change to the Clinton presidency in the US. The strategic calculus also radically changed under the Clinton presidency, as the US sought to exploit for its own interest the collapse of the USSR and Yugoslavia under the guise of "democracy promotion". The secessionist crises in the communist federations were then treated under international customary law as akin to decolonisation, with the principle of *uti possidetis iuris* used to recognise only the highest constituent administrative level in the federations as new states (Cassese, 1995). International recognition stopped at that level, leaving all the other secessionist units, irrespective of other legal and moral claims, as ambiguous 'entities' in the international system, and many of these entities were forged out of civil wars post-collapse.

The most radically politicised Western intervention on the secession question was felt in Yugoslavia (Woodward, 1995). Germany held the then EC presidency at the time of the declarations of independence by Slovenia and Croatia in June 1991, and was proactive in pushing a divided EC into favouring recognition (Glaurdić, 2011). The EC had two main instruments for managing the Yugoslav crisis: the London "Peace Conference", headed by UK foreign secretary Lord Carrington; and the "Arbitration Commission", headed by French socialist party luminary Robert Badinter (thus usually termed the Badinter Commission). Nominally the Badinter Commission was composed of a panel of leading constitutional lawyers of EC states, but they were also ruling-party politicians from France, Germany, Italy, Spain, and Belgium. The Badinter Commission declared in its famous Opinion One of November 1991 that Yugoslavia was a state "in the process of dissolution". The basis in law for the decision is controversial. The Opinion stated that the "factual" basis for the decision was that federal institutions were not functioning, and referendums in favour of independence had been held (even though these did not have federal government sanction) (Radan, 2001). The decision ignored the fact that the Yugoslav federation was only in crisis because Croatia and Slovenia were attempting to secede in the first place (Weller, 2005). The consequence was that the political question was transformed from one of evaluating the claims for secession to the criteria for legitimating by recognition the new states according to the principle of *uti possidetis iuris* and any other conditions favoured by the Western powers. In December 1991 the EC foreign ministers' meeting in Brussels issued two significant declarations: "On the Guidelines on the Recognition of the New States in Eastern Europe and in the Soviet Union" and "On Yugoslavia" (Rich, 1993: Annex 2). The declarations made selective references to the Helsinki Final Act and the Charter of Paris, stressing the "principle of self-determination", while omitting the principles of respect for national sovereignty and respect for borders. The "Guidelines" asserted that recognition would be restricted to those new states which were constituted on a "democratic basis" and respected the rule of law, human rights, and the inviolability of borders, and provided guarantees for the rights of ethnic and national groups and minorities, among other conditions. The EC countries committed themselves to not recognising "entities which are the result of aggression". The criteria provided a rationale for even greater Western intervention (Caplan, 2005). Later, Carrington spoke of how "that man" (Badinter) had "torpedoed" his efforts to keep Yugoslavia united (Glaurdić, 2011).

Federalism in Eastern Europe after communism

The refederalisation of Russia

The institutional theory of collapse also tends to ignore the existence of a fourth communist-era federation within a federation, namely, the RSFSR within the USSR. The fact that Russia successfully refederalised itself as an ethnofederal state is a serious challenge to the hypothesis that ethnofederalism causes state instability. Moreover, Russia's territorial integrity has been preserved and has been challenged by only one major ethnic secessionist conflict, that of Chechnya in 1991–2005. What factors account for the exceptionalism of Russian federalism?

Several structural constraints have been important limitations on secessionism. Demographic composition is an important difference with the USSR. At the time of the 1989 census, Russians constituted a bare majority (50.78 per cent) of the USSR's 286.7 million population. In contrast, in the Russian Federation ethnic Russians were an overwhelming majority (81.5 per cent) of the 147 million population (SSSR, 1990). Of the eighty-eight constituent units of the Russian Federation in late 1991, thirty-one had a titular ethnic designation, of which twenty were republics and the rest autonomous districts. Of these only four (Ossetiya, Tuva, Chechnya, and Chuvashiya) had an absolute majority of the titular ethnic group. In three republics (Tatarstan, Kabardino-Balkar, and Kalmykia), the titular ethnic group constituted a simple majority. For example, the largest ethnic minority in the Russian Federation, the Tatars (6.64 million), are a minority within their own titular ethnic homeland, the Republic of Tatarstan (Tatars are 48 per cent of the population, Russians 43 per cent). In twelve republics ethnic Russians are an absolute majority or the majority group. It is not, therefore, simply numerical superiority at the state level that makes ethnic Russian homogeneity such an important factor in limiting ethnic separatism, but also the spatial dispersion of Russians in strength throughout the bulk of the territory of the federation. Resource interdependencies are another factor. Most ethnic republics are net beneficiaries of federal budgetary transfers. Only four ethnic republics are economically important or have significant natural resources: Tatarstan (oil/military-related manufacturing), Bashkortostan (oil/transit), Sakha-Yakutia (diamonds), and Chechnya (oil, refining capacity). Geography is a further constraint. Chechnya's peripheral/border location gave it more capacity to attempt secession, but Tatarstan and Bashkortostan are landlocked by ethnic Russian regions, and Sakha (Yakutia) is effectively landlocked in remote Eastern Siberia (Hughes, 2001).

The sheer size of Russia and its ethnic, cultural, and economic diversity arguably demands regional autonomy and some form of fiscal federalism. Russia's elites inherited a federal structure from the USSR but they engaged in a process of experimentation with the whole federal institutional design in the 1990s in an effort to balance the demands for greater autonomy with an effective central state. Yeltsin had been pivotal in undermining Gorbachev's efforts to preserve the USSR, and in August 1990 had famously exhorted Russia's ethnic leaders to "take as much sovereignty as you can swallow". At first, in the Federal Treaty of March 1992, this was achieved by empowering the asymmetric federal arrangement inherited from the Soviet constitution. The six types of federal subjects, with differing powers, were retained (regions, territories, republics, cities of federal jurisdiction, autonomous regions, and autonomous districts). A special status and powers were given to the twenty ethnic republics on taxation, culture, and control of natural resources (neither Tatarstan nor Chechnya signed this treaty). Later, in the 1993 constitution, an equalisation of the status and powers of republics and regions was imposed by Yeltsin. The thornier issues of separatism that were most serious in just two republics, Tatarstan and Chechnya, were consistently postponed. Under its wily president Mintimer Shaimiev, Tatarstan held a referendum on the republic's sovereignty in March 1992: 62 per cent voted in favour. In November 1992 it adopted its own constitution and declared itself "a subject of international law".

From early 1994 the experimentation changed as the Yeltsin administration focused on a more selective asymmetric federalism. A hierarchical framework of bilateral asymmetric power-sharing treaties between the federal government and republics and regions was developed. The basis for this policy was Yeltsin's unilateral imposition of strong presidential rule in the December 1993 constitution in the aftermath of the violent clashes between president and parliament in October 1993. Yeltsin's management of federal relations was bound up with the nature of his autocratic presidential style, which rested on a combination of coercion, co-option, and charismatic populism. US scholars, in particular, have viewed the asymmetric federalism as being intrinsically destabilising Lapidus, 1999; Solnick, 1996). For others, the non-transparent executive patrimonial federalism that developed from early 1994 based on the bilateral treaties helped to stabilise Russia by co-opting the most important elites in Russia's regions and ethnic republics (Hughes, 2001). Yeltsin's patrimonial federalism was the key to the negotiated and mutually agreed accommodations with President Mintimer Shaimiev of Tatarstan, President Murtaza Rakhimov of Bashkortostan, and President Nikolaev of Sakha. Equally, however, it proved to be the main stumbling block to an accommodation with the other significant challenge to an integral Russian Federation – President Dzhokar Dudaev's secessionist Chechnya. By summer 1998, forty-six subject units of the Russian Federation had signed federal treaties, but most were symbolic and only a few gave any significant concessions. These treaties were not formally constitutionalised, which made them vulnerable to a change of president, and that was precisely what followed when Putin came to power in January 2000.

There were also external constraints on secessionism in Russia. No Western country recognised secessionist Chechnya, although there was much sympathy for the Chechen cause. Rather, the Western Alliance, led by Clinton, developed a "special relationship" with Yeltsin, who was regarded as compliant with Western interests, and sought to bolster him against all of his domestic opposition. Clinton even compared Yeltsin to Lincoln justly battling separatists.

Much of the criticism of the asymmetric arrangements focused on two aspects: first, whether the ethnified federalism would mean that Russia "would go the way of the USSR" and second, that the patrimonial ties between Yeltsin and regional leaders embedded local authoritarianism and resistance to a progressive transition in Russia. Charges of clientelism within Russia and from outside were often levelled at Shaimiev in Tatarstan (Matsukato, 2001). Shaimiev, like Yeltsin, was a communist party *Obkom* (that is, oblast-level committee) secretary who had successfully reinvented himself as an ethnic nationalist entrepreneur, and someone who was embedded in the new business oligarchy that emerged after the fall of communism. Furthermore, the bilateral treaty between the federal government and Tatarstan was by far the most constitutionally perverse. It established a co-sovereignty arrangement whereby relations were regulated by the Russian constitution and the constitution of Tatarstan, and the treaty. Tatarstan had its own citizenship, tax arrangements, banking, customs, education, symbols, and controls on natural resources, and Tatar was equal with Russian as a state language in the republic. There was also a power to conduct foreign relations. The lessons of Chechnya, which was devastated by two costly wars with Russia, made Shaimiev and the Tatar elite approach these arrangements with a great deal of caution and conservativism.

Yeltsin himself seems to have started the backlash against his own variant of asymmetric federalism by appointing Vladimir Putin de facto as his federal supremo – in May 1998 as first deputy chief of presidential staff for regions, and then in July 1998 as head of the "commission for the preparation of agreements on the delimitation of power of regions and the federal centre" of the presidential administration. Under Putin the commission completed no further agreements. In June 1999 a new federal law stipulated that all treaties had to comply with the Russian constitution by 2002. After Putin became president in January 2000, he launched a blitzkrieg to revive Russia as a great power. He embarked on a federal territorial restructuring/recentralisation in May 2000 (dividing the country into seven overarching federal districts headed by directly appointed presidential plenipotentiaries). The assault on the treaties was formally approved by a constitutional court ruling in June 2000 that instituted a judicial review process. In August 2000 a new federal law reformed the structure of the upper chamber of parliament, the Federation Council, replacing elected governors by nominees selected by the regional parliaments then approved by the president. After the Beslan School massacre in September 2004, the structure was changed again so that the president made the nomination for approval by the regional parliaments. During his second term as president (2004–2008), Putin also oversaw the amalgamation of a few regions and the number of federal regions dropped from eighty-nine to eighty-three due to mergers. Five regions in the Urals, Siberia, and Far East absorbed small ethnic (in population) autonomous *okrugi*. The recentralisation of Russian federalism under Putin's policy of rebuilding a "power vertical" to "pull the state together" has led some to suggest that Russia is no longer a federal state but a hybrid state with more unitary features than federal ones (Ross, 2010).

Putin also devised a more sophisticated neo-imperialist divide-and-rule strategy to manage the Chechen insurgency, which is generally termed "Chechenisation". It required the co-option of a former rebel group, the Kadyrovtsy clique, and then its installation as a collaborationist regime, first under its elder Ahmad Kadyrov until his assassination in 2004, and then under his son Ramzan Kadyrov, who was appointed president of Chechnya by Putin in 2007 (Hughes, 2007). Putin views Kadyrov not only as the key to stabilisation in Chechnya but also as a pivotal, special, regional client in Russia (Russell, 2008; Souleimanov, 2015). By "Chechenisation" Putin accepted what has been termed "separatism without secession" – a higher degree of self-rule for Chechnya than any other Russian federal subject, and a form of authoritarian Islamisation that sets Chechnya de facto outside the Russian constitutional order in a kind of "dual state" (Sakwa, 2010). The Putin-Kadyrov tandem has successfully crushed the Islamist insurgency in the North Caucasus, at the price of a special autonomy for the Kadyrov regime, and massively disproportional fiscal subsidies to stabilise and reconstruct Chechnya (Hughes and Sasse, 2016).

The federalisation of Bosnia and Herzegovina

The Dayton Agreement of December 1995, mediated by the US on the basis of an International Contact Group plan, brought to an end one of the bloodiest civil wars to occur in modern Europe. Conservative estimates are that of a pre-war population of 4.4 million, an estimated 100,000 died, and about 50 per cent of the population migrated, many through ethnic cleansing (about 1.5 million became refugees, and almost 1 million persons were internally displaced). The Agreement affirmed that Bosnia and Herzegovina (BiH) would be preserved as a single state within the borders that it held under Yugoslavia, but it was to be constitutionally reconstructed on a complex ethnofederal concept. The new state would be confederal in its composition with two "entities": the Federation of Bosnia and Herzegovina that was further sub-divided into ethnic cantons, and the Bosnian Serb Republika Srpska. The Agreement divided BiH spatially roughly equally between the former (51 per cent) and the latter (49 per cent). The ceasefire borders were essentially maintained by the agreement.

The powers of the state government and those of the entities were intricately demarcated in the Agreement's Annex 4 which set out the new constitution (Dayton, 1995). There was some continuity with the ethnofederalism of the communist era, including in the ambiguous constitutional language used. Bosniaks, Croats, and Serbs were defined as "constituent peoples", and there were consociational-type provisions for ethnic self-government, mutual vetoes, and constitutional checks. There was to be external cooperation from the two regional powers (The Federal Republic of Yugoslavia and Croatia), but oversight and guarantees came mainly from the Western Alliance through a NATO peacekeeping force (initially 60,000-strong, but after various restructurings the mission became an EU-led one, and after 2012 EUFOR had fewer than 600 troops in BiH); a Western-dominated Peace Implementation Council (PIC) composed of fifty-five countries and international organisations which appointed a High Representative (HR) as a kind of Western proconsul; and international representation on the constitutional court. BiH would have three armies and a weak central government (with no defence competence), and a cumbersome rotating tripartite ethnically denominated presidency. As a condition of the NATO membership process, the army was later unified by a reform in 2005, but it retained its ethnic units (three ethnic battalions in three regiments, one located in each ethnic area). The upper chamber of parliament, the House of Peoples, was composed of fifteen members (five from each of the three ethnic "constituent peoples", though there were other minorities in BiH). Annex VII of the Agreement made provisions for the return of property and displaced persons to their locale of origin but it embedded a high degree of de facto segregation; it also allowed for compensation in lieu of return, which appears to have become the norm. In many ways, the Agreement replicated the ethnofederal structures of Yugoslavia which had led to gridlock, which itself was considered by Badinter as grounds for declaring the state to be "in dissolution".

President Clinton and the US diplomats involved in its negotiation, notably Richard Holbrooke, considered the Agreement a great success, while regretting the use of the term "Republika Srpska" (Holbrooke, 1998). However, the ethnofederal character of the Agreement stirred much Western liberal criticism about the stability and sustainability of the peace, as well as normatively driven opposition on the grounds that (1) there was no moral distinction made between signatories considered to be war criminals and those on the "right side"; (2) the new state was ethnically grounded, not liberal; (3) there was insufficient focus on the "humanitarian" and "civil society" dimensions; (4) there was no systematic reversal of ethnic cleansing; (5) there were no conflict transformation mechanisms for transcending the divisions; and (6) there were no incentives for change. Questions about the sustainability of the peace have lost some of their edge over time, as the Agreement has now been in place for more than twenty years without a renewal of conflict. The normative critique about the ethnofederal character of the state, however, has endured.

A Western liberal agenda to reform Dayton "from above" was enacted from the late 1990s, using the so-called Bonn Powers approved by the PIC in 1997 (Belloni, 2008). The powers, which exceeded those allowed to the HR under the Agreement, included the right to impose decrees/laws, sack public officials (including elected ones), overturn entity decisions, and even those of the constitutional court. The aim was to override deadlocked decisions between the entities, strengthen the confederal level over the entities, remove BiH politicians considered to be "spoilers" for the Western agenda, and circumvent locally elected politicians by relying more on Western-funded civil society actors. The effort was criticised as "liberal imperialism" and peaked during the tenure of British politician and ex-special forces officer Paddy Ashdown as HR in 2002–2006. Some have called this period the "Ashdown Raj" because of his propensity to bulldoze over the wishes of recalcitrant local politicians by frequent use of the Bonn Powers, behaving in ways reminiscent of the British imperialism of a bygone age (Knaus and Martin, 2003). The agenda was pursued under a classic imperial guise of promoting "progress", and the rational-technical goals of reducing "dysfunctionality" and promoting interdependence and cooperation between the entities. Ashdown's behaviour led to a Venice Commission report of 2005 which recommended the closure of the Office of the HR and a speedy transition to greater legal oversight of its arbitrary decree powers and power of removal of elected officials (Venice Commission, 2005).

Judicial review of the constitution by the constitutional court in several judgements between 2000 and 2005 also significantly moderated the trend for a deepening of ethnically segregated constitutional spaces in BiH and enhanced the role of the HR. One of the most important decisions was the so-called Decision on the Constituency of Peoples, which was actually a set of decisions during 2000. The court decided that the constitutions of the entities must conform to that of the state, and in so doing the territorial division of BiH into two entities by the Agreement could not serve as "constitutional legitimacy for ethnic domination, national homogenisation or the right to maintain results of ethnic cleansing" (BiH Constitutional Court, 2000). Consequently, the designation of Bosniaks, Croats, and Serbs as constituent peoples in the Preamble of the Constitution of BiH was to be understood as an all-inclusive principle for the entities as well as the state itself. In 2000–2001 the court judged that it could not review the exercise of powers by the HR granted by the Agreement and the Bonn PIC decisions, but it could review the constitutionality of laws enacted by the HR. The Agreement had also imposed international supervision on the multi-ethnic Brčko District of BiH, and over a fifteen-year period (to the end of international supervision in 2012) a major effort was made to transform the area into a model for interethnic cooperation and development.

From 2000, the EU assumed a steadily increasing role in assuming the lead responsibility for the external management of BiH. Ashdown was the first HR to simultaneously hold the office of EU Special Representative. After Ashdown, HRs became more nuanced and took a much less proactive interventionist role in BiH government. The current HR, Austrian Slovene Valentin Inzko, was the former EU Special Representative prior to becoming HR, and he is one of the least interventionist, arguing that it is for the politicians of BiH to resolve their differences themselves (Inzko, 2016). The government of BiH submitted its membership application to the EU in February 2016, but the reform of Dayton by the ethnic blocs has been made a condition by the EU for progress in accession, and in implementing the Stabilisation and Association Agreement of 2005, which came into force only in June 2015. It provides the EU road map towards membership. However, interethnic negotiations on broader constitutional reform, notably internationally mediated talks in 2005 and in Butmir in 2009, stalled over EU and US proposals to create a unified presidency and the strengthening of the central government. Elections in BiH have consistently consolidated the power of the respective ethnic parties and blocked progress on reform (Sebastián-Aparicio, 2014). BiH's accession to the EU has also been made conditional by the EU on the implementation of the European Court of Human Rights (ECHR) decision in the case of *Sejdić and Finci v. Bosnia and Herzegovina* (2009). The applicants were a Bosnian Roma (Sejdić) and a Bosnian Jew (Finci) who were barred under the Agreement (as non-members of one of the "constituent peoples") from being elected to the upper house of parliament and to the tripartite presidency. The ECHR ruled that their human rights are infringed. So far, there has been no progress in implementing the decision in BiH.

BiH has been a grand project for Western state-building. With over $14 billion in international aid in the 1990s, 60,000 troops, seventeen different foreign governments, eighteen UN agencies, twenty-seven intergovernmental organisations, and about 200 non-governmental organisations, BiH was probably the most expensive per capita and most extensive peace-building and democratisation experiment in history (McMahon and Western, 2009). The refrain among many Western actors, even those involved in its negotiation, has been consistent almost from the outset: the settlement seemed "morally wrong and politically impracticable" (Weller and Wolff, 2006). Yet, HRs have come and gone in BiH, yet Dayton endures, as does peace in BiH.

Conclusion

Despite the extensive theoretical speculation about the relationship between ethnofederalism and political instability arising from the collapse of three of four communist-era ethnofederations, the concept of federalism persists in state-building in Eastern Europe. It is a form of state-building that has been implemented both by the elite successors of the communist era in countries such as Russia and BiH, but has also been proposed and implemented by Western states as a conflict management device. Federalism and regional autonomy, often asymmetric, are widely proposed solutions for many of the protracted "frozen conflicts" in the broader Eastern European region as a method of conflict management and state-building in multi-ethnic societies. Regional autonomy and federal-type relations were the basis of the Boden Plan (2002) for resolving the Georgia-Abkhazia conflict and the Kozak Memorandum (2003) for resolving the Transnistria-Moldova conflict, and were embodied in the decentralisation provisions for Kosovo Serbs from 2005 and in the EU-mediated agreement between Kosovo and Serbia in 2015. That none of these proposals has been implemented should not distract from the fact that the major powers involved in these proposals – Germany, France, and Russia – do not avoid ethnofederalism and autonomy as vital conflict management devices.

The post-communist federal types of state-building or refederalisation offer a testing ground for research into first, whether the federal concept remains a viable one in the region for managing the political problems arising from multinational and multi-ethnic societies, and second, whether the theoretical claims linking ethnofederalism to state collapse will be affirmed. Fundamentally, the critique of ethnofederalism has less to do with state stability and is rooted, in essence, in a normative repulsion among Western liberals at the institutionalisation of ethnic power. Few could argue that ethnofederalism offers an attractive vision of the "Good Life" for any state seeking to build an integrated democratic civic culture. However, the realities of divided societies, in particular where they have endured ethnic discrimination and been broken by violent conflict, make for the necessity for a trade-off between peace and stability and ethnofederalism (and other forms of consociational and regional autonomy) on the one hand, and liberal forms of state-building on the other hand.

References

Armstrong, J. A. (1982). *Nations Before Nationalism.* Chapel Hill: University of North Carolina Press.

Beissinger, M. R. (2002). *Nationalist Mobilization and the Collapse of the Soviet State.* Cambridge: Cambridge University.

Belloni, R. (2008). *State Building and International Intervention in Bosnia.* London: Routledge.

BiH Constitutional Court (2000). *Decision on the Constituency of Peoples.* Available at http://miris.eurac.edu/mugs2/do/blob.html?type=html&serial=1042801884091

Bookman, M. Z. (1993). *The Economics of Secession.* London: St Martin's Press.

Brown, A. (2004). The Soviet Union: Reform of the System or Systemic Transformation? *Slavic Review*, 63(3), pp. 489–504.

Brubaker, R. (1996). *Nationalism Reframed: Nationhood and the National Question in the New Europe.* Cambridge: Cambridge University Press.

Bunce, V. (1999a). Peaceful Versus Violent State Dismemberment: A Comparison of the Soviet Union, Yugoslavia and Czechoslovakia. *Politics and Society*, 27(2), pp. 217–237.

Bunce, V. (1999b). *Subversive Institutions: The Design and the Destruction of Socialism and the State*. Cambridge: Cambridge University Press.

Caplan, R. D. (2005). *Europe and the Recognition of New States in Yugoslavia*. Cambridge: Cambridge University Press.

Cassese, A. (1995). *Self-Determination of Peoples: A Legal Reappraisal*. Cambridge: Cambridge University Press.

Czechoslovakia (1968). *143/1968 Sb. Ústavní zákon ze dne 27. října 1968 o československé federacy* [*Constitutional Law of 27 October 1968 on the Federation of Czechoslovakia*]. Available at www.psp.cz/docs/texts/constitution_1968.html

Dallin, A. (1992). Causes of the Collapse of the USSR. *Post-Soviet Affairs*, 8(4), pp. 279–302.

Dayton Agreement (1995). *General Framework Agreement for Peace in Bosnia and Herzegovina*. Available at http://peacemaker.un.org/sites/peacemaker.un.org/files/BA_951121_DaytonAgreement.pdf

Ellman, M. and Kontorovich, V. (1992). Overview. In: M. Ellman and V. Kontorovich (eds). *The Disintegration of the Soviet Economic System*. London: Routledge, pp. 1–39.

Glaurdić, J. (2011). *The Hour of Europe: Western Powers and the Break-Up of Yugoslavia*. New Haven, London: Yale University Press.

Holbrooke, R. (1998). *To End a War: From Sarajevo to Dayton and Beyond*. New York: Random House.

Hough, J. F. (1997). *Democratization and Revolution in the USSR 1985–1991*. Washington, DC: Brookings Institution.

Hughes, J. (2001). Managing Secession Potential in the Russian Federation. *Regional & Federal Studies*, 11(3), pp. 36–68.

Hughes, J. (2007). *Chechnya: From Nationalism to Jihad*. Philadelphia: University of Pennsylvania Press.

Hughes, J. and Sasse, G. (2001). Conflict and Accommodation in the Former Soviet Union: The Role of Institutions and Regimes. *Regional and Federal Studies*, 11(3), pp. 220–240.

Hughes, J. and Sasse, G. (2016). Power Ideas and Conflict: Ideology, Linkage, and Leverage in Crimea and Chechnya. *East European Politics*, 32(3), pp. 314–334.

Innes, A. (2001). *Czechoslovakia: The Short Goodbye*. New Haven, CT: Yale University Press.

Inzko, V. (2016). *Xinhua: Interview With HR Valentin Inzko*, 14 April. Available at www.ohr.int/?p=68949&lang=en

Knaus, G. and Martin, F. (2003). Lessons From Bosnia and Herzegovina: Travails of the European Raj. *Journal of Democracy*, 14(3), pp. 60–73.

Kraus, M. and Stanger, A. (2000). *Irreconcilable Differences?: Explaining Czechoslovakia's Dissolution*. Lanham, MD: Rowman & Littlefield.

Lapidus, G. (1999). Asymmetrical Federalism and State Breakdown in Russia. *Post-Soviet Affairs*, 15(1), pp. 74–82.

Linz, J. and Stepan, A. (1992): Political Identities and Electoral Sequences: Spain, the Soviet Union and Yugoslavia. *Daedalus*, 121(2), pp. 123–139.

MacMillan, M. (2002). *Paris 1919: Six Months That Changed the World*. New York: Random House.

Martin, T. (2001). *The Affirmative Action Empire: Nations and Nationalism in the Soviet Union, 1923–1939*. Ithaca, NY: Cornell University Press.

Matsukato, K. (2001). From Ethno-Bonapartism to Centralized Caciquismo: Characteristics and Origins of the Tatarstan Political Regime, 1990–2000. *Journal of Communist Studies and Transition Politics*, 17(4), pp. 43–77.

McGarry, J. and O'Leary, B. (2009). Must Plurinational Federations Fail? *Ethnopolitics*, 8(1), pp. 5–25.

McMahon, P. C. and Western, J. (2009). The Death of Dayton: How to Stop Bosnia From Falling Apart. *Foreign Affairs*, 88(5), pp. 69–83.

Radan, P. (2001). *The Break-Up of Yugoslavia and International Law*. London: Routledge.

Rich, R. (1993). Recognition of States: The Collapse of Yugoslavia and the Soviet Union. *European Journal of International Law*, 4(1), pp. 36–65.

Riker, W. H. (1964). *Federalism: Origin, Operation, Significance*. Boston, MA: Little, Brown.

Roeder, P. G. (1991). Soviet Federalism and Ethnic Mobilization. *World Politics*, 43(2), pp. 196–232.

Roeder, P. G. (1993). *Red Sunset: The Failure of Soviet Politics*. Princeton, NJ: Princeton University Press.

Ross, C. (2010). Federalism and Inter-governmental Relations in Russia. *The Journal of Communist Studies and Transition Politics*, 26(2), pp. 165–187.

Russell, J. (2008). Ramzan Kadyrov: The Indigenous Key to Success in Putin's Chechenization Strategy? *Nationalities Papers*, 36(4), pp. 659–687.

Sakwa, R. (2010). The Revenge of the Caucasus: Chechenization and the Dual State in Russia. *Nationalities Papers*, 38(5), pp. 601–622.

Sebastián-Aparicio, S. (2014). *Post-war Statebuilding and Constitutional Reform: Beyond Dayton in Bosnia*. Basingstoke: Palgrave Macmillan.

Skalnik-Leff, C. (1999). Democratization and Disintegration in Multinational States: The Breakup of the Communist Federations. *World Politics*, 51(2), pp. 205–235.

Snyder, T. (2003). *The Reconstruction of Nations: Poland, Ukraine, Lithuania, Belarus, 1569–1999*. New Haven, CT: Yale University Press.

Solnick, S. (1996). The Political Economy of Russian Federalism: A Framework for Analysis. *Problems of Post-Communism*, 43(6), pp. 13–25.

Souleimanov, E. (2015). An Ethnography of Counterinsurgency: Kadyrovtsy and Russia's Policy of Chechenization. *Post-Soviet Affairs*, 31(2), pp. 91–114.

SSSR v tsifrakh v 1989g. [USSR in Figures in 1989] (1990). Moscow: Finansy i statistika.

Stalin, I. V. (1913). *Marxism and the National Question*. Available at www.marxists.org/reference/archive/stalin/works/1913/03.htm

Suny, R. (1993). *The Revenge of the Past: Nationalism, Revolution, and the Collapse of the Soviet Union*. Stanford, CA: Stanford University Press.

USSR (1977). *The Constitution of the Union of Soviet Socialist Federal Republics*. English Language Version. Available at www.departments.bucknell.edu/russian/const/1977toc.html

Venice Commission (2005). The Council of Europe. European Commission for Democracy Through Law (Venice Commission). *Opinion on the Constitutional Situation in Bosnia and Herzegovina and the Powers of the High Representative*, 11 March 2005. Available at www.venice.coe.int/webforms/documents/default.aspx?pdffile=CDL-AD%282005%29004-e

Weller, M. (2005). The Self-Determination Trap. *Ethnopolitics*, 4(1), pp. 3–28.

Weller, M. and Wolff, S. (2006). Bosnia and Herzegovina Ten Years After Dayton: Lessons for Internationalized State Building. *Ethnopolitics*, 5(1), pp. 1–13.

Wolchik, S. L. (1994). The Politics of Ethnicity in Post-Communist Czechoslovakia. *East European Politics and Societies*, 8(1), pp. 159–167.

Woodward, S. (1995). *Balkan Tragedy: Chaos and Dissolution After the Cold War*. Washington, DC: Brookings Institution.

Yugoslavia (1974). Ustav Socijalističke Federativne Republike Jugoslavije [Constitution of the Socialist Federal Republic of Yugoslavia]. *Constitution of 1974*. English Language Imprint. Belgrade: Dopisna Delavska Univerza.

PART III

Elections and political participation

11

ELECTIONS AND ELECTORAL PARTICIPATION

Sarah Birch

The peoples of Central and Eastern Europe have participated in elections for over a hundred years; most of them have participated in truly democratic elections for no more than twenty-five years. Elections were first introduced in the Austro-Hungarian and Russian empires in the late nineteenth century. These elections employed weighted suffrages, however, and they were largely indirect. Following the First World War, elections of varying quality were held throughout Eastern Europe in the new and newly reconfigured states that emerged from this conflict and its aftermath, though open electoral competition was curtailed in much of the region as right-wing authoritarian governments assumed power.

In the aftermath of the Second World War, communist regimes modelled on the Soviet Union emerged in Central and South Eastern Europe. Elections were regularly held under communism, but they were either entirely uncompetitive, as in the Soviet Union, or they involved effectively non-partisan choice, as in Yugoslavia. Elections in communist Europe were all governed by absolute majority rules, and implemented in single-member or multi-member districts. Turnout was nowhere formally compulsory, but the citizenries of these states experienced varying degrees of pressure to turn out at the polls. With the exception of late-communist Poland (which experienced grassroots electoral boycotts), turnout during this period was high. Rather than being mechanisms through which citizens held their leaders to account, elections were mobilising devices through which the communist states indoctrinated, monitored, and manipulated their populations (Birch, 2013; Furtak, 1990; Pravda, 1978).

Only following the momentous events of 1989–1991 were free, fair, and credible elections attempted across the Eastern European region, and these attempts have been of varying quality (Herron, 2009; Way, 2005). Today Eastern Europe displays perhaps the greatest variation in electoral integrity of any region of the world, from Belarus, which holds some of the most problematic elections, to Estonia, which has some of the most democratic.

The first major shift in the post-communist move towards competitive elections involved the introduction of multi-party politics and the adoption of electoral systems suited to fostering political party development. The result of this process was in most cases the rapid abandonment of communist-era absolute majority systems in favour of proportional representation (PR) and mixed systems. The dynamics of so-called founding elections – the first elections held after the inauguration of a transition from communism – proved fertile ground for scholarly analysis (for example, Colomer, 1995; Ishiyama, 1996; Turner, 1993). Once their transitions from communism

Table 11.1 Electoral systems in Eastern Europe (most recent parliamentary elections)

State	Year of most recent election	Size of chamber	Electoral system	Single-party threshold (first tier PR seats)*	Preferences in PR list voting?	Success requirement in single-member seats
Albania	2013	140	PR	3%*	No	–
Belarus	2012	110	SMD	–	–	Absolute majority
Bosnia and Herzegovina	2014	42	PR	None	Yes	–
Bulgaria	2014	240	Mixed (87% PR)	4%	Yes	–
Croatia	2015	151	PR	5%	No	–
Czech Republic	2013	200	PR	5%*	Yes	–
Estonia	2015	101	PR	None**	Yes	–
Hungary	2014	199	Mixed (47% PR)	5%	No	Plurality
Kosovo	2014	120	PR	5%	Yes	
Latvia	2014	100	PR	5%	Yes	–
Lithuania	2012	141	Mixed (50% PR)	5%*	Yes	Absolute majority
Macedonia	2014	123	PR	None	No	–
Moldova	2014	101	PR	6%*	No	–
Montenegro	2012	81	PR	3%	No	–
Poland	2015	460	PR	5%*	Yes	–
Romania	2012	412	Mixed (24%PR)	5%*	Yes	–
Russia	2011	450	PR	7%	No	–
Serbia	2014	250	PR	5%	No	–
Slovakia	2016	150	PR	5%	Yes	–
Slovenia	2014	90	PR	4%	Yes	–
Ukraine	2014	450	Mixed (50% PR)	5%	No	Plurality

* Graduated threshold structure; higher levels for coalitions.
** A 5 per cent threshold is imposed for seat distribution in the upper tier.

Sources: Aceproject at http://aceproject.org; Inter-parliamentary Union Parline database, www.ipu.org; OSCE (2012); Venice Commission (2015).

were complete, Eastern European states entered into a new phase of post-communist politics which varied considerably from country to country. Table 11.1 displays electoral system characteristics of the states in the region. As can be seen from this data, about three quarters have adopted proportional representation, with closed lists in the former Soviet Union and Yugoslavia and open lists in most of the rest of the region. There are also a handful of mixed systems, and one single-member district system, in Belarus.

The post-communist period has thus been characterised by political divergence, which has had both substantive implications for political developments in the area, and methodological implications for scholars studying states in this region. On the one hand, emerging variations across Eastern Europe in political institutions and behaviours has afforded scholars the opportunity for fruitful comparative analysis; on the other hand, the growing political heterogeneity within the region also means that those working in this area are continually confronted with definitional questions about the core characteristics that define the Eastern European political space. These intellectual dynamics pervade scholarship on post-communist elections.

Salient themes in the study of Eastern European elections

An overarching question that perfuses the literature on elections in Eastern Europe is the extent to which empirical regularities established by canonical studies of elections in established democracies 'travel' eastwards. A wave of research comparing elections East and West sought to demonstrate that theories that derived from the voluminous study of democratic elections have indeed found considerable evidence to support them – with minor variations – in the emerging electoral practices of the post-communist states (e.g. van der Brug, Franklin and Toka, 2008; Evans, 2006; Evans and Whitefield, 1993; Pacek, 1994; Rose and Mishler, 1998; Rose, Mishler and Haerpfer, 1998; Tavits, 2005, 2008; Tucker, 2001, 2006; Whitefield and Rohrschneider, 2009).

Other scholarship has instead emphasised the importance of the communist legacy and the mode of transition itself in conditioning electoral and political developments in the region (e.g. Bunce, 2003; Bustikova and Kitschelt, 2009; Ekiert, 1991; Grzymała-Busse, 2002; Kitschelt, Mansfeldová, Markowski and Toka, 1999; Miller, White and Heywood, 1998; Pop-Eleches, 2007). Research of this sort has focused on the way in which communist-era attitudes and cleavages shaped post-communist voting patterns, as well as the learning process through which post-communist voters began to explore the possibilities inherent in representative politics.

Another source of potential insight for students of Eastern European elections is the democratisation literature that grew out of the study of transition from authoritarian rule in Southern Europe in the 1970s and Latin America in the 1980s. When Eastern Europe began to democratise in the late 1980s and 1990s, many scholars seized on the paradigms established in the existing literature on democratisation and sought to extend them to Eastern Europe (e.g. Linz and Stepan, 1996; Kubicek, 1994; Schmitter and Karl, 1994).

Others pointed to the limits of the democratisation literature in explaining post-communist transitions. A particularly influential statement of such critiques was in Bunce (1995), followed eight years later by Bunce (2003). Bunce argues that the post-communist Eastern European experience has been distinct from prior democratisation experiences, in that the most successful democratisations involved a decisive break with the communist past rather than a 'pacting' process that granted concessions to representatives of the former authoritarian regime. The challenge of combined economic and political transition, the precariousness of state boundaries, and widespread mass involvement in the democratisation process there are also factors that the previous democratisation literature has established as threats to successful democratic consolidation, but Bunce argues that the Eastern European experience does not support these arguments, as none of these factors obviously impeded democratisation in Eastern Europe (Bunce, 1995, 2003).

As Bunce and others have demonstrated, the post-communist electoral order has a number of features that distinguish it from electoral contexts following other transitions. These features can be summed up under several useful rubrics, including weak party identification and attendant party system fluidity, the appeal of populism, and the importance of electoral institutions in channelling political developments.

According to the standard literature on party identification (e.g. Campbell, Converse, Miller and Stokes, 1960; Lazarsfeld, Berelson and Gaudet, 1948), attachment to parties is something that is established relatively early in life and reinforced over one's life. Given that the majority of the parties competing in post-communist political fora were established well after the majority of those eligible to vote had achieved the age of electoral majority, it is not surprising that party identification in this region should be weak. There is, however, an additional factor that also accounts for the particularly weak ties between political parties and voters in Eastern Europe: post-communist scepticism with parties in general, which can be traced back to the coercive and nondemocratic role played by the overbearing communist parties which dominated the political stage of these countries for so many decades. Even in Western Europe, anti-party sentiment has been riding relatively high in recent years (van der Brug, Fennema and Tillie, 2000; Norris, 2011); in Eastern Europe such sentiment is even higher (Pop-Eleches, 2010; Rose and Mishler, 1998). Linked to weak attachment to political parties is the relatively high propensity of Eastern European voters to opt for newly established parties. Party volatility in post-communist Europe has generally been high by Western European standards (see Enyedi and Deegan-Krause in this volume). Propensity to protest against incumbents has varied according to several factors, including economic conditions, reform trajectories, civil society organisation, and trust in government, which have all varied considerably across the region (Kopecký and Mudde, 2003; March, 2013; Beissinger and Sasse, 2014).

The attraction of right-wing populist parties in Eastern Europe is a phenomenon that has been identified by a number of scholars (e.g. Bustikova, 2014; Bustikova and Kitschelt, 2009; Hockenos, 1993; Kopecký and Mudde, 2003; Mudde, 2005; Vachudova, 2008; also Mudde in this volume). Such parties include the Movement for a Better Hungary (Jobbik); the Greater Romania Party, the Self-Defence Party, and the League of Polish Families in Poland. Eastern Europe is of course not the only part of the world where right-wing populism has gained in strength in recent years; anti-immigrant, anti-establishment parties have been found to be popular in many contexts where large sectors of the population have suffered the economic effects of globalisation (including European integration) and multiculturalism. In Eastern Europe, the 'losers from globalisation' are also in many cases the same people who have lost status and economic position in the protracted transition from communism to capitalism.

Another branch of Eastern European electoral studies has focused on the development of electoral systems and their consequences. The aforementioned move from majority to proportional-representation electoral systems which occurred relatively early in the post-transitional years launched a spate of scholarly works devoted to electoral reform. Studies of the determinants of electoral reform in the region have in some cases examined the early institutional settlements that took place during the transition from communism (Birch, Millard, Williams and Popescu, 2002; Elster, 1996; Elster, Offe and Preuss, 1998), whereas other studies have examined electoral system change over a longer period (Herron, 2009). The two and a half decades since the collapse of communism have witnessed a number of further revisions to electoral provisions, as the emerging democracies and semi-democracies in the region sought to fashion electoral institutions fit for their societies. The abandonment of pure absolute majority systems was nearly universal; only Belarus retains this electoral system. All the other states in Eastern Europe have adopted either list proportional representation – the most common electoral system type in Western Europe – or some type of mixed system combining proportional representation with single-member constituencies (see Table 11.1). A number of states – Albania, Bulgaria, Croatia, Macedonia, Romania, Russia, and Ukraine – have switched between proportional representation and mixed systems, while others (e.g. the Czech Republic, Hungary, Poland, Slovakia, and Estonia) have altered features of systems they adopted relatively early in the post-transitional period (Bol, Pilet and Riera, 2015; Herron, 2009; Nikolenyi, 2011). There appears to be a tendency for states in this region (as elsewhere in Europe) to seek an electoral system 'sweet spot' that is largely proportional but with thresholds, limited constituency sizes, and other devices that limit party system fragmentation (Bol et al., 2015; cf. Nikolenyi, 2011; Renwick, 2011).

The results of the elections held under the new more proportional post-communist electoral systems have also been subject to scrutiny by electoral systems scholars in the aim of determining the effects of the various different systems adopted (e.g. Bielasiak, 2002; Birch, 2003; Bochsler, 2010; Herron, 2009; Ishiyama, 1996; Kostadinova, 2002; Moser, 1999; 2001; Shvetsova, 1999). This research has found that while proportional representation electoral systems – often accompanied by high thresholds – fostered party system institutionalisation, the plurality systems that remained in the early post-communist period and the plurality components of mixed electoral systems have tended to operate somewhat differently in the post-communist region from the way in which they typically operate in established democracies. In states such as Russia, Ukraine, and Macedonia, single-member districts were associated with party system fragmentation due to geographic heterogeneity in patterns of political support and lack of nationalised political parties. Several studies have found a strong interaction effect between electoral systems and party nationalisation (Birch, 2003; Bochsler, 2010; Herron, 2009; Moser, 1999, 2001).

Electoral participation is an additional major topic which has occupied many scholars of Eastern European politics. The region has relatively low level of electoral participation, at least compared to the levels generally achieved in Western Europe. The post-communist period was accompanied by declines in electoral participation across the post-communist region. Though voting had not been compulsory under communism, pressure on citizens to take part in communist civic rituals was great. Far from being enthusiastic about the prospect of taking an active part in the new multi-party electoral competitions held falling communism's collapse, many of the region's people simply wanted to pursue their private interests and relax in the knowledge that the state would no longer pressure them to go to the polls.

There were, of course, variations in turnout declines across the region, and these have been subjected to analysis by a number of authors who have identified structural, economic, and institutional causes for differences in rates of post-communist electoral participation (Birch, 2003; Ceka, 2013; Kostadinova, 2003, 2009; Pacek, Pop-Eleches and Tucker, 2009). Table 11.2 provides an overview of turnout across the region. As can be seen from the data in this table, the decline in rates of participation has been greatest in Romania and Kosovo, and least in Belarus and Montenegro.

The generally low turnouts across the region have been explained in terms of citizens frustrated with politics tending to withdraw from the electoral realm, exercising their right to 'exit' rather than voicing their discontent at the ballot box (though as noted above, vote choice prompted by frustration has also been manifest in the region). Vigorous political competition actually appears to stifle electoral participation in Eastern Europe, as the cut and thrust of electoral competition reduces trust and turns people away from political life (Ceka, 2013).

The final major topic of study in the sub-field of Eastern European electoral studies is the use of referendums in political life. Referendums first saw widespread use in Eastern Europe during the interwar period, when they were used as part of the state-formation process and to resolve territorial disputes (Brady and Kaplan, 1994). In recent years, referendums have been used across the region for a variety of purposes, including confirming sovereign statehood and ratifying European Union accession (Brady and Kalpan, 1994; Tverdova and Anderson, 2004). Other typical uses vary by sub-region.

The Soviet constitution of 1977 made provision for referendums, though this possibility was not acted on until the late Soviet period. The all-Union referendum on the future of the Soviet Union in March 1991 was the first significant opportunity for Soviet citizens to express their views in this type of electoral exercise. At the time of the collapse of the Soviet Union later that same year, independence referendums took place in nine of the fifteen Soviet republics. During the post-Soviet period, referendums have been employed in all of the Soviet successor states. In

Table 11.2 Turnout in Eastern Europe

State	Last communist-era election	First multi-party election	Most recent parliamentary election
Albania	~99%	98.9%	53.3%
Belarus	~99%	N/A	74.6%
Bosnia and Herzegovina	N/A	80%	54.1%
Bulgaria	99.9%	90.8%	51.0%
Croatia	~95%	84.5%	60.1%
Czech Republic	99.4%	96.8%	59.5%
Estonia	~99%	78.2%	64.2%
Hungary	93.9%	65.1%	61.7%
Kosovo	N/A	N/A	42.6%
Latvia	~99%	81.3%	58.9%
Lithuania	~99%	71.7%	52.9%
Macedonia	~90%	77.2%	63.0%
Moldova	~99%	83.4%	58.9%
Montenegro	N/A	75.8%	70.6%
Poland	78.9%	62.1%	50.9%
Romania	99.9%	86.2%	41.8%
Russia	~99%	77.0%	60.1%
Serbia	N/A	71.5%	53.1%
Slovakia	99.4%	95.4%	59.8%
Slovenia	~90%	83.5%	51.7%
Ukraine	~99%	84.7%	52.4%

Sources: Birch (2003); Election Guide database at electionguide.org; Inter-parliamentary Union Parline database at www.ipu.org; OSCE (2012).

states such as Belarus, Russia, and Ukraine they have served to extend the terms of presidents and to push through controversial constitutional reforms (Herron, 2009: chap. 7; Qvortrup, 2002: 90–91). The most controversial such event in recent times has undoubtedly been the referendum on the future of Crimea that Russian occupying forces held on Ukrainian territory in 2014. The Baltic republics and Moldova have employed referendums for more democratic purposes. According to Herron (2009), Lithuania was the most enthusiastic user of this tool, holding eight referendums during the 1992–2008 period.

Starting in 1990, Yugoslavia witnessed what Kaplan and Brady describe as a 'parade of referendums' on sovereignty (Brady and Kaplan, 1994: 207). Not all of these polls were official electoral procedures, and the territories on which they held overlapped, leading to confusing interpretations of their democratic authority. It is perhaps not surprising that this series of popular consultations failed to stop war from breaking out. Since the Dayton Peace Accords of 1995, the use of referendums has been more restrained, though this device has been employed by all states in the former Yugoslavia to decide constitutional, moral, and other issues.

Central European states have used referendums to decide a variety of policy issues, as well as changes to constitutions, electoral laws, and citizenship rights. It is also worth noting contexts in which referendums have *not* been used, such as to adjudicate the break-up of Czechoslovakia in 1992, which was decided by elites alone even after much discussion of the possibility of a referendum (Brady and Kaplan, 1994). Low turnouts in some referendums have stymied this type of poll as a mechanism for making decisions, including a 1990 referendum in Hungary on the direct election of the president in which only 14 per cent voted. This poll was declared invalid due to its failure to pass the turnout threshold of 50 per cent.

The foregoing overview of the main branches in the field of post-communist electoral studies in Eastern Europe has demonstrated that there is considerably diversity in this area, both in terms of the objects of study which scholars have chosen, and also in terms of the theoretical perspectives they have adopted.

New and emerging themes

The study of elections in Eastern Europe remains an important topic, given the centrality of elections to the workings of both democratic and authoritarian regimes. The considerable political variety now evident in the region means that Eastern Europe constitutes an excellent natural laboratory in which to study the impact of different factors on political trajectories. As noted earlier, the communist electoral systems displayed a marked degree of similarity; despite minor differences, they all employed the same type of electoral system and they all precluded genuine multi-party competition. Since then, electoral systems and electoral patterns have diverged widely in the twenty-odd states that make up this part of the world.

The role of elections in paths of democratic and authoritarian development remains an under-explored topic. In this context, elections can be seen both as an independent and a dependent variable. Scholars tend to view elections as motors of democracy (Lindberg, 2009), though a number of recent analyses have also noted that elections can serve the ends of authoritarianism (Gandhi and Lust-Okar, 2009; Gandhi and Przeworski, 2007; Geddes, 2006; Lust-Okar, 2009), and this can certainly be seen to have been the case in Belarus where elections have been heavily staged and controlled events that have served to shore up the domestic legitimacy of president Alexandr Lukashenko. Elections can also be seen as outcomes of political processes, however. Competing claims to legitimacy and challenges to those claims have led to numerous pre-term elections in the Eastern European region, as well as to referendums designed to resolve fundamental issues of state identity and the direction to be taken by state-building initiatives. Now that we have twenty-five years' worth of electoral data, which in most states includes at least six full electoral cycles, there is considerable scope for detailed longitudinal analyses that might tease out the role of electoral politics in the dynamics of post-communist political change.

Another area in which Eastern Europe lends itself to scholarly investigation is the emerging field of electoral integrity studies. The rapid recent emergence of electoral integrity as a scholarly sub-field suggests that analyses of electoral integrity will loom larger in Eastern European electoral studies in future years. Electoral integrity is a topic that has come to the fore in the past decade due largely to renewed interest by the international community in election observation and electoral assistance as tools of democratisation. The academic community is only just beginning to form a consensus on the fundamental drivers of electoral integrity and the factors associated with electoral malpractice. Eastern Europe provides an excellent context in which to explore issues related to electoral integrity, given the great variety of electoral practices across the region.

The studies that have been carried out in this area point to the role of electoral system design in facilitating abuse, and in particular to the higher degree of electoral malpractice under single-member district electoral systems in this region (Birch, 2007; Herron, 2009). Other studies have noted high levels of electoral abuse in special voting facilities such as those found in hospitals, prisons, ships, and so forth (Herron, 2009). In addition to institutional factors, scholars have also pointed to the role of fraud as a signalling mechanism among elites keen to demonstrate their power to manipulate the population (Myagkov, Ordeshook and Shakin, 2009; Simpser, 2013).

The study of electoral malpractice in Eastern Europe received a boost from the series of 'colour revolutions' that ripped across the region in the early years of the twenty-first century. The 'Bulldozer revolution' in Serbia, the 'Rose revolution' in Georgia, and the 'Orange revolution' in Ukraine were all triggered by electoral fraud. The ensuing protests and the regime changes they brought about provided much opportunity for students of contentious politics and election specialists alike to examine the dynamics of mass mobilisation for electoral reform (Beissinger, 2007; Bunce and Wolchik, 2010; Kalandadze and Orenstein, 2009; Lane and White, 2010; O Beacháin and Polese, 2010; Tucker, 2007). In these cases, fraud served to heighten awareness of authoritarianism and ultimately to bring about moves towards greater democracy.

In other states, however, electoral malpractice has persisted for extended periods of time, helping 'competitive authoritarian' regimes in Belarus and Russia to control their populations. The Russian case has been subject to the most intensive scrutiny in the literature, as scholars have sought to delineate the various ways in which electoral abuse has been undertaken and its role in the structuring of power (e.g. Goodnow, Moser and Smith, 2014; Lukinova, Myagkov and Ordeshook, 2011; Myagkov, Ordeshook and Shakin, 2005, 2007; Smyth, Sobolev and Soboleva, 2013; White, 2014).

Critical reflections on East European electoral studies

Criticisms of existing approaches to the study of elections in Eastern Europe include the aforementioned allegation that Western-derived theories are not necessarily relevant in the post-communist sphere. This is a debate that has largely taken place *within* the field of post-communist politics, and is thus not a criticism of the field itself, but it is an important argument to review. The universalist propensity of much contemporary comparative political analysis has in the sphere of post-communist studies encountered the rather different research trajectory of traditional area studies specialists. For comparativists, Eastern Europe is yet another piece of academic real estate that has become available for comparative analysis. While such comparativists acknowledge that the region many have its own specificities, they tend to see these as factors that can be controlled for in empirical studies or analysed as phenomena in their own right; they do not typically see these differences as impediments to the extension of Western-derived theoretical paradigms to the Eastern European terrain. As noted earlier, area studies specialists tend to question whether the theoretical apparatus of comparative political science is well-suited to the study of elections in Eastern Europe. Criticisms they make of such endeavours often point to the assumptions that subtend such intellectual projects, such as the common subjective understanding of elections across democratic states and emerging democracies, and voting that takes place on the basis of sincere preferences, rather than being guided by clientelistic ties and vote-buying or other considerations not directly linked to voters' 'genuine' preferences for parties. It may also be problematic to assume that elections have the same meaning to citizens in the post-communist region as they have in the established democracies of the West (Pammett and DeBardeleben, 1996; Birch, 2011).

Another potentially problematic characteristic of much of the Eastern European electoral studies literature is the assumption of geographically defined 'regions' (Chen and Sil, 2007; King, 2000). 'Eastern Europe' itself is a concept that is potentially less relevant than it was twenty-five years ago, now that there has been such divergence in trajectories of post-communist political development. The neat East-West dichotomy is no longer necessarily applicable; elections in those states that have joined the European Union are in many respects more similar to elections held in older EU member states than they are to elections held in, for example, Russia or Belarus (van der Brug et al., 2008; Birch, 2011).

Also potentially problematic is the tendency of scholars to group states together into sub-regional categories such as 'Baltic republics', former Soviet states', and 'former Yugoslav states'. Although it is clear from a number of important and valuable studies of path dependency in the region that the legacy of communist regime type and mode of transition loomed large in the political developments of the early post-communist years (Bunce, 2003; Grzymała-Busse, 2002; Kitschelt et al., 1999), these paths have by now been punctuated with many post-communist developments, and the relevance of such categories is no longer so clear. This is especially true now that new institutional legacies have formed, such as that of European Union accession and membership.

Conclusion

The two and a half decades that have elapsed since the collapse of communism in Eastern Europe may represent a small fraction of modern European history, but it is a period during which the Eastern part of the continent has undergone rapid and profound change. It is rare that so many states have experienced simultaneously such fundamental transformation of their electoral practices. For scholars of electoral politics, Eastern Europe thus offers a rich terrain of political development. The rapid development of electoral studies is testimony to the academic excitement generated by the advent of multi-party elections in this part of the world. Eastern Europe has offered comparativists a number of new states on which to test existing theories, and the concentration of political activity that attends elections in any state has afforded scholars researching Eastern Europe with a powerful lens through which to examine the politics of the states they study. Even with the fragmentation of Eastern Europe into a range of very different states, Eastern European elections promise to offer political scientists ample material for critical analysis well into the future.

References

Beissinger, Mark R. (2007), 'Structure and Example in Modular Political Phenomena: The Diffusion of Bulldozer/Rose/Orange/Tulip Revolutions', *Perspectives on Politics* 5(2), pp. 259–76.

Beissinger, Mark R. and Gwendolyn Sasse (2014), 'An End to "Patience"? The Great Recession and Economic Protest in Eastern Europe', in Nancy Bermeo and Larry M. Bartels (eds.), *Mass Politics in Tough Times: Opinions, Votes and Protest in the Great Recession*, Oxford: Oxford University Press, pp. 334–70.

Bielasiak, Jack (2002), 'The Institutionalisation of Electoral and Party Systems in Post-communist Europe', *Comparative Politics* 34(2), pp. 189–210.

Birch, Sarah (2003), *Electoral Systems and Political Transformation in Post-communist Europe*, One Europe or Several? Series, Basingstoke: Palgrave-Macmillan.

Birch, Sarah (2007), 'Electoral Systems and Electoral Misconduct', *Comparative Political Studies* 40(12).

Birch, Sarah (2011), 'Post-Soviet Electoral Practices in Comparative Perspective', *Europe-Asia Studies* 63(4), pp. 707–29.

Birch, Sarah (2013), 'Elections and Voters', in Stephen White, Paul G. Lewis and Judy Batt (eds.), *Developments in Central and East European Politics 5*, Basingstoke: Palgrave-Macmillan, pp. 156–70.

Birch, Sarah, Frances Millard, Kieran Williams and Marina Popescu (2002), *Embodying Democracy: Electoral System Design in Post-communist Europe*, One Europe or Several? Series, Basingstoke: Palgrave-Macmillan.

Bochsler, Daniel (2010), *Territory and Electoral Rules in Post-Communist Democracies*, Basingstoke: Palgrave-Macmillan.

Bol, Damien, Jean-Benoit Pilet and Pedro Riera (2015), 'The International Diffusion of Electoral Systems: The Spread of Mechanisms Tempering Proportional Representation Across Europe', *European Journal of Political Research* 54(2), pp 384–410.

Brady, H. E. and C. S. Kaplan (1994), 'Eastern Europe and the Former Soviet Union', in D. Butler and A. Ranney (eds.), *Referendums Around the World: The Growing Use of Direct Democracy*, Basingstoke: Macmillan, pp. 174–217.

Bunce, Valerie (1995), 'Should Transitologists Be Grounded?', *Slavic Review* 54(1), pp. 111–27.

Bunce, Valerie (2003), 'Rethinking Recent Democratization: Lessons From the Postcommunist Experience', *World Politics* 55(2), pp. 167–92.

Bunce, Valerie J. and Sharon L. Wolchik (2010), 'Defeating Dictators: Electoral Change and Stability in Competitive Authoritarian Regimes', *World Politics* 62(1), pp. 43–86.

Bustikova, Lenka (2014), 'Revenge of the Radical Right', *Comparative Political Studies* 47(12), pp. 1738–65.

Bustikova, Lenka and Herbert Kitschelt (2009), 'The Radical Right in Post-communist Europe: Comparative Perspectives on Legacies and Party Competition', *Communist and Post-Communist Studies* 42(4), pp. 459–83.

Campbell, Angus, Philip Converse, W. Miller and Donald Stokes (1960), *The American Voter*, New York: Wiley.

Ceka, Besir (2013), 'The Perils of Political Competition Explaining Participation and Trust in Political Parties in Eastern Europe', *Comparative Political Studies* 46(12), pp. 1610–35.

Chen, Cheng and Rudra Sil (2007), 'Stretching Postcommunism: Diversity, Context, and Comparative Historical Analysis', *Post-Soviet Affairs* 23(4), pp. 275–301.

Colomer, Josep (1995), 'Strategies and Outcomes in Eastern Europe', *Journal of Democracy* 6(2), pp. 74–85.

Ekiert, Grzegorz. 1991. "Democratization Processes in East Central Europe: A Theoretical Reconsideration." *British Journal of Political Science* 21(3), pp. 285–313.

Elster, Jon (ed.) (1996), *The Roundtable Talks and the Breakdown of Communism*, Chicago and London: University of Chicago Press.

Elster, Jon, Claus Offe and Ulrich K. Preuss (1998), *Institutional Design in Post-Communist Societies: Rebuilding the Ship at Sea*, Cambridge: Cambridge University Press.

Evans, Geoffrey (2006), 'The Social Bases of Political Divisions in Post-Communist Eastern Europe', *Annual Review of Sociology* 32, pp. 245–70.

Evans, Geoffrey and Stephen Whitefield (1993), 'Identifying the Bases of Party Competition in Eastern Europe, *British Journal of Political Science* 23(4), pp. 521–48.

Furtak, Robert K. (ed.) (1990), *Elections in Socialist States*, New York and London: Harvester Wheatsheaf.

Gandhi, Jennifer and Ellen Lust-Okar (2009), 'Elections Under Authoritarianism', *Annual Review of Political Science* 12, pp. 403–22.

Gandhi, Jennifer and Adam Przeworski (2007), 'Authoritarian Institutions and the Survival of Autocrats', *Comparative Political Studies* 40(11), pp. 1279–301.

Geddes, Barbara (2006), *Why Parties and Elections in Authoritarian Regimes?*, Presented at the Annual Meeting of the American Political Science Association, Washington, DC.

Goodnow, Regina, Robert G. Moser and Tony Smith (December 2014), 'Ethnicity and Electoral Manipulation in Russia', *Electoral Studies* 36, pp. 15–27.

Grzymała-Busse, Anna (2002), *Redeeming the Communist Past*, Cambridge: Cambridge University Press.

Herron, Erik S. (2009), *Elections and Democracy After Communism?* Basingstoke: Palgrave Macmillan.

Hockenos, P. (1993), *Free to Hate: The Rise of the Right in Post-Communist Eastern Europe*, London: Routledge.

Ishiyama, John T. (1996), 'Electoral Systems Experimentation in the New Eastern Europe: The Single Transferable Vote and the Additional Member System in Estonia and Hungary', *East European Quarterly* 29(4), pp. 487–507.

Kalandadze, Katya and Mitchell A. Orenstein (2009), 'Electoral Protests and Democratization Beyond the Color Revolutions', *Comparative Political Studies* 42(11), pp. 1403–25.

King, Charles (2000), 'Post-Postcommunism: Transition, Comparison, and the End of "Eastern Europe"', *World Politics* 53(1), pp. 143–72.

Kitschelt, Herbert, Zdenka Mansfeldová, Radoslaw Markowski and Gabor Toka (1999), *Post-Communist Party Systems: Competition, Representation and Inter-Party Cooperation*, Cambridge: Cambridge University Press.

Kopecký, Petr and Cas Mudde (eds.) (2003), *Uncivil Society? Contentious Politics in Post-Communist Europe*, New York and London: Routledge.

Kostadinova, Tatiana (2002), 'Do Mixed Electoral Systems Matter?: A Cross-National Analysis of Their Effects in Eastern Europe', *Electoral Studies* 21(1), pp. 23–34.

Kostadinova, Tatiana (2003), 'Voter Turnout Dynamics in Post-Communist Europe', *European Journal of Political Research* 42(6), pp. 741–59.

Kostadinova, Tatiana (2009), 'Abstain or Rebel: Corruption Perceptions and Voting in East European Elections', *Politics & Policy* 37(4), pp. 691–714.

Kubicek, Paul. 1994. "Delegative Democracy in Russia and Ukraine." *Communist and Post-Communist Studies* 27(4), pp. 423–441.

Lane, David and Stephen White (eds.) (2010), *Rethinking the 'Coloured Revolutions'*, New York and London: Routledge.

Lazarsfeld, P. F., B. Berelson and Hazel Gaudet (1948), *The People's Choice: How the Voter Makes Up His Mind in a Presidential Campaign*, New York: Columbia University Press.

Lindberg, Staffan (2009), 'Democratization by Elections: A New Mode of Transition?', in Staffan Lindberg (ed.), *Democratization by Elections: A New Mode of Transition?* Baltimore, MD: Johns Hopkins University Press, pp. 1–21.

Linz, Juan J. and Alfred Stepan (1996), *Problems of Democratic Transition and Consolidation: Southern Europe, Latin America, and Post-Communist Europe*, Baltimore, MD: Johns Hopkins University Press.

Lukinova, Evgeniya, Mikhail Myagkov and Peter C. Ordeshook (2011), 'Metastasised Fraud in Russia's 2008 Presidential Election', *Europe-Asia Studies* 63(4), pp. 603–21.

Lust-Okar, Ellen (2009), 'Legislative Elections in Hegemonic Authoritarian Regimes: Competitive Clientelism and Resistance to Democratization', in Staffan I. Lindberg (ed.), *Democratization by Elections: A New Mode of Transition*, Baltimore, MD: Johns Hopkins University Press, pp 226–45.

March, Luke (2013), *Radical Left Parties in Europe*, London and New York: Routledge.

Miller, William L., Stephen White and Paul Heywood (1998), *Values and Political Change in Post-communist Europe*, Basingstoke: Palgrave-Macmillan.

Moser, Robert G. (1999), 'Electoral Systems and the Number of Parties in Post-Communist States', *World Politics* 51(3), pp. 359–84.

Moser, Robert G. (2001), *Unexpected Outcomes: Electoral Systems, Political Parties, and Representation in Russia*, Pittsburgh, PA: University of Pittsburgh Press.

Mudde, Cas (ed.) (2005), *Racist Extremism in Central and Eastern Europe*, London: Routledge.

Myagkov, Mikhail, Peter C. Ordeshook and Dimitri Shakin (2005), 'Fraud or Fairytales: Russia and Ukraine's Electoral Experience', *Post-Soviet Affairs* 21(2), pp. 91–131.

Myagkov, Mikhail, Peter C. Ordeshook and Dimitri Shakin (2007), 'The Disappearance of Fraud: The Forensics of Ukraine's 2006 Parliamentary Elections', *Post-Soviet Affairs* 23(2), pp. 218–39.

Myagkov, Mikhail, Peter C. Ordeshook and Dimitri Shakin (2009), *The Forensics of Election Fraud: Russia and Ukraine*, Cambridge: Cambridge University Press.

Nikolenyi, Csaba (2011), 'When Electoral Reform Fails: The Stability of Proportional Representation in Post-communist Democracies', *West European Politics* 34(3), pp. 607–25.

Norris, Pippa (2011), *Democratic Deficit: Critical Citizens Revisited*, Cambridge: Cambridge University Press.

O Beacháin, Donnacha and Abel Polese (eds.) (2010), *The Colour Revolutions in the Former Soviet Republic: Successes and Failures*, New York and London: Routledge.

Organization for Security and Cooperation in Europe [OSCE] (2012), *Republic of Belarus Parliamentary Elections 23 September 2012 OSCE/ODIHR Election Observation Mission Final Report*, Warsaw: Organization for Security and Cooperation in Europe.

Pacek, Alexander (1994), 'Macroeconomic Conditions and Electoral Politics in East Central Europe', *American Journal of Political Science* 38(3), pp. 723–44.

Pacek, Alexander C., Grigore Pop-Eleches and Joshua A. Tucker (2009), 'Disenchanted or Discerning: Voter Turnout in Post-Communist Countries', *Journal of Politics* 71(2), pp. 473–91.

Pammett, Jon H. and Joan DeBardeleben (1996), 'The Meaning of Elections in Transitional Democracies: Evidence From Russia and Ukraine', *Electoral Studies* 15(3), pp. 363–81.

Pop-Eleches, Grigore (2007), 'Historical Legacies and Post-Communist Regime Change', *Journal of Politics* 69(4), pp. 908–26.

Pop-Eleches, Grigore (2010), 'Throwing Out the Bums: Protest Voting and Unorthodox Parties After Communism', *World Politics* 62(2), pp. 221–60.

Pravda, Alex (1978), 'Elections in Communist Party States', in Guy Hermet, Richard Rose, and Alain Rouquié (eds.), *Elections Without Choice*, London: Macmillan, pp. 169–95.

Qvortrup, M. (2002), *A Comparative Study of Referendums: Government by the People*, Manchester and New York: Manchester University Press.

Renwick, Alan (2011), 'Electoral Reform in Europe Since 1945', *West European Politics* 34(3), pp. 456–77.

Rose, Richard and William Mishler (1998), 'Negative and Positive Party Identification in Post-Communist Countries', *Electoral Studies* 17(2), pp. 217–34.

Rose, Richard, William Mishler and Christian Haerpfer (1998), *Democracy and Its Alternatives: Understanding Post-communist Societies*, Baltimore, MD: Johns Hopkins University Press.

Schmitter, Philippe C. and Terry Lynn Karl (1994), 'The Conceptual Travels of Transitologists and Consolidologists: How Far to the East Should They Attempt to Go?', *Slavic Review* 53(1), pp. 173–85.

Shvetsova, Olga (1999), 'A Survey of Post-Communist Electoral Institutions, 1990–1998', *Electoral Studies* 18, pp. 397–409.

Simpser, Alberto (2013), *Why Governments and Parties Manipulate Elections: Theory, Practice, and Implications*, Cambridge: Cambridge University Press.

Smyth, Regina, Anton Sobolev and Irina Soboleva (2013), 'A Well-Organized Play', *Problems of Post-Communism* 60(2), pp. 24–39.

Tavits, Margit (2005), 'The Development of Stable Party Support: Electoral Dynamics in Post-Communist Europe', *American Journal of Political Science* 49(2), pp. 283–98.

Tavits, Margit (2008), 'Policy Positions, Issue Importance, and Party Competition in New Democracies', *Comparative Political Studies* 41(1), pp. 48–72.

Tucker, Joshua (2001), 'Economic Conditions and the Vote for Incumbent Parties in Russia, Poland, Hungary, Slovakia and the Czech Republic From 1990–1996', *Post-Soviet Affairs* 17(4), pp. 309–31.

Tucker, Joshua (2006), *Regional Economic Voting: Russia, Poland, Hungary, Slovakia and the Czech Republic, 1990–1999*, Cambridge: Cambridge University Press.

Tucker, Joshua (2007), 'Enough! Electoral Fraud, Collective Action Problems, and Post-Communist Colored Revolutions', *Perspectives on Politics* 5, pp. 534–51.

Turner, Arthur W. (1993), 'Postauthoritarian Elections: Testing Expectations About "First" Elections', *Comparative Political Studies* 26(3), pp. 330–49.

Tverdova, Y. V. and C. J. Anderson (2004), 'Choosing the West? Referendum Choices on EU Membership in East-Central Europe', *Electoral Studies* 23(2), pp. 185–208.

Vachudova, Milada A. 2008. "Tempered by the EU? Political Parties and Party Systems before and after Accession." *Journal of European Public Policy*, 15(6), pp. 861–879.

van der Brug, Wouter, Meindert Fennema and Jean Tillie (2000), 'Anti-immigrant Parties in Europe: Ideological or Protest Vote?', *European Journal of Political Research* 37(1), pp. 77–102.

van der Brug, Wouter, Mark Franklin and Gabor Toka (2008), 'One Electorate or Many? Differences in Party Preference Formation Between New and Established European Democracies', *Electoral Studies* 27(4), pp. 589–600.

Venice Commission (2015), 'Proportional Electoral Systems: The Allocation of Seats Inside the Lists (Open/Closed Lists)', Adopted by the Council for Democratic Elections at Its 50th Meeting (Venice, 19 March 2015) and by the Venice Commission at its 102nd Plenary Session (Venice, 20–21 March 2015).

Way, Lucan (2005), 'Authoritarian State Building and the Sources of Regime Competitiveness in the Fourth Wave: The Cases of Belarus, Moldova, Russia, and Ukraine', *World Politics* 57(2), pp. 231–61.

White, Stephen (2014), *Russia's Authoritarian Elections*, New York and London: Routledge.

Whitefield, Stephen and Robert Rohrschneider (2009), 'Understanding Cleavages in Party Systems Issue Position and Issue Salience in 13 Post-Communist Democracies', *Comparative Political Studies* 42(2), pp. 280–313.

12

VOTERS AND PARTIES IN EASTERN EUROPE

Zsolt Enyedi and Kevin Deegan-Krause

Introduction

Although the voters and parties of Eastern Europe are different from those of Western Europe, the differences are smaller than they were at the beginning of post-communism. Not all of the change came from the East, however. In some ways, the East and West have converged towards new patterns that do not conform to past experiences of political parties in the West or to Western expectations of the East.

In the second half of the twentieth century, an era of political stability in Western Europe coincided with the rise of a new generation of scholars and new research tools to produce an unprecedented number of landmark studies on political parties. As new democracies emerged elsewhere in the 1980s and 1990s, much of this scholarship found its way into Western advice on transitions and became incorporated into what might be termed a "Western standard model" of party politics in consolidated democracies. In line with Western European patterns of the 1960s and 1970s, this model makes a series of implicit prescriptions for the health of democracy, including low to moderate fragmentation of the party system, stable programmatic positions of parties relative to one another, and a nearly fixed roster of major parties and inter-party alliances. The Western standard model also prescribed a strong linkage between parties and voters, built on low voter volatility, party preferences shaped by programmatic offerings on the most salient issues, stable party roots in society, and a relatively coherent socio-demographic identity and group consciousness among party voters (Bartolini and Mair 1990; Kitschelt 1992; Lipset and Rokkan 1967; Mair 1989; Pedersen 1979; Sartori 1976).

In the early 1990s, party politics in Eastern Europe was as far removed from this model as possible. The region's politics featured constant party entry and exit, lack of stability in party attachments, a weak role of standard socio-demographic categories in shaping party choice, continuous emergence of new issues (and new combinations of issues), and fundamental instability in the ideological and demographic profile of most parties.

Today, Eastern Europe appears much less deviant on some of these indicators. Most countries in the region have settled down into competition over relatively recognisable political issues among a reasonable number of political parties, most of which maintain at least some connection to particular demographic groups. In many ways, however, the East has remained quite different from the Western standard model: the issues and issue combinations are often different than in Western Europe; the frequent entry and exit of parties continues as do the unexpected combinations within government coalitions; and electoral behaviour is characterised by the marginal impact of social class and by an amount of vote switching that is unknown in established democracies.[1]

But the lack of frozen party systems with identifiable reservoirs of loyal voters does not mean that there are no other patterns in the relationships between parties and voters. These patterns are worthy of study, not only to understand Eastern Europe for its own sake but also to understand it as a laboratory for party systems across the globe. Indeed, in some ways the weakness and instability of the early years of party politics in Eastern Europe have now become apparent on all continents, including even North America and Western Europe. The jury may still be out on whether these new norms are consistent with long-term democracy as the West has known it, but there can be little doubt that the experiences of Eastern European political systems are useful in answering this question and have developed a relevance far beyond their own region boundaries.

Parties within party systems

Individual parties cannot be understood outside the context of their competitors. In many Eastern European countries, that context evolved relatively quickly into systems with a reasonably compact and relatively stable array of programmatic offerings, but in some countries the roster of parties making those offerings continued to change, sometimes abruptly.

Party system fragmentation: towards a happy medium

The number and relative sizes of political parties are the most visible and observable aspects of party systems. In the standard model, systems raise concerns when the number of effective parties falls below two or rises above five or six. After the collapse of communism, the number and relative sizes of political parties changed rapidly. In some cases, the binary oppositions between Communist Party successors and democratic initiatives shattered into fragments, but even in the most extreme cases the number of viable competitors soon returned to a reasonable number. As Figure 12.1 shows, by the late 1990s the mean number of parties had declined to levels indistinguishable from those of Western Europe, both hovering around 4.0. In the late 2000s, Eastern European levels fell narrowly below those of Western Europe, whose party system sizes have shown a slight upward trend.

There is also a degree of differentiation *within* Eastern Europe. Among the Eastern European countries that acceded to the European Union in 2004 – those in the Baltics and Central Europe – party system sizes were a full point higher (among the Baltic states it was higher still). In most of the other countries in the region, however, the fragmentation levels were lower. Ethnic complexity clearly plays a role in explaining some cases of fragmentation – Bosnia and Herzegovina may be better understood as assembly of two or three formally distinct party systems – and some studies suggest that electoral rules (especially high electoral thresholds) play a discernible role (Casal Bértoa 2013; Rashkova 2014). Nevertheless, the range of values within the sub-region and the significant changes within countries over time, some rising and some falling, resist easy explanation based purely on historic traditions or socio-economic development.

Although measures of the effective number of parties do adjust for party weight, it is also necessary to look at the *relative sizes* of parties. Single-party majorities were relatively rare in the region, and except in Montenegro in the 2000s and Hungary in the 2010s (and Russia during a period when the country had arguably ceased being a democracy), these rarely endured beyond a single term. Although a single party's possession of a parliamentary majority was

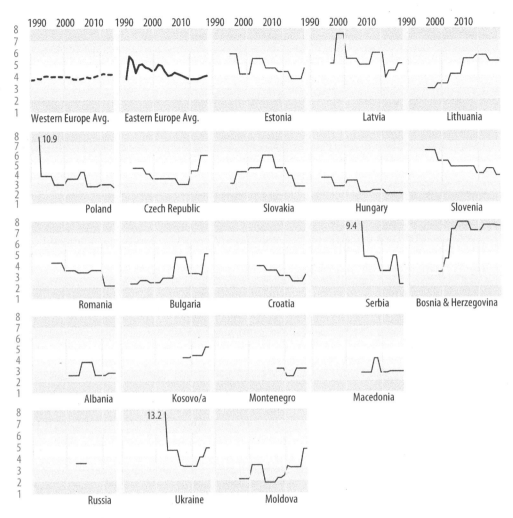

Figure 12.1 Effective number of parliamentary parties in Eastern and Central Europe over time

Source: Casal Bértoa (2016) for all countries except Bosnia and Herzegovina; Gallagher (2015) for Bosnia and Herzegovina.

neither a necessary condition for weakened democracy (Slovakia in the mid-1990s) nor a sufficient condition (Hungary, Bulgaria, and Lithuania during the mid-1990's), one party-dominated governments often undermined institutional accountability, particularly in countries such as Montenegro, Russia, and post-2010 Hungary.

Party system ideological patterns: new configurations and different dimensions

Ideology and programme played a consistent role in shaping the positions of and interactions within Eastern European party systems, though not to the same extent or in the same way as in the West. In the early 1990s, many scholars saw the political party oppositions in the region as a tabula rasa that was wide open to many potential forms of competition, but even these authors did not expect the openness to endure forever (Elster, Offe and Preuss 1998). Subsequent scholarship (Evans and Whitefield 1993, 2000; Kitschelt, Mansfeldová, Markowski and Tóka 1999; Whitefield 2002; Tavits 2008; Rohrschneider and Whitefield 2012) from a wide range of methods – expert studies, mass surveys, and the analyses of party manifestos, as well as elite surveys, content analysis of mass media, and scrutiny of parliamentary roll call records and legislative debates – has produced considerable agreement concerning the fundamental nature and degree of Eastern Europe's ideological divides.

While some of these studies indicate that Eastern European parties have less clearly defined policy profiles than their Western counterparts (Schmitt, van der Eijk and Wessels 2013; Wessels and Schmitt 2012), two large-scale expert surveys covering EU member states in the region nevertheless found similar (and similarly coherent) results regarding the main dimensions of competition. In spite of the fact that the strong push towards economic liberalisation after the collapse of communism limited parties' ability to take clear economic positions (Innes 2002; Wessels and Klingemann 2006), factor analysis of both expert surveys detected a strong dimension of competition regarding economic distribution and the role of the state in the economy (this divide appears in particularly robust form in the Czech Republic, Slovakia, Bulgaria, and Lithuania). In most countries, an additional factor emerged on questions of cultural norms and lifestyle.[2] The cultural conflicts in the region differ in important ways from those in the West with more emphasis on conflict over nation, religious norms, and authoritarian traditional practices, and less on post-materialist questions of environment, gender, and sexuality.

An even more significant difference is the way in which these two dimensions align. As Figure 12.2 indicates, Western European parties tend to combine free-market attitudes with cultural conservatism, whereas a preference for government intervention in the economy in Eastern Europe tends to coincide with a more restrictive view of cultural freedoms, stronger opposition to European integration, and more restrictive attitudes towards immigration (Marks, Hooghe, Nelson, and Edwards 2006; Rohrschneider and Whitefield 2009, 2012; Kitschelt 1992; Vachudova and Hooghe 2009; Bustikova and Kitschelt 2009). Eastern Europe also exhibits more variation than the West in the specific country patterns. Bakker, Jolly and Polk (2012) argue that unlike other countries in the region, Slovenia, Estonia, and Latvia more closely resemble the Western pattern combining markets and conservatism, and that Slovakia shows no alignment between the two dimensions.

While East and West can be analysed through the lens of the same fundamental ideological dimensions, left-right orientation is less helpful for understanding policy positions in the East, largely because the economic and the cultural dimensions diverge. Consequently, the RILE index used to analyse party programmes produce less valid results in the East (Mölder 2013).

There is also a discrepancy between the content of the ideological orientations and the labels used to denote political actors. Parties that elsewhere would claim to be libertarian or classical liberal may accept in Eastern Europe the "left-wing" label due to their relatively cosmopolitan and modernist approach to family values or religious norms. In the most Eastern part of the region, on the other hand, a reference to socialism or communism in the name or ideology of a party often implies an anti-globalisation and anti-Western approach, the suspicion of capitalist market economy and organisational links with post-communist political forces. The region cannot even rely on the customary association between "left" and "change" since its own *ancien régime* had a self-proclaimed leftist ideology. Furthermore, many countries in the region have subsequently undergone repeated mini-regime changes, obscuring the locus of change itself.

The profile of regional patterns is further complicated by the fact that even these broadly formulated dimensions do not address all of the significant issue positions that shape politics

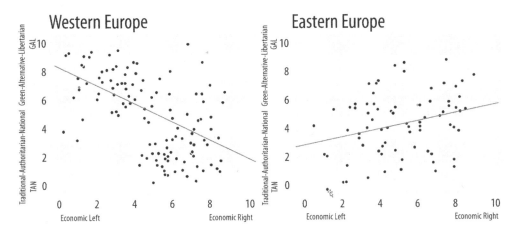

Figure 12.2 Positions of political parties on economic and cultural questions in Eastern and Western Europe according to expert surveys, 2006

Source: Rovny and Edwards (2012, 64).

in specific countries of the region. At least four other dimensions merit discussion, though for different reasons:

- *Communism*. Observers expected competition related to the communist regime to fade away after the regime change, but in fact it continues to divide parties, even though no significant political actors advocate the restoration of the communist regime. Nor does this issue dimension simply replicate the dimensions discussed earlier; anti-communism may focus on both moral and religious aspects and on economic ones, but it can also focus on only one or the other and can shift its emphasis depending on circumstances.

- *Ethnicity and nationalism*. Ethnic differences obey a logic different from questions about economic or cultural regulation. In countries where distinct ethnic groups are fairly evenly matched in size, such as Bosnia and Herzegovina or Ukraine, these issues quickly emerge to dominate political competition, but these countries are unfortunately absent from most cross-regional studies which offer systematic comparative data on ethnic competition. In better covered countries, such as Bulgaria, Romania, and Slovakia, as well as the Baltics, ethno-linguistic minorities tend to constitute a smaller fraction of the voting population. These latter countries, furthermore, often experience a two-level effect that does not register easily: the majority-minority opposition is complemented by a more subtle but equal conflict that occurs *among* majority political representatives who may differ among themselves in a more symmetric conflict over how to deal with the minority. These intertwined dimensions interact in complex ways with other issues. In many countries where minorities originate from the centre of a collapsed communist federation (Soviet Union and Yugoslavia), parties supporting the minority ethnic group tend to have a statist orientation; the opposite pattern tends to prevail where the origin of the minority is different (Rovny 2015). Ethnic parties also differ in their availability for forming coalitions. In some countries in the region such as Slovakia, Bulgaria, and Romania, ethnic minority parties have emerged as pro–status quo forces which take centrist positions on nearly all issues except minority rights questions and promote minority interests by a willingness to bargain in other areas. The opposite pattern prevails in countries such as Latvia and Montenegro, where a large part of the legislature is excluded from the government-building process due to its association with the identities and interests of minorities and of large, neighbouring states (Russia and Serbia, respectively).

- *Democracy.* In many Eastern European countries, competition has emerged between parties regarding their willingness to set aside the basic principles of democratic competition in the interest of a higher goal (most often a national or cultural one), though these differences are often obscured by both sides claiming that their position is the only truly democratic one. Threats to the democratic systems have coincided with these kinds of alignments: Croatia under Tudjman, Yugoslavia under Milošević, and Slovakia under Mečiar in the 1990s, and Hungary under Orbán in the 2010s (Haughton 2005; Fisher 2006). Romania, Macedonia, Moldova, Montenegro, Croatia, and Bulgaria have also occasionally evoked concern in this regard, as has Slovakia under Fico and Poland under Kaczyński. Eastern Europe has also produced a significant number of parties (such as People's Party–Our Slovakia in Slovakia, Jobbik in Hungary, Ataka in Bulgaria, and the League of Polish Families in Poland) that reject liberal democracy in an even more explicit and unequivocal way than do most radical left-wing or right-wing parties in Western Europe, though these parties have been actively excluded from participation in government for the most part.

- *Corruption.* The question of corruption dominates political debate in many Eastern European countries but poses a difficult classification challenge, because it seems to lack ideological or programmatic characteristics. Since every party claims to oppose corruption, the question seems to fall in the category of "valence" issues related to effectiveness and trustworthiness, but corruption actually has a systemic character that makes it worthy of consideration as a programmatic conflict in its own right. The difference among parties emerges not necessarily in the specific anti-corruption policies, but rather in the salience of those policies for party campaigns and the degree to which leaders can point to systematic reasons for doubting the claims of the incumbents. Parties in Eastern Europe have had an advantage in this regard, since the claim that the ruling parties are corrupt has had (until recently at least) greater plausibility among Eastern than Western voters. Given the widespread corruption-related frustration in the electorate, parties such as the Party of National Resurrection in Lithuania, the Alliance of Dissatisfied Citizens in the Czech Republic, Ordinary People in Slovakia, the Party of Miro Cerar in Slovenia, and Bridge in Croatia may not feel any need to take extreme positions on questions other than corruption and may in fact adopt centrist positions on the other dimensions.

The issue dimensions listed can thoroughly reshape a country's politics when they emerge in parallel with other configurations described earlier. The ethnic dimension has shaped political competition, particularly in Estonia, Latvia, Slovakia, Bulgaria, Macedonia, and Bosnia and Herzegovina, and the corruption dimension has recently produced major shifts in the governing balance of Czech Republic and Slovenia. The coincidence of a political divide over democracy and a single-party majority (or near-majority), coupled with high polarisation and populist party strategies, has periodically affected the democratic trajectory in Slovakia, Albania, Montenegro, Romania, Croatia, and Macedonia, and most recently in Hungary.

Party system change: ongoing instability of party system components

Responses to corruption also relate closely to perhaps the most noteworthy characteristic of Eastern European political parties: the degree of institutional change. From the post-communist

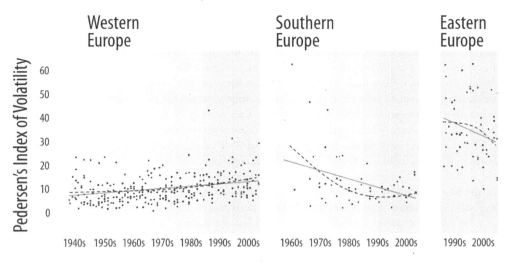

Figure 12.3   Dassonneville and Hooghe findings regarding Pedersen Index in parliamentary elections in Western, Southern, and Eastern Europe adapted to a single horizontal and vertical scale

Source: Dassonneville and Hooghe (2011, 18, 21, 23).

decade to today, observers have expressed wonder and concern at the high degree of electoral volatility in the region and the proliferation of party splits, mergers, deaths, and births (Tóka 1998; Tavits 2008; Sikk 2012).

Recent work by Dassonneville and Hooghe (2011, reprinted here in Figure 12.3) and Ersson (2012) confirms numerous other studies showing high rates of volatility in Central and Eastern Europe, a level more than three times higher than in Western Europe and twice as high as the average rate in the newer democracies of Southern Europe. Indeed, even the lowest volatility rates in the Eastern and Central European region are higher than all but the highest volatility rates in Western Europe. Dassonneville and Hooghe (2011) and Powell and Tucker (2013) find a decreasing trend for the first decade of the 2000s, but more recent results in many countries (including spectacularly high volatility in elections in Slovenia and the Czech Republic) point to a return to higher levels of volatility in the 2010s.

Of course, the volatility itself is inextricably bound both to party system offerings and voter preferences. Recent nuanced analyses of volatility look as closely as possible into the different kinds of change including exchange of voters among existing parties and the party system change related to party entries and exits. Measures of the role of new parties in volatility (Powell and Tucker 2013) and the average age of parties in the party system (Haughton and Deegan-Krause 2015) show consistent patterns: the occasional breakthroughs of new parties at the expense of older ones, the constant churn among new parties frequently replaced by newer parties, and the relatively stable performance of more established parties. While in the West the shifts among established parties are four times more common than those related to party entry and exit, in Eastern Europe the entry of new parties and departure of existing ones produces almost the same amount of change as the shift of preferences within the universe of established parties (Mainwaring, Gervasoni and España 2016).

The most relevant reasons for the overall instability are the ones that were identified already at the beginning of the democratic era: fragile organisational structures, weak (or non-existent) inherited party loyalties, the shallow embeddedness of parties in civic organisations, media-oriented (and now social media–oriented) politics, and fuzzy class identities. Some parties were successful in building a reliable clientele. Social and organisational rootedness can characterise both niche (ethnic, religious, pensioner, or peasant) and more mainstream parties such as the Czech Republic's Social Democrats, Bulgaria's and Romania's Socialists, Slovenia's Democrats, or Hungary's Young Democrats. Even many of these parties, however, are in constant danger of being squeezed or entirely overrun by new rivals that lack their deep roots but are also free from the deep antipathies to these parties that have developed over time among some voters. Disappointment with economic performance and corruption scandals have triggered the collapse of many major parties in the region and new parties have proven capable of taking advantage of loose, flexible structures, celebrity candidates, fuzzy identities, and corruption-related grievances to gain election. Of course, these characteristics favour party emergence more than sustainability, and only a few of the newer parties have managed to stabilise themselves by building party organisation, offering solid governmental performance, building networks of auxiliary organisations, and rallying around a single charismatic leader (though this last mechanism offers mixed blessings since the party's long-term survival becomes overly dependent on one person).

Change in party system components also concerns the coalitional units that parties create together and the positional relationships that parties hold in relationship to one another. Coalition governments are still the most common path to power in both Eastern and Western Europe (Bågenholm, Deegan-Krause and Weeks 2015), and the nature of coalition interaction is critical for understanding the political party systems in both regions. Building on the "party system closure" approach of Mair (1997), recent research (Casal Bértoa 2013; Enyedi and Casal Bértoa 2013) finds that the institutionalisation of coalition patterns is lower in Eastern Europe than in the West, due to the frequency of changes in coalition partners and relative ease with which newcomers participate in the government-building process. At the same time, the fact that some Eastern European countries (Albania, Montenegro, Hungary, Georgia, and Macedonia) have developed relatively closed systems indicates that it may actually be easier for parties to close ranks in the governmental arena than to stabilise their electorates (Enyedi 2016).

Voters in party systems

The relationship between voters and parties has three tightly interrelated but conceptually distinct aspects: the relationship of voters' choices to their past preferences, their current political attitudes, and their socio-demographic positions.

Voter loyalty: stable and unstable electorates

Although party entry and exit, discussed earlier, are a primary source of electoral volatility in Eastern Europe, even shifts among existing parties are several times more common than in the West (Mainwaring et al. 2016). Party identification is also a less powerful predictor of electoral choice (Schmitt and Scheuer 2012). In line with these weaknesses of structural anchors, Roberts (2008) found that voters in Eastern Europe are exceptionally sensitive to variations in economic results. The resulting "hyper-accountability" leads them to punishing incumbents, even if it means giving up on parties they once supported.

The aforementioned focus on corruption issues (especially in the region's EU member states) also undermines habitual voting because new parties in power are unlikely to maintain a reputation for purity. The pattern of endorsing outsiders can be a self-reinforcing one and create the possibility of voters who are not merely de-aligned but who are actually unalignable, habituated not to a stable party choice but to a stable preference for doing something different in each election. Exit polls give some evidence for the paradoxical emergence of a relatively stable core of unstable voters who alternate between not voting, voting for new parties, and voting for even newer parties (Haughton and Deegan-Krause 2015). At the same time, surveys also give evidence that next to segments characterised by habitual volatility, there are other groups which remain committed over time to one preferred party, and some new parties even manage to convert their novelty-seeking electorates into loyalists.

At the same time, where partisan loyalty does exist, it is not without its drawbacks. While partisanship in the West tends to lead to satisfaction with democracy and thereby play an integrative role, in the East this beneficial mechanism is overshadowed by the potential of party identification to facilitate ideological radicalism (Enyedi and Todosijević 2009).

While there is less clear survey evidence from the Western Balkans and the former Soviet Union, the electorally fluid segment of the voting population in those regions of Eastern Europe appears to be considerably smaller than in the EU member states. Some of this quiescence may be due to the stronger role of socio-demographic identity in voting, but much of the immobility can be explained by a smaller range of party choices and the lack of plausible newcomer parties which in turn result from established parties' greater control of institutional rules and clientelist resources.

Voter attitudes: stable issue preferences in unstable systems

As a consequence of the factors considered earlier, electoral behaviour is more idiosyncratic in Eastern Europe than in the West (Van der Brug, Franklin, Popescu and Tóka 2009), and voters have more difficulty identifying the position of parties (Kritzinger and McElroy 2012). This difference, while relatively minor, has significant effects, especially because lack of clarity in the programmatic profile of parties often advantages the most radical forces, the only ones that appear to voters as transparent and predictable (Ezrow, Tavits and Homola 2014). At the same time, and in spite of the often changing and unorthodox character of the individual parties, the quality of party-based representation (understood as the similarity of electorates and parties in terms of major ideological dimensions) is not radically lower than in the West. The positions of the region's voters map quite closely onto the positions of the parties they voted for. On some topics, such as European integration, there is even more issue voting in East Central Europe than in the West (De Vries and Tillman 2011). It seems that the historical trajectory of the East, which triggered a focus on cultural matters and on sovereignty-related concerns, prepared the public well for the twenty-first century's values-based conflicts, at least on topics of globalisation and European integration.

Voter demographics: ethnicity, religion, and location instead of class

To the extent that the party systems of Eastern and Central Europe demonstrate a reasonably strong and moderately regular political competition on economic and cultural questions, it is possible to ask how closely those conflicts link social class, denomination, religiosity, age, and other socio-demographic characteristics. Most studies find a relatively small but still statistically significant relationship between these characteristics, policy preferences (such as redistribution or cultural norms), and party choice. Knutsen's (2013) study, for example, detects links between party choice and religious denomination, church attendance, rural residence, and certain measures of class (but not the Alford Index of "working class versus all others"). Ecological and survey-based studies suggest that while the party systems among EU members in the East have weaker roots than those of Western Europe as a whole, they are more strongly linked to religion, urban-rural divide, or class than in Southern Europe.

Ethnicity plays a particularly strong role in shaping political choice (Whitefield 2002). Almost without exception, in the swathe of territory stretching from Estonia to Macedonia, members of ethnolinguistic minority communities share similar opinions on group-salient political questions and vote for particular minority ethnic parties on the basis of identity and attitudes. Religiosity also has an impact but mainly in predominantly Roman Catholic societies such as Poland, Hungary, Slovenia, and Croatia; in the Protestant countries of the Baltics and many Orthodox countries in the former Soviet Union and southern Balkans, religion has less structuring power.

Across the region, citizens with geographical locations and skills that facilitate integration into global markets or into the supranational administrative structures turned out to be the winners of market reforms, globalisation, and the post-communist transition, while low-educated, blue-collar, and administrative workers, together with the employees of non-competitive sectors and the members of the Roma minority, ended up as the losers. And yet, few parties unequivocally represent the winners' or the losers' side. In spite of the rapid increase of social inequalities, the transition has not led to the crystallisation of robust class-based identities, at least not those familiar to Western European modes of analysis. The most relevant socio-political units are not the working class subcultures or the self-conscious middle-class milieux. The level of education and the degree of connection to large cities, and thereby to the global economy, seems more important to many voters than actual income or any sense of class solidarity. The relative importance of rural-urban divisions also seems to be more embedded in different lifestyles and cultural sensitivities than in organised and economy-focused interest representation.

The relatively low explained variance of social structure on electoral choices found in most studies may also be due to the fact that existing methods simply fail to tap the deeper or less easily quantifiable structures that might actually explain voter behaviour. A more detailed classification of occupational groups (Kitschelt and Rehm 2014) or the integration of family histories may bring us closer to understanding electoral behaviour. The post-communist divide is, for example, largely based on family memories and on the related diverging interpretations of history. Similarly, qualitative evidence suggests that family- or community-rooted clientelist networks play a substantial role in shaping party choice. But such factors have little chance to show up in standard surveys.

Cleavages that divide large groups that recognise their internal common interests and are closed off from other groups – the model for Lipset and Rokkan (1967) and Bartolini and Mair (1990) – are rare in Eastern Europe. Applying such high standards for "cleavage" would lead us to ignore many of the region's most important divisions, while relaxing the expectations of group closure and group symmetry allows closer consideration of the broader array of divisions that shape party politics. Figure 12.4 presents this array in graphic form. The figure presents deep cleavages (in the upper left) but also examples that depart from this model in terms of symmetry (top to bottom) or closure (left to right). The greatest degree of closure in the region – deep divides between rival groups and their party representatives – appears on ethnic questions. The few cases in this category that are relatively symmetrical, such as Ukraine and Bosnia and Herzegovina, have proven difficult to reconcile within the institutions of a single state (and many of the new states of the region are the result of previously internal cleavages that could not be accommodated within common borders). More common are the less symmetrical but high-closure circles of minority ethnic populations such as Russians in Latvia and Estonia and Albanians in Macedonia, along with smaller but still significant groups of Hungarians in Romania and Slovakia, as well as Turks in Bulgaria. The asymmetry may sometimes keep the minority's political parties and its issues on the margins of political life, but such parties nevertheless frequently shape coalition formation and the resulting policy options. Non-ethnic cultural conflicts, particularly religious ones in Roman Catholic countries, tend to occupy a middle ground that ranges from

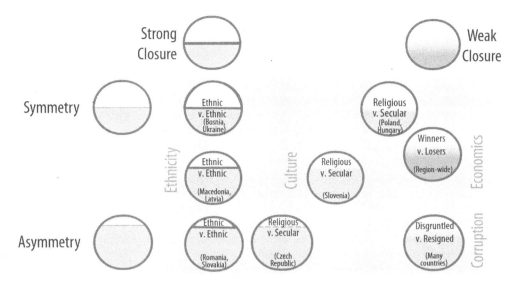

Figure 12.4   Examples of Eastern and Central European political divides according to degree of symmetry and closure

Source: Adapted from Deegan-Krause (2013, 831).

the Czech Republic's small and relatively devout religious community with its own Christian Democratic party to Poland's full-scale culture clash with multiple gradations between (and sometimes within) parties.

As indicated earlier, the differences between transition winners and losers, while universal within the region (right hand side of the graph), is rarely well articulated, partly because demographic differences are not tightly connected to values and party choice. The lower right quadrant in Figure 12.4 is populated by amorphous concerns such as corruption, which do not necessarily divide the population into equal shares or develop deeper roots. However, the lack of closure and symmetry does not make such conflicts irrelevant, at least in instances when, as in the case of the Baltics in the 2000s or Slovenia and the Czech Republic in the 2010s, these generate parties that use such issues to gain election victories and shape the course of government and society.

Conclusion: Eastern European party systems, voters and the future of parties everywhere

Readers from 1989 might, at first glance, find little interest in a chapter from the future that emphasises East-West convergence. Indeed, most observers in the late 1980s and early 1990s expected that many Eastern European party systems and voters would eventually come to look more like their Western counterparts. The same readers, however, would likely be shocked at the specific *ways* in which the two halves of the continent have moved closer together: the declining relevance of traditional class divides (eroded in the West, weakly established in the East), the emergence of sovereignty and corruption as major issues that can reshape entire party systems, and the rise of a large societal segment that appears not only unanchored but perhaps even unanchorable.

Readers from the future, by contrast, might be surprised that this chapter still uses Western Europe as the appropriate baseline for comparison. Of course, the West's long research legacy along with historical connections and proximity make it an obvious reference point and encourage cross-regional research projects, but in many ways it is the East that more closely resembles party system and voter developments across the rest of the globe. In two decades of quantitative and qualitative research across twenty countries, scholarship on Eastern Europe has done more than simply demonstrate the similarities and differences between East and West. It has gone further to produce new insights and conceptual tools that have enriched the study of parties by clarifying phenomena that have not (yet) been integrated into models of party systems and voting behavior. In particular, scholarship on Eastern European parties has forced the attention to new kinds of social groups, and new (kinds of) issues that do not fit comfortably into the programmatic, clientelist, or charismatic categories. Furthermore, scholarship about Eastern Europe that integrates social structures, voter demands, and the supply side of party competition (Kreuzer and Pettai 2004; Deegan-Krause and Enyedi 2010; Sikk 2012; Raymond 2014) has demonstrated not only that party systems can exhibit a relatively autonomous logic but also that political parties can actively and purposefully shape social dynamics.

In conjunction with the literature on Latin America, published research on Eastern European political parties has also helped to refine the concept of institutionalisation, revealing differences between institutionalisation at the party-level and at the party-system level, and demonstrating that electoral volatility does not always serve as a stable proxy for institutionalisation. Turbulence in Eastern Europe's party politics has also produced new tools that can better account for splits and mergers, for changes of name, personnel and programme, and for the differences between volatility that is intra-system or extra-system and mass-driven or elite-driven (Rose and Munro 2003; Powell and Tucker 2013). Finally, research on politics in Eastern Europe also reminds us of the twin existence of the Scylla and Charybdis of party system institutionalisation: rapid party system and voter change can weaken the quality of governance and democracy, but so can the combination of institutionalisation with polarisation, and the entrenchment of parties that are willing to manipulate rules for their own benefit.

The study of the parties and voters in Eastern Europe does not yet possess a well-integrated narrative comparable to the one provided by Lipset and Rokkan and others for Western Europe. Nor is it as compartmentalised into various sub-fields as the US electoral behaviour literature. Developing a homogeneous framework or achieving American-style specialisation are neither realistic nor attractive goals, but the strengths of these approaches can help improve our understanding of Eastern Europe, especially if they reflect the existing strengths of scholarship on the region including sensitivity to historical and cultural differences, and acute awareness of the key role played by political actors. The impossibility of producing a single homogeneous framework for all countries in the region should not, on the other hand, hold back from theorising about the most fundamental conflict lines that divide the societies. These conflicts may be overshadowed by repeated waves of protest vote, fuelled by cycles of disillusionment and poor economic performance, but even these reactions will be socially and culturally conditioned. Understanding the interaction between these structures and the choices made by political actors will require more and better information. Research in the region will benefit from finer-grained research on occupational groups, education specialisations, and other demographic categories; the assembly of richer time series of attitudinal data and the gathering where possible of panel data; the integration of party manifesto data with data on campaign materials, speeches, and elite interviews; and the linkage of candidates, elite surveys, and mass surveys. These efforts may never produce an "Eastern standard model", but they will shed light on the most important political questions in a region which, it seems, is ever more typical of the world as a whole.

Notes

1 This description does not apply to Russia, where the concentration of power in the executive office and the intimate links between politicians and business groups relegate parties to the fringes of political life (Hale 2007).
2 Rohrschneider and Whitefield (2012) find the cultural conflict to be considerably weaker in Eastern Europe than in Western Europe, while the Chapel Hill Expert Survey detects a relatively strong and independent cultural dimension.

References

Bågenholm, A., K. Deegan-Krause, and L. Weeks. (2015). Political Data in 2014. *European Journal of Political Research Political Data Yearbook*, 54(1): 1–18.

Bakker, R., S. Jolly, and J. Polk. (2012). Complexity in the European Party Space: Exploring Dimensionality With Experts. *European Union Politics*, 13(2): 219–245.

Bartolini, S. and P. Mair. (1990). *Identity, Competition, and Electoral Availability: The Stabilisation of European Electorates 1885–1985.* Cambridge: Cambridge University Press.

Bustikova, L. and H. Kitschelt. (2009). The Radical Right in Post-communist Europe. Comparative Perspectives on Party Competition. *Communist and Post-Communist Studies*, 42(4): 459–483.

Casal Bértoa, F. (2013). Post-communist Politics: On the Divergence (and/or Convergence) of East and West. *Government and Opposition*, 48(3): 398–433.

Casal Bértoa, F. (2016). *Who Governs in Europe and Beyond.* Database. Available at: whogoverns.eu

Dassonneville, R. and M. Hooghe. (2011). *Mapping Electoral Volatility in Europe. An Analysis of Trends in Electoral Volatility in European Democracies Since 1945.* Paper presented at the 1st European Conference on Comparative Electoral Research, Sofia (Bulgaria).

Deegan-Krause, K. (2013). Full and Partial Cleavages. In *The Handbook of Political Change in Eastern Europe.* Eds. Sten Berglund, Terje Knutsen, Joakim Ekman, and Kevin Deegan-Krause. Cheltenham: Edward Elgar: 35–50.

Deegan-Krause, K. and Z. Enyedi. (2010). Agency and the Structure of Party Competition. *West European Politics*, 33(3): 686–710.

De Vries, C. E. and E. R. Tillman. (2011). European Union Issue Voting in East and West Europe: The Role of Political Context. *Comparative European Politics*, 9(1): 1–17.

Elster, J., C. Offe, and U. K. Preuss. (1998). *Institutional Design in Post-Communist Societies: Rebuilding the Ship at Sea.* Cambridge: Cambridge University Press.

Enyedi, Z. (2016). Populist Polarization and Party System Institutionalization: The Role of Party Politics in De-Democratization. *Problems of Post-Communism*, 63(4): 210–220.

Enyedi, Z. and F. Casal Bértoa. (2013). *Elite and Mass Dynamics: The East Central European Example.* Paper presented at the 41st ECPR Joint Sessions of Workshops in Mainz, 11–16 March.

Enyedi, Z. and B. Todosijević. (2009). Adversarial Politics, Civic Virtues and Party Identification in Eastern and Western Europe. In *Political Parties and Partisanship: Social Identities and Individual Attitudes.* Eds. John Bartle and Paolo Bellucci. London: Routledge: 246–284.

Ersson, S. (2012). *Electoral Volatility in Europe: Assessments and Potential Explanations for Estimate Differences.* 2012 Elections, Public Opinion and Parties (EPOP) Conference. Oxford University, September 7–9.

Evans, G. A. and S. Whitefield. (1993). Identifying the Bases of Party Competition in Eastern Europe. *British Journal of Political Science*, 23(4): 521–548.

Evans, G. A. and S. Whitefield. (2000). Explaining the Formation of Electoral Cleavages in Post-Communist Democracies. In *Elections in Central and Eastern Europe: The First Wave.* Eds. Hans-Dieter Klingemann, Ekkehard Mochman, and Kenneth Newton. Berlin, Germany: Sigma.

Ezrow, L., M. Tavits, and J. Homola. (2014). Voter Polarization, Strength of Partisanship, and Support for Extremist Parties. *Comparative Political Studies*, 47(11): 1558–1583.

Fisher, S. (2006). *Political Change in Post-Communist Slovakia and Croatia.* New York: Palgrave Macmillan.

Gallagher, M. (2015). *Election Indices Dataset.* Available at: www.tcd.ie/Political_Science/staff/michael_gallagher/ElSystems/index.php

Hale, H. (2007). *Why Not Parties in Russia? Democracy, Federalism, and the State.* Cambridge: Cambridge University Press.

Haughton, T. (2005). *Constraints and Opportunities of Leadership in Post-communist Europe.* Aldershot: Ashgate.

Haughton, T. and K. Deegan-Krause. (February 6, 2015). Hurricane Season: Systems of Instability in Central and East European Party Politics. *East European Politics and Society*, 29(1), 61–80.

Innes, A. (2002). Party Competition in Post-communist Europe: The Great Electoral Lottery. *Comparative Politics*, 35(1): 85–104.

Kitschelt, H. (1992). The Formation of Party Systems in East Central Europe. *Politics & Society*, 20(1): 7–50.

Kitschelt, H., Z. Mansfeldová, R. Markowski, and G. Tóka. (1999). *Post-Communist Party Systems: Competition, Representation and Inter-Party Cooperation*. New York: Cambridge University Press.

Kitschelt, H., and P. Rehm. (2014). Occupations as a Site of Political Preference Formation. *Comparative Political Studies*, 47(12): 1670–1706.

Knutsen, O. (2013). Structural Determinants of Party Choice: The Changing Impact of Socio-Structure Variables on Party Choice in Comparative Perspective. In *Party Governance and Party Democracy*. Eds. W. Müller and H. M. Narud. New York: Springer: 175–204.

Kreuzer, M., and V. Pettai. (2004). Political Parties and the Study of Political Development: New Insights From the Postcommunist Democracies. *World Politics*, 56(4): 608–633.

Kritzinger, S. and G. McElroy. (2012). Meaningful Choices? Voter Perceptions of Party Positions in European Elections. In *An Audit of Democracy in the European Union*, Eds. S. A. Banducci, M. Franklin, H. Giebler, S. Hobolt, M. Marsh, W. Van Der Brug, and C. Van der Eijk, Florence: European University Institute: 169–192.

Lipset, S. M., and S. Rokkan. (1967). Cleavage Structures, Party Systems, and Voter Alignments: An Introduction. In *Party Systems and Voter Alignments: Cross-National Perspectives*. Eds. S. M. Lipset and S. Rokkan. New York: Free Press.

Mainwaring, S., P. Gervasoni, and A. España. (2016). Extra – And Within-system Electoral Volatility. *Party Politics*. Forthcoming.

Mair, P. (1989). Continuity, Change and the Vulnerability of Party. *West European Politics*, 12(4): 169–187.

Mair, P. (1997). *Party System Change: Approaches and Interpretations*. Oxford: Clarendon Press.

Marks, G., L. Hooghe, M. Nelson, and E. Edwards. (2006). Party Competition and European Integration in East and West: Different Structure, Same Causality. *Comparative Political Studies*, 39(2): 155–175.

Mölder, M. (2013). The Validity of the RILE Left – Right Index as a Measure of Party Policy. *Party Politics*, 22(1): 37–48.

Pedersen, M. (1979). The Dynamics of European Party Systems: Changing Patterns of Electoral Volatility. *European Journal of Political Research*, 7(1): 1475–6765.

Powell, E. N. and J. Tucker. (2013). Revisiting Electoral Volatility in Post-Communist Countries: New Data, New Results and New Approaches. *British Journal of Political Science*, 44(1): 123–147.

Rashkova, E. R. (2014). Learning the Game: Explaining Party System Convergence in European Democracies. *Political Studies*, 62(4): 804–823.

Raymond, C. (2014). Party Agency and the Religious – Secular Cleavage in Post-Communist Countries: The Case of Romania. *Political Studies*, 62(2): 292–308.

Roberts, A. (2008). Hyperaccountability: Economic Voting in Eastern Europe. *Electoral Studies*, 27(3): 533–546.

Rohrschneider, R. and S. Whitefield. (2009). Understanding Divisions in Party Systems: Issue Position and Issue Salience in 13 Post-Communist Democracies. *Comparative Political Studies*, 42(2): 280–313.

Rohrschneider, R. and S. Whitefield. (2012). *The Strain of Representation: How Parties Represent Diverse Voters in Western and Eastern Europe*. Oxford: Oxford University Press.

Rose, R. and N. Munro. (2003). *Elections and Parties in New European Democracies*. Glasgow: CQ Press.

Rovny, J. (2015). Party Competition Structure in Eastern Europe: Aggregate Uniformity Versus Idiosyncratic Diversity? *East European Politics & Societies*, 29(1): 40–60.

Rovny, J. and E. Edwards. (2012). Struggle Over Dimensionality: Party Competition in Western and Eastern Europe. *East European Politics & Societies*, 26(1): 56–74.

Sartori, G. (1976). *Parties and Party Systems: A Framework for Analysis*. Cambridge: Cambridge University Press.

Schmitt, H. and A. Scheuer. (2012). Wahlen und Parteien. In *Metamorphosen*. Eds. Silke Keil and Jan van Deth. Baden-Baden: Nomos: 209–236.

Schmitt, H., C. van der Eijk, and B. Wessels. (2013). Parties, Candidates and Voters in the 2009 Election to the European Parliament. In *An Audit of Democracy in the European Union*. Eds. Susan Banducci et al. Florence: European University Institute: 221–240.

Sikk, A. (2012). Newness as a Winning Formula for New Political Parties. *Party Politics*, 18(4): 465–486.

Tavits, M. (2008). On the Linkage Between Electoral Volatility and Party System Instability in Central and Eastern Europe. *European Journal of Political Research*, 47(5): 537–555.

Tóka, G. (1998). Party Appeals and Voter Loyalty in New Democracies. *Political Studies*, 46(3): 589–610.

Vachudova, M. A. and L. Hooghe. (2009). Postcommunist Politics in a Magnetic Field: How Transition and EU Accession Structure Party Competition on European Integration. *Comparative European Politics*, 7(2): 179–212.

Van der Brug, W., M. Franklin, M. Popescu, and G. Tóka. (2009). Towards a European Electorate: One Electorate or Many? In *The Legitimacy of the European Union After Enlargement*. Ed. J. Thomassen. Oxford: Oxford University Press: 65–92.

Wessels, B., and H.-D. Klingemann. (2006). Parties and Voters – Representative Consolidation in Central and Eastern Europe? *International Journal of Sociology*, 36(2): 11–44.

Wessels, B. and H. Schmitt. (2012). Meaningful Choices: Does Party Supply Matter. In *Elections and Democracy*. Ed. J. Thomassen. London: Oxford University Press: 38–59.

Whitefield, S. (June 2002). Political Cleavages and Post-Communist Politics. *Annual Review of Politics*, 5: 181–200.

13

SOCIAL MOVEMENTS AFTER COMMUNISM

Ondřej Císař

Introduction: why study social movements after communism?

In spring 2016, demonstrations took place in Prague in opposition to public displays of xeno-phobia in the Czech Republic. Warsaw and other Polish cities were engulfed by demonstrations against the winning party in the 2015 parliamentary elections and its conservative policies. Anti-government protests marked Bulgarian politics in 2013–2014. These are just some examples, but there are dozens of protest events going on everywhere all the time against or in support of various causes. From the perspective of the political system as a whole, the mobilisation of the populace is believed to have contributed to the demise of the pre-1989 communist regimes in some East European countries, most notably Poland, but in a different manner also, for example, Czechoslovakia (Glenn 2003) and Romania (Nistor 2016). Social movements and mobilisation also played an important political role after 1989. In countries such as Slovakia (1998) and Serbia (2000), they were able to help topple populist leaders and dictators (Bunce and Wolchik 2011); in others, such as Hungary (2010), they helped install populist rulers aspiring to become dictators in a new post-liberal age (Greskovits and Wittenberg 2016). Although civil society and social movements in post-communist countries have often been regarded as weak, they have neverthe-less existed in all of them and have evolved in different forms (see Ekiert and Kubik 2014, and later). Along with other political agents such as political parties, they have been visible actors in both supporting and resisting democratisation in the post-communist region. And even though they continue to be overlooked or downplayed in some branches of political science, it is impos-sible to make sense of political developments without examining social movements (Císař 2015).

Movements and mobilisations did not appear out of the blue at the end of the 1980s when the old regimes collapsed. Fully-fledged social movements, such as Solidarity in Poland, and unofficial and quasi-official platforms in other communist countries existed and received some scholarly attention even before 1989 (e.g. Holzer 1984, Bugajski 1987, Bakuniak and Nowak 1987; after 1989: Kubik 1994, Hicks 1996, Sarre and Jehlička 2007). At that time, autonomous non-state collective actors were discussed in the work of dissident (anti-regime) authors, such as Václav Havel (Czechoslovakia), György Konrád (Hungary), and Adam Michnik (Poland), and were discussed from the perspective of an embryonic or immanent *civil society*. Simply put, civil society presented a radical alternative to the oppressive power of the communist state. As such, the idea of civil society served more of a normative/political than an analytical function; it challenged the official regimes' monopoly over the many aspects of communist citizens' lives. In some contexts, such as Poland, this notion of dissident civil society turned into an open opposition (Bernhard 1993).

With the end of communism academic freedom made possible relatively unrestricted inquiry into any social phenomena, including social movements. Many aspects and instances of social movement mobilisation in Eastern Europe after 1989 have been addressed in analyses of many movements and social movement organisations (SMOs). Since 1989, studies have emerged on: anti-communist resistance and especially the Solidarity movement in Poland (Kubik 1994, Osa 2003); anti-communist mobilisation that accompanied the end of the communist regimes in 1989 (Lomax 1997, Glenn 2003, Nistor 2016); nationalism (Beissinger 2002); trade unions (Ost 2000, 2005); environmentalism (Hicks 1996, Fagan 2004, 2005, Jehlička et al. 2005, Carmin and VanDeveer 2005, Fagan and Carmin 2011); and feminist and minority (Einhorn 1993, McMahon 2001, Flam 2001, Jacobsson and Saxonberg 2013), human rights (Vermeersch 2006), right-wing (Kopecký and Mudde 2003, Zakharov 2013, Greskovits and Wittenberg 2016), and anti-globalisation and anti-war movements (Navrátil 2010, Navrátil and Císař 2014). It is also possible to find country-specific protest event analyses (e.g. Szabó 1996, Ekiert and Kubik 2001, Beissinger 2002, Robertson 2010).

This chapter focuses on the most important debates in research on social movements in post-communist countries. It also looks at this research from the perspective of its potential contribution to more general research on social movement mobilisation. Post-communist Europe has in fact come to be understood as a unique 'laboratory' not just by students of democratisation in general, but also in other areas of the social sciences, social movement studies included.

Weak movements, democracy, and post-communist transformation

After the communist regimes collapsed, there were relatively high expectations that Eastern European populations would turn into democratic citizens participating in civil society and engaged in social and political activism (see Barnes et al. 1998). However, this never came about in reality; on the contrary, civil societies were largely overtaken by a particular advocacy-based form of activism not driven by broad participation (see Carothers 1999, Petrova and Tarrow 2007, Císař 2013c). In terms of both political participation and group membership, Eastern European citizens displayed lower rates than citizens in established democracies (Howard 2003, Bernhagen and Marsh 2007). On the basis of the 1995–1997 World Values Survey, Howard (2003) documented that the average number of members in voluntary organisations per person in post-communist countries was significantly lower than in the older democracies and post-authoritarian countries. Low membership in SMOs, and civil society organisations generally, and the inability of these organisations to mobilise, have been regarded as indicators of weak social movements in the region (McMahon 2001, Henderson 2003). At best, they have been seen as providing a democratic façade for unresponsive governments (Ost 2000).

In the early 1990s, Eastern Europe faced a double challenge, namely, to transform both its politics and its economy (further compounded by a state-building process in post-USSR, post-Yugoslavia, and former Czechoslovakia). While democratic institutions were expected to replace the undemocratic ones in the political arena, capitalism was to take over centrally planned economies. At the same time, economic restructuring produced groups of impoverished people who were now able to express their grievances via newly established democratic institutions. All the conditions for large-scale political protest seemed to be in place: the grievances produced by structural changes and the opportunities provided by democratisation of political institutions

(Snow and Soule 2010). Based on the logic of mainstream social movement theories, an outburst of protest was the expected outcome, but contrary to initial fears it never occurred. The strange absence of protest during the first transition decade became one of the most prominent theoretical puzzles in the transitional political economy. Why did East Europeans not protest en masse when faced with economic hardships? The academic literature offers three explanations: *institutional, grievance-based*, and *policy-based*.

From an *institutional* perspective, Ekiert and Kubik (1998, 2001), whose area of interest is Poland, Hungary, Slovakia, and former East Germany, argue that limited access to tripartite institutions and the fragmentation of the labour movement are what chiefly account for the lack (except to some extent in Poland) of protest in these four countries. They claim that contentious politics in the early 1990s (1989–1993) was strongest in Poland owing to the country's pre-1989 tradition of such activity. Employing a *grievance-based* approach, Greskovits (1998) finds possible explanations in a host of structural characteristics of post-communist countries, such as the lack of extreme inequality (the source of relative deprivation and thus grievances), a lack of an established protest culture (the source of the protest repertoire), and a lack of young people in urban areas ready to be mobilised (the social base of protest). He also cites the rise of social expenditures, which is at the heart of the third explanation. Focusing on the Czech Republic, Hungary, and Poland, Vanhuysse (2004, 2006) adopts a *policy-based* approach to explain the absence of significant protest. He argues that the subdued populations in these transforming countries were the result of a 'divide and pacify' style of social policies, which was designed to prevent any potential social disquiet. While there were different paths across the region, such as strategic retirement, that is, laying productive workforce off the labour market, and pro-employment labour market policies, they all resulted in decreasing protest potential. It took twenty years for this patience to run out.

With the recession hitting some East European countries after the 2008 financial crisis, the growing sense of impatience started to be discussed in connection with the study of varieties of contention triggered by different configurations of political economy or capitalism (Bohle and Greskovits 2012). Drawing on data from eighteen East European countries after 2007, Beissinger and Sasse (2014) claim that the recession did indeed bring about the political mobilisation of East European populations and that this mobilisation was fuelled by socioeconomic deprivation. They contend that while it is easier to endure economic hardships for an initial period of time and under conditions of optimistic expectations (such as in the 1990s), it is much more difficult to do so for a second time while simultaneously lacking prospects for a brighter future. In the same volume, Kriesi (2014) shows that extra-institutional protest mobilisation was universally triggered by the adoption of austerity policies. Most importantly, Kriesi concludes that protest has important implications for elections, an observation that draws attention to the interplay between party and protest politics.

Focusing on the whole political spectrum in post-1989 Central and Eastern Europe (Poland, Hungary, Czech Republic, and Slovakia), Císař and his colleagues (Císař and Navrátil 2015a, Císař and Vráblíková 2015) demonstrated the existence of a countervailing relation between the arenas of party and protest politics, which means that issues articulated by political parties are not articulated by social movements and vice versa. For instance, while 69 per cent of protest events in Hungary in the 1990s and 2000s were related to economic issues, such issues were behind only 16 per cent of protest in the Czech Republic (Císař and Vráblíková 2015: 12). From this perspective, the structure of party competition determines what issues are articulated in the protest field. If the party field's main conflict line is economic left-right, extra-institutional collective action driven by economic issues is crowded out. If a socio-cultural dimension (social conservatism vs. liberalism) is what primarily defines the political party field, economic issues are more represented in the protest field (Hungary). However, there are moments when the two fields align and become closely intertwined. Greskovits and Wittenberg (2016) show how the Hungarian right took roots in civil society after 2003 to prepare the ground for its electoral offensive in 2010, which was accompanied by extra-parliamentary mobilisation in the streets. In general, their research not only highlighted the variability of issues articulated in civil society and the interplay between them, but also the general variety of activist forms.

Varieties of activism

After recognising the existence of different forms of activism in Eastern Europe, activism in the region was systematically mapped and its main characteristics identified (see e.g. Jacobsson and Saxonberg 2012, Jacobsson and Saxonberg 2013, Ekiert and Kubik 2014). Further, conceptualisations of activism were formulated. For example, drawing on the definition of two types of activism – participatory and transactional – put forth by Petrova and Tarrow (2007; see also later), Císař (2013a) proposed seeing them as two dimensions of a new typology of political activism. As depicted in Table 13.1, the participatory dimension refers to the mobilisation capacity of political activists. It describes the capacity of activists to engage citizens in collective action, that is, to induce them to participate in politics. The transactional dimension describes the capacity of activists and their organisations to engage in 'transactional activism', that is, to network, cooperate, and communicate with other activists and organisations and public institutions, and make claims that bear on someone's interests.

In effect, the two dimensions differentiate between an activism's mobilisation and advocacy capacities. If combined, we get four basic types. Two types are characterised by relatively well-developed transactional capacity, which means that they are based on capable organisations. One of them contains the combination of high transactional and high mobilisation capacities that is typical of 'old' organisations such as trade unions. These organisations, representing a *participatory activist type*, are based on broader membership and are better able to cooperate, network, and communicate with their counterparts than other types, and they are recognised as legitimate partners by the political system. The second type has the high transactional capacity and low mobilisation capacity that characterise the *transactional activist type* originally described by Petrova and Tarrow, who focus on what Diani (2011) has labelled *transactions* or 'weak organisational ties' largely based on resource exchange and synonymous with inter-organisational cooperation, and not on 'social bonds' established through shared membership. In fact, focusing on post-communist countries, Petrova and Tarrow seem to draw on the well-established resource-mobilisation argument about the substituting 'thick mobilisation infrastructures' with their 'thin' versions, which are unable to tap into existing pools of potential followers (McCarthy 1987; see also Císař and Navrátil 2015b).

Table 13.1 Varieties of activism

		Mobilisation	Capacity
		High	Low
Transactional capacity	**High**	participatory activism	transactional activism
	Low	episodic mass mobilisation	radical activism; civic self-organisation

Source: Adopted from Císař (2013a: 142).

As a result, this activist type primarily takes the form of advocacy organisations (Flam 2001, Fagan 2004, 2005, Toepler and Salamon 2003, Fagan and Carmin 2011, Ekiert and Kubik 2014). Issues associated with the environment and with human and civil rights and freedoms usually form the basis of transactional activists' political demands (Císař 2013b).

The third type, *episodic mass mobilisation*, is defined by a high mobilisation capacity and low transactional capacity. Protests of this type are able to win strong popular support for a period, but they are unable to sustain themselves over time and translate their mobilisation success into a lasting organisational legacy. The last type involves a combination of low mobilisation and low transactional capacities and includes two sub-types: *radical activism* and *self-organisation*. Although radical right-wing and left-wing activism is based on the active involvement of devoted activists and organisational platforms, these are unable to mobilise anything close to a wide following, while at the same time they either fail or refuse to take the path of institutionalisation, that is, the path of organisational capacity-building that is a precondition for a high advocacy capacity. Self-organisation does not mobilise many citizens and, like mass mobilisation, does not survive organisationally over time. Local, small-scale, and informal protests would belong under this type (see Jacobsson 2015b and later). Five different types of activism can therefore be distinguished (see Table 13.1).

Movement activism explained? Three diffusion debates

Foreign involvement in the development of social movements and mobilisation in Eastern Europe is widely covered in the literature. The link between exogenous funding and the emergence of transnational activist networks is explained from three distinct perspectives: The *advocacy model* argues that, after the fall of communism, American foundations began to search for citizen representatives to be supported by their pro-democracy civil society-building programmes and they found them in professionalised organisations that started to emerge right after 1989 (Carothers 1999). There is a broad consensus that by signalling to East Europeans that formally registered and more or less professionally managed organisations are most likely to actually receive funding, they helped professionalised advocacy organisations to spread across the region (McMahon 2001, Fagan 2004, 2005, Aksartova 2006, Císař 2013c). In this sense, they created connections, that is, brokered between their home country's model of civic life, based on advocacy organisations, and post-communist states, and by favouring funding for officially registered advocacy groups contributed to the spread of this model. While in the first half of the 1990s, the US and US-based private foundations were the most important brokers, though individual European states and foundations also played a role, they had scaled down their programmes by the end of the decade. At that time, the European Union (EU) overtook their role as the primary source of funding, and as a result the 'Americanisation' of activist groups was replaced by their 'Europeanisation'.

The *Europeanisation model* describes the impact of accession on social movements and interest organisations in candidate countries (e.g. Carmin and VanDeveer 2005, Stark et al. 2006, Císař and Vráblíková 2010, Fagan and Carmin 2011, Buzogány 2011, Císař and Vráblíková 2013, Bruszt and Vedrés 2013). This impact has been felt and studied from three perspectives. First, the accession requirements exerted a transformative impact on the domestic political opportunity structures of post-communist states, opening up new possibilities for social movements and their strategies of influence. Second, SMOs have been progressively influenced by their increased reliance on European funding, which since the end of the 1990s forced them to become more formalised and professionalised (Börzel and Buzogány 2010, Císař and Vráblíková 2010, Bruszt and Vedrés 2013). Third, the accession of post-communist countries to the EU provided local SMOs with a new level of policymaking, thus opening for them a transnational political opportunity structure to be utilised, albeit to a limited extent, in their multi-level political strategies (see Císař and Vráblíková 2013).

The *electoral model* can be seen as a continuation of the aforementioned advocacy model. The electoral model captures the variety of forms of mobilisation relating to elections that emerged in eight post-communist countries from 1996 to 2005 and resulted in the replacement of undemocratic political leaders with representatives of the democratic opposition, even though this had only a limited long-term impact in many of them (Bunce and Wolchik 2010). This wave of election-related protests swept across Serbia, Bulgaria, Romania, Slovakia, Croatia, Georgia, Ukraine, and Kyrgyzstan. These 'colour revolutions', as they are commonly called, and their aftermath have become an important topic in the study of post-communist mobilisation and social movements (e.g. Beissinger 2007, Ó Beacháin and Polese 2010, Bunce and Wolchik 2011, Petrova, 2014, Ishchenko 2015). According to Bunce and Wolchik (2010), the diffusion of electoral model of activism was facilitated by the structural similarities between post-communist countries, the self-interest of the opposition forces in these countries and their common goal to topple authoritarian leaders, the closed domestic political opportunity structure, the existence of (at least) semi-competitive elections, and transnational networking. The latter in particular has been thoroughly analysed, and it was found to have been facilitated by Western and regional agencies and donors, which played a role in this model very similar to the one they played in the advocacy model in the beginning of the 1990s (Bunce and Wolchik 2011). They acted as resourceful brokers, forging connections between previously unconnected social sites, and helped produce 'messengers of revolution' by training activists who, after completing their mission in their home country, often became involved in educating activists in another country (Petrova 2014). Ultimately, this training was not only passed on to other post-communist activists, but some Eastern European activists even trained future leaders of the Arab Spring.

Movement activism lost? Three co-optation debates

Democratic co-optation

The inability to mobilise people meant that SMOs in Eastern Europe were forced to rely on external – mostly American and EU – sources of funding. One group of scholars has pointed out this reliance on external patronage as the reason for the general weakness of social movements and their co-optation by donors and political elites (McMahon 2001, Fagan 2004). According to this narrative, by providing institutional support external donors not only directly influenced agendas pursued by these organisations, but also redirected their activities away from the domestic mobilisation of their constituencies to (transnational) grant-seeking (Mendelson and Glenn 2002, Henderson 2003). Instead of empowering and making these organisations able to become means of participation, patronage created in them dependency and caused them to be trapped in an endless vicious circle of grant applications. According to the harshest critics (McMahon 2001), these programmes actually prevented East Europeans from creating indigenous social movements, and imposed on them instead a particular organisational pattern that was inimical to the idea of popular movements.

An alternative view has identified external patronage as a source of the political autonomy of SMOs in the post-communist semi-democratic and democratising regimes that were unable to provide indigenous support for many types of SMOs, especially those focused on 'new politics' issues such as the environment and human rights (Aksartova 2006, Císař 2010, Císař and Navrátil 2015b). Owing to the somewhat conservative political culture and the lack of a conscious constituency in East European states, the autonomy and often the very existence of these SMOs was ensured only by the availability of external resources. According to this argument, although foreign patrons steered local organisations towards professionalisation and formalisation, these changes were not necessarily accompanied by co-optation. SMOs dependent on foreign support became relatively effective advocates capable of challenging the prevailing social norms not in spite of but rather because of their foreign dependency, which liberated them from the domestic political and cultural context non-conducive to their goals (Stark et al. 2006, Vermeersch 2006, Císař 2010). We can call this process a particular type of democratic channelling.

Authoritarian co-optation

This similar process, but one animated by explicitly non-democratic forces, has been analysed in relation to hybrid regimes, especially Russia. In this case, the co-optation effect was not the unintended by-product of the original intention to empower civil society, as in the case of Western-based donors, but was the primary goal of state strategies aimed at containing protest. In his seminal study of Russian protest, Robertson (2010) differentiates between coercive strategies used to limit protest by the imposition of repressive conditions and measures intended to channel protest in another directions. While direct repression involves deploying police forces and exercising strict control over the protesters on the ground, channelling means diverting the attention of the potential supporters of the protests by controlling visual, print, and even electronic media.

These channelling strategies put in place to quash the political articulation of social problems achieve this by introducing a firm distinction between acknowledging these problems as something to be dealt with by legitimate authorities and the politicisation and 'misuse' of these problems by political forces inimical to the establishment. In other words, while the regime accepts the existence of problems, it at the same time tries to scare citizens away from actively articulating them. It leaves no room for either autonomous political action or any action challenging the elite. Political action is on the contrary monopolised by public officials, who interpret any protests as a direct challenge to their monopoly over the definition and resolution of problems.

Robertson also points out that additional strategies have been used in post-Soviet Russia that all originated in the style of politics practised in the preceding non-democratic Soviet regime. Thus, this repertoire consists of organising pro-government protest events to demonstrate the legitimacy of power holders. The post-Soviet authorities also used blame-shifting (from the very top to the lower levels of decision-making), partial concessions, and protest bureaucratisation. For example, Vladimir Putin has employed the first-mentioned tactic by seeking to blame his own ministers and officials for errors and mismanagement and offered at times almost miraculous solutions to them that were duly publicised in the official media. Under Putin, this repertoire of strategies has been expanded by the addition of long-forgotten Brezhnev-style tactics of preventive detention.

These strategies have resulted in efforts by the state to acquire broader discretion over which groups and activists can operate in Russia. In this context, the law on foreign agents (2012) has even made international headlines and has generated a large public outcry (see e.g. Turbine 2015). The two processes discussed in this chapter thus came head to head in the case of post-Soviet Russia. Transactional activists supported from abroad were directly challenged by the authoritarian Russian state. The regime was well aware of the *liberating effect* of foreign money, which gave at least some autonomy to the supported activist organisations. Although they might have been perceived as donor-dependent and co-opted, in the eyes of Western-based researchers, they in fact enjoyed comparative autonomy within their immediate local environment. It was for this reason that the state made efforts to sever their transnational connections and fully co-opt their activities by starving these organisations out.

Consentful contention

The third co-optation debate strives to navigate away from the distinction between the manipulative external environment, be it international donors or the authoritarian state, on one hand, and independent movement actors on the other, and not to focus primarily on 'dissentful' varieties of contention (see Cheskin and March 2015a). While the first two debates contend that social movements often use contentious strategies to challenge authorities, scholars engaged in the third debate seek to distinguish also the less visible *consentful strategies of claims-making*. In other words, the fact that there is not very much visible protest action in Russia does not mean there is no action. On the contrary, some very important citizen action may be taking place on the local level or in areas that are no direct threat to the power holders in the centre. Distinguishing such practices challenges the simplified picture of 'Russian-style civil society as bad and undemocratic' (Cheskin and March 2015b: 267).

The main asset of distinguishing examples of consentful strategies of claims-making is that doing so captures the variegated forms of citizen coordination that may exist under semi-democratic conditions. While the scholars who are interested in this form of claims-making do not dispute the existence of mechanisms of hard and soft repression listed by Robertson, they also want to take into account examples of 'non-dissentful' contention, which is less visible and not aimed against the state authorities (see Fröhlich 2012 and the contributions in Cheskin and March 2015a). While a clear-cut black and white distinction between the powerful state and movements drives us to see the end of action autonomy and independent contention whenever some form of state repression is employed, this approach makes it possible to see also the 'grey zones' in which co-optation 'allows a certain level of challenge and contention' (Cheskin and March 2015b: 267).

In order to see this, it is important to distinguish between explicitly political and social forms of activism. While the former may be steered, cut down, and manipulated by hybrid regimes, the latter can flourish and even provide the population with valuable services. In a nutshell, consentful contention overlaps with service provision much more than with advocacy. In this respect, while this new approach can bring a much-needed nuance to the study of forms of social activism, it may be less interesting to social movement scholars, since they have traditionally been interested in acts of (political and/or cultural) dissent and advocacy for or against social change. One can welcome the contribution of consentful contention scholars for the light this approach sheds on the hard-to-see civic activities in contemporary Russia (and other hybrid regimes) without necessarily embarking on conceptual stretching. Consentful contention and movement action are two different concepts that relate to two different phenomena.

Conclusion: movement activism found?

Focusing explicitly on movement actors, recent additions to the literature on East-European social movements include studies that indicate a revival of movement activism, although probably not exactly in the expected form. In response to the 2008 financial crisis, the post-accession depression, and the recent migrant crisis, there has been a visible mobilisation of nationalist forces across East European countries (Greskovits 2015). Some authors even claim that the thin liberal façade that national political cultures in countries such as Bulgaria, Hungary, Poland, Slovakia, and the Czech Republic erected in the EU accession process has withered away in the years since accession (Dawson and Hanley 2016). As Greskovits and Wittenberg (2016) have demonstrated in the case of Hungary, civil society activism can be supportive of not only democratic development, but also populist and illiberal forces.

On the other hand, some scholars have identified recent examples of 'islands of positive deviations' where a more progressive form of political activism can be observed inside an environment that is otherwise becoming more and more conservative. According to this view, while there have been debates about the (non)existence of truly participatory social movements in Eastern Europe, they have tended to be overly focused on organised forms of activism on the national level. However, some research on East European cities has shown that grassroots movements are able to emerge in urban settings in relation to disputes over public spaces, non-corrupted urban planning mechanisms, or opposition to gentrification (see Kerény 2010, and most notably Jacobsson 2015a). This type of research suggests that 'local, grassroots-driven, small-scale, low-key forms of activism – such as much of urban grassroots activism – represent an important component of post-socialist civil society as well as an important new phase of post-socialist civil society making' (Jacobsson 2015b: 275).

Urban centres in Eastern Europe have also served as fertile ground for various subcultures and subcultural movements, which to some extent overlap with urban movements, most notably squatters (see Kurti 2003, McKay et al. 2009, Císař and Koubek 2012, Polanska and Piotrowski 2015). In this respect, post-socialist cities seem to be a space of substantial contention, but one that has so far been somewhat cut off mainstream research on social movements. Only recently have efforts been made to explicitly connect the two fields (Císař and Koubek 2012, Jacobsson 2015a). When some of the debates summarised in this chapter (see Table 13.1) are applied to urban activism, it is often interpreted as the manifestation of self-organisation (and radicalism) in an urban context, examples of which include squatters, bike activism, environmentalism, tenants' movements, and rehousing initiatives to combat homelessness.

Acknowledgement

This chapter was prepared as part of work on the research project 'Activism in Hard Times' funded by the Czech Science Foundation (no. 16–10163S). It was also supported by the P17 research framework programme of Charles University.

References

Aksartova, Sada. 2006. "Why NGOs? How American Donors Embrace Civil Society After the Cold War." *The International Journal of Non-for-Profit Law* 8(3): 15–20.

Bakuniak, Grzegorz and Krzysztof Nowak. 1987. "The Creation of a Collective Identity in a Social Movement: The Case of Solidarnosc in Poland." *Theory and Society* 16(3): 401–429.

Barnes, Samuel H., Janos Simon and Hans-Dieter Klingemann, eds. 1998. *The Postcommunist Citizen*. Budapest: Erasmus Foundation and IPS of HAS.

Beissinger, Mark R. 2002. *Nationalist Mobilization and the Collapse of the Soviet State*. Cambridge: Cambridge University Press.

Beissinger, Mark R. 2007. "Structure and Example in Modular Political Phenomena: The Diffusion of Bulldozer/Rose/Orange/Tulip Revolutions." *Perspectives on Politics* 5(2): 259–276.

Beissinger, Marc R. and Gwendolyn Sasse. 2014. "An End to 'Patience'? The Great Recession and Economic Protest in Eastern Europe." pp. 334–370 in *Mass Politics in Tough Times*, edited by Nancy Bermeo and Larry M. Bartels. Oxford: Oxford University Press.

Bernhagen, Patrick and Michael Marsh. 2007. "Voting and Protesting: Explaining Citizen Participation in Old and New European Democracies." *Democratization* 14(1): 44–72.

Bernhard, Michael. 1993. "Civil Society and Democratic Transition in East Central Europe." *Political Science Quarterly* 108(2): 307–326.

Bohle, Dorothee and Béla Greskovits. 2012. *Capitalist Diversity on Europe's Periphery*. Ithaca and London: Cornell University Press.

Börzel, Tanja A. and Aron Buzogány. 2010. "Governing EU Accession in Transition Countries: The Role of Non-state Actors." *Acta Politica* 45(1): 158–182.

Bruszt, László and Balász Vedrés. 2013. "Associating, Mobilizing, Politicizing: Local Developmental Agency From Without." *Theory and Society* 42(13): 1–23.

Bugajski, Janusz. 1987. *Czechoslovakia: Charter 77's Decade of Dissent.* New York: Praeger.

Bunce, Valerie and Sharon Wolchik. 2010. "Transnational Networks, Diffusion Dynamics, and Electoral Change in the Postcommunist World." pp. 140–162 in *The Diffusion of Social Movements: Actors, Mechanisms, and Political Effects*, edited by Rebecca Kolins Givan, Kenneth M. Roberts and Sarah Soule. Cambridge: Cambridge University Press.

Bunce, Valerie and Sharon Wolchik. 2011. *Defeating Authoritarian Leaders in Postcommunist Countries.* Cambridge: Cambridge University Press.

Buzogány, Aron. 2011. "Stairway to Heaven or Highway to Hell? Ambivalent Europeanization and Civil Society in Central and Eastern Europe." pp. 69–85 in *Protest Beyond Borders*, edited by Hara Kouki and Eduardo Romanos. New York: Berghahn Books.

Carmin, JoAnn and Stacy VanDeveer, eds. 2005. *EU Enlargement and the Environment: Institutional Change and Environmental Policy in Central and Eastern Europe.* London: Routledge.

Carothers, Thomas. 1999. *Aiding Democracy Abroad: The Learning Curve.* Washington, DC: Carnegie Endowment for International Peace.

Cheskin, Ammon and Luke March, eds. 2015a. State-society Relations in Contemporary Russia: New Forms of Political and Social Contention [special issue]. *East European Politics* 31(3).

Cheskin, Ammon and Luke March. 2015b. "State-society Relations in Contemporary Russia: New Forms of Political and Social Contention." *East European Politics* 31(3): 261–273.

Císař, Ondřej. 2010. "Externally Sponsored Contention: The Channelling of Environmental Movement Organisations in the Czech Republic After the Fall of Communism." *Environmental Politics* 19(5): 736–755.

Císař, Ondřej. 2013a. "A Typology of Extra-parliamentary Political Activism in Post-Communist Settings: The Case of the Czech Republic." pp. 139–167 in *Beyond NGO-ization: The Development of Social Movements in Central and Eastern Europe*, edited by Kerstin Jacobsson and Steven Saxonberg. Farnham: Ashgate.

Císař, Ondřej. 2013b. "Post-Communism and Social Movements." pp. 994–999 in *Encyclopedia of Social and Political Movements*, vol. 3, edited by David Snow, Donatella Della Porta, Bert Klandermans and Doug McAdam. London: Blackwell.

Císař, Ondřej. 2013c. "The Diffusion of Public Interest Mobilization: A Historical Sociology View on the Advocates Without Members in the Post-Communist Czech Republic." *East European Politics* 29(1): 69–82.

Císař, Ondřej. 2015. "Social Movements in Political Science." Pp. 50–67 in *Oxford Handbook of Social Movements*, edited by Donatella Della Porta and Mario Diani. Oxford: Oxford University Press.

Císař, Ondřej and Martin Koubek. 2012. "Include 'Em All? Culture, Politics and a Local Hardcore/Punk Scene in the Czech Republic." *Poetics: Journal of Empirical Research on Literature, the Media and the Arts* 40(1): 1–21.

Císař, Ondřej and Jiří Navrátil. 2015a. "At the Ballot Boxes or in the Streets and Factories: Economic Contention in the Visegrád Group." pp. 35–53 in *Austerity and Protest: Popular Contention in Times of Economic Crisis*, edited by Marco Giugni and Maria Grasso. Farnham: Ashgate.

Císař, Ondřej and Jiří Navrátil. 2015b. "Promoting Competition or Cooperation? The Impact of EU Funding on Czech Advocacy Organizations." *Democratization* 22(3): 536–559.

Císař, Ondřej and Kateřina Vráblíková. 2010. "The Europeanization of Social Movements in the Czech Republic: The EU and Local Women's Groups." *Communist and Post-Communist Studies* 43(2): 209–219.

Císar?, Ondřej and Kateřina Vráblíková. 2013. "Transnational Activism of Social Movement Organizations: The Effect of European Union Funding on Local Groups in the Czech Republic." *European Union Politics* 14(1): 140–160.

Císař, Ondřej and Kateřina Vráblíková. 2015. "At the Parliament or in the Streets? Issue Composition of Contentious Politics in the Visegrád Countries." *Paper Presented at the ECPR General Conference, Université de Montréal*, 26–29 August 2015 (https://ecpr.eu/Filestore/PaperProposal/63bb4d92-87b0-49ef-ae49-0e1d69e17048.pdf).

Dawson, James and Seán Hanley. 2016. "The Fading Mirage of the 'Liberal Consensus'." *Journal of Democracy* 27(1): 20–34.

Diani, Mario. 2011. "Social Movements and Collective Action." pp. 223–235 in *The Sage Handbook of Social Network Analysis*, edited by Peter Carrington and John Scott. London: Sage.

Einhorn, Barbara. 1993. *Cinderella Goes to Market: Citizenship, Gender and Women's Movements in the East Europe*. London, New York: Verso.

Ekiert, Grzegorz and Jan Kubik. 1998. "Contentious Politics in New Democracies: East Germany, Hungary, Poland, and Slovakia, 1989–93." *World Politics* 50(4): 547–581.

Ekiert, Grzegorz and Jan Kubik. 2001. *Rebellious Civil Society: Popular Protest and Democratic Consolidation in Poland, 1989–1993*. Ann Arbor: University of Michigan Press.

Ekiert, Grzegorz and Jan Kubik. 2014. "Myths and Realities of Civil Society." *Journal of Democracy* 25(1): 46–58.

Fagan, Adam. 2004. *Environment and Democracy in the Czech Republic: The Environmental Movement in the Transition Process*. Cheltenham, Northampton: Edward Elgar.

Fagan, Adam. 2005. "Taking Stock of Civil-Society Development in Post-Communist Europe: Evidence From the Czech Republic." *Democratization* 12(4): 528–547.

Fagan, Adam and JoAnn Carmin, eds. 2011. *Green Activism in Post-Socialist Europe and the Former Soviet Union*. London: Routledge.

Flam, Helen, ed. 2001. *Pink, Purple, Green: Women's, Religious, Environmental, and Gay/Lesbian Movements in Central Europe Today*. Boulder, CO: East European Monographs.

Fröhlich, Christian. 2012. "Civil Society and the State Intertwined: The Case of Disability NGOs in Russia." *East European Politics* 28(4): 371–389.

Glenn, John. 2003. *Framing Democracy: Civil Society and Civic Movements in Eastern Europe*. Palo Alto, CA: Stanford University Press.

Greskovits, Béla. 1998. *The Political Economy of Protest and Patience: East European and Latin American Transformations Compared*. Budapest: CEU Press.

Greskovits, Béla. 2015. "Hollowing and Backsliding of Democracy in East Central Europe." *Global Policy* 6(1): 28–37.

Greskovits, Béla and Jason Wittenberg. 2016. "Civil Society and Democratic Consolidation in Hungary in the 1990s and 2000s." *Working Paper* (www.jasonwittenberg.org/wp-content/uploads/2016/02/Greskovits_Wittenberg_Civil-Society_Democratic_Consolidation_Feb_2016_final_draft.pdf).

Henderson, Sarah. 2003. *Building Democracy in Contemporary Russia: Western Support for Grassroots Organizations*. Ithaca and London: Cornell University Press.

Hicks, Barbara. 1996. *Environmental Politics in Poland: A Social Movement Between Regime and Opposition*. New York: Columbia University Press.

Holzer, Jerzy. 1984. *Solidarnosc, 1980–1981: Geneza i historia [Solidarity, 1980–1981: Origins and History]*. Paris: Instytut Literacki.

Howard, Marc Morjé. 2003. *The Weakness of Civil Society in Post-Communist Europe*. Cambridge: Cambridge University Press.

Ishchenko, Volodymyr. 2015. *The Ukrainian Left During and After the Maidan Protests*. Study requested by the DIE LINKE delegation in the GUE/NGL (http://cslr.org.ua/en/the-ukrainian-left-during-and-after-the-maidan-protests-2/).

Jacobsson, Kerstin, ed. 2015a. *Urban Grassroots Movements in Central and Eastern Europe*. Farnham: Ashgate.

Jacobsson, Kerstin. 2015b. "Conclusion: Towards a New Research Agenda." pp. 273–287 in *Urban Grassroots Movements in Central and Eastern Europe*, edited by Kerstin Jacobsson. Farnham: Ashgate.

Jacobsson, Kerstin and Steven Saxonberg. 2012. Symposium: A New Look At Social Movements and Civil Society in Post-Communist Russia and Poland. *East European Politics* 28(4): 329–408.

Jacobsson, Kerstin and Steven Saxonberg, eds. 2013. *Beyond NGO-ization: The Development of Social Movements in Central and Eastern Europe*. Farnham: Ashgate.

Jehlička, Petr, Philip Sarre, and Juraj Podoba. 2005. "The Czech Environmental Movement's Knowledge Interest in the 1990s: Compatibility of Western Influences With Pre-1989 Perspectives." *Environmental Politics* 14(1): 64–82.

Kerény, Szabina. 2010. "Using Pollution to Frame Collective Mobilization in Budapest." pp. 144–162 in *Urban Pollution: Cultural Meanings, Social Practices*, edited by Eveline Dürr and Rivke Jaffe. New York: Berghahn Books.

Kopecký, Petr and Cas Mudde, eds. 2003. *Uncivil Society? Contentious Politics in Post-Communist Europe*. London: Routledge.

Kriesi, Hanspeter. 2014. "The Political Consequences of the Economic Crisis in Europe: Electoral Punishment and Popular Protest." pp. 297–333 in *Mass Politics in Tough Times*, edited by Nancy Bermeo and Larry M. Bartels. Oxford: Oxford University Press.

Kubik, Jan. 1994. *The Power of Symbols Against the Symbols of Power: The Rise of Solidarity and the Fall of State Socialism in Poland*. University Park: Pennsylvania State University Press.

Kurti, László. 2003. "The Uncivility of a Civil Society: Skinhead Youth in Hungary." pp. 35–51 in *Uncivil Society? Contentious Politics in Post-Communist Europe*, edited by Petr Kopecký and Cas Mudde. London: Routledge.

Lomax, Bill. 1997. "The Strange Death of 'Civil Society' in Post-communist Hungary." *Journal of Communist Studies and Transition Politics* 13(1): 41–63.

McCarthy, John D. 1987. "Pro-Life and Pro-Choice Mobilization: Infrastructure Deficits and New Technologies." pp. 49–66 in *Social Movements in an Organizational Society*, edited by Mayer N. Zald and John D. McCarthy. New Brunswick, NJ: Transaction.

McKay, George, Christopher Williams, Michael Goddard, Neil Foxlee, and Egidija Ramanauskaite, eds. 2009. *Subcultures and New Religious Movements in Russia and East-Central Europe*. Oxford: Peter Lang.

McMahon, Patrice. 2001. "Building Civil Societies in East Central Europe: The Effects of American Non-governmental Organizations on Women's Groups." *Democratization* 8(2): 45–68.

Mendelson, Sarah and John Glenn, eds. 2002. *The Power and Limits of NGOs*. New York: Columbia University Press.

Navrátil, Jiří. 2010. "Between the Spillover and the Spillout: Tracing the Evolution of the Czech Global Justice Movement." *Sociologický časopis / Czech Sociological Review* 46(6): 913–944.

Navrátil, Jiří and Ondřej Císař. 2014. "Towards a 'Non-Global Justice Movement'? Two Paths to Re-scaling the Left Contention in the Czech Republic." pp. 227–252 in *Spreading Protest in Social Movements of the Crisis*, edited by Donatella Della Porta and Alice Mattoni. Colchester: ECPR Press.

Nistor, Laura. 2016. "Social Movements in Pre – And Post-December 1989 in Romania." pp. 419–437 in *Social Movement Studies in Europe: The State of the Art*, edited by Olivier Fillieule and Guya Accornero. New York: Berghahn Books.

Ó Beacháin, Donnacha and Abel Polese, eds. 2010. *The Color Revolutions in the Former Soviet Republics: Successes and Failures*. London: Routledge.

Osa, Maryjane. 2003. *Solidarity and Contention: Networks of Polish Opposition*. Minneapolis: University of Minnesota Press.

Ost, David. 2000. "Illusory Corporatism in Eastern Europe: Neoliberal Tripartism and Postcommunist Class Identities." *Politics and Society* 28(4): 503–530.

Ost, David. 2005. *The Defeat of Solidarity: Anger and Politics in Postcommunist Europe*. Ithaca, NY: Cornell University Press.

Petrova, Tsveta. 2014. *From Solidarity to Geopolitics: Support for Democracy Among Postcommunist States*. Cambridge: Cambridge University Press.

Petrova, Tsveta and Sidney Tarrow. 2007. "Transactional and Participatory Activism in the Emerging European Polity: The Puzzle of East Central Europe." *Comparative Political Studies* 40(1): 74–94.

Polanska, Dominika and Grzegorz Piotrowski. 2015. "The Transformative Power of Cooperation Between Social Movements. Squatting and Tenants' Movements in Poland." *City* 12(2–3): 274–296.

Robertson, Graeme B. 2010. *The Politics of Protest in Hybrid Regimes: Managing Dissent in Post-Communist Russia*. Cambridge: Cambridge University Press.

Sarre, Philip and Petr Jehlička. 2007. "Environmental Movements in Space-Time: The Czech and Slovak Republics From Stalinism to Post-Socialism." *Transactions of the Institute of British Geographers* 32(3): 346–362.

Snow, David and Sarah Soule. 2010. *A Primer on Social Movements*. New York: W. W. Norton.

Stark, David, Balász Vedrés, and László Bruszt. 2006. "Rooted Transnational Publics: Integrating Foreign Ties and Civic Activism." *Theory and Society* 35(3): 323–349.

Szabó, Máté. 1996. "Repertoires of Contention in Post-Communist Protest Cultures: An East Central European Comparative Survey (Hungary, Slovakia, Slovenia)." *Social Research* 63(4): 1155–1183.

Toepler, Stefan and Lester M. Salamon. 2003. "NGO Development in Central and Eastern Europe: An Empirical Overview." *East European Quarterly* 37(3): 365–378.

Turbine, Vikki. 2015. "Women's Human Rights in Russia: Outmoded Battlegrounds, or New Sites of Contentious Politics?" *East European Politics* 31(3): 326–341.

Vanhuysse, Pieter. 2004. "East European Protest Politics in the Early 1990s: Comparative Trends and Preliminary Theories." *Europe-Asia Studies* 56(3): 412–438.

Vanhuysse, Pieter. 2006. *Divide and Pacify. Strategic Social Policies and Political Protests in Post-Communist Democracies*. Budapest: Central European University Press.

Vermeersch, Peter. 2006. *The Romani Movement: Minority Politics and Ethnic Mobilization in Contemporary Central Europe.* New York, Oxford: Berghahn Books.

Zakharov, Nikolay. 2013. "The Social Movement against Immigration as the Vehicle and Agent of Racialization in Russia." pp. 169–189 in *Beyond NGO-ization: The Development of Social Movements in Central and Eastern Europe,* edited by Kerstin Jacobsson and Steven Saxonberg. Farnham: Ashgate.

14

THE STUDY OF PROTEST POLITICS IN EASTERN EUROPE IN THE SEARCH OF THEORY

Grzegorz Ekiert and Jan Kubik

Spectacular and sometimes tragic in their consequences, waves of contention have swept Eastern Europe since the end of the Second World War with remarkable regularity. From the initial armed resistance through manifold forms of everyday disobedience to spectacular outbursts of rebellious anger, the people of Eastern Europe have periodically challenged reigning regimes. Protest under communism came from oppressed and voiceless social groups challenging powerful authorities through weakly institutionalised mobilisations that in turn provoked extremely repressive responses from the state. After 1989, protests have become routinised, highly institutionalised and organised by political movements and civil society organisations. Today, contention is a constant feature of post-communist politics generating a high number of significant protest events.

Western theory of contention and protest politics in Eastern Europe

There is a large, diverse social science and history literature on protest, contention, and oppositional activities in Eastern Europe both before and after 1989. We review the scholarship on the later period, focusing in particular on its theoretical trajectory. The goal is to identify and briefly characterize the main stages in the development of the literature on protest in Eastern Europe and to trace down mutual influences between this literature and theories of contentious politics developed in the Western social sciences.

There are four distinctive stages in the scholarly literature on post-1945 protest in the region. They correspond roughly to the four historical phases of contention. A series of early rebellions against the new communist rule across the region constitutes the first stage. Largely descriptive analyses of this period are interspersed with theoretical strands inspired by the idea of totalitarianism and some elements of collective behaviour and mass society theories (Zinner 1962, Baring 1972, Lewis 1958).

The second phase is marked by the emergence of dissident movements, counter hegemonic discourses, and open political opposition, rooted in the defeat of communist reformers of the Prague Spring and made possible by the Helsinki Accords of 1975.[1] The rise and defeat of the Solidarity movement in Poland was its central event. Scholars studying the second phase at that time (and often later) rely mostly on case studies and employ several broad interpretative approaches popular in the social science of the period: historical and political sociology, political anthropology, and critical Marxism combined with the resurrected concept of civil society (see also Císař in this volume). Their work is informed by a broad liberal stance centred on the idea of pluralism and inalienable human rights and freedoms.

The revolutions of 1989–1991, treated here as the third phase in the history of post-1945 contention in Eastern Europe, were massive upheavals across the entire region leading to the collapse of communist regimes, the dissolution of the Soviet bloc, and the emergence of new nation states. These revolutions immediately attracted scholarly attention and have never ceased to fascinate scholars representing various disciplines and theoretical orientations (Ash 1990; Mueller, Gehler, and Suppan 2015; Eisenstadt 2015; Della Porta 2014), including the practitioners of game theoretic approaches to contention (Kuran 1991; Lohmann 1994; Opp 1994). Existing analyses range from micro-level studies of protest participation to sweeping accounts of regional dynamics of contention, and there is a bifurcation between studies of the dissolution of the Soviet Union and the overthrow of communist regimes elsewhere.

Finally, in the fourth phase, stretching from 1989 to today, the entire range of contentious behaviours characteristic of modern political regimes have appeared. Researchers who study this period come from all disciplines and employ all theoretical and methodological approaches of contemporary social science, with its classic division between rationalist, institutionalist, and culturalist schools of thought and use all contemporary theories of contention (Lichbach 1995, 1998; McAdam, McCarthy, and Zald 1996). As contention in the region has become normalised, so have ways of studying it.

Thus, until the end of 1970s, the study of contention in Eastern Europe was largely disconnected from Western theories of social movements, revolutions, and protest politics. Communism was considered to be a system sui generis, its politics unique, and best understood through the prism of a totalitarian paradigm. While most of the earlier works are to a large degree descriptive in nature, some of them echo distinct theoretical claims derived from the theories of collective behaviour (Smelser 1963), mass society (Kornhauser 1959), or totalitarianism that were influential roughly up to the mid-1960s.

During the 1980s but particularly after 1989, the field of study of East European contention expanded rapidly, as several distinct patterns of contention, characteristic of the increasingly divergent sub-regional situations, have emerged. Data and research opportunities have become widely available and all major theoretical orientations proposed in the field of contentious politics have made their appearance. Some authors have embedded their empirical work within other theoretical frameworks, including critical Marxism, comparative politics, historical and political sociology, or political anthropology (Ost 1990; Bernhard 1993; Ekiert 1996; Kubik 1994). At the same time, a new wave of scholars (mostly younger historians from the region) has entered the newly opened archives and proposed novel, sometimes revisionist, historical analyses of the past and current cases of protest (McDermott and Stibbe 2006; Paczkowski 2003; Kamiński, Małkiewicz, and Ruchniewicz 2004).

Revolutions of 1989 and 1991

The revolutions of 1989 came largely as a surprise, yet the intensity of surprise varied among scholars (Tarrow 1991). Those who observed Poland and the activities of underground Solidarity were arguably less startled, as they studied the country where an accumulated legacy of rebellions had earlier culminated in the Solidarity movement (1980–1981) and where, since 1981, manifold clandestine activities had periodically led to eruptions of open protest (Ash 1983; Bernhard 1993; Cirtautas 1997; Ekiert 1996; Kubik 1994). The 1988 wave of strikes, that constituted the decisive factor pushing the communist authorities to enter a path of negotiations (Paczkowski 2015), did not materialise spontaneously; it was preceded by years of patient organising and massive clandestine work on cultural, political, and even economic levels (with underground publishing houses and networks of distribution).

The literature on 1989 is thus divided into two strands. The more prominent one continues the tradition of earlier approaches to contention in the region (descriptive/historical and interpretative). Its theoretical competitor draws on the approaches to contentious politics that are inspired by game theory (Ash 2011). Historians, historically minded sociologists and political scientists, and journalists are most influential in the literature on Poland, Hungary, and Czechoslovakia, where the revolutionary wave of protest in 1988–1989 came as the culmination of years of contentious challenges to the communist monopoly of power, often emanating from the domain of culture. These writers emphasise historical legacies and reconstruct long-term trajectories of resistance and rebellion, but primarily provide detailed accounts of multiple oppositional activities by the Polish Solidarity or the Czechoslovak Charter 77 and a constellation of organisations associated with them. The widely read works range from witness accounts (Ash 1990; Gwertzman and Kaufman 1991) to more systematic and comparative accounts (Banac 1992; Stokes 1993; Joppke 1995; Bruszt and Stark 1991). This tradition of analysing the 1989 revolutions as a complex social and cultural phenomenon with long historical roots continues not only among historians (Kenney 2003; Pleshakov 2009; Sebestyen 2010; Mueller et al. 2015), but also among social scientists (Eisenstadt 2015; della Porta 2014).

On the other hand, for the students of other countries, particularly East Germany, where the end of communism is usually associated with the fall of the Berlin Wall, the element of surprise and rapid mobilisation have become phenomena needing explanation. It is no wonder, therefore, that this literature is dominated by models designed to explain individuals' calculus to join or not join the unanticipated but rapidly rising tide of contention.

However, the studies written within the rationalist paradigm are not uniform. They differ in their choice of concepts, issues, modelling techniques, and the robustness of empirical verification. For example, Kuran (1991) offers a model based on the modified assumptions of the rational choice school in which he distinguishes between private and public preferences (the latter are "for show") and analyses the dynamic of simulating support for the unwanted regime that he calls preference falsification (hiding private preferences). Once the first challengers publicly express their discontent, "there comes a point where [one's] external cost of joining the opposition falls below his internal cost of preference falsification" (1991: 18). This is a person's "revolutionary threshold." As a growing number of people cross their individual thresholds and join a "revolutionary bandwagon," the protest wave gathers strength. But in addition to individual calculations, Kuran emphasises also the mobilising power of internal and external factors that are beyond actors' control (e.g. Gorbachev's liberalization) that served as triggers setting off the revolutionary bandwagon, mostly in East Germany.

Karklins and Petersen (1993) set out to "explain how individual citizens made their decisions to demonstrate against their powerful governments, . . . why the regimes failed to suppress the demonstrations, and . . . why the process occurred so rapidly and thoroughly" (1993: 588). To answer these questions, they build a model of strategic game played by the people and the government. What is particularly important in the model is that the "masses" are not seen as an homogeneous entity, but rather as a set of distinct groups, dissidents, students, workers, and party supporters, each of which has a different tipping point beyond which its members are ready to demonstrate (assumption very similar to Kuran's). Individuals' calculations of protection and prediction (e.g. the probability of the regime's fall) are central to their model of the situation construed as an n-person assurance game. The models are then tested with empirical data from Czechoslovakia, East Germany, Romania, and China (a negative case).

Lohmann produced a detailed study of several waves of mobilization mostly in Leipzig, East Germany, using painstakingly collected empirical evidence and a sophisticated "dynamic threshold model [that] interprets a sequence of mass protest activities as an informational cascade" (1994: 49). Similar to Kuran and Karklins and Petersen, she emphasizes the significance of heterogeneity within the set of potential protesters. In her conceptualisation there are four categories, ranging from anti-status quo extremists to pro-status quo extremists. Lohmann manages "to show that individual participation decisions may depend on changes in aggregate turnout over time because people extract benefit-cost information from turnout numbers" (1994: 91).

Opp (1994, 1998) offers the fourth influential rational choice model that he tests by using survey data. The central puzzle that drives the analysis does not concern the protest participants, but rather the actions of the tyrannical regime. Opp asks why the powerful and oppressive regime failed to prevent the challenge in 1989, and why it had been successful earlier. The main tool such regimes rely on is repression, and Opp shows that its impact on the probability of protest is not linear; the intensification of repression may actually encourage people to protest under certain circumstances. To argue this, and in contrast to other rational choice scholars, Opp and his colleagues (see Opp, Voss, and Gern 1995) assume that incentives such as public goods incentives, moral incentives ("moral indignation"), and social incentives (social pressure within friendship networks) matter, under certain circumstances, in mobilising people for collective protest action at least as much as selective benefits. One of the key findings of this study is that the perception of the changing political environment in the Soviet Bloc had a powerful influence on the potential protesters (1994: 129).

While rational choice explanations (CARP) are prominent in the literature on 1988–89 in East Central Europe, works belonging to another research program, Synthetic Political Opportunity Structure (SPOT) are increasingly present as well.[2] These include the authoritative study on the role of protest in the breakup of the Soviet Union by Beissinger, who – relying on the method of event analysis – produced an exhaustive study "on the role of the contentious event in the politics of nationalism" (2002: 11) and the way the nationalist mobilisations contributed to the collapse of the Soviet system. Gorenburg (2003) used this approach to analyse minority ethnic mobilisation in the Russian Federation, Glenn (2003) to examine 1989 in Poland and Czechoslovakia, and Vladisavljević (2008) to determine the contribution of popular mobilisation to the fall of communism and the breakup of Yugoslavia.

Post-1989 contention: empirical access, theoretical embarrassment of riches, and diverging regions

Freedom of research that followed the fall of state socialism has attracted to the region scholars from all corners of the social sciences. They expanded the disciplinary range of the study of Eastern Europe and often engaged in productive collaborations with the earlier generation of area studies scholars. In what has become a multi-stranded literature on the post-1989 protest politics of the region we detect three approaches that had earlier helped to interpret contention in Eastern Europe. First is the line of thought indebted to critical social science, inspired by Marxism. It has produced studies on labour unions and working class protests, and on the "losers" of post-communist transformations more generally. The second broad school belongs to comparative politics, as it focuses on the *role protest plays in the consolidation of post-communist political regimes* and on the interaction between institutionalised and contentious forms of politics. Scholars belonging to the third group study *bottom up, popular mobilisation among specific groups and sectors of the post-1989 society*, ranging from ethnic minorities, ecologists, to women and LGBT people. Their work is often anchored in the tradition of political and historical sociology, and political anthropology.

Critical social science

Researchers continuing the tradition of critical social science often study what may be called a *puzzle of low working class contentiousness*. Why do workers in post-communist countries, often experiencing detrimental changes in their professional and private lives, not protest more vigorously? There are several explanations. Greskovits compares Eastern Europe and Latin America, observes that the transformations in the former were accompanied by less violence and contention, and concludes that the main reason for that East European "patience" is that:

> Communism left behind societies lacking in the structural, institutional, and cultural factors associated with violent collective action. The lack of extreme income inequality, the smaller number of marginalized poor, the relatively lower degree of urbanization of the population, and the absence of recent, violent experiences with coups and riots may all have contributed a stabilizing influence under post-Communism.
>
> *(1998: 85)*

Vanhuysse emphasises a different set of factors to explain the relative quiescence of workers: high levels of exit into the informal economy, the decline of unionised jobs, the ineptness of union leadership, ideological "delusions" (such as the attraction of illiberal and populist ideas), but primarily well-designed governmental strategies of "divide and pacify" (2006: 137).

Crowley, Ost, and their colleagues argue that the main cause of labour weakness is its "own anti-union ideas, or what might be called a crisis of class identity, that contributes powerfully to union weakness" (2001: 7) and see this crisis as a legacy of state socialism, under which labour unions functioned mostly as "transmission belts" of communist party power. Bohle and Greskovits (2012) dispute some of the conclusions in Crowley and Ost (2001), particularly that unions in South Eastern Europe were created "as weak actor." They argue that in many cases they started relatively strong and only weakened over time (2012: 184–191). Ost (2005) develops the argument about Solidarity activists "betraying" their unionist identity, replacing it with nationalistic and religious ideology and in the process losing their effectiveness as labour's champions.

Sil's "second generation" argument (2014) is that labour in Eastern Europe is not particularly weak and the unions are not inconsequential (after the initial decline), though their influence varies across the region. He offers a complex, context-sensitive explanation for the difference in the effectiveness of labour unions in Poland and the Czech Republic, and concludes that in the latter the unions are less divided and more successful in defending workers' interests because they form more effective alliances with left-wing parties. Wenzel (forthcoming) studies labour union activities in Poland, particularly their protest actions, and – much like Sil – concludes that the unions have had significant influence on the course of post-communist transformations in that country. Ashwin (1999) examines the relative quiescence of the Russian working class.

Beissinger and Sasse (2013), who studied the massive protest wave that swept the post-communist countries after the crisis of 2008, ask whether *the end of this patience is coming*. They refer to the relative quiescence of the labour class in post-communist countries. They conclude that it is context-dependent:

> In Tolstoyan fashion, those "happy" countries that continued to experience economic growth in the midst of global crisis were all little affected by protest, while those "unhappy" countries that experienced significant economic contractions were all "unhappy" in their own ways, displaying quite varied protest responses to economic decline.
>
> *(2013: 363–364)*

Comparative politics: regimes, institutions, and contention

The literature in this area can be usefully grouped into four, occasionally overlapping, strands. They include studies of (1) contentious politics in new democracies (including right-wing contentious challenges to liberal democracy and protests against democratic backsliding), (2) the role of protests in semi-authoritarian and authoritarian states, (3) "colour revolutions", and (4) contentious dimensions of ethnic politics.

There is a group of post-communist countries that at some point began negotiating membership in the EU and eventually became members of this elite club, and made the best progress on the path of democratisation. Most work on these countries concentrates on top-down mechanisms of change, such as institutional reforms, the emergence and evolution of political systems and political parties, and the political economy of transformations. Studies of bottom-up mobilisations have been far less common. Building on an assumption that protest is a legitimate mode of political behaviour in a democracy, Ekiert and Kubik (1998a, 1998b, 1999) propose a systematic study of the role of bottom-up contention in the consolidation of democracy in Poland, Hungary, Slovakia, and the former East Germany. Their method is event analysis based on systematic data collection from newspaper sources, often used by the scholars working within the SPOT paradigm. Other scholars of contention *and* democratisation studied the role of "corrective" bottom-up protests in Bulgaria (Ganev 2014), Romania (Margarit 2016), or, comparatively, in Bulgaria, Hungary, and Romania (Margarit 2015, see also Szabó 1996).

Democratic backsliding in the new EU member states has recently attracted scholarly attention, also among scholars of contention. The problem, observed at least since least 2008, is particularly pronounced in Hungary where the right-wing populist parties – often relying on mass mobilisation – have challenged liberal democracy (Krasztev and Van Til 2016). The rise of right-wing populist movements in Eastern Europe and the increasing visibility of their contentious actions is captured in the large comparative project, "The Logic of Civil Society in New Democracies: Hungary, Poland, South Korea and Taiwan" (Greskovits, Várhalmi, and Wittenberg 2013; Ekiert, Kubik, and Wenzel 2013). Using the method of event analysis, Płatek and Płucienniczak (2016) conducted a detailed study of Polish right-wing protests in 2003–2014. More generally, right-wing mobilisation in the region is well-documented in several collections, Kopecký and Mudde (2003), Melzer and Serafin (2013) and Langenbacher and Schellenberg (2011). These works analyse a broad range of organisations in several East and Central European countries, though they did not study protest actions per se.

The second distinct body of work is devoted to the study of protest politics in countries where political transformations stalled and the outcome has been more or less repressive authoritarianism. Here, the dominant problem areas include periodic outburst of discontent, most famously *colour revolutions* (discussed as a separate phenomenon later), protest actions directed against the abuses of electoral process (*electoral protests*) and de-democratization, and protest under authoritarian regimes. Bunce and Wolchik (2011) study eleven electoral episodes in nine countries to comparatively examine the electoral model of democratic transition in mixed (hybrid) regimes. They do not focus on protest per se, but examine its role as the major factor of political change, alongside and in interaction with elections. Their work examines also the role of diffusion, also of protest repertoires, in challenging non-democratic regimes (particularly in Bunce and Wolchik 2010). Several influential works focus explicitly on the role of protest in hybrid regimes (conceptualised often as competitive or electoral authoritarianism). Robertson (2007, 2010), using the method of event analysis and relying partially on his own database constructed from the daily reports prepared by the Russian Interior Ministry, builds a densely textured analysis of the Russian case (during three periods: Yeltsin, 1997–2000; the first Putin term, 2000–2004;

and the second Putin term, 2005–2008). He generalises that within hybrid regimes "variations in protest patterns are likely to be driven by three key variables: *organizational ecology, state mobilization strategies*, and *elite competition*" (2010: 6). Specific combinations of the values of these three dummy variables account for eight specific patterns of contention (2010: 204). For the students of mixed regimes, including Russia, the most important finding is that in such regimes "competition is less something that authoritarians have failed to eliminate, but rather something that they consciously allow and try to control" (2010: 217). Lankina and Voznaya (2015) study "multiple protest arenas" in a large hybrid regime state (Russia) and demonstrate that regional variation influences both the intensity of protest and the type of demands. Greene (2014) shows the post-communist system in Russia increasingly relies on "disconnecting" the political world of the elite from society. Russian society is not suppressed, but rather it is just made irrelevant, since the state/government/elite has managed to form a system in which it is relatively isolated from "bottom-up" pressures of protest. The society is not as passive as it is portrayed in most standard studies; it is active but the system's configuration prevents this activity from being effective. Smyth (2014) and Smyth, Soboleva, Shimek, and Sobolev (2015), building on their original database (including interviews with the protestors), analyse the competing mobilisations (and narratives) of Putin's opponents and supporters, often clashing in the streets after the December 2011 presidential elections. Smyth, Sobolev, and Soboleva (2013) study the manufactured mobilisation of Putin's supporters and its political impact.

Two books deal with the periodic outburst of protest in the most authoritarian post-communist states. Navumau (2016) studies "the Belarussian Maidan" of 2006 in a rare study of protest in the most oppressive regime in Europe. He provides a detailed account of what transpired, but also an original interpretation, partially driven by an effort to assess the applicability of Western models to the specific realities of post-Soviet Belarus. Radnitz (2010), in a book "subverting" the chief idea of James Scott's influential study (1985), shows that protest in Kyrgyzstan was to a large degree manufactured by a part of the elite that achieved influence over some segment of the populace through a mechanism he calls "subversive clientelism."

The literature on colour revolutions, a fascinating cross-national protest wave, deserves to be discussed as a distinct strand. The 2000 "Bulldozer Revolution" in Serbia was the first in a series of revolts against new authoritarian rulers in the region. As in other cases, the success was predicated on massive mobilisation of civil society and its coordinated actions (Bieber 2003). Revolutions in Georgia (2003), Ukraine (2004), and Kyrgyzstan (2005) followed. Their origins, mechanisms, and consequences have been interpreted and explained in several ways. Wilson (2005) offers a description and day-to day analysis of the Orange Revolution in Ukraine, while Onuch (2014), comparing this revolt with the Argentinian upheaval of 2001, provides a comprehensive history of Ukrainian revolts since 1920, develops her own theoretical frames inspired predominantly by SPOT, uses her own multifaceted database, and as a result is able to "map" a very comprehensive picture of the revolution. Hypotheses derived from the SPOT program are mixed with several CARP ideas in Beissinger's analysis of the Orange Revolution (2013). Relying on the results of two surveys, he shows that the revolutionaries in Ukraine (as in Tunisia and Egypt) were not driven by a strong commitment to democratic ideals; rather, people with disparate preferences formed "negative coalitions" and their actions were "fueled predominantly by extreme rejection of the incumbent regime, with no dominant, overarching grievance" (2013: 17). For Tucker (2009), who works within the CARP paradigm, the free-riding dilemma is one of the central concerns. He argues that the most important factor that helped to overcome this dilemma in Ukraine and trigger mobilisation was information about vote-rigging. Lane (2009), by contrast, believes that most people assumed that the information about the rigged elections was manufactured (2009: 132). Lane focuses also on "democracy promotion" that he sees as a misguided strategy, because counter-elites use the ideology of democracy to win power from incumbents, not to justify and underpin democratic reforms. He also confirms a widely accepted view that while relative deprivation predisposes people to rebel, it is not a sufficient cause of insurgency (2009: 125).

Beissinger (2007) sets out to determine whether the external (such as diffusion of ideas and democracy promotion) or internal factors (that is, structural conditions and elite behaviour) are more important in triggering "modular" revolutions and in increasing the probability of their success. He convincingly demonstrates that while the power of example can help to overcome adverse structural conditions and trigger protest, the success of the revolt is more difficult to achieve if favourable internal, structural, and institutional factors are not properly aligned. Beissinger mixes elements of SPOT and CARP, as he models the impact of both structural factors and mobilisation thresholds, calculated by the elites, to model the shape of protest waves. Way (2008) gives primacy to structural factors (political opportunity structure in SPOT's terminology) emphatically in a study in which he tries to explain differential successes of various colour revolutions.

The fourth subset of works in comparative politics deals with national and ethnic mobilisations that often take highly contentious forms. Beissinger's seminal work (2002) set the standard for this body of literature. Building on his own sophisticated theorising of the relationship between structure and agency (firmly embedded within the SPOT tradition) and a painstakingly collected protest event database, he argued that although the collapse of the Soviet Union was caused by a complex set of factors, the dominant role was played by contentious events that accumulated over time and ultimately overwhelmed the ostensibly unmovable power structure. In a study that also relies heavily on the SPOT analytical apparatus, Gorenburg (2003) examines four ethnic republics of the Russian Federation and shows that the success of bottom-up nationalist mobilisation does not depend on the existence of propitious economic conditions, but is rather brought about by the strengthening of ethnic loyalties by "friendly" institutions that are often provided by the state. Stroschein (2012; also in this volume), another practitioner of SPOT, observes that the literature on the rise of ethnic politics and ethnic mobilisations does not always articulate with the field of study of contentious politics. She sets out to rectify this problem and, relying on her own database (built by protest event analysis), she studies contentious actions of the Hungarian minority in Slovakia and Romania to demonstrate "how ethnic protest served to incorporate Hungarians into polities in which that are permanent minorities, by providing an extra-institutional means for them to confluence policies" (2012: 10).

Sociology of discontent: protests of the excluded

This literature, anchored in the historical and political sociology, is concerned with identifying, understanding and explaining *patterns of mobilisation per se*, and assessing their role in politics though not always explicitly their impact on regime consolidation. The studies belonging to this strand deal predominantly with contentious politics driven by *identity issues*, ranging from religion to sexual orientation. Members of many social groups and categories struggle for the full recognition of their identities and interests and/or protest against the high costs of transformations, unjustly – in their judgment – impacting their members. There are works on protests by farmers (Foryś 2008), women (Regulska and Grabowska 2013), environmentalists (Fagan and Carmin 2011), homeless and urban activists (Jacobsson 2015), and sexual minorities (Vermeersch 2006; Holzhacker 2012; O'Dwyer 2012; Sperling 2014; O'Dwyer in this volume). Some scholars have focused on the study of left-wing (often radical) movements and their weakness in postcommunist Europe, for example, alterglobalists (Piotrowski 2013).

Summary

Collective protests and contentious mobilisations have been permanent features of East European politics since 1945 to the present, although over time they have changed considerably. There are four distinct periods in the evolution of contentiousness in the region: (1) mostly spontaneous rebellions against the imposition of communist rule and policies of the new regimes; (2) the period of reforms and opposition movements lasting from the Prague Spring in 1968 until 1989, with the Prague Spring and the rise and suppression of the Solidarity movement as its dominant events; (3) the 1989–1991 revolutions that involved widespread contentious mobilisation, contagion and diffusion, and an enormous range of protest strategies from peaceful demonstration to bloody civil wars; and (4) the post-1989 period, characterised by the "normalisation" of contention shaped by diverging regime types, spanning the entire range from consolidated democracies to various forms of authoritarian rule.

In this review we did not set out to present protest and contentious mobilisation in Eastern Europe, but rather to reconstruct the evolution of approaches used to describe, interpret, and explain contention. We focus in particular on the post-1989–1991 period characterised by an impressive diversity of interpretative and explanatory strategies. Inspirations of critical Marxism are clearly reflected in the continuing interest in the absence of class-based mobilisation and weakness of the left-wing radicalism. The second broad research programme belonging mostly to comparative politics is preoccupied with the role of contention in democratisation and authoritarian backsliding, while the third strand focuses on patterns of mobilisation related to social cleavages and identities. While many studies of contention in the region are descriptive and interpretive, there is an equally significant body of work employing more "positivistic" explanatory strategies focused on identifying causal mechanisms and based on large, systematic, and comparative data sets.

Notes

1 The Helsinki Accords (or Helsinki Final Act) were signed on 1 August 1975, at the conclusion of the first Conference on Security and Co-operation in Europe. They legitimated the post-Second-World-War borders of Europe. The thirty-five signatory states (including the Soviet Union and all its satellite states, except Albania) agreed, *inter alia*, to respect human rights and basic political freedoms. From that point on, the Soviet Bloc governments had a much more difficult time suppressing political opposition (dissident movements) that would invoke the Accords when faced with persecution.
2 Since the 1970s, two research programmes have come to dominate the field of study on contentious politics: Synthetic Political Opportunity Theory (SPOT) and Collective Action Research Programme (CARP), as they were dubbed by Lichbach (1998). SPOT's dominant tenor is structuralist and historical (its leading scholars are Tilly, Tarrow, and McAdam), while CARP focuses on individual decisions and relies on rational choice and game theory. See also Lichbach (1995).

Bibliography

Ash, Konstatin. 2011. "A Game-theoretic Model of Protest in the Context of Post-communism." *Communist and Post-Communist Studies* 44: 1–15.
Ash, Timothy Garton. 1983. *The Polish Revolution: Solidarity.* New York: Charles Scribner's Sons.
Ash, Timothy Garton. 1990. *Magic Lantern: Revolution of '89.* New York: Random House.
Ashwin, Sarah. 1999. *Russian Workers: The Anatomy of Patience.* Manchester: Manchester University Press.
Banac, Ivo. ed. 1992. *Eastern Europe in Revolution.* Ithaca, NY: Cornell University Press.
Baring, Arnulf. 1972. *Uprising in East Germany: June 17, 1953.* Ithaca, NY: Cornell University Press.
Beissinger, Mark R. 2002. *Nationalist Mobilization and the Collapse of the Soviet State.* Cambridge: Cambridge University Press.

Beissinger, Mark R. 2007. "Structure and Example in Modular Political Phenomena: The Diffusion of Bulldozer/Rose/Orange/Tulip Revolutions." *Perspectives on Politics* 5, 2: 259–276.

Beissinger, Mark R. 2013. "The Semblance of Democratic Revolution: Coalitions in Ukraine's Orange Revolution." *American Political Science Review* 107, 3: 574–592.

Beissinger, Mark R. and Gwendolyn Sasse. 2013. "An End to Patience? The 2008 Global Financial Crisis and Political Protest in Eastern Europe." In Larry Bartels and Nancy Bermeo, eds. *Mass Politics in Tough Times: Opinions, Votes and Protest in the Great Recession.* New York: Oxford University Press, 334–370.

Bernhard, Michael H. 1993. *The Origins of Democratization in Poland.* New York: Columbia University Press.

Bieber, Florian. 2003. "The Serbian Opposition and Civil Society: Roots of the Delayed Transition in Serbia." *International Journal of Politics, Culture, and Society*, 17, 1 [Studies in the Social History of Destruction: The Case of Yugoslavia]: 73–90.

Bohle, Dorothee and Béla Greskovits. 2012. *Capitalist Diversity on Europe's Periphery.* Ithaca, NY: Cornell University Press.

Bruszt, László and David Stark. 1991. "Remaking the Political Field: From the Politics of Confrontation to the Politics of Competition." *Journal of International Affairs*, 45, 1: 201–245.

Bunce, Valerie and Sharon Wolchik. 2010. "Transnational Networks, Diffusion Dynamics, and Electoral Change in the Postcommunist World." In Rebecca Kolins Givan, Kenneth M. Roberts, and Sarah Soule, eds. *The Diffusion of Social Movements: Actors, Mechanisms, and Political Effects.* Cambridge: Cambridge University Press, 140–162.

Bunce, Valerie and Sharon Wolchik. 2011. *Defeating Authoritarian Leaders in Postcommunist Countries.* Cambridge: Cambridge University Press.

Cirtautas, Arista M. 1997. *The Polish Solidarity Movement: Revolution, Democracy and Natural Rights.* London: Routledge.

Crowley, Stephen and David Ost, eds. 2001. *Workers After Workers' States: Labor and Politics in Postcommunist Eastern Europe.* Lanham, MD: Rowman & Littlefield.

Della Porta, Donatella. 2014. *Mobilizing for Democracy: Comparing 1989 and 2011.* Oxford: Oxford University Press.

Eisenstadt, Shmuel N. 2015. "The Velvet and the Classical Revolutions – A Comparative Analysis in the Framework of the Dynamics of Modernity." In Andrzej Rychard and Gabriel Motzkin, eds. *The Legacy of Polish Solidarity: Social Activism, Regime Collapse, and Building of a New Society.* Frankfurt am Main: Peter Lang, 203–213.

Ekiert, Grzegorz. 1996. *The State Against Society: Political Crises and Their Aftermath in East Central Europe.* Princeton, NJ: Princeton University Press.

Ekiert, Grzegorz and Jan Kubik. 1998a. "Contentious Politics in New Democracies: East Germany, Hungary, Poland, and Slovakia, 1989–1994." *World Politics*, 50: 547–581.

Ekiert, Grzegorz and Jan Kubik. 1998b. "Collective Protest in Postcommunist Poland, 1989–1993." *Communist and Post-Communist Studies*, 31, 2: 91–117.

Ekiert, Grzegorz and Jan Kubik. 1999. *Rebellious Civil Society: Popular Protest and Democratic Consolidation in Poland, 1989–1993.* Ann Arbor: University of Michigan Press.

Ekiert, Grzegorz, Jan Kubik, and Michal Wenzel. 2013. *Civil Society in Poland After the Fall of Communism: A Diachronic Perspective.* Presented at the Council for European Studies' (CES) Twentieth International Conference of Europeanists, June 25–27, 2013, Amsterdam.

Fagan, Adam and JoAnn Carmin, eds. 2011. *Green Activism in Post-Socialist Europe and the Former Soviet Union.* London: Routledge.

Foryś, Grzegorz. 2008. *Dynamika sporu. Protesty rolników w III Rzeczpospolitej* [*The Dynamics of Dispute: The Farmers' Protests in the Third Republic*]. Warszawa: Wydawnictwo Naukowe SCHOLAR.

Ganev, Venelin. 2014. "Bulgaria's Year of Civic Anger." *The Journal of Democracy*, 25, 1: 33–45.

Glenn, John. 2003. *Framing Democracy: Civil Society and Civic Movements in Eastern Europe.* Stanford, CA: Stanford University Press.

Gorenburg, Dmitry P. 2003. *Minority Ethnic Mobilization in the Russian Federation.* Cambridge: Cambridge University Press.

Greene, Samuel A. 2014. *Moscow in Movement: Power and Opposition in Putin's Russia.* Stanford, CA: Stanford University Press.

Greskovits, Béla. 1998. *The Political Economy of Protest and Patience: East European and Latin American Transformations Compared.* Budapest: Central European University Press.

Greskovits, Béla, Zoltán Várhalmi, and Jason Wittenberg. 2013. *Contentious Civil Society and Democratic Consolidation: Hungary in the 1990s and 2000s*. Presented at the Council for European Studies' (CES) Twentieth International Conference of Europeanists, 25–27 June 2013, Amsterdam.

Gwertzman, Bernard and Michael F. Kaufman, eds. 1991. *The Collapse of Communism*. New York: Times Book.

Holzhacker, Ronald. 2012. "National and Transnational Strategies of LGBT Civil Society Organizations in Different Political Environments: Modes of Interaction in Western and Eastern Europe for Equality." *Comparative European Politics*, 10, 1: 23–47.

Jacobsson, Kerstin, ed. 2015. *Urban Grassroots Movements in Central and Eastern Europe*. Farnham: Ashgate.

Joppke, Christian. 1995. *East German Dissidents and the Revolution of 1989: Social Movement in a Leninist Regime*. Houndmills: MacMillan Press.

Kamiński, Łukasz, Andrzej Małkiewicz, and Krzysztof Ruchniewicz. 2004. *Opór społeczny w Europie Środkowej w latach 1948–1953 na przykładzie Polski, NRD i Czechosłowacji [Social Resistance in Central Europe in 1948–53: Cases of Poland, German Democratic Republic and Czechoslovakia]*. Wrocław: Atut.

Karklins, Rasma and Roger Petersen. 1993. "Decision Calculus of Protesters and Regimes: Eastern Europe 1989." *Journal of Politics*, 55, 3: 588–614.

Kenney, Padraic. 2003. *A Carnival of Revolution: Central Europe 1989*. Princeton, NJ: Princeton University Press.

Kopecký, Petr and Cas Mudde. 2003. *Uncivil Society? Contentious Politics in Post-communist Europe*. London: Routledge.

Kornhauser, William. 1959. *The Politics of Mass Society*. New York: Free Press.

Krasztev, Péter and Jon Van Til, eds. 2016. *The Hungarian Patient: Social Opposition to an Illiberal Democracy*. Budapest: Central European University Press.

Kubik, Jan. 1994. *The Power of Symbols Against the Symbols of Power: The Rise of Solidarity and the Fall of State Socialism in Poland*. College Park, PA: Penn State Press.

Kuran, Timor. 1991. "Now Out of Never. The Element of Surprise in the East European Revolution." *World Politics*, 44, 1: 7–48.

Lane, David. 2009. " 'Coloured Revolution' as a Political Phenomenon." *Journal of Communist Studies and Transition Politics*, 25, 2–3: 113–135.

Langenbacher, Nora and Britta Schellenberg, eds. 2011. *Is Europe on the "Right" Path? Right-wing Extremism and Right-wing Populism in Europe*. Berlin: Friedrich Ebert Stiftung.

Lankina, Tomila V. and Alisa Voznaya. 2015. "New Data on Protest Trends in Russia's Regions." *Europe-Asia Studies*, 67, 2: 327–342.

Lewis, Flora. 1958. *A Case History of Hope: The Story of Poland's Peaceful Revolution*. New York: Doubleday.

Lichbach, Mark I. 1995. *The Rebel's Dilemma*. Ann Arbor: University of Michigan Press.

Lichbach, Mark I. 1998. "Contending Theories of Contentious Politics and the Structure-Action Problem of Social Order." *Annual Review of Political Science*, 1: 401–424.

Lohmann, Susanne. 1994. "The Dynamics of Informational Cascades. The Monday Demonstrations in Leipzig, East Germany, 1989–91." *World Politics*, 47: 42–101.

Margarit, Diana. 2015. "Ideology and Social Movements: A Comparative Analysis of the 2013 Protests in Bulgaria, Hungary, and Romania." In Geoffrey Pleyers and Ionel N. Sava, eds. *Social Movements in Central and Eastern Europe: A Renewal of Protest and Democracy*. Bucharest: Editura Universitatii din Bucuresti, 13–26.

Margarit, Diana. 2016. "Civic Disenchantment and Political Distress: The Case of the Romanian Autumn." *East European Politics*, 32, 1: 46–62.

McAdam, Doug, John D. McCarthy, and Mayer N. Zald, eds. 1996. *Comparative Perspectives on Social Movements: Political Opportunities, Mobilizing Structures, and Cultural Framing*. Cambridge: Cambridge University Press.

McDermott, Kevin and Matthew Stibbe, eds. 2006. *Revolutions and Resistance in Eastern Europe: Challenges to Communist Rule*. Oxford: Berg.

Melzer, Ralf and Sebastian Serafin, eds. 2013. *Right-wing Extremism in Europe: Country Analyses, Counter-Strategies and Labor-Market Oriented Exit Strategies*. Berlin: Friedrich Ebert Foundation.

Mueller, Wolfgang, Michael Gehler, and Arnold Suppan, eds. 2015. *The Revolutions of 1989: A Handbook*. Vienna: Verlag der Osterreichischen Akademie der Wissenschaften.

Navumau, Vasil. 2016. *The Belarussian Maidan in 2016: A New Social Movement Approach to the Tent Camp Protest in Minsk*. Frankfurt am Main: Peter Lang.

O'Dwyer, Conor. 2012. "Does the EU Help or Hinder Gay-Rights Movements in Postcommunist Europe? The Case of Poland." *East European Politics*, 28, 4: 332–352.

Onuch, Olga. 2014. *Mapping Mass Mobilization: Understanding Revolutionary Moments in Argentina and Ukraine*. London: Palgrave Macmillan.

Opp, Karl-Dieter. January 1994. "Repression and Revolutionary Action: East Germany in 1989." *Rationality and Society*: 101–138.

Opp, Karl-Dieter. 1998. "Explaining Revolutions From Below: East Germany in 1989. A Reply." *The Independent Review* III, 1: 91–102.

Opp, Karl-Dieter, Peter Voss, and Christiane Gern. 1995. *Origins of a Spontaneous Revolution: East Germany, 1989*. Ann Arbor: University of Michigan Press.

Ost, David. 1990. *Solidarity and the Politics of Anti-politics: Opposition and Reform in Poland Since 1968*. Philadelphia, PA: Temple University Press.

Ost, David. 2005. *The Defeat of Solidarity: Anger and Politics in Postcommunist Europe*. Ithaca, NY: Cornell University Press.

Paczkowski, Andrzej. 2003. *Strajki, bunty, manifestacje jako "polska droga" przez socjalizm* [*Strikes, Rebellions, Manifestations as the "Polish Road" Through Socialism*]. Poznań: Wydawnictwo Poznańskiego Towarzystwa Przyjaciół Nauk.

Paczkowski, Andrzej. 2015. *Revolution and Counterrevolution in Poland, 1980–89*. Warsaw: ISP PAN/University of Rochester Press.

Piotrowski, Grzegorz. 2013. "Social Movement or Subculture? Alterglobalists in Central and Eastern Europe." *Interface: A Journal for and About Social Movements*, 5, 2: 399–421.

Płatek, Daniel and Piotr P. Płucienniczak. 2016. *Civil Society and the Extreme Right Collective Actions in Poland, 1990–2013*. Unpublished Paper.

Pleshakov, Constantine. 2009. *There Is No Freedom Without Bread: 1989 and the Civil War That Brought Down Communism*. New York: Farrar, Straus and Giroux.

Radnitz, Scott. 2010. *Weapons of the Wealthy Predatory Regimes and Elite-Led Protests in Central Asia*. Ithaca, NY: Cornell University Press.

Regulska, Joanna and Magdalena Grabowska. 2013. "Social Justice, Hegemony, and Women's Mobilizations." In Jan Kubik and Amy Linch, eds. *Postcommunism From Within: Social Justice, Mobilization, and Hegemony*. New York: New York University Press, 139–190.

Robertson, Graeme. 2007. "Strikes and Protest in Hybrid Regimes." *American Political Science Review*, 101, 4: 781–798.

Robertson, Graeme. 2010. *The Politics of Protest in Hybrid Regimes: Managing Dissent in Post-Communist Russia*. Cambridge: Cambridge University Press.

Scott, James C. 1985. *Weapons of the Weak: Everyday Forms of Peasant Resistance*. New Haven, CT: Yale University Press.

Sebestyen, Victor. 2010. *Revolution 1989: The Fall of the Soviet Empire*. New York: Vintage.

Sil, Rudra. 2014. *Liberalization and Labor Incorporation in Postcommunist Europe: A Paired Comparison of Poland and the Czech Republic*. Presented at the Annual Meeting of the International Studies Association, March 2014, Toronto, Canada.

Smelser, Neil. 1963. *Theory of Collective Behavior*. New York: Free Press.

Smyth, Regina. 2014. "The Putin Factor: Personalism, Protest, and Regime Stability in Russia." *Politics & Policy*, 42, 4: 567–592.

Smyth, Ragina, Anton Sobolev, and Irina Soboleva. 2013. "A Well-Organized Play." *Problems of Post-Communism* 60, 2: 24–39.

Smyth, Regina, Irina Soboleva, Luke Shimek, and Anton Sobolev. 2015. "Defining Common Ground: Collective Identity in Russia's Post-Election Protests and Rallies." In Cameron Ross, ed. *Civil Society Awakens? The Systemic and Non-Systemic Opposition in the Russian Federation: National and Regional Dimensions*. Aldershot: Ashgate Press, 51–75.

Sperling, Valerie. 2014. *Sex, Politics, and Putin: Political Legitimacy in Russia*. New York: Oxford University Press.

Stokes, Gale. 1993. *The Walls Came Tumbling Down*. New York: Oxford University Press.

Stroschein, Sherrill. 2012. *Ethnic Struggle, Coexistence, and Democratization in Eastern Europe*. Cambridge: Cambridge University Press.

Szabó, Máté. 1996. "Repertoires of Contention in Post-Communist Protest Cultures: An East Central European Comparative Survey (Hungary, Slovakia, Slovenia)." *Social Research*, 63, 4: 1155–1183.

Tarrow, Sidney. 1991. " 'Aiming at the Moving Target': Social Science and the Recent Rebellions in Eastern Europe." *PS: Political Science and Politics*, 24, 1: 12–20.

Tucker, Joshua. 2009. "Enough! Electoral Fraud, Collective Action Problems, and Post-Communist Colored Revolutions." *Perspectives on Politics*, 5, 3: 535–551.

Vanhuysse, Pieter. 2006. *Divide and Pacify: Strategic Social Policies and Political Protests in Post-Communist Democracies*. Budapest: Central European University Press.

Vermeersch, Peter. 2006. *The Romani Movement: Minority Politics and Ethnic Mobilization in Contemporary Central Europe*. New York, Oxford: Berghahn Books.

Vladisavljević, Nebojša. 2008. *Serbia's Anti-bureaucratic Revolution: Milošević, the Fall of Communism and Nationalist Mobilization*. London: Palgrave.

Way, Lucan. 2008. "The Real Causes of The Color Revolutions." *Journal of Democracy*, 19, 3: 55–69.

Wenzel, Michal. 2016. *Labour Protest in Poland: Trade Unions and Employee Interest Articulation After Socialism*. Frankfurt am Main: Peter Lang.

Wilson, Andrew. 2005. *Ukraine's Orange Revolution*. New Haven, CT: Yale University Press.

Zinner, Paul. 1962. *Revolution in Hungary*. Freeport: Books for Libraries Press.

PART IV

Minorities and identity politics

15

UNDERSTANDING ETHNIC MINORITIES IN EASTERN EUROPE

Sherrill Stroschein

Introduction

This chapter presents a summary examination of ethnic minorities in Eastern Europe. The chapter first provides a historical overview of the development of the concept of ethnic minorities, which will show how the emergence and change of state borders in the region have produced ethnically diverse states out of empires. Politically mobilised ethnic groups first truly emerged during the 1800s in the region. Ethnicity was then subsumed within the socialist political structures but emerged as a strong political force in post-1989 democratisation processes. Following this historic and demographic overview, the chapter then sketches some of the key ideas on how ethnic groups matter in society and politics. The discussion outlines general dynamics of ethnic relations, mobilisation, and group goals, and then turns to ethnic minority parties, elections, and decentralisation. The piece concludes with a consideration of the promise and limitations of these general ideas in the complex ethnic context of Eastern Europe.

Ethnic minorities in Eastern Europe

The geographical area known as Eastern Europe has been a place of population movements, wars, and border changes spanning over a thousand years. The way in which the mixing of these diverse populations has been understood has changed across time, in relation to different political events. Up until 1050, many parts of the region were included in empires, such as the Roman, Byzantine, and Bulgarian empires (Magocsi 1993: 6–11, Hupchick and Cox 2001a, 2001b). For the next few hundred years, the region featured medieval kingdoms such as those of Poland, Hungary, Croatia, Bulgaria, Serbia, and Kievan Rus', as well as the Holy Roman Empire (Magocsi 1993: 13–15, Hupchick and Cox 2001a, 2001b). In the 1400s the Ottoman Empire began to advance into the region, and by the late 1500s the Ottomans controlled lands as far north and west as Hungary and Croatia (Magocsi 1993: 47, Szakály in Sugar et al. 1990: 87, Lendvai 2003: 98). The Habsburgs regained control of Hungary and Croatia by 1683, but the Balkan lands including Bosnia, south Serbia, south Romania, and Bulgaria remained under Ottoman control until the late 1800s (Hupchick and Cox 2001b: map 26). A long period of declining Ottoman powers in the region was then followed by the First World War (Magocsi 1993: 63–65, 68, 85; Kann and David 1984: 6–13, Carnegie Endowment 1993).

The peace agreements following the war carved the region into states that are familiar to us today, although the region's border was moved westward with the Soviet Union's acquisition of some eastern territories after the Second World War, changing the shapes of the states to a map that we can recognise today (Rothschild 1989: 2; Rothschild 1992: 2, Hupchick and Cox 2001a). However, after 1991 modifications were also made to the borders of the post-war map, with the collapse of Soviet, Czechslovak, and Yugoslav federal states into smaller units.

This extremely complex history has aligned with shifts in what it means to be a minority, including an ethnic minority. For several hundred years, minority status was often tied to a religious identity. To be a Serb in the Ottoman Empire meant to be an Orthodox Christian rather than a Muslim, though this difference also came with economic implications (Jelavich 1983: 91–92, Banac 1984: 59–69). Identity was retained through language to some degree. However, as the business of empires was conducted in a common language, languages that were not used for official purposes, such as Czech, tended to be more common in domestic spheres during the age of empires (Glassheim 2005).

An understanding of ethnicity and nationalism as motivations in politics that is similar to today's understanding began to emerge in the 1800s (Banac 1984: 79). Some of the uprisings of Serbs against the Ottoman Empire in the early 1800s featured an aspect of ethnic identity, though Serbian grievances also reflected their economic circumstances (Jelavich 1983: 196–203). Jelavich (1983) links this nationalist development to the ideas of the German philosopher Johann Gottfried Herder, who outlined the *Volk*, or people, as being a crucial unit of society that took priority over individual interests. These ideas also contained an explicit link to language and culture (Jelavich 1983: 172–174).

In 1848, there was a series of popular uprisings against the Austro-Hungarian Empire (the Habsburgs). The notion of a national identity linked to language and culture was clearly reflected in these mobilisations. There are several lines of thought about the emergence of nationalism as a political identity that implied a connection between a national group and governance of that group. Some historians, such as Smith (1986), noted that while this particular manifestation of identity might be modern, elements of nations such as their ethnic roots and myths were in fact ancient. The view that nations have deeply historical roots is also often reflected in interviews with self-identified nationalists in the region.

A contrasting view focuses on nations as being constructed by modern forces, beginning in the 1800s in particular. Anderson (1991) posited that national identities became salient along with the advent of newspapers and print capitalism. Newspapers presented faraway events as connected to individuals because of their shared language, culture, and identity, and they thus created "imagined communities" of nations. As he describes, "[T]he members of even the smallest nation will never know most of their fellow-members, meet them, or even hear of them, yet in the minds of each lives the image of their communion" (Anderson 1991: 6). Gellner saw nationalism, or the political notion that nations and states should align, as a kind of secular religion that was instilled by state governments through an education system, an inherently modern trait of an industrial society (1983). A somewhat similar perspective is outlined by Hobsbawm (1992), who emphasises how the idea of nationalism is used by governing elites to ensure popular mobilisation.

Is nationalism connected more to ethnicity, language, religion, culture, or other traits? In Connor's (1994) useful breakdown, nationalism is often confused with a number of these traits. Like Gellner, Connor instead focuses on the way in which it can be used for political ends. The claim that nations and states go together is one that both authors question. The term nation state is an especially problematic example of a lack of careful language with regard to these concepts. The notion that nations and states should be "congruent" (Gellner 1983: 1) is a political project, one that should be critically examined by observers.

For conceptual clarity, it is useful to consider traits such as ethnicity, language, religion, and culture as potential items on the menu of nations. One trait is sufficient to demarcate a nation, but a combination of traits may also be present. In addition, to avoid muddling concepts, it can be useful to think of nations in terms of Anderson's imagined communities, with nationalism as a political manifestation of the national identity. In terms of sentiment towards a state, patriotism is a more appropriate word. Ethnic minorities, then, exhibit specific traits of descent (Chandra 2006) that differ from that of the state's titular group, or the ethnicity reflected in the state's name (Laitin 1998: xiv). For example, ethnic Slovaks are the titular group in Slovakia, while ethnic Hungarians are an ethnic minority there. The degree to which these ethnic traits matter for politics will vary according to the political context. More is said about these latent versus mobilised differences later.

During the period of socialism in Eastern Europe, political mobilisations outside of the Socialist Party line were discouraged. Ethnic minorities were allowed to participate in activities that took place within the government regime, but were prohibited from any activities that regimes perceived as challenging their rule. Minority cultural organisations such as dance groups were often encouraged and even funded by the state. In addition, in most states ethnic minorities were allowed to attend schools in their own language, even at university level in some cases. There were some exceptions to this rule. For example, the practice of ethnicity was more problematic in the context of the former Yugoslavia, where Josip Broz Tito's regime emphasised a common "Yugoslav" identity in the wake of a brutal civil war between groups during the Second World War.

Separate religious identities were more complicated in terms of their relationship to the state. Socialism tended to be secular, but religious officials exhibited varied types of relationships with the state in different contexts. Some religious officials were jailed for their beliefs or actions, as was the case for some Hungarian leaders in Romania – a treatment sometimes linked to their status as ethnic minorities. Ethnic minority mobilization in religious terms was antithetical to the Socialist regimes, and thus was treated with suspicion by these governments. Ethnic minorities might have their own newspapers and separate Socialist organizations – as was the case for Hungarian minorities throughout the region – but all of these institutions had to stay within the official party line to continue their operations (Stroschein 2012: 83–84). With the collapse of the Socialist regimes in 1989, ethnic minorities quickly became politically mobilised, often forming their own parties.

Ethnic minorities, regime change, and democracy

The political upheavals in 1989 included mobilisation by ethnic Hungarians in Timişoara, Romania, when the government attempted to arrest an ethnic Hungarian protestant minister (Gati 1990: 183–184, Stokes 1993: 163). Romania's December 1989 transition involved significant violence between protesters and government forces. Violence also erupted in March 1990 between ethnic Hungarians and Romanians in the mixed city of Târgu Mureş, originating in a conflict over the language of instruction in local schools. In spite of tensions and disagreements, however, there was no further inter-group violence on this scale in Romania (Stroschein 2012: 97–102).

By the spring and summer of 1991, there were skirmishes and then violence between Serbs and Croats in relation to the Croat and Slovene declarations of independence from Yugoslavia

(Glenny 1992). When Bosnia and Herzegovina declared independence in 1992, it became the site of a brutal civil war between mixed ethnic/religious groups. It was in the course of this conflict that the term "ethnic cleansing" was frequently used – the notion that group mixing should be reversed through violence, with the aim of creating ethnically homogenous populations. This conflict was only brought to an end with the internationally brokered Dayton Peace Agreement in November 1995. Ethnic mixing became "unmixed" in both Croatia and Bosnia and Herzegovina. Bosnia had been particularly demographically mixed before these wars, and as a result of the violence a large portion of the Bosnian population was displaced (Glenny 1992, Woodward 1995).

The Yugoslav conflicts are often described as ethnic, between ethnic Serbs, Croats, and Bosnians (see also Bieber in this volume). However, they might be better understood as an effort to establish political control over territories by elites invoking a national identity. Yugoslavia first started to unravel with Slovenia and Croatia declaring independence in 1991. These declarations were followed by a Yugoslav National Army (JNA) response that produced limited violence in homogenous Slovenia. However, the JNA response and the new Croatia's counter-response produced more protracted violence in Croatia, with initial Yugoslav attempts to stop its secession and then the Croatian government's efforts to pressure its Serbian population to leave (Glenny 1992). When heavily mixed Bosnia and Herzegovina declared independence in 1992, a three-way civil war between Serbs, Croats, and Bosniaks (or Muslims), embroiled the country until 1995 (Woodward 1995). Religion was often invoked during the wars, and victims were sometimes identified by religious markers, including their ability to recite certain prayers. Serbs tend to be Christian Orthodox, Croats tend to be Catholic, and Bosnians have become known as Muslim – although there are certainly secular individuals in each group. The complexity of the Bosnian conflict produced a small academic industry from attempts to explain these and related events.

Yugoslavia was one of three states to fragment into component parts as a result of ethnic mobilisation. The federation of Czechoslovakia also dissolved into its Czech and Slovak component parts in 1993, but did so in a non-violent fashion. Eastern Europe today is also generally considered to contain the Baltic states of Estonia, Latvia, and Lithuania, which declared independence from the Soviet Union in 1991 and have established themselves as sovereign states. Latvia and Estonia in particular contain large Russian populations.

Table 15.1 gives a breakdown of the ethnic composition of the region's countries in the wake of these events.

The sections that follow outline some key understandings on ethnic minority politics that relate to the East European mobilisations. The chapter then presents an overview of ethnic politics considerations in democracies, including parties, elections, and constitutional options.

Ethnic mobilisation

During the 1990s, a common phrase used in relation to ethnicity and Eastern Europe was that the collapse of the socialist regimes had "taken the lid off of the cauldron" of ethnic conflicts that were simmering underneath Socialist rule. Robert Kaplan's book *Balkan Ghosts* became a popular book due to its rich description of some of the cultural traditions that the author had found during his travels in the region. Likely intended to simply be a travel book, it was also used by some policymakers in an attempt to avoid intervention in Bosnia and Herzegovina because the region was a morass of "ancient hatreds". During the Yugoslav wars of the early 1990s, many scholars approached this view as a foil, and instead tried to draw attention to the nuanced motivations for ethnic political mobilisations.

Table 15.1 Ethnic minority groups in East European countries

Country	Titular ethnic group	Significant current ethnic minorities, 3% or more of one group*
Estonia	Estonians	Russians
Latvia	Latvians	Russians
Lithuania	Lithuanians	Poles, Russians
Poland	Poles	(only small groups recorded)
Czech Republic	Czechs	Moravians
Slovakia	Slovaks	Hungarians
Hungary	Hungarians	Roma
Slovenia	Slovenes	(only small groups recorded)
Croatia	Croats	Serbs
Bosnia and Herzegovina	Bosnians	Serbs, Croats[2]
Serbia	Serbs	Hungarians
Macedonia[3]	Macedonians	Albanians, Turks
Kosovo	Kosovar Albanians	Serbs[4]
Albania	Albanians	(only small groups recorded)
Romania	Romanians	Hungarians, Roma
Moldova	Moldovans	Ukrainians, Russians, Gagauz[5]
Bulgaria	Bulgarians	Turks, Roma

Sources: Sebök 1998, Rothschild 1992, Senn 1997, Muiznieks 1997, Raun 1997, cross-checked with current census data.

* Roma are vastly under-recorded in this kind of data, and thus in the table. But there is a visible Roma presence in most countries of the region.

One set of ideas that appeared fruitful to theorists trying to explain the ethnic mobilisation and conflict of the 1990s came from the 1950s. One long-standing line of thought on ethnic relations regards the question of whether increased contact between individuals of different groups produces more tolerance or more conflict. The contact hypothesis reflects a view indicated in Allport (1954), which posits that increased contact between individuals of different groups provides increased information that should promote tolerance. An opposing view, the conflict hypothesis, posits that the more one learns about the other, the less one may like the other. This notion was also reflected in survey work by Massey et al. (1999: 670) in Yugoslavia before the onset of war, which indicated the highest levels of ethnic intolerance to lie in ethnic enclaves, where there were concentrations of "similarly identified people". The contact hypothesis ideas are oriented to a focus of ties and networks between individuals.

A contrasting view is a focus on individual cost-benefit calculations, as emphasised by rational-choice and strategic models. Fearon (1994) explained the unfolding of the Serb-Croat skirmishes in 1991 with this approach, informed by international relations theories on security. He outlined that a security dilemma existed between the groups in which it became rational to attack first. His work on the inability of groups to make credible commitments to each other (the "commitment problem") became part of the standard language applied to explain the conflict. A later development of rationalist theory by Fearon and Laitin (1996) outlined that leaders of groups might punish individuals who engage in conflicts, and thus that a strong role for leaders is crucial to maintain inter-group peace – and not contact between individuals of those groups, which is to be discouraged in their model.

Another approach to explaining ethnic conflict in the region is the elite manipulation hypothesis, put forward by Snyder (2000). In this view, elites eager to gain support in new democracies will take an extreme ethnic or nationalist stance in order to win votes. This theory became very popular in the policy community in their approach to the region, as it presented a set of achievable tasks. If elites and a nationalist rhetoric were the source of the problem, various projects could counter these elites and this rhetoric. In addition to the war in Yugoslavia, ethnic clashes between Romanians and Hungarians began to be explained as due to the machinations of elites. Several non-governmental organisation (NGO) projects funded by Western donors attempted to address these issues. Some NGOs arranged meetings between elites of different groups, or between ordinary people of different groups in an effort to get them to talk with each other. In addition, a number of efforts to write "true" and "neutral" histories of the region emerged as well, but with little resonance within populations. It is noteworthy that these theories did not fully consider why populations might respond to these machinations of elites.

Another line of focus in the literature examines transnational aspects of ethnic minority group mobilisation. Brubaker (1996) proposed the term "triadic nexus" to illustrate the political dynamics that take place between ethnic minorities and their state governments – as well as their "external national homelands," or the states with which they do share a title. As one example, the dynamics of politics between the Hungarian ethnic minority in Romania and the Romanian government also involve the external Hungarian "homeland" state. Later work began to describe this external state as a "kin-state" with a strong interest in policies towards their ethnic kin living as minorities in other states (Venice Commission 2001, Caspersen 2008, Waterbury 2010, Udrea 2014).[6] Within the region, Hungary serves as a kin-state for Hungarians living in Romania, Slovakia, Serbia, and Croatia – as well as in Ukraine and Austria. Another frequent kin-state example used is that of Russia and the ethnic Russians living in Estonia and Latvia, as ethnic politics in those countries are inevitably linked to Russia. In addition, Turkey remains very interested in the fate of Turks in Bulgaria. Most kin-states in Eastern Europe have passed legislation that grants some legal status to their ethnic kin, and Hungary formally established dual citizenship in 2010.

In addition to kin-states, another external focus point with regard to minority politics in the region has been the European Union (EU). There has been a debate regarding the degree to which minority policies in the region have been affected by EU institutional conditionality (Vachudova 2001) or by Europeanisation, a process of socialisation to EU norms (Schimmelfennig and Sedelmeier 2005). With regard to policies on ethnic minorities, there is some debate on the degree to which the EU was in fact able to influence minority policy. There is some evidence that political elites were most likely to align with EU policies when they suited their own domestic goals (Csergo 2007). The next section focuses on these domestic political dynamics.

Ethnic minorities in democratic politics

One of the early features of the post-1989 democracies in Eastern Europe was the emergence of ethnic parties, or parties defined according to an ethnic principle (Horowitz 1985). As many ethnic minorities had their own cultural and socialist organisations in the previous regimes, these institutions provided a base structure from which parties could arise. In addition, most of the East European states adopted proportional electoral systems during the 1990s.[7] In such systems, voters cast their votes for parties, and the parliamentary share reflects the proportion of the vote given to each. Proportional representation encourages smaller parties, unlike the majoritarian electoral systems in the US and the UK. Ethnic parties have become a standard feature of the political landscape in many states, particularly for ethnic minorities. These ethnic parties tend to focus on identity-related issues, such as policies on language use and education, symbols, and increased governance powers for minorities (Horowitz 1985, Stroschein 2001, 2012).

Ethnic parties exhibit some traits that differ from parties as generally understood. Several minority groups throughout the region have well-organized ethnic parties, particularly within the Hungarians in Romania and Serbia, and previously among Hungarians in Slovakia. Albanians in Serbia and Macedonia also have quite institutionalised parties. Turks in Bulgaria have a party that is officially a multi-ethnic party, but which de facto is a party for their group.

Systems with strong ethnic parties may feature "census" voting, in which the proportional voting percentages reflect the census data for particular ethnic groups (Horowitz 1985: 326). The fact that ethnic parties can only mobilise support within one ethnic group means that they do not tend to focus on broad appeals or issue-areas, but rather tend to have a focus on policies that affect the identity of their group. As outlined by Horowitz (1985), this internal focus tends to produce "outbidding" in ethnic parties. In the mechanism of outbidding, would-be party elites each attempt to be more "ethnic" than the others in an effort to gain support from within the limits of the ethnic population. For this reason, and informed by his work on Asia and Africa, Horowitz viewed ethnic parties as potentially dangerous political units that should be discouraged because they produce polarisation.

There are particular institutional rules that can affect the strength and behaviour of ethnic parties. In proportional representation systems, it is common to establish a percentage threshold of electoral support that parties must achieve in order to be included in parliaments. Thresholds are intended to exclude very small parties and to reduce the number of parties in such systems. They can also be designed to affect the ability of ethnic minority parties to obtain parliamentary representation. For example, Slovakia's electoral threshold was 5 per cent in the 2012 elections, which led to the exclusion of some ethnic parties that had been long-standing political actors: the Hungarian Coalition Party and the Slovak National Party, a Slovak ethnic party. One ethnic group that has been less successful in mobilising throughout the region are the Roma. While there are some successful Roma elites across different countries, Roma populations tend to be fragmented in most of the countries in a way that is not conducive to strong ethnic party positioning (Vermeersch 2009; see also Vermeersch in this volume).

In addition to the electoral system and officeholder aspects, ethnic minority political dynamics also relates to levels of decentralisation within states in the region. Ethnic minorities may have some concentrations in enclaves, where they are the local ethnic majority. Some countries feature large and politically mobilised enclaves, such as the Hungarians in the Secuime region of Romania or Hungarians in the ŽitnýOstrov region of south Slovakia, as well as Albanians in north-western Macedonia. Claims for increased governance powers in enclaves often emerge, because key actors in such regions would often prefer more self-government over their own affairs – particularly in relation to identity-related policies on language and education. Ethnic majorities are often reluctant to agree to decentralisation or to grant autonomy, due to fears of loss of political control for the central state as well as the potential for autonomous units to become platforms for secession.

There has been an ongoing debate in the literature regarding whether decentralisation (including autonomy) might appease ethnic minorities; or whether it might encourage secession (Rothchild and Hartzell 1999, Mozaffar and Scarritt 1999, Cornell 2002). Academic consensus on this question remains elusive. Much of the current literature on decentralisation for ethnic minorities has now turned to focus on more specific conditions in each place, such as local demography (Hale 2004: 475–476) or the role of parties (Brancati 2006). It has also been observed that the process of contesting potential decentralisation and autonomy may in fact lead to conflict, as ethnic minorities and majorities will tend to disagree on this issue (Sasse 2002).

Much literature on the design of democratic institutions has included a consideration of how to best address the question of ethnic minorities in democracy (Lijphart 1977, Horowitz 1985, Sisk 1999, and Reilly 2001 are some examples). Different approaches to electoral systems and to the degree of decentralisation or autonomy can be grouped according to two categories: (1) segmented or consociational; and (2) integrative (Sisk 1999: 34–45). A segmented or consociational approach reflects Lijphart's (1977) understanding of consociationalism, in which ethnic groups in society remain separated to ensure representation. The main work of politics in a consociational structure is conducted by elites, who are envisioned to negotiate and cooperate with each other (Lijphart 1977). This echoes the logic of Fearon and Laitin's (1996) elite-led model outlined in the previous section, as well as the ideas of the conflict hypothesis. Groups are separate to ensure that their voices are heard, but there is also a latent assumption that it is unproductive for them to fully engage with each other – the business of politics across groups is thus left to elites.

In contrast, the integrative approach envisions that groups should mix in politics. Thus, separate structures for different groups, including perhaps ethnic parties and potential autonomies, should be avoided. Rather, electoral systems should encourage political actors to make appeals across groups for votes, reducing the salience of ethnicity in the process, as do majoritarian and alternative vote ranked systems (Reilly 2001). This resonates with the contact hypothesis here – the notion that more mixing is healthy for a diverse society to stay together. The institutional approach favoured often depends on one's diagnosis of the problem: whether one thinks that more contact or less contact is the cause of potential ethnic conflicts and political stalemates.

Questioning principal contributions on ethnic minorities and democracy

The biggest problem lurking in the contributions on ethnic minorities is that they reify minority groups as unified entities. Much work carries the assumption that ethnic groups are stable and unified entities, and this assumption simplifies the execution of statistical work that codes groups in this way in databases that assess the state of ethnicity across the globe. However, any time spent on the ground in Eastern Europe reveals that individuals within the same ethnic group will display vastly different political opinions and goals.

One of the most exciting recent developments in the study of ethnic minorities in fact relates to the way in which individuals within the same nominal ethnic group might exhibit quite different political stances, including towards ethnic policies. For example, the political claims of ethnic minorities that are concentrated in enclaves may differ greatly from the interests of other members of the ethnic minority who live dispersed outside of the enclave (Birnir 2006; Stroschein 2011). Thus, claims for political autonomy for an ethnic enclave may be opposed by the titular majority, but also may not find favour from dispersed members of the same ethnic group who will fall outside of its proposed boundaries. In addition, interviews show that although individuals of the same group may have access to kin-state benefits, their individual propensities will produce varying degrees of engagement with those benefits (Brubaker et al. 2006, Knott 2015). People may share the same ethnic name, but we may simply assume that means they engage in the same type of politics.

Ethnic minorities and the future

If ethnic minorities do not act as cohesive units, one might rightly ask why we should still study them. The answer lies in relation to the outline of historical developments at the beginning of this chapter. Ethnic minorities have especially salient identities in an environment of democratic political competition and ethnic parties. Ethnicity is politically salient in the contemporary context in a way that it could not be under socialism or under autocratic empires. This salience has been intertwined with episodes of violence in the 1990s that have consolidated identities in the region. Although Bosnia and Herzegovina and Croatia were the most extreme cases of inter-group violence, an ethnic riot also took place in Romania, and there are ongoing stories of skirmishes between ethnic groups.[8]

Recent political events also indicate that ethnicity remains a salient political mobilizer. Nearly all of the states in the region have passed kin-state legislation in which ethnic minorities in other states can access benefits from their "homeland" or kin-states. Dual citizenship, including voting rights, has also been introduced by Hungary in 2010, and Romania allows Moldovan citizens to become Romanian citizens and vote in elections (Knott 2015). Those individuals that benefit from these policies do not need to have ever lived in the kin-state, thus many of these benefits are applied in a cross-border manner that violates what some understand to be principles of state sovereignty established in 1648 (Deets and Stroschein 2005). However, a normative argument can also be made for the duties of states towards their ethnic kin (Udrea 2014).

In what may be an even more serious set of developments, the recent movement of refugees and migrants through Eastern Europe led to some strident reactions by political elites. In many instances, leaders are using a rhetoric of ethnic identity to justify blocking them on their journeys westward. Other types of attempts are also made to deny them entry or support. It may be the case that domestic ethnic minorities and majorities have normalized their interactions into democratic channels. But national identity remains potentially salient when faced with persons from an unfamiliar culture such as Syria, or an unfamiliar religion such as Islam. Some of the aggressive anti-other rhetoric of the 1990s has begun to re-emerge in light of these population flows. In Hungary, claims have been made that some ethnic minority Roma have aligned with Islamist groups among the refugees. Will more such links be made in other states, as hysteria is a powerful political force? More will certainly remain to be explained, using some of the literature insights outlined in this chapter.

Conclusion

In this chapter, I have summarized some of the primary discussions on the concept of ethnic minorities in Eastern Europe. The historical discussion indicates that ethnicity first became politically salient in the region during the 1800s. Within the context of democracy and ethnic parties, ethnicity has become a particularly salient political force. It is important to understand ethnic mobilization and ethnic group goals, as well as the notion of whether increased group contact leads to tolerance or to conflict. I have also considered literature on the dynamics of ethnic minority parties and elections, as well as political debates on ethnic minorities and decentralization and autonomy. While the chapter has emphasized general theories on ethnic minorities, I have concluded with some questions about the goal of general theories, and made a plea for some added nuance and specificity for the methods we use to examine these questions. In addition, the literature may need to expand to include a consideration of immigrants, migrants, and refugees in a more cohesive manner. Recent events indicate that group differences will remain a salient force in the region, in meaningful and perhaps disturbing ways.

Notes

1 Wikipedia data on these censuses is useful, but should be cross-checked with other sources.
2 Bosniaks are the titular group here in name, but Serbs and Croats are also treated as constituent nations that are part of the government structure established by Dayton Peace Agreement (1995).

3 Due to a name dispute with Greece, the formal name of this country is the Former Yugoslav Republic of Macedonia (FYR Macedonia or FYROM).
4 Due to a boycott of the latest census by many Serbs, this percentage is not clear.
5 Due to some changes, the percentage of Romanians may increase in the 2014 census, to be released between late 2016 and 2017. I am grateful to Eleanor Knott for this note, via correspondence.
6 The Venice Commission document emerged to respond to a Hungarian state law passed in 2001 (The Status Law) that allocated benefits to ethnic Hungarians living in neighbouring states. I am grateful to Steve Saideman and Andreea Udrea for pointing me to some of this literature.
7 There has been some institutional change, and Romania adopted a more majoritarian system for the 2008 elections.
8 Participant observation in the region by the author has involved stories of Hungarians being thrown off of trains in Slovakia, bar fights between Hungarians and Romanians in Romania, and continued suspicion of other groups in Bosnia and Herzegovina.

References

Allport, G. (1954) *The Nature of Prejudice*. New York: Basic Books, 1979 edition used.
Anderson, B. (1991) [1983] *Imagined Communities: Reflections on the Origin and Spread of Nationalism*. New York: Verso.
Banac, I. (1984) *The National Question in Yugoslavia: Origins, History, Politics*. Ithaca, NY: Cornell University Press.
Birnir, J. (2006) *Ethnicity and Electoral Politics*. New York: Cambridge University Press.
Brancati, D. (2006) "Decentralization: Fueling the Fire or Dampening the Flames of Ethnic Conflict and Secessionism?" *International Organization* 60 (3): 651–686.
Brubaker, R. (1996) "National Minorities, Nationalizing States, and External National Homelands in the New Europe," Chapter 3 in *Nationalism Reframed: Nationhood and the National Question in Europe*. New York: Cambridge University Press: 55–76.
Brubaker, R., M. Feischmidt, J. Fox, and L. Grancea (2006) *Nationalist Politics and Everyday Ethnicity in a Transylvanian Town*. Princeton, NJ: Princeton University Press.
Carnegie Endowment for International Peace (1993) *The Other Balkan Wars: A 1913 Carnegie Endowment Inquiry in Retrospect With a New Introduction and Reflections on the Present Conflict by George F. Kennan*. Washington, DC: The Carnegie Endowment for International Peace.
Caspersen, N. (2008) "Between Puppets and Independent Actors: Kin-State Involvement in the Conflicts in Bosnia, Croatia and Nagorno Karabakh," *Ethnopolitics* 7 (4): 357–372.
Chandra, K. (2006) "What Is Ethnic Identity and Does It Matter?" *Annual Review of Political Science* 9: 397–424.
Connor, W. (1994) "A Nation Is a Nation, Is a State, Is an Ethnic Group, Is a . . .," In *Ethnonationalism: The Quest for Understanding*. Princeton, NJ: Princeton University Press.
Cornell, S. (2002) "Autonomy as a Source of Conflict: Caucasian Conflicts in Theoretical Perspective," *World Politics* 54 (2): 245–276.
Csergo, Zs. (2007) *Talk of the Nation: Language and Conflict in Romania and Slovakia*. Ithaca, NY: Cornell University Press.
Deets, S., and S. Stroschein (2005) "Dilemmas of Autonomy and Liberal Pluralism: Examples Involving Hungarians in Central Europe," *Nations and Nationalism* 11 (2): 285–305.
Fearon, J. (1994) "Ethnic War as a Commitment Problem," paper presented at the American Political Science Association, New York, August 30-September 2, 1994. 1995 version online, available at: https://web.stanford.edu/group/fearon-research/cgi-bin/wordpress/wp-content/uploads/2013/10/Ethnic-War-as-a-Commitment-Problem.pdf
Fearon, J., and D. Laitin (1996) "Explaining Interethnic Cooperation," *American Political Science Review* 90 (4): 715–735.
Gati, C. (1990) *The Bloc that Failed: Soviet-East European Relations in Transition*. Bloomington: Indiana University Press.
Gellner, E. (1983) *Nations and Nationalism*. Ithaca, NY: Cornell University Press.
Glassheim, E. (2005) *Noble Nationalists: The Transformation of the Bohemian Aristocracy*. Cambridge, MA: Harvard University Press.
Glenny, M. (1992) *The Fall of Yugoslavia: The Third Balkan War*. New York: Penguin Books.

Hale, H. (2004) "Explaining Ethnicity," *Comparative Political Studies* 37 (4): 458–485.

Hobsbawm, E. J. (1992) *Nations and Nationalism Since 1780: Programme, Myth, Reality*. London: Cambridge University Press.

Horowitz, D. (1985) *Ethnic Groups in Conflict*. Berkeley: University of California Press.

Hupchick, D., and H. Cox (2001a) *The Palgrave Concise Historical Atlas of Eastern Europe*. New York: Palgrave.

Hupchick, D., and H. Cox (2001b) *The Palgrave Concise Historical Atlas of the Balkans*. New York: Palgrave.

Jelavich, B. (1983) *History of the Balkans: Eighteenth and Nineteenth Centuries*, Volume I. Cambridge: Cambridge University Press. 1995 edition used.

Kann, R., and Z. David (1984) *The Peoples of the Eastern Habsburg Lands, 1526–1918*. Seattle and London: University of Washington Press.

Kaplan, R. (1994) [1993] *Balkan Ghosts: A Journey Through History*. New York: St. Martin's Press. 1994 edition used.

Knott, E. (2015) *Kin-States and Kin Majorities From the bottom-up: Testing a Model of Nested Integration in Crimea and Moldova*. PhD thesis, London School of Economics and Political Science.

Laitin, D. (1998) *Identity in Formation: The Russian-Speaking Populations in the Near Abroad*. Ithaca, NY: Cornell University Press.

Lendvai, P. (2003) *The Hungarians: 1000 Years of Victory in Defeat*. London: Hurst.

Lijphart, A. (1977) *Democracy in Plural Societies: A Comparative Explanation*. New Haven, CT: Yale University Press.

Magocsi, P. R. (1995) [1993] *Historical Atlas of East Central Europe*. Seattle and London: University of Washington Press. 1995 edition used.

Massey, G., R. Hodson, and D. Sekulić (1999) "Ethnic Enclaves and Intolerance: The Case of Yugoslavia," *Social Forces* 78 (2): 669–693.

Mozaffar, S., and J. Scarritt (1999) "Why Territorial Autonomy Is Not a Viable Option for Managing Ethnic Conflict in African Plural Societies," *Nationalism and Ethnic Politics* 5 (3–4): 230–253.

Muiznieks, N. (1997) "Latvia: Restoring a State, Rebuilding a Nation," In Ian Bremmer and Ray Taras, eds., *New States New Politics: Building the Post-Soviet Nations*. New York: Cambridge University Press: 376–403.

Raun, T. (1997) "Estonia: Independence Redefined," In Ian Bremmer and Ray Taras, eds., *New States New Politics: Building the Post-Soviet Nations*. New York: Cambridge University Press: 405–433.

Reilly, B. (2001) *Democracy in Divided Societies: Electoral Engineering for Conflict Management*. New York: Cambridge University Press.

Rothchild, D., and C. Hartzell (1999) "Security in Deeply Divided Societies: The Role of Territorial Autonomy," *Nationalism and Ethnic Politics* 5 (3–4): 254–271.

Rothschild, J. (1989) *Return to Diversity: A Political History of East Central Europe Since World War II*. Oxford: Oxford University Press.

Rothschild, J. (1992) [1974] *East Central Europe Between the Two World Wars*. Seattle and London: University of Washington Press. 1992 edition used.

Sasse, G. (2002) "Conflict-Prevention in a Transition State: The Crimean Issue in Post-Soviet Ukraine," *Nationalism and Ethnic Politics* 8 (2): 1–26.

Schimmelfennig, F., and U. Sedelmeier, eds. (2005) *The Europeanization of Central and Eastern Europe*. Ithaca, NY: Cornell University Press.

Sebök, L. (1998) *Nationality Map of East Central and Southeast Europe*. Budapest: Teleki László Foundation, published by Südost Institut Munich.

Senn, A. (1997) "Lithuania: Rights and Responsibilities of Independence," In Ian Bremmer and Ray Taras, eds., *New States New Politics: Building the Post-Soviet Nations*. New York: Cambridge University Press: 353–375.

Sisk, T. (1999) *Power Sharing and International Mediation in Ethnic Conflicts*. Washington, DC: US Institute of Peace.

Smith, A. (1986) *The Ethnic Origins of Nations*. Cambridge: Blackwell.

Snyder, J. (2000) *From Voting to Violence: Democratization and Nationalist Conflict*. New York: W. W. Norton.

Stokes, G. (1993) *The Walls Came Tumbling Down: The Collapse of Communism in Eastern Europe*. London: Oxford University Press.

Stroschein, S. (2001) "Measuring Ethnic Party Success in Romania, Slovakia, and Ukraine," *Problems of Post-Communism* 48 (4): 59–69.

Stroschein, S. (2011) "Demography in Ethnic Party Fragmentation: Hungarian Local Voting in Romania," *Party Politics* 17 (2): 189–204.

Stroschein, S. (2012) *Ethnic Struggle, Coexistence, and Democratization in Eastern Europe.* New York: Cambridge University Press.

Szakály, F. (1990) "The Early Ottoman Period, Including Royal Hungary, 1526–1606," In P. Sugar, P. Hanák, and T. Frank, eds., *A History of Hungary.* Bloomington: Indiana University Press: 83–99.

Udrea, A. (2014) "A Kin-State's Responsibility: Cultural Identity, Recognition, and the Hungarian Status Law," *Ethnicities* 14 (2): 324–346.

Vachudova, M. (2001) *Europe Undivided: Democracy, Leverage, and Integration After Communism.* London: Oxford University Press.

Venice Commission. (2001) *Preferential Treatment of National Minorities by Their Kin-State, Draft Report.* Strausbourg: Council of Europe, 16 October. CDL (2001) 097-e.

Vermeersch, P. (2009) "In Search of a Movement: The Opportunities and Limits of Romani Political Solidarity," *Südosteuropa Mitteilungen* 49 (2): 88–94.

Waterbury, M. (2010) *Between State and Nation: Diaspora Politics and Kin-State Nationalism in Hungary.* New York: Palgrave.

Woodward, S. (1995) *Balkan Tragedy: Chaos and Destruction After the Cold War.* Washington, DC: The Brookings Institution.

16

THE PLIGHT OF EASTERN EUROPE'S ROMA

Peter Vermeersch

Background: the historical and intellectual development of the study of the Roma in Central and Eastern Europe

How the Roma historically emerged as a topic of academic study

The Roma, a population group that includes many of Central and Eastern Europe's most socio-economically vulnerable citizens (see EU Agency for Fundamental Rights 2012: 80–81, OSCE 2013, World Bank 2013), are not a new topic of study in the social sciences. For a long time, however, the plight of the region's Roma populations did not receive much attention from either politicians or academicians. In anthropology, for example, the Roma were often the subject of amateurish folklore (Stewart 2013), a fact that may have been related to the particular image attached to them – they were depicted as 'social outcasts and scapegoats, or, in a flattering but far from illuminating light, as romantic outsiders' in many accounts (Lucassen, Willems and Cottaar 1998: 1). In the 1970s and 1980s more sophisticated anthropological and sociological accounts of Romani communities (Acton 1979, Okely 1983, Puxon 1977, Ulč 1988) increased the profile of what came later to be known as 'Romani studies', which is now a broad interdisciplinary field attracting attention from scholars from a variety of specialisations from across the social sciences and the humanities (Acton 2000, Guy 2001, Matras 2012). Current research efforts include not only small-scale ethnographic investigations but also large-scale studies focusing on the socio-economic position of the Roma, which highlight, for example, issues of employment (e.g. Kertesi and Kézdi 2011), housing and residential segregation (e.g. Sýkora 2009), migration and mobility (e.g. Grill 2012, Matras 2000, Vidra 2013, Vullnetari 2012), poverty and social mobility (e.g. van Baar 2012a, Szalai and Zentai 2014), education (e.g. Kling and Brüggemann 2012, Brüggemann 2012), culture and language (e.g. Mundy and Acton 1997), political activism and participation (Barany 2002, Kovats 2000, McGarry and Agarin 2014, Vermeersch 2006), and discrimination (e.g. Fox and Vidra 2014). In recent years there has been a surge of country case studies, policy reports, and efforts by international governmental and non-governmental organisations (NGOs) to collect reliable socio-economic data.

In this chapter, I will provide a very brief introduction to some of the main discussions in the field, pointing out how a topic at the margins of social science research has gradually begun to occupy a more important position. Yet, while there is now a broad literature available, stereotypical views of the Roma persist – also in academic writing – and there continues to be a lack of reliable empirical data on many of the problems that face the Roma. There continues to be a need for high-quality studies on issues related to the Roma since such research may influence current policy debates on local, national, and European levels.

Prior to considering in some detail the existing social science literature that analyses the plight of the Roma (the socio-economic situation of the Roma, the politics around Romani identity, migration and mobility of Roma, and European Roma-related policy formation), it is instructive to consider briefly the history of how the Roma have become a subject of growing scholarly attention. This development has itself been the topic of some research.

Van Baar (2012b), for example, goes back to the time of the Enlightenment to examine how researchers and governments have discovered, addressed, and 'problematised' this population – and how this research has always somehow been implicated in state practices of population control. He discusses pioneering Central European 'Gypsy scholars' Johann Rüdiger (1751–1822) and Heinrich Grellmann (1753–1804), who attempted to prove scientifically that the Roma have Indian roots and, on the basis of that discovery, formulated opinions about how governments should deal with them – Rüdiger was critical of the assimilationist approaches of the Habsburg rulers, while Grellmann praised them. So even in those times, research on Roma happened in response to or in preparation of policy development. In later times, the link between research and policy would sometimes become problematic up to the point of tragedy. Willems (1997) has written extensively about the detrimental role of the German youth psychiatrist Robert Ritter and his associates in the latter half of the 1930s. Ritter tried to establish a causal connection between biological traits of Roma and antisocial behaviour. Inspired by Nazi ideology, he argued that 'Romani genes' had affected the German 'race' and in this way had led to the creation of people 'of mixed blood.' Eugenic and racial hygiene arguments were used to provide license to state practices of sterilisation, deportation, and mass murder (Burleigh 2000: 372–374, Nečas 1999).

Careful and detailed reflection on the history of how the Roma have been conceptualised as a subject of scholarly study is needed to understand the sensitivities underlying the discussions about this in current Romani studies. Contemporary scholars working on Roma are often well aware of the fact that the dominant (though by no means unanimous) view is that there is a tight, even inherent, link between the name 'Roma' and socio-economic marginalisation. This link is reinforced by politicians and the media when they focus on Romani poverty and the social ills it begets (often blaming the Roma for their own predicament) (Stewart 2013, Vermeersch 2012, Sigona 2005). Those who do not fit the socio-economic mould are often not even 'visible' as Roma (van Baar and Vermeersch 2015).

In a context where stigma is both historically and socio-economically prevalent, it is not a surprise that a lot of scholars working on Roma spend considerable time discussing how to define the group they want to study. Current views about how to conceptualise Roma diverge not only on terms of whether it make sense to talk about common descent as the basis of Romani identity, and how to read, against this background, the problematic influence of earlier researchers who defined them on the basis of biological, cultural, or socio-economic traits. They are also about broader epistemological questions (How do we understand ethnicity?) and normative strategies (Which analytic approach to Romani identity best prevents the reinforcement of a colonial 'orientalising' gaze?). The work of Matras (2012), on the one hand, highlights the importance of linguistic commonality not only because language can (and in his view should) be regarded as the basis on which Romani identity has historically been formed, but also because the current recognition of common linguistic origins may be a good way towards claiming rights for Roma and counteracting negative stereotypes (which usually presume typical forms of social behaviour). Lucassen et al. (1998), on the other hand, have focused on the labelling practices of authorities (their empirical research mostly pertains to Germany), which over the course of the eighteenth and nineteenth centuries has lumped together different groups with a similar lifestyle under one overarching ethnic label (*Zigeuner*). They suggest that it makes little sense – historically and politically – to think about Romani identity in terms of common descent or linguistic commonality; we should see this identity instead as a constructed category to which authorities have assigned negative meaning.

Scholars who propagate the linguistic and cultural approach might find themselves in agreement with the ultimate concern of those who highlight socio-economic and political factors of identity formation – both sides seek to free up Romani identity from the stigmatising images that are usually associated with it – but the debate remains. Should the Roma be regarded as a group constructed by internal processes of identity formation on the basis of common language and culture, or should they be seen as a group formed by external forces, including categorisation schemes imposed on them by authorities and scholars? That the discussion on this continues is to some extent related to the particular puzzle that researchers seem to be faced with when they undertake empirical research on the situation of the Roma – although there are clearly patterns of mutual identification among the Roma across national borders (and indeed, one could say, a sense of common belonging), such identity exists and persists 'without shared religion, without any form of ritual or political leadership, and without overarching or underpinning political organization' (Stewart 2013: 418). Many have seen in this persistence a sign of the continuing discrimination against the Roma: socio-economic exclusion solidifies them as a single group, and *ethnifies* or *racialises* them. Others have rather understood this persistence as proof of a strong common culture and belief in common descent, which survives even in the face of external forces stigmatizing their identity. They have argued that the political recognition of such cultural commonalities will bring emancipatory power.

Although the problem of essentialising (and exoticising) the Roma – that is, seeing them as a historically unchanged and unadapted group whose members wilfully refuse the norms and values of society at large – is still present in some (certainly the most stereotypical) writings about Roma, there is among students of the plight of the Roma (including those who argue for the public recognition of common Romani descent and culture) a growing agreement that it makes sense to view Romani identity – as any form of ethnicity – not simply as a matter of isolated group characteristics, but rather as the product of complex classification processes involving both classifiers and those classified as Roma (Emigh, Fodor and Szelényi 2001: 6). In this way, it is also easier to make sense of prevailing exonyms that are used to refer to more or less the same population (such names as Gypsy, Zigeuner, and Tsigane); their equivalents in the Eastern European languages (such as cigán, cikán, cigány, etc.), and the self-appellations that serve as subidentities (such as Kalderash, Manush, Caló, Vlach, Rómungro, Beash, Sinto, etc.). All these categories relate in some way to the overarching term Roma – a term that has historically served as a self-appellation for speakers of the Romani language (sometimes called Romanes) but is now used to encompass a wider group of people, including those who do not speak Romanes but for socio-cultural or political reasons still identify themselves, or are identified by others, as belonging to this group.

Eastern Europe and the discovery of the Roma as a topic of social scientific study

Since a large majority of the estimated 8–12 million Roma in the world live in Central and Eastern Europe, it should not come as a surprise that a lot of the research has taken place in this region. Some of that work predates 1989. There have been sociological studies of varying quality about the position of the Roma in several Central and Eastern European countries throughout the communist era. Such scholarship has often been dependent on specific interests and traditions at certain academic institutions. In Bulgaria, for example, Marushiakova and Popov (1997) have done a lot of work before 1989 that perhaps can be called historical ethnography. There have been important strands of sociological and anthropological research in communist Hungary (Havas and Kemény 1999) and Czechoslovakia (Davidová 1995). For much of the time, however, the topic did retain a certain obscurity. When in 1975, the Czech exiled photographer Josef Koudelka published a selection of sixty photographs taken in various Roma settlements around East Slovakia, he could still have been considered a pioneer – someone who brought the topic from the margins to the centre of serious attention. He chose to accompany his expressive black and white photography with a social scientific essay documenting the situation of the Roma in Czechoslovakia (Koudelka 2011).

In 1971, survey research by Hungarian sociologists found that the socio-economic situation of those who were called 'Gypsies' was highly problematic. They found, for example, that housing was extremely poor. 'Nearly two thirds (65.1 per cent) of Gypsy households were located in separate colonies. In 1971, the majority of these could be described as spontaneously erected, family-built shanties, traditionally situated away from, or on the fringe of, towns or villages. They lacked even the most basic facilities (Havas and Kemény 1999: 366). The survey was replicated in 1993, and the conclusion then was that the problem was getting worse. Thus, in the Hungarian case it is clear that policies to alleviate the problems facing the Roma predate 1989 but also that some of the misconceptions about how to help Roma date from those earlier periods. While the Roma were in some cases slightly better off during the communist era – they were sometimes even seen as 'beneficiaries' of the planned economy – the policies that were directed at them were not implemented in such a way that remedied the structural inequality (Emigh et al. 2001). During the communist era, social scientists in Hungary, as in other Central and Eastern European countries, might have had an idea of the extent of the socio-economic plight of the Roma, but they were limited in their opportunities to communicate their conclusions with the wider world.

The topic rose to prominence internationally in the social sciences in the 1990s, in the wake of growing concern about discrimination and stark socio-economic exclusion of large sections of the Roma in the context of democratisation and market transition. Journalist accounts of extremism and the fate of vulnerable groups (e.g. Hockenos 1993) and publications by human rights organisations – international NGOs like Human Rights Watch, Amnesty International, Project on Ethnic Relations, and the European Roma Rights Centre (ERRC) – helped to raise awareness about the alarming levels of discrimination and marginalisation. It became clear that marginalised Roma had become trapped in urban slums or isolated ghettos in rural areas where a situation had arisen that is likely to perpetuate exclusion and poverty (Sobotka and Vermeersch, 2012: 813). Over the years many anti-Roma initiatives, policies, and mobilisations have been documented. Examples include the building of walls separating Roma neighbourhoods from other sections of a town (as happened, for example, in the Czech town of Ústí nad Labem in 1999), the illegal registration of the ethnic background of clients and potential employees at private companies and the public sector (in 2006, ERRC documented several cases of this across Europe [Hyde 2006]), the practice in several countries of segregating Roma children in special schools or classes (in 2007, the Czech Republic was convicted for this type of discrimination in a landmark judgment of the European Court of Human Rights [*D.H. and Others v. The Czech Republic*]), and the expulsion and ethnic resettlement campaigns directed at Roma migrants in the EU (e.g. France decided in 2010 to shut down a large number of irregular Roma dwellings and single out Bulgarian and Romanian Roma for an expulsion campaign) (Vermeersch 2011). Growing scholarly attention also went hand in hand with greater concern from some governmental actors, a fact that was arguably stimulated by the international concern for interstate conflict around national minorities. New reporting on the situation of the Roma happened at a time when the violent conflicts in the Balkans had broken out, and fear of territorial secessions by national minorities in response to majority nationalism was generally regarded as a troubling dynamic that could lead to war and migration. The risk that an ethnic conflict involving Roma would develop into a war between two or more states was deemed minimal, yet growing media coverage of all kinds of tensions around the lack of protection for this group, and the growth of a 'racialised' underclass (Emigh et al. 2001), did lead to some important new texts and initiatives by international institutions such as the Council of Europe, the European Parliament, and the High Commissioner on National Minorities.

Where we are now: studies of Roma in Eastern Europe after 1989

Understanding exclusion and discrimination

In 2000 and 2001, research by the World Bank concluded that, overall, poverty among Roma is closely linked to four main factors: (1) regional economic conditions; (2) the size and concentration of the Romani population in a settlement; (3) the percentage of Roma in a settlement; and (4) the degree of geographic integration or segregation of the settlement and its proximity to a neighbouring village or town (Ringold 2002). We have now come to a point in time when research is increasingly responding to the need for more detailed figures and analysis related to Roma exclusion. Several attempts at more specific mapping and data collection have been undertaken (e.g. EU Agency for Fundamental Rights 2012, Kósa et al. 2007, Milcher 2006, Molnár, Adány, Adám, Gulis and Kósa 2010, UNDP Bratislava 2013, Vuksanović-Macura 2012) and various studies have now developed detailed indicators to confirm that Romani communities across Europe live on average in more dire economic circumstances than their co-citizens. These studies also allow for a better understanding of how socio-economic marginalisation affects multiple spheres of life and how problems of ill health, poverty, unemployment, and segregation are interconnected. Particularly telling are the data on the socio-economic conditions, experiences of discrimination, and rights awareness of Roma that have been compiled in eleven EU member states in 2011 through the 'pilot survey' of the EU's Fundamental Rights Agency (FRA) (in collaboration with the World Bank and UNDP). The survey interviewed 10,811 Roma and 5,508 non-Roma living nearby, and the results are made available the website of the FRA (http://fra.europa.eu/en/theme/roma). It might seem puzzling that the situation on the ground continues to deteriorate. Scholars and activists have argued that underlying the failure of social policies to remedy this situation is a lack of will of national politicians to prioritise the issue and the persistence of discriminatory attitudes among the majority of their voters. Even if welfare and social inclusion policies mostly stay under the control of the individual states (Schall 2012), it has become clear that the social inclusion of Roma is a matter on which the EU cannot remain passive.

In recent years the issue of persistent discrimination against the Roma seems to have become an even more vexing puzzle for social scientists. Over the last few years the Roma appear to have become increasingly politicised and as such have become the focus of populism and extremism throughout Central and Eastern Europe (Stewart 2012). In Hungary, for example, the level of negative stereotypical attitudes about the Roma now appears to exceed that of the 1990s, which was quite high even then (Csepeli, Fábián and Sik 1998). Since far-right and populist parties gained strength in 2006, anti-Roma discourse and behaviour have even become more popular, with authorities remarkably reluctant to provide any form of counteraction. Local governments, in particular, seem to have become largely permissive to the language of hatred and incitement against Roma (for example, Zolnay 2012).

In several countries in the region not only is the lack of clear and implemented anti-discrimination policies to blame, or the fact that politicians use anti-Romani discourse as a way to gain votes; the economic inequality is perpetuated by other types of exclusion as well. Education is a case in point, and some researchers have focused their work on this specific subdomain. There are several studies discussing, mapping, and demonstrating the problematic character of pervasive educational segregation across several Central and Eastern European countries – from schools in poor Romani neighbourhoods or the placement of Romani pupils in so-called special schools for children with developmental disabilities or in separate classrooms (e.g. Rostas 2012). Up to this date, there has been little to report in terms of change. While the legality of selection practices has been severely contested – the European Court of Human Rights issued ground-breaking judgements against the Czech Republic (2007) and Greece (2008) – many actors in the education systems of several countries are not interested in reform, and Romani parents often remain uninformed about the consequences of segregation or see the short-term benefits of not having to seek acceptance among majority populations in a more diverse schooling system.

While the educational segregation persists, there have been international initiatives that have tried to make some progress in changing general attitudes. The Roma Education Fund, for example, is an international foundation that runs the largest tertiary education scholarship programme for Roma in Central and Eastern Europe. The Fund operates four scholarship schemes in fifteen countries. Since their inception in 2004, the programmes have provided support to about 5,000 Roma students. Some of these students may, in the future, themselves become active in research on the inclusion of Roma in education.

The study of Roma minority politics, activism, and participation

There is a branch of research in Romani studies that focuses on how Romani activists and their supporters respond to the Roma's grievances (e.g. Vermeersch 2006, McGarry 2010, Kovats 2000). A growing number of Roma are involved in various forms of political and social activism, often in self-organised civil society groups. There are no exact figures on the number of Roma civil society organisations in Central and Eastern Europe – ERRC has collected dozens of links to Roma civil society organisations and organizations supportive of Roma in about thirty countries (www.errc.org/links-to-ngos-and-roma-media), but that list is far from exhaustive since it only includes active websites run by organisations that have submitted a link to the ERRC. It is likely that in about every municipality where a substantive part of the population is Roma, there exists some form of Roma organisation. The most effective Roma organisations, however, are internationally organised, such as the European Roma and Travellers Forum (established in France in 2004 with the support of the Council of Europe) or umbrella organisations and networks of NGOs. Examples of the latter are the European Roma Grassroots Organizations Network (ERGO), located in Brussels and bringing together twenty-six organizations from different European countries, and the International Roma Youth Network (ternYpe) in Berlin, gathering at least ten Roma youth organisations from across Europe. Many of these international civil society initiatives are supported by international donors, such as the National Democratic Institute or the Open Society Foundation. Romani organisations have also increasingly been part of a transnational advocacy networks on Romani inclusion that has had some impact on the development of EU policies in this field. Romani communities are also active with regards to protest. Throughout Europe, some of the most visible demonstrations in response to targeted expulsion and migration control strategies have been led by Roma and supporting non-Roma organisations and groups.

Some of the findings in this strand of research relate to the quantitative growth of Romani political participation. For example, the number of Roma who participate in local elections as candidates has markedly increased over the recent years. In Slovakia, for example, the number of Romani candidates increase with each local, regional, or parliamentary election – the local is especially significant (for example, Degro 2015).

Some of the research in this field is concerned with the quality of participation. Various international institutions have written reports to emphasise that Romani participation and consultation are critical in the design and implementation of policy programmes meant to address the problems facing Roma. Nevertheless, studies point out that growing attention for Romani policy input is not necessarily a sign of the real acceptance of a Romani voice in mainstream politics and policymaking. McGarry and Agarin (2014), for instance, have argued that, although policymakers often talk about Romani participation in policy design and implementation, they usually refrain from specifying what exactly this means in practice (van Baar and Vermeersch 2015). Such forms of Romani participation often turn out to be 'thin' and may be a form of tokenism.

The study of Romani migration

Roma have often been associated with intra-national mobility and cross-border migration. This has at several times been prominent in the academic writing about Roma. Being a complex and multi-faceted topic, it has also led to confusion with the larger audience. Two popular but faulty assumptions persist: that Romani migration from east to west is massive; and that Roma are culturally and inherently inclined towards mobility. Especially in Central and Eastern Europe Roma are usually not nomadic. As Matras (2000) has argued, what is remarkable about much of the Romani migration in Europe is that it has happened despite a lack of nomadic traditions. In addition, the extent of Romani migration is often exaggerated, which may be caused by a number of other factors: lack of precise official numbers, for example, and arguably also the high visibility, the relatively high level of internal cohesion, and the severe poverty of the Romani communities who are on the move (Vermeersch 2013: 347). For example, it has been pointed out that, according to estimates, the number of Roma in France has remained between 15,000 and 20,000 since the early 2000s (Muiznieks 2015); opportunities for internal mobility within the EU did not change that figure substantially. While in some areas there has been a visible influx of Roma, the overall Roma migration tends to follow the extent of general East-West migration in Europe. It is useful to consider the results of the Roma Pilot Survey of the EU Fundamental Rights Agency on attitudes towards migration. The average number of Roma respondents who said they would consider to move to another country was 15 per cent, while that of non-Roma living nearby was 12 per cent. The urge to move was not that different from non-Roma populations in the same areas, despite highly different experiences at home. The share of Roma respondents who had experienced discrimination in the previous five years was much higher than that of non-Roma living nearby (on average, 46 per cent among Roma and 4 per cent among non-Roma) (see http://fra.europa.eu/en/publications-and-resources/data-and-maps/survey-data-explorer-results-2011-roma-survey).

It is important to make a distinction between various forms of Roma migration. On the one hand, itinerant groups in Western Europe, such as the Gens du Voyage in France, are national citizens of the countries in which they travel and usually migrate across a limited number of national borders as part of their normal travel routes. On the other hand, Romani citizens who do not live in caravans, and do not have (or do not seek) an itinerant lifestyle, may still migrate within a country to seek economic improvement, but usually they do not have the means to do this. They lack opportunities both for territorial or social mobility. In turn, these groups are not to be confused with another, third, category: those Roma who are citizens of an EU member state and make use of the opportunities for free movement within the EU to go to another member state with a plan to live there for a longer stretch of time (Grill 2012). Some of them seek to migrate further to North America (Vidra 2013). Another category comprises those individuals who seek asylum in the EU.

Some of the research on Roma has intersected with studies on general patterns of migration in and from Central and Eastern Europe (see Morosanu, Szilassy and Fox 2012). Concerns about increasing numbers of asylum claimants have led individual EU member states to adopt ethnically framed migration control or highly restrictive immigration policies aimed at discouraging the entry of Roma (Cahn 2003). Visa regulations for countries in Eastern and South Eastern Europe have had a particular impact on the experience of migrating Roma, independently of whether they intend to apply for asylum.

Europe-wide policy formation

An important part of current scholarly attention has focused on policy formation, especially on the EU level (Vermeersch 2013, van Baar 2012b). In the context of enlargement, the EU demanded that candidate states enact and implement laws to protect Romani citizens as well as deal with their political, social and economic isolation. In the run-up to the enlargement, NGO reports directed EU attention to the precarious position of the Roma in otherwise successful candidate countries like the Czech Republic or Slovakia. European policymakers became increasingly concerned about the poverty facing many Roma in the region, the increasing spate of racist attacks against them, the apparent lack of protection by the police, the Roma's experiences of unequal treatment in education and the justice system, and the issue of unequal access to public services. Both a legacy of poverty and problematic social policies of the past as well as more recent failures to remedy the situation had created social and spatial segregation between non-Roma and Roma, the results of which became now all the more visible both in urban areas and in the countryside. Important criticism of the Central European governments was included, for example, in the European Commission's key document 'Agenda 2000' (European Commission 1997), which pointed out that the treatment of minorities in the region was in general satisfactory, except for the situation of the Roma (Vermeersch 2002). The EU included the topic of the Roma in its discussions on preconditions for EU accession. However, as such pre-accession conditionality appears not to have led to progressive change within the new member states of Central and Eastern Europe, the EU has developed other methods in this field. Most recently, the European Commission has urged member state governments to draw up 'national Roma integration strategies' (NRISs). The idea has been to bring the NRISs together under the umbrella of a coordinated European effort, which would make it easier to compare national policy ideas, practices and commitments, and create new pathways towards more robust monitoring by independent agencies and civil society actors. The European Commission's 2013 assessment report coming out of the first phase of this exercise focused specifically on the structural preconditions needed in each country. In the coming years, such yearly reports will use information provided by each country, NGOs, international organisations and FRA to review further policy progress. The European Commission also seeks to examine more closely the ways in which member states have used (or failed to use) European Structural and Investment Funds for projects in which Roma are involved – all of this in order to ensure that the budgetary opportunities for Romani inclusion policies that come with European membership are not squandered. Through the European Social Fund (ESF), the European Regional Development Fund (ERDF) and the European Agricultural Fund for Rural Development (EARDF), relatively large budgets have been made available for tackling various aspects of the problems facing the Roma, and conditions have been put into place in order to avoid such funds being used to segregate the Roma even further (as it happened in the past). In the case of the ERDF, for example, projects that are not explicitly aimed at desegregation – such as those that seek to improve housing conditions in a segregated area – will not be eligible for funding (Sobotka and Vermeersch 2012). In response to such monitoring and reviewing efforts by the European Commission, several member states have revised their national strategies or action plans and set up consultation forums on the implementation of these plans. Expert reports and independent shadow monitoring by NGOs have helped many member states in this regard (e.g. Rorke 2012).

Looking forward: what can we expect from the field?

In the field of politics and policy studies relating to Roma, we can expect continued attention on developments at EU level and the ensuing responses (or non-responses) of national governments. These developments are likely to be monitored not only by a growing number of independent scholars but also by international institutions and NGOs. An important new development is that more scholars from a Romani background are participating in this field as researchers.

There will be a continuing need for a critical look at what governments can do about the plight of the Roma across Europe. Reflection will be needed on how matters are implemented on the ground and how the politics around these new policies evolve. Obviously a long list could be drawn up of key themes and sub-topics that can and should be studied to push the discussion forward. By way of conclusion, three key issues can be highlighted:

1   How are policies implemented locally? The EU's strategic framework for Romani inclusion has led to a growth of policy plans by national governments, but policies will need to interact with specific socio-economic and political configurations on the local level. The responses to such local circumstances will need to be the subject of further detailed empirical research.

2   What will happen with anti-Romani discourse? Government policies aimed to help the Roma might unwittingly provide ammunition for those who seek to push Roma away. The current backlash is in some ways perhaps comparable to that created by some communist policies, which failed to alleviate the plight of the Roma but still reinforced hatred against them by suggesting that the Roma were 'privileged' beneficiaries of government help. There will be a continued need to observe how the Roma are politically framed and reframed. Will they be portrayed as a burden on the national economy, or can they claim their position as co-citizens who deserve economic support and may, in turn, become contributors to Europe's future.

3   What will the long-term effects be of the EU's efforts at overseeing national policies for the social inclusion of Roma? The European Commission wants to compel national governments to devise and implement better social policies using the available EU funding mechanisms. Such EU-led efforts, however, might give domestic politicians an opportunity to evade their own country's responsibility.

For academicians interested in the topic of the Roma more broadly, it is clear that their field of research is likely to continue to grow in the coming years, attracting interest from even more disciplines. In a context where stigma is both historically and socio-economically prevalent, it is important that these studies examine the situation of the Roma in a unbiased and balanced way – for example, through providing research that not only focuses on the dynamics of marginalisation and exclusion but also on social mobility and diversifying life experiences among certain sections of the Roma population, internal and external framing processes, and changing inter-actions between Roma and non-Roma populations in a variety of political and socio-economic circumstances.

References

Acton, T. (1979), 'Academic Success and Political Failure: A Review of Modern Social Science Writing in English on Gypsies', *Ethnic and Racial Studies*, 2(2), 231–241.

Acton, T. (ed.) (2000), *Scholarship and the Gypsy Struggle: Commitment in Romani Studies*, Hatfield: University of Hertfordshire Press.

Barany, Z. (2002), *The East European Gypsies: Regime Change, Marginality, and Ethnopolitics*, Cambridge: Cambridge University Press.

Brüggemann, C. (2012). 'Roma Education in Comparative Perspective. Analysis of the UNDP/World Bank/EC Regional Roma Survey 2011', *Roma Inclusion Working Papers*, Bratislava: United Nations Development Programme.

Burleigh, M. (2000), *The Third Reich: A New History*, New York: Hill and Wang.

Cahn, C. (2003), 'Racial Preference, Racial Exclusion: Administrative Efforts to Enforce the Separation of Roma and Non-Roma in Europe Through Migration Controls', *European Journal of Migration and Law*, 5(4), 479–490.

Csepeli, G., Z. Fábián, and E. Sik (1999), 'Xenophobia and Opinions about the Roma', in: *Social Report 1998*, ed. by T. Kolosi, G. I. Tóth, and G. Vukovich, Budapest: TÁRKI, Social Research Informatics Center, 452–482.

Davidová, E. (1995), *Romano Drom: Cesty Romů 1945–1990 (The Way of the Roma, 1945–1990)*, Olomouc: Vydavatelství Univerzity Palackého.

Degro, M. (2015), 'Engaging the Roma Community in the Political Party Process in Slovakia', *European View*, 14(1), 1–8.

Emigh, J., E. Fodor and I. Szelényi (2001), 'The Racialization and Feminization of Poverty', in: *Poverty, Ethnicity and Gender in Eastern Europe During the Market Transition*, ed. by J. Emigh and I. Szelényi, Westport: Praeger, 1–32.

EU Agency for Fundamental Rights (FRA) (2012), *The Situation of Roma in 11 EU Member States*, Vienna: EU Agency for Fundamental Rights.

European Commission (1997), *Agenda 2000: For a Stronger and Wider Union* [COM(97) 2000], http://ec.europa.eu/agriculture/cap-history/agenda-2000/com97-2000_en.pdf

Fox, J. and Z. Vidra (2014), 'Mainstreaming of Racist Anti-Roma Discourses in the Media in Hungary', *Journal of Immigrant & Refugee Studies*, 12(4), 437–455.

Grill, J. (2012). '"Going Up to England": Exploring Mobilities Among Roma From Eastern Slovakia', *Journal of Ethnic and Migration Studies*, 38(8), 1269–1287.

Guy, W. (ed.) (2001), *Between Past and Future: The Roma of Central and Eastern Europe*, Hatfield: University of Hertfordshire Press.

Havas, G. and I. Kemény (1999), 'The Statistics of Deprivation', in: *Encounters: A Hungarian Quarterly Reader*, ed. by Z. Zachár, Budapest: The Hungarian Quarterly Society, Balassi Kiadó, 361–370.

Hockenos, P. (1993), *Free to Hate: The Rise of the Right in Post-Communist Eastern Europe*, London and New York: Routledge.

Hyde, A. (2006), 'Systematic Exclusion of Roma From Employment', *Roma Rights*, 11(1), 3–8.

Kertesi, G. and G. Kézdi (2011), 'Roma Employment in Hungary After the Post-communist Transition', *Economics of Transition*, 19(3), 563–610.

Kling, J. and C. Brüggemann (2012), 'Measuring Results? Education Indicators in Roma Integration Strategies', *Development and Transition*, June 2012, 26–28.

Kósa, Z., G. Széles, L. Kardos, K. Kósa, R. Németh, S. Országh, G. Fésüs, M. McKee, R. Adány and Z. Vokó (2007), 'A Comparative Health Survey of the Inhabitants of Roma Settlements in Hungary', *American Journal of Public Health*, 97(5), 853–859.

Kovats, M. (2000), 'The Political Significance of the First National Gypsy Minority Self-government in Hungary', *Contemporary Politics*, 6(3), 247–262.

Koudelka, J. (2011), *Gypsies*, London: Thames & Hudson (afterword by Will Guy).

Lucassen, L., W. Willems and A. Cottaar (1998), *Gypsies and Other Itinerant Groups*, London: MacMillan.

Marushiakova, E. and V. Popov (1997), *Gypsies (Roma) in Bulgaria*, Frankfurt am Main: Peter Lang.

Matras, Y. (2000), 'Romani Migrations in the Post-Communist Era: Their Historical and Political Significance', *Cambridge Review of International Affairs*, 13(2), 32–50.

Matras, Y. (2012), 'Scholarship and the Politics of Romani Identity: Strategic and Conceptual Issues', *European Yearbook of Minority Issues*, 10, 211–247.

McGarry, A. (2010), *Who Speaks for Roma? Political Representation of a Transnational Minority Community*, New York: Continuum.

McGarry, A. and T. Agarin (2014), 'Unpacking the Roma Participation Puzzle: Presence, Voice and Influence', *Journal of Ethnic and Migration Studies*, 40(12), 1–19.

Milcher, S. (2006), 'Poverty and the Determinants of Welfare for Roma and Other Vulnerable Groups in Southeastern Europe', *Comparative Economic Studies*, 48(1), 20–35.

Molnár, A., R. Adány, B. Adám, G. Gulis, and K. Kósa (2010), 'Health Impact Assessment and Evaluation of a Roma Housing Project in Hungary', *Health Place*, 16(6), 1240–1247.

Morosanu, L., E. Szilassy and J. Fox (2012), 'The Racialization of the New European Migration to the UK', *Sociology*, 46(4), 680–695.

Mui nieks, N. (2015), *Report by Nils Mui nieks, Council of Europe Commissioner for Human Rights following his visit to France from 22 to 26 September 2014, CommDH(2015)1*, Strasbourg: Council of Europe.

Mundy, G. and T. Acton (1997), *Romani Culture and Gypsy Identity*, Hatfield: University of Hertfordshire Press.

Nečas, C. (1999), *The Holocaust of Czech Roma*, Prague: Prostor.

Okely, J. (1983), *The Traveller-Gypsies*, Cambridge: Cambridge University Press.

OSCE (Organization for Security and Cooperation in Europe) (2013), *Implementation of the Action Plan on Improving the Situation of the Roma and Sinti Within the OSCE Area: Renewed Commitments, Continued Challenges*, Warsaw: OSCE ODIHR (Office for Democratic Institutions and Human Rights).

Puxon, G. (1977), 'Forgotten Victims: Plight of the Gypsies', *Patterns of Prejudice*, 11(2), 23–28.

Ringold, D. (2002), 'Poverty and Roma in Central and Eastern Europe: A View From the World Bank', *European Roma Rights Centre*, www.errc.org/article/poverty-and-roma-in-central-and-eastern-europe-a-view-from-the-world-bank/710

Rorke, B. (2012), *Review of EU Framework National Roma Integration Strategies (NRIS): Open Society Foundations Review of NRIS Submitted by Bulgaria, the Czech Republic, Hungary, Romania and Slovakia*, Budapest: Open Society Foundations.

Rostas, I. (ed.) (2012), *Ten Years After – A History of Roma School Desegregation in Central and Eastern Europe*, Budapest and New York: REF and CEU Press.

Schall, C. E. (2012), 'Is the Problem of European Citizenship a Problem of Social Citizenship? Social Policy, Federalism, and Democracy in the EU and United States', *Sociological Inquiry*, 82(1), 123–144.

Sigona, N. (2005), 'Locating "The Gypsy Problem": The Roma in Italy. Stereotyping, Labelling and "Nomad Camps"', *Journal of Ethnic and Migration Studies*, 31(4), 741–756.

Sobotka, E. and P. Vermeersch (2012), 'Governing Human Rights and Roma Inclusion: Can the EU Be a Catalyst for Local Social Change?', *Human Rights Quarterly*, 34(3), 800–822.

Stewart, M. (ed.) (2012), *The Gypsy 'Menace': Populism and the New Anti-Gypsy Politics*, London: Hurst.

Stewart, M. (2013). 'Roma and Gypsy "Ethnicity" as a Subject of Anthropological Inquiry', *Annual Review of Anthropology*, 42, 415–432.

Sýkora, L. (2009), '"New Socio-spatial Formations: Places of Residential Segregation and Separation in Czechia', *Tijdschrift voor economische en sociale geografie*, 100, 417–435.

Szalai, J. and V. Zentai (eds), *Faces and Causes of Roma Marginalization in Local Contexts*, Budapest: Center for Policy Studies, Central European University.

Ulč, O. (1988), 'Gypsies in Czechoslovakia: A Case of Unfinished Integration', *East European Politics & Societies*, 2(2), 306–332.

UNDP (United Nations Development Programme) Bratislava (2013), 'Atlas rómskych komunít na Slovensku 2013' (Atlas of Romani Communities in Slovakia 2013), *UNDP*, www.employment.gov.sk/files/slovensky/rodina-socialna-pomoc/socialne-sluzby/atlasrom-kom.pdf

van Baar, H. (2012a), 'Socio-Economic Mobility and Neo-Liberal Governmentality in Post-Socialist Europe: Activation and the Dehumanisation of the Roma', *Journal of Ethnic and Migration Studies*, 38(8), 1289–1304.

van Baar, H. (2012b), *The European Roma: Minority Representation, Memory and the Limits of Transnational Governmentality*, PhD Dissertation, University of Amsterdam.

van Baar, H. and P. Vermeersch (2015), 'Hypervisibility and the Limits of Operational Representations: "Ways of Seeing Roma" Beyond the Recognition-Redistribution Paradigm', paper presented at the 22nd

International Conference of European Studies, Council for European Studies (CES), Paris, July 8–10, 2015.

Vermeersch, P. (2002), 'Ethnic Mobilisation and the Political Conditionality of EU Accession', *Journal of Ethnic and Migration Studies*, 28(1), 83–101.

Vermeersch, P. (2006), *The Romani Movement: Minority Politics and Ethnic Mobilization in Contemporary Central Europe*, New York and Oxford: Berghahn Books.

Vermeersch, P. (2011), 'Roma and Mobility in the European Union', in: *Roma and Traveller Inclusion in Europe*, ed. by K. Pietarinen, Brussels: Green European Foundation, 91–97.

Vermeersch, P. (2012), 'Reframing the Roma: EU Initiatives and the Politics of Reinterpretation', *Journal of Ethnic and Migration Studies*, 38(8), 1195–1212.

Vermeersch, P. (2013), 'The European Union and the Roma: An Analysis of Recent Institutional and Policy Developments', *European Yearbook of Minority Issues*, 9, 341–358.

Vidra, Z. (2013), *Roma Migration to and From Canada: The Czech, Hungarian and Slovak Case*, Budapest: Center for Policy Studies.

Vuksanović-Macura, Z. (2012), 'The Mapping and Enumeration of Informal Roma Settlements in Serbia', *Environment and Urbanization*, 24(2), 685–705.

Vullnetari, J. (2012), 'Beyond "Choice or Force": Roma Mobility in Albania and the Mixed Migration Paradigm', *Journal of Ethnic and Migration Studies*, 38(8), 1305–1321.

Willems, W. (1997), *In Search of the True Gypsy: From Enlightenment to Final Solution*, New York: Routledge.

World Bank (2013), *Reducing Vulnerability and Promoting the Self-employment of Roma in Eastern Europe Through Financial Inclusion*, Washington, DC: World Bank.

Zolnay, J. (2012), 'Abusive Language and Discriminatory Measures in Hungarian Local Policy', in: *The Gypsy 'Menace'*, ed. by M. Stewart, London: Hurst, 25–41.

17

THE REPRESENTATION OF WOMEN

Frank C. Thames

The end of communism in Eastern Europe created new opportunities for citizens to participate more widely in politics. For women, democratisation offered not only fresh prospects for political participation, but also for increasing gender equality in all spheres of life. The broader, comparative politics literature, however, points out that the extension of suffrage to women and the creation of participation rights do not, in and of themselves, guarantee gender equality, much less equality in representation. Even in countries with long democratic histories such as the US and the UK, women's legislative representation remains low.

Given that democracy does not guarantee equal representation of women in legislatures, what should we expect in Eastern Europe with its limited democratic history? Many scholars have attempted to explain the dynamics of women's representation in Eastern Europe. Much of this research tries to answer two questions. First, why did women's legislative representation drop so precipitously during the initial post-communist elections in Eastern European countries? Second, what caused women's representation to rebound in many countries after these initial losses? For answers to these questions, scholars borrowed heavily from the existing, broader literature on women's representation in comparative politics. Consequently, much of the research on women's representation in Eastern Europe tests arguments based on theories developed through the analysis of cases from across the globe. Specifically, scholars have pointed to the impacts of political culture, electoral systems, political parties, and party gender quotas on women's representation in Eastern Europe.

In 1988, East European Communist legislatures averaged over 25 per cent women (International Parliamentary Union, 2015). By 1994, the situation changed dramatically. The average percentage of female representation in the newly post-communist states had fallen to just over 9 per cent. (International Parliamentary Union, 2015). Existing research identifies several major factors to explain the significant decrease in women's representation – a common communist legacy of gender policies, a patriarchal political culture, the weakness of the women's movement, the electoral system, and the resistance of political parties.

Efforts to explain women's representation in Eastern Europe universally identify the impact of a unique communist legacy. Communist ideology espoused gender equality. Several communist-era policies did aid equality such as access to education, legal guarantees for equality, limits on religious rules that limited women's empowerment, child allowances, state-sponsored childcare, and mandatory maternity leave (LaFont, 2001; Verdery, 1994). The goal of many of these policies was to encourage women to enter the labour force (Rueschemeyer and Wolchik, 2009a). Labour force participation has long been an indicator associated with women's representation. Access to work provides women with resources that make political participation more possible. In addition, work outside the home can raise consciousness about gender inequalities. Thus, women's labour force participation is thought to increase women's representation. Though communist regimes were committed to increasing women's labour force participation, in many cases the job opportunities offered to women were low-skill positions in low-tech sectors of the economy (LaFont, 2001; Titkov, 1998; Fodor, 1998; Chimiak, 2003). Moreover, without an open civil society in these regimes, women's access to the labour force did not lead to the development of an autonomous women's movement. Thus, it did not form the basis for feminist or other women's organisations. In addition, the closed nature of the regimes meant that women lacked the exposure to outside influences or ideas from Western democracies such as second-wave feminism (Miroiu, 2010).

While communism did provide opportunities for women in the economic sphere, the emphasis on work outside the home did not free women from domestic responsibilities. Communist ideology still emphasised women's traditional roles as mothers and homemakers (Chimiak, 2003). Thus, the party reinforced the "double" burden of women as both workers outside the home and the primary workers within the home (Fisher, 1998).

The educational and economic advantages enjoyed by East Europeans did not translate into political equality. As discussed earlier, the percentage of women in East European Communist legislatures was relatively high. This high level was achieved through quotas for women in national legislatures, created by the Communist Party to perpetuate the myth of women's equality (Kunovich, 2003). Of course, the real power in communist systems remained within the higher organs of the party. Women were underrepresented in the party hierarchies. Without power in the party, women would remain largely outside of policymaking decisions in East European Communist states.

For women in newly democratised Eastern Europe, the legacy of communist gender relations complicated the expansion of women's representation. The desire to increase the number of women in the workforce did give women access to education and job opportunities that could have created a foundation for women's representation. In the East European cases, the limitations on autonomous political organisations, however, restricted women's opportunities to organise and push for greater equality. In addition, the party's goal to push women into the economy was coupled with another goal that reinforced women's roles in the home and as mothers. This solidified typical gender stereotypes in Eastern Europe.

The end of communism in Eastern Europe replaced the centrally planned economy with a new, fledgling market economy. The costs of the transition to the market disproportionately fell on women. Unemployment particularly hurt women, who were often locked into low-skill jobs (Titkov, 1998; Wolchik, 1998). The reduction of state support in terms of child care and other subsidised public goods also undermined the economic position of women, still burdened by the inequality in family responsibilities (Fodor, 1998). As women's economic position weakened, the ability to form women's organisations and act politically also weakened.

One of the main explanations for the decline in women's representation after the end of communism was Eastern Europe's patriarchal political culture. Survey data suggested that even after the transition political culture remained highly patriarchal (Matland, 2003; Titkov, 1998; Montgomery and Ilonszki, 2003; Ristova, 2003; Saxonberg, 2003). Among the population, voters and elites embraced the view that politics was a "man's" world (Wilcox et al., 2003). In addition, in some cases there was a lack of recognition by men and women that gender equality was necessary (Chimiak, 2003). In Slovakia and the Czech Republic, for example, women appeared less interested in politics and gender equality than in family, health, and welfare issues (Wolchik, 1998).

Thus, women's groups often championed economic issues at the expense of gender equality. For some, gender equality was part and parcel of the discredited communist ideology (Rueschemeyer and Wolchik, 2009a). A focus on gender equality was a communist ideal that did not have a place in the new post-communist Eastern Europe.

This patriarchal attitude was, in some cases, reinforced by important political actors. In Poland, for example, the Catholic Church reinforced traditional, conservative roles for women that emphasised home and family (Titkov, 1998). In many cases, new political actors arose who did not embrace gender equality. The rise of conservative and nationalist parties opposed to greater gender equality in many East European states undermined support for greater women's representation (Verdery, 1994; Wolchik, 1998; LaFont, 2001; Chiva, 2005).

One of the main findings of existing research is that autonomous women's organisations were weak during the initial period after communism. Strong women's movements can push political actors to adopt policies that aid gender equality. They can help create an environment to elect more women to political office. Certainly, the communist legacy of weak civil society certainly complicated matters. In many cases, women did play important roles in the democratic transitions; however, this did not translate into an autonomous, organised women's movement (Wolchik, 1998; Chiva, 2005). One issue that consistently arose in studies was the lack of reliable support for Western feminism among the groups that did exist (Matland and Montgomery, 2003). In Bulgaria, for example, women's political mobilisation was undermined by a hostility towards Western feminism and negative attitudes about women's affirmative action (Rashkova and Zankina, 2013). More broadly, this created tension in women's organisations between those who wanted to support home and hearth versus Western feminist conceptions of gender equality (Sloat, 2005; Matland and Montgomery, 2003).

Another major area of focus was the impact of the electoral system. The general conclusion of the gender literature on electoral systems is that proportional representation systems create greater incentives for party leaders to nominate women increase women's representation. While the drop in women's representation occurred in many states, early evidence suggested that proportional representation systems elected, on average, more women than did other systems (Matland, 2003; Kunovich, 2003). Though, in some cases like Hungary, the incentives to balance tickets was limited by the ability to place candidates on multiple lists, low district magnitudes on some tiers, and the difficulty of predicting the competitiveness of different slots on lists (Montgomery and Ilonszki, 2003).

Research also suggests that the behaviour of political parties and their leaders undermined women's representation after the end of communism. Several studies point out that parties simply failed to nominate a significant number of women for election across many different cases (Kostadinova, 2003; Saxonberg, 2003; Kunovich, 2003; Wolchik, 1998). Communist policies that offered women access to higher education and opened the labour force to them created a significant number of well-educated women with resources. This should have created a strong pool of candidates for elective office. Yet, in the majority of post-communist Eastern European countries parties did not exploit this resource and, instead, nominated few women for office (Matland and Montgomery, 2003). Why did parties fail to nominate women? Part of the explanation may be cultural – party leaders simply viewed politics as a "man's" game and women were not suitable candidates (Gaber, 1999). In some cases, Poland for example, party leaders saw female candidates as "riskier" than male candidates (Siemienska, 2003). In addition, the weakness of women's organisations within and outside parties meant little pressure on party leaders to nominate women (Saxonberg, 2003; Matland and Montgomery, 2003; Montgomery and Ilonszki, 2003). Parties often had weak, poorly institutionalised nominations procedures that worked against female nominations (Saxonberg, 2000). Party ideology did appear to matter. Even during this early period, left parties were more likely to nominate women than were other parties (Montgomery and Ilonszki, 2003; Siemienska, 2003; Chiva, 2005).

While the overall level of women's representation fell during the initial post-communist elections, the situation changed over time. By 2014, the level of women's representation on average reached 22 per cent (International Parliamentary Union, 2015). This level is lower than that of Western Europe; however, it does represent a significant increase in women's representation. What explains this turnaround in women's representation? To answer this question, gender scholars again used arguments well-grounded in the broader comparative literature on women's representation.

One of the factors noted for the low level of women's representation previously was the existence of a political culture that did not support women's entrance into the political sphere. More recent evidence from some countries suggests changing attitudes towards the participation of women in politics (Siemienska, 2009). More actors and voters appear to have accepted women as political actors. As acceptance for women in politics grew, the perceived costs of nominating women fell. In Poland, party leaders responded to voters who increased the list positions of women by increasing the number and rankings of women (Kunovich, 2012). In one study of the Czech Republic, a significant number of female candidates report being approached by parties to run for office (Wolchik, 2009). The encouragement of women to run for office by parties is a significant step forward for women's representation. Yet, the changes in political culture do not appear uniform; moreover, there remained popular attitudes that discouraged gender equity in some countries (Rashkova and Zankina, 2013). In Estonia, for example, public opinion was solidly against the creation of legislative quotas for women in 2004 (Laas, 2005).

More recent research also highlights the important role played by electoral institutions. One study of mixed-member systems found that women fared better in proportional representation systems, but that mixed-member systems outperformed majoritarian systems (Kostadinova, 2007). In Bulgaria, women found much more success in the proportional representation lists than in individual nominations (Ghodsee, 2009). A 2001 reform in Poland that increased party magnitude by reducing the number of constituencies and increasing district magnitude successfully increased women's representation (Siemienska, 2005). There are contrasting findings on the impact of open-list proportional representation systems. One study of Bosnia and Herzegovina found that the move to open lists reduced women's representation (Borić, 2005); however, it did not impact women's representation in Poland (Kunovich, 2012). Another study finds that the success of women in populist parties in Poland and Bulgaria is due to their centralised structures that reduced the power of party gatekeepers and the importance of loyalty over other factors (Kostadinova and Mikulska, 2015).

The early decline in women's representation was blamed, in part, on the weakness of the women's movement in many Eastern European states. More recent research finds that improvements in the organisation and strength of the women's movement has led to increases in women's representation (Rueschemeyer and Wolchik, 2009b). In some cases, improvements were made due to the efforts of women's organisations within political parties. In Slovenia, for example, the demand by women's organisations in political parties led to more nominations for female candidates (Gaber, 1999).

One area where the power of women's organisations mattered the most was in the adoption of quotas for female candidates. Pressure by female activists was essential to the adoption of party quotas in countries such as Poland (Siemienska, 2009; Siemienska, 2005), Bosnia and Herzegovina (Borić, 2005), and Croatia (Leakovi, 2005). Organised women's groups pushed for both party and national quotas in Macedonia (Dimitrievska, 2005). In Hungary, women's organisations in left parties worked with left-wing non-governmental organisations for more women in leadership positions as well as quotas (Bonifert and Gurmai, 2005). In Bulgaria, women's groups saw quotas as the only way to increase women's representation given the significant obstacles to gender equality in the country (Rashkova and Zankina, 2013).

The increased presence of women in Eastern European legislatures begs the question of whether this increased presence led to changes in government policy. On the whole, there is little research on women's substantive representation in Eastern Europe. The general conclusion of most of the existing studies is that women, as a group, have not been able to impact policy significantly, and remain relatively weak forces in the legislature. Several studies of legislative committees reveals that female legislators rarely serve in leadership positions and often sit on committees dealing with stereotypically women's issues and not on more powerful committees (Siemienska, 2009; Gaber, 2009; Rueschemeyer and Wolchik, 2009b). In addition, the sense among many is that women have not successfully achieved a "critical mass" sufficient to influence policy (Gaber, 2009; Wolchik, 2009; Ghodsee, 2009).

On the whole, the research on women's representation has produced a number of important studies that add much to our understanding of gender equality in Eastern Europe and, to an extent, more broadly. The record, however, is not without its weaknesses. Much of the research concentrates specifically on legislatures. More work needs to be done on other representative institutions, such as the executive, judiciary, and bureaucracy. In one recent study of cabinets, the percentage of women in ministerial posts was found to be associated with the number of women with higher education degrees (Bego, 2013). While there are, perhaps, few women with such posts, we do see variation across the region in the number of female executives. Given the importance of executives in policymaking, we need to understand those factors that explain female representation in the executive in Eastern Europe. Moreover, the dynamics of female executive representation might give us insights on the role of women within East European political parties.

Much of the existing research relies on case studies or studies of a small number of cases. Such work provides us with important information about the dynamics of women's representation at particular times and in particular places. However, such approaches make it difficult to isolate those factors that explain variation across the region. Matland (2003) points out that studies of the region often cite a common, patriarchal culture that undermines women's representation; however, given that we see variation in women's representation, a common, cross-national culture cannot explain this variation. Many studies, for example, elucidate how parties, at times, discourage women and electoral systems vary in their impact on women's representation. There are few, however, large-N studies of electoral or party system effects in the region. Kostadinova (2007), which analyses the impact of mixed-member systems, is a notable exception.

Many of the theoretical approaches used to study women's representation are based on the broader comparative literature on women's representation. This is a very helpful strategy, since it allows us to understand the Eastern European cases in a larger frame of reference. Yet, there are few if any empirical comparisons of Eastern Europe with Western Europe or other regions. Thus, it is often difficult to determine how "different" these cases are from others. Given the significant literature on the communist legacy, one wonders whether this legacy created important differences between Eastern Europe and other cases. This seems plausible; however, it is difficult to isolate the effects of this legacy without comparing East European cases to ones that did not experience this communist legacy. Much can be learned by comparing East European cases with those outside the region. In one prominent example, Jacquette and Wolchik (1998) compares the experiences of women in newly democratising Latin American with the experience of women in the newly democratising Eastern Europe. It concluded that after the transition, the women's movements in Eastern Europe did not mobilise around gender issues because women lacked experience organising, of concerns among East European women about the goals of Western feminism, and the association of women's equality with the communist agenda. By comparing the East European experience to broader contexts, we can better understand those factors that determine the level of women's representation in Eastern Europe.

Another potentially critical factor that remains under-investigated is the impact of European Union (EU) membership on East European member nations. Entrance into the EU required aspiring states to meet entrance requirements that could, theoretically, influence women's representation, both descriptively and substantively. Yet, there are few empirical studies of this impact. Avdeyeva (2010) finds variation in how well new East European members met these requirements. Another study found that EU incentives impacted the presence of women in East European cabinets (Bego, 2013). These are important first steps; however, we need more research on this question.

Since the initial decrease in women's representation, Eastern Europe has experienced significant increases in the number of women elected to the legislature in many countries. Yet, the existence of variation among Eastern European states, the absence of levels of women's representation approaching equality, and the potentially interesting differences between East European countries and other countries makes the further study of women's representation important. East European countries differ not only in terms of the overall level of representation, but in electoral system effects, party behaviours, and other institutional factors such as quotas. These differences need to be explored further. In addition, important differences between the East European experiences, such as the communist legacy or the patriarchal political culture, and other countries provides a unique opportunity to understand better those factors that drive gender equality. By comparing Eastern European cases with others more broadly, we can better isolate the impact of these and other influences on women's representation. We should expect differences between regions; however, the best way to understand those differences is to continue to compare Eastern Europe with other cases. This provides us with one of the best justifications for the continued study of women's representation in Eastern Europe.

Of course, the best reason to continue our analysis of women's representation in Eastern Europe is to understand better the causes of the continued inequality between men and women in the political realm. Eastern Europe, as in many other regions of the world, has seen an increasing trend in women's representation. The improvements, however, leave all countries in the region well below gender equality. Until women are able to translate their policy preferences into outcomes, we will continue to see gender inequality not only in politics but in other spheres.

While questions about the cause of gender inequality remain, the existing research has certainly pushed us closer to more definitive answers. Thanks to the efforts of scholars asking important questions and undertaking important research we certainly understand more about women's representation in Eastern Europe than we did in the past. As more scholars conduct research using new methods, approaches, and data, we will move even closer to understanding why women remain underrepresented in Eastern Europe.

Bibliography

Avdeyeva, O., 2010. States' Compliance With International Requirements Gender Equality in EU Enlargement Countries. *Political Research Quarterly*, 63(1), pp. 203–217.

Bego, I., November 2013. Accessing Power in New Democracies: The Appointment of Female Ministers in Postcommunist Europe. *Political Research Quarterly*, 67(2), pp. 347–360.

Bonifert, M. and Gurmai, Z., 2005. Advancement of Women's Issues Through Political Mobilization in Hungary: Impact of the Hungarian Socialist Party Quota. In: *The Implementation of Quotas: European Experiences.* Stockholm, Sweden: IDEA.

Borić, B., 2005. Application of Quotas: Legal Reforms and Implementation in Bosnia and Herzegovina. In: *The Implementation of Quotas: European Experiences.* Stockholm, Sweden: IDEA.

Chimiak, G., 2003. Bulgarian and Polish Women in the Public Sphere. *International Feminist Journal of Politics*, 5(1), pp. 3–25.

Chiva, C., 2005. Women in Post-Communist Politics: Explaining Under-Representation in the Hungarian and Romanian Parliaments. *Europe-Asia Studies*, 57(7), pp. 969–994.

Dimitrievska, D., 2005. Quotas: The Case of Macedonia. In: *The Implementation of Quotas: European Experiences.* Stockholm, Sweden: IDEA.

Fisher, M. E., 1998. From Tradition and Ideology to Elections and Competition: The Changing Status of Women in Romanian Politics. In: M. Rueschemeyer, ed. *Women in the Politics of Postcommunist Eastern Europe, Revised and Expanded.* Armonk, NY: M. E. Sharpe.

Fodor, E., 1998. Political Woman? Women in Politics in Hungary. In: M. Rueschemeyer, ed. *Women in the Politics of Postcommunist Eastern Europe, Revised and Expanded.* Armonk, NY: M. E. Sharpe.

Gaber, M. A., 1999. Slovene Political Parties and Their Influence on the Electoral Prospects for Women. *Journal of Communist Studies and Transition Politics*, 15(1), pp. 7–29.

Gaber, M. A., 2009. Women in the Slovene Parliament: Working Toward a Critical Mass. In: *Women in Power in Post-Communist Parliaments.* Bloomington: Indiana University Press.

Ghodsee, K., 2009. Reflections on the Return of the King: Women in the Bulgarian Parliament. In: *Women in Power in Post-Communist Parliaments.* Bloomington: Indiana University Press.

International Parliamentary Union, 2015. *Women in National Parliaments: Statistical Archive.* [Online] Available at: www.ipu.org/wmn-e/classif-arc.htm [Accessed 24 October 2015].

Jacquette, J. and Wolchik, S. eds., 1998. *Women and Democracy: Latin America and Eastern Europe.* Baltimore, MD: Johns Hopkins University Press.

Kostadinova, T., 2003. Women's Legislative Representation in Post-Communist Bulgaria. In: R. Matland and K. Montgomery, eds. *Women's Access to Political Power in Post-Communist Europe.* New York: Oxford University Press, pp. 304–321.

Kostadinova, T., June 2007. Ethnic and Women's Representation Under Mixed Election Systems. *Electoral Studies*, 26(2), pp. 418–431.

Kostadinova, T. and Mikulska, A., 2015 (forthcoming). The Puzzling Success of Populist Parties in Promoting Women's Political Representation. *Party Politics.*

Kunovich, S., 2003. The Representation of Polish and Czech Women in National Politics: Predicting Electoral List Position. *Comparative Politics*, 35(3), pp. 273–291.

Kunovich, S., 2012. Unexpected Winners: The Significance of an Open-List System on Women's Representation in Poland. *Politics & Gender*, 8(2), pp. 153–177.

Laas, A., 2005. To Suspect or Respect? Quota Discourse in Estonia. In: *The Implementation of Quotas: European Experiences.* Stockholm, Sweden: IDEA, pp. 104–111.

LaFont, S., 2001. One Step Forward, Two Steps Back: Women in the Post-communist States. *Communist and Post-Communist Studies*, 34(2), pp. 203–220.

Leakovi, K., 2005. Political Party Quotas in the Croatian Social Democratic Party. In: J. Ballington and F. Binda, eds. *The Implementation of Quotas: European Experiences.* Stockholm, Sweden: IDEA, pp. 72–74.

Matland, R., 2003. Conclusion. In: R. Matland and K. Montgomery, eds. *Women's Access to Political Power in Post-Communist Europe.* New York: Oxford University Press, pp. 321–342.

Matland, R. and Montgomery, K., 2003. Recruiting Women to the National Legislatures. In: R. Matland and K. Montgomery, eds. *Women's Access to Political Power in Post-Communist Europe.* New York: Oxford University Press, pp. 19–42.

Miroiu, M., September 2010. Not the Right Moment: Women and the Politics of Endless Delay in Romania. *Women's History Review*, 19(4), pp. 575–593.

Montgomery, K. and Ilonszki, G., 2003. Weak Mobilization, Hidden Majoritarianism, and Resurgence of the Right: A Recipe for Female Under-Representation in Hungary. In: R. Matland and K. Montgomery, eds. *Women's Access to Political Power in Post-Communist Europe.* New York: Oxford University Press, pp. 105–129.

Rashkova, E. R. and Zankina, E., November 2013. Does Party Exist in the 'Macho' World? Party Regulation and Gender Representation in the Balkans. *Representation*, 49(4), pp. 425–438.

Ristova, K., 2003. Establishing a Machocracy: Women and Elections in Macedonia (1990–1998). In: R. Matland and K. Montgomery, eds. *Women's Access to Political Power in Post-Communist Europe.* New York: Oxford University Press, pp. 196–216.

Rueschemeyer, M. and Wolchik, S., 2009a. Women in Power: The Issues. In: *Women in Power in Post-Communist Parliaments.* Bloomington: Indiana University Press.

Rueschemeyer, M. and Wolchik, S., 2009b. Women in Power: Concluding Thoughts. In: *Women in Power in Post-Communist Parliaments*. Bloomington: Indiana University Press, pp. 251–266.

Saxonberg, S., 2000. Women in East European Parliaments. *Journal of Democracy*, 11(2), pp. 145–158.

Saxonberg, S., 2003. Czech Political Parties Prefer Male Candidates to Female Votes. In: R. Matland and K. Montgomery, eds. *Women's Access to Political Power in Post-Communist Europe*. New York: Oxford University Press, pp. 245–266.

Siemienska, R., 2003. Women in the Polish Sejm: Political Culture and Party Politics Versus Electoral Rules. In: R. Matland and K. Montgomery, eds. *Women's Access to Political Power in Post-Communist Europe*. New York: Oxford University Press, pp. 217–244.

Siemienska, R., 2005. Gender Party Quotas in Poland. In: *The Implementation of Quotas: European Experiences*. Stockholm, Sweden: IDEA, pp. 80–85.

Siemienska, R., 2009. Women's Representation in the Polish Parliament and the Determinants of Their Effectiveness. In: *Women in Power in Post-Communist Parliaments*. Bloomington: Indiana University Press, pp. 61–92.

Sloat, A., November 2005. The Rebirth of Civil Society: The Growth of Women's NGOs in Central and Eastern Europe. *European Journal of Women's Studies*, 12(4), pp. 437–452.

Titkov, A., 1998. Polish Women in Politics: An Introduction to the Status of Women in Poland. In: M. Rueschemeyer, ed. *Women in the Politics of Postcommunist Eastern Europe, Revised and Expanded*. Armonk, NY: M. E. Sharpe, pp. 24–32.

Verdery, K., 1994. From Parent-state to Family Patriarchs: Gender and Nation in Contemporary Eastern Europe. *East European Politics & Societies*, 8(2), pp. 225–255.

Wilcox, C., Stark, B. and Thomas, S., 2003. Popular Support for Electing Women in Eastern Europe. In: R. Matland and K. Montgomery, eds. *Women's Access to Political Power in Post-Communist Europe*. New York: Oxford University Press, pp. 43–62.

Wolchik, S. L., 1998. Women and the Politics of Transition in the Czech and Slovak Republics. In: M. Rueschemeyer, ed. *Women in the Politics of Postcommunist Eastern Europe, Revised and Expanded*. Armonk, NY: M. E. Sharpe, pp. 116–141.

Wolchik, S. L., 2009. Women in Power in the Czech Republic: Problems and Prospects. In: *Women in Power in Post-Communist Parliaments*. Bloomington: Indiana University Press, pp. 111–130.

18

THE STRUGGLE FOR LGBT RIGHTS

Conor O'Dwyer

Introduction: why study LGBT rights after communism?

Seen from the perspective of scholars of both comparative politics and Eastern Europe, lesbian, gay, bisexual, and transgender (LGBT) politics and gay rights are particularly instructive as lenses for considering the region's development since the epochal changes of 1989. The following is a list of just some of the broader questions that this issue touches on. How liberal are post-communist democracies really? Is robust rights activism possible in weak civil societies? How much influence do transnational institutions such as the European Union, which has come to be seen as a promoter of gay rights, really wield? How much like the rest of Europe has post-communist Europe become? What is the role of religion in post-communist politics? We could go on, but the point is clear: the question of LGBT rights brings each of these questions, which have purchase across a range of social and political issues in the region's development since the fall of communism, into sharp focus. One might also point out, of course, that problems of majority-minority relations have historically very closely linked with the region's democratic development – most dramatically in the interwar period.[1] In this chapter, I seek not to answer these questions but to provide a brief orientation as to how the scholarship on LGBT politics in post-communist Europe has evolved over the course of grappling with them.

A note on terminology

Before going any further, however, a brief caveat about terminology, in particular the terms "LGBT" and "gay rights," is in order. First LGBT – for lesbian, gay, bisexual, and transgender – is an umbrella term that is now well-known in the region. It is used by both supporters and detractors alike. Nevertheless, it must be applied with care when describing even recent history. The problem is not only that it was not always much used by activists and others. It is that some of the categories contained within it did not really exist for all practical purposes. For example, in the early 1990s, and certainly before, there were very few, if any, transgender people. One of the first transgender activist groups in the region, Poland's *Transfuzja* (Transfusion), was only established in 2008. To speak, then, of LGBT activism in the 1990s is somewhat anachronistic. Likewise, the category "bisexual" seems very much underrepresented if one looks at the organisational composition of social movements. In general, the composition of these movements in the early years after the fall of communism was dominated by gay men, with a much smaller number of lesbians. Over time, these proportions have shifted. A further problem is that even the language of activists and politicians (on both sides of the rights question) is not consistent over time. In the early 1990s, rights activists favoured the term "homosexuals" in naming their organisations. Later the preferred usage was "gay" or "lesbian." Most recently, the term "queer" is presented as an alternative.

Likewise, the term "gay rights," though commonly used on the ground and among analysts as a kind of shorthand, presents similar difficulties. First, following on the comments above, these are rights not just of gay men. Second, just what rights are included? Same-sex marriage? The right to adopt children? Or do we have in mind more basic rights such as labour laws to protect against discrimination in employment? Or, taking into account the backdrop of deep repression – and, in some cases, criminalisation – of homosexuality under communism, should we employ a more basic concept of "gay rights" in this region than we are accustomed to in the US? Even today, citizenship rights such as free speech, the right to organise collectively, and protection from overt discrimination are at issue.

After all, recent history has brought threats to even these more basic liberal freedoms in a number of countries in the region. In recent years, these has included unconstitutional bans of Pride marches in Poland and Latvia; violent attacks on parades in Hungary in 2007, Serbia in 2010, and Croatia in 2011; the passage of laws against "homosexual propaganda" in schools in Lithuania; and a surge in the mobilisation of the hard right, from electoral breakthroughs of openly antigay parties in Poland and Hungary to the street mobilisation of Ukraine's *Pravyi Sektor* (Right Sector). Then, of course, there is Russia, which in the last several years has taken on the mantle of defender of traditional and conservative (read antigay) values on the international stage.

Rather than try to capture the gradually blurring boundaries between the movement's constituents or its shifting boundaries and goals, we use the encompassing terms "gay rights" and "LGBT rights" interchangeably here to refer to the movement, its members, and its goals. Just as "gay rights" has become a blanket term for the goals of the broader LGBT movement, we will use it to cover the gamut of policies and goals from ensuring basic citizen rights to more ambitious goals such as same-sex registered partnerships, antidiscrimination protection, adoption rights, and even same-sex marriage. Likewise, the term gay-rights movement will be used to encompass the varieties of activism. In both cases, we recognise that meaning shifts not only across place but over time.[2]

An overview of a literature struggling to catch up

Having laid out some of the central questions that LGBT rights raise for scholars of the region and the term's various levels of meaning, we now provide a brief overview of the scholarship by first discussing the salience of this issue in comparative politics scholarship over time and then identifying the main thematic orientations within this scholarship. It should be emphasised at the outset that the relatively recent explosion of LGBT issues onto the political scene in countries from Poland to Croatia represents another instance of political scientists being taken by surprise by real-world events. Scholars of comparative politics, at least those writing for an English-language audience, are still struggling to catch up with events on the ground – which is another way of saying that this literature remains underdeveloped compared with that on other aspects of post-communism. This section outlines the chronology of this development beginning with the communist period and ending with the current day.

To a large degree, the development of scholarship on homosexuality in Eastern Europe and the former Soviet Union has followed the politics of the issue itself. Just as the issue was long socially taboo and politically invisible in the region, likewise it was largely overlooked by scholars, at least political scientists. There were, of course, some notable exceptions, as described later. Academic interest, especially among scholars based outside of the region, has greatly increased, but only really in the last decade – which was also the point at which the issue began making headlines.

As was the case in the US and Western Europe, the appearance of HIV/AIDS led to new visibility, if not notoriety, for homosexuality in the 1980s. For Eastern Europe and the Soviet Union, this was late-stage communism, a period during which country-specific factors made for a highly varied map of state-society relations and ideological rigour in the application of the Soviet model. These differences were reflected in the official treatment of homosexuality, though not always in the same way as other aspects of state-society relations. For example, Poland's regime was generally considered much less repressive than Czechoslovakia's in the 1980s (Ekiert 1996); however, in the area of homosexuality, the situation was reversed. Polish social scientists treated homosexuality as a perversion likely to lead to socially deviant, even criminal behaviour (Owczarzak 2009, 2010). By contrast, Czechoslovak social scientists, especially those in the field of sexology, treated homosexuality as an innate condition, which, because of social stigma, would likely lead to social problems (Long 1999; Seidl 2012). Thus, Czechoslovak sexologists sought to use therapy to ameliorate these adverse consequences. To offer a third example of the variation in the authorities' treatment of homosexuality, in Romania homosexuality was a criminal offense punishable by imprisonment of up to five years (Buzogány 2008; Kligman 1998).[3] Yet even as we note these differences in how the region's states treated homosexuality under communism, we should not allow them to obscure the deeper similarities among communist states and societies in this area. Namely, homosexuality was deeply taboo in society – reflecting a still largely traditional political culture reinforced by what Janos (2001) has called communism's "neo-Victorian" morality. Consequently, gay and lesbian life was deeply underground. One consequence of this was that across the region the secret police threatened to "out" suspected gays as a means of trying to recruit them as informants.

Interest in the politics of homosexuality from comparative politics scholars outside of the region came in the aftermath of the fall of communism. Here we can think of the work of Gessen (1994), Long (1999), Flam (2001), and Ramet (1999). As the brevity of this list indicates, however, the politics of homosexuality was far from the attention of most scholars and observers of the region in the 1990s (Kulpa and Mizielińska 2011). Instead the paradigms of transition, with its triple-transition of democratisation, economic reform, and state-building, were the topics of the day. These triple-transitions constituted the yardsticks for assessing political development after communism. As a caveat, it should be noted that minority rights did find a niche within this first wave of post-communist scholarship. They did so, however, in the form of ethnic minority conflict and the gendered character of economic transition.[4] The politics of both are arguably quite different than those of "sexual minorities." Even recognising these differences, one can find certain themes that would later be picked up on by the post-2000 scholarship on LGBT politics, as described later. First, the connection between transnational pressure and minority-rights policies – inspired by the earlier application of Europeanisation literature to ethnic minority rights and citizenship policy in the Baltics (Kelley 2003) – became a theme in the later scholarship. Second, in the field of gender politics, a number of first-wave scholars sought to account for the surprising weakness of women's movements after 1990 – surprising, that is, given the disproportionately harsh consequences of the economic transition on women (Sperling 1999).

Following the EU's enlargement to Eastern Europe beginning in 2004, the question of LGBT identity and rights began to generate much more scholarly attention, especially in the West. We may divide this literature into three thematic streams: focusing on communism's legacy; dealing with the formation of new identities after communism, which tends to identify with the broader discipline of queer studies; and analysing the changing politics of homosexuality through the lens of transnational norm diffusion, which draws heavily on the Europeanisation literature. These boundaries can be porous at times, but they are useful in identifying the different emphases in the scholarship: legacy, identity, or transnational pressure.

The legacies branch focuses on the attitudinal and political cultural inheritance of communism. The persistence of such neo-traditionalism can be seen, these scholars typically argue, in the weakness of civil society, on the one hand, and in the church's re-entry into politics after 1989. The former draws on the work of Jowitt (1992) and Howard (2003) to argue that social attitudes towards homosexuality in Eastern Europe reflect the persistence of communism's neo-Victorian political culture. Štulhofer and Rimac (2009) argue, for example, that homosexuality is probably the most telling indicator of political cultural divides between Eastern and Western Europe.[5] More case-oriented research on the legacies of communist-era attitudes towards homosexuality include Chetaille (2011), Graff (2006, 2010), and Owczarzak (2009, 2010) on Poland; Renkin (2007) on Hungary; Gould (2015) on Slovakia; Gould and Moe (2015) on Serbia; and Sperling (2014) on Russia – to offer a partial list. We may also consider scholarship on the reassertion of church authority in the political sphere under the rubric of legacies approach. After all, as Grzymała-Busse (2015) and Turcescu and Stan (2005) have shown, the fate of the various "national" churches under communism has shaped how they engage with homosexuality since 1989. Grzymała-Busse argues that the immense moral authority that communism (unintentionally) endowed on the Polish Catholic church did not lead it to engage as actively in antigay mobilisation, as might have been expected.[6] Poland certainly did have an antigay backlash in the mid-2000s, but its chief fomenters were hard-right political parties such as the League of Polish Families. Romania offers a contrast here; the Romanian Orthodox church was decimated under communism, but it has since re-energized, using much of its new vigour to combat what it sees as the threat of homosexuality (Buzogány 2008; Turcescu and Stan 2005).

A second major approach among scholars is that focusing on the construction of LGBT identities, a perspective that takes its inspiration from Queer Studies. The use of the plural ("identities") here is not only necessary but deserves special emphasis. Especially in Eastern Europe, the term LGBT is contested and does not constitute one identity. As noted earlier, even using the terms "lesbian" and "gay" is relatively new, though they have now largely replaced the previous term of choice, "homosexual." Though transgender identity exists and can claim its own activism and scholarship, it is not universally accepted by gays and lesbians in the region. Kuhar and Takács (2007) serves as a good example of this approach.[7] This book brings together a diverse field of contributors from academia (mainly in sociology and anthropology) to activists. The chapters are diverse in choice of sources, which span from film to personal testimonials to the print news media, and in methodologies, which range from participant observation to content analysis to survey analysis. Most, though not all, of the contributors are based in the countries that they analyse.

Despite this diversity, it is possible to identify a few common propositions across the contributors. First, there is a consensus that a distinctive "local" framing (or set of framings) of LGBT identity has emerged in the region since 1989. Though these scholars acknowledge the considerable role of European integration processes in raising the issue's salience, they consistently and strongly argue that local identities are not the same as Western European or even US ones. This claim highlights the role of legacy, and especially communist legacy, in the formation of identity. To highlight the communist legacy is not, of course, to trace contemporary identities to the communist period. Scholars of this school typically stress how today's LGBT movements overcame "medicalised" definitions of sexual orientation prevalent under communism to adopt LGBT (even queer) ones today (Sokolová 2005).

The third major approach evident in the scholarship is that focusing on the transnational dimension of LGBT politics. As noted earlier, this branch focuses primarily on LGBT politics through the lens of European integration. Among political scientists based outside of the region, it is fair to say, this has become the predominant approach. Ayoub and Paternotte (2014) is an excellent example of this EU perspective and illustrates some of its primary themes and contributions (see also Ayoub 2016; Ayoub and Paternotte 2012; Buzogány 2008; Graff 2008; Holzhacker 2012; Kochenov 2007; O'Dwyer and Schwartz 2010; O'Dwyer 2010, 2012; Slootmaeckers, Touquet and Vermeersch 2016). First, there is the question of how the EU itself came to be associated with LGBT rights. Given the strength of this association, it is useful to be reminded that the EU is in fact relatively new to this issue, and it is important to distinguish between actual EU influence and perceived EU influence. As Ayoub and Paternotte write in their introduction to the volume, they aim to explain the origins of

> the "special relationship" that unites issues of sexuality and Europe . . . addressing the paradox that, while being marginal within EU policies, LGBT rights have become a powerful symbol of Europe, featuring centrally in debates ranging from foreign relations to economic trade.
>
> *(2014, 3)*

While defining what counts as marginal from a policy perspective may be debatable, the larger point of the symbolic importance of gay rights to the EU's image is unquestioned. It is so often argued by gay-rights opponents that the EU is responsible for foisting a homosexual agenda on them that one might imagine the EU's commitment to this issue to be absolute and its tools for promoting this agenda vast. In the more paranoid versions of this thinking, the promulgation of gay rights is seen as a central EU objective, as in the remarks of Alexei Pushkov, chairman of the Russian Parliament's Foreign Affairs Committee, regarding Ukraine's Maidan protesters: "Of course, this means the expansion of the sphere of the so-called gay culture, which has now turned into the official policy of the EU" (quoted in Ayoub and Paternotte 2014, 1).

In reality, the EU's own path to the issue of gay rights is relatively recent, and its instruments of influence are circumscribed. First, explicit mention of sexual orientation within the EU's governing treaties did not occur until 1997, with the Treaty of Amsterdam. In 2000, EU Directive 2000/78 mandated the adoption of antidiscrimination policies in the labour market in member-states and applicants, with explicit mention of sexual orientation. In addition, the principle of non-discrimination on the basis of sexual orientation received explicit mention in the Charter of Fundamental Rights of the European Union, also enacted in 2000 (Waaldijk, 2006). The legal codification of gay-rights norms by European institutions has since broadened through the jurisprudence of the European Court of Justice (van der Vleuten, 2014), but protections against discrimination on the basis of sexual orientation are still at root primarily a labour-market issue. Especially in the new post-communist member-states, such antidiscrimination provisions often proved politically controversial; however, the arguments against them always had a "slippery-slope" quality – as being a first step on the road to gay marriage, adoption, and so on.

In addition to promoting gay-rights norms through legal conditionality in the accession process, the EU also promoted such norms indirectly through support for the European Region of the International Lesbian, Gay, Bisexual, Trans and Intersex Association (ILGA-Europe).[8] This transnational advocacy group is headquartered in Brussels and produces what are now highly detailed monitoring reports on the legal frameworks and societal atmosphere in member-states and potential member-states. The most visible form of this monitoring is the now yearly Rainbow Index, which serves as a kind of clearinghouse for ranking LGBT-rights frameworks as the Freedom House does for democracy.[9] ILGA-Europe also consults with and coordinates LGBT groups throughout Europe, serving as a resource for tactics and expertise. For example, ILGA-Europe provided strategic advice to Slovak rights groups in the run-up to the February 2015 referendum on same-sex marriage. In this way, it functions very much as the kind of epistemic community that scholars of norms diffusion such as Keck and Sikkink (1998) have analysed. It should also be emphasised, however, that ILGA-Europe is a relatively new organisation (established in 1996), which has only received direct EU funding since 2000 (Ayoub and Paternotte 2012). Thus, a certain caution must be exercised in analysing the EU's influence over the politics of homosexuality in Eastern Europe. It is often difficult to separate *de jure* EU influence from perceived EU influence. Or to put it slightly differently, "Gayropa" is more a construction by critics of homosexuality than it is a description of reality.

This tension is reflected in the scholarly literature. While academics were quick to appreciate the relevance of the Europeanisation framework for gay rights – and especially antidiscrimination norms – it is also hard not detect an almost palpable sense of disappointment in much of this scholarship.[10] One need not read any further than the title of Kochenov's (2007) analysis of the EU's eastern enlargement – "Democracy and Human Rights – Not for Gay People?" – as a reflection of this disappointment. Further examples of this disappointment may be found in a number of other studies of the politicisation of homosexuality in the years immediately before and after EU accession – (see Buzogány [2008] on Romania and Hungary and O'Dwyer and Schwartz [2010] on Poland and Latvia). The thrust of this scholarship is that EU conditionality was a powerful instrument for forcing legal change (albeit primarily in the labour market), but that, since post-communist states gained membership, the leverage via conditionality has largely evaporated – and with it the impetus for further legal change.

Conclusion

Gay rights highlight the tension between traditional conceptions of national identity, which typically are hostile to homosexuality, and transnational (especially EU) discourses on minority rights. Examining the debate over homosexuality provides a new and compelling perspective on the rapidly changing conceptions of national identity, citizenship, and belonging in post-communist societies. As I have argued here, the literature on LGBT rights and rights activism in Eastern Europe is still very much a nascent one. This situation is all the more striking given how politicized this once taboo issue has become in the region over the last decade. Nevertheless, the outlines of at least three strands of theorizing are emerging: a legacies approach, an identity-based approach, and a transnational diffusion approach. Each has generated important insights; however, as yet most of the scholarship has taken the form of single-country studies.[11]

Integrating these insights and applying them in a more explicitly comparative framework is the next step for scholars. This will be important not just for a better understanding of the politics of homosexuality after communism but also for theorizing the causal pathways by which European integration continues to alter domestic politics both after accession and over different waves of accession. The former Yugoslav republics serve as particularly rich sites for considering the latter point, as they include examples of first-wave post-communist EU entrants (Slovenia), more recent ones (Croatia), and ongoing applicants (the rest). Recent work by Ayoub (2016), Bilić (2016), Mikuš (2011), and O'Dwyer (2012) has begun to tackle this challenge by focusing more narrowly than Europeanisation scholars usually do on the nature of activism and social movements in the context of integration. Such research directly engages the gap between international norms and the everyday practice of rights, contributing to a broader comparative literature on transnational activism (Bob 2012; Tarrow 2005). Those scholars focusing on the former Yugoslav republics tend to draw pessimistic conclusions about the impact of transnational advocacy on local rights activism. As Bilić provocatively put it, the post-Yugoslav space forms

> a kind of imperialist "laboratory" for contemporary social, economic, and political engineering and in that sense it offers us an important, but understudied, perspective for exploring both the affinities and the tensions between "new" social movements and EU accession.
>
> *(2016, 7)*[12]

Scholarship on the East Central European cases, on the other hand, tends to see more positive effects on local activism from contact with transnational norms (Ayoub 2016; O'Dwyer 2012). Common across these newer works, however, is the view that the EU is a disruptor of patriarchal and homophobic norms; the debate continues as to whether its sponsorship of rights norms ultimately empowers or alienates local gay-rights movements.

Notes

1 See for example, Rothschild (1977) and Walicki (2000). This historical echo is not lost on contemporary gay-rights activists in the region, who have likened the position of today's LGBT with that of interwar Jews. See Czarnecki (2007).
2 Similarly, I will follow the increasingly common convention of using the term "antigay" to include all forms of prejudice based on sexual orientation.
3 In this way, Romania resembled the Soviet Union and Serbia (Kahlina 2015), which also criminalized homosexual relations (Gessen 1994).
4 As examples, consider Barany's work on the Roma (2002) and Sperling's (1999) on the Russian women's movement.
5 For similar cross-national attitudinal research, see also Gerhards (2010) and Takács and Szalma (2011).
6 See also Ramet (2006).
7 See also Kulpa and Mizielińska (2011).
8 Another transnational organisation active in supporting LGBT groups in the region was the Open Society Institute, now called the Open Society Foundations.
9 The index can be found at http://rainbow-europe.org.
10 Probably the most concise statement of this framework and the one that has informed its application to gay rights in Eastern Europe is Schimmelfennig and Sedelmeier (2005).
11 Ayoub (2016) is a notable exception.
12 See also Mikuš (2011).

Bibliography

Ayoub, Phillip M. 2016. *When States Come Out: Europe's Sexual Minorities and the Politics of Visibility*. New York: Cambridge University Press.

Ayoub, Phillip M. and David Paternotte. 2012. "Building Europe: The International Lesbian and Gay Association (ILGA) and LGBT Activism in Central and Eastern Europe." *Perspectives on Europe* 42(1): 50–56.

Ayoub, Phillip M. and David Paternotte. 2014. *LGBT Activism and the Making of Europe: A Rainbow Europe?* Basingstoke, UK: Palgrave Macmillan.

Barany, Zoltan. 2002. *The East European Gypsies: Regime Change, Marginality, and Ethnopolitics*. New York: Cambridge University Press.

Bilić, Bojan, ed. 2016. *LGBT Activism and Europeanisation in the Post-Yugoslav Space: On the Rainbow Way to Europe*. London: Palgrave Macmillan.

Bob, Clifford. 2012. *The Global Right Wing and the Clash of World Politics*. New York: Cambridge University Press.

Buzogány, Aron. 2008. "Joining Europe, Not Sodom: LGBT Rights and the Limits of Europeanization in Hungary and Romania." Paper presented at the National Convention of the American Association for the Advancement of Slavic Studies (AAASS), Philadelphia, PA, November 20–23.

Chetaille, A. (2011). "Poland: Sovereignty and Sexuality in Post-Socialist Times." In M. Tremblay, D. Paternotte and C. Johnson (eds) *The Lesbian and Gay Movement and the State: Comparative Insights Into a Transformed Relationship.* Farnham, Ashgate: 119–133.

Czarnecki, Gregory. (2007). "Analogies of Pre-War Anti-Semitism and Present-Day Homophobia in Poland." In Roman Kuhar and Judit Takács (eds) *Beyond the Pink Curtain: Everyday Life of LGBT People in Eastern Europe.* Ljubljana, Slovenia: Peace Institute: 327–344.

Ekiert, Grzegorz. 1996. *The State Against Society: Political Crises and Their Aftermath in East Central Europe.* Princeton, NJ: Princeton University Press.

Flam, Helena, ed. 2001. *Pink, Purple, Green: Women's, Religious, Environmental and Gay/Lesbian Movements in Central Europe Today.* Boulder, CO: East European Monographs.

Gerhards, J. 2010. "Non-Discrimination Towards homosexuality: The European Union's Policy and Citizens' Attitudes Towards Homosexuality in 27 European Countries." *International Sociology* 25(1): 5–28.

Gessen, Masha. 1994. *The Rights of Lesbians and Gay Men in the Russian Federation.* Report of the International Gay and Lesbian Human Rights Commission. San Francisco, California.

Gould, John. 2015. "From Gay Grocer to Rainbow Activist: Uncovering Slovakia's Hidden LGBTQ Politics." Paper presented at the annual convention of the American Political Science Association. San Francisco, CA. September 5, 2015.

Gould, John and Edward Moe. 2015. "Nationalism and the Struggle for LGBTQ Rights in Serbia, 1991–2014." *Problems of Post-Communism* 62(5): 273–286.

Graff, Agnieszka. 2006. "We Are (Not All) Homophobes: A Report From Poland." *Feminist Studies* 32(6): 434–449.

Graff, Agnieszka. 2008. "The Land of Real Men and Real Women: Gender and EU Accession in Three Polish Weeklies." In Carolyn M. Elliott (ed) *Global Empowerment of Women: Responses to Globalization and Politicized Religions.* New York: Routledge: 191–212.

Graff, Agnieszka. 2010. "Looking at Pictures of Gay Men: Political Uses of Homophobia in Contemporary Poland." *Public Culture* 22(3): 583–603.

Grzymała-Busse, Anna. 2015. *Nations Under God: How Churches Use Moral Authority to Influence Policy.* Princeton, NJ: Princeton University Press.

Holzhacker, Ronald. 2012. "National and Transnational Strategies of LGBT Civil Society Organizations in Different Political Environments: Modes of Interaction in Western and Eastern Europe for Equality." *Comparative European Politics* 10(1): 23–47.

Howard, Marc Morjé. 2003. *The Weakness of Civil Society in Post-Communist Europe.* New York: Cambridge University Press.

Janos, Andrew C. 2001. "From Eastern Empire to Western Hegemony: East Central Europe Under Two International Regimes." *East European Politics and Societies* 15(2): 221–249.

Jowitt, Kenneth. 1992. *New World Disorder: The Leninist Extinction.* Berkeley: University of California Press.

Kahlina, Katja. 2015. "Local Histories, European LGBT Designs: Sexual Citizenship, Nationalism, and 'Europeanisation' in Post-Yugoslav Croatia and Serbia." *Women's Studies International Forum* 49: 73–83.

Keck, Margaret and Kathryn Sikkink. 1998. *Activists Beyond Borders: Advocacy Networks in International Politics.* Ithaca, NY: Cornell University Press.

Kelley, Judith. 2004. *Ethnic Politics in Europe: The Power of Norms and Incentives.* Princeton, NJ: Princeton University Press.

Kligman, Gail. 1998. *The Politics of Duplicity: Controlling Reproduction in Ceausescu's Romania.* Berkeley: University of California Press.

Kochenov, Dimitry. 2007. "Democracy and Human Rights – Not for Gay People?: EU Eastern Enlargement and Its Impact on the Protections of the Rights of Sexual Minorities." *Texas Wesleyan Law Review* 13(2): 459–495.

Kuhar, Roman and Judit Takács, eds. 2007. *Beyond the Pink Curtain: Everyday Life of LGBT People in Eastern Europe.* Ljubljana, Slovenia: Peace Institute.

Kulpa, Roman and J. Mizielińska, eds. 2011. *De-Centering Western Sexualities: Central and Eastern European Perspectives.* Farnham: Ashgate.

Long, Scott. 1999. "Gay and Lesbian Movements in Eastern Europe: Romania, Hungary, and the Czech Republic." In Barry D. Adam, Jan Willem Duyvendak, and André Krouwell (eds) *The Global Emergence of Gay and Lesbian Politics: National Imprints of a Worldwide Movement.* Philadelphia, PA: Temple University Press: 242–265.

Mikuš, Marek. 2011. " 'State Pride': Politics of LGBT Rights and Democratisation in 'European Serbia'." *East European Politics and Societies* 25(4): 834–851.

O'Dwyer, Conor. 2010. "From Conditionality to Persuasion? Europeanization and the Rights of Sexual Minorities in Postaccession Poland." *Journal of European Integration* 32(3): 229–247.

O'Dwyer, Conor. 2012. "Does the EU Help or Hinder Gay-Rights Movements in Postcommunist Europe? The Case of Poland." *East European Politics* 28(4): 332–352.

O'Dwyer, Conor and Katrina Z. S. Schwartz. 2010. "Minority Rights After EU Enlargement: A Comparison of Antigay Politics in Poland and Latvia." *Comparative European Politics* 8(2): 220–243.

Owczarzak, Jill. 2009. "Defining Democracy and the Terms of Engagement With the Postsocialist State: Insights From HIV/AIDS." *East European Politics and Societies* 23(3): 421–445.

Owczarzak, Jill. 2010. "Activism, NGOs, and HIV Prevention in Postsocialist Poland: The Role of 'Anti-Politics'." *Human Organization* 69(2): 200–211.

Ramet, Sabrina P., ed. 1999. *Gender Politics in the Western Balkans: Women and Society in Yugoslavia and the Yugoslav Successor States.* University Park: Pennsylvania State University Press.

Ramet, Sabrina P. 2006. "Thy Will Be Done: The Catholic Church and Politics in Poland Since 1989." In T. Byrnes and P. Katzenstein (eds) *Religion in an Expanding Europe.* Cambridge: Cambridge University Press: 117–147.

Renkin, Hadley. 2007. "Skeletons in the National Closet: Sexuality, History, and the Ambiguities of Belonging in Post-socialist Hungary." In Catherine Baker et al. (eds) *Nation in Formation: Inclusion and Exclusion in Central and Eastern Europe.* London: School of Slavonic and East European Studies, University College London: 43–58.

Rothschild, Joseph. 1977. *East Central Europe Between the Two World Wars.* Seattle: University of Washington Press.

Schimmelfennig, Frank and Ulrich Sedelmeier, eds. 2005. *The Europeanization of Central and Eastern Europe.* Ithaca, NY: Cornell University Press.

Seidl, Jan. 2012. *Od žaláře k oltáři. Emancipace homosexuality v českých zemích od roku 1867 do současnosti* [*From the Dungeon to the Altar: Homosexual Emancipation in the Czech Lands From 1867 to the Present*]. Brno: Host.

Slootmaeckers, Koen, Heleen Touquet, and Peter Vermeersch, eds. 2016. *The EU Enlargement and Gay Politics: The Impact of Eastern Enlargement on Rights, Activism and Prejudice.* Basingstoke, UK: Palgrave Macmillan.

Sokolová, Věra. 2005. "Identity Politics and the (B)Orders of Heterosexism: Lesbians, Gays and Feminists in the Czech Media After 1989." In J. van Leuween and N. Richter (eds) *Mediale Welten in Tschechien nach 1989: Genderprojektionen und Codes des Plebejismus* [*Media Worlds in the Czech Republic After 1989: Gender Projections and Codes of Conventionality*]. München: Kubon und Sagner: 29–44.

Sperling, Valerie. 1999. *Organizing Women in Contemporary Russia: Engendering Transition.* New York: Cambridge University Press.

Sperling, Valerie. 2014. *Sex, Politics, and Putin: Political Legitimacy in Russia.* New York: Oxford University Press.

Štulhofer, A. and I. Rimac. 2009. "Determinants of Homonegativity in Europe." *Journal of Sex Research* 46(1): 24–32.

Takács, Judit and Ivett Szalma. 2011. "Homophobia and Same-sex Partnership Legislation in Europe." *Equality, Diversity and Inclusion* 30(5): 356–378.

Tarrow, Sidney. 2005. *The New Transnational Activism.* New York: Cambridge University Press.

Turcescu, Lucian and Lavinia Stan. 2005. "Religion, Politics and Sexuality in Romania." *Europe-Asia Studies* 57(2): 291–310.

van der Vleuten, Anna. 2014. "Transnational LGBTI Activism and the European Courts." In Phillip M. Ayoub and David Paternotte (eds) *LGBT Activism and the Making of Europe: A Rainbow Europe?* Basingstoke: Palgrave Macmillan.

Waaldijk, K. 2006. "Legislation in Fifteen EU Member States Against Sexual Orientation Discrimination in Employment: The Implementation of Directive 2000/78/EC." In A. Weyembergh and S. Carstocea (eds) *The Gays' and Lesbians' Rights in an Enlarged European Union.* Brussels: Institut d'Etudes Européennes: 17–47.

Walicki, Andrzej. 2000. "The Troubling Legacy of Roman Dmowski." *East European Politics and Societies* 14(1): 12–46.

19

POLITICS AT THE FRINGES?

Eastern Europe's populists, racists, and extremists

Cas Mudde

Eastern Europe has long been associated with nationalism, more specifically nasty "ethnic" or "racial" types of civil wars and pogroms. As soon as the Berlin Wall came down, the discourse on post-communist Eastern Europe was divided between the optimistic "return to Europe" and the pessimistic "return to the past." Although the divisions were never as clear-cut as in these simplistic narratives, this chapter mainly focuses on the forces associated with the return to the dark past of ethnic nationalism. It will chronicle the most important developments within the East European far right, introduce and critically assess the scholarship on the topic, and lay out avenues for future research.

As Minkenberg (2002, p. 361), the prime scholar on the topic, noted at the turn of the century, "studying the radical right in transformation countries in Central and Eastern Europe not only resembles shooting at a moving target but also shooting with clouded vision". Almost 15 years later, his observation still rings true. Particularly compared to Western Europe, there is remarkably little academic research on the far right in Eastern Europe.[1] Moreover, existing scholarship quickly becomes out of date, as parties come and go with blistering speed. Most East European far-right parties that were relevant at the time Minkenberg made this observation are no longer relevant, while the two most successful parties today, the Movement for a Better Hungary (Jobbik) and the Conservative People's Party of Estonia (EKRE), were both founded after 2002.

Despite the continuing electoral volatility of the region, there is one important constant with regard to the topic at hand: far-right *politics* have always been much more important than far-right *parties*. With few exceptions, far-right parties have been relatively small and isolated, but many other political actors have promoted far-right politics, including established political parties and rogue mainstream politicians. This was so in the turbulent days of the democratic transition of the early 1990s and it is so in the turbulent days of the Great Recession and the "refugee crisis" of today. Understanding the differences and similarities of far-right parties and politics has profound importance for gaining a better understanding of politics inside and outside of the region.

History

While far-right groups were marginal under communism, they were not completely absent. In Soviet Russia, groups that claimed to help "preserve Russian culture" had existed since the

1970s, with the most well-known being *Pamyat* (Memory). One year before the breakup of the Soviet Union, in 1990, Vladimir Zhirinovsky founded the Liberal Democratic Party of the Soviet Union, later renamed Liberal Democratic Party of the Russian Federation (LDPR). Both were at least protected by high-ranking members within the Communist Party and tolerated by the communist regime. Despite significant state repression, small neo-fascist and neo-Nazi groups existed in several satellite states, particularly in the German Democratic Republic (see Wagner 2002).

With the fall of communism a plethora of new far-right groups emerged within the region, taking their main inspiration from a variety of historical periods (see Mudde 2000; also Shafir 2000). Pre-communist far-right groups located their identity in the pre-communist period, most notably in the local or international fascist organisations of the early twentieth century. These groups often profited from far-right elements within émigré communities in the West, who provided expertise and money at a time that most other groups lacked both. However, with the exception of some parties and organisations in Croatia and Slovakia, most notably, pre-communist far-right groups remained fairly irrelevant and have, by now, largely ceased to exist. Even the two parties that continue to exist, the Croatian Party of Rights (HSP) in its many varieties and the Slovak National Party (SNS), use their historical identity mainly as a veneer of authenticity, as their political programme addresses primarily contemporary issues.

So-called communist far-right groups based their identity on the nationalist streams of some communist regimes, most notably in Bulgaria, Romania, Russia, and Serbia. They were sometimes referred to as "red-brown" alliances (see e.g. Ishiyama 2009, 1998; Vujačić 2003), even though the communism was much more of a personal than ideological nature – with the notable exception of the Communist Party of the Russian Federation (KPRF), but there the far-right aspect has become much less relevant with time. Parties like the Party of Romanian National Unity (PUNR) and the Bulgarian Fatherland Party of Labour (OPT) were led by people who had been active within the communist party and wanted to return to the communist regime's repressive policies towards ethnic minorities (Hungarian and Turkish speakers, respectively). The communist far right was a marginal and transitional phenomenon, which had largely disappeared from the region by the late 1990s.

Today virtually all far-right groups are post-communist and, increasingly, post-post-communist. The post-communist parties are new organisations, not claiming an institutional identity or link to a past period, and addressing contemporary issues. For much of the first two decades, the issues were mostly related to the post-communist transformation process, including the ethnic make-up of the (new) state, the (alleged) corruption of the privatisation process, and membership of the European Union (EU). A unifying discourse of post-communist populist groups throughout the region was centred on the "stolen revolution," which claimed that the former communist elite and the new democratic elite had made a secret deal to divide the national riches at the expense of the people (see Mudde 2001).

Table 19.1 provides an overview of the main far-right party of each East European country for the period 1989–2015, listing the year and score of the highest electoral results as well as the results in the most recent national parliamentary elections (both in percentage of the national vote). What stands out are the following: (1) far-right parties have been relatively small in most East European countries; (2) most far-right parties had their highest result many years ago; and (3) the far right is almost completely absent from the region today. In fact, compared to Western Europe, far-right parties are much less successful. Hungary is the only country with a really successful far-right party (Jobbik), whereas Austria, Denmark, and Switzerland have parties with similar levels of support in Western Europe – while far-right parties in France, Netherlands, and Sweden poll at comparable levels.

Table 19.1 Electoral results of main far-right parties in Eastern Europe in percentage of national vote, 1989–2015

Country	Party	Highest Result (year)	Latest Result (year)
Bulgaria	National Union Attack (Ataka)	9.4 (2009)	4.5 (2014)
Croatia	Croatian Democratic Union (HDZ)	45.2 (1995)	n/f
	Croatian Rights Party (HSP)	7.1 (1992)	3.0 (2011)
Czech Republic	Coalition for Republic – Republican	8.0 (1996)	n/c
	Party of Czechoslovakia (SPR-RSČ)	6.9 (2013)	6.9 (2013)
	Dawn – National Coalition (Dawn)		
Estonia	Conservative People's Party of Estonia (EKRE)	8.1 (2015)	8.1 (2015)
	Estonian National Independence Party (ERSP)	8.8 (1992)	n/c
Hungary	Hungarian Justice and Life Party (MIÉP)	5.5 (1998)	0.0 (2014)
	Movement for a Better Hungary (Jobbik)	20.5 (2014)	20.5 (2014)
Latvia	People's Movement for Latvia (TKL)	15.0 (1995)	n/c
Lithuania	Lithuanian Nationalist Union (LTS)	2.0 (1992)	n/c
Poland	League of Polish Families (LPR)	8.0 (2005)	n/c
Romania	Greater Romania Party (PRM)	19.5 (2000)	1.5 (2012)
Russia	Liberal Democratic Party of Russia (LDPR)	22.9 (1993)	11.7 (2011)
Serbia	Serbian Radical Party (SRS)	29.5 (2008)	2.0 (2014)
Slovakia	Slovak National Party (SNS)	11.6 (2006)	4.6 (2012)
Slovenia	Slovene National Party (SNS)	10.2 (1992)	n/f

Notes:
n/c = did not contest last election (in some cases no longer exists)
n/f = no longer a far right party

Table 19.2 Participation in government by far-right parties, 1989–2015

Country	Party	Period(s)	Coalition Partner(s)
Bulgaria	Ataka	2013–2014[1]	BSP + DPS
Croatia	HDZ	1990–2000	
Estonia	ERSP	1992–1995	Isamaa
Poland	LPR	2005–2006	PiS & Samoorona
Romania	PUNR	1994–1996	PDSR & PSM
	PRM	1995	PDSR & PSM
Serbia	SRS	1998–2000	SPS & JUL
Slovakia	SNS	1994–1998	HZDS & ZRS
		2006–2010	HZDS & Smer

[1]Minority governments in which far-right party functions as the official support party.

A similar story can be told about the far right's participation in national government in the region (see Table 19.2). Whereas these parties were involved in various national governments in the 1990s, this has become increasingly rare and short-lived in the twenty-first century. At the end of 2015 no far-right party was part of a government coalition. In Latvia the National Alliance (NA) has been an official member of the coalition government since 2011. While the NA itself is not a far-right party, and seems to defend relatively mainstream right-wing positions in the government, one of its constituent parties, All for Latvia! (VL), was a far-right party.

The year 2015, Europe's *annus horribilis*, might be a turning point for the far right in Eastern Europe. The Greek crisis, terrorist attacks in Paris, and particularly the so-called refugee crisis have significantly shifted the far-right landscape in the region. First and foremost, Hungarian Prime Minister Viktor Orbán and his Fidesz-Hungarian Civic Alliance have become the main voice of far-right politics in Europe, even eclipsing Marine Le Pen and the French National Front (FN) in their zeal to defend Europe's "Christian values" against an "army" of Syrian refugees (e.g. see Mudde 2016; Müller 2015). Second, the EU plan to resettle refugees more or less proportionately across the Union has led to an unprecedented anti-Muslim backlash in the region. In all Visegrád countries, leading politicians (including premiers and a president) have spoken out against the refugees in often Islamophobic language, while thousands of people have taken to streets to oppose "Islam" and "Muslims." These mostly spontaneous protests could give birth to new far-right groups, ranging from new single-issue organisations like the Bloc against Islam (BPI) in the Czech Republic to older far right parties like the National Movement (RN) in Poland.

Major works

Given the association of Eastern Europe with "nasty" nationalism in much of the academic and popular understanding of the region, there is a remarkable lack of systematic scholarship on the far right in Eastern Europe. While academic articles and books on the far right in Western Europe number in the thousands, those on Eastern Europe do not go much beyond one hundred.

Early scholarship on the far right in Eastern Europe took a very broad approach, focusing on an amorphous phenomenon captured by the vague and ominous term "ultranationalism," which was believed to be dominating the region. A popular myth was that the communist regimes had been able to repress the natural destructive nationalist urges of the Eastern Europeans, but with the fall of the Berlin Wall, "ultra-nationalist feelings are back with a vengeance, like genies from the bottles in which they were so long confined" (Merkl 1997, p. 6). In short, the region had returned to the pre-communist period, in which nationalism was once again "the sine qua non for political success" (Fischer-Galati 1993, p. 12). This broad-brush approach focused not so much on far-right actors per se, but on anything that could be related to (ultra)nationalism, most notably alleged communist-nationalist hybrids like Serbian-Yugoslav dictator Slobodan Milošević and Slovak strongman Vladimír Mečiar. Consequently, the far right was both everywhere and nowhere in Eastern Europe.

Most studies published in the 1990s were anecdotal and pessimistic, considering Eastern Europe more or less historically determined towards "ultranationalism" and seeing the far right as a major threat to democratisation in the region and even security in the world (see Braun and Scheinberg 1996; Hockenos 1993). The most influential book in this tradition was Tismaneanu (1998), which was already quite outdated by the time it finally came out. It was more a contribution to the (essayist) literature on democratisation, rather than to far-right parties in Europe, and was (too) strongly influenced by the rather unique situation in Romania in the early 1990s (see also Shafir 2000).

Ramet (1999) was the first book that more or less mirrored the many edited volumes on the far right in Western Europe. It consisted mainly of country chapters, preceded by a conceptual and theoretical chapter that merged democratisation and far-right literature, and ended with a somewhat esoteric afterword by fascism scholar Roger Griffin. Given the warp-speed of the life cycle of East European parties in the 1990s, many chapters were already completely or partly outdated by the time of publication, but the book did at least identify the main far-right move-ments and parties of the first decade of post-communist politics. Moreover, it discussed the far right not exclusively in the framework of democratisation, making it more accessible to scholars of the far right in Western Europe.

Mudde (2005) was the next comprehensive study of the far right in the region, although its approach and origins were not strictly academic. The book originated within the Open Society Foundation and includes chapter by both academic and non-academic authors. Following a strict outline, each chapter identifies the key "extremist groups" (that is, political parties, organisations, and subcultures), legal framework to deal with "racist extremism," racist extremist incidents, and state and civic responses. While the scope of the book is very broad, spanning all East European countries that joined the EU in 2004 and 2007, many of the groups covered were or are now marginal. Still, for almost 10 years, it remained the only (English language) book on the topic.

Ironically, at a time that the electoral success of far-right parties in the region is at a post-communist low, scholarship is finally increasing and improving. Just in the past few years the *Routledge Studies in Extremism and Democracy* has published three volumes on the far right in Eastern Europe. Pirro (2015) looks at the ideology, impact, and electoral performance of far-right parties in Bulgaria, Hungary, and Slovakia, while Pytlas (2016) focuses on the interaction between mainstream and far-right parties in Hungary, Poland, and Slovakia. Both studies extend the conceptual and theoretical frameworks of the study of far-right parties in Western Europe to the East, without losing sight of the region's unique character and history. This is also the case for Stojarová (2013), who applies a theoretical framework inspired by Mudde (2007) to her comparative study of far-right parties in the Balkans – a region reduced to Bulgaria and Romania in many other studies of the far right in Eastern Europe.

Finally, the edited volume by Minkenberg (2015) is the most comprehensive political science study of the topic to date. It combines country studies of East Central Europe, the Balkans, and the post-Soviet space with comparative and theoretical chapters, introduced and concluded by an updated version of Minkenberg's powerful conceptual and theoretical framework. The volume is not just comprehensive in approach and scope, but also in its inclusion of many younger scholars from the region, who have so far lacked a voice in much of the English-language debate.

Principal contributions

Given the rather limited scholarship on the far right in Eastern Europe, there are not too many major contributions to report, let alone those with consequences for different, related, fields of study. Much of the early scholarship was merely an extension of the broader democratisation literature (e.g. Tismaneanu 1998), while more recent work is deeply rooted in the literature on far-right parties in Western Europe. If there is anything specific to the literature on Eastern Europe, compared to the dominant work on the western part of the continent, it is a much bigger focus on the non-party far right and on the far right's relationship to democracy/democratisation and religion.

Some of the best scholarship of the early period tried to integrate the far right into the democratisation paradigm, seeing it, unsurprisingly, as a hindrance or threat. Williams (1999) developed a remarkably elaborate and complex theoretical framework, building upon both fas-cism and democratisation literature, which was unfortunately ignored by most other scholars. In a range of articles in English and German Minkenberg (2002, 2009) adjusted his earlier theoretical framework to explain the far right in Western Europe (2000) to the specific post-communist conditions of Eastern Europe (also Beichelt and Minkenberg 2002). This framework was applied, to some extent, in case studies by his colleagues and (former) PhD students, which were published in special issues of *Osteuropa* (March 2002) and *Communist and Post-Communist Studies* (December 2009), as well as the edited volume mentioned earlier (Minkenberg 2015).

Minkenberg's theoretical framework is an updated version of modernisation theory, seeing the far right in Eastern Europe as a response to the economic and social changes of the post-communist period. Going beyond the simple "losers of transformation" paradigm, he includes historical legacies that distinguish different types of post-communist societies and explain both the electoral success and the ideological sub-type of the far-right party in a country (see, in particular, Minkenberg 2009, p. 452). Of particular interest is the conceptual framework, which distinguishes far-right actors on the basis of both ideological and organisational features. While Minkenberg developed this framework initially for the far right in Western Europe, his application to Eastern Europe has been much more influential. Ideologically, three types of far-right groups are distinguished: fascist-authoritarian, racist-ethnocentrist, and religious-fundamentalist. Organisationally, he again differentiates between three types: party/campaign organisation, social movement organisation, and subcultural milieu. In various publications, he has categorised the main far-right groups in the region on the basis of this three-by-three grid (see, for example, in Minkenberg 2002, p. 347). The combined theoretical framework is both comprehensive and complex and will require a long-term, integrated, multi-author research project to be fully tested – ideally at a pan-European, rather than merely East European, scale.

Reflecting the bigger emphasis on historical legacies (see also Bustikova and Kitschelt 2009; Ishiyama 2009; Pirro 2015), studies of the far right in Eastern Europe have put more emphasis on the relationship with mainstream society in general. Of particular interest is the issue of religion, largely ignored in the scholarship on the far right in Western Europe. Unsurprisingly, all work on the far right in Poland focuses on the close relationship between nationalism and religion, exemplified in the strong ties between the far-right party League of Polish Families (LPR) and the Catholic-nationalist subculture around Radio Maria (e.g. De Lange and Guerra 2009). Despite decades of (more and less) enforced atheism, religion seems to play a more important role in the far right in Eastern Europe than in the West. There are strong ties between Orthodox Christianity and myriad far-right groups, for example, in Romania (Andreescu 2015) and Russia (Verkhovsky 2002).

For quite obvious reasons, there is more attention paid to anti-Semitism, Romaphobia, and conspiracy theories in the scholarship on the far right in Eastern Europe (Dymerskaya-Tsigelman and Finberg 1999; Mudde 2005; Schnirelman 1998). Most studies on the far right in Western Europe create an artificial distinction between the far right and the political mainstream, consistent with the "normal pathology" thesis (Scheuch and Klingemann 1967), which holds that the far right constitutes a pre-modern aberration in contemporary Western societies. In sharp contrast, most studies of the far right in Eastern Europe highlight the similarities with the political mainstream, particularly with regard to anti-Semitism and Romaphobia (see, for example, Shafir 2002; Stewart 2012; Volovici 1994), consistent with the "pathological normalcy" thesis (Mudde 2010). Interestingly, Pytlas's new comparative study of the strategic relationships between mainstream and far-right parties in East Central Europe also explicitly works within the pathological normalcy paradigm.

While research on the far right in Eastern Europe has become increasingly influenced by concepts and theories of the much more voluminous scholarship on Western Europe, it is still less dominated by quantitative studies of electoral success of political parties. Moreover, one of the few cross-national quantitative studies published in a major mainstream political science journal to date, goes well beyond the narrow approach so common in studies on far-right parties in Western Europe. Bustikova (2014) introduces and tests an original theory that sees the success of far-right parties in Eastern Europe as a backlash against the political successes of minorities and concessions extracted on their behalf. This theory could also make an important contribution to the literature on the far right in Western Europe, which so far has not paid too much attention on this particular backlash (though see Dancygier 2010; Koopmans et al. 2005).

Main criticisms

Given the limited scholarship on the far right in Eastern Europe, much of the criticism is aimed at what is *not* done rather than what is done. Like most literatures, including on the far right in Western Europe, there is much too much focus on only a small group of countries (notably Hungary, Poland, Romania, and Russia). This notwithstanding, even in these countries we know relatively little about the key far-right actors, including the political parties, which tend to be described in fairly general terms in most studies. Some countries and parties lack almost any scholarship, most notably the Baltic countries. While there is an obvious positive correlation between the political relevance of the far right and the scholarship on it, it is far from perfect. Overall, we simply do not know much about the far right in Eastern Europe, parties, social movement organisations, and subcultures alike.

Moreover, research on the far right in Eastern Europe is rarely embedded in a broader theoretical framework or comparative approach. Hence, we are left with either broad and vague essays on "nationalism" in a specific country or the region as a whole, or with narrow case studies of specific far-right groups, such as neo-Nazis in the Czech Republic (Vejvodová 2014), skinheads in Hungary (Kürti 2003), the Slovak National Movement in Slovakia (Malová 2003), or Alexander Dugin (Ingram 2001) and the Eurasian movement in Russia (Laruelle 2015). This is particularly problematic, because the far-right scene in Eastern Europe is even more fluid than that in the West, making many studies dated, if not largely irrelevant, by the time they are published.

Much of this criticism is a consequence of the lack of infrastructure in the study of the far right in Eastern Europe. There are very few scholars on the topic, in sharp contrast to the abundance of scholars of the far right in Western Europe. This is not just the case in the region itself, but also among Western scholars of Eastern Europe. In addition, the few scholars cannot profit from the same academic infrastructure, being marginal(ised) within the scholarly communities of both East European politics and far-right politics. In fact, there are only a few places that have a critical mass of scholars of the East European far right, most notably at the International Institute of Political Science at Masaryk University in Brno (Czech Republic) and the Mirovni Institute at the University of Ljubljana (Slovenia), and they have very limited resources.

Future developments

Paradoxically, there are many good reasons to assume that the real success of the far right in Eastern Europe is yet to come. As Greskovits (1998) already argued more than twenty years ago in his original but not much cited comparative study of political protest in democratising Latin America and Eastern Europe, populist politics tends to only become successful *after* a transformation process has come to an end. This is in line with insights from Western Europe, where far-right parties have, on average, done better in more affluent countries and during economically good times (see Mudde 2016). Moreover, the various political crises of 2015 have shaken the European continent to its core, and nowhere more so than in Eastern Europe, particularly the Visegrád countries. All of this should make Eastern Europe of particular interest to students of far-right politics. I will discuss four specific issues that deserve much more academic study, preferably from scholarly collectives rather than individual scholars.

The first major issue is the fundamental differences and similarities between the far right in Eastern Europe and Western Europe. While this question has been at the forefront of virtually all concerted studies on the far right in Eastern Europe, dividing those who believe they are essentially similar (e.g. Mudde 2007) and different (e.g. Minkenberg 2002, 2009; Pirro 2015), it needs, at the very least, clarification and updating. Most East European countries are more than twenty-five years "post" communism, of which more than ten were spent within the EU, which makes the post-communist framework increasingly dated. After all, the majority of East European citizens have *not* been socialised during communism. This is not to argue that there are no "Leninist legacies," which after all are constantly created and recreated, but these legacies compete with contemporary narratives and practices, many of which are shared with the rest of the continent. Consequently, scholarship should try to more accurately determine the precise relevance of the Leninist legacies for the far right in Eastern Europe: which aspects of far-right politics are post-communist and which are post-post-communist?

Related to this is the second issue, which is the impact of the *annus horribilis* 2015 on the far right in Eastern Europe. The combination of two favourite issues of the far right, European integration and immigration, in the ill-conceived policy of forced distribution of refugees across the continent, has profoundly impacted the politics of all EU member states. However, whereas Euroscepticism and anti-immigration sentiments have been part and parcel of the far right, as well as the broader population, in many West European countries for many years now, they are more recent phenomena in many Eastern European countries. It is likely that the popular resentment will strengthen the support of the few more or less established far-right organisations and parties in the region, like in Western Europe, but will it also give way to new far-right parties, which will resemble their brethren in the West even more?

Again connected to this is the third, and most important, issue that confronts Eastern Europe even more profoundly than Western Europe: the radicalisation of mainstream politics. While the effect of far-right parties on mainstream parties has been studied for over a decade now (e.g. Bale 2003; Minkenberg 1998; Schain 2006), and recently also in East Central Europe (Pytlas 2016), recent developments point to a more fundamental issue: the differences between far-right *parties* and far-right *politics* (see Mudde 2016). Essentially, how relevant is it if a political party or politician meets the various criteria to be labelled far right, if it not just advocates but even implements far-right policies? This is most acutely relevant to Hungarian premier Orbán and his Fidesz party, but the Law and Justice (PiS) party in Poland and Slovak premier Robert Fico (Smer) have also expressed nativist, authoritarian, and populist tendencies that go well beyond mere strategic countering of far-right challengers.

Rather than citing regional exceptionalism, as is too common in East European studies, scholars should look for insights from studies on Western European countries as well as comparative studies across the East-West divide. While there might be a broader acceptance of populist radical-right politics in Eastern Europe, although this has not really been empirically proven, it still needs to be explained under which conditions it becomes prevalent within a political system (that is, the early 1990s and the current period). Related to that, more in-depth and systematic studies of "borderline parties" like Fidesz, PiS, and Smer are necessary to establish in which party family they truly fit – the new category of "national conservatism" seems mainly a cop-out to avoid having to classify them as far right.

Finally, studies of the East European far right have to be much more sensitive to the huge variety of far-right actors and successes in the region. Some countries had only successful far-right parties in the 1990s (e.g. Slovenia), while others only in the twenty-first century (e.g. Bulgaria). Some have weak parties and strong subcultures (e.g. Czech Republic and Poland), while other countries have strong parties, social movement organisations, and subcultures (e.g. Hungary and

Russia). It is particularly in this cross-national and cross-temporal diversity *within the region* that scholars can find deeper insights into the complexity of the far-right phenomenon in Eastern Europe.

Note

1 Although the observation holds true for all scholarship, I will focus almost exclusively on English-language studies of the far right in Eastern Europe in this chapter. To be fair, few important studies have been published in other languages, not even in the various local languages of the region.

Bibliography

Andreescu, G., 2015. The emergence of a new radical right power: the Romanian Orthodox Church. *In:* M. Minkenberg, ed. *Transforming the transformation? The East European radical right in the political process.* London: Routledge, 255–277.

Bale, T., 2003. Cinderella and her ugly sisters: the mainstream and extreme right in Europe's bipolarizing party systems. *West European Politics*, 26 (3), 67–90.

Beichelt, T., and Minkenberg, M., 2002. Rechtsradikalismus in Transformationsgesellschaften. Entstehungsbedingungen und Erklärungsmodell. *Osteuropa*, 52 (3), 247–262.

Braun, A., and Scheinberg, S., 1996. *The extreme right: freedom and security at risk.* Boulder, CO: Westview.

Bustikova, L., 2014. Revenge of the radical right. *Comparative Political Studies*, 47 (12), 1738–1765.

Bustikova, L., and Kitschelt, H., 2009. The radical right in post-communist Europe: comparative perspectives on legacies and party competitions. *Communist and Post-Communist Studies*, 42 (2), 459–483.

Dancygier, R. M., 2010. *Immigration and conflict in Europe.* Cambridge: Cambridge University Press.

De Lange, S. L., and Guerra, S., 2009. The league of Polish families between east and west, past and present. *Communist and Post-Communist Studies*, 42 (2), 527–549.

Dymerskaya-Tsigelman, L., and Finberg, L., 1999. *Antisemitism of the Ukrainian radical nationalists: ideology and policy.* Trans: Yisrael Cohen. Jerusalem: Vidal Sassoon International Center for the Study of Anti-semitism, Hebrew University.

Fischer-Galati, S., 1993. The political right in Eastern Europe in historical perspective. *In:* J. Held, ed. *Democracy and right-wing politics in Eastern Europe.* Boulder, CO: East European Monographs, 1–12.

Greskovits, B., 1998. *The political economy of protest and patience: East European and Latin American transformations compared.* Budapest: Central European University Press.

Hockenos, P., 1993. *Free to hate: the rise of the right in post-communist Eastern Europe.* London: Routledge.

Ingram, A., 2001. Alexander Dugin: geopolitics and neo-fascism in post-Soviet Russia. *Political Geography*, 20 (8), 1029–1051.

Ishiyama, J. T., 1998. Strange bedfellows: explaining political cooperation between communist successor parties and nationalists in Eastern Europe. *Nations and Nationalism*, 4 (1), 61–85.

Ishiyama, J. T., 2009. Historical legacies and the size of the red-brown vote in post-communist politics. *Communist and Post-Communist Studies*, 42 (2), 485–504.

Koopmans, R., Statham, P., Giugni, M., and Passy, F., 2005. *Contested citizenship: immigration and cultural diversity in Europe.* Minneapolis: University of Minnesota Press.

Kürti, L., 2003. The uncivility of a civil society: skinhead youth in Hungary. *In:* P. Kopecký and C. Mudde, eds. *Uncivil society? Contentious politics in post-communist Europe.* London: Routledge, 37–54.

Laruelle, M., ed., 2015. *Eurasianism and the European far right: reshaping the Europe-Russia relationship.* Lanham, MD: Lexington.

Malová, D., 2003. The Slovak national movement: a case of successful contention. *In:* P. Kopecký and C. Mudde, eds. *Uncivil society? Contentious politics in post-communist Europe.* London: Routledge, 55–73.

Merkl, P. H., 1997. Why are they so strong now? Comparative reflections on the revival of the radical right in Europe. *In:* P. H. Merkl and L. Weinberg, eds. *The revival of right-wing extremism in the nineties.* London: Cass, 17–46.

Minkenberg, M., 1998. Context and consequence: the impact of the new radical right on the political process in France and Germany. *German Politics & Society*, 16 (3), 1–23.

Minkenberg, M., 2000. The renewal of the radical right: between modernity and anti-modernity. *Government and Opposition*, 35 (2), 170–188.

Minkenberg, M., 2002. The radical right in postsocialist Central and Eastern Europe: comparative observations and interpretations. *East European Politics and Societies*, 16 (2), 335–362.

Minkenberg, M., 2009. Leninist beneficiaries? Pre-1989 legacies and the radical right in pos-1989 Central and Eastern Europe: some introductory observations. *Communist and Post-Communist Studies*, 42 (2), 445–458.

Minkenberg, M., ed., 2015. *Transforming the transformation? the East European radical right in the political process*. London: Routledge.

Mudde, C., 2000. Extreme-right parties in Eastern Europe. *Patterns of Prejudice*, 34 (1), 5–27.

Mudde, C., 2001. In the name of the peasantry, the proletariat, and the people: populism in Eastern Europe. *East European Politics and Societies*, 15 (1), 33–53.

Mudde, C., ed., 2005. *Racist extremism in Central and Eastern Europe*. London: Routledge.

Mudde, C., 2007. *Populist radical right parties in Europe*. Cambridge: Cambridge University Press.

Mudde, C., 2010. The populist radical right: a pathological normalcy. *West European Politics*, 33 (6), 1167–1186.

Mudde, C., 2016. *On extremism and democracy in Europe*. London: Routledge.

Müller, J.-W., 2015. Hungary: 'sorry for our prime minister'. *The New York Review of Books* [online], 14 October. Available from: www.nybooks.com/blogs/nyrblog/2015/oct/14/orban-hungary-sorry-about-prime-minister/ [Accessed 25 November 2015].

Pirro, A.L.P., 2015. *The populist radical right in Central and Eastern Europe: ideology, impact, and electoral performance*. London: Routledge.

Pytlas, B., 2016. *Radical right parties in Central and Eastern Europe: mainstream party competition and electoral fortune*. London: Routledge.

Ramet, S., ed., 1999. *Radical right in Central and Eastern Europe since 1989*. University Park: Pennsylvania State University Press.

Schain, M., 2006. The extreme-right and immigration policy-making: measuring direct and indirect effects. *West European Politics*, 29 (2), 270–289.

Scheuch, E. K., and Klingemann, H. D., 1967. Theorie des Rechtsradikalismus in westlichemn Industriegesellschaften. *Hamburger Jahrbuch für Wirtschafts – und Sozialpolitik*, 12, 11–19.

Schnirelman, V. A., 1998. *Russian neo-pagan myth and anti-Semitism*. Jerusalem: Vidal Sassoon International Center for the Study of Antisemitism, Hebrew University.

Shafir, M., 2000. Marginalization or mainstream? the extreme right in post-communist Romania. *In*: P. Hainsworth, ed. *The politics of the extreme right: from the margins to the mainstream*. London: Pinter, 247–267.

Shafir, M., 2002. *Between denial and "comparative trivialization": Holocaust negationism in post-communist East Central Europe*. Jerusalem: Vidal Sassoon International Center for the Study of Antisemitism, Hebrew University.

Stewart, M., ed., 2012. *The Gypsy 'menace': populism and the new anti-Gypsy politics*. London: Hurst.

Stojarová, V., 2013. *The far right in the Balkans*. Manchester: Manchester University Press.

Tismaneanu, V., 1998. *Fantasies of salvation: democracy, nationalism and myth in post-communist Europe*. Princeton, NJ: Princeton University Press.

Vejvodová, P., 2014. *Transnational forms of contemporary neo-Nazi activity in Europe from the perspective of Czech neo-Nazis*. Brno: MUNI Press.

Verkhovsky, A., 2002. The role of the Russian Orthodox Church in nationalist, xenophobic, and antiwestern tendencies in Russia today: not nationalism, but fundamentalism. *Religion, State and Society*, 30 (4), 333–345.

Volovici, L., 1994. *Antisemitism in post-communist Eastern Europe: a marginal or central issue?* Jerusalem: Vidal Sassoon International Center for the Study of Antisemitism, Hebrew University.

Vujačić, V., 2003. From class to nation: left, right, and the ideological and institutional roots of post-communist "national socialism". *East European Politics and Societies*, 17 (3), 359–392.

Wagner, B., 2002. Rechtsradikalismus in Ostdeutschland. *Osteuropa*, 52 (3), 305–319.

Williams, C., 1999. Problems of transition and the rise of the radical right. *In*: S. P. Ramet, ed. *The radical right in Central and Eastern Europe*. University Park: Pennsylvania State University Press, 29–47.

PART V

Policy issues and policy choices

20

VARIETIES OF CAPITALISM IN EASTERN EUROPE

Dorothee Bohle

Introduction

It was not before the late 1990s that the diversity of post-socialist political economies became a major issue for scholars studying Eastern Europe. Before that time discussions had been dominated by the essential problems the East European countries had to master in order to transition from a planned to a market economy. Implicitly or explicitly, the literature assumed that there were best practices for this endeavour. As a consequence, Eastern Europe's new market economies were considered to differ in degree rather than in kind. Countries were ranked according to how close they came to the ideal of a market economy without further qualification, characterised by private property rights, and liberalized financial, capital, and labour markets, as well as free foreign trade.

This "transition paradigm" (Stark 1994) has, however, been challenged, as it became increasingly clear that despite partly similar reforms, post-socialist countries exhibit significant differences in the organisation of the economy, production profile, skill level of their populations, social security systems, and state capacities. Thus, for instance, in the eyes of many Russia has morphed into a typical "petrol state" (Karl 1999), while the four Visegrád countries Poland, the Czech Republic, Slovakia, and Hungary have turned into veritable "manufacturing miracles" (Bohle and Greskovits 2012: 161), which increasingly compete with advanced capitalist countries in complex industrial segments. The second section of this chapter will take a closer look at the East European varieties of capitalism identified in the literature.[1] It will show that the literature offers a large number of classifications, but there is also agreement that a deep dividing line exists between capitalism in the former republics of the Soviet Union (with the exception of the Baltic states), and the East Central European (ECE) countries. Further distinction are often made between resource-rich and manufacturing-based former Soviet republics and between capitalisms in the Baltic and the Visegrád countries.[2]

The literature has identified three major explanations for this capitalist diversity after the breakdown of communism: legacies and path dependency, early economic and social reforms, and international integration. While most approaches focus only on one of these explanations, in the third section of the chapter I will argue that it is precisely the combination of all these factors that explain capitalist diversity in Eastern Europe. The fourth section assesses the merits of the research agenda on East European varieties of capitalism and points to directions for future research.

The worlds of East European capitalism

During the first decade after the breakdown of socialism, transition research mostly focused on essential problems of liberalisation, privatisation, and the building of capitalist institutions, and it ranked countries according to how close they came to the ideal of a Western-type market economy. By the end of the 1990s, however, it became clear that transition had resulted in rather different types of capitalism. Drawing on diverse theoretical traditions, authors started to compare East European capitalisms with each other. This section gives an overview over existing approaches and typologies.

Neoclassical sociology

The earliest systematic comparative analyses of East European capitalisms develop what Eyal, Szelényi and Townsley (1998) call a neoclassical sociological perspective. As they explain,

> [n]eoclassical sociology, much like the classics of sociological theorizing, will primarily be concerned with the origins and character of modern capitalism. With the fall of communism, however, there is an important shift in emphasis. For Marx and Weber, the question was: what are the preconditions which give rise to modern capitalism? . . . Neoclassical sociology is less concerned with preconditions. . . . What neoclassical sociology emphasizes is the diversity of modern capitalism – in short the subject matter of neoclassical sociology is comparative capitalism.

Drawing on Szelényi's earlier work on class power under socialism (Konrád and Szelényi 1979, Szelényi 1988), and more broadly on classical notions of capital and class as developed by Marx, Weber, and Bourdieu, this perspective argues that what sets East European capitalism apart from its Western counterpart is that it is created without capitalists. The question then is who the new capitalists are, and which resources they build on. Eyal et al. (1998) identified a dividing line between East Central Europe and the former Soviet republics. In ECE, the former technocracy in alliance with intellectuals successfully transformed their inherited cultural capital into economic capital and thus became top of the new capitalist hierarchy. However, "the former communist technocracy do not hold ultimate decision making powers as owners, . . . rather they exercise power as experts and managers" (Eyal et al. 1998: 14). Hence, in this part of the post-socialist world, marketisation outpaced the creation of a private propertied class and thus a managers' "capitalism without capitalists" emerged. Later work argues that subsequently, foreign capitalists were invited to become the new owners, and the variety of capitalism was called liberal capitalism (King and Szelényi 2005, King 2007, Szelényi 2015). In contrast, the former Soviet republics exhibited the opposite mismatch. Here, new "capitalists" expropriated state property "without capitalism," that is, before all the core institutions of a market economy were put in place (Eyal et al. 1998: 4–5). Thus, the former nomenklatura was busy liberalizing and privatizing the economy and turning it into an economic opportunity for itself and its clients. This form of capitalism is labelled political capitalism, patrimonial capitalism, or capitalism from above (King and Szelényi 2005, Szelényi 2015, see also Robinson 2013).

The most encompassing typology of East European capitalism building on the conceptual tools developed by Szelényi et al. is that by Norkus (2012). Norkus distinguishes between a rational entrepreneurial capitalism in the Baltic states, Visegrád countries and Slovenia; a political oligarchic capitalism in some Central Asian countries, Russia, Ukraine, and the Eastern and Western Balkans; and a state capitalism in Belarus, Uzbekistan, China, and Vietnam.

While accounts of East European varieties of capitalisms developed by Szelényi et al. focus on the trajectory of various elites who convert their endowed capital into new forms of capital and power, another early influential approach that also falls into the neoclassical sociological paradigm concentrates on networks and informal structures and asks about how these influence the new capitalist institutions (Stark and Bruszt 1998, Stark and Grabher 1997, Chavance 2008, for a recent analysis see Schoenman 2014). Arguably, however, the major contribution of this approach is not so much the identification of different types of capitalism within Eastern Europe. Rather, especially the early work in this tradition compares selected East Central European countries with the aim of identifying a "distinctively East European variant of capitalism" (Stark and Bruszt 1998: 4). The major claim is that informal structures and networks that had emerged as a reaction to the inadequacies of state socialism and in the early phase of post-socialism have left their distinctive marks on East European capitalisms. Different ECE countries exhibit different networks. However, beneath these differences lies a commonality: economic coordination in these capitalisms is based neither on markets nor hierarchies, but on networks.

"Varieties of Capitalism" travels east

During the second half of the 2000s, the influential "Varieties of Capitalism" (VoC) research agenda as developed by Hall and Soskice (2001) increasingly superseded the neoclassical approach to East European comparison. Hall and Soskice distinguish between a liberal market economy (LME), which is characterised by the prevalence of market relations in capitalisms' core institutions, and a coordinated market economy (CME) which relies on consensual and cooperative relations between major economic actors. Furthermore, Hall and Soskice argue that in each capitalist model, institutions are complementary in the sense that the efficiency of one institution is reinforced by the functioning of other institutions.

A number of authors have tested whether Hall and Soskice's classification can be transferred to Eastern Europe (for an overview see Bluhm 2010, the contributions in Lane and Myant 2007, King 2007, Mykhnenko 2007, Feldmann 2007, Crowley and Stanojević 2011). Thus, Feldman (2007) and Buchen (2007) were among the first to suggest that two tiny countries on Eastern Europe's western rim – Estonia and Slovenia – are clear cases of LMEs and CMEs respectively, even if they do not fit the models in all respects. Other western rim countries however do not seem to fit as neatly the Hall and Soskice typology. Some authors, for instance, classify Poland, Hungary, and Bulgaria as liberal capitalisms (e.g. Knell and Srholec 2007), while others see Hungary, Poland, and the Czech Republic much closer to the CMEs (e.g. Lane 2007). Mykhnenko (2007) argues instead that post-communist countries are best analysed as mixed-market economies with weak coordination capacity.

An original application of the VoC framework to Eastern Europe was developed by Nölke and Vliegenthart (2009). Departing from a more complex reading of the VoC literature, and also drawing on dependency theory (Cardoso and Faletto 1979, Schneider 2009), they add a third category – the dependent market economy (DME) – to the original classification, and demonstrate its presence in the Visegrád region. In Nölke and Vliegenthart's view, the Visegrád economies are largely coordinated by transnational corporations (TNCs). Taking advantage of an abundance of skilled labour, TNCs have turned these economies in export platforms of semi-standardised industrial goods.

Another interpretation of ECE's dependent capitalism draws on more heterodox approaches, especially the French Regulations School (Aglietta 2000, Boyer 2000). Becker and Jäger (2010, 2012, see also Becker et al. 2010) introduce an important difference between "dependent industrialisation", which is characteristic for the Visegrád countries and Slovenia, and "dependent financialisation", characteristic for the Baltic states and to a lesser degree Romania and Bulgaria. This difference is crucial for understanding the growth patterns during the 2000s and also the different crisis experiences in Eastern Europe (Becker and Jäger 2010, 2012, Becker et al. 2010, Myant and Drahokoupil 2012, Bohle and Greskovits 2012).

Polanyian varieties of capitalism

As the preceding section shows, a number of authors posit that it is possible to analyse some features of Eastern Europe's most successful and advanced capitalist political economies with the VoC approach. In this view, the difficulty of classifying countries is not unique to Eastern Europe, as witnessed by the rich literature on "mixed market economies" (Molina and Rhodes 2007), "state capitalism" (Schmidt 2003), or the identification of several instead of two varieties of capitalism (Amable 2003) for advanced capitalist economies. A number of authors, however, doubt the usefulness of the VoC approach for analysing East European capitalisms. An important alternative is articulated by Bohle and Greskovits (2007a, 2007b, 2012).

Bohle and Greskovits argue that a major flaw in the VoC literature is that it does not take cognizance of the fact that Hall and Soskice's approach has explicitly been developed for advanced capitalist economies, and that it is an open question in how far it can be simply transposed to peripheral societies. A second criticism relates to the fact that all attempts at applying the original or enlarged VoC concept to Eastern Europe suffer from VoC's shortcomings when it comes to understanding the emergence of institutions; a crucial issue in post-socialist economies where the market order has only recently taken shape and its consolidation cannot yet be taken for granted. In the context of the radical change that has occurred across the region, the origins of the post-socialist order must partly be located outside of the realm of existing institutions. Any meaningful conceptualisation of the new configurations must therefore include propositions about transformative political agents and their interplay with transnational and supranational actors.

Bohle and Greskovits (2007a, 2012) propose an alternative, Polanyian approach to studying ECE varieties of capitalism. Building on Karl Polanyi's (1957 [1944]) idea of the development of capitalism as a conflictual *double movement* towards liberalisation and social protection, they classify the new regimes according to the vigour with which and the forms in which transformative actors have used state power to build market economies pursuing the goals of liberalisation, and to simultaneously preserve social cohesion and political legitimacy in line with the agendas of welfare capitalism and industry protection. Concretely, they trace the emergence of three capitalisms: a neoliberal type in the Baltic states, Romania and Bulgaria; an embedded neoliberal type in the Visegrád countries and Croatia; and a neo-corporatist type in Slovenia.

Sectoral varieties of capitalism

A number of authors have taken Eastern Europe's increasing international openness and integration as an analytical starting point for their inquiry and ask how concrete forms of international integration have shaped the new capitalist order. To answer this question, they draw on a diverse body of developmental theories and develop them into comparative capitalism frameworks. One early influential formulation stems from Greskovits (2005). Combining sectoral political economy (Shafer 1994) and world system theory (Wallerstein 1979, Gereffi 1996), he analyses the leading industrial sectors through which a number of East Central European countries have been integrated in the international economy. Greskovits identifies four "sectoral varieties of capitalist political economies". The *heavy basic* sectoral political economy originates from state socialisms' specific industrialisation path in heavy industries. The *light basic* sectoral political economy is populated by traditional labour-intensive industries, such as textile and clothing. The *heavy complex* political economy is the result of foreign direct investment penetration in a number of capital intensive industrial sectors that rely on skilled labour and sophisticated production methods, such as car, pharmaceuticals machinery, or chemistry. Finally, the *light complex* political economy, made up of relatively skilled but labour-intensive leading sectors, such as the electronics sector, has also emerged as a result of trans-nationalization strategies of foreign companies. While these sectoral varieties of capitalism was developed for the new EU member states, with the Visegrád countries being characterised by different complex leading sectors, and the Baltic states, Romania and Bulgaria by basic ones, Bohle and Greskovits (2007b) extended this framework to a number of former republics of the Soviet Union characterised by a traditional peripheral insertion in the world economy, where international integration is shallow, and trade is overwhelmingly based on raw material exports and industrial goods imports.

The most comprehensive mapping of East European capitalisms from a sectoral political economy perspective to date is the one proposed by Myant and Drahokoupil (2011). They distinguish complex product exporters, financial flow dependent economies, commodity exporters, and remittance- and aid-based economies, and analyse the institutional requisites that account for the different insertion in international markets. Thus, political and social stability, a functioning legal and business system, as well as a pool of skilled labour has allowed the Visegrád and Slovenia's unique complex specialisation, and these institutional features have been reinforced by the EU accession and the geographic proximity to Germany. These features were present to a somewhat lesser extent in the Baltic states, Romania, and Bulgaria, which consequently exhibit lower competitiveness and a stronger dependence on financial flows. Competition in commodity markets, especially gas and oil, allows substantial earnings without requiring institution-building, and therefore often works at the expense of other export sectors. This also reflects the interests of oligarchs who built their wealth from resource exports, and are not concerned with developing other segments of the economy. Russia and a number of Central Asian countries have followed this path. Finally, a few countries have not developed the capacity to build an economic system that would allow them to generate significant resources other than from remittances. Myant and Drahokoupil also complement this taxonomy with an analysis of welfare state configurations and the enterprise sector. Based on all of this, they distinguish five East European varieties of capitalism: FDI-based; peripheral market economies; oligarchic-clientelistic capitalism; order states; and remittance-based economies.

Taken together, the literature offers a wide array of typologies, and diverse set of criteria that allow to distinguish between East European capitalisms. Table 20.1 summarises the main approaches and typologies.

Table 20.1 Typologies of East European varieties of capitalism

Approach	Types	Distinguishing variables	Geographical scope	Main authors
Neoclassical sociology	Liberal vs. patrimonial capitalism	Elite's conversion of endowed capital into new forms of power and capital	Selected fSU and ECE countries	Iván Szelényi, Lawrence King
	Rational-entrepreneurial; political-oligarchic, and state capitalism	Origin of entrepreneurs, state-entrepreneur relationship	Entire post-socialist world	Zenonas Norkus
	East European "network capitalisms"	Characteristics of networks between economic and political actors	Selected ECE countries	David Stark, László Bruszt, Roger Schoenman
VoC	Liberal vs. coordinated Mixed market economies	Coordinating mechanisms	Selected ECE countries, sometimes selected fSU	Martin Feldmann, David Lane, Martin Myant, Vlad Mykhnenko
	Dependent market economy Dependent industrialisation vs dependent financialisation	Coordinating role of transnational capital	Visegrád countries Visegrád vs. Baltic states	Andreas Nölke, Arjan Vliegenthart Joachim Becker, Johannes Jäger
Polanyian varieties of capitalism	Neoliberal, Embedded neoliberal, neo-corporatist	Conflictual double movement towards liberalisation and social protection	All ECE countries	Dorothee Bohle, Béla Greskovits
Sectoral political economy	Heavy basis, light basic, heavy complex, light complex	Characteristics of the leading export sector	ECE countries	Béla Greskovits
	FDI – based; peripheral market economies, oligarchic clientelistic capitalism, order states, and remittance- or aid-based economies	Leading export sector and other forms of external revenues	Whole post-socialist world	Jan Drahokoupil, Martin Myant

Explaining East European varieties of capitalism

The literature has developed a number of explanations for the capitalist diversity in Eastern Europe. Authors have focused on historical legacies, and argued that these have shaped the paths post-communist states could embark on. Early reform choices constitute a second important explanation, while a third explanation looks at the form of international embeddedness. While different authors typically focus on one of these explanations, I will combine them into an encompassing explanatory framework.[3]

Legacies and path dependency

Legacy explanations of East European capitalist diversity originate in the early research agenda formulated by evolutionary and institutional approaches to transformation (Chavance and Magnin 1997, Stark 1994, Stark 1996, Stark and Grabher 1997, Stark and Bruszt 1998). Arguably the most influential formulation is that of Stark, who outlined his research agenda as follows:

> instead of *transition* we examine *transformation*, in which the new emerges through adaptations, rearrangements, permutations and reconfigurations of existing organizational forms. Instead of *institutional vacuum* we examine *institutional legacies* rethinking the metaphor of collapse to ask whether differences in how the pieces fell apart have consequences for rebuilding new institutions.

(Stark 1994: 3)

The major contributions of this research agenda has been to "bring history back" in to the transformation debate. East European transformations are seen as path-dependent, in that the development paths a system could embark on was limited by inherited institutional and organisational legacies, and that different societies followed different development paths. Instead of moving towards one "optimal" model of market economy, path dependency also suggests multiple ways or national trajectories.

The views on which legacies matter and how for capitalist diversity differ (Beissinger and Kotkin 2014). Stark and Bruszt (1998, see also Stark and Grabher 1997, Schoenman 2014) look at how informal structures and networks that had emerged as a reaction to the inadequacies of state socialism have been put to use during the phase of transition, and how this has shaped the developmental potential and institutions of the new capitalisms. Others focus on the differences among socialist systems (e.g. Chavance and Magnin 1997). They argue that countries with reform socialist legacies – such as Hungary, former Yugoslavia or Poland – allow the incorporation of past elements in the capitalist system, whereas more orthodox legacies required a cleaner break with the past. Bohle and Greskovits (2012) and Greskovits (2014) stress the importance of socialist and pre-socialist industrialisation, state- and nation-building. These legacies favoured the ECE countries over the rest of the post-socialist world. ECE countries had the longest history of industrial development, as well as longer or shorter spells of independent statehood and democratic regimes. All of this enabled their capitalist breakthrough, compared to the much more problem-ridden patrimonial capitalism further east. Thus, whereas the former Soviet republics have mostly been constrained by their unfavourable legacies, ECE countries mostly had enabling legacies. To understand how legacies matter, we need however to probe further in the relationship between legacies and early reforms.

Early reforms

Early reforms aimed at establishing a market economy, privatisation, institution-building, and social protection are another important element in the explanation of capitalist diversity. While legacies had an impact on early reform choices, the latter were not predetermined. Rather, the impact is mediated by how actors relate to the legacies. For instance, Stark (1996) famously brought attention to the ongoing *bricolage* which resulted in peculiar ownership patterns. Bricolage refers to how economic actors recombine elements of the past with those of the present to create something entirely new. With respect to the new ownership patterns, this "recombinant property" (Stark 1996) in some places resulted in hybrids between states and markets more reminiscent of East Asian conglomerates than Western corporations.

However, not all East European capitalisms are characterised by this recombinant property. Also, as we have seen, East European capitalisms differ by how marketised they are, how robust their institutions are, and how much they protect their populations against social hardship, all of which is the results of early reforms (Frye 2010). To explain how ECE countries, which had similar legacies yet embarked on different reform paths, Bohle and Greskovits (2012) argue that this is the result of how policy-makers perceived existing legacies. Thus, policy makers in the Baltic states perceived existing legacies as a threat to their newly acquired independent statehood. Rather than "building capitalisms with the ruins of socialism" (Stark 1994), they opted for radical reforms and established institutions that secured a radical neoliberal order, such as currency boards, flat tax rates, or a commitment to balanced budgets. In contrast, reformers in the Visegrád countries and Slovenia perceived existing legacies more positively, and embarked on more gradual reforms. This allowed economic actors to recombine their inherited and new economic resources much in the way that Stark (1996) analysed. In contrast, as argued above, legacies were constraining rather than enabling for most of the former Soviet republics. Most importantly, these countries lacked capable states which resulted in inconsistent reforms, stop-and-go policies, and de-institutionalisation. These countries entered a vicious circle, in which the former nomenklatura expropriated state property for private gains. The result were captured states and "industrial involution" (Burawoy 1996, see also Ganev 2007) and eventually patrimonial capitalism.

Internationalisation

A further factor in the explanation of capitalist diversity in Eastern Europe is the role played by transnational actors and institutions. From the early 2000s onwards, scholars have recognised the initially ignored salience of transnational aspects of ECE transformations (Jacoby 2006a, Orenstein et al. 2008). Especially in the early years of transformation, international policy advisers and institutions such as the International Monetary Fund and the World Bank played a major role in shaping reforms (Greskovits 1998, Pop-Eleches 2009). It is not least due to their advice and policy conditionality that almost all post-socialist reformers embraced neoliberal policy ideas focusing on privatisation and creating market economies. Neoliberal international policy advice however did not result in convergence on a single model of capitalism, as it interacted with different legacies and capacities to reform. Thus, neoliberal reforms were clearly detrimental to economic development in most of the former republics of the Soviet Union, while they seemed to serve the ECE countries comparatively well. Furthermore, the existence of diverse neoliberal capitalisms in ECE – pure neoliberal in the Baltic states and embedded neoliberal in the Visegrád countries – also shows that there is room for diversity within the neoliberal paradigm.

A second major international actor that has helped to consolidate existing varieties of capitalism is the European Union (EU). Eastern enlargement of the EU has initially been highly contested because of the large number of countries, their socialist legacies, their comparatively poor and backward yet potentially competitive economies, and their unconsolidated political systems. Core EU actors perceived these countries as threats to their established economic and social compacts. Consequently, they sought to "attenuate, weaken and manage" the threat potential (Jacoby 2014: 10) by setting a hitherto unprecedented amount of requirements to the new entrants. Compliance with the EU's requirements was assured through accession conditionality, painstaking monitoring of the applicant's progress, and measures that aimed at the socialisation of the new members into the EU (Schimmelfennig and Sedelmeier 2005). How have these conditions shaped Eastern Europe's emerging capitalisms and their variation? The literature makes two claims. First, it argues that the EU has overall helped especially the weaker economies to strengthen their core economic institutions and capacities. Thus, many authors (Bruszt 2002, Vachudova 2005, Jacoby 2006b, Bruszt and Vukov 2014) have shown that the EU has used its influence in ECE to create strong and capable regulatory states. This has helped them to develop and upgrade their economies.

Second, the EU had an important impact on shaping ECE's policies towards foreign direct investment (FDI), as well as the FDI inflow. In its accession partnerships, the EU specifically promoted privatisation via foreign ownership in a number of strategic sectors, and openness to FDI crystallised as one important condition for membership (Medve-Bálint 2014). In addition, the EU sponsored national investment promotion agencies, and initially trained their staff (Medve-Bálint 2014: 41–2, see also Bandelj 2008). From the late 1990s onwards, these agencies have played a major role in attracting FDI (Drahokoupil 2008). However, it was not only industrial capital that entered the region. From the 2000s onwards, investment in services, particular financial services, started to also play a major role. Once again, it is the interaction of legacies, early reforms, and international influences which explain why some countries – the Visegrád countries and to a lesser extent Slovenia – have turned into veritable foreign-dominated manufacturing miracles, whereas the Baltic states have mostly profited from FDI in their service sector, and especially the financial sector (Bohle and Greskovits 2012, Greskovits 2014, Becker and Jäger 2012). Based on the foregoing, it can be argued that the EU served mostly to reinforce the different pathways the ECE countries have embarked upon earlier by strengthening their state capacities and encouraging FDI inflows, while the shallow international integration experienced by the countries further east also reinforces their specific patrimonial variety of capitalism (Bruszt and Greskovits 2009).

All in all then, it is the interplay of legacies, early reforms and different forms of international integration which explain the varieties of capitalism in Eastern Europe. Table 20.2 summarises the main arguments.

Table 20.2 Explaining East European varieties of capitalism

Explanatory factors	Mechanism	Outcome		
		Patrimonial Capitalism (PC)	*Neoliberal capitalism (NLC)*	*Embedded neoliberal capitalism (ENC)*
Legacies	Path dependency	Legacies constrain reform capabilities	Legacies enable reforms	
Early reforms	Interaction with legacies • Reforms undermine inherited institutions and empower the former nomenklatura (PC) • Reformers reject legacies (NLC) • Reformers build on legacies (ENC)	Inconsistent reforms Emergence of oligarchs and state capture	Radical neoliberal reforms and institutions De-industrialisation	Gradual reforms, recombinant property
Internationalisation	Policy advice and conditionality	Neoliberal policy advice reinforces weakening of institutions	Neoliberal advice combines with domestic radicalism	Neoliberal advice combines with domestic gradualism
	EU accession conditionality anchors reforms and channels capital inflow	Absence of external reform anchor reinforces patrimonial features	Reinforces NLC: • Strengthening of regulatory state capacity • FDI inflow, esp. in financial sector	Reinforces ELC • Strengthening of regulatory state capacity • FDI inflow, esp. in manufacturing

Assessment and future research

The research on East European capitalist diversity has produced important insights in the origin, pathways, international constitution, and specific characteristics of East European capitalisms. It has done so by drawing on an eclectic body of literature, which includes institutionalist, structuralist, mainstream and heterodox approaches, and theories developed for advanced as well as peripheral capitalist countries. By doing so, it has started to overcome its original status as "area studies", where processes of economic transformation have been perceived so peculiar that they defied concepts developed in the analysis of other parts of the world.

Compared to the literature on advanced capitalist countries, eclecticism might seem a disadvantage. This is particularly true in comparison to the original contributions of the VoC approach. Thus, Hall and Soskice's (2001) approach is appealing precisely because of its parsimony and rigour, its focus on micro-foundations, skilful incorporation of economic concepts and tools, and its neat predictions about institutional reproduction and change (Bohle and Greskovits 2009, Streeck 2011). Literature on East European capitalism typically lacks these qualities. Arguably, however, what it lacks in rigour, parsimony, and capacity of generating testable hypotheses makes it better equipped to deal with some of the challenges that the VoC approach has faced. Thus, VoC has often been criticised for its inability to conceptualise transformative change, its dichotomous understanding of capitalist models which leaves most of the OECD world in the under-conceptualised grey zone of "mixed regimes", its methodological nationalism, and, more fundamentally, its inadequate conceptualisation of capitalism as a fragile, contradictory and crisis-prone social system (Bohle and Greskovits 2009, Streeck 2011, Bruff et al. 2015).

Given that fundamental change was at the origin, and that transnational factors and actors have played a constitutive role in the emergence of East European capitalisms, it is no small wonder that these issues play a more prominent role in the East European comparative capitalism literature. Scholars studying Eastern Europe are in general also more sensitive to the fragile nature of capitalist settlements, as is shown in a rich literature on the crisis. What sets the East European capitalism literature apart is that it perceives crisis vulnerability as endogenous to the respective capitalist models, rather than as a random external effect. In this respect it pays off that the literature has been somewhat less blind to the role of finance in diverse capitalist models than the core VoC (Becker and Jäger 2010, 2012, Becker et al. 2010, Drahokoupil and Myant 2015, Bohle and Greskovits 2012, see also Epstein in this volume). However, the difference between finance-led and industry-led models is still far too broad brushed to genuinely account for the role of finance in each of the capitalist varieties. Future research thus needs to develop a more fine grained understanding of East European "varieties of financialisation", with due consideration of the role of private, household, and public debt.

While there are advantages in eclecticism, this comes at a price. In the eyes of many scholars focusing on the West, researchers examining Eastern Europe seem to be preoccupied with overly general and complex questions, and not immersed enough in any sub-fields such as industrial relations, monetary policy, or welfare states. Their perceived lack of proficiency in up-to-date and specialised academic debates has been an obstacle to their participation in cutting-edge debates. Their impact is also limited by the fact that their knowledge is still sometimes viewed as hardly generalisable. As a consequence, theoretical innovations developed in the study of East European capitalisms have not made inroads to the study of Western capitalisms. The fallout from the global financial crisis however might well serve as a catalyser for a closer integration of the research on Eastern and Western capitalism. Especially with the crisis of the Eurozone, it has become clear that a fault line also exists between core and peripheral European countries in the West, which begs for comparative research on Eastern and Western peripheral capitalisms.

An important lacuna of the research agenda on East European varieties of capitalism is the scant attention it pays to politics proper, the interaction of politics and the economy, and the relationship between economic and political regimes. The lack of sensitivity to political aspects of diverse capitalist regimes has become particularly noticeable with the turn towards "illiberal democracies" in a number of countries in the region. Comparative capitalism research could potentially make an important contribution to studying illiberal democracies by asking whether and how these are grounded in socio-economic cleavages and power constellations.

Notes

1 This chapter uses varieties of capitalism and capitalist diversity interchangeably. When it refers to the specific varieties of capitalism approach as developed by Hall and Soskice (2001), it uses the abbreviation VoC.
2 This chapter uses former republics of the Soviet Union as an umbrella term for the following twelve countries: Armenia, Azerbaijan, Belarus, Georgia, Kazakhstan, Kyrgyzstan, Moldova, Russia, Tajikistan, Turkmenistan, Ukraine, and Uzbekistan. East Central Europe (ECE) refers to the eleven East European EU member states: Bulgaria, Croatia, the Czech Republic, Estonia, Hungary, Latvia, Lithuania, Poland, Romania, Slovakia, and Slovenia. Baltic States refers to Estonia, Latvia and Lithuania, and Visegrád countries to Hungary, Poland, the Czech Republic, and Slovakia.
3 For the sake of simplicity, this section will focus on explaining three major distinctive models of capitalism: patrimonial capitalism (predominant in many former republics of the Soviet Union), and the two major sub-groups of ECE capitalism: the embedded neoliberal and the neoliberal varieties.

References

Aglietta, Michel. 2000. *A Theory of Capitalist Regulation: The US Experience.* London: Verso.
Amable, Bruno. 2003. *The Diversity of Modern Capitalism.* Oxford: Oxford University Press.
Bandelj, Nina. 2008. *From Communists to Foreign Capitalists: The Social Foundations of Foreign Direct Investment in Postsocialist Europe.* Princeton, NJ: Princeton University Press.
Becker, J., and J. Jäger. 2010. "Development Trajectories in the Crisis in Europe." *Debatte* 18 (1): 5–27.
Becker, J., and J. Jäger. 2012. "Integration in Crisis: A Regulationist Perspective on the Interaction of European Varieties of Capitalism." *Competition & Change* 16 (3): 169–87.
Becker, Joachim, Johannes Jäger, Bernhard Leubolt, and Rudy Weissenbacher. 2010. "Peripheral Financialization and Vulnerability to Crisis: A Regulationist Perspective." *Competition & Change* 14 (3–4): 3–4.
Beissinger, Mark, and Stephen Kotkin. 2014. *Historical Legacies of Communism in Russia and Eastern Europe.* New York: Cambridge University Press.
Bluhm, Katharina. 2010. "Theories of Capitalism Put to the Test: Introduction to a Debate on Central and Eastern Europe." *Historical Social Research/Historische Sozialforschung* 35 (2): 197–217.
Bohle, Dorothee, and Béla Greskovits. 2007a. "Neoliberalism, Embedded Neoliberalism and Neocorporatism: Towards Transnational Capitalism in Central-Eastern Europe." *West European Politics* 30 (3): 443–66.
Bohle, Dorothee, and Béla Greskovits. 2007b. "The State, Internationalization, and Capitalist Diversity in Eastern Europe." *Competition & Change* 11 (2): 89–115.
Bohle, Dorothee, and Béla Greskovits. 2009. "Varieties of Capitalism and Capitalism "tout Court"." *European Journal of Sociology* 50 (3): 355–86.
Bohle, Dorothee, and Béla Greskovits. 2012. *Capitalist Diversity on Europe's Periphery.* Ithaca, NY: Cornell University Press.
Boyer, Robert. 2000. "Is a Finance-Led Growth Regime a Viable Alternative to Fordism? A Preliminary Analysis." *Economy and Society* 29 (1): 111–45.
Bruff, Ian, Matthias Ebenau, and Christian May. 2015. "Fault and Fracture? The Impact of New Directions in Comparative Capitalisms Research on the Wider Field." In *New Directions in Comparative Capitalisms Research*, 28–44. Springer. http://link.springer.com/chapter/10.1057/9781137444615_3
Bruszt, László. 2002. "Making Markets and Eastern Enlargement: Diverging Convergence?" *West European Politics* 25 (2): 121–40.

Bruszt, László, and Béla Greskovits. 2009. "Transnationalization, Social Integration, and Capitalist Diversity in the East and the South." *Studies in Comparative International Development* 44 (4): 411–34.

Bruszt, László, and Visnja Vukov. 2014. "European Integration and the Evolution of State Capacities in the Southern and Eastern Peripheries of Europe." Unpublished manuscript, available at https://works.bepress.com/laszlo_bruszt/2/download

Buchen, Clemens. 2007. "Estonia and Slovenia as Antipodes." In *Varieties of Capitalism in Post-Communist Countries*, edited by David Stuart Lane and Martin R. Myant, 65–89. Basingstoke: Palgrave Macmillan.

Burawoy, Michael. 1996. "The State and Economic Involution: Russia through a China Lens." *World Development* 24 (6): 1105–17.

Cardoso, Fernando Henrique, and Enzo Faletto. 1979. *Dependency and Development in Latin America*. Berkeley: University of California Press.

Chavance, Bernard. 2008. "Formal and Informal Institutional Change: The Experience of Postsocialist Transformation." *The European Journal of Comparative Economics* 5 (1): 57–71.

Chavance, Bernard, and Eric Magnin. 1997. "Emergence of Path-Dependent Mixed Economies in Central Europe." In *A Modern Reader in Institutional and Evolutionary Economics*, edited by Geoffrey M. Hodgson, 168–200. Edward Elgar, Cheltenham, UK: Northampton, MA, USA.

Crowley, S., and M. Stanojević. 2011. "Varieties of Capitalism, Power Resources, and Historical Legacies: Explaining the Slovenian Exception." *Politics & Society* 39 (2): 268–295.

Drahokoupil, Jan. 2008. *Globalization and the State in Central and Eastern Europe: The Politics of Foreign Direct Investment*. Abingdon: Routledge.

Drahokoupil, Jan, and Martin Myant. 2015. "Putting Comparative Capitalisms Research in Its Place: Varieties of Capitalism in Transition Economies." *New Directions in Comparative Capitalisms Research: Critical and Global Perspectives*, 155.

Eyal, Gil, Iván Szelényi, and Eleanor R. Townsley. 1998. *Making Capitalism Without Capitalists: Class Formation and Elite Struggles in Post-Communist Central Europe*. London: Verso.

Feldmann, Magnus. 2007. "The Origins of Varieties of Capitalism: Lessons From Post-Socialist Transition in Estonia and Slovenia." In *Beyond Varieties of Capitalism: Conflict, Contradictions, and Complementarities in the European Economy*, edited by Bob Hancké, Mark Thatcher, and Martin Rhodes, 328–349. Oxford; New York: Oxford University Press.

Frye, Timothy. 2010. *Building States and Markets After Communism: The Perils of Polarized Democracy*. New York: Cambridge University Press.

Ganev, Venelin I. 2007. *Preying on the State: The Transformation of Bulgaria After 1989*. Ithaca, NY: Cornell University Press.

Gereffi, Gary. 1996. "Global Commodity Chains: New Forms of Coordination and Control among Nations and Firms in International Industries." *Competition & Change* 1 (1): 427–39.

Greskovits, Béla. 1998. *The Political Economy of Protest and Patience: East European and Latin American Transformations Compared*. Budapest: Central European University Press.

Greskovits, Béla. 2005. "Leading Sectors and the Variety of Capitalism in Eastern Europe." *Actes Du Gerpisa* 39: 113–28.

Greskovits, Béla. 2014. "Legacies of Industrialization and Paths of Transnational Integration After Socialism." In *Historical Legacies of Communism in Russia and Eastern Europe*, edited by Mark Beissinger and Stephen Kotkin, 68–89. Cambridge: Cambridge University Press.

Hall, Peter A., and David Soskice, eds. 2001. *Varieties of Capitalism: The Institutional Foundations of Comparative Advantage*. Oxford; New York: Oxford University Press.

Jacoby, Wade. 2006a. "Inspiration, Coalition, and Substitution: External Influences on Postcommunist Transformations." *World Politics* 58 (4): 623–51.

Jacoby, Wade. 2006b. *The Enlargement of the European Union and NATO: Ordering From the Menu in Central Europe*. Cambridge: Cambridge University Press.

Jacoby, Wade. 2014. "The EU Factor in Fat Times and in Lean: Did the EU Amplify the Boom and Soften the Bust?" *JCMS: Journal of Common Market Studies* 52 (1): 52–70.

Karl, Terry Lynn. 1999. "The Perils of the Petro-State: Reflections on the Paradox of Plenty." *Journal of International Affairs* 53 (1): 31–52.

King, Lawrence P. 2007. "Central European Capitalism in Comparative Perspective." In *Beyond Varieties of Capitalism: Conflict, Contradictions, and Complementarities in the European Economy*, edited by Bob Hancké, Mark Thatcher, and Martin Rhodes, 307–27. Oxford: Oxford University Press.

King, Lawrence, and Iván Szelényi. 2005. "The New Capitalism of Eastern Europe." In *Handbook of Economic Sociology*, edited by Neil J. Smelser and Richard Swedberg, 205–33. Princeton, NJ: Princeton University Press.

Knell, Mark, and Martin Srholec. 2007. "Divergent Pathways in Central and Eastern Europe." In *Varieties of Capitalism in Post-Communist Countries*, edited by David Stuart Lane and Martin R. Myant, 40–62. Basingstoke: Palgrave Macmillan.

Konrád, György, and Ivan Szelényi. 1979. *The Intellectuals on the Road to Class Power*. New York: Harcourt.

Lane, David Stuart. 2007. "Post-state Socialism. A Diversity of Capitalisms?" In *Varieties of Capitalism in Post-Communist Countries*, edited by David Stuart Lane and Martin R. Myant, 13–39. Basingstoke: Palgrave Macmillan.

Lane, David Stuart, and Martin R. Myant, eds. 2007. *Varieties of Capitalism in Post-Communist Countries*. Basingstoke: Palgrave Macmillan.

Medve-Bálint, Gergö. 2014. "The Role of the EU in Shaping FDI Flows to East Central Europe." *JCMS: Journal of Common Market Studies* 52 (1): 35–51.

Molina, Oscar, and Martin Rhodes. 2007. "The Politics of Adjustment in Mixed Market Economies: A Study of Spain and Italy." In *Beyond Varieties of Capitalism: Conflict, Contradictions, and Complementarities in the European Economy*, edited by Bob Hancké, Mark Thatcher, and Martin Rhodes, 223–52. Oxford, New York: Oxford University Press.

Myant, Martin, and Jan Drahokoupil. 2011. *Transition Economies: Political Economy in Russia, Eastern Europe, and Central Asia*. Hoboken, NJ: John Wiley and Sons.

Myant, Martin, and Jan Drahokoupil. 2012. "International Integration, Varieties of Capitalism and Resilience to Crisis in Transition Economies." *Europe-Asia Studies* 64 (1): 1–33.

Mykhnenko, Vlad. 2007. "Strength and Weaknesses of Weak Coordination: Economic Institutions, Revealed Comparative Advantages and Socio-Economic Performance of Mixed Market Economies in Poland and Ukraine." In *Beyond Varieties of Capitalism: Conflict, Contradictions, and Complementarities in the European Economy*, edited by Bob Hancké, Mark Thatcher, and Martin Rhodes, 352–75. Oxford; New York: Oxford University Press.

Nölke, Andreas, and Arjan Vliegenthart. 2009. "Enlarging the Varieties of Capitalism: The Emergence of Dependent Market Economies in East Central Europe." *World Politics* 61 (4): 670–702.

Norkus, Zenonas. 2012. *On Baltic Slovenia and Adriatic Lithuania: A Qualitative Comparative Analysis of Patterns in Post-Communist Transformation*. Budapest: Central European University Press.

Orenstein, Mitchell Alexander, Stephen R. Bloom, and Nicole Lindstrom. 2008. *Transnational Actors in Central and East European Transitions*. Pittsburgh, PA: University of Pittsburgh Press.

Polanyi, Karl. 1957 [1944]. *The Great Transformation: The Political and Economic Origins of Our Time*. Boston: Beacon Press.

Pop-Eleches, Grigore. 2009. *From Economic Crisis to Reform: IMF Programs in Latin America and Eastern Europe*. Princeton, NJ: Princeton University Press.

Robinson, Neil. 2013. "Economic and Political Hybridity: Patrimonial Capitalism in the Post-Soviet Sphere." *Journal of Eurasian Studies* 4 (2): 136–45.

Schimmelfennig, Frank, and Ulrich Sedelmeier. 2005. *The Europeanization of Central and Eastern Europe*. Ithaca, NY: Cornell University Press.

Schmidt, Vivien. 2003. "French Capitalism Transformed, Yet Still a Third Variety of Capitalism." *Economy and Society* 32 (4): 526–54.

Schneider, Ben Ross. 2009. "Hierarchical Market Economies and Varieties of Capitalism in Latin America." *Journal of Latin American Studies* 41 (3): 553–71.

Schoenman, Roger. 2014. *Networks and Institutions in Europe's Emerging Markets*. Cambridge: Cambridge University Press.

Shafer, D. Michael. 1994. *Winners and Losers: How Sectors Shape the Developmental Prospects of States*. Cornell Studies in Political Economy. Ithaca, NY: Cornell University Press.

Stark, David. 1994. "Path Dependence and Privatization Strategies in East Central Europe." In *Transition to Capitalism? The Communist Legacy in Eastern Europe*, edited by János Mátyás Kovács, 63–100. New Brunswick, NJ: Transaction.

Stark, David. 1996. "Recombinant Property in East European Capitalism." *American Journal of Sociology* 101(4): 993–1027.

Stark, David, and László Bruszt. 1998. *Postsocialist Pathways: Transforming Politics and Property in East Central Europe*. Cambridge Studies in Comparative Politics. Cambridge and New York: Cambridge University Press.

Stark, David, and Gernot Grabher, eds. 1997. *Restructuring Networks in Post-Socialism: Legacies, Linkages, and Localities*. Oxford; New York: Oxford University Press.

Streeck, Wolfgang. 2011. "Taking Capitalism Seriously: Towards an Institutionalist Approach to Contemporary Political Economy." *Socio-Economic Review* 9 (1): 137–67.

Szelényi, Iván. 1988. *Socialist Entrepreneurs: Embourgeoisement in Rural Hungary*. Madison: University of Wisconsin Press. http://agris.fao.org/agris-search/search.do?recordID=US8922109.

Szelényi, Iván. 2015. "Capitalisms after Communism." *New Left Review*, II, 96 (December): 39–51.

Vachudova, Milada Anna. 2005. *Europe Undivided: Democracy, Leverage, and Integration after Communism*. Oxford; New York: Oxford University Press.

Wallerstein, Immanuel Maurice. 1979. *The Capitalist World-Economy: Essays*. Cambridge and New York: Cambridge University Press.

21

DEALING WITH THE PAST

Post-communist transitional justice

Vello Pettai and Eva-Clarita Pettai

The politics of post-communist Central and Eastern Europe (CEE) features a number of phenomena that arguably have very clear parameters and straightforward ways of measuring change and progress.[1] Whether it is economic reform, party system consolidation, European Union (EU) accession, voter behaviour, or ethnic relations, political science offers many different analytical tools and benchmarks with which to assess transformation in these various realms.

Transitional justice (TJ) is decidedly not one of those fields. In this chapter we will show how the rubric of 'transitional justice' constitutes a dizzying array of meanings and foci (Bell 2009, Fletcher and Weinstein 2015). Moreover, we will argue that scholars would do well to first map out this range of phenomena before simply selecting a single measure and seeing it as the incarnation of TJ.

A further occupational hazard of TJ research is that it is eminently about how individuals, groups, and whole countries take an explicit, normative stance towards a particular period of the past. Transitional justice is often about dictating the permitted narratives regarding that past, about determining the socialisation of future generations in relation to this past, and about making certain people culpable for the past although this culpability is rarely clear-cut.

It is no wonder, therefore, that TJ lacks a third essential parameter, which is a yardstick for determining when countries have reached an adequate level of transitional justice, sometimes declared as 'reconciliation'. Hence, not only do we not have good measurement tools for our work, but we also have no intrinsic standards for when enough transitional justice has achieved tangible objectives or outcomes. Because the phenomenon of transitional justice concerns such core political issues as legitimacy, accountability, and recognition, it is perhaps impossible to define absolute values or justifiable thresholds of 'justice'. This, however, only exacerbates the ambiguities the field must deal with now and in the future.

We will endeavour to illustrate these claims by presenting an overview of the field that is structured largely along methodological grounds. We echo in this respect the approach taken by Stan and Nedelsky (2015), who organise their work (as we will) around determinants and impacts of transitional justice along with some supplementary phenomena such as temporal waves of TJ policy and memory issues. However, what is missing in their volume is a more rigorous mapping out of what exactly the term 'transitional justice' encompasses. In this sense, our first analytical section aims at conceptualising the field as such in order to fill this gap more meticulously. We will compare how different scholars have conceptualised the notion of transitional justice, particularly the range of empirical phenomena that authors have decided to encompass when they have dealt with truth and justice issues.

Second, we will show how, depending on an author's empirical delineation of the phenomenon, the independent variables chosen across time or across countries have also varied. This is crucial, since if we as scholars each shoot at different targets (phenomena), it is no wonder that our arrows (methods) will be different, and we end up lamenting the fact that there is no consensus in the field or that we have no universal explanations for what has taken place.

Third, we will turn the methodological equation around and examine those (albeit far fewer) scholars who have examined transitional justice as a causal phenomenon and sought to answer what transitional justice (in whatever form it is conceptualised) actually bring to society. These approaches often pose the most important normative topics, such as whether transitional justice has achieved 'closure', greater rule of law, deeper societal trust, or more consolidated democracy. Here again we face important challenges regarding the conceptualisation and operationalisation of these phenomena. Yet, for obvious reasons these also remain some of the most vital questions surrounding the field.

Lastly, we will present a set of sub-themes in the field of post-communist transitional justice, namely the comparative study of institutions devoted to TJ, the growing importance of international influences on TJ, and the place of specifically post-conflict TJ in the context of former Yugoslavia.

The meaning of 'transitional'

It is widely believed that the first scholar to actively employ the term 'transitional justice' was Neil J. Kritz, who pioneered the concept in the early 1990s in connection with a path-breaking international comparative project on how newly democratising countries were dealing with their repressive past (Kritz 1995, see also Bell 2009). The timing of his scholarly revolution underscores two points about how TJ in CEE has been studied. On the one hand, Kritz and other participants in that project were clearly drawn to the topic by the explosion of justice issues facing the recently freed countries of post-communist Europe. In other words, post-communist Europe has driven an important part of the overall field thanks to its wide-ranging empirical set of cases and the simultaneity with which all of these countries began to engage with their past.

At the same time, much of the study of post-communist transitional justice stands apart from the broader international comparative scene, with few if any scholars venturing outside the conventional area-studies context. To do a comparative study of, say, Bulgaria and Bolivia would seem almost unthinkable, even though 'transitional justice' as a subject designation ostensibly applies to both (exceptions are Kaminski and Nalepa 2006, Curry 2007). Scholars of post-communist transitional justice have rarely sought to speak to the wider field. Instead, the focus has been on understanding the particularities of what seemed to be a separate genus of political processes: dealing with the legacies of repression carried out during totalitarian and/or post-totalitarian regimes as opposed to authoritarian ones.

Needless to say, if we take as important this distinction between political regimes (going back to Linz 1975), then the quiet separation of post-communist transitional justice as a sub-field was entirely warranted in analytical terms (see e.g. Killingsworth 2010). The magnitude of communist-era repression, its infiltration into all aspects of social life through agents and informants, and the much greater degree of ambiguity between perpetrators and victims made the cases of TJ in post-communist Europe somehow distinct from those encountered even in nearby Greece or Spain. Some scholars even aimed to characterise the phenomenon in a particularly contextual manner by speaking of 'decommunization' (Sadurski 2005, Czarnota 2009).

Still, it has taken time to build bridges across regions and phenomena. Some scholars, most prominently Elster (2004: 3), undertook this by extending the analytical focus of transitional justice back in time, not only to recast our understanding of earlier justice moments such as the Nuremberg trials, but also to stretch the lineage as far back as ancient Greece (see also Teitel 2003). Stan and Nedelsky (2013) have also expanded our horizons greatly by editing the first encyclopaedia of TJ that examines measures and institutions of TJ around the globe.

A second ambiguity about how the field has evolved concerns how scholars have semantically understood the word 'transitional' in transitional justice. In his pioneering work, Kritz established much of the conventional interpretation of 'transitional' as representing the political process by which new democratic regimes seek to find a balance between seeking revenge against past rulers and at the same time establishing democratic credibility by adhering to and fostering rule of law. This understanding that transitional justice writ large has something to do with 'coming to terms' with past repression is widespread and largely unproblematic. At the same time, writers like Teitel (2000) have treated 'transitional justice' from a more legal-philosophical perspective, examining how law and justice are thrown into uncertainty during times of political transformation. While Teitel clearly erected a landmark in the field by entitling her treatise *Transitional Justice*, her approach needs to be understood as above all a normative reflection on the meaning of justice amid political change.

Further semantic nuance to the notion of transitional justice has been given by the meaning of transitional that is 'temporary' or intended at some point to come to an end (Rožič and Grodsky 2015: 169). While many policies adopted by governments to deal with past wrongs have indeed been time-delimited, this understanding of TJ as simply an intermediate reform process has ultimately not proven to be true. Many countries have explicitly prolonged TJ measures when their initial mandates had expired. Transitional justice has rarely been seen as something that is confined to the period of democratic consolidation. It has generally been an open-ended political arena, where time and again the past is reignited as an object of contention.[2]

A final perspective on transitional justice has come to the fore only in the last decade or so, as struggles over the past have indeed resurfaced years after the regime change. These examples have led several authors to talk about 'protracted transitional justice' and in particular 'late lustration' (Horne 2009, Szczerbiak 2015). This phenomenon is certainly widespread across CEE, where many political elites have sought to revise previous TJ settlements and to reshape the narratives surrounding the erstwhile democratic transition. The most prominent case discussed in this regard has been Poland, where the first lustration law was adopted as late as 1999 and efforts to revise both it and the narratives of the anti-communist struggle have recurred repeatedly in the 2000s. An analytically more nuanced interpretation of this phenomenon has been put forward by Raimundo (2013) and further developed by Pettai and Pettai (2015), who define these latter-day struggles as 'post-transitional justice'. With this they not only clearly delineate the temporal boundaries of transitional justice as being confined to the immediate regime transition, they also point to the substantive difference between the TJ politics that surrounds transition as opposed to that which develops later.

Conceptualizing transitional justice

Against the backdrop of this terminological multiplicity, it is perhaps no surprise that the empirical content of what scholars have studied under the rubric of transitional justice in the post-communist context has also greatly varied. By far the most frequent object of analysis has been lustration policy or the adoption of laws aimed at either exposing, vetting and screening, or altogether removing current and/or future members of the political elite or state administration based on individuals' possible prior involvement with repression under the erstwhile regime (Nalepa 2009, 2010, 2012, 2015, David 2011, Appel 2005, Letki 2002, Haughton 2013, Williams et al. 2005, Calhoun 2002). Since practically every country in CEE has considered enacting this kind of legislation at one point or another, the phenomenon has come to dominate much of the discussion surrounding transitional justice.

This predisposition to reduce TJ to a single legal domain is understandable to the extent that policies in this area are often controversial and attract public attention. However, it can also detract from a multitude of other justice issues that may be pursued in post-communist society and that more often than not are happening in parallel with this question about what to do with former members of the security services (Grodsky 2009). Therefore, scholars such as Stan have pursued a more comprehensive approach to the topic by examining multiple truth and justice dimensions and demonstrating interlinkages between them. Beginning with an initial volume covering the entire post-communist space and later producing a separate case-study of Romania, Stan (2009a, 2013) has shown the way in which post-communist societies have often had to grapple with numerous truth and justice issues at once. In her profile of Romania, Stan covers no less than eight different truth and justice domains, including court trials, access to former regime files, lustration policies, property restitution and rehabilitation/compensation for former political prisoners. She also deals with symbolic or mnemonic aspects of truth and justice, including official condemnations of the former communist regime, the rewriting of history textbooks, and various 'unofficial projects' such as the changing of place names or grassroots campaigns to put communism as an ideology on trial. As an overview of topics relating to post-communist transitional justice, Stan's work is a key point of reference. Other comprehensive country studies include Tamm (2013) on Estonia and Kim and Swain (2015) on Hungary.

However, if we are to make progress in explaining the causes and effects of transitional justice, more conceptually driven frameworks are needed. Many scholars have sought to move in this direction by structuring transitional justice along sub-categories. This approach often begins with the classic distinction between measures that are aimed at punishing perpetrators and those that are aimed at helping victims. Tucker (2006a, 2006b), for example, writes in this vein about negative and positive justice (see also Tucker 2015). Meanwhile, David (2012) distinguishes in a review of transitional justice in the Czech Republic between 'retribution, reparation, and revelation' as forms of TJ. And most recently Rožič and Grodsky (2015) survey the field in terms of three sub-categories: retributive justice, administrative justice, and restorative/reparatory justice. The first area examines criminal cases or legal proceedings brought against leaders or operatives of the communist regimes; the second encompasses not only lustration, but also more symbolic measures such as opening former security files to the public and allowing everyone to see who was in them; and the third turns attention to the victims of repression by profiling policies that deal with rehabilitation, property restitution, apologies, and overall memorialisation. Some of this approach draws on Grodsky's (2011) earlier synthesis of truth and justice measures into a spectrum of policies that politicians can adopt depending on their costliness in terms of political capital. In that one-dimensional model, Grodsky ranked measures as ranging from simply a cessation of human rights abuses (as being lenient) to full-scale prosecution of commanders of repression. Within this scale, one could find measures relating to both victims and perpetrators.

Hence, many of these works have remained relatively taxonomical. A third level of conceptualisation, pioneered by Offe, draws explicitly on typologies and conceptual models. Offe (1992) highlighted very early in the literature that truth and justice measures should be distinguished not only by the perpetrator/victim dimension, but also by the level at which measures are adopted (see also Calhoun 2004). Whereas Offe worked with only two levels of measures, criminal law and civil law, others have added a third, symbolic level in order to separate out those measures that may be codified in legislative acts, but do not have direct effects on either perpetrators or victims. In this manner, opening up old security files is distinguished from other more retributive forms of lustration, since the former merely shames individuals, while the latter may force them legally to resign or be banned from office. Likewise, within the realm of victim-oriented policies, having a separate category devoted to symbolic measures helps to delineate acts such as commemorative activities or truth commissions from more personalised measures such as compensation schemes or legal rehabilitation.

A genuinely conceptual understanding of transitional justice would therefore look like Table 21.1. All of the different measures generally associated with post-communist TJ can easily be located within this matrix, and in so doing we can begin to compile a more complete picture of the *patterns* of transitional justice that one or another country may have used over the last quarter-century. Pettai and Pettai (2015) illustrate the utility of this framework by comparing Estonia, Latvia, and Lithuania in terms of the justice measures these countries have adopted in relation to both repression during the late Soviet era as well as that which was inflicted during the Stalinist period (something they differentiate as transitional vs. retrospective justice). They find that when looking at composite patterns of transitional justice, we can distinguish between étatist countries, where the state takes the lead in promoting measures across the full range of TJ domains, and inactive countries, where governments leave transitional justice to civil society to deal with or get involved only with temporary measures. Replicating this kind of comprehensive overview of transitional justice in other post-communist countries represents one of the future research trajectories of the field.

The three approaches to TJ conceptualisation outlined in this section admittedly entail certain epistemological choices to be made by any scholar interested in contributing to the field. Those who seek to limit the meaning of transitional justice to just one or two TJ measures (for example, lustration) gain from a high degree of analytical precision and specification, especially if the phenomenon can be reduced to a dichotomous variable (e.g. the presence or absence of a lustration law), which in turn lends itself well to comparative quantitative testing (Letki 2002). However, what is lost in this approach is not only terminological consistency (especially when transitional justice is used as a synonym for lustration), but also a broader appreciation of the complexities of post-communist *Vergangenheitsbewältigung*, or coming to terms with the past. Meanwhile, empirical case studies that cover many TJ measures at once help to advance scholarship, but at the same time can imply an epistemological belief that ultimately each country has its own unique communist legacy to manage, and that over-generalised conceptual frameworks can end up being artificial or distortive of reality. Frameworks that seek to map out full-scale patterns of transitional justice argue in favour of both comprehensiveness and comparison, but require the largest amount of empirical data collection as well as a more intricate aggregation model when summing up precise patterns of TJ in order to be fully effectual.

Table 21.1 An integrated conceptual framework for examining transitional justice

	Perpetrators	*Victims*
criminal-judicial	trials	rehabilitation
political-administrative	purges/vetting	compensation, property restitution
symbolic-representational	voluntary self-reporting	recognition/truth-telling

Source: Pettai and Pettai (2015: 21).

Explaining variation in post-communist transitional justice

Continuing our methodological analysis of post-communist transitional justice, it is again no surprise that where scholars have decided to focus on only one aspect of truth and justice, the explanatory variables that they have put forward to explain variation across countries have not always been the same that more multi-dimensional studies have proffered. Across studies that aim to explain the specific phenomenon of lustration across CEE, explanatory variables have included both structural and actor-based factors (Welsh 1996). Structural determinants begin with the type of communist regime, often drawing on Kitschelt's (1995) famous distinction between national-accommodative, bureaucratic-authoritarian, and patrimonial regimes in the communist world. This distal variable is subsequently linked to the type of democratic transition that eventually took place in the late 1980s, the argument being that bureaucratic-authoritarian regimes were generally more rigid than national-accommodative ones and therefore collapsed more quickly. This, in turn, led to a different *rapport de force* between pro-lustration and anti-lustration groups with former bureaucratic-authoritarian countries (like the Czech Republic) implementing harsher lustration measures, while erstwhile national-accommodative countries (like Poland or Hungary) saw roundtable talks that (at least initially) thwarted the tendency towards harsh measures (and might even have set the stage for a reprise of these issues later).

At the same time, lustration can also be seen as driven by 'present politics' or political calculations made by different actors depending on the degree to which they or their opponents have 'skeletons in their closet'. This approach helps to explain more proximate variations in terms of how individual politicians or political parties have behaved in pushing lustration issues or avoiding them. It can also be very fruitfully modelled using rational choice and game theory (Nalepa 2010). Somewhat in between these structural and individual levels of explanation lie more circumstantial explanations that draw attention simply to the amount of reliable information (e.g. files) available to the democratic regime about individuals' past involvement with the security services. This pertains particularly to some of the post-Soviet cases, where KGB files were removed to secure areas in Russia before the USSR collapsed.

In terms of research design, most explanations for lustration come from qualitative comparative studies, some constructed in explicit Millian terms, others more casually. Among the former is Nedelsky's (2004) structured comparison of the Czech Republic and Slovakia, taking as its point of departure the common political origin of these two countries (Czechoslovakia), yet highlighting the remarkable disparity between the two states' lustration policies. Meanwhile, Nalepa (2010) and David (2011) each draw on Hungary, the Czech Republic, and Poland to test their (albeit very different) hypotheses regarding lustration. Several other studies (Appel 2005, Ellis 1997, Stan 2009a) attempt to examine almost all of the countries of the region, but as a consequence tend to be descriptive and draw few causal conclusions.

Among our other types of truth and justice policies, comparative and inferential research is scant. One reason is that the measures themselves have sometimes been too rarely enacted to allow for multi-case testing. For example, within the realm of criminal prosecutions, very few countries in CEE have attempted to put their erstwhile repressive leaders on trial. Fijalkowski and Grosescu (2015) have put forth the notion of 'transitional criminal justice', but no generalised hypotheses exist for explaining when democratic governments seek such prosecutions, much less what types of criminal paragraphs are used.

Studies of truth-seeking commissions in CEE are likewise limited. On the one hand, some scholars have lamented the absence of real truth commissions in the region (akin to the famous truth and reconciliation commission in South Africa), explaining this with the fact that in some countries the 1989 roundtable talks between regime and opposition already served as a necessary moment of catharsis (Garton Ash 2002, Mink 2013). At the same time, where certain investigative commissions have been created (e.g. in Germany, Romania, and the Baltic states), scholars have tried to treat these nevertheless as truth commissions (Stan 2009b, Ciobanu 2009, Beattie 2015). However, the question remains whether in conceptual terms these officially appointed commissions can fruitfully be considered as truth commissions in line with well-established definitions for such bodies (Hayner 2002, see also Brahm 2009). Because these post-communist commissions have often had a historical and highly academic focus (looking back at Stalinist-era crimes), they have lacked the strong victim-oriented, restorative justice component usually associated with truth commissions (Pettai 2015). Moreover, in the Romanian case Ciobanu (2009) has shown how the so-called Tismaneanu commission was mostly a product of political manoeuvring by the president at the time in order to discredit political opponents and reanimate anti-communist sentiment. In this respect, it has been difficult to generalise across the region.

Other restorative justice measures such as rehabilitation, compensation, or property restitution for victims have all, of course, been widely practised in the post-communist world. Rehabilitation began already in the post-Stalinist era (McDermott and Stibbe 2015), while compensation or special social benefits for political prisoners or deportees were often added after 1989 (see in particular Schroeder and Küpper 2010). Communist-era nationalisation of property was also righted through large-scale restitution policies implemented throughout the 1990s and often stretching out into the 2000s (Blacksell and Born 2002, Kuti 2009). However, we do not have truly explanatory comparisons across any of these domains as yet, since individual case studies or broad-brush overviews predominate in the literature.

Finally, hypothesis testing has remained limited among works that offer truly composite studies of transitional justice, since these studies have either focused on single cases (Offe and Poppe 2005), they deal with arguably too diverse cases (Grodsky 2011), or they remain analytically very preliminary (Pettai and Pettai 2015). Nevertheless, for studies that adopt this perspective, we see that the explanatory variables tend to be structural. For example, Pettai and Pettai find that Lithuania's more activist pattern of transitional justice as opposed to Estonia's more hands-off stance can be explained by historical-contextual circumstances such as the fact that the post-1945 partisan war was much more intense in Lithuania, leading to not only many more latter-day criminal trials of former KGB officials, but also more victim rehabilitation, compensation, and memorialisation. Likewise, they show how emerging party systems have a decisive impact on truth and justice policies across all domains. Thus, where the post-communist party system is defined by ethnic cleavages (as in Latvia) or ex-communist/anti-communist divisions (as in Lithuania), the resulting polarization of the political field has a tangible effect on the degree to which elites have engaged in issues of retrospective justice (see also Bernhard and Kubik 2014).

Effects of transitional justice

Wherever post-communist truth and justice measures have been advocated or adopted, their predicted effects have included any number of normative, behavioural, or attitudinal goals. First and foremost, transitional justice is said to underpin a firm commitment to rule of law in democratising countries. Both perpetrator-oriented and victim-oriented TJ policies should contribute to a restored ethos of legalism, respect for human and civil rights, and confidence in the judicial system. Additionally, many have maintained that transitional justice will prevent future politicians from abusing power or engaging in repressive activities. It is also argued that the new political system as a whole will perform better without the influence of those compromised or tainted by the former regime. Lastly, truth and justice policies should increase citizens' overall satisfaction with democracy or their feelings of trust towards politics, political institutions, or in each other (generalised trust) (for a general review of these issues, see Thoms, et al. 2010).

True empirical research into TJ as an independent variable has been rather preliminary until now, not least because of the same methodological issues already mentioned involving conceptualisation and operationalisation. How can outcomes such as improved rule of law or enhanced human rights be properly assessed or measured? Global datasets such as the Transitional Justice Data Base project have been used to test the effects of a tripartite conceptualisation of TJ (based on the existence of trials, amnesties, and/or truth commissions) on broadly defined variables such as democracy and human rights (Olsen et al. 2010). In these studies, CEE countries have been included alongside post-authoritarian and post-conflict TJ cases. Meanwhile, more focused research on post-communist Europe has been presented by Lynch and Marchesi (2015) drawing on another dataset prepared by the Transitional Justice Research Collaborative. In this dataset, numerous truth and justice policies are measured, including domestic criminal prosecutions, amnesty policies and lustration policies; moreover, lustration is operationalised into separate sub-categories depending on the severity of a country's policy. However, in a preliminary analysis of the data, Lynch and Marchesi look mostly at the effects of lustration on subsequent levels of political and civil rights in a country, and they find very few statistically significant relationships. A composite variable of TJ measures also yields no statistically significant results.

Studies of the attitudinal effect of lustration have been led by Horne (2012, 2015), who has attempted to test the impact of lustration on trust in public institutions and national government. Although her basic measure of lustration is limited to just three levels (no lustration, 'insufficiently lustrated', and 'sufficiently lustrated'), she runs numerous statistical models controlling for the timing of lustration, the degree of other TJ measures present, as well as additional political and economic factors. Her findings indicate that 'countries with more extensive lustration programs, more severe lustration programs, and more extensive transitional justice measures have higher levels of trust in public institutions', whereas the impact on trust in national government is inconclusive (2012: 433).

Choi and David (2012) take a unique experimental approach to testing the effects of lustration on public trust. First, drawing on the cases of the Czech Republic, Hungary, and Poland, the authors operationalise lustration as a categorical variable involving three types of lustration systems: dismissal, exposure, and confession. They then embed these variants directly into a survey questionnaire by developing fictional vignettes about a former informant being subjected either to dismissal or no dismissal, exposure or no exposure, confession or no confession. When one or the other narrative is read to a respondent, one can compare the respondent's subsequent degree of trust in government along with his/her trust in the fictional official in order to arrive at a controlled, individual-level measurement of attitudinal change. While David and Choi hypothesise that all three types of lustration should increase trust in government, only respondents exposed to dismissal and confession showed higher levels of trust as opposed to being told that there would be no dismissal or no confession. Moreover, the effect of being told there would be a dismissal policy (versus no dismissal) was much stronger than the effect of confession, hinting that respondents generally welcomed dismissal more than any other option in terms of increasing their trust in government. Meanwhile, the study showed that trust in the tainted officials was likely to improve if the officials went through a process of confession, while exposure would decrease this trust. These results clearly represent one of the more sophisticated and original research designs concerning the effects of transitional justice. In separate work, David and Choi (2006) also examined victims' readiness to forgive perpetrators using similarly original survey data. While such endeavours are costly and require meticulous preparation, they do exhibit how important empirical and comparative results can be achieved in the field.

Sub-fields of research

As studies of post-communist transitional justice have evolved, a number of sub-themes have developed as additional focal points for different clusters of scholars. The first concerns the comparative study of national institutions established to deal with different TJ policies. Whether it is individual government offices set up to review secret police files (e.g. the German *Stasi-Unterlagenbehörde* [Stasi Records Agency]) or full-scale institutes for national remembrance (including in countries like Ukraine and Moldova), the way in which transitional justice policies have spawned entire administrative structures in some countries arguably constitutes a corollary field to TJ policies themselves. On a conceptual level, these institutions represent an interesting link between TJ and the politics of memory. Many of them, like the Polish Institute of National Remembrance or the Lithuanian Genocide and Resistance Research Centre work in close cooperation with state prosecutors in tracking down surviving perpetrators of Stalin-era atrocities, or they assist victims of past repression in seeking rehabilitation and compensation. At the same time, these institutions are often home to extensive museums and other commemorative activities aiming at much larger audiences and actively shaping collective perceptions of the communist past (Mink 2013). In the past decade, moreover, these institutions have become increasingly inter-connected through transnational networks, the aim of which is to lobby for greater recognition and scrutiny of communist crimes on a pan-European level. While these new actors and constellations concerned with the politics of memory pose an interesting field for the study of transnational practices and agency, the networks also play a role in the field of transitional justice, as they push for lustration in different countries, examine best practice, or serve as watchdogs for ongoing justice processes in different states.

Related to the study of transnational memory actors is an emerging field of study that looks at how domestic transitional justice processes have traversed borders of nation states and national jurisdictions into European judicial and political institutions. Thus, on several occasions the European Court of Human Rights has been asked to cast judgments on the legal permissibility of certain national TJ measures such as lustration or the criminal trials of former secret police agents. Several scholars have used these rulings to compare different legal and historical perceptions of communist-era crimes and to theorise about the politics of memory through criminal law (Brems 2011, Mälksoo 2014). Additionally, attention has been paid to how memory institutions in CEE (mentioned earlier) and individual politicians from new EU member states have lobbied European representative bodies (such as the European Parliament or the Parliamentary Assembly of the Council of Europe) to condemn the crimes of communism and raise awareness about those crimes. The objective of these efforts has been to secure the adoption of not only landmark declarations denouncing the communist regimes, but also financing for civil society programs aimed at the commemoration and remembrance of past sufferings. In analytical terms, authors have established a connection between the degree to which states have previously engaged in public remembrance and transitional justice and their ability to secure European resources for further activities in these areas. Although arguably many of these studies relate more to the study of memory politics than to transitional justice, they have shed light on new areas of contestation around TJ issues beyond individual national contexts (Gledhill 2011, Neumayer 2015).

Lastly, when we examine the place of transitional justice in Eastern Europe outside the overriding backdrop of former communism, it is necessary to note that there has been considerable transitional justice also in the context of war-torn ex-Yugoslavia (Simić and Volčič 2012). Much research in this context has gone into examining 'the politics of cooperation' with the International Criminal Tribunal for the Former Yugoslavia (Ostojić 2014; see also Subotić 2015), raising interesting questions about the impact of international judicial bodies on domestic TJ processes more broadly, and of the Milošević trial on domestic debates in particular (Dragović-Soso 2014). Indeed, an important outcome of these studies has been the realisation that courts have a rather mixed impact on transitional societies. Studies on Serbia in particular show how the international discourses on TJ contributed more to 'silencing' critical public and political debates on the conflict and related responsibilities than to their opening (Obradović-Wochnik, 2013). Some authors have, moreover, argued that by linking compliance with the Tribunal's demands to the EU accession negotiations, Brussels often did more to constrain rather than strengthen domestic truth and justice policies (Spoerri 2011). Ultimately, however, this particular area of research is concerned with processes of coming to term with an ethnic conflict, rather than with the pre-war communist regime and its human rights violations. As Subotić (2015) shows, the Yugoslav case involves many legacies that other CEE countries do not have such as ethnic warfare, multiple transitions to democracy, and strong international intervention. This makes a meaningful cross-regional comparison of TJ, including the former Yugoslavia, rather difficult.

Conclusion

This chapter began with a claim that transitional justice in CEE was different from other subject areas in political science because it was more dispersed in its conceptual landscape and analytical approaches. We end with an observation that although truth and justice remains a salient issue in many CEE countries, it does have a half-life and in phenomenological terms it fades at some point into memory studies and history. The political incentive or imperative to continue investigations of octogenarian perpetrators, to enact supplementary social benefits for aging political prisoners, to complete the processing of property restitution claims, or to issue recurrent parliamentary declarations condemning the communist past is bound to become less acute over time. Certainly, rhetoric and controversy surrounding the legacies of communism will continue, but transitional justice as policy will gradually diminish.

This leaves the field with a challenge. With new analytical material appearing to ebb, research on transitional justice should focus on integrating what we know into a broader international context. In what ways do countries with long authoritarian regimes resemble those of communism and how might the lessons of transition justice in CEE serve these newly democratizing countries? Consider countries such as Egypt, Iran, or Myanmar. How can strong internal security services be dismantled, former perpetrators prosecuted, past human rights abuses investigated, and victims acknowledged in these countries when and if democratic leaders come to power? Irrespective of the conceptual distinctions we may hold between communist and authoritarian regimes, there may be useful lessons to be drawn from the policy structure and political sequencing of truth and justice measures that have been adopted in Central and Eastern Europe. This requires a broader comparative approach.

Another dimension of future research focuses on the place of *Vergangenheitsbewältigung* in many of the still-democratising countries of the region such as Ukraine, Georgia, and Moldova, not to mention authoritarian regimes in Russia, Belarus, Azerbaijan, and Central Asia. While the lack of democratisation in these societies in the 1990s can be explained by any number of different factors, the lack of any real processes of transitional justice should also be looked into as a counterfactual set of cases to CEE. This would make the field likewise more balanced and integrative.

Notes

1 This research was made possible by institutional research grant (IUT) no. 20–39 from the Estonian Research Council.

2 Indeed, the notion of transitional justice has become particularly stretched when it has been applied to regional and political contexts that have nothing to do with democratic transition and involve measures (such as truth and reconciliation commissions, official apologies or reparations) intended to redress past human rights violations against aboriginal groups (Winter 2014).

References

Appel, Hilary. 2005. "Anti-Communist Justice and Founding the Post-Communist Order: Lustration and Restitution in Central Europe." *East European Politics & Societies* 19(3): 379–405.

Beattie, Andrew H. 2015. "Post-Communist Truth Commissions: Between Transitional Justice and the Politics of History." In *Post-Communist Transitional Justice: Lessons From Twenty-Five Years of Experience*, eds. Lavinia Stan and Nadya Nedelsky. Cambridge: Cambridge University Press. 213–232.

Bell, Christine. 2009. "Transitional Justice, Interdisciplinarity and the State of the 'Field' or 'Non-Field'." *International Journal of Transitional Justice* 3(1): 5–27.

Bernhard, Michael, and Jan Kubik. 2014. *Twenty Years After Communism: The Politics of Memory and Commemoration*. Oxford: Oxford University Press.

Blacksell, Mark, and Karl Martin Born. 2002. "Private Property Restitution: The Geographical Consequences of Official Government Policies in Central and Eastern Europe." *Geographical Journal* 168(2): 178–190.

Brahm, E. 2009. "What Is a Truth Commission and What Does It Matter?" *Peace and Conflict Review* 3(2): 1–14.

Brems, Eva. 2011. "Transitional Justice in the Case Law of the European Court of Human Rights." *International Journal of Transitional Justice* 5(2): 282–303.

Calhoun, Noel. 2002. "The Ideological Dilemma of Lustration in Poland." *East European Politics & Societies* 16(2): 494–520.

Calhoun, Noel. 2004. *Dilemmas of Justice in Eastern Europe's Democratic Transitions*. New York: Palgrave Macmillan.

Choi, Susanne Y. P., and Roman David. 2012. "Lustration Systems and Trust: Evidence from Survey Experiments in the Czech Republic, Hungary, and Poland." *American Journal of Sociology* 117(4): 1172–1201.

Ciobanu, Monica. 2009. "Criminalising the Past and Reconstructing Collective Memory: The Romanian Truth Commission." *Europe-Asia Studies* 61(2): 313–336.

Curry, Jane L. 2007. "When an Authoritarian State Victimizes the Nation: Transitional Justice, Collective Memory, and Political Divides." *International Journal of Sociology* 37(1): 58–73.

Czarnota, Adam. 2009. "Lustration, Decommunisation and the Rule of Law." *Hague Journal on the Rule of Law* 1(2): 307–336.

David, Roman. 2011. *Lustration and Transitional Justice: Personnel Systems in the Czech Republic, Hungary, and Poland*. Philadelphia: Pennsylvania University Press.

David, Roman. 2012. "Twenty Years of Transitional Justice in the Czech Lands." *Europe-Asia Studies* 64(4): 761–784.

David, Roman, and Susanne Y. P. Choi. 2006. "Forgiveness and Transitional Justice in the Czech Republic." *Journal of Conflict Resolution* 50(3): 339–367.

Dragović-Soso, Jasna. 2014. "Collective Responsibility, International Justice and Public Reckoning With the Recent Past: Reflections on a Debate in Serbia." In *The Milošević Trial: An Autopsy*, ed. Timothy Waters. Oxford: Oxford University Press. 389–408.

Ellis, Mark S. 1997. "Purging the Past: The Current State of Lustration Laws in the Former Communist Bloc." *Law and Contemporary Problems* 59(4): 181–196.

Elster, Jon. 2004. *Closing the Books: Transitional Justice in Historical Perspective*. Cambridge: Cambridge University Press.

Fijalkowski, Agata, and Raluca Grosescu. 2015. *Transitional Criminal Justice in Post-Dictatorial and Post-Conflict Societies*. Amsterdam: Intersentia.

Fletcher, Laurel E., and Harvey M. Weinstein. 2015. "Writing Transitional Justice: An Empirical Evaluation of Transitional Justice Scholarship in Academic Journals." *Journal of Human Rights Practice* 7(2): 177–198.

Garton Ash, Timothy. 2002. "Trials, Purges and History Lessons: Treating a Difficult Past in Post-Communist Europe." In *Memory and Power in Post-War Europe. Studies in the Presence of the Past*, ed. Jan-Werner Müller. Cambridge: Cambridge University Press. 265–282.

Gledhill, John. 2011. "Integrating the Past: Regional Integration and Historical Reckoning in Central and Eastern Europe." *Nationalities Papers* 39(4): 481–506.

Grodsky, Brian K. 2009. "Beyond Lustration Truth-Seeking Efforts in the Post-Communist Space." *Taiwan Journal of Democracy* 5(2): 21–43.

Grodsky, Brian K. 2011. *The Costs of Justice: How New Leaders Respond to Previous Rights Abuses*. Notre Dame, IN: University of Notre Dame Press.

Haughton, Tim. 2013. "Battlefields, Ammunition and Uniforms: The Past and Politics in Post-Communist Central and Eastern Europe." *Comparative European Politics* 11(2): 249–260.

Hayner, P. 2002. *Unspeakable Truths: Facing the Challenge of Truth Commissions*. London: Routledge.

Horne, Cynthia M. 2009. "Late Lustration Programmes in Romania and Poland: Supporting or Undermining Democratic Transitions?". *Democratization* 16(2): 344–376.

Horne, Cynthia M. 2012. "Assessing the Impact of Lustration on Trust in Public Institutions and National Government in Central and Eastern Europe." *Comparative Political Studies* 45(4): 412–446.

Horne, Cynthia M. 2015. "The Timing of Transitional Justice Measures." In *Post-Communist Transitional Justice: Lessons From Twenty-Five Years of Experience*, eds. Lavinia Stan and Nadya Nedelsky. Cambridge: Cambridge University Press. 123–147.

Kaminski, Marek M, and Monika Nalepa. 2006. "Judging Transitional Justice a New Criterion for Evaluating Truth Revelation Procedures." *Journal of Conflict Resolution* 50(3): 383–408.

Killingsworth, Matt. 2010. "Lustration and Legitimacy." *Global Society* 24: 71–90.

Kim, Dae Soon, and Nigel Swain. 2015. "Party Politics, Political Competition and Coming to Terms with the Past in Post-Communist Hungary." *Europe-Asia Studies* 67(9): 1445–1468.

Kitschelt, Herbert. 1995. "Formation of Party Cleavages in Post-Communist Democracies." *Party Politics* 1(4): 447–472.

Kritz, Neil J. 1995. *Transitional Justice: How Emerging Democracies Reckon With Former Regimes*. Vol. 1. Washington DC: US Institute of Peace Press.

Kuti, Csongor. 2009. *Post-Communist Restitution and the Rule of Law*. Budapest: Central European University Press.

Letki, Natalia. 2002. "Lustration and Democratisation in East-Central Europe." *Europe-Asia Studies* 54(4): 529–552.

Linz, Juan J. 1975. "Totalitarian and Authoritarian Regimes." In *Handbook of Political Science*, Vol. 3, eds. Fred Greenstein and Nelson Polsby. Reading, MA: Addison Wesley. 175–411.

Lynch, Moira, and Bridget Marchesi. 2015. "The Adoption and Impact of Transitional Justice." In *Post-Communist Transitional Justice: Lessons From Twenty-Five Years of Experience*, eds. Lavinia Stan and Nadya Nedelsky. Cambridge: Cambridge University Press. 73–96.

Mälksoo, Maria. 2014. "Criminalizing Communism: Transnational Mnemopolitics in Europe." *International Political Sociology* 8(1): 82–99.

McDermott, Kevin, and Matthew Stibbe. 2015. *De-Stalinising Eastern Europe: The Rehabilitation of Stalin's Victims After 1953*. London, New York: Palgrave Macmillan.

Mink, Georges. 2013. "Institutions of National Memory in Post-Communist Europe: From Transitional Justice to Political Uses of Biographies (1989–2010)." In *History, Memory and Politics in Central and Eastern Europe: Memory Games*, eds. Georges Mink and Laure Neumayer. Basingstoke: Palgrave Macmillan. 155–170.

Nalepa, Monika. 2009. "Lustration and the Survival of Parliamentary Parties." *Taiwan Journal of Democracy* 5(2): 45–68.

Nalepa, Monika. 2010. *Skeletons in the Closet: Transitional Justice in Post-Communist Europe*. Cambridge: Cambridge University Press.

Nalepa, Monika. 2012. "Tolerating Mistakes How Do Popular Perceptions of Procedural Fairness Affect Demand for Transitional Justice?" *Journal of Conflict Resolution* 56(3): 490–515.

Nalepa, Monika. 2015. "The Institutional Context of Transitional Justice." In *Routledge Handbook of Comparative Political Institutions*, eds. Jennifer Gandhi and Ruben Ruiz-Rufino. Oxford: Routledge. 389–403.

Nedelsky, Nadya. 2004. "Divergent Responses to a Common Past: Transitional Justice in the Czech Republic and Slovakia." *Theory and Society* 33(1): 65–115.

Neumayer, Laure. 2015. "Integrating the Central European Past into a Common Narrative: The Mobilizations around the 'Crimes of Communism' in the European Parliament." *Journal of Contemporary European Studies* 23(3): 344–363.

Obradović-Wochnik, Jelena. 2013. "The 'Silent Dilemma' of Transitional Justice: Silencing and Coming to Terms With the Past in Serbia." *The International Journal of Transitional Justice*, 7(2): 328–347.

Offe, Claus. 1992. "Coming to Terms With Past Injustices." *European Journal of Sociology* 33(1): 195–201.

Offe, Claus, and Ulrike Poppe. 2005. "Transitional Justice After the Breakdown of the German Democratic Republic." In *Rethinking the Rule of Law After Communism*, eds. Adam Czarnota, Martin Krygier and Wojciech Sadurski. Budapest: Central European University Press. 153–189.

Olsen, Tricia D, Leigh A Payne, and Andrew G Reiter. 2010. "The Justice Balance: When Transitional Justice Improves Human Rights and Democracy." *Human Rights Quarterly* 32(4): 980–1007.

Ostojić, Mladen. 2014. *Between Justice and Stability. The Politics of War-Crime Prosecutions in Post-Milošević Serbia*. Farnham: Ashgate.

Pettai, Eva-Clarita. 2015. "Negotiating History for Reconciliation: A Comparative Evaluation of the Baltic Presidential Commissions." *Europe-Asia Studies* 67(7): 1079–1101.

Pettai, Eva-Clarita, and Vello Pettai. 2015. *Transitional and Retrospective Justice in the Baltic States*. Cambridge: Cambridge University Press.

Raimundo, Filipa. 2013. "Dealing With the Past in Central and Southern European Democracies: Comparing Spain and Poland." In *History, Memory and Politics in Central and Eastern Europe*, eds. Georges Mink and Laure Neumayer. London: Palgrave Macmillan. 136–154.

Rožič, Peter, and Brian Grodsky. 2015. "Transitional Justice in Central and Eastern Europe." In *Central and East European Politics: From Communism to Democracy*, eds. Sharon L. Wolchik and Jane Leftwich Curry. Lanham, MD: Rowman & Littlefield. 169–188.

Sadurski, Wojciech. 2005. " 'De-Communization', 'Lustration' and Constitutional Continuity: Dilemmas of Transitional Justice in Central Europe." Paper presented at the EUI Working Paper LAW 15, 2005, Florence.

Schroeder, Friedrich-Christian and Herbert Küpper, eds. 2010. *Die rechtliche Aufarbeitung der kommunistischen Vergangenheit in Osteuropa* [Legal reckoning with the communist past in Eastern Europe]. Frankfurt: Peter Lang.

Simić, Olivera, and Zala Volčič. 2012. *Transitional Justice and Civil Society in the Balkans*. New York: Springer Science & Business Media.

Spoerri, Marlene. 2011. "Justice Imposed: How Policies of Conditionality Effect Transitional Justice in the Former Yugoslavia." *Europe-Asia Studies*, 63(10): 1827–1851.

Stan, Lavinia. 2009a. *Transitional Justice in Eastern Europe and the Former Soviet Union: Reckoning With the Communist Past*. London: Routledge.

Stan, Lavinia. 2009b. "Truth Commissions in Post-Communism: The Overlooked Solution?" *Open Political Science Journal* 2: 1–13.

Stan, Lavinia. 2013. *Transitional Justice in Post-Communist Romania*. Cambridge: Cambridge University Press.

Stan, Lavinia, and Nadya Nedelsky, eds. 2013. *Encyclopedia of Transitional Justice*. New York: Cambridge University Press.

Stan, Lavinia, and Nadya Nedelsky, eds. 2015. *Post-Communist Transitional Justice: Lessons From Twenty-Five Years of Experience*. New York: Cambridge University Press.

Subotić, Jelena. 2015. "Out of Eastern Europe Legacies of Violence and the Challenge of Multiple Transitions." *East European Politics & Societies* 29(2): 409–419.

Szczerbiak, Aleks. 2015. "Explaining Late Lustration Programs: Lessons From the Polish Case." In *Post-Communist Transitional Justice: Lessons From Twenty-Five Years of Experience*, eds. Nadya Nedelsky and Lavinia Stan. Cambridge: Cambridge University Press. 51–70.

Tamm, Marek. 2013. "In Search of Lost Time: Memory Politics in Estonia, 1991–2011." *Nationalities Papers* 41(4): 651–674.

Teitel, Ruti G. 2000. *Transitional Justice*. Oxford: Oxford University Press.

Teitel, Ruti G. 2003. "Transitional Justice Genealogy." *Harvard Human Rights Journal* 16: 69–94.

Thoms, Oskar NT, James Ron, and Roland Paris. 2010. "State-Level Effects of Transitional Justice: What Do We Know?". *International Journal of Transitional Justice* 4: 329–354.

Tucker, Aviezer. 2006a. "Paranoids May Be Persecuted: Post-Totalitarian Transitional Justice." In *Retribution and Reparation in the Transition to Democracy*, ed. Jon Elster. Cambridge: Cambridge University Press. 181–205.

Tucker, Aviezer. 2006b. "Rough Justice: Rectification in Post-Authoritarian and Post-Totalitarian Regimes." In *Retribution and Reparation in the Transition to Democracy*, ed. Jon Elster. Cambridge: Cambridge University Press. 276–298.

Tucker, Aviezer. 2015. *The Legacies of Totalitarianism: A Theoretical Framework*. Cambridge: Cambridge University Press.

Welsh, Helga A. 1996. "Dealing with the Communist Past: Central and East European Experiences After 1990." *Europe-Asia Studies* 48(3): 413–428.

Williams, Kieran, Brigid Fowler, and Aleks Szczerbiak. 2005. "Explaining Lustration in Central Europe: A 'Post-Communist Politics' Approach." *Democratization* 12(1): 22–43.

Winter, Stephen. 2014. *Transitional Justice in Established Democracies: A Political Theory.* London: Palgrave Macmillan.

22

"THE WEST, THE EAST AND THE REST"

The foreign policy orientations of Central Eastern European countries

Elsa Tulmets

Introduction[1]

After over four decades of communist domination, Central Eastern European (CEE) countries have claimed their "return to Europe" through European Union (EU) and North Atlantic Treaty Organisation (NATO) accessions in the 1990s and 2000s (cf. Drulák 2001; Lindstrom 2003; Batt 2007; Tulmets 2009, 2014; Cadier 2012). Given CEE countries' varied national histories, a thorough analysis of their foreign policies has to rely on older as well as more recent aspects of their nations' external relations. Many CEE nations have gone through years of occupation or fights against occupation by Germany, Russia, and Sweden in the North and East, but also by the Austro-Hungarian and Ottoman Empires in the East and South. Only a few of them have been independent states in recent history, contrary to other European countries like France, Germany, the UK, or Spain, which claim long foreign policy traditions. The first part of the chapter will show how the past of each nation and country affects the way to analyse CEE countries' external relations. Difficulties to draw on past foreign policy traditions and resources partly explain why the "modern" foreign policies of the CEE countries, as defined in the 1990s and 2000s, decided to focus on "the West", "the East", and sometimes "the rest".

This chapter claims that theoretical approaches towards CEE country foreign policies are missing despite drastic empirical evolutions on this topic. In order to make the link between past analytical works and more recent ones on CEE countries' foreign policies, one needs to not only rely on literature from foreign policy analysis (FPA), international relations (IR), and European Studies, but also from history and area studies. As a matter of fact, since the early 1990s, foreign policies were mainly studied by groups of experts in each of the CEE countries, but less in the Anglo-Saxon field of FPA (cf. Hill and Wong 2011; Baun and Marek 2013). It is mainly in IR and European Studies that CEE country foreign policies have been dealt with, although mainly through the perspective of EU and NATO accessions, thus focusing more on sectoral and technical negotiations and positions of the countries (cf. Schimmelfennig and Sedelmeier 2005; Bulmer and Lequesne 2004, 2012). However, history and area studies are instructive when approaching bilateral actions defined in the framework of national foreign policies (Kanet 1983; Sodaro and Wolchik 1983), mainly during and after EU and NATO accessions (Fawn 2003;

Batt 2007; Ehin and Berg 2009). It is indeed at this time that political priorities and historical obligations or path dependencies started to merge, but also sometimes to clash, thus explaining some of the continuities and contradictions in CEE foreign policies (cf. Tulmets 2012, 2014).

Historical and intellectual developments on CEE foreign policies

Analyses of the foreign policies of CEE countries are generally difficult to trace back to before the interwar period (1918–1939), which represents the only time in history where almost all CEE countries enjoyed sovereignty before the end of the Cold War. Only a few states, like Poland, the Czech Republic (in fact Bohemia), Lithuania, Hungary, and Romania may claim to have a long foreign policy past, though not always as a nation state, like the periods of the Polish-Lithuanian Commonwealth, the Austro-Hungarian Empire, and Czechoslovakia show. CEE countries' foreign relations have therefore mainly been studied from the perspective of national awakening or nation-building (Kiss 2000). The focus on nationalism as a vital element of foreign policy formation was, however, generally avoided by specialists of FPA given the uneasy legacy of nationalism in Europe, which, for example, strongly contributed to justifying the Holocaust during the Second World War (cf. Prizel 1998; Kiss 2000: 82).

In comparison, a few authors have written about the foreign policies of CEE countries under communism (e.g. Sodaro and Wolchik 1983; Kanet, 1983; Mareš 2001, 2007; Batt 2007; Zając and Zięba 2010), although here again, not all countries had a foreign policy. In practice, the foreign policy relations of communist countries varied from relative independence from Moscow, like in the case of ex-Yugoslavia or Romania, to inexistence, like for the Baltic states. Furthermore, like Kiss writes, the communist ideology and the Soviet Union were dominated by "denationalised regionalism" (Kiss 2000: 90). It was therefore more the official communist ideology which guided foreign policy than national feelings, thus explaining the development of relations with countries situated in Asia (like China and Vietnam), in Africa (like Angola, Egypt, Ethiopia, Mozambique, and Zambia), and other places of the world (such as Cuba and Nicaragua) sharing a similar ideology. Analytical point of views, however, differ if one considers relations through the neo-realist perspective of military events, like the Cuban Missile Crisis (Allison 1971), which shows the importance of limited-rationalism in decision-making processes, or through the more liberal economic and cultural aspects, which highlight more exchange between actors, even between the countries of the two blocs (cf. Sodaro and Wolchik 1983: 20; Mareš 2001).

The fall of the Berlin Wall in 1989 and of the Soviet Union in 1991 again opened up the expression of national discourses and actions as guidance of foreign policy. The Baltic states took the path of a peaceful independence process to regain their sovereignty in 1991, and Czechoslovakia divided into two states, the Czech and the Slovak republics, after the Velvet Revolution of 1992. Conflictual events and civil war, however, brought Yugoslavia to fall apart into several small states throughout the 1990s and 2000s (see Bieber in this volume). On the whole, despite dramatic events in ex-Yugoslavia, nationalist trends were rather successfully canalised in the 1990s and 2000s through multilateral structures designed by the international community. As a matter of fact, the accession to international organisations and regional structures, mainly NATO and the EU, represented one of the main foreign policy goals of all CEE states (see Webber and Dimitrova in this volume). It is therefore mainly in this perspective that CEE foreign policies were defined and studied after 1989, which explains academic focus on specific concepts linked to multilateralism, like Europeanisation and NATO-isation, and the neglect of more theoretical approaches from an FPA perspective. In the 1990s, however, part of the FPA literature on CEE drew on past reflections often coming from the interwar period, which cultivated the definition of new foreign policy identities.

New foreign policy identities and priorities

Academic and mainly "grey" literature[2] developed exponentially in each of the CEE countries, and also partly abroad, to shape and analyse the new foreign policy priorities adopted after the events of 1989 and 1991 (cf. Hill and Reuben 2011; Drulák and Šabič 2012; Baun and Marek 2013; Tulmets 2014). They mainly served the purpose of accompanying reflections of policy makers who needed to draft new foreign policy orientations for governments looking for the support of "the West": in all CEE states, accession to the EU and NATO was thus defined as the top priority. In a constructivist sense, the CEE states embraced the norms and values defended and promoted by the EU, which are democracy and human rights, the rule of law, an open market economy, and solidarity. They constructed a foreign policy identity oriented against a communist or Soviet past, which is particularly evident in Poland and the Baltic states (for example Longhurst and Zaborowski 2007; Made 2011), but also against the Yugoslavian past, like in Slovenia and to a lesser extent Croatia (Hansen 1996; Šabič and Brglez 2002; Lindstrom 2003). For several CEE states, Russia is still considered as the other against which national identity is being developed (cf. Ehin and Berg 2009; Made 2011). This also had an important impact on the definition of EU-Russia relations in the 2000s (Leonard and Popescu 2007; DeBardeleben 2008; Kanet 2009; Spruds 2009; Delcour 2011).

It is not possible to mention the many authors who contributed to redefine and suggest initial analyses of foreign policy in CEE states, but a few names are worth citing for some of these countries. In Poland, foreign policy orientations were defined in taking over some of the key ideas developed in the interwar period, like the ones of president General Józef Piłsudski and conservative politician Roman Dmowski, and also relied on the approach designed by Polish intellectuals in exile, like Jerzy Giedroyc, who conceived Polish foreign policy in a way that it could avoid being caught between Germany and Russia (Kuźniar 2008, 2009; Longhurst and Zaborowski 2007; Szczepanik 2011). Multilateralism, thus joining the EU, NATO, and other international organisations, is seen as an opportunity to escape such a situation, and to also work on "good neighbourly relations" with Germany and Russia, as well as with the Eastern neighbours, especially those where Polish minorities are present (Gerhardt 2007: 79; Kuźniar 2008).

In the Czech Republic, humanist ideas expressed during the interwar period, mainly those of the first Czechoslovak president Tomáš Garrigue Masaryk, were taken over again to define the Czech foreign policy of the 1990s (Drulák 2005). Drawing on Václav Havel's ideas, Czech foreign policy discourse mainly focuses on the promotion of human rights and democracy, a trend which was maintained throughout the years despite ongoing debates (cf. Weichsel 2007; Kořan 2007, 2007ff, 2010; Weiss 2011). In Hungary, foreign policy priorities of the 1990s reflected the need to compensate the trauma of the Trianon Treaty of 1920, which deprived Hungary of a large part of its territory and population. All strategies thus highlight the need to join the EU and NATO, alongside the development of an active policy towards Hungarian minorities mainly situated in Romania, Slovakia, Serbia and Ukraine, either through multilateral or bilateral channels (Kiss 2000, 2003; Andor 2000; Rácz 2011).

Romania, which, also declared accession to the EU and NATO as a core foreign policy priority, was active in shaping a policy in the Black Sea region, and in reinforcing its relations with Moldova. The fact that Bessarabia[3] used to belong to Romania in the early twentieth century and that there is strong language proximity, launched passionate debates in the 1990s on the possibility of a unification of Moldova with Romania (Vogel 2002; Gallagher 2005; Angelescu 2011). Slovenia represents an example of a country which first sought a clean break from its past by constructing the Balkan region and ex-Yugoslavia as its foreign policy *other*, then used its foreign policy in this region to be visible in EU and NATO policies (Kajnč 2011; Šabič and Brglez

2002; Šabič and Burkowski 2002). Estonia, like Latvia and Lithuania, represents a good example of an ex-Soviet republic which managed to define a new foreign policy, initially separated from its Soviet past and Russia, and then in accordance with its international engagements (Ehin and Berg 2009; Kesa and Tulmets 2012). While some reflections on sovereignty were taken over from the interwar period, the core priorities of this small nation, which was almost always under foreign rule, were to integrate multilateral cooperation frameworks which would allow it to gain a voice on the European and international stages. The yearbook on Estonian foreign policy, which is edited each year since 2003 by the Estonian Foreign Policy Institute (cf. Kasekamp 1996ff), documents rather well evolutions and reflections on this country's foreign policy priorities.

In the 1990s, CEE states had few opportunities to cooperate on foreign policy issues, as they were often in competition with each other. Some exceptions were the non-institutionalised Visegrád Group created in 1991 and institutional cooperation between the Baltic states, through which minimal coordination allowed the countries to enhance negotiation positions with the EU and NATO (Vykoukal et al. 2003; Kořan 2007; Cadier 2008; Dangerfield 2009; Tulmets 2014: 185ff.). The Visegrád Group, in particular, which was deemed to disappear once its advocacy role would be over, in fact remained after the CEE accession to Western institutions: its core purpose in the field of foreign policy became to support other countries in coming closer to the EU and NATO (Dangerfield 2009; Tulmets 2014: 185ff.). In the context of the 1990s and early 2000s, academic literature thus mainly focused on the adaptation processes which took place in each CEE country to come in line with the EU and NATO requirements.

A focus on Europeanisation and NATO-isation

During the EU and NATO accession processes, a large literature developed on the Europeanisation and NATO-isation of CEE states. In practice, the EU accession process focused on around thirty very detailed and technical chapters, the chapter on foreign policy being in fact dealt with rather quickly and without long negotiations. It mainly consisted of an alignment to EU foreign policy declarations and priorities, and a requirement to participate in EU's development policy. On the EU side, core defence and security issues were considered to have been addressed within the framework of NATO accession, and other issues were negotiated in coordination with other organisations, like the Council of Europe and the Organisation for Security and Co-operation in Europe (OSCE) regarding human rights and minority issues.

Several CEE authors focused in the 1990s and 2000s on changes in their country "on their road to the EU" (e.g. Kasekamp 1996ff; Ágh 1999; Andor 2000; Drulák 2001; Kajnč 2011). Some authors tried to theorise the process and described it as asymmetrical, therefore looking at all forms of legislative and institutional reforms which would be in conformity with the conditions posed by the EU at the political, socio-economic, and security levels (Linden 2002; Schimmelfennig 2003; Jacoby 2004; Schimmelfennig and Sedelmeier 2005). The research agenda was mainly set by the work of Schimmelfennig and Sedelmeier (2005), who applied the extensive literature on Europeanisation (Radaelli 2000; Caporaso, Green-Cowles and Risse 2001; Bulmer and Lequesne 2004/2012) and the IR debate on constructivism versus rationalism to the EU accession process. Studies along these lines therefore focused on the details of chapter negotiations and legislative reforms, thus opting mainly for an institutionalist approach of Europeanisation (Ágh 1999; Andor 2000; Jacoby 2004; Bulmer and Lequesne 2004/2012; Braun 2013; also Dimitrova in this volume).

Regarding NATO, Schimmelfennig (2003) and Jacoby (2004) formed the academic foundation which some scholars used to develop case studies linked to reforms and modernisation of foreign policy and armed forces (cf. Linden 2009). Several authors, however, focused on specific moments where CEE country positions on issues related to NATO activities. These were, for example, the war in Kosovo (1999) and in Iraq (2003), which exemplified the CEE states' will to show commitment towards NATO and sometimes also US foreign policy priorities (for example, Kasekamp 1996ff; Larrabee 2000; Kuźniar 2008, 2009; Kořan 2007ff; Zaborowski and Wojna 2011; also Webber in this volume). For example, the "letter of the eight" of 30 January of 2003 titled "Europe and America Must Stand United", urging UN action against Saddam Hussein, and the letter of the Vilnius group of 5 February 2003, supporting an UN resolution asking Iraq to comply with its disarmament obligations, were signed among others by the Czech, Polish, and Hungarian governments. The latter demonstrated their alignment with the US approach of the war in Iraq, despite German and French opposition to it and intra-EU tensions around the issue (cf. Tulmets 2014: 66, 75). This prompted US Secretary of Defence Donald Rumsfeld to speak of a divided continent, thus of differences between "old Europe" and "new Europe". The recognition of the independence of Kosovo in 2008 is a further divisive issue, as some CEE countries, like Romania and Slovakia, refused to recognise this country (Tulmets 2014: 161ff.).

The Europeanisation and NATO-isation approaches reveal useful to understand the role played by the EU and NATO in shaping some of the new foreign policy priorities of CEEs, like their support to further candidates to EU and NATO, and their will to promote their experience of transition and accession to these organisations (Balfour 2005; Balcer 2010; Tulmets 2014). They are also useful when one looks at the way EU institutions and practices, like participation in EU institutions (Kuus 2011; Ban 2013) and the preparation of EU presidencies (cf. Tulmets 2014), have impacted on the way coordination takes place on foreign policy issues within the EU and NATO. To some extent, these approaches contributed to theorise and legitimise part of the "grey" literature in FPA which accompanied the transition and accession processes led by policy makers. While some of the leading work insisted on the rationalist and constructivist aspects of EU and NATO accession (for example, Schimmelfennig and Sedelmeier 2005; Baun and Marek 2013), others clearly inscribed themselves in line with the constructivist agenda interested in the evolution of foreign policy identity (Hansen 1996; Fawn 2004; Fürst 2008; Drulák and Šabič 2012; Andrespoke and Kasekamp 2012), thus offering a different picture than classical FPA work on states of middle or small size had offered so far.

In fact, the core of the literature on Europeanisation and NATO-isation focused on the short-term approach needed to attest the capacity of candidates to fulfil the Copenhagen criteria, but implementation aspects were very often neglected, although it is at this level that one can judge the countries' capacities to maintain sustainable changes. Work by Epstein and Sedelmeier (2008), Trauner (2009), Braun (2013), and others have shown, indeed, that reforms have not always been sustained in several policy fields. These findings are important, but foreign policy aspects were often barely mentioned, although a similar trend can be observed in this field: while a relative consensus among national political parties existed on foreign policy issues until EU and NATO accessions, this consensus often disappeared after accessions.

While a core aspect of CEE foreign policies remains the will to support further candidates to EU and NATO (Balfour et al. 2005; Bartovic and Král 2010; Zięba 2010; Balcer 2010; Tulmets 2014), foreign policy issues increasingly reveal different worldviews among CEE representatives. Several aspects of foreign policy, maybe the more problematic ones due to a "freezing" of old regional conflicts during the Cold War, were often set aside in academic work focusing on EU and NATO accessions, although they constitute salient issues to take into account in the future developments of CEE foreign policies. For example, the relations towards Russia and positions to adopt regarding conflictual events and frozen conflicts (energy issues, war in Georgia in 2008, in Ukraine in 2014, and Transnistria) often reveal divisive, not only among political parties, but also within political parties and, furthermore, among CEE states. The members of the Visegrád

Group, for example, strongly disagreed over Ukraine in 2014, although differences of views are common, and the objective of the Group is to reach consensus on such complex issues (Dostál 2015). In the context of the war in Syria and the migration crisis, the Visegrád countries have found a common ground again, but their strict positions regarding refugees and the protection of borders have become a divisive issue, this time, at the European level (Dostál 2015). One way to understand these differences thus consists in recasting foreign policy positions in the longer history of relations between CEE nations and Europe, but also between nations and sub-regional integration. Therefore, not only multilateral integration, but also the evolution of bilateral relations to specific strategic partners, like to France and Germany in the European Union, and to the US or Russia in general, remain interesting to explore.

CEE foreign policies: an area in need of further exploration and developments

As CEE countries are sometimes still perceived as a homogeneous bloc in the Western-led academic community, differences between national approaches are often downplayed in the analysis of CEE foreign policies. Difficulties to take decisions in an EU with a growing number of member states is in fact symptomatic and an expression of these various approaches (cf. Král and Pachta 2005). In practice, the foreign policy of Poland, the largest country in CEE, is often considered representative of CEE foreign policy by policy-makers and in EU decision-making processes.

The literature on EU and NATO accessions often neglects the differentiated engagement of CEE states in their commitments towards these communities, and also the different positions taken within the countries in the political, economic, and social levels. While "grey" literature is often prolific on salient topics, the academic literature is largely silent on the common positions and debates regarding events such as participation in the wars in the Western Balkans, Iraq, and Afghanistan, as well as the conflicts in Georgia and in Ukraine both at the national and multilateral levels. Common actions of CEE representatives, like their support to the Orange revolution in Ukraine, their presence in Tbilisi during the negotiation of the ceasefire with Russia, or their engagement in the Ukrainian Maidan movements of 2013–2014, are often better known than, for example, the divisions among political parties and the Czech population regarding the project of the missile defence shield (Hynek and Střítecký 2010) and the "pro-European" Polish reaction after the withdrawal of the US radar project. The redefinition of security approaches, of relations to Russia, as well as national reactions to conflicts like the one in Syria are also issues which will need to be better understood from an academic point of view when exploring the Western engagement with the CEE states, and where knowledge of history can be very useful.

New CEE foreign policy orientations defined towards "the East" and "the rest" of the world are, at the national and regional levels, still not well coordinated and also not documented sufficiently in academic research. Under Polish influence, the CEE countries indeed managed to shape part of EU foreign policy in Eastern Europe, but other countries like Slovenia and Hungary contributed to also put the Western Balkans high on the EU's agenda. In general, all CEE states support further EU accession processes and closer relations with the Eastern countries of the European Neighbourhood Policy (ENP), including the Eastern Partnership (EaP) inaugurated in 2009 (Copsey 2007; DeBardeleben 2008; Dangerfield 2009; contributions in Ehin and Berg 2009, and in Tulmets 2011, 2012; Cadier 2012; contributions in Baun and Marek 2013; also Korosteleva in this volume). Differences in the preferences in bilateral relations and the way the EU policy was influenced are, however, less researched. While it is generally known that some CEE states, like Poland, the Czech Republic, and Lithuania were key in the launching period of the ENP and EaP (Natorski 2008; Copsey and Pomorska 2014), it is still less known which role representatives of these countries exactly played in the negotiations of the association agreements with Ukraine, Moldova, and Georgia; the nature of economic relations with the EaP countries; and the depth of cultural and historical links with these countries. Some of the later aspects, however, started to be tackled through research which was initiated in the field of development policy and the way EU accession impacted on the definition of CEE bilateral and multilateral strategies.

The impact of accession, which required active participation by CEE states in EU development policy and democracy promotion towards other regions like Africa or Asia only recently started to be presented and explained by European and Anglo-Saxon academicians (Lightfoot 2010; Szczepanik 2011; Najšlova 2011; Petrova 2011; Andrespoke and Kasekamp 2012; Timofejevs Henriksson 2013; Lightfoot and Horký-Hlucháň 2013; Lightfoot and Szent-Iványi 2014; Tulmets 2011, 2014). Beside the countries of the Western Balkans and EaP, Central Asia, some African countries with which political and economic relations are inherited from communist times (e.g. Egypt and Zambia), other countries like Vietnam and Myanmar in Asia, and Cuba are among key priority countries of CEE foreign assistance. Despite the increasing number of analyses which focus on CEE current duties in the field of development, there is still some space to explore, for example, the links between past and present activities. There are various ways to do so. Some of the publications mentioned earlier indeed started showing the role played by the communist past in the rediscovery of bilateral relations between former "ideological brothers" in the 1990s and especially 2000s. Others insisted rather on the way the issue of democracy promotion, through the export of a unique transition experience, has become an opportunity for CEE states to find their place in the Western community and to develop an original foreign policy (Petrova 2011; Kesa 2011). The constructivist literature on small states, which mainly developed in the field of FPA (e.g. Šabič and Bukowski 2002), also mentions that the accession of small states to multilateral frameworks, like the EU, NATO, or the UN, reinforced their foreign policy identity. Small CEE states thus became able to promote their own view in these structures (Kuus 2011) and to seize for themselves an international shape (Andrespoke and Kasekamp 2012).

The role of multilateral groups within the EU is also a topic which is still not sufficiently researched or known. Several authors already highlighted the lack of interest from the (Western European) research community for the Visegrád Group or its subsequent evolution, although there were several attempts from other CEE countries, like Slovenia and Romania, to define themselves as Central European states (Šabič and Brglez 2002; Vogel 2002; Kajnč 2011) and to join this attractive coordination framework (cf. Kořan 2007; Cadier 2008; Dangerfield 2009; Tulmets 2013, 2014; see also contributions in the *Visegrád Revue*). Little is also known about the evolution of cooperation between the Baltic states, the exact role of Romania and Bulgaria in the Black Sea region, or CEE positions on the independence of Kosovo (cf. Tulmets 2014). And although the Weimar Triangle (that is, France, Germany, and Poland) was prominent in the framework of mediation processes at the start of the war in Ukraine in March 2014, it is in search of new legitimacy since it was superseded by the Normandy format led by France and Germany in the following months. Many other informal coordination frameworks including CEE states nevertheless contribute to shape EU foreign policy, like the Groups of Friends of Georgia, of Ukraine, of the Eastern Partnership, and so forth which are also important to mention and to maybe study (cf. Fürst 2008; Kesa 2011).

The impact of external events on the foreign policy of CEE states and also on EU Common Foreign and Security Policy (CFSP) and Common Security and Defence Policy (CSDP) is interesting to take into account (Neuhold and Sucharipa 2003; Fürst 2008; Hill and Wong 2011), also in terms of new orientations regarding security and defence policies (Cadier 2008; Baun and Marek 2013). In the context of recent events, they tend to be tackled by authors producing policy advice and "grey" literature, while more theoretical explanations of these developments are missing. The wars in Georgia and Ukraine, but also gas crises, are in fact important periods to consider in the evolution of the EU's foreign policy and especially CEE security strategies. One needs to observe how events will develop in the future to identify longer explanatory trajectories beyond differential discourses and actions of successive CEE governments represented by different political parties or coalitions.

One notices that the war in Georgia prompted some CEE states, like Poland and the Czech Republic, to define new foreign policy strategies as well as to again prioritise their security and defence policies, beyond the aims to be more active in, and find ways for better dialogue between EU and NATO – as finally enshrined in the NATO summit declaration of Warsaw of 8–9 July 2016. The war in Ukraine even contributed to a reconfiguration of coalitions among CEE countries, with the Visegrád Group partly losing coherence and Poland coming much closer to the Baltic states in its critical assessment of the situation and its relations to Russia (Fuksiewicz and Łada 2015). It also prompted CEE states to ask for reassurance regarding NATO and the US concerning their territorial security and, as such, reveals the existence of different perceptions of threats and security conceptions among NATO members (Dostál 2015). Cooperation in the Visegrád format nevertheless reinforced again in the context of the migration crisis of summer 2015. All of these developments therefore open new avenues for research on CEE foreign policies, and require analysis of twenty-five years of activity. This necessitates to adapt FPA tools developed so far for "Western" countries or at least to consider the role of the CEE past in a different way than for nation states which can rely on longer foreign policy traditions (Baun and Marek 2013; Tulmets 2011, 2014). In this context, it is for example particularly useful to link these research fields with IR traditions highlighting the role of culture, history, and identity in foreign policy and world politics (Katzenstein 1996; Hansen 1996; Hudson 1997; Prizel 1998; Drulák 2001; Kiss 2003; Ehin and Berg 2009; Tulmets 2014).

Conclusion

After the fall of the Berlin Wall in 1989 and of the Soviet Union in 1991, the CEEs focused on their "return to Europe", thus to "the West", while relegating their relations to the East as belonging to the past. Once their EU and NATO integrations were accepted, they started defining new foreign policy priorities and mainly oriented them towards the "East", thus post-communist or still communist countries. Given their engagement in international structures, they also defined approaches for "the rest" of the world, focusing on key countries and regions for the EU and NATO (such as Afghanistan and the Middle-East) and including other regions like Asia and Africa in their foreign development strategies.

Despite these changes, comparative academic work remained rather scarce and there is a growing need to better conceptualise CEE foreign policies. Interestingly, one has seen for several years the publication of yearbooks which is a sign of this will to list priorities, but also, over time, to have a more analytical approach of CEE foreign policies (e.g. Kasekamp 1996ff; Zaborowski and Wojna 2011; Kořan 2007ff). There is therefore some space for the development of comparative research in this field, which necessitates crossing different approaches and insights coming from FPA, IR, European Studies, but also history and area studies. This way, one may hope for a normalisation of the analysis of CEE foreign policies, maybe along other analytical lines which would show that there is no "old" and "new" Europe, but rather foreign policy positions and networks which evolve less through an East/West than a North/South divide, and more according to the issues studied.

Notes

1 I would like to thank the editors of the book and a lector for their excellent comments and edition suggestions. I also thank the IIR in Prague and Palgrave MacMillan for allowing me to draw on some ideas and sentences from Tulmets (2012, 2014).
2 "Grey" literature generally refers to publications coming from outside traditional academic channels. It includes government reports, white papers, as well as think tank and civil society organisation analyses and studies.
3 According to the *Encyclopaedia Britannica*, Bessarabia is a

"region in eastern Europe that passed successively, from the 15th to 20th century, to Moldovia, the Ottoman Empire, Russia, Romania, the Soviet Union, and Ukraine and Moldova. It is bounded by the Prut River on the west, the Dniester River on the north and east, the Black Sea on the southeast, and the Chilia arm of the Danube River delta on the south". (www.britannica.com/place/Bessarabia, accessed 30 August 2016)

References

Ágh, Attila (1999) "Europeanisation of Policy-Making in East Central Europe: The Hungarian Approach to EU Accession", *Journal of European Public Policy*, 6 (5): 839–854.

Allison, Graham T. (1971) *Essence of Decision. Explaining the Cuban Missile Crisis*, Boston: Little, Brown.

Andor, László (2000) *Hungary on the Road to the European Union: Transition in Blue*, Westport: Praeger.

Andrespoke, Evelin and Kasekamp, Andres (2012) "Development Cooperation of the Baltic States: A Comparison of the Trajectories of Three New Donor Countries", *Perspectives on European Politics and Society*, 13 (1): 117–130.

Angelescu, Irina (2011) "New Eastern Perspectives? A Critical Analysis of Romania's Relations with Moldova, Ukraine and the Black Sea Region", *Perspectives*, 19 (2): 123–142, www.perspectives.cz/upload/Perspectives/2011/Perspectives02_11.pdf

Balcer, Adam (ed.) (2010) *Poland and the Czech Republic: Advocates of the EU Enlargement?*, Warsaw: Demos Europa.

Balfour, Rosa et al. (2005) "One Year On. The Foreign Policy of the Enlarged EU. An Overview of the New Member States' Contribution to European Foreign Policy", *CeSPI Working Paper*, 21. www.cespi.it/WP/WP21%20Balfour.pdf

Ban, Carolyn (2013) *Management and Culture in an Enlarged European Commission: From Diversity to Unity?*, Basingstoke: Palgrave MacMillan.

Bartovic, Vladimír and Král, David (2010) "The Czech Republic and the EU Enlargement: Supportive but not Enough?", in Balcer Adam (ed.) *Poland and the Czech Republic: Advocates of the EU Enlargement?*, Warsaw: Demos Europa, 36–56.

Batt, Judy (2007) "Introduction: Defining Central and Eastern Europe", in White Stephen, Batt Judy and Lewis Paul G. (eds.) *Developments in Central and East European Politics 4*, Houndmills, Basingstoke: Palgrave Macmillan, 1–19.

Baun, Michael and Marek, Dan (eds.) (2013) *The New Member States and the European Union: Foreign Policy and Europeanization*, London: Routledge (Routledge Advances in European Politics).

Braun, Mats (2013) *Europeanisation of Environmental Policy in the New Europe: Beyond Conditionality*, Surrey/Burlington: Ashgate.

Bulmer, Simon J. and Lequesne, Christian (eds.) (2004, 2012) *Member States and the European Union*, Oxford: Oxford University Press.

Cadier, David (2008) "CFSP and Central European Strategic Cultures: The Visegrád Countries and the Georgian Crisis", *EU-Consent Paper*, Brussels, February.

Cadier, David (2012) "Après le retour à l'Europe: la politique étrangère des pays d'Europe centrale" [After the Return to Europe: The Foreign Policy of the Countries of Central Europe], *Politique étrangère*, 3: 573–584.

Caporaso, James, Green-Cowles, Maria and Risse, Thomas (eds.) (2001) *Transforming Europe: Europeanisation and Domestic Change*, Ithaca, NY: Cornell University Press.

Copsey, Nathaniel (2007) "The Member States and the European Neighbourhood Policy", *European Research Working Paper Series*, 20, Birmingham: European Research Institute.

Copsey, Nathaniel and Pomorska, Karolina (2014) "The Influence of Newer Member States in the European Union: The Case of Poland and the Eastern Partnership", *Europe-Asia Studies*, 66 (3): 421–443.

Dangerfield, Martin (2009) "The Contribution of the Visegrád Group to the European Union's 'Eastern' Policy: Rhetoric or Reality?", *Europe-Asia Studies*, 61 (10): 1735–1755.

DeBardeleben, Joan (ed.) (2008) *The Boundaries of EU Enlargement: Defining a Place for Neighbours*, Houndmills: Palgrave.

Delcour, Laure (2011) *Shaping the Post-Soviet Space? EU Policies and Approaches to Region-Building*, Aldershot: Ashgate.

Dostál, Vít (2015) *Trends of Visegrád Foreign Policy*, Prague: Association for International Affairs.

Drulák, Petr (ed.) (2001) *National and European Identities in EU Enlargements. Views From Central and Eastern Europe*, Prague: Institute of International Relations.

Drulák, Petr (2005), "Probably a Regime, Perhaps a Union: European Integration in the Czech and Slovak Political Discourse", in Sjursen, Helene (ed.) *Enlargement in Perspective*, Oslo: ARENA Report No 2/05, 209–246.

Drulák, Petr and Šabič, Zlatko (eds.) (2012) *Regional and International Relations of Central Europe*, Basingstoke: Palgrave Macmillan.

Ehin, Piret and Berg, Eiki (eds.) (2009) *Identity and Foreign Policy: Baltic-Russian Relations and European Integration*, Burlington: Ashgate.

Epstein, Rachel and Sedelmeier, Ulrich (2008) "Beyond Conditionality: International Institutions in Post-communist Europe After Accession", *Journal of European Public Policy*, 15 (6): 795–805.

Fawn, Rick (2003) "Ideology and National Identity in Post-Communist Foreign Policies", *Communist Studies and Transition Politics*, 19 (3), special issue.

Fawn, Rick (2004) *Ideology and National Identity in Post-Communist Foreign Policies*, London and Portland: Frank Cass.

Fuksiewicz, Aleksander and Łada, Agnieszka (2015) *Baltic Group. Poland, Lithuania, Latvia and Estonia in Search of Common Interests*, Warsaw: Institute of Public Affairs.

Fürst, Heiko (2008) *Europäische Außenpolitik zwischen Nation und Union. Die Konstruktion des polnischen, rumänischen und ungarischen Diskurses zur GASP* [European Foreign Policy Between Nation and Union. The Construction of Polish, Romanian and Hungarian Discourse on CFSP], Baden-Baden: Nomos.

Gallagher, Tom (2005) *Theft of a Nation: Romania Since Communism*, London: Hurst.

Gerhardt, Sebastian (2007) *Polska Polityka Wschodnia. Die Außenpolitik der polnischen Regierung von 1989 bis 2004 gegenüber den östlichen Nachbarstaaten Polens (Russland, Litauen, Weißrussland, Ukraine)* [Polish Eastern Policy: The Foreign Policy of the Polish Government Towards Poland's Eastern Neighbour Countries (Russia, Lithuania, Belarus, Ukraine) from 1989 to 2004], Marburg: Herder Institut.

Hansen, Lene (1996) "Slovenian Identity: States-Building on the Balkan Border", *Alternatives* 21 (4): 473–496.

Hill, Christopher and Wong, Reuben (eds.) (2011) *National and European Foreign Policy: Towards Europeanisation*, London: Routledge.

Hudson, Valerie (1997) *Culture and Foreign Policy*, Boulder, CO: Lynne Rienner.

Hynek, Nik and Střítecký, Vít (2010) "The Fortunes of the Czech Discourse on the Missile Defense", in Drulák Petr and Braun Mats (eds.) *The Quest for the National Interest: A Methodological Reflection on Czech Foreign Policy*, Frankfurt/Main: Peter Lang, 87–103.

Jacoby, Wade (2004) *The Enlargement of the EU and NATO: Ordering From the Menu in Central Europe*, Cambridge: Cambridge University Press.

Kajnč, Sabina (2011) "Slovenia. Searching for a Foreign Policy Identity via the EU", in Hill Christopher and Wong Reuben (eds.) *National and European Foreign Policy: Towards Europeanization*. London: Routledge, 189–209.

Kanet, Roger E. (ed.) (1983) "Eastern Europe and the Third World: The Expanding Relationship", in Sodaro Michael J., Wolchik Sharon L. (eds.) *Foreign and Domestic Policy in Eastern Europe in the 1980s: Trends and Prospects*, New York: St Martin's Press, 234–259.

Kanet, Roger E. (ed.) (2009) *A Resurgent Russia and the West: The European Union, NATO and Beyond*, Dordrecht: Republic of Letters.

Kasekamp, Andres (ed.) (1996ff) *The Estonian Foreign Policy Yearbook 2003*, Tallinn: The Estonian Foreign Policy Institute (yearly edition from 1996 until 2015)

Katzenstein, Peter J. (ed.) (1996) *The Culture of National Security: Norms and Identity in World Politics*, New York: Columbia University Press.

Kesa, Katerina (2011) "Latvian and Lithuanian Policy in the Eastern Neighbourhood: Between Solidarity and Self Promotion", *Perspectives*, 19 (2): 81–100, www.perspectives.cz/upload/Perspectives/2011/Perspectives02_11.pdf

Keša, Katerina and Tulmets, Elsa (2012) "Les Etats baltes et le voisinage oriental de l'Union européenne. Une solidarité renouvelée?" [The Baltic States and the Eastern Neighbourhood of the European Union. A Renewed Solidarity?], in Bayou Céline, Chillaud Matthieu (eds.) *Les Etats baltes en transition. Le retour à l'Europe* [The Baltic States in Transition. Back to Europe], Brussels: Peter Lang, 221–238.

Kiss, László (2000) "Nation and Integration at the Turn of Millennium: Duality of Hungary's Foreign Policy", *Foreign Policy Review*, 6: 82–102.

Kiss, László (2003) "Foreign Policy and National Identity in East-Central Europe", *Foreign Policy Review*, 2 (1): 115–130.

Kořan, Michal (2007) "Domestic Politics in Czech Foreign Policy: Between Consensus and Clash", *International Issues & Slovak Foreign Policy Affairs*, XVI (2): 23–45.

Kořan, Michal (2007ff) *Česká zahraniční politika v roce 2007* [Czech Foreign Policy in 2007], Prague: Institute of International Relations (yearly editions from 2007 until 2013)

Kořan, Michal et al. (eds.) (2010) *Czech Foreign Policy in 2007–2009: Analysis*, Prague: Institute of International Relations.

Král, David and Pachta, Lukáš (2005) *Enlarged European Union and Its Foreign Policy: Issues, Challenges, Perspectives*, Prague: Europeum, Institute for European Policy.

Kuus, Marje (2011) "Whose Regional Expertise? Political Geographies of Knowledge in the European Union", *European Urban and Regional Studies*, 25 May. doi:10.1177/0969776411406034

Kuźniar, Roman (2008) "Poland at the Time of Global Turbulence", *The Polish Quarterly of International Affairs*, 17 (4): 25–40.

Kuźniar, Roman (2009) *Polish Foreign Policy After 1989*, Warsaw: Wydawnictwo naukowe.

Larrabee, Stephen (2000) "The Kosovo Conflict and the Central European Members of NATO: Lessons and Implications", *Foreign Policy Review*, special issue: 24–30.

Leonard, Mark and Popescu, Nicu (2007) *A Power Audit of EU-Russian Relations*, London: European Council on Foreign Relations.

Lightfoot, Simon (2010) "The Europeanisation of International Development Policies: The Case of Central and Eastern European States", *Europe-Asia Studies*, 62 (2): 329–350.

Lightfoot, Simon and Horký-Hlucháň, Ondřej (eds.) (2013) *Development Policies of Central and Eastern European States*, London: Routledge.

Lightfoot, Simon and Szent-Iványi, Balázs (2014) "Reluctant Donors? The Europeanization of International Development Policies in the New Member States", *Journal of Common Market Studies*, 52 (6): 1257–1272.

Linden, Ronald H. (ed.) (2002) *Norms and Nannies: The Impact of International Organisations on the Central and East European States*, Lanham, MD: Rowman & Littlefield.

Linden, Ronald H. (2009) "The Burden of Belonging: Romanian and Bulgarian Foreign Policy in the New Era", *Journal of Balkan and Near Eastern Studies*, 11 (3), September: 269–291.

Lindstrom, Nicole (2003) "Between Europe and the Balkans: Mapping Slovenia and Croatia's 'Return to Europe' in the 1990s", *Dialectical Anthropology*, 27 (3–4): 313–329.

Longhurst, Kerry and Zaborowski, Marcin (2007) *A New Atlanticist: Poland's Foreign and Security Policy Priorities*, Oxford: Blackwell/Chatham House.

Made, Vahur (2011) "Shining in Brussels? The Eastern Partnership in Estonian Foreign Policy", *Perspectives*, 19 (2): 62–83.

Marès, Antoine (ed.) (2001) *Les politiques étrangères des Etats satellites de l'URSS, 1945–1989* [The Foreign Policies of the USSR Satellite States, 1945–1989], Prague: CEFRES.

Marès, Antoine (ed.) (2007) *Culture et politique étrangère des démocraties populaires* [Culture and Foreign Policy of People's Democracies], Paris: Institut des études slaves.

Najšlova, Lucia (2011) "Slovakia in the East: Pragmatic Follower, Occasional Leader", *Perspectives*, 19 (2): 101–122.

Natorski, Michał (2008) "National Concerns in the EU Neighbourhood: Spanish and Polish Policies on the Southern and Eastern Dimensions", in Delcour Laure, Tulmets Elsa (eds.) *Pioneer Europe? Testing EU Foreign Policy in the Neighbourhood*, Baden-Baden: Nomos, 57–75.

Neuhold, Hans-Peter and Sucharipa, Ernst (eds.) (2003) *The CFSP/ESDP After Enlargement: A Bigger EU = A Stronger EU*, Vienna: Diplomatische Akademie.

Petrova, Tsveta (2011) "The New Role of Central and Eastern Europe in International Democracy Support", *The Carnegie Papers*, June, http://carnegieendowment.org/files/east_eur_democracy.pdf

Prizel, Ilya (1998) *The National Identity and Foreign Policy. Nationalism and Leadership in Poland, Russia and Ukraine*, Cambridge: Cambridge University Press.

Rácz, Andras (2011) "A Limited Priority: Hungary and the Eastern Neighbourhood", *Perspectives*, 19 (2): 143–164.

Radaelli, Claudio (2000) "Whither Europeanisation? Concept Stretching and Substantive Change", *European Integration online Papers* (EIoP), 4 (8). http://eiop.or.at/eiop/texte/2000-008a.htm

Šabič, Zlatko and Brglez, Milan (2002) "The National Identity of Post-Communist Small States in the Process of Accession to the European Union. The Case of Slovenia", *Communist and Post-Communist Studies*, 35 (1): 67–84.

Šabič, Zlatko and Bukowski, Charles (eds.) (2002) *Small States in the Post-Cold War World. Slovenia and NATO Enlargement*, Westport and London: Praeger.

Schimmelfennig, Frank (2003) *The EU, NATO and the Integration of Europe: Rules and Rhetoric*, Cambridge: Cambridge University Press.

Schimmelfennig, Frank and Sedelmeier, Ulrich (2005) *The Europeanisation of Central and Eastern Europe*, Ithaca, NY and London: Cornell University Press.

Sodaro, Michael J. and Wolchik, Sharon L. (eds.) (1983) *Foreign and Domestic Policy in Eastern Europe in the 1980s. Trends and Prospects*, New York: St. Martin's Press.

Spruds, Andris (2009) "Entrapment in the Discourse of Danger? Latvian-Russian Interaction in the Context of European Integration", in Ehin Piret and Berg Eiki (eds.) *Identity and Foreign Policy: Baltic-Russian Relations and European Integration*, Burlington, VT: Ashgate, 101–116.

Szczepanik, Melchior (2011) "Between a Romantic 'Mission in the East' and Minimalism: Polish Policy Towards the Eastern Neighbourhood", *Perspectives*, 19 (2): 45–66, www.perspectives.cz/upload/Perspectives/2011/Perspectives02_11.pdf

Timofejevs Henriksson, Péteris (2013) *The Europeanisation of Foreign Aid Policy: Slovenia and Latvia 1998–2010*, Umeå: Umeå Universitet.

Trauner, Florian (2009) "Post-accession compliance with EU law in Bulgaria and Romania: A Comparative Perspective", *European Integration online Papers (EIoP)*, 13 (Special Issue 2). http://eiop.or.at/eiop/pdf/2009-021.pdf

Tulmets, Elsa (2009) "Les 'nouveaux' Etats membres et la politique européenne de voisinage" ['New' Member States and the European Neighbourhood Policy], *Annuaire français de relations internationales*, X: 595–612.

Tulmets, Elsa (ed.) (2011) "Identity and Solidarity in Foreign Policy: Investigating East Central European Relations with the Eastern Neighbourhood", *Perspectives*, 19 (2): 5–26.

Tulmets, Elsa (ed.) (2012) *Identities and Solidarity in Foreign Policy: East Central Europe and the Eastern Neighbourhood*, Prague: Institute of International Relations.

Tulmets, Elsa (2013) "Is Weimar Plus a Copy of the Visegrád Plus?", *Visegrad Revue*, 16 April. http://visegradrevue.eu/is-weimar-plus-a-copy-of-the-visegrad-plus/

Tulmets, Elsa (2014) *East Central European Foreign Policy Identity in Perspective: Back to Europe and to EU's Neighbourhood*, Basingstoke and New York: Palgrave Macmillan.

Vogel, Sándor (2002) "The Euro-Atlantic Integration and Romania's Central-Europe-Concept", *Foreign Policy Review*, 1: 193–207.

Vykoukal, Jiří et al. (eds.) (2003) *Visegrád, možnosti a meze středoevropské spolupráce* [Visegrád, possibilities and limits of Central European cooperation], Prague: Dokořan.

Weichsel, Volker (2007) *Tschechien in Europa. Nationalpolitische Traditionen und integrationspolitische Konzepte* [The Czech Republic in Europe. National-Political Traditions and Political Integration Concepts], Berlin: LIT Verlag.

Weiss, Tomáš (2011) "Projecting the Re-Discovered: Czech Policy Towards Eastern Europe", *Perspectives*, 19 (2): 27–44, www.perspectives.cz/upload/Perspectives/2011/Perspectives02_11.pdf

Zaborowski, Marcin and Wojna, Beata (eds.) (2011) *Yearbook of Polish Foreign Policy (2005–2010)*, Warsaw: Polish Institute of International Affairs. www.pism.pl/publications/journals/Yearbook

Zając, Justyna and Zięba, Ryszard (2010) *Polska w stosunkach międzynarodowych 1945–1989* [Poland in International Relations 1945–1989], Warsaw: Wydawnictwa Akademicjie i Profesjonalne.

Zięba, Ryszard (2010) *Głównie kierunki polityki zagranicznej Polski po zimnej wojnie* [The Milestones of Polish Foreign Policy After the Cold War], Warsaw: Wydawnictwa Akademicjie i Profesjonalne.

23

COMBATTING CORRUPTION

Tatiana Kostadinova and Maria Spirova

Corruption in post-communist Europe has been a common topic in both popular and academic literature. Scandals about politicians taking kick-backs and bribes, appointing party loyalists, business connections, or friends to important positions in the state administration, and buying and controlling votes have brought governments out of power, caused concern in Brussels, and lowered public trust in democratic politics throughout the region. The academic literature on corruption, and combatting corruption specifically, naturally reflects the development of this process. As corruption came to be seen as a ubiquitous phenomenon taking various forms in post-communist Europe, attempts at explaining it focused mostly on the legacy of the previous regimes (Sajó 1998; Karklins 2002, 2005; Holmes 2006). Further variation in the practice of corruption and criticisms of the overzealous theorising linking current levels of malfeasance to the nature of the old regimes (Sajó 1998, 37–38) ushered in a plethora of new, more specific arguments. They emphasise the role of democratic institutional reform, liberalisation and privati-sation, party competition, EU accession, and new political actors in curbing and preventing cor-ruption. More recently, scholars turned their attention to the possible consequences of the abuse of public office in Eastern Europe for political culture and participation (Kolarska-Bobinska 2002; Anderson and Tverdova 2003; Tavits 2008; Kostadinova 2009).

This chapter will present the main arguments in the literature on combatting corruption as it developed through these stages, its findings and conclusions, as well as the methodological challenges faced by those researching corruption. It begins with a review of the more concep-tual and descriptive literature on the extent and type of corruption in post-communist Europe and then moves on to introduce the major hopefuls of combatting corruption with attention to specific arguments and approaches. The chapter concludes by outlining the major lessons from the literature and a potential research agenda. The main argument of this piece is that despite significant achievements, research on combatting corruption in Eastern Europe is often driven by the anti-corruption policy agenda and remains limited by data quality and availability.

It should be noted, however, that in addition to the academic literature, numerous interna-tional bodies such as Transparency International (TI), the World Bank (WB) and the European Union (EU) have taken on a major role in defining the study of corruption in the region. They have commissioned a variety of reports on its nature, causes, and consequences and engaged scholars in their anti-corruption efforts (Kaufmann et al. 1999; World Bank 2000; Mungiu-Pippidi et al. 2013). While complete separation of these two strands of the literature is impossible given the use of TI and WB indicators and measures in a large part of the literature, the present focus will remain on academic approaches to the study of corruption and the ways to curb it in post-communist Europe.

The ubiquitous nature of corruption

That post-communist states are arenas for diverse and extensive corrupt exchanges, and that their omnipresence is an accepted reality of political life, has become a truism in academic and policy research on corruption (Holmes 2013, 1163). A series of books and articles have outlined the pervasive nature of political corruption, while attempting to define its features and mechanisms. A lot has been achieved, yet deficiencies in the general literature on the topic challenge the research effort and continue to present scholars with certain methodological challenges.

The definition of political corruption continues to trouble political theorists and practitioners, almost as much as its practice troubles international and national political organisations. Probably the most commonly used understanding of corruption is the one also applied by the biggest anti-corruption advocacy organisation, Transparency International – "the misuse of public office for private gain" – but what exactly *office* and *gain* may mean remains subject to various interpretations (Kostadinova 2012, 6–7; Philp 2015, 20–22). While such a definition clearly includes the act of taking bribes in exchange for public decisions and is quite appropriate for comparative research, it might leave other forms of corrupt exchange out. Therefore, some researchers prefer to use more specific definitions relevant to the research question addressed in a particular study. For example, studying state capture in Hungary, Fazekas and Tóth (2016) specify grand corruption as "the allocation and performance of public procurement contracts by bending prior explicit rules."

For Eastern Europe, corruption has been well documented by a plethora of works and reports (e.g. Holmes 2006, 109–111; Kostadinova 2012, 29; Mungiu-Pippidi et al. 2013, 14–15), but popular and academic accounts of post-1989 politics also point to phenomena such as party patronage and clientelism as widespread practices across the region. Further, academic research has shown a high proclivity of political parties to engage in appointing party candidates to various administrative positions and to the jobs in public companies (e.g. Gwiazda 2008; Kopecký and Spirova 2011a; Xhaferaj 2013; Dragojević and Konitzer 2013; Volintiru 2015; also Meyer-Sahling in this volume), significant levels of party politicization of ministerial bureaucracies (e.g. Meyer-Sahling 2008; Dimitrov, Goetz and Wollmann 2006), and a general trend towards the use and misuse of the state and its resources for partisan purposes (e.g. Kopecký 2006; O'Dwyer 2006; Grzymała-Busse 2007). Understanding and identifying ways to combat corruption must thus also consult works that incorporate a wider conception of corrupt exchange and its determinants.

Overall, conceptual and operational definitions of corruption may vary across the actors involved and the forms it takes (Neshkova and Rosenbaum 2015, 99). Given the importance of phenomena such as patronage, influence peddling, clientelism, and institutional capture in the region, much of the influential scholarship in the field includes them as corrupt activities, without applying a broader definition as a starting point (Karklins 2005; Holmes 2006). This review will incorporate a similar approach; it will cover both the literature that deals specifically with corruption (however defined) and the literature that deals with notions such as patronage (political appointments in the state apparatus) and clientelism (the exchange of monetary and non-monetary rewards for electoral benefits such as votes). We believe that this choice is justified because these phenomena are often conceptually and empirically overlapping, and because they all have been extremely relevant to the political development of Eastern Europe.

The legacy of communism

One trend throughout the early literature has to do with the inevitable nature of corruption in post-communist Europe. It was assumed that links to the previous one-party regime in terms of inherited structures of interaction and citizen-state relationships, make people consider corruption inevitable and continue to engage in bribe-giving as part of everyday life. This literature focuses on describing the different types of corruption that seemed rampant in the region and on identifying their roots. Most influential in this regard is probably Rasma Karklins's work that develops a typology of post-communist corruption (Karklins 2002, 2005). In her book *The System Made Me Do It* (2005, 25), she differentiates several types of corruption: everyday interactions between officials and citizens (e.g. bribery); interactions between public institutions (e.g. profiteering from privatisation or public procurement); and influence on political institutions (e.g. state capture and buying votes). Her detailed description and illustrations clearly link current rates of malfeasance with features inherited from the previous regimes, a politicised and all-powerful bureaucracy, and uncontested political elite.

In a similar vein, Holmes (2006) defines and describes corruption as omnipresent in Eastern Europe and attributes some of its persistence to the legacy of the communist regimes. In terms of both political culture and path dependent institutional developments, the post-communist world, in his view, emerges as particularly prone to sustain corruption. The hierarchical nature of the regimes, the blurred borders between state and party and private and public, the development logic of the state, and the absence of any alternatives to power are among the strongest legacies of the communist era that potentially lead to a "rotten state" (Holmes 2006, 179–187). A similar line of thought is followed by Kostadinova in her discussion of the sources of corruption in post-communist Europe, although then she moves on to identify more significant explanations in the current institutional and political context (Kostadinova 2012, 26–28). Focusing on party patronage, a path dependency pattern is observed by Kopecký and Spirova, who link the nature of the communist regimes – patrimonial in Bulgaria and bureaucratic in Czechoslovakia – to the extent and nature of post-1989 party patronage (Kopecký and Spirova 2011b, 900–904).

Such arguments, of course, made corruption an almost self-fulfilling prophecy in the new democracies of Eastern Europe, but do not reveal much about the causal mechanisms leading to corruption. The transition from communism to democracy opened up these political systems to myriad new factors and influences with a potential to also affect the likelihood of political elites and the public to engage in corrupt behaviour.

The promise of institutional reform

Institutions and legislation supporting integrity and the rule of law were among the first weapons chosen in the struggle against corruption (Lederman et al. 2005). The post-communist countries implemented numerous institutional reforms in the late 1990s and the early 2000s in order to reduce corruption, partly driven by domestic forces and partly by the need to comply with EU and other international requirements. After the start of the democratic transition, various legislative acts were passed to provide for more transparency and integrity in public life (Batory 2012, 66–68; Holmes 2006, 223–229). Legal codes were adapted to penalise activities such as conflict of interest and bribery, and to improve financial supervision and regulate party finance and public procurement (Ikstens et al. 2002, Grzymała-Busse 2007, Kostadinova 2012, 169–173). New civil service legislation set professionalisation and political autonomy as core principles in the reform of the East European bureaucracies (Nunberg 1999, Neshkova and Kostadinova 2012;

also Meyer-Sahling in this volume); state subsidies were provided for political parties in most states of the region (Casal Bertoa and Spirova, forthcoming). In fact, as Karklins argues "by late 2003 many states in the region had adopted most of the recommended anti-corruption laws and institutions" (Karklins 2005, 125).

Despite the intense legislating and establishment of various anti-corruption bodies, evidence for institutional effectiveness in the fight against corruption remains scarce. In their study on post-1989 administrative reform, Neshkova and Kostadinova (2012) confirm that the very adoption of a civil service act affects the opportunity structure of party patronage and hence, reduces corruption in the political system. Yet, many scholars conclude that the existence of relevant legislation "appears to have had little effect," as Karklins (2005, 125–145) puts it. She provides a rich and multifaceted discussion of accountability and the different degrees to which it had been instituted in ten post-communist states, to just conclude that the ultimate challenge everywhere was implementation and not absence of strict provisions (Karklins 2005, 125–145). In a similar vein, Batory argues that despite a coherent set of anti-bribery laws in Hungary, "citizens have a multitude of reasons not to comply with anti-graft laws, and relatively few do comply, on either instrumental or normative grounds" (Batory 2012, 78).

The big question for practitioners and scholars is whether the reason for the lack of a satisfactory effect of the numerous structures created in the name of reducing corruption is in their design or in the level of compliance by politicians, bureaucrats, and ordinary people. Looking at a larger number of countries, Bugaric maintains that the institutions of the rule of law remain simply underdeveloped and non-institutionalised, partly because the institutional process ignored local culture, norms and traditions, and copied Western traditions instead (Bugaric 2015). Further, researchers who assess the role of party finance regulation warn that insufficient enforcement of the requirements for disclosure is the biggest problem for the failure to increase transparency (van Biezen and Kopecký 2001, Walecki 2005). The common conclusion of these studies points to the need of developing context-relevant institutions supported by strong and empowered social and political actors, if corruption is to be curbed for good.

The promise of liberalisation

The introduction of the free market in Eastern Europe was another reform that gave hope in fighting corruption. As the previous state monopoly over politics and the economy was seen as the main culprit for cementing corruption in the new democratic systems, liberalisation and privatisation were expected to generate new incentives and subject corruption to the control of competition. That this was not going to work out became evident rather quickly, as the challenges of the triple political/economic/social transition emerged.

New economic practices co-existing with old habits at a time when political structures were fragile and legal frameworks in flux, opened up new spaces for corrupt exchange (Holmes 2006, 187–191; Schmidt 2007, 210–212; Jordan 2002, 20). Mafia-like criminal networks emerged in several post-communist countries, most notably Russia, and engaged in high-level corruption (Glinkina 1998; Ledeneva 1998; Volkov 2002; Varese 1997). Similar but less intense trends were also observed in Bulgaria, where shady economic interests took over state structures and "predatory" elites weakened the capacity of the state to resist malfeasance (Ganev 2007, 178–180, Kostadinova 2012, 97–106). As market economies developed and institutionalised, so did suspicious links between business and politics. The simpler models of bribery and embezzlement of the 1990s were transformed into more structured clientelistic networks that maintained a stable system of corrupt exchanges in many post-communist states (Kostadinova 2012, 95–125; Jordan 2002; Engler 2016).

The literature on the interplay between market economy and political corruption of various forms remains somewhat limited in terms of comparative span, while rich in detailed discussion of single cases. Exactly because of the nature of the relationship between economic groups and political elites, one that requires an intimate knowledge of who does what, when, and how during a covert exchange, research is often limited to single case studies. While there are enough studies on some states, we lack a good understanding of how the same process evolved in other places. This trend has been partially countered by research in the area of petty corruption. For example, recent scholarship analyses the impact of market competition on bribe-paying from a comparative perspective in Eastern Europe. Using survey data from fifteen post-communist states, Diaby and Sylwester (2015) conclude that greater market competition among firms is associated with greater bribe payments, a conclusion also supported partially by Duvanova (2014). Overall, this lacuna, arguably identifiable in most research on corruption, still remains urgent to fill, especially with regards to the role of both domestic and international economic liberalisation.

The promise of political competition

Competition of a different kind – within the party system – is, arguably, an important mechanism of control over corruption, because political parties are often the main loci of corrupt exchanges. This argument, popular in the general literature on political corruption, has certainly reverberated in the post-communist scholarship as well. Competition is supposed to limit political corruption in two ways. First, competitive elections motivate political parties to refrain from engagement in improper activities, fearing that voters may punish such behaviour at the ballot box, and second political parties may also "keep each other in check," thus lowering the overall levels of political corruption (Della Porta 2004; Johnston 2002).

With regard to post-communist politics, the impact of party competition on reducing corruption has been examined, qualified, and challenged on several – theoretical and empirical – grounds. Grzymała-Busse (2007) sees strong, "robust" party competition as a major constraint on corruption. Based on empirical evidence from nine Eastern European countries, she specifies that none but only a well-organised and effective opposition can discourage party elites inclined to engage in corrupt exchanges. Analysing the Bulgarian case, however, Krastev and Ganev (2004) argue that the political urgency of anti-corruption may have counterproductive results, as allegations of systemic office abuse can be used for unfair political competition by political opponents. They maintain that this was the case during the 2001 electoral competition between incumbents and newcomers in Bulgaria, in line with what Smilov has argued might be case in Eastern Europe overall (Smilov 2007).

It is the unstable nature of the young party systems in Eastern Europe that have made researchers quite sceptical. Their central argument is that the potential of political competition to curb corruption is conditioned by the degree to which such competition is "stable" or "institutionalised" (Johnston 2002; O'Dwyer 2004, 2006). This has been evident throughout the region, as Grzymała-Busse's (2007) analysis on the temptation of elites to exploit the post-1989 state and other scholarship show. In party systems that are constantly in flux, with parties disappearing and new parties arising before every election, the disciplining function of elections declines, and political parties attempt to maximize their short-term benefits by engaging in corruption while in power. Moreover, such "under-institutionalized" or "unstable" party systems are also characterised by a high degree of fragmentation, which renders effective competition between political parties more difficult due to coordination costs. Hence, party systems in which the opposition is fragmented, consisting of a multitude of political formations, coordinated and effective contestation vis-à-vis the incumbent party or parties becomes less likely (O'Dwyer 2004, 2006). Party competition as such does not need to and has not produced less corrupt governments.

More recently, Meyer-Sahling and Veen (2012) have challenged the role of party competition to control corrupt activities even more fundamentally. Focusing on the impact of government alternation on senior civil service politicisation, they argue that it is party alternation in government, a direct result of the pattern of competition that made senior civil service politicisation possible (Meyer-Sahling and Veen 2012, 17–18). In a systematic study of the politicisation of corruption in electoral campaigns from 1981 to 2011 in Europe, Bågenholm and Charron (2014) still find out that the use of corruption for campaign purposes has been increasing in Eastern Europe and that "parties have benefited electorally from politicizing corruption – in particular in more highly corrupt settings." Thus, the utility of competition as an effective deterrent of corruption remains a disputed topic with empirical results pointing in different directions.

The promise of EU membership

A lot of hope was put in the ability of the EU accession process to impact reforms in various spheres of political and economic life in the post-communist countries, and combatting corruption is not an exception. Somewhat reflecting the European accession process itself, the main arguments advanced in the literature in the 2000s focus on "conditionality," and in the 2010s on "backsliding."

It should be noted that the conditionality mechanism – imposing the reduction of malfeasance as a condition for accession to the EU – could not be applied directly in this case, since corruption control was not part of the *acquis* of the EU.[1] Still, conditionality could impact the level of corruption in indirect ways, and earlier literature remained moderately optimistic about the ability of the EU integration process to facilitate change (Mungiu-Pippidi 2006; Kopecký and Spirova 2011b). In this regard, the imposition of the Control and Verification Mechanism on Bulgaria and Romania after their 2007 accession was the first notable illustration that fighting corruption is taking a more centre stage in the accession process (Vachudova 2009, 48–51).

How effective has this new policy tool been so far? The evidence for the promise of the EU accession process can be characterized as mixed. Batory (2010) finds no "substitute for the impact of the EU in instigating corruption related reforms" but does remain sceptical about the sustained impact of conditionally in post-2004 Hungary. Spendzharova and Vachudova (2012), on their part, stress the important incentives generated through the monitoring exercised by the European Commission over the performance of post-communist governments. The question they raise is whether the possibility for EU sanctions due to lack of results in controlling corruption would be an effective instrument forcing governing elites to expose and sanction malpractice. Finally, Kostadinova's work incorporates comparative analysis of six Balkan countries at various stages of EU integration over the period 1996–2008. Her regression results confirm that advancement towards accession did help limit the spread of corruption, independent from the influence of economic liberalisation and the material and technological capacity of states (Kostadinova 2012).

Later on, "backsliding" became as popular of a term as conditionality had been before. The expectation was that following accession, the control impact of EU membership would subside and new member states will slide back into old habits. Ivanov (2010) describes how after accession, "Romania regressed from its previous achievements against corruption, and Bulgaria remained reluctant to prosecute senior officials or confront organised crime" (Ivanov 2010, 210). Levitz and Pop-Eleches (2010) find little evidence of backsliding, but later, Kartal's (2014) systematic analysis of longitudinal data on corruption control in the post-communist EU members showed that in that aspect, state behaviour changed significantly after accession. He concludes that integration encouraged the formation of anti-corruption coalitions in the candidate states but in the absence of further incentives, the commitment subsided fast after achievement of full membership (Kartal 2014, 953–954).

The promise of anti-system parties

Parallel to the EU integration process in the 2000s, Eastern Europe experienced a surge of numerous anti-establishment political parties. One of their major grievances against the establishment was the high level of (perceived) corruption in the respective countries (Hanley and Sikk 2014). Two major questions have been addressed by research on anti-system parties and corruption: whether the focus on corruption and anti-corruption helps these new parties do well electorally; and whether if successful, parties that build their electoral base by using anti-establishment and anti-corruption rhetoric, act to curb corruption. The answers to both of these questions have, to say the least, not been equivocal.

Anti-establishment parties appeared throughout all of Europe in the 2000s but those have been particularly popular in post-communist Eastern Europe. There, they have also made the biggest electoral gains, arguably because of the high levels of corruption and the high politicization of the issue (Bågenholm and Charron 2014). Hanley and Sikk (2014) and Ecker et al. (2015) qualify as direct the positive link between high corruption and support for anti-establishment parties. In their study which focuses only on East Central Europe, Hanley and Sikk find that relative *levels* of perceived corruption are important in explaining the electoral breakthrough of anti-establishment parties in post-communist Europe, but the impact of the absolute (high or low) levels remains unclear (Hanley and Sikk 2014, 8–9). In a broader comparative study of support for anti-establishment parties in Europe, including all post-communist EU member states, Ecker et al. (2015, 16–17) find that voters do support newcomers because of widespread corruption among the ruling elite. This trend is strongly influenced by partisan feelings and the belief that a turnover would bring change, thus echoing some of the caveats identified in the discussion of political competition and corruption in more general terms.

Most recently, Engler (2016) and Klašnja et al. (2016) challenged the links between rising levels of corruption and success of new parties even more, developing the argument further theoretically and testing it empirically on both party and voter level. Engler argues that while new parties certainly benefit from the mass distrust in established parties driven by a relative rise of perceived corruption, long-standing corruption may actually have a negative impact on the chances of new players to win. Clientelistic practices – part of real life that shapes the corruption perceptions – allow parties with access to state resources to maintain a strong electoral base. In contrast, "[n]ew parties have access neither to existing clientelist structures nor to state resources that could help to develop such structures, it is more difficult for them to succeed" (Engler 2016, 289). Empirically, Engler's statistical analysis provides enough evidence to support her argument about the counteracting effects of corruption. Klašnja et al. (2016) argues that corruption influences voting in two distinct ways: experiences of corruption at the individual level and the perception of corruption at the social level impact electoral behaviour through different channels. Personal experiences (which they call pocketbook corruption voting) seem to have a more direct impact on support for the incumbent party (Klašnja et al. 2016, 80).

If anti-corruption appeals have helped anti-establishment parties gain electorally, have they done anything to curb corruption? Early on, Krastev (2004) expressed pessimism about the potential success of such crusader parties to curb corruption and several country examples pointed to the failures of such formations to achieve meaningful results (Spirova 2012; Holmes 2013, 1180). Still, cross-national research by Bågenholm draws a more complicated picture by examining the emergence and impact of what he calls "anti-corruption parties" from several perspectives. Both Bågenholm (2013, 181) and Bågenholm and Charron (2015) explore the impact anti-corruption parties have had on subsequent levels of corruption and good government. This research (Bågenholm 2013, 177) identifies eighteen parties that focus "on fighting corruption in the election campaign, either by addressing the issue in general terms, . . . or more specifically by accusing the opponents," and studies their ability to carry out the anti-corruption promise. Two major findings stand out: first, a positive impact for parties such as NDSV in Bulgaria, Res Publica in Estonia, New Era and Law and Justice in Poland, which managed to secure strong positions at the first, breakthrough election. Over the years of their governments, the corruption scores of the countries improved significantly, although this observation remains difficult intuitively since the impact of anti-corruption policies is usually only felt in the medium or longer term. Second, and equally interestingly, "only one of the parties repeated its anti-corruption strategy in the second election," implying that corruption is a difficult issue to explore for electoral purposes more than once, and even more so from the position of power (Bågenholm 2013, 192–193).

In sum, while the literature devoted to the anti-system parties has made some contributions, a lot more remains to be done to fully explore the potential for fighting corruption. Establishing that contexts characterised by systemic abuse of public office are favourable to the election of populist formations, is relatively easier and has already been done. It is more challenging to validate the causal link between anti-system parties and reducing corruption, because the thrill of electing a new party that vigorously rejects the corrupt incumbents might simply affect the perception measures used to gauge malfeasance. The attention has to now turn to the question of what policies, if at all, the East European anti-system parties formulate once they win office, and what explains their success/failure in constraining malfeasance.

Conclusion: what have we learned?

Several broad conclusions emerge from this brief review of the literature on combatting corruption in the post-communist world. To begin with, research on corruption and anti-corruption remains limited because of the nature and practice of the phenomenon. The challenge is common for all scholarship on the subject, regardless of geographic area and period under investigation.

Corruption is, by nature, a secretive process, and data on it remains difficult to come by (Lambsdorff 2007, 236–237). A lot of the comparative academic research has relied on various indices based on perceptions of the spread and magnitude of corruption developed by experts, the general public, or the business elite. At the very best, these measures are subjective and proxies of the real phenomenon, not direct measures of it for which they have received a healthy dose of criticism (Sik 2002). In contrast, detailed examinations of corrupt practices in particular country contexts provide a very specific account of malfeasance in practice but limit the ability to generalize about the causes and consequences of corruption. The data pitfall remains probably more evident in corruption research than in any other area of political science.

These methodological challenges notwithstanding, certain research questions can still be better analysed by using measures of perceived rather than actual corruption. For example, research on public attitudes and political participation has helped us understand the harmful impact of corruption on institutional confidence and voting in young democracies such as the Eastern European ones (Anderson and Tverdova 2003; Kostadinova 2012). In these research designs, how people assess the threat of malfeasance is justifiably a more valid measure because the perception (as biased as it could be sometimes) drives the formation of attitudes and motivation for engagement.

The literature on anti-corruption is also driven by the agenda and activities of various international organisations engaged in the cause of fighting corruption. As the number of experts is limited, however, researchers often end up doing the work in both the applied and the more scientific areas. They become engaged in the policy assessment and revision of anti-corruption policies and simultaneously in their academic exploration. Caught in what Krastev (2004, 5) dubbed an "anti-corruptions consensus," academic research on the topic is therefore likely to consist of self-fulfilling prophecies.

The focus of the corruption and anti-corruption literature has been shifting over the last two decades to reflect actual policies and the major actors involved. Democratisation, political and economic competition, EU accession, and new anti-corruption parties have all been in the academic spotlight at some point in time, but none of them have been able to provide workable solutions to the "problem of corruption" in post-communist Europe. The results of the scholarly effort remain contradictory, just as in practice the levels of corruption do not seem to decline everywhere and as fast as desired.

What is then to be done? One suggestion drawn upon results of recent empirical analyses points at the need to increase the capacity of the state to reduce corruption among public officials by increasing their salaries and reforming the civil service (Kostadinova 2012, 144; Neshkova and Kostadinova 2012). Others maintain that we need to "focus on the situations rather than on the participants" (Miller 2006). Regardless of how honest officials may be and how critical of corruption citizens are, both would be tempted to engage in a corrupt exchange if they find themselves in situations where it is hard to resist. The probability for such circumstances can be reduced through offering multiple options for service to people and enhancing the ability for appeal before the courts. However, if domestic politics and international actions have failed so far, Mungiu-Pippidi (2013) argues, only collective actions at the grassroots societal levels can help further. In the Eastern European context, such a development would be hampered by a legacy of weak civil societies and a serious deficit of credible leadership. Political science research on corruption will then need to follow suit and refocus its attention on such less traditional foci of anti-corruption activities.

Note

1 Except in limiting the politicisation of the state administration since civil service reform was part of the entry criteria. See the contribution of Meyer-Sahling to this volume.

References

Anderson, C. and Tverdova, Y. (2003) Corruption, political allegiances, and attitudes toward government in contemporary democracies. *American Journal of Political Science* 47(1), 91–109.

Bågenholm, A. (2013) The electoral fate and policy impact of "anti-corruption parties" in Central and Eastern Europe. *Human Affairs* 23(2), 174–195.

Bågenholm, A. and Charron, N. (2014) Do politics in Europe benefit from politicizing corruption? *West European Politics* 37(5).

Bågenholm, A. and Charron, N. (2015) Anti-corruption parties and good government. In C. Dahlström and L. Wängnerud (eds.), *Elites, Institutions and the Quality of Government*. New York: Palgrave Macmillan, 263–282.

Batory, A. (2010) Post-accession malaise? EU conditionality, domestic politics and anti-corruption policy in Hungary. *Global Crime* 11(2), 164–177.

Batory, A. (2012) Why do anti-corruption laws fail in Central eastern Europe? A target compliance perspective. *Regulation and Governance* 6 (1), 66–82.

Bugaric, B. (2015) Law derailed: Lessons from the post-communist world. *Hague Journal on the Rule of Law* 7(2), 175–197.

Casal Bertoa, F. and Spirova, M. (2016) Parties between thresholds. unpublished manuscript (maybe forthcoming)

Della Porta, D. (2004) Political parties and corruption: Ten hypotheses on five vicious circles. *Crime, Law & Social Change* 42(1), 35–60.

Diaby, A. and Sylwester, K. (2015) Corruption and market competition: Evidence from post-communist countries. *World Development* 66(1), 487–499.

Dimitrov, V., Goetz, K. and Wollmann, H. (2006) *Governing After Communism Institutions and Policymaking.* Lanham, MD: Rowman & Littlefield.

Dragojević, M. and Konitzer, A. (2013) The forensics of patronage: Identifying the linkage between parties and public sector employment in Serbia. Социолошки преглед (Sociological Review) XLVII (1), 3–22.

Duvanova, D. (2014) Economic regulations, red tape, and bureaucratic corruption in post-communist economies. *World Development* 59(2), 298–312.

Ecker, A., Glinitzer, K. and Meyer, T. M. (2015) Corruption performance voting and the electoral context. *European Political Science Review*, available on CJO2015. doi:10.1017/S1755773915000053.

Engler, S. (2016) Corruption and electoral support for new political parties in Central and Eastern Europe. *West European Politics* 39(2), 278–304.

Fazekas, M. and Tóth, J. I. (2016) From corruption to state capture: A new analytical framework with empirical implications from Hungary. *Political Research Quarterly*, doi:10.1177/1065916639137.

Ganev, V. (2007) *Preying on the State: The Transformation of Bulgaria After 1989.* Ithaca, NY: Cornell University Press.

Glinkina, S. P. (1998) The ominous landscape of Russian corruption. *Transitions* (March), 16–23.

Grzymała-Busse, A. (2007) *Rebuilding Leviathan: Party Competition and State Exploitation in Post-Communist Democracies.* Cambridge: Cambridge University Press.

Gwiazda, A. (2008) Party patronage in Poland. The democratic left alliance and law and justice compared. *East European Politics and Societies* 22(4), 802–827.

Hanley, S. and Sikk, A. (2014) Economy, corruption or floating voters? Explaining the breakthroughs of anti-establishment reform parties in eastern Europe. *Party Politics*, first published on September 18, 2014 doi:10.1177/1354068814550438

Holmes, L. (2006) *Rotten States? Corruption, Post-communism and Neoliberalism.* Durham and London: Duke University Press.

Holmes, L. (2013) Postcommunist transitions and corruption: Mapping patterns. *Social Research* 80(4), 1163–1186.

Ikstens, J., Smilov, D. and Walecki, M. (2002) *Party and Campaign Funding in Eastern Europe: A Study of 18 Member Countries of the ACEEEO.* Washington, DC: International Foundation for Election Systems. http://ifes.org/sites/default/files/brijuni18countryreport_finaledited1_0.pdf, accessed 4 May 2016.

Ivanov, K. (2010) The 2007 accession of Bulgaria and Romania: Ritual and reality. *Global Crime* 11(2), 210–219.

Johnston, M. (2002) Party systems, competition, and political checks against corruption. In A. J. Heidenheimer and M. Johnston (eds.), *Political Corruption: Concepts and Contexts.* New Brunswick, NJ: Transaction, 777–797.

Jordan, J. M. (2002) Patronage and corruption in the Czech Republic. *SAIS Review* 22(2), 19–52.

Karklins, R. (2002) Typology of post-communist corruption. *Problems of Post Communism* 49(4), 22–32.

Karklins, R. (2005) *The System Made Me Do It.* Armonk, NY: M. E. Sharpe.

Kartal, M. (2014) Accounting for the bad apples: The EU's impact on national corruption before and after accession. *Journal of European Public Policy* 21(6), 941–959.

Kaufmann, D., Kraay, A., and Zoido-Lobaton, P. (1999) *Governance Matters.* World Bank Policy Research, Working Paper No. 2196. Washington, DC: The World Bank.

Klašnja, M., Tucker, J. A. and Deegan-Krause, K. (2016) Pocketbook vs. sociotropic corruption voting. *British Journal of Political Science* 46(1), 67–94.

Kolarska-Bobinska, L. (2002) The impact of corruption on legitimacy of authority in new democracies. In S. Kotkin and A. Sajó (eds.), *Political Corruption in Transition.* Budapest: Central European University Press, 314–325.

Kopecký, P. (2006) Political parties and the state in post-communist Europe: The nature of symbiosis. *Journal of Communist Studies and Transition Politics* 22(3), 251–273.

Kopecký, P. and Spirova, M. (2011a) 'Jobs for the boys'? Patterns of party patronage in post-communist Europe. *West European Politics* 34(5), 897–921.

Kopecký, P. and Spirova, M. (2011b) Party management and state exploitation in post-communist Europe: The ambiguous impact of the European Union. In P.G. Lewis and R. Markowski (eds.), *Europeanizing Party Politics: Comparative Perspectives on Central and Eastern Europe*. Manchester: Manchester University Press, 25–44.

Kostadinova, T. (2009) Abstain or rebel: Corruption perceptions and voting in East European elections. *Politics & Policy* 37(4, August), 691–714.

Kostadinova, T. (2012) *Political Corruption in Eastern Europe, Politics After Communism*. Boulder and London: Lynne Rienner.

Krastev, I. (ed.) (2004) *Shifting Obsessions: Three Essays on the Politics of Anticorruption*. Budapest: Central European University Press.

Krastev, I. and Ganev, G. (2004) The missing incentive: Corruption, anti-corruption, and reelection. In I. Krastev (ed.), *Shifting Obsessions: Three Essays on the Politics of Anticorruption*. Budapest: Central European University Press, 75–108.

Lambsdorff, J.G. (2007) *The Institutional Economics of Corruption and Reform: Theory, Evidence, and Policy*. Cambridge: Cambridge University Press.

Ledeneva, A.V. (1998) *Russia's Economy of Favours: Blat, Networking and Informal Exchange*. Cambridge: Cambridge University Press.

Lederman, D., Loayza, N. and Soares, R. (2005) Accountability and corruption: Political institutions matter. *Economics & Politics* 17(1), 1–150.

Levitz, P. and Pop-Eleches, G. (2010) Monitoring, money and migrants: Countering post-accession backsliding in Bulgaria and Romania. *Europe-Asia Studies* 62(3), 461–479.

Meyer-Sahling, J.-H. (2008) The changing colours of the post-communist state: The politicisation of the senior civil service in Hungary. *European Journal of Political Research* 47(1), 1–33.

Meyer-Sahling, J.-H. and Veen, T. (2012) Governing the post-communist state: Government alternation and senior civil service politicisation in Central and Eastern Europe. *East European Politics* 28(1), 1–19.

Miller, William L. (2006) Corruption and corruptibility. *World Development* 34(2), 371–380.

Mungiu-Pippidi, A. (2006) Corruption: Diagnosis and treatment. *Journal of Democracy* 17(3), 86–99.

Mungiu-Pippidi, A. (2013) Controlling corruption through collective action. *Journal of Democracy* 24(1), 101–115.

Mungiu-Pippidi, A., Bratu, R., Charron, N., Dimulescu, V., Doroftei, M., Fazekas, M., Kasemets, A., King, L.P., Martinez Barranco Kukutschka, R., Pop, R. and Tóth, I.J. (2013) *Controlling Corruption in Europe*. Toronto: Barbara Budrich.

Neshkova, M. and Kostadinova, T. (2012) The effectiveness of administrative reform in new democracies. *Public Administration Review* 72(3), 324–333.

Neshkova, M.I. and Rosenbaum, A. (2015) Advancing good government through fighting corruption. In J.L. Perry and K. Christensen (eds.), *Handbook of Public Administration*, third edition. San Francisco: Jossey-Bass, 97–118.

Nunberg, B. (1999) *The State After Communism: Administrative Transitions in Central and Eastern Europe*. Washington, DC: The World Bank.

O'Dwyer, C. (2004) Runaway state building: How political parties shape states in post-communist Eastern Europe. *World Politics* 56(4), 520–553.

O'Dwyer, C. (2006) *Runaway State-Building: Patronage Politics and Democratic Development*. Baltimore, MD: Johns Hopkins University Press.

Philp, M. (2015) The definition of political corruption. In P. Heywood (ed.), *The Handbook of Political Corruption*. London and New York: Routledge.

Sajó, A. (1998) Corruption, clientelism, and the future of the constitutional state in Eastern Europe. *East European Constitutional Review* 7(2), 37–46.

Schmidt, D. (2007) Anti-corruption: What do we know? Research on preventing corruption in the post-communist world. *Political Studies Review* 5, 202–232.

Sik, E. (2002) The bad, the worse, and the worst: Guesstimating the level of corruption. In S. Kotkin and A. Sajó (eds.), *Political Corruption in Transition: A Sceptic's Handbook*. Budapest: Central European University Press, 91–113.

Smilov, S. (2007) Introduction. In D. Smilov and J. Toplak (eds.), *Political Finance and Corruption in Eastern Europe: The Transition Period*. London and New York: Routledge, 1–32.

Spendzharova, A.B. and Anna Vachudova, M. (2012) Catching up? Consolidating liberal democracy in Bulgaria and Romania after EU accession. *West European Politics* 35(1), 39–58.

Spirova, M. (2012) 'A tradition we don't mess with': Party patronage in Bulgaria. In P. Kopecký, P. Mair and M. Spirova (eds.), *Party Government and Party Patronage in European Democracies*. Oxford: Oxford University Press, 54–73.

Tavits, M. (2008) Representation, corruption, and subjective well-being. *Comparative Political Studies*, 41(12), 1607–1630.

Vachudova, M. A. (2009) Corruption and compliance in the EU's Post-communist members and candidates. *Journal of Common Market Studies Annual Review*, 47, 43–62.

Van Biezen, I. and Kopecký, P. (2001) On the predominance of state money: Reassessing party financing in the new democracies of Southern and Eastern Europe. *Perspectives on European Politics and Society* 2(3), 401–429.

Varese, F. (1997) The transition to the market and corruption in post-socialist Russia. *Political Studies* 45(3), 579–596.

Volintiru, C. (2015) The exploitative function of party patronage: Does it serve the party's interest? *East European Politics* 31(1), 39–55.

Volkov, V. (2002) *Violent Entrepreneurs: The Use of Force in the Making of Russian Capitalism*. Ithaca, NY: Cornell University Press.

Walecki, M. (2005) *Political Money and Corruption*. International Foundation for Election Systems (IFES). Political Finance White Paper Series. Washington, DC: IFES.

World Bank (2000) *Anticorruption in Transition: A Contribution to the Policy Debate*. Washington, DC: The World Bank.

Xhaferaj, A. (2013) Appointed elites in the political parties – Albania case. *Academic Journal of Interdisciplinary Studies* 2(3), 307.

24

EAST EUROPEAN EXCEPTIONALISM

Foreign domination in finance

Rachel A. Epstein

By 2007, Eastern Europe had the highest penetration of foreign bank ownership of any region in the world. Nine of the 10 post-communist countries that had joined the European Union (EU) in 2004 or after had foreign bank ownership approaching 70 per cent or above.[1] In several cases, foreign ownership in banking neared 100 per cent (EBRD 2009). Foreign domination in finance to this degree was unusual in global perspective and also represented a major structural difference between East and West Europe. In the latter case, most countries had protected their banking markets from large numbers of foreign entrants, preferring instead to maintain preponderant domestic control (Epstein 2014a; Claessens and van Horen 2015).

East European exceptionalism with respect to permitting foreign domination in finance is important for allowing us to test the developmental and political consequences of high levels of foreign bank ownership. A range of prominent academics and practitioners has warned against yielding to foreign entrants in banking markets, citing the extent to which banks inevitably have home biases, which in turn leads to host market vulnerability (Block 1996; Wade 2007; Ortiz 2012). In the 1990s and early 2000s when East European bank privatisation with foreign capital was underway, it was controversial. For proponents of banking nationalism (that is, keeping banks under domestic control) too much foreign bank ownership threatened to limit economic opportunity, curb macroeconomic policy discretion, and introduce economic volatility – not to mention political vulnerability. Debates about bank privatisation therefore mirrored larger transition disagreements about the appropriate role of the state in the economy.

Interestingly, on the question of volatility, East European banking markets mostly *do not* bear out these arguments regarding the dangers of foreign domination in finance (Bonin 2010; Epstein 2014c; Bonin and Louie 2015; Epstein 2017). Equally important, however, East European market openness, including in banking, has limited the pathways for economic catching-up in the European and global economies (Nölke and Vliegenthart 2009; Epstein 2014b).

The developmental and political consequences of unprecedentedly high foreign bank ownership levels there are intrinsically compelling – especially if one considers the heated controversies at the origins of banking market openness (Epstein 2008a) and more recent attempts in the region to claw back some national control over finance (Naczyk 2015). However, there are also broader, comparative concerns at stake. For one, foreign bank ownership levels across the globe are up sharply, even as most industrialised and major emerging economies have preserved preponderant domestic control (Claessens and van Horen 2012 and 2015; Epstein 2014a). Thus

Table 24.1 Eastern Europe, new member states of the EU: foreign bank ownership

Country	Percentage of Foreign-Owned Banks, Assets: 2008 and 2013	
Bulgaria	84	70
Croatia (joined the EU in 2013)	91	90
Czech Republic★	84	85
Estonia	98	97
Hungary	84	84
Latvia	66	65
Lithuania	92	93
Poland	77	68
Romania	88	89
Slovakia	99	85
Slovenia	31	34

★Source for Czech Republic is Claessens and van Horen 2015 because the country exited European Bank for reconstruction and Development (EBRD) programmes before this data was collected.

Source: EBRD 2009 and EBRD Banking Survey for 2013.

lessons from Eastern Europe on volatility and development stemming from foreign domination in finance have salience in a growing number of countries (see Table 24.1 for foreign bank ownership levels in Eastern Europe).

Second, a core problem in the European debt and currency crisis was West European insistence on domestic bank control, which had been predicted to undermine a common currency (Eichengreen 1993), and ultimately did through bank-state ties that led to national regulatory forbearance as well as bank-state "doom loops" (Epstein 2014a; Epstein and Rhodes 2016; Epstein 2017).[2] The point is that very high levels of foreign bank ownership in Eastern Europe are probably also required across Eurozone states in order to sustain the common currency. The European Banking Union is indeed structured for this very purpose. Thus in what could be an unusual reversal of fortunes, East European economic organisation today, with foreign domination in finance, could be West European states' futures, if the European Banking Union succeeds in weakening bank-states ties, harmonising regulation, and mutualising bank insurance. Thus, not only do "emerging" economies around the world have something to learn from East Europe's experiment with extreme economic openness, but so too do the West European economies that have only recently been forced to cede bank governance to supranational authorities in the EU.

The origins of foreign domination in finance in Eastern Europe

The political foundations and purposes of banks have been inescapable for states, which means that it has never been easy for states to contemplate ceding control over banks (Pauly 1988; Epstein 2014a; Calomiris and Haber 2014). Banks have historically served as creditors to states. They have been an important tool of macroeconomic management through credit provision or restriction, have been critical to securing domestic political support, and to achieving economic competitiveness. Banks have therefore contributed to (or detracted from) states' power positions in the world economy. Indeed, financial systems have long been at the root of economic organisation, leading to longer-term or shorter-term time horizons among actors in an economy, with consequences for numerous other national institutions, including firms, labour markets, educational systems, and welfare states (Gerschenkron 1962; Katzenstein 1978; Zysman 1983; Hall and Soskice 2001; Hancké, Rhodes and Thatcher 2007; Grittersová 2014; Bohle and Greskovits 2012; Bohle this volume). Banks have also relied on states – for bail-outs in crises and for various other kinds of subsidies, regulatory forbearance, or restricted competition in normal times (see e.g. Pérez 1997; De Cecco 2009; Clarke and Hardiman 2013; Donnelly 2014; Goyer and Valdivielso del Real 2014).

Given the traditional centrality of banks to states' political and economic fortunes, it is little wonder that the privatisation of formerly state-owned banks coming out of communism should have proven controversial during Eastern Europe's transition (Epstein 2008a; Bonin, Hasan and Wachtel 2014). And so it was. Even as post-communist states were transforming their socialist-era "monobanks" into conventional two-tier banking systems more familiar to capitalist economies, they sought initially to retain control over their banks, not least so that favoured enterprises could continue to receive credit. Just as commercial banking was being reorganised under these sometimes conflicting objectives of greater efficiency alongside economic sustenance, central banks too were caught between accommodating the international push for political independence and the perceived domestic imperative to limit the ravages of the transition downturn (Epstein 2008a; Epstein and Johnson 2010; Johnson 2016). Outright collapse of banking sectors was the result in some post-communist countries, while very high non-performing loan volumes were the problem in others. Either way, banking sector crises, in addition to international institutional pressure, paved the way not just for bank privatisation, but also for bank privatisation with foreign capital, mostly from Western Europe, and secondarily from North America.

If there is controversy in the literature about the causes of overwhelming levels of foreign bank ownership in Eastern Europe, it centres on two issues. First is the weight of banking crises against other drivers, including pressure from international organisations; second is the nature of that international pressure – whether materially or socially coercive. Banking crises certainly narrowed the range of appealing policy options (Bonin, Hasan and Wachtel 2014; Grittersová 2016) and in some cases brought new political parties to power who used crises to change policy course – including towards more liberalisation (Vachudova 2005; Epstein 2008a). On the other hand, even states without severe banking crises opted to liberalise the bulk of their banking assets with foreign capital, including in Poland. Moreover, in two important cases, banking crises did not precipitate broad openness to foreign bank investors – in Russia and Slovenia (see Johnson 2000; Lindstrom and Piroska 2007; Epstein 2008b; Spendzharova 2014). These findings point to the scope for choice among states, with the important caveat from the crisis literature that banking failures change the balance of power (see Martinez-Diaz 2009; Stein 2010), and in Eastern Europe, outside advisors were often the chief beneficiaries (Epstein 2008a).

If it was crisis together with international pressure that led to high levels of foreign bank ownership in Eastern Europe, then the second area of disagreement one detects in the literature is the nature of that pressure. A number of scholars point to the power of EU conditionality in general (Schimmelfennig and Sedelmeier 2005; Vachudova 2005) and with specific reference to bank privatisation (Bohle 2014; Medve-Bálint 2014). By contrast, international institutions' social pressure was more important to securing high levels of foreign bank ownership. While the *acquis* certainly puts limits on state aid, it is nevertheless restrained with respect to requiring certain forms of bank ownership – it would have to be given that in 2002, over 42 per cent of German bank assets were held by government-owned banks (Barth, Caprio and Levine 2006: 149). A process-tracing strategy revealed instead that a host of institutions, including the International Monetary Fund (IMF), EBRD, and even the US Treasury persuaded East European policy-makers that state intervention in their economies through banks was too resonant with central planning of the past, and that moreover these transition states would benefit from the capital and know-how that foreign entrants would bring (Epstein 2008a, 2008b; see also Ban 2016). Two cases stand out as exceptions to this: Romania, which did come under more direct EU pressure to privatise with foreign capital (Epstein 2008a); and Slovenia, which, for reasons linked to the continuity in its leadership class, ignored international institutions' urgings to jettison state control, even in the context of EU enlargement (Lindstrom and Piroska 2007; Epstein 2008b; Spendzharova 2014).

The developmental consequences of high levels of foreign bank ownership

More than a decade after foreign investors took over the bulk of Eastern Europe's banking assets, it was still not clear whether, on balance, such high levels of foreign bank ownership enhanced the region's chances for catching up with Western Europe, or were a hindrance. An extensive literature had long focused on the European East-West divide and the sources of political and economic variation (e.g. Gerschenkron 1962; Brenner 1989; Bunce 2000; Janos 2000; Epstein 2014b; Epstein and Jacoby 2014). While every new EU member state had increased its per capita income relative to the "old" EU-15[3] between 2000 and 2013, even the richest post-communist accession state – Slovenia – was only at half the EU-15 average by 2013, measured in absolute terms (Epstein 2014b: 22). In addition, the US financial crisis and later the European debt and currency crisis had slowed or reversed convergence trends (Farkas 2013).

On the one hand, the upside of foreign bank ownership was that it had been one conduit though which capital arrived in Eastern Europe – to such an extent that for the first time, the expectation that richer countries would fund development in poorer ones was confirmed on a broad scale (EBRD 2009: 63–64). The problem was that much of the funding was not sustainable or not leading to longer-term sources of economic growth, such as indigenous innovation (Deuber 2011; Bohle 2014; Jacoby 2014). Moreover, since many of the most dramatic cases of catching up around the world had relied upon political control over credit allocation (for example, Zysman 1983; Wade 1990; Woo-Cumings 1997; Kohli 2004), sceptics have concluded that between high levels of foreign bank ownership and EU state aid limitations, developing pathways for accelerated growth and away from "dependent capitalism", had not been achieved in Eastern Europe (Nölke and Vliegenthart 2009; Böröcz 2012; Epstein 2014b).

On the other side of this debate is the argument that foreign direct investment (FDI), including in banking, can be just as an effective catching-up strategy as political control over finance. In support of FDI, there are several countries outside of Europe that have moved into the World Bank's "middle income" category, largely by attracting FDI (Stallings with Studart 2006).[4] Ireland had, before the European debt crisis, become among the world's wealthiest countries through a low-tax, high-FDI strategy, and as such became an explicit model for Eastern Europe (Ornston 2012; see also Appel 2011). The World Bank also has argued the Eastern Europe can "innovate through osmosis" and need not "invest much more in R&D [research and development] and the production of knowledge" (World Bank 2012: 16; for the fuller theoretical debate on FDI, see Bàndelj 2008).

To a certain extent, work by Bohle and Greskovits (2007, 2012), Bohle (in this volume) and Bruszt and Vukov (2015) support the claim that FDI can lead to substantial upgrading in receiving countries, which in turn leads to growth and supports convergence. Two caveats are in order, however. First, Bohle and Greskovits make it clear that the kind of FDI matters. The greater the share of FDI in tradable sectors, the better it is for upgrading, skills development, growth and convergence. But second, as Bruszt and Vukov point out, the fact that Hungary's share of medium-tech to high-tech activity in manufacturing exports is bigger than Germany's, relative to the respective size of these economies, probably does not reveal the true extent of where value has been added (2015: 27). In other words, returning to Nölke and Vliegenthart (2009), medium-skilled workers in Eastern Europe are labouring on what are essentially assembly platforms. Moreover, there is limited evidence for the "indirect" effects of FDI – that is, the extent to which foreign investment leads not just to greater competitiveness of the receiving firm, but also in the sector overall, including among host-owned firms (Hanousek, Kočenda and Maurel 2011; Farkas 2013: 16–17).

However, scepticism towards Eastern Europe's prospects for catching up in light of foreign domination in banking should not be interpreted as a call to renationalise majorities of banking assets in the region – at least not outside the context of other, major institutional reforms. The reason is that although domestically controlled banks have been critical to catching up around the world, it is not also the case that all countries with domestically controlled banks have advanced in the global economy. There are as many cases of developmental failure as success. Looking at both foreign and domestic banks in Eastern Europe through the US financial crisis, and then the European debt and currency crisis, for example, it was domestic banks in Latvia and Slovenia that caused the greatest chaos. Meanwhile, domestically controlled banks in Hungary and especially in Poland acted more as counter-cyclical stabilisers (Epstein 2013; Epstein 2017).

Although there is not significant variation in the structure of new member states' banking structures, there is nevertheless some variation in the performance of still domestically controlled banks, as the previous paragraph points out. But one can see, from Table 24.1, that in all countries except Slovenia, foreign owners dominate. Thus, for broad trends in production profile development, the legacies and policies highlighted in the Varieties of Capitalism literature may be more important than bank ownership (see Bohle, this volume).

Other kinds of bank variation do exist, however, in other dimensions of ownership and regulatory and monetary regimes. Slovenia and Poland stand out for the continued role of significant state ownership. Hungary's largest bank, OTP, is also domestically managed, but differs from the largest banks in both Poland and Slovenia insofar as it is actually majority foreign-owned – albeit through dispersed shareholdings, so there is no single foreign strategic stakeholder with overriding management power. The fact that all three Baltic states, Slovenia, and Slovakia were in the Eurozone by 2016 also had implications for bank governance in those countries. These five post-communist countries were automatically included in European Banking Union, which required the conferral of bank supervisory and licensing authority from the national level to the European Central Bank (ECB). While Romania and possibly also Bulgaria would opt in to banking union, Poland, the Czech Republic, and Hungary elected instead to retain domestic supervisory authority over banks operating in their jurisdictions.

Limiting volatility: the "second home market" versus the Vienna initiative

Very high levels of foreign bank ownership in Eastern Europe gave rise to fears that the region would fall victim to "cutting and running" during the US financial crisis, whereby foreign banks repatriate capital and liquidity to their "home" markets at the expense of host ones. Hypothesised vulnerability relates back to banks' presumed home biases, referred to by Block (1996), Wade (2007) and Ortiz (2012) at the beginning of this article. Funding reversals had had devastating effects over the last twenty years in East Asia, Turkey, Brazil, Argentina, and elsewhere (Roubini and Setser 2004). Given the history of foreign bank retrenchment, East European watchers were writing headlines in late 2008 and early 2009 such as "Eastern European Crisis May Put Us All in the Goulash" (King 2009) and "Next Wave of Banking Crisis to Come from Eastern Europe" (Engdahl 2009). Everyone from journalists to industry analysts to Paul Krugman believed Eastern Europe was headed for disaster given the confluence of crisis and foreign domination in finance (Epstein 2014c).

Despite the dire forecasts about Eastern Europe in late 2008 and early 2009, the largest foreign banks did not abruptly cut and run from the region as had been widely expected. Instead, scholars and journalists were writing, by the end of 2009, about the banking crisis that never was (Åslund 2010). But herein lies the controversy: while most analysts had concluded that it was a voluntary bank rollover agreement, the "Vienna Initiative" (also known as the European Bank Coordination Initiative), that forced foreign banks to maintain their exposures to Eastern Europe to avoid calamity (e.g. EBRD 2009: 18; IMF 2010a: 63; De Haas et al. 2012; Blyth 2013; Kudrna and Gabor 2013: 556), a minority view held that banks never intended, could, or wanted to leave (Epstein 2014c; Bonin and Louie 2015; Epstein 2017). In support of the Vienna Initiative side of this debate was the fact that the US financial crisis created a collective action problem among foreign bank investors in Eastern Europe. Given the historically well-established propensity of foreign banks to cut and run from their host markets in crises, which in turn reduces currency and asset values and raises non-performing loan volumes in host states, if banks were going to jump ship, it would make sense to be first to leave rather than last. From the international financial institutions' perspective, then, the trick was to provide reassurance that everyone would stay so that capital flight and all the attending negative economic repercussions could be contained.

A process-tracing research strategy revealed a number of problems with the argument outlined earlier about the power of the Vienna Initiative (VI), however. First, the VI technically only covered five countries, and a number of the commitment letters signed by banks, in which those banks pledged to maintain particular exposures, were signed after the critical crisis period had passed. Second, the commitment letters were voluntary, which had never proved to be a robust guard against capital flight in previous crises. The literature arguing on behalf of the VI's effectiveness did not specify what set the East European context apart in 2009 from previous rollover agreements that had failed. Third, it turns out that the six largest west European banking groups invested in Eastern Europe were at the origins of the VI.[5] These large banks' evident desire to improve coordination casts doubt on the notion that international institutions reigned in banks' worst impulses, and instead points to a very different causal logic in which the banks themselves were running the international financial institutions, and not the other way around.

Thus, the alternative explanation to the VI was that large banks invested in Eastern Europe were operating under a "second home market" model characterised by long time horizons, competition for mass market share and tolerance for high volatility (Epstein 2014c). The second home market model was a reflection of the extent to which, underappreciated by many observers in the run-up to the crisis, Eastern Europe truly was exceptional with respect to the uniqueness of its economic model that had foreign domination in finance at its centre. What was unusual, in addition to very high foreign ownership levels, was that foreign investors had overwhelmingly expanded through subsidiaries instead of branches (Cerutti, Dell'Ariccia and Pería 2007). This meant that foreign banks were as or more subject to host regulatory authority as to home. East European states used their supervisory and regulatory authority over foreign-owned bank subsidiaries in the crisis to tighten capital and liquidity requirements and in some cases to restrict the payment of bank bonuses and dividends, leading foreign bankers in the region to declare that "capital mobility in Eastern Europe is dead" (Epstein 2014c; also see Spendzharova 2014 on regulatory measures). In addition, since foreign banks had been in search of mass market share, many of their loans were long-term and could not be called in. Third and perhaps most important, since banks like UniCredit of Italy and Raiffeisen of Austria were coming from over-banked and relatively small home markets, they had no desire to retreat from a newly established market of millions of consumers back to a comparatively miniscule home one, especially after having spent two decades (in Raiffeisen's case) building their business and brand in the post-communist world. They were in Eastern Europe for the long term and had no desire to "cut and run" from their markets there.

One might wonder then, why there was a Vienna Initiative. If big banks had no intention of leaving, why sign undisclosed commitment letters promising to stay? By late 2008, the likes of Raiffeisen, Erste Bank, UniCredit, and others had a problem. Because of all the catastrophic reporting referred to earlier, including a blog post by Paul Krugman in October 2008 equating Eastern Europe to Southeast Asia in 1997, there was widespread fear among global investors that Eastern Europe was going to implode.[6] This created funding problems for the big banks invested in Eastern Europe – that is, other financial institutions did not want to extend credit to banks dependent on East European markets. In addition, East European countries were using their regulatory authority over foreign-owned subsidiaries in their jurisdictions to "ring-fence" resources (referred to earlier) – that is, to restrict foreign banks in their use (and particularly their removal) of capital and liquidity (Kudrna and Gabor 2013). The six big banks sent the letter to international organisations in November 2008 to begin a process, the Vienna Initiative, which would ultimately serve as an important signalling device to international markets that East European markets were not on the brink of collapse. The banks also used Vienna to win additional leverage vis-à-vis host regulatory authorities to get them to lighten up. The strategy worked. Fears were alleviated, funding returned, and the IMF used its bailouts in the region to secure macroeconomic and regulatory policies favourable to the large foreign bank investors (see Kudrna and Gabor 2013; Epstein 2014c, especially p. 865).

What is instructive about the East European experience through the US financial crisis is that while states have long been reluctant to allow high levels of foreign bank ownership, they should probably be more concerned about the institutional channels through which funding flows. In other words, states should be more concerned about funding through branches and cross-border bank lending than foreign ownership of bank subsidiaries because there is little "financial friction" in those former instances to prevent large-scale funding retreat. And in fact, comparing Eastern Europe in 2008 to Southeast Asia in 1997–1998, funding reversals in the latter case were largely the result of cross-border borrowing, not foreign bank ownership. Bank subsidiaries owned by the biggest outside investors, over which hosts had regulatory and supervisory authority, proved a relatively stable model of funding in Eastern Europe through the US financial crisis, and even after.

Conclusions: Eastern Europe as Europe's future

Three main arguments about foreign bank ownership in Eastern Europe were explored in this chapter. The first is that foreign bank ownership levels are unprecedentedly high stemming from the peculiar pressures of banking crises together with international institutions and EU enlargement. The second is that in historical comparative perspective, foreign domination in finance limits the pathways through which Eastern Europe can catch up, in terms of per capita income, to its West European counterparts. The third, however, is that the particular institutional form that foreign bank ownership has taken in Eastern Europe, through preponderant foreign ownership of subsidiaries and a "second home market model", has been a relatively stable source of funding. Linking points two and three is the fact that to a greater degree than at any previous juncture, neoclassical expectations that rich countries should fund economic growth in poorer ones has been confirmed on a broad scale.

The findings outlined in this chapter are not completely settled, however. In particular, the developmental consequences of foreign domination in finance require further investigation. One general observation is that foreign-owned banks are not as good as their domestic counterparts at locating and funding promising local entrepreneurs, which may hinder economic growth – especially if indigenous innovation is stifled by inadequate access to finance. A rival hypothesis, however, is that funding to small and medium-sized enterprises in Eastern Europe has been weak because entrepreneurship is limited. A second but related pair of questions is that given high levels of foreign bank ownership in Eastern Europe, where has indigenous high value-added innovation nevertheless taken place and how was it financed. Further research along these lines would tell us whether Eastern Europe has better prospects to catch up through channels other than control over finance. It would also suggest constructive policies going forward – including whether more domestic control over banking would serve any of the post-communist countries well, or whether more political influence over credit allocation would simply increase related-party lending and excessive risk-taking.

By way of conclusion, it is important to stress that lessons from Eastern Europe about high levels of foreign bank ownership are not confined to the region, or even to other middle-income or "emerging" economies around the world. Rather, the effects of foreign bank ownership are increasingly pertinent to the rich industrialized states of Western Europe, and especially to those in the Eurozone. This relevance is generated by the notable role that banking sector protectionism there played in extending and exacerbating the European debt and currency crisis (Epstein 2014a; Epstein and Rhodes 2016; Epstein 2017). In brief, West European insistence on domestic control over banking sectors, very much *unlike* the East European posture during post-communist transition, allowed the introduction of a common currency in the context of still nationally fragmented banking systems. Political ties between banks and states in the run-up to and during the US and Eurozone crises led to multiple problems. These included the linked economic vulnerabilities of banks and states referred to earlier as "doom-loops"; national regulatory forbearance in the interest of protected domestic bank consolidation and outward bank expansion; domination by banks in funding at the expense of other, more diverse sources, which limited economic recovery; and national retrenchment in funding during the crisis, undermining the effectiveness of the ECB's monetary policy setting for the Eurozone.

Here again, there is debate – about whether the European Banking Union, which relocates regulatory and supervisory authority over banks from the national to the supranational level in the ECB – sufficiently weakens the bank-state ties that undermined the euro in the crisis (see Epstein and Macartney 2016; Howarth and Macartney 2016). Supposing that it does, however, as some analysts speculate (Véron 2015; Epstein and Rhodes 2016), the entire point would be to limit political impulses for protectionism. It means, particularly with centralised bank supervision, licensing, and the mutualisation of bank insurance schemes linked to deposits and resolution, that foreign bank ownership levels are likely to rise, also in Western Europe. Judging from Eastern Europe, cross-penetration in banking markets is likely to limit economic policy autonomy and make economic adjustment more difficult (Hardie and Howarth 2013). On the other hand, intra-European volatility might well be curbed – both because national retrenchment in funding would be less pervasive and because the euro and the ECB would be on firmer, single-market footing. In this sense, high levels of foreign bank ownership in Eastern Europe could well be indicative of all of Europe's economic future.

Notes

1 Croatia, another post-communist new member state that joined the EU in 2013 also followed this pattern, with foreign bank ownership over 90 per cent.

2 A "doom loop" during the European debt and currency crisis refers to the linked vulnerabilities of states and banks that emerged because banks were lending disproportionately to their own sovereigns. While this strategy was intended to keep states' borrowing costs down, it was failing to do so in Italy, Spain, and Slovenia by 2011 and 2012. Thus when bank lending to governments was insufficient to control borrowing costs, banks' balance sheets also suffered because of previously accumulated government debt. The dynamic effectively pushed governments' borrowing costs higher because of investor fears that states would again have to bail out their banks (Gros 2013).

3 The "Old EU 15" refers to those member states who had joined the EU prior to 2004.

4 Note that all of the new member states from Eastern Europe under consideration here are already either "high income" or "high middle income" countries by the World Bank's categorisations. Thus, the outcome of interest in the literature described is really convergence on West European levels of wealth.

5 See the letter from 27 November 2008 addressed to the European Commission, among others, which resulted from a meeting among the six largest bank investors in Eastern Europe at the Raiffeisen headquarters earlier that month: www.ebrd.com/downloads/research/economics/events/Banks_letter.pdf.

6 Krugman's blog post can be found here: http://krugman.blogs.nytimes.com/2008/10/31/eastern-europe-2008-southeast-asia-1997/?_r=0.

References

Appel, H 2011, *Tax Politics in Eastern Europe: Globalization, Regional Integration and the Democratic Compromise*, Ann Arbor, University of Michigan Press.

Åslund, A 2010, *The Last Shall Be The First: The East European Financial Crisis*, Washington, DC, Peterson Institute for International Economics.

Ban, C 2016, *Ruling Ideas: How Global Neoliberalism Goes Local*, Oxford, Oxford University Press.

Bandelj, N 2008, *From Communists to Foreign Capitalists: The Social Foundations of Foreign Direct Investment in Postsocialist Europe*, Princeton, NJ, Princeton University Press.

Barth, JR, Caprio, G Jr, and Levine, R 2006, *Rethinking Bank Regulation: Till Angels Govern*, New York, Cambridge University Press.

Block, FL 1996, *The Vampire State: And Other Myths and Fallacies About the U.S. Economy*, New York, The New Press.

Blyth, M 2013, 'The Austerity Delusion: Why a Bad Idea Won Over the West', *Foreign Affairs*, 92(3), pp. 41–56.

Bohle, D 2014, 'Post-socialist Housing Meets Transnational Finance: Foreign Banks, Mortgage Lending, and the Privatization of Welfare in Hungary and Estonia', *Review of International Political Economy*, 21(4), pp. 913–948.

Bohle, D and Greskovits, B 2007, 'Neoliberalism, Embedded Neoliberalism and Neocorporatism: Towards Transnational Capitalism in Central-East Europe', *West European Politics*, 30(3), pp. 443–466.

Bohle, D and Greskovits, B 2012, *Capitalist Diversity on Europe's Periphery*, Ithaca, NY, Cornell University Press.

Bonin, JP 2010, 'From Reputation amidst Uncertainty to Commitment under Stress: More than a Decade of Foreign-Owned Banking in Transition Economies'. *Comparative Economic Studies*, 52(4), pp. 465–494.

Bonin, JP, Hasan, I and Wachtel, P 2014, 'Banking in Transition Countries', eds AN Berger, P Molyneux, and JOS Wilson, *The Oxford Handbook of Banking*, New York, Oxford University Press, pp. 963–982.

Bonin, JP and Louie, D 2015, 'Did foreign banks "cut and run" or stay committed to Emerging Europe during the crises?' BOFIT Discussion Papers, No. 31. Bank of Finland (April 11). Helsinki, Finland, Bank of Finland, Institute for Economies in Transition.

Böröcz, J 2012, 'Notes on the Geopolitical Economy of Post-Socialism', eds N Bandelj and DJ Solinger, *Socialism Vanquished, Socialism Challenged: Eastern Europe and China, 1989–2009*, Oxford, Oxford University Press, pp. 103–124.

Brenner, R 1989, 'Economic Backwardness in Eastern Europe in Light of Developments in the West', ed D Chirot, *The Origins of Backwardness in Eastern Europe*, Berkeley, University of California Press, pp. 15–52.

Bruszt, L and Vukov, V 2015, "Managing Core-Periphery Relations in Europe", Paper presented at the conference on "European Integration and Pathways away from the Periphery in Europe", European University Institute, Florence, 28–29 May 2015.

Bunce, V 2000, 'The Historical Origins of the East-West Divide: Civil Society, Political Society, and Democracy in Europe', eds N Bermeo and PG Nord, *Civil Society Before Democracy*, Lanham, MD, Rowman & Littlefield, pp. 209–236.

Calomiris, CW and Haber, SH 2014, *Fragile By Design: The Political Origins of Banking Crises and Scarce Credit*, Princeton, NJ, Princeton University Press.

Cerutti, E, Dell'Ariccia, G and Pería, MSM 2007, 'How Banks Go Abroad: Branches or Subsidiaries?' *Journal of Banking and Finance*, 31(6), pp. 1669–1692.

Claessens, S and van Horen, N 2012, 'Foreign Banks: Trends, Impacts and Financial Stability', IMF Working Paper No. 12/10, Washington, DC, International Monetary Fund.

Claessens, S and van Horen, N 2015, 'The Impact of the Global Financial Crisis on Banking Globalization', *IMF Economic Review*, 63(4), pp. 868–918.

Clarke, B and Hardiman, N 2013, 'Ireland: Hubris and Crisis', eds SJ Konzelmann and M Fovargue-Davies, *Banking Systems in Crisis*, pp. 107–133, London and New York, Routledge.

De Cecco, M 2009, 'Italy's Dysfunctional Political Economy', eds M Bull and M Rhodes, *Italy – A Contested Polity*, London and New York, Routledge, 107–127.

De Haas, R, Korniyenko, Y, Loukoianova, E and Pivovarsky, A 2012 'Foreign Banks and the Vienna Initiative: Turning Sinners into Saints', EBRD Working Paper No. 143, London, European Bank for Reconstruction and Development.

Deuber, G 2011, 'Post-Crisis Banking Sector Outlook in CEE', *Osteuropa Wirtschaft*, 56(3–4), pp. 169–194.

Donnelly, S 2014, 'Power Politics and the Undersupply of Financial Stability in Europe', *Review of International Political Economy*, 21(4), pp. 980–1005.

Eichengreen, B 1993, 'European Monetary Unification', *Journal of Economic Literature*, 31(3), 1321–1357.

Engdahl, WF 2009, 'New Wave of Banking Crisis to come from Eastern Europe', *Global Research*, 18 February. Available from: www.globalresearch.ca/next-wave-of-banking-crisis-to-come-from-eastern-europe/12339.

Epstein, RA 2008a, *In Pursuit of Liberalism: International Institutions in Postcommunist Europe*, Baltimore, MD, Johns Hopkins University Press.

Epstein, RA 2008b, 'The Social Context in Conditionality: Internationalizing Finance in Postcommunist Europe', *Journal of European Public Policy*, 15(6), pp. 880–898.

Epstein, RA 2013, 'Central and East European Bank Responses to the Financial 'Crisis: Do Domestic Banks Perform Better in a Crisis than their Foreign-Owned Counterparts?' *Europe-Asia Studies*, 65(3), pp. 528–547.

Epstein, RA 2014a, 'Assets or Liabilities? The Politics of Bank Ownership', *Review of International Political Economy*, 21(4), pp. 765–789.

Epstein, RA 2014b, 'Overcoming "Economic Backwardness" in the European Union', *Journal of Common Market Studies*, 52(1), pp. 17–34.

Epstein, RA 2014c 'When Do Foreign Banks "Cut and Run"? Evidence from West European Bail-outs and East European Markets', *Review of International Political Economy*, 21(4), pp. 847–877.

Epstein, RA 2017, *Banking on Markets: The Transformation of Bank-State Ties in Europe and Beyond*, Oxford, Oxford University Press.

Epstein, RA and Jacoby, W 2014, 'Eastern Enlargement Ten Years On: Transcending the East-West Divide?' *Journal of Common Market Studies*, 52(1), pp. 1–16.

Epstein, RA and Johnson, J 2010, 'Uneven Integration: Economic and Monetary Union in Central and Easter Europe', *Journal of Common Market Studies*, 48(5), pp. 1235–1258.

Epstein, RA and Macartney, H (eds) 2016, 'Dilemmas in post-crisis bank regulation: Supranationalization versus retrenchment', *Journal of Banking Regulation*, 17(1/2), pp. 1–145.

Epstein, RA and Rhodes, M 2016, 'International in Life, National in Death? Banking Nationalism on the Road to Banking Union', eds. JA Caporaso and M Rhodes, *The Political and Economic Dynamics of the Eurozone Crisis*, pp. 200–232. Oxford, Oxford University Press.

European Bank for Reconstruction and Development [EBRD] 2009, *Transition Report 2009: Transition in Crisis?* London: EBRD.

Farkas, B 2013, 'Changes in the European Convergence Model', Monthly Report: 1/13, Vienna, The Vienna Institute for International Economic Studies, pp. 14–19.

Gerschenkron, A 1962, *Economic Backwardness in Historical Perspective*, Cambridge, MA, Belknap Press.

Goyer, M and Valdivielso del Real, R 2014, 'Protection of Domestic Bank Ownership in France and Germany: The Functional Equivalency of Institutional Diversity in Takeovers', *Review of International Political Economy*, 21(4), 790–819.

Grittersová, J 2014, 'Non-Market Cooperation and the Variety of Finance Capitalism in Advanced Democracies', *Review of International Political Economy*, 21(2), 339–371.

Grittersová, J 2016, *Borrowing Credibility: Foreign Financiers and Monetary Regimes*, Ann Arbor, University of Michigan Press.

Gros, D 2013, 'Banking Union with a Sovereign Virus', *Intereconomics*, 48(2), 93–97.

Hall, PA and Soskice, D (eds) 2001, *Varieties of Capitalism: The Institutional Foundations of Comparative Advantage*, New York, Oxford University Press.

Hancké, B, Rhodes, M and Thatcher, M (eds) 2007, *Beyond Varieties of Capitalism: Conflict, Contradictions, and Complementarities in the European Economy*, New York, Oxford University Press.

Hanousek, J, Kočenda, E and Maurel, M 2011, 'Direct and Indirect Effects of FDI in Emerging European Markets: A Survey and Meta-Analysis', *Economic Systems*, 35(3), pp. 301–322.

Hardie, I and Howarth D (eds) 2013, *Market-Based Banking and the International Financial Crisis*, Oxford, Oxford University Press.

Howarth, D and Macartney H (eds) 2016, 'The Politics of Supranational Banking Supervision in Europe', *West European Politics*, 39(3), pp. 415–604.

International Monetary Fund [IMF] 2010a, *Regional Economic Outlook: Europe: Building Confidence*, Washington, DC, International Monetary Fund.

International Monetary Fund [IMF] 2010b, *Romania: Letter of Intent and Technical Memorandum of Understanding*, 5 February. Available from: www.imf.org/external/np/loi/2010/rou/020510.pdf. Accessed 2 September 2016.

Jacoby, W 2014, 'The EU Factor in Fat Times and Lean: Did the EU Amplify the Boom and Soften the Bust?' *Journal of Common Market Studies*, 52(1), 52–70.

Janos, AC 2000, *East Central Europe in the Modern World: The Politics of the Borderlands From Pre – to Postcommunism*, Stanford, CA, Stanford University Press.

Johnson, J 2000, *A Fistful of Rubles: The Rise and Fall of the Russian Banking System*, Ithaca, NY, Cornell University Press.

Johnson, J 2016, *Priests of Prosperity: How Central Bankers Transformed the Postcommunist World*, Ithaca, NY, Cornell University Press.

Katzenstein, P (ed) 1978, *Between Power and Plenty: Foreign Economic Policies of Advanced Industrialized States*, Madison, University of Wisconsin Press.

King, I 2009, 'Eastern European Crisis May Put Us All in the Goulash', *The Times*, 19 February. Available from: www.thetimes.co.uk.

Kohli, A 2004, *State-Directed Development: Political Power and Industrialization in the Global Periphery*, New York, Cambridge University Press.

Kudrna, Z and Gabor, D 2013, 'The Return of Political Risk: Foreign-Owned Banks in Emerging Europe', *Europe Asia Studies*, 65(3), 548–566.

Lindstrom, N and Piroska, D 2007, 'The Politics of Privatization and Europeanization in Europe's Periphery: Slovenian Banks and Breweries for Sale?', *Competition & Change*, 11(2), pp. 115–133.

Martinez-Diaz, L 2009, *Globalizing in Hard Times: The Politics of Banking-Sector Opening in the Emerging World*, Ithaca, NY, Cornell University Press.

Medve-Bálint, G, 2014, 'The Role of the EU in Shaping FDI Flows to East Central Europe', *Journal of Common Market Studies*, 52(1), 35–51.

Naczyk, M, 2015, 'Budapest in Warsaw: Central European Business Elites and the Rise of Economic Patriotism since the Crisis', Paper presented at the 26th Annual SASE Conference (Society for the Advancement of Socioeconomics) 10–12 July 2014, Chicago.

Nölke, A and Vliegenthart, A 2009, 'Enlarging the Varieties of Capitalism: The Emergence of Dependent Market Economies in East Central Europe', *World Politics*, 61(4), pp. 670–702.

Ornston, D 2012, *When Small States Make Big Leaps: Institutional Innovation and High-Tech Competition in Western Europe*, Ithaca, NY, Cornell University Press.

Ortiz, G 2012, 'Emerging Markets Must Lead Bank Reform', *Financial Times*, 5 March, p. 9.

Pauly, LW 1988, *Opening Financial Markets: Banking Politics on the Pacific Rim*, Ithaca, NY, Cornell University Press.

Pérez, SA 1997, *Banking on Privilege: The Politics of Spanish Financial Reform*, Ithaca, NY, Cornell University Press.

Roubini, N and Setser, B 2004, *Bailouts or Bail-Ins? Responding to Financial Crises in Emerging Economies*, Washington, DC, Institute for International Economics.

Schimmelfennig F and Sedelmeier, U (eds) 2005, *The Europeanization of Central and Eastern Europe*, Ithaca, NY, Cornell University Press.

Spendzharova, A 2014, *Regulating Banks in Central and Eastern Europe: Through Crisis and Boom*, Houndmills, Palgrave Macmillan.

Stallings, B with Studart, R 2006, *Finance for Development: Latin America in Comparative Perspective*, Washington, DC, Brookings Institution Press.

Stein, H 2010, 'Financial Liberalization, Institutional Transformation and Credit Allocation in Developing Countries: The World Bank and the Internationalisation of Banking', *Cambridge Journal of Economics*, 34(2), pp. 257–273.

Vachudova, MA 2005, *Europe Undivided: Democracy, Leverage and Integration after Communism*, New York and Oxford, Oxford University Press.

Véron, N 2015, 'Europe's Radical Banking Union', *Bruegel Essay and Lecture Series*, Brussels, Bruegel.

Wade, R 1990, *Governing the Market: Economic Theory and the Role of Government in East Asian Industrialization*, Princeton, NJ, Princeton University Press.

Wade, R 2007, 'The Aftermath of the Asian Financial Crisis: From "Liberalize the Market" to "Standardize the Market" and Create a "Level Playing Field" ', *Ten Years After: Revisiting the Asian Financial Crisis*, ed B Muchhala, Washington, DC, Woodrow Wilson International Center for Scholars, pp. 73–94.

Woo-Cumings, M 1997, 'Slouching toward the Market: The Politics of Financial Liberalization in South Korea', eds M. Loriaux et al., *Capital Ungoverned: Liberalizing Finance in Interventionist States*, Ithaca and London, Cornell University Press, pp. 57–91.

World Bank 2012, *Golden Growth: Restoring the Lustre of the European Economic Model*, Washington, DC, World Bank.

Zysman, J 1983, *Governments, Markets, and Growth: Financial Systems and the Politics of Industrial Change*, Ithaca, NY, Cornell University Press.

PART VI

International relations and actors

25

ENLARGEMENT AND EUROPEANISATION IN CENTRAL AND EASTERN EUROPE

Accession and beyond

Antoaneta L. Dimitrova

Introduction

The EU enlargement incorporating the post-communist states of Central and Eastern Europe (CEE) was completed in 2004–2007 and represented the culmination of more than a decade of negotiations and preparations by the candidate countries and adaptation of policies and decision-making by the Union itself. It was a momentous and difficult undertaking that changed the size and character of the EU, but despite the challenges it brought, it was hailed by many as the true unification of Europe (Avery and Cameron 1997; Dimitrova 2004; Friis 1998; Maniokas 2005; Vachudova 2005; Vassiliou 2007).

The process that we refer to as 'enlargement' consists of intergovernmental negotiations between the member states (as the EU's Council of Ministers) and the candidates. An equally important aspect of enlargement, without which negotiations do not progress, are the candidates' preparations to fulfil the obligations of membership and adopt the existing policies, legislation, and case law of the Union (the *acquis*). As the Union's Eastern or 'big bang' enlargement involved the largest number of potential members – ten post-communist states plus Cyprus and Malta – it required not only the transformation of the candidates, but also the adaptation of the Union's decision making and policies, in particular the Common Agricultural Policy (CAP), the structural funds, and the budget (Vassiliou and Christoffersen 2007:103–105). Enlargement can be thus seen as a set of processes including, but not limited to, EU reforms, negotiations, domestic transformation of the candidates, and the resolution of outstanding bilateral issues and regional conflicts. The domestic transformations that candidates underwent, adopting EU rules in their own legislation and creating new institutions in order to comply with the EU's criteria for accession, are often referred to as Europeanisation. Europeanisation, a concept as used and as contested as 'democratisation', has been defined in the context of the Eastern enlargement as 'a process in which states adopt EU rules' (Schimmelfennig and Sedelmeier 2005a:7).

Almost a decade after enlargement, each of these processes deserves a reassessment with the benefit of hindsight. In this chapter, I will first outline briefly the most important features of the Eastern enlargement as a process of negotiation and adaptation and the policy tools the EU developed to support the CEE countries' transformation to democracies and market economies.

The second section will look at the CEE states as full EU members and discuss how enlargement has been absorbed by member states and their citizens. The following sections will discuss compliance with the EU's *acquis* and economic and political aspects of Europeanisation of the CEE states. I will argue that post-enlargement, the record of CEE countries as EU member states presents a certain paradox, namely that they simultaneously performed much better and much worse as EU member states than expected. To develop this argument, I will highlight key findings in compliance research in CEE and the Europeanization of the polities and politics of CEE states. In terms of complying with the *acquis* of the Union in key policy areas such as the internal market, environmental policy, transport, agriculture, and other 'classic' community policies, CEE states performed much better than expected (Toshkov, 2008; Sedelmeier 2008). Yet in terms of core democratic principles, norms and values, Europeanisation has been more uneven: not only Bulgaria and Romania, seen as the laggards with respect to rule of law and quality of democracy, but also Hungary and more recently Poland have developed their political systems in unexpected ways, evaluated by many as backsliding from democratic achievements (Ágh 2014; Rupnik and Zielonka 2013). The next section will discuss what instruments and tools the EU has used to cope with post-accession democratic backsliding. The last section will highlight crisis responses of the CEE member states and argue that the economic, geopolitical, and refugee crises affecting the EU have put the unity of the enlarged Union to the test.

The EU's unprecedented 'big bang' enlargement

When CEE states applied to join the EU in the early and mid-1990s, the challenge they represented meant that the EU had to formulate clear conditions and guidelines not only for the adoption of the *acquis*, but also for defining the institutional and governance characteristics essential for a member state, such as democratic institutions, rule of law, and market economy. Therefore, meeting in Copenhagen in 1993, the European Council (at the time, the heads of state and government of the twelve EU member states) agreed to offer the CEE states emerging from communist rule a membership perspective and formulated a set of criteria for membership that came to be known as the Copenhagen criteria (European Council in Copenhagen 1993).[1]

Accession negotiations, in contrast to other kinds of international negotiations between the Union and third parties, have been first and foremost about the conditions under which candidates take the *acquis* on board (Avery and Cameron, 1998:31–33). Starting with the Copenhagen criteria, the EU introduced a number of innovations to this traditional method of enlargement (Preston 1997; Maniokas 2004; Dimitrova 2011). These additional conditions are sometimes referred to as the 'enlargement *acquis*', while the policy tools, such as the regular progress reports have become an integral part of the Union's enlargement policy.

After a candidate has officially applied for membership, the European Commission provides a detailed opinion of its political and economic situation. With CEE candidates, this required a detailed process of 'screening' their legislation prior to negotiations to establish their compatibility with the EU's policies (Avery and Cameron 1998; Christoffersen 2007). The EU *acquis* is divided into chapters for the purpose of the negotiations and these chapters are opened and provisionally closed in the Intergovernmental Conferences between the candidates, the Council of the Union, and the European Commission.

Having opened the door to enlargement at the Copenhagen European Council, the Union had to come to grips with the institutional and policy changes needed to make enlargement work. In 1997, the European Commission prepared an important set of proposals presented in the Agenda 2000, detailing the necessary policy reforms in key areas as well as opinions on the membership applications of each of the ten CEE candidates (European Commission 1997).

Following the Commission's opinions and after negotiations at the Luxembourg European Council, the EU decided to open enlargement negotiations with Cyprus, the Czech Republic, Estonia, Hungary, Poland, and Slovenia. A second group of candidates was to be screened and open negotiations when deemed sufficiently prepared (Christoffersen 2007: 31–32; Friis 1998). Deciding which candidates could start negotiations was difficult, as the Union had recently emerged from an Intergovernmental Conference negotiating the Amsterdam Treaty in 1997. Furthermore, various member states were sceptical about the ability of all the candidates to fulfil the obligations of membership, since they were neither fully-fledged democracies nor market economies when they applied. The European Commission, together with member states committed to enlargement, managed to promote an 'objective' approach to enlargement, emphasising candidates' preparation instead of political considerations (Friis 1998). Thus, candidates would move together in the negotiations, but each would progress according to its own speed of preparation, an approach the EU dubbed 'the regatta principle'. In the end, the EU offered all candidates an inclusive process whereby the Council adopted Accession partnerships detailing the reforms needed in each country and the Commission started monitoring progress with regular reports. The five remaining candidates – Bulgaria, Malta, Latvia, Lithuania, Romania, and Slovakia – started negotiating in 2000 after a decision by the Helsinki European Council. The Union proceeded with its own internal negotiations and institutional reforms, reaching a (partial and imperfect) solution for the inclusion of the future members in its institutions embodied in the Nice Treaty in 2000. Ultimately, ten countries joined in 2004, while Bulgaria and Romania were deemed not to have developed market economies. They were able to join later, in 2007. Since the ten CEE states applied and went through key stages of the process approximately at the same time, the 2004–2007 enlargement is seen as a single enlargement round, sometimes called the 'big bang' enlargement.

The Accession Partnerships and the regular yearly reports of the European Commission became institutionalized enlargement policy tools, used not only for measuring progress, but also providing a roadmap of the reforms needed in fundamental areas of governance such as electoral process, public administration, the judiciary, nuclear safety, and many others. The continuous demands for candidates to reform institutions and policies in order to move closer to accession became known as conditionality, a policy tool that emerged as the linchpin of the EU's approach to the 2004–2007 and subsequent enlargements (Schimmelfennig and Sedelmeier 2005a, Dimitrova 2002, 2011). When it emerged that Bulgaria and Romania had serious deficiencies in the area of rule of law and problems with organised crime and corruption, the EU instituted another monitoring tool just before their accession, the Cooperation and Verification Mechanism (CVM). Furthermore, realising the weaknesses in fundamental areas of democratic governance in the whole region and taking the lessons from the 2004–2007 enlargement on board, the EU has shifted the emphasis of its enlargement strategy in the Western Balkans towards fundamental reforms and rule of law. This emphasis on the fundamentals has been reflected in a new sequencing of negotiation chapters, a more elaborate system of benchmarks, and use of financial assistance as an instrument facilitating reforms.

Having adopted wide-ranging reforms in governance and policies in response to the EU's conditionality, the CEE candidates essentially underwent a process of Europeanisation before joining the EU. Europeanisation of the CEE states should be evaluated both in the narrow sense, defined by Schimmelfennig and Sedelmeier (2005b: 7), as the adoption of EU rules and compliance with the *acquis* of the Union and in the broader sense, as institution-building and support for democratic principles and rule of law (Dimitrova 2002, 2010).

Arguably the most important aspect of Europeanisation as institution-building was the anchoring of democratic changes and moderation of political behaviour of political parties and leaders in response to the EU's leverage and conditionality (Schimmelfennig and Sedelmeier 2005a; Vachudova 2005). Alongside democratic consolidation and market reforms, the adaptation of key policy areas to the *acquis* became a form of policy modernisation in many areas and sectors, reflecting the ideas, bargains, and technical solutions the EU had adopted.

Given this extensive adaptation in response to EU conditionality and the requirements of the accession process in all areas, including both domestic and foreign policy, it is fair to say that the enlargement negotiations defined the relations between the EU and the post-communist states in CEE in the 1990s and early 2000 and that they currently define the relations between the EU and the Western Balkans. But what has happened with the new member states after enlargement?

Adapting to enlargement: compliance and decision-making

The CEE countries that took part in EU's big bang enlargement cannot be called new member states any more: the Czech Republic, Estonia, Hungary, Latvia, Lithuania, Poland, Slovakia and Slovenia have been members for more than a decade, Bulgaria and Romania for eight years and even Croatia, which joined on the 1st of July 2013, can look back at more than two years of membership. The CEE member states participate fully in decision-making and implementation of EU policies, and five of them – Estonia, Latvia, Lithuania, Slovakia, and Slovenia – have also joined the Eurozone.

Despite the success of enlargement, worrying trends and developments have emerged suggesting the Cold War divide of Europe has not been overcome. Perceptions of the timing, process, and effects of the Eastern enlargement vary considerably between member states. Among politicians and citizens of the EU–15, arguments that the post-communist states of Eastern Europe joined the EU too fast, before they were ready, are common (Verheugen 2013; Dimitrova et al. 2015). Politicians and commentators from the CEE member states, on the other hand, perceived their countries' road to the Union as too long (Telička and Bartak 2007: 144; Maniokas 2005). The divide between the east and west of the EU is still reified in research, as exemplified by the fact that most analyses of public opinion in the EU examine either the EU–15 (that is, pre-2004 EU members) or the 'new member states', but hardly ever both (Toshkov et al. 2014). Taken together with the divergent responses to the multiple crises the Union has recently encountered, it can be argued that we witness today the unfinished unification of Europe.

The moment when CEE states achieved the status of 'normal' EU members was therefore marked by a historical irony. Just as CEE states gained the confidence and experience to behave as equal partners to the older member states, the EU has been beset by multiple crises, subjecting it to powerful centrifugal forces and overshadowing the historical achievements of Eastern enlargement.

This contradiction between past achievement and current strains make it important to assess the performance of CEE states as member states and their compliance with EU rules, as well as democratic record.

Much of the research before and after CEE accession focused on whether candidates from CEE could function properly as EU members, in terms of transposition of existing *acquis* and compliance with EU rules. Their transposition and implementation record has been investigated in great depth, both quantitatively, across candidates and sectors (Toshkov 2008; Sedelmeier 2008) and qualitatively, through comparative case studies of compliance within certain sectors (Toshkov et al. 2010; Falkner and Treib 2008). Even before they entered, CEE member states had already reached levels of transposition of the EU *acquis* which were equal to and in many cases better than the transposition records of existing member states (Toshkov 2008; Sedelmeier 2008). As they became EU members, the 2004–2007 entrants established a more mixed record, dividing between implementation leaders (Lithuania, Latvia, Slovakia, even, for a while, Bulgaria) and (relative) implementation laggards (the Czech Republic and Poland).

In general, fears that CEE member states would lag behind dramatically in compliance have not materialised. The EU did not suffer from bad implementation, or at least no more than it did before the CEE countries joined. The relative success of the CEE states in transposition of the EU *acquis* should be attributed to a great extent to the substantial upgrades in administrative capacity during the pre-accession period (Dimitrova 2002; Dimitrova and Toshkov 2009; Meyer-Sahling 2004; Zubek 2005; Zubek and Staronova 2010). Next to adopting and adapting to the EU *acquis*, CEE member states have also adjusted to decision-making procedures in the EU and have become increasingly confident as they have organised and conducted successful presidencies of the Council of Ministers (Vandecasteele et al. 2015).

Despite the good transposition record of CEE member states, there have been widespread expectations that transposition would not lead to proper implementation. EU rules have remained 'dead letters' in some policy areas (Falkner and Treib 2008), which has raised questions as to the real Europeanisation of policies in CEE. As research in specific policy areas in CEE has progressed and the number of implementation studies has slowly grown, a more nuanced picture has emerged. In some sectors and some member states, lack of resources and weak rule of law lead to a situation where the EU rules indeed remain dead letters (Falkner and Treib, 2008 Buzogány 2009). There are, however, areas where implementation has worked well and EU rules have led to the Europeanisation of policies (Dimitrova and Steunenberg 2013, Zhelyazkova et al. 2017). There is a considerable sectoral-level difference in implementation, one that can be attributed not only to country-level factors, but also to a number of structural and actor-related factors such as the configuration and preferences of relevant veto players (Dimitrova 2010), state capacity and resources (Buzogány 2009; Falkner and Treib 2008, Dimitrova and Toshkov 2009, Martinsen and Vasev 2015), the configuration of non-state actors, and their capacity and organisation (Börzel and Buzogány 2010).

EU decision-making – measured as the Union's legislative output – has not slowed down as a result of enlargement (Toshkov 2015). Despite complaints that the initial statement of positions (*'tour de table'*) at the Council of Ministers has become unworkably long with twenty-eight member states, this has not translated, on average, to less legislative output from the enlarged EU. This is partly, however, the result of preparation and adjustment in all decision-making for an enlarged Union. Member states and the European Commission embarked on several rounds of institutional and treaty changes (finalised with the Amsterdam, Nice, and Lisbon Treaties), to a great extent driven by the anticipation of larger number of member states (Steunenberg 2002).

Negotiating institutional changes to prepare for enlargement has been anything but easy. EU member states and institutions used enlargement as an opportunity for renegotiating core bargains (Steunenberg 2002). The agreement to limit the number of commissioners once member states reached twenty-five is an example of an enlargement driven adjustment enshrined in the Nice Treaty, but one that remained contentious and was ultimately rejected. Post-Lisbon, informal rules have slowly evolved to supplement the new formal rules governing decision-making in the enlarged Union. As shown by Reh et al. (2013), for example, there have been many more early agreements in co-decision (reached through the so-called trilogues) after enlargement, a development they attribute to the need to alleviate functional pressures on decision-making. There has also been a trend of increasing differentiation between member states (Leuffen et al. 2013), although arguably it is an effect of the division between Eurozone members and the rest of the EU, rather than enlargement.

Core-periphery dynamics: has enlargement led to economic convergence?

When contemplating the success of the Eastern enlargement and the challenges of post-enlargement integration, it is easy to overlook the other enlargement objective of unifying and integrating Europe economically and ending the division between core and periphery (Epstein and Jacoby 2014). As Buzogány and Korkut (2013) have rightly noted, convergence in policies such as structural funds should lead to development and economic convergence. Europeanised policies are not an end in themselves, but rather are the means for the desired increase in prosperity and economic growth in CEE.

A growing body of research investigating trajectories of economic development in CEE after communism has attributed some credit to the EU for economic stabilization, growth and increase in foreign direct investment (FDI) in CEE. While it is clear that the EU's market-liberal orientation and its nature of a regulatory rather than redistributive union have prevented large-scale transfers to CEE states to stimulate development, the EU did support the candidate states' economies in the hardest years of transition. EU support alleviated some of the negative externalities arising from the economic restructuring, which the Union required during pre-accession (Bruszt and Langbein 2017). The EU pre-accession support and structural funds did make a difference for both growth (Epstein and Jacoby 2014) and FDI (Medve-Bálint 2014; Langbein 2015). Attracting FDI, however, was initially a question of low production costs for CEE states, sometimes leading to a 'bidding war' for foreign investment and tensions between candidates and existing member states (Drahokoupil 2009; Medve-Bálint 2014).

As Epstein and Jacoby argued, growth in CEE is not in itself sufficient to change the status of CEE states as European periphery (Epstein and Jacoby 2014). A noticeable increase of complex manufacturing as a share of CEE economies can be seen as the true measure for development and sustainable growth in the region (Bohle and Greskovits 2012; Langbein 2015). In addition, EU structural fund spending has, to a certain extent, softened the impact of the 2008 economic crisis for CEE states (Jacoby 2014) and limited CEE states' vulnerability in the international system (Epstein 2014). However, as Epstein (2014) warns, to achieve sustainable growth under crisis conditions of more limited FDI, the CEE states would need to develop more innovation in their economies.

The generally positive assessment of policy Europeanisation and economic growth following CEE accession to the EU changes when we turn to more recent developments in politics and polities in CEE. Research on Europeanisation East, as Héritier has rightfully noted, has developed contemporaneously with transition research, but the two should be seen as analytically separate (Héritier 2005:204; see also Dimitrova 2004:4–5). The processes of post-communist democratisation and Europeanisation have coincided in time and brought effects of mutual reinforcement for those states that took part in the Eastern enlargement. Nowadays, however, we need to reassess the EU's effects on the polity and politics of CEE states in the light of the illiberal turn in several Central European states.

Polity and politics: backsliding in CEE and the EU

While Bulgaria and Romania have been criticised for weaknesses in their democratic institutions ever since their entry in the EU and continue to suffer serious deficiencies with respect to democracy and the rule of law (Ganev 2013; Dimitrov et al. 2016, 2015; Spendzharova and Vachudova 2012), the backsliding in democratic quality in Hungary and Poland has taken many by surprise.

The constitutional, legislative, and personnel changes made in Hungary by the Fidesz government led by Prime Minister Orbán have affected negatively key democratic and state institutions such as the electoral system, the judiciary and administration, and the media (Ágh 2013; Meyer-Sahling and Jaeger 2012; Rupnik 2012). Elements of Orbán's approach of taking control of state institutions, and limiting judicial independence and media freedom appear to be emulated by the government of the Law and Justice Party (PiS) in Poland, confirming fears of an 'authoritarian turn' in the region (Rupnik and Zielonka 2013:3). The PiS government, in power since 2015, explicitly referred to Orbán's 'illiberal democracy' as a model to emulate (The Economist 2015).

While it is not the task of this chapter to delve into analyses of the causes and mechanisms underlying the illiberal turn in some CEE states, the question what, if anything, the EU can do about it, should be addressed. There are three possible avenues of inquiry: first, to compare the EU's role as an actor engaging with democratisation in CEE before and after accession. Second and connected to the first, the tools that the Union has at its disposal in dealing with backsliding member states should be evaluated. Third, scholars have started asking questions whether the economic model the EU has promoted affects the political economy and thereby the political systems in CEE states (Greskovits 2015; Innes 2014). These three directions will be explored in turn.

Comparing EU leverage before and after accession, scholars note a diminishing power of conditionality: what the EU can do for candidates in terms of encouraging democratic reforms and discouraging backsliding, it cannot do for its full members (Sedelmeier 2008; Epstein and Sedelmeier 2008; Dimitrova 2010). Before accession, the EU was considered by many to have a kind of transformative power, based on the tools discussed earlier, underpinned by incentives and socialisation mechanisms (Dimitrova 2002; Grabbe 2006; Schimmelfennig and Sedelmeier 2005a; Vachudova 2005). There is near universal agreement among scholars that the EU conditionality and pre-accession support were beneficial for democratic institutions (Dimitrova 2004, Grabbe 2006; Ekiert 2008; Jacoby 2006; Levitz and Pop-Eleches 2010; Vachudova 2005). It must be noted, however, that there are some important disagreements with the story of the EU's transformative power; for example, Mungiu-Pippidi (2014) has argued that the EU was able to promote democracy only to a limited extent and has failed to promote good governance. Yet while most scholars claimed the EU's pre-accession tools played a positive role for consolidation of democracy, post-accession the Union's role was found to be weaker (Levitz and Pop-Eleches 2010). The Union has limited instruments and even more limited will to deal with what Ganev dubbed 'post-accession hooliganism' of CEE members (2013).

The instruments the EU has at its disposal to affect democratic backsliding in member states, can be divided into those explicitly targeting specific states – the CVM for Bulgaria and Romania – and the tools available for all member states, such as Article 7 of the Treaty on the European Union (TEU). The CVM's record is mixed and opinions of its effectiveness and usefulness are divided (Dimitrov et al. 2014, 2016; Dimitrova 2015; Toneva-Metodieva 2014; Spendzharova and Vachudova 2012). The European Commission itself did not appear to find the CVM an effective mechanism, as evidenced by the fact that it changed enlargement strategies for Croatia and the Western Balkan candidates respectively in 2011, 2013, and 2015 to put fundamental democratic governance reforms and their implementation at the centre of accession negotiations.

With respect to EU sanctions beyond the CVM, existing studies show mixed results as well. Sedelmeier's (2014) comparative study of the EU's post-accession efforts to contain democratic backsliding in Romania and Hungary sought to establish whether and under what conditions the EU had an influence. Sedelmeier qualified the EU's efforts to address breaches in liberal democracy in Hungary as highly selective and partially effective. He found that transnational partisan politics had a negative impact on the EU's ability to mobilise and impose sanctions, with party groups in the EP supporting or denying sanctions instrumentally depending on the party affiliation of those violating democratic principles (Sedelmeier 2014:133). Both Sedelmeier (2014) and Spendzharova and Vachudova (2012) highlighted the importance of issue linkages (e.g. with Schengen membership) for successful leverage from the EU on non-*acquis* matters such as media or judicial independence. Using issue linkages, Bulgarian environmentalists have used EU rules in some policy areas to challenge lack of transparency in other, related policy areas (Dimitrova and Buzogány 2014).

The effectiveness of article 7 of the TEU, created to address fundamental breaches of democratic principles in member states, has also been questioned (Sedelmeier, 2014; van Hüllen and Börzel, 2013). Article 7 is known as 'the nuclear option', referring to the demanding voting threshold required to make it work and its far-reaching consequences of suspending voting rights, both making it near impossible to apply. To create a more nuanced approach, the EU adopted a mechanism in 2014 to address systematic violations of rule of law and democratic principles, which relies on a European Commission opinion and reflection and ultimately may lead to the activation of Article 7 TEU (European Commission 2014).

The experience with Hungary seems to have had an impact on EU institutions with regard to other potential cases of backsliding. When the new Law and Justice (PiS) government in Poland started 'remaking the state in a hurry' in the last days of 2015 (The Economist 2015), the European Commission and European Parliament took a series of highly visible steps suggesting the possibility of sanctioning Poland under the new mechanism for breaches of democratic principles and rule of law. The Polish government and parliament were addressed in two letters by Commission Vice President Frans Timmermans. Commission President Jean-Claude Juncker and Commissioner Günther Oettinger hinted the letters could be the first steps in triggering the mechanism addressing violations of the rule of law and democratic principles (Rettman 2015; Reuters 2016). The European Parliament (EP) invited Polish Prime Minister Beata Szydło for a hearing in early 2016 (Zalan 2016). The proactive approach from the Commission and the EP towards the law amendments affecting the constitutional court and media in Poland can be explained with the lessons from earlier confrontations with Hungary's Fidesz government, in which the EU was considered rather weak and ineffective.

It is too early to evaluate whether the EU's more proactive approach will have an effect in Poland, but it is clear that the governments in Poland and Hungary, backed by large parliamentary majorities, do not shy away from a confrontation with 'Brussels'. The lingering social effects of decades of reforms combined with the expectation of prosperity thwarted by the economic crisis allow anti-EU rhetoric to flourish and resonate with the public, as shown by some citizens' discourses regarding enlargement (Dimitrova et al. 2015).

The effects of EU supported economic policies are seen by some authors as a major cause for democratic backsliding (Greskovits 2015; Ágh 2013). Greskovits has argued that the development of neoliberal economies in Latvia, Lithuania, Slovakia, or Bulgaria has led to hollowing of democracy in these states (Greskovits 2015). However, Greskovits has also found that more welfare-oriented policies and an active civil society in Hungary have not led to democratic resilience. Instead, the rollback of democracy in Hungary occurred in the context of mobilized and vibrant civil society (Greskovits 2015).

The rules of the EU's single market and Economic and Monetary Union have limited the space for different domestic economic policies and taken over some competences from the national level. In some CEE states this may exacerbate existing problems and contribute to the rise of populist and illiberal political forces. To establish whether this is indeed the case, future research would need to investigate the potential link between inequality, EU policies, and illiberal politics.

Responses to the crises: no longer trying to be the best pupils in the class

Just like the older member states in the North and South of Europe, CEE member states have been affected in varying degrees by the series of major crises: the Eurozone and sovereign debt crisis; the Greek debt crisis; the Ukraine crisis and the annexation of the Crimea in 2013–2014; the migration and refugee crisis in 2014–2016; and the terrorist attacks in Europe in 2015–2016. The fact that member states are affected in different ways and degrees has meant that common solutions have been hard to develop (Lefkofridi and Schmitter 2014).

Slovakia's stance towards the Greek bailout and crisis was an example of the divergent domestic and European pressures affecting domestic politics. Slovaks have argued that a state as poor as Slovakia should not be required to fund the bailout of much richer Greece. Slovakia's centre-right government, led by Prime Minister Iveta Radičová, lost a parliamentary vote of confidence linked to the Slovak contribution to the Greek bailout (Haughton 2014). Not only for Slovakia, but also for Latvia, the Greek bailout stood in contrast to the costs of the transformations they had gone through. In opposition to the Greek left that presented the Greek crisis as a confrontation between the rich North and the poor South, Slovaks and Latvians argued that it was not about austerity, but rather about much needed reforms Greece needed to undertake, just as CEE states had done.

During the most severe of the multiple crises that beset the EU, the refugee crisis, the Czech Republic, Hungary, and Slovakia challenged measures proposed by Germany. A rare coordinated response from the Visegrád Group opposed the EU plan for quotas for refugee distribution (Vlada.cz 2015). For the first time since enlargement, member states preferences seemed to cluster along the East-West divide (although Poland, Bulgaria, and the Baltic states voted in favour of the quota plan). In addition, in December 2015, Slovakia announced it would challenge the EU's decision on migrant quotas in front of the European Court of Justice. Such actions hint at a possible negative future scenario: the formation of an illiberal alliance between the current governments of the Visegrád Group of states, further increasing the gap between East and West in Europe (The Economist 2015). Ultimately, the Eurozone crisis or the refugee crisis did not have much to do with the effects of enlargement. Nevertheless, decreasing solidarity and a lack of common response to these crises exacerbates and exaggerates the differences between member states.

CEE states are far from being the only ones to exhibit short-sighted or nationalist behaviour in response to Europe's multiple crises. As Rupnik and Zielonka noted, the EU as a whole has not set a great example: 'If old European democracies find it extremely difficult to cope with the damaging implications of the current crisis, can new democracies be expected to do any better?' (2013:4). There has been hardly any leader in the EU – bar German Chancellor Angela Merkel – that has shown the way for a different, less self-interested approach to dealing with each other in the Union. Neither then UK Prime Minister David Cameron's push of negotiating a deal for the UK in February 2016 to the detriment of non-discrimination principles, nor the mix of scepticism, pragmatism and efficiency of the Danish or the Dutch, can serve as an example for CEE leaders of how to approach the EU as more than a zero-sum game.

In conclusion

The previous sections have shown that the integration of CEE states into the EU was quite successful and exceeded the rather pessimistic expectations at the start of the enlargement process, at least with respect to the classical areas of European integration and the absorption of the *acquis*.

Participation in the Union's decision-making institutions – the Council of the European Union, the European Commission, and the European Parliament – has also been less problematic than expected. Not only have CEE states become more adept and vocal at defending their positions in the EU, but they have also become more focused on their national interests. They can be seen as 'normal' members, less inclined to take a back seat and avoid confrontation with older member states. This normalisation is not a problem in itself, but it has put additional stress on a Union battered by crises and centrifugal forces. Public opinion studies show a perceived gap between East and West of Europe, making it painfully clear that European unification is still far from complete. Nationalist rhetoric and chaotic responses to the multiple crises affecting Europe have been driving member states further apart.

For the moment at least, the gap between East and West is one of rhetoric and perception rather than implementation and decision-making. The EU's big bang enlargement has been a challenging, but successful project, making the EU a bigger economic and geopolitical player and ameliorating some of the effects of global economic downturn. We can only hope that the enlarged EU will find a way to complete its unification and uphold the values and principles that made the Eastern enlargement a success.

Note

1 According to these, membership requires that

'a candidate has achieved stability of institutions guaranteeing democracy, the rule of law, human rights and respect for and protection of minorities, the existence of a functioning market economy as well as the capacity to cope with competitive pressure and market forces within the Union. Membership presupposes the candidate's ability to take on the obligations of membership including adherence to the aims of political, economic and monetary union.'

References

Ágh, A. (2013) The triple crisis in Hungary: The backsliding of Hungarian democracy after twenty years. *Romanian Journal of Political Science*, 13(1): 25–51.
Ágh, A. (2014) The fall of the Berlin Wall and European politics: Perspectives of new Europe in the early twenty first century, in Magone, J. (ed.) *Routledge Handbook of European Politics*. London: Routledge, pp. 116–131.
Avery, G. and Cameron, F. (1998) *The Enlargement of the European Union*, Sheffield: Sheffield Academic Press.
Bohle, D. and Greskovits, B. (2012) *Capitalist Diversity on Europe's Periphery*. Ithaca, NY: Cornell University Press.
Börzel, T. and Buzogány, A. (2010) Governing EU accession in transition countries: The role of non-state actors. *Acta Politica*, 45(1–2): 158–182.
Bruszt, L. and Langbein, J. (2017) Varieties of disembedded liberalism: EU integration strategies in the Eastern peripheries of Europe. *Journal of European Public Policy*, 24(2): 297–315.
Buzogány, A. (2009) Romania: Environmental governance: Form without substance, in Börzel, T. (ed.) *Coping with accession to the European Union*. Basingstoke, Hampshire: Palgrave Macmillan, pp. 169–191.
Buzogány, A. and Korkut, U. (2013) Administrative reform and regional development discourses in Hungary. Europeanisation going NUTS? *Europe-Asia Studies*, 65(8): 1555–1577.
Christoffersen, P.S. (2007) The preparation of the fifth enlargement, in Vassiliou, G. (ed.) *The Accession Story: The EU from 15 to 25 Countries*. Oxford: Oxford University Press, pp. 24–33.
Dimitrov, G., Haralampiev, K. and Stoychev, S. (2016) The adventures of the CVM in Bulgaria and Romania. *MAXCAP Working Paper Series*, No. 29, "Maximizing the integration capacity of the European Union: Lessons of and prospects for enlargement and beyond" (MAXCAP), Berlin. Available at: http://userpage. fu-berlin.de/kfgeu/maxcap/system/files/maxcap_wp_29.pdf [Accessed 22 August 2016].
Dimitrov, G., Haralampiev, K., Stoychev, S. and Toneva-Metodieva, L. (2014) *The Cooperation and Verification Mechanism: A Shared Political Irresponsibility Between European Commission and the Bulgarian Governments*. Sofia: St Kliment Ochridski University Press.

Dimitrova, A. (2002) Enlargement, institution building and the EU's administrative capacity requirement. *West European Politics* 25(4): 171–190.

Dimitrova, A. (2004) Enlargement driven change and post-communist transformations: A new perspective, in Dimitrova, A. L. (ed.) *Driven to Change: The European Union's Enlargement Viewed from the East*. Manchester University Press, Manchester, pp. 1–17.

Dimitrova, A. (2010) The new member states of the EU in the aftermath of enlargement: Do new European rules remain empty shells? *Journal of European Public Policy*, 17(1): 137–148.

Dimitrova, A. (2011) Speeding up or slowing down? Lessons from the last enlargement on the dynamics of enlargement-driven reform. *South European Society and Politics*, 16(2): 221–235.

Dimitrova, A. (2015) The effectiveness and limitations of political integration in Central and Eastern European member states: Lessons from Bulgaria and Romania. *MAXCAP Working Paper Series*, No. 10, "Maximizing the integration capacity of the European Union: Lessons of and prospects for enlargement and beyond" (MAXCAP). Berlin. Available at: http://userpage.fu-berlin.de/kfgeu/maxcap/system/files/maxcap_wp_10.pdf [Accessed 21 August 2016].

Dimitrova, A. and Buzogány, A. (2014) Post accession policy making in Bulgaria and Romania: Can non-state actors use EU rules to promote better governance? *Journal of Common Market Studies*, 52(1): 139–157.

Dimitrova, A., Kortenska, E. and Steunenberg, B. (2015) Comparing discourses about past and future EU enlargements: Core arguments and cleavages. *MAXCAP Working Paper Series*, No. 13, "Maximizing the integration capacity of the European Union: Lessons of and prospects for enlargement and beyond" (MAXCAP). Berlin. Available at: http://userpage.fu-berlin.de/kfgeu/maxcap/system/files/maxcap_wp_13_2.pdf

Dimitrova, A. and Steunenberg, B. (2013) Living in parallel universes? Implementing European movable cultural heritage policy in Bulgaria. *Journal of Common Market Studies*, 51(1): 246–263.

Dimitrova, A. and Toshkov, D. (2009) Post-accession compliance between administrative co-ordination and political bargaining, *European Integration Online Papers* (EIoP), 2.

Drahokoupil, J. (2009). *Globalization and the state in Central and Eastern Europe*. London: Routledge.

The Economist (2015) *Europe's New Headache* [online]. Available at: www.economist.com/news/leaders/21679470-new-government-poland-has-made-awful-start-europes-new-headache [Accessed 10 January 2016].

Ekiert, G. (2008) Dilemmas of Europeanization: Eastern and Central Europe after the EU enlargement. *Acta Slavica Japonika*, 25: 1–28.

Epstein, R. A. (2014) Overcoming 'economic backwardness' in the European union. *Journal of Common Market Studies*, 52(1): 17–34.

Epstein, R. A. and Jacoby, W. (2014) Eastern enlargement ten years on: Transcending the East-West divide? *Journal of Common Market Studies*, 52(1): 1–17.

Epstein, R. and Sedelmeier, U. (2008) Beyond conditionality: International institutions in postcommunist Europe after enlargement. *Journal of European Public Policy*, 15(6): 795–805.

European Commission (1997) *Agenda 2000: For a Stronger and Wider Union*. Available at: http://ec.europa.eu/agriculture/cap-history/agenda-2000/com97-2000_en.pdf [Accessed 31 March 2016]

European Commission (2014) *Communication from the Commission to the European Parliament and the Council: A New EU Framework to Strengthen the Rule of Law*. COM(2014) 158 final/2.

European Council in Copenhagen (1993) *Conclusions of the Presidency*. Available at: www.consilium.europa.eu/en/european-council/conclusions/1993-2003/ [Accessed 31 March 2016].

Falkner, G. and Treib, O. (2008) Three worlds of compliance or four? The EU-15 compared to new member states. *Journal of Common Market Studies*, 46(2): 293–313.

Friis, L. (1998) The end of the beginning of Eastern enlargement – Luxembourg Summit and agenda-setting. *European Integration Online Papers* 2(7); http://eiop.or.at/eiop/texte/1998-007a.htm.

Ganev, V. (2013) Post-accession hooliganism – Democratic governance in Bulgaria and Romania after 2007. *East European Politics & Societies* 27(1): 26–44.

Grabbe, H. (2006) *The EU's Transformative Power: Europeanization through Conditionality in Central and Eastern Europe*. Basingstoke and New York: Palgrave Macmillan.

Greskovits, B. (2015) The hollowing and backsliding of democracy in East Central Europe. *Global Policy* 6(1): 28–37.

Haughton, T. (2014) Money, margins and the motors of politics: The EU and the development of party politics in Central and Eastern Europe. *Journal of Common Market Studies* 52(1): 71–87.

Héritier, A. (2005) Europeanization research East and West: A comparative assessment, in Schimmelfennig, F. and Sedelmeier, U. (eds) *The Europeanization of Central and Eastern Europe*. Ithaca, NY: Cornell University Press.

Innes, A. (2014) The political economy of state capture in Central Europe. *Journal of Common Market Studies*, 52(1): 88–104.

Jacoby, W. (2006) Inspiration, coalition and substitution: External Influences on postcommunist transformations. *World Politics*, 58(4): 623–651.

Jacoby, W. (2014) The EU factor in fat times and in lean: Did the EU amplify the boom and soften the bust? *Journal of Common Market Studies*, 52(1): 52–70.

Langbein, J. (2015) *Transnationalization and regulatory change in the EU's eastern neighbourhood*. London: Routledge.

Lefkofridi, Z. and Schmitter, P. (2014). Transcending or descending? European integration in times of crisis. *European Political Science Review*, 7(1): 3–22.

Leuffen, D., Rittberger, B. and Schimmelfennig, F. (2013). *Differentiated Integration*. Houndmills, Basingstoke: Palgrave Macmillan.

Levitz, P., and Pop-Eleches, G. (2010). Why no backsliding? The European Union's impact on democracy and governance before and after accession. *Comparative Political Studies*, 43(4): 457–485.

Maniokas, K. (2004) The method of EU enlargement: A critical appraisal, in Dimitrova, A. L. (ed.) *Driven to Change: The European Union's Enlargement Viewed from the East*. Manchester: Manchester University Press, pp. 17–37.

Maniokas, K. (2005) Road to negotiations: Enlargement instruments and the development of Lithuania's status, in Maniokas, K., Vilpišauskas, R. and Žeruolis, D. (eds.) *Lithuania's Road to the European Union: Unification of Europe and Lithuania's EU Accession Negotiation*. Vilnius: Eugrimas, pp. 19–59.

Martinsen, D. and Vasev, N. (2015). A difficult encounter – National health care models and the EU. *Social Policy & Administration*, 49(4): 427–444.

Medve-Bálint, G. (2014). The role of the EU in shaping FDI flows to East Central Europe. *Journal of Common Market Studies*, 52(1): 35–51.

Meyer-Sahling, J. H. (2004) Civil service reform in post-communist Europe: The bumpy road to depoliticisation. *West European Politics*, 27(1): 69–101.

Meyer-Sahling, J. H., and Jaeger, K. (2012). Capturing the state: Party patronage in Hungary, in Kopecký, P., Mair, P. and Spirova, M. (eds.) *Party Patronage and Party Government: Public Appointments and Political Control in European Democracies*. Oxford: Oxford University Press.

Mungiu-Pippidi, A. (2014) The transformative power of Europe revisited. *Journal of Democracy*, 25(1): 2–32.

Preston, C. (1997) *Enlargement and integration in the European Union*. London: Routledge.

Reh, C., Héritier, A., Bressanelli, E. and Koop, C. (2013) The informal politics of legislation: Explaining secluded decision making in the European Union. *Comparative Political Studies*, 46(1): 1112–1142.

Rettman, A. (2015) EU urges Poland to halt constitutional reform. *EU Observer*. Available at: https://euobserver.com/justice/131665 [Accessed 5 January 2016].

Reuters UK (2016) *German Commissioner to Push for EU Action over Poland's Media Law*, 3 January. Available at: http://uk.reuters.com/article/uk-poland-eu-media-germany-idUKKBN0UH0CJ20160103 [Accessed 6 January 2016].

Rupnik, J. (2012). How things went wrong. *Journal of Democracy*, 23(3): 132–137.

Rupnik, J. and Zielonka, J. (2013). Introduction: The state of democracy 20 years on: Domestic and external factors. *East European Politics & Societies*, 27(1): 3–15.

Schimmelfennig, F. and Sedelmeier, U. (2005a) *The Europeanization of Central and Eastern Europe*. Ithaca, NY: Cornell University Press.

Schimmelfennig, F. and Sedelmeier, U. (2005b) Conceptualizing the Europeanization of Central and Eastern Europe, in Schimmelfennig, F. and Sedelmeier, U. (eds.) *The Europeanization of Central and Eastern Europe*. Ithaca, NY: Cornell University Press, pp. 1–29.

Sedelmeier, U. (2008) After conditionality: Post accession compliance with EU Law in East Central Europe. *Journal of European Public Policy*, 15(6): 806–825.

Sedelmeier, U. (2014) Anchoring democracy from above? The European Union and democratic backsliding in Hungary and Romania after accession. *Journal of Common Market Studies*, 52(1): 105–121.

Spendzharova, A. and Vachudova, M. A. (2012) Catching up? Consolidating Liberal democracy in Bulgaria and Romania after EU accession. *West European Politics*, 35(1): 20–38.

Steunenberg, B. (2002) *Widening of the European Union: The Politics of Institutional Change and Reform*. London: Routledge.

Telička, P. and Bartak, K. (2007) The accession of the Czech Republic to the EU, in Vassiliou, G. (ed.) *The Accession Story: The EU from 15 to 25 Countries*. Oxford: Oxford University Press, pp. 144–156.

Toneva-Metodieva, L. (2014) Beyond the carrots and sticks paradigm: Rethinking the cooperation and verification experience of Bulgaria and Romania. *Perspectives on European Politics and Society* 15(4): 1–18.

Toshkov, D. (2008) Embracing European law: Compliance with EU directives in Central and Eastern Europe. *European Union Politics*, 9(3): 379–342.

Toshkov, D. (2015) The effects of the Eastern enlargement on the decision-making capacity of the European Union. *MAXCAP Working Paper Series*, No. 5, March 2015.

Toshkov, D., Kortenska, E., Dimitrova, A., Fagan, A. (2014) The 'old' and the 'new' Europeans: Analyses of public opinion on EU enlargement in review. *MAXCAP Working Paper Series*, No. 02, "Maximizing the integration capacity of the European Union: Lessons of and prospects for enlargement and beyond" (MAXCAP). Berlin. Available at: http://userpage.fu-berlin.de/kfgeu/maxcap/system/files/maxcap_wp_02.pdf [Accessed 18 August 2016].

Toshkov, D., Knoll, M. and Wewerka, L. (2010) Connecting the dots: A review of case studies of compliance and application of EU law. *Working Paper* 10/2010. Institute for European Integration Research, Vienna.

Vachudova, M. A. (2005), *Europe Undivided: Democracy, Leverage and Integration After Communism*. Oxford: Oxford University Press.

van Hüllen, V. and Börzel, T. A. (2013) The EU's governance transfer. From external promotion to internal protection? *SFB Governance Working Paper Series*, No. 56, Berlin: Collaborative Research Center (SFB).

Vandecasteele, B., Bossuyt, F. and Orbie, J. (2015). A fuzzy-set qualitative comparative analysis of the Hungarian, Polish and Lithuanian Presidencies and European Union eastern partnership policies. *European Politics and Society*, 16(4): 556–580.

Vassiliou, G. (2007) The public attitude to enlargement in EU, in Vassiliou, G. (ed.) *The Accession Story: The EU from 15 to 25 Countries*. Oxford: Oxford University Press, pp. 108–116.

Vassiliou, G. and Christoffersen, P. S. (2007) Financing the enlargement, in Vassiliou, G. (ed.) *The Accession Story: The EU from 15 to 25 Countries*. Oxford: Oxford University Press, pp. 100–108.

Verheugen, G. (2013) *Enlargement since 2000: Too much too soon? The Crisis of EU enlargement, LSE ideas special report, SR018*; http://www.lse.ac.uk/IDEAS/publications/reports/pdf/SR018/Verheugen.pdf [Accessed 15 May 2017].

Vlada.cz (2015). *Statement of the Heads of Governments of the Visegrad Group | Government of the Czech Republic*, 4 September. Available at: www.vlada.cz/en/media-centrum/aktualne/statement-of-the-heads-of-governments-of-the-visegrad-group-134161/ [Accessed 7 January 2016].

Zalan, E. (2016). 'We will continue' with changes, Polish PM tells EU. *EUobserver*, 19 January. Available at: https://euobserver.com/political/131910 [Accessed 31 March 2016].

Zhelyazkova, A., Kaya, C. and Schrama, R. (2017) Notified and substantive compliance with EU law in enlarged Europe: Evidence from four policy areas. *Journal of European Public Policy* 24(2): 216–238.

Zubek, R. (2005) Complying with transposition commitments in Poland: Collective dilemmas, core executive and legislative outcomes. *West European Politics* 28(3): 592–619.

Zubek, R. and Staronova, K. (2010) Ministerial transposition of EU Directives: Can oversight improve performance? *Institute for European Integration Research Working Paper*, 9, Vienna: EIF. Available at: https://eif.univie.ac.at/downloads/workingpapers/wp2010-09.pdf [Accessed 20 August 2016].

26

NATO ENLARGEMENT AND THE POST-COMMUNIST STATES

Mark Webber

Introduction

The North Atlantic Treaty Organization (NATO), so the cliché goes, was created 'to keep the Russians out, the Americans in and the Germans down' (quote by Lord Ismay cited in Medcalf 2005: 3). This blunt (and probably apocryphal) characterisation conveys, nonetheless, an important meaning. NATO's overt purpose, to defend against a known adversary, has necessarily entailed transatlantic support and the co-option of continental Europe's major power. In other words, as with all alliances, NATO's strength is in numbers. What is striking is by how much that number has increased. NATO has grown from an original twelve members to twenty-eight (likely to become twenty-nine in 2017). Growth, moreover, has occurred in the midst of other profound changes. Since the termination of the Cold War, the alliance has acquired a range of new functions. Collective defence has remained significant, but equal standing has also been given to two other 'core tasks': 'crisis management' and 'cooperative security' (NATO 2010: para. 4). NATO has thus seen action in places as far apart as the Balkans, Libya, and Afghanistan. All this, moreover, has been accompanied by an ongoing process of institutionalisation (standardisation, defence planning, and command coordination), an emphasis on political solidarity, and creative efforts in the realm of doctrinal and strategic thinking.

None of this is to idealise NATO's recent (or, indeed, longer) history. The alliance has been troubled by internal division during all six decades of its existence. Questions have been regularly posed about the wisdom and efficacy of its operations, as well as the structural weakness occasioned by European dependency on American military power. NATO, nonetheless, has confounded expectations that its demise is imminent (Thies 2009: 1–24). Prognostications of collapse (or, at least, irrelevance) following the end of the Cold War, 9/11, or the 2003 Iraq crisis do not bear scrutiny when set against the reorientation of NATO purpose each of these historical watersheds occasioned. And while a certain scepticism of NATO's roles in Bosnia and Herzegovina, Kosovo, Libya, and Afghanistan may be justified, here NATO's defenders can still point to the alliance's resilience in the face of demanding security challenges (Webber 2013: 28–29). If, as Tetrais (2004; 139) has argued, 'permanent multinational alliances appear increasingly to belong to the past', then it is clear that NATO has bucked the trend. NATO has outlived its Cold War contemporaries (the Warsaw Pact, the Southeast Asia Treaty Organization, ANZUS, and the Western European Union), and has provided a framework of cooperative effort much more substantial than its putative post–Cold War rivals (the Russian-led Collective Security Treaty Organisation, for instance).

Enlargement was emblematic of NATO's 'reinvention' in the years immediately after the Cold War (Asmus 2005); an exercise in NATO's repurposing as well as Europe's reordering. It played with the rhetoric of the time – of creating 'a Europe whole and free', in partnership not competition with post-Soviet Russia, in accordance with America's continued engagement in the continent, and in alignment with a unified Germany's new eastern agenda. During the 1990s, enlargement, therefore, promised much. But even then it competed with NATO's other more urgent priority of managing conflict in the Balkans. Order, in other words, was as much about operational deployment and reconfiguration as it was adding new members. This was much more the case with NATO's post-9/11 involvement in Afghanistan (outside of Europe and detached entirely from the enlargement agenda). With the Crimean and Ukraine crises of 2014, meanwhile, NATO has been required to refocus on Europe and so pay greater attention to the security interests of its new eastern members.

NATO enlargement is considered in this chapter with this background in mind. The premise of the chapter is that the consequences of enlargement for post-communist Europe are inseparable from how the policy has affected NATO. That interaction informs the chapter's structure. The first two sections are largely descriptive, offering a short chronological account and an overview of enlargement's geographic scope. The chapter then moves to an analysis of the reasoning (and debates) behind the policy and the attendant scholarly explanations. This is followed by consideration of enlargement's consequences and then some reflections on its future course.

A short history of enlargement

Formed in April 1949, NATO was first established with twelve members. Article 10 of the North Atlantic Treaty made possible a future expansion of alliance membership, but the scope of enlargement was necessarily constrained by the geopolitical reality of the emerging Cold War. This ruled out membership for East European countries then under Soviet occupation (the Soviet invasion of Hungary in 1956 put paid to any notion that East European states enjoyed latitude in their security policy) as well as for independent socialist states such Albania and Yugoslavia. Over the subsequent four decades, NATO enlargement conformed to Europe's bipolar division. Greece and Turkey obtained membership in 1952 – these countries' strategic significance outweighing the reservations held by some in NATO on their democratic credentials (Smith 2000: 62–95). Geopolitical logic was starker still in the case of Germany. Accession of the Federal Republic of Germany to NATO in 1955 was intended to accommodate German rearmament and to subordinate the West German military to a multilateral (but US-led) defence framework. It also entrenched Germany and Europe's division. The formation of the Warsaw Pact, incorporating the German Democratic Republic (GDR) alongside the Soviet Union and six other East European states, was announced less than two weeks after West Germany's move into the alliance. Following these events, NATO membership remained static for nearly three decades. Spain joined the alliance in 1982 and this proved to be the last enlargement of the Cold War period.

Although these instances were significant, NATO expended little political energy on enlargement. During the period of *détente* in the late 1960s and early 1970s, NATO did favour 'eliminating the [. . .] unnatural barriers between Eastern and Western Europe' in service of a 'just and lasting peaceful order' on the continent (NATO 1967a: para. 1; NATO 1967b: para. 7). How such an achievement would affect NATO's core functions and size remained, however, unspecified (and unexplored) as the exigencies of coping with ongoing East-West competition remained uppermost in NATO priorities. This state of affairs changed dramatically between 1989 and 1991. German unification in 1990 brought the territory of the former GDR into NATO. NATO's London Declaration of July 1990, meanwhile, extended a 'hand of friendship' to 'the countries of the East' and, in parallel, called for a declaration of non-aggression with the Warsaw Pact (NATO 1990). The November 1991 'New Strategic Concept' (replacing a document which had stood since 1968) made clear that amid uncertainty in Europe, NATO had an ongoing purpose – to guard against emerging, 'multi-faceted [. . .] and multi-directional' risks (NATO 1991a: para. 8). This meant a reconfiguration of NATO's military tasks, as well an elevation of its political role; addressing new challenges would require dialogue and cooperation with the still extant Soviet Union and former Warsaw Pact countries. In a groundbreaking move, NATO thus established the North Atlantic Cooperation Council ushering in what it suggested was 'a new era of partnership' (NATO 1991b: para. 11).

With the exception of GDR (which was an unusual case), several years would elapse before NATO's openness to former communist countries translated into membership. That this process took so long ought not to be a surprise given how drawn out enlargement had been in previous decades. Explanations of enlargement will be considered below, but at this point it is worth noting its contextual circumstances. In the 1990s, Goldgeier (1999: 1) noted that the policy of extending NATO membership was 'highly controversial, and [. . .] by no means inevitable.' It enjoyed no natural constituency within the alliance and was opposed by Russia. In that light, the story of how enlargement came to policy prominence has been told largely in reference to the US's conversion to the cause. But American advocacy alone did not determine the outcome. The institutional 'architecture' of European security in the 1990s and early 2000s seemed predisposed to NATO enlargement in that no other body (be that the EU or the Organisation for Security and Cooperation in Europe) had, after the Cold War, developed the combined functions of collective defence, conflict management, and coercive power (Croft 2000). The demand for membership was thus considerable, and in order to manage it NATO developed a variety of mechanisms – Partnership for Peace, and Membership Action Plans (MAP) being the best known – aimed at moving aspiring members towards NATO military (and perhaps less obviously, political) standards. Sometimes criticised for being overly bureaucratic, these arrangements (with some notable exceptions considered later in this chapter) have not impeded the alliance's enlargement. In 1999, NATO took in the Czech Republic, Hungary, and Poland; it went on in 2004 to incorporate seven further states – Bulgaria, Estonia, Latvia, Lithuania, Romania, Slovakia, and Slovenia. Following that wave, Albania and Croatia acceded to NATO in 2009; Montenegro concluded accession talks in May 2016 and was expected to join the Alliance in 2017.

The limits of enlargement

NATO enlargement, it was noted earlier, has been determined by geopolitical constraints. Equally important has been a geographic delimitation. Article 10 of the North Atlantic Treaty allows for accession by European states only. During the Cold War, such a position reflected NATO's focus on European defence. As operations moved 'out-of-area' from the 1990s, so this operational pre-occupation underwent revision. After 9/11, commentators thus began to talk seriously of a 'global NATO'. Australia, Japan, South Korea, Brazil, India, and South Africa were all considered to be in the frame for membership. By this point, NATO had already constructed an expansive network of partnerships stretching across North Africa, the Gulf Region, and the Asia-Pacific. Elevating those states with the more developed of these partnerships did not seem inconsistent with a vision of a 'truly global alliance' able to 'address the global challenges of the day' (Daalder and Goldgeier 2006). Enlarging NATO in this manner did not, however, obtain traction among NATO's existing members (Hallams 2009), and talk of an extra-European enlargement faded once NATO had made clear from 2012 that it was to scale down its mission in Afghanistan.

The geographic boundary of enlargement has thus remained intact. Enlargement has taken in states from Northern Europe (the Baltics), East Central Europe, and the Balkans. Significantly, every one of NATO's new entrants since 1990 has been a former communist state – once part, in most cases, of the dissolved communist federations of the Soviet Union and Yugoslavia. This redrawing of Europe's geopolitical map is not complete. But while there remain areas of Europe where NATO membership is hypothetical, these are often highly problematic.

The most obvious instance in this regard is Russia. As we shall see, Moscow has been a strident critic of enlargement, but it is worth recalling that NATO membership for Russia itself has been a subject of periodic attention. The high point here was the so-called honeymoon period of NATO-Russia relations of the early 1990s (Smith 2002: 59–60). The leadership of President Boris Yeltsin alluded on more than one occasion to the possibility of Russian accession, part of a hoped-for association with the Atlantic world that would break Russia's connection to its Soviet past, give Moscow a greater say in pan-European security matters, and affirm its modern (as opposed to Asiatic and economically underdeveloped) identity (Webber 2007: 151). This position chimed with official American thinking. The concept of enlargement held by the Clinton administration was one which, according to Deputy Secretary of State Strobe Talbott (2002: 131–132), 'always included [. . .] the idea of Russia's eventual eligibility and indeed its entry.' As Talbott argued, to rule the country out as a matter of principle would be both a 'gratuitous insult to Russia and would belie [any] claim that NATO enlargement served the larger cause of inclusive integration.' Further, as former US Secretary of State James Baker (2002: 99) pointed out, incorporating Russia was in keeping with NATO's character as a 'coalition of former adversaries', such as France and Germany, and Greece and Turkey. In a similar vein, Russia would now be added and would sit alongside its erstwhile Cold War adversaries. Here, however, was the rub. The process of reconciliation that NATO membership would bring about required Russian commitment to NATO's conditions of membership (stable democracy, harmonious relations with neighbours, conformity to NATO military standards, and a willingness to submit to NATO's internal decision-making process), something it was unable or unwilling to effect. It also meant a parallel acceptance that membership ought to be open to other former communist countries as well – something Moscow increasingly regarded as unwelcome. Squaring this circle meant, on Russia's part, that membership was only agreeable if NATO was somehow transformed and Russia was given a privileged position in the revamped body. But objections to this within the alliance rendered Russian accession less and less likely. As relations soured between NATO and Russia on other matters (the 1999 Kosovo war, differing interpretations of the Conventional Forces in Europe [CFE] Treaty, and US/NATO missile defence deployment), then so the possibility receded still further. Moscow's antipathy to NATO's enlargements of 1999 and 2004 effectively put paid to the idea of Russian membership. Thereafter, the leadership tandem of Vladimir Putin and Dimitri Medvedev in Moscow came to see NATO in largely negative terms with its vision of European security governance now involving a subordination of the alliance to a pan-European security treaty (Nopens 2009). A growing discord was also evident on the NATO side with Russia being cited as culpable in the 2008 war with Georgia and, following the annexation of Crimea in the spring of 2014, for the destabilisation of Ukraine. NATO's position on these matters, led by the US, was also shaped by the new East European members, some of whom (Poland most obviously) had imported into NATO a distinct scepticism of Russian behaviour.

Wherever blame may lie for the deterioration of NATO-Russia relations (Forsberg and Herd 2014), Russia's absence from the alliance rendered a reversion to a posture of collective defence and mutual suspicion increasingly likely on both sides. Moscow had since the late 1990s regarded enlargement as directed against Russia. NATO's reassurances to the contrary along with a significant effort towards institutional partnership has failed to overcome the view that enlargement is a tool of US influence building (Antonenko and Giegerich 2009: 14). This position has been conditioned by a feeling of mistrust. Russia has argued that understandings reached between the Western powers and Moscow at the time of German unification in 1990 obliged NATO to refrain from enlargement. The weight of published evidence does not seem to support this contention (Kramer 2009), but it is the perception (or misperception) that matters. That such a pledge might have been broken has reinforced a view among Russia's political elite that their country has been treated 'as an adversary and an outsider' (Wolff 2015: 1106).

Enlargement has thus become a major bone of contention between NATO and Russia. The dangers which follow have been clearly evident in the cases of Georgia and Ukraine. Of these two states, Georgia has been the most forthright in its claim to NATO membership. Accession has been an explicit objective of its foreign policy since the early 2000s. To that end, Tbilisi has made itself a valuable NATO partner, providing a significant number of troops to NATO's missions in Afghanistan, hosting NATO exercises, and participating in rotations of the NATO Response Force. Georgia has not, however, been rewarded with a clear path to membership. At its 2008 summit in Bucharest, NATO stated that Georgia would become a member but demurred from granting it a MAP, the concrete mechanism by which accession would be achieved (NATO 2008: para. 23). In the years since, Georgia has been the beneficiary of various NATO initiatives (the NATO-Georgia Commission established in 2008, and a 'substantial package' of measures agreed at NATO's 2014 summit in Wales), but a MAP has proven elusive. The progress of political and military reform has been less important in the eyes of NATO members than considerations of Georgia's geopolitical vulnerability. The Russo-Georgian war of 2008 and the subsequent decoupling of Abkhazia and South Ossetia from the jurisdiction of the government in Tbilisi have made clear that a Georgia in NATO would be highly provocative to Russia. Indeed, according to some (Asmus 2010: 221), Russia provoked the war precisely to deter Georgia from seeking membership and to prevent NATO from offering it. Such a strategy appears to have worked. Georgia's cause has been supported by some new NATO members but not by the states which matter in pushing through NATO decisions. The patronage which Georgia enjoyed under the Bush administration lapsed under Obama. France and Germany, meanwhile, had been wary of Georgia's credentials from the outset. NATO has formally stuck to its commitment to Georgian membership, but officials, not least in the US, have publicly acknowledged that any decision must not antagonise Russia (Babayan 2016: 14). Georgia has, in short, been 'knocking on a closed door' (German 2015: 613).

NATO's qualified commitment to Georgia has been repeated in the case of Ukraine (it too was mentioned in the Bucharest Declaration). Kiev, unlike Tbilisi, has however, been inconsistent in its own claims to membership. President Leonid Kuchma raised the possibility in 2002, but in practice he steered towards a close relationship with Moscow. His star, in any case, quickly waned with the US and the NATO allies owing to allegations of Ukrainian arms transfers to Saddam Hussein's Iraq. Following Ukraine's Orange Revolution in late 2004, new President Viktor Yushchenko pursued a more overtly pro-NATO position and made a bid paralleling that of Georgia for access to a MAP. This position was, however, reversed by Yushchenko's successor, Viktor Yanukovych, who in 2010 signed a law requiring Ukraine's 'non-participation in military-political alliances' (Pop 2010). The Euromaidan protests which ousted Yanukovych from power in February 2014 then triggered Russia's annexation of Crimea and subsequent support of Ukrainian separatism in the Donbass region. The newly installed Ukrainian government revived its ambition to join NATO in response. In December 2014, the Ukrainian parliament repealed the legal commitment to non-alignment. Both President Petro Poroshenko and Prime Minister Arseny Yatsenyuk came out in support of NATO membership as a means of countering Russian military destabilisation. The alliance offered some limited material support to the Ukrainian military, but enlargement has remained off the agenda. This is, in part, because of Ukraine's chronic political instability, but it has flowed also from geopolitical realities. To begin the accession process would mean having to face the possibility that at some future point NATO would be called upon to defend a new ally in the face of Russian military preponderance.[1]

NATO enlargement, seemingly expansive in scope, has been delimited on two occasions – by the retreat from globalism and by the buffer put up by Russia in Georgia and Ukraine. The first of these hardly compromises the enlargement project as there had never been any serious expectation that membership would be extended beyond Europe (with the exception of a few voices in the Bush administration, this was a cause supported more by think tanks than policy makers). Georgia and Ukraine are different because here NATO had raised expectations, only to backtrack in the face of internal division and Russian bellicosity. NATO's level of ambition has been curtailed accordingly. Within NATO, enlargement is now only seriously considered in relation to Finland and Sweden (two easy cases from the point of view of preparedness) and the Balkans – although progress is likely to be slow in the region following Montenegro's accession. Macedonian entry is opposed by Greece; Bosnia and Herzegovina has languished for years in various NATO partnership schemes; and Serbia lacks the political desire to orientate itself towards the alliance (Wolff 2015).

Explaining enlargement

Played out on more than one occasion over many years, enlargement has come to be seen as the outcome of a series of complex, diplomatic, and political interactions involving allies, aspirants, interested third parties (whether hostile such as Russia or friendly such as the EU) and influential opinion formers in the press, think-tanks and domestic politics.

NATO's first post–Cold War enlargement, given its unique and precedent-setting character, was the subject of greatest debate. The invitation extended to the Czech Republic, Hungary, and Poland balanced a number of considerations. First, it took account of the position of Germany, the first NATO state to advocate enlargement, and the ally most acutely concerned at possible instability to its east (Hyde-Price 2000: 149–151). Second, it reflected the view of the Clinton administration that NATO remained the best means of projecting stability in Europe. Enlargement also demonstrated the ability of the US to exercise transatlantic leadership, and allowed Washington an ongoing influence in Europe at a time when the EU was beginning to develop a security competence (Goldgeier 1999: 9). France and the UK, meanwhile, had initially been lukewarm on enlargement (the former fearing it would entrench US dominance, the latter that it would dilute NATO's military purpose and drag the organisation into unwanted disputes), but fell in line behind the German and US positions (Brown 1999: 21–22, 31–33). As for the choice of new members, across the alliance there was strong support for the Czech Republic, Hungary, and Poland. These three states all viewed NATO membership as a means of guarding against regional instability, orienting their foreign policies and political development westwards, and pre-empting the re-emergence of a threat from Russia (*Transitions* 1997). Slovakia, Romania, and Slovenia were favoured by some, but not all allies, and so fell afoul of NATO's consensus rule. NATO's internal discussions ran in parallel to an external diplomatic track. NATO delayed its decision on enlargement in order to work out a settlement with Russia. The 1997 NATO summit in Madrid thus saw the unveiling of the NATO-Russia Founding Act, which, while it did not remove Moscow's objections, temporarily blunted them.

A similar interplay of factors helps to account for enlargement in the mid-2000s. A process which resulted in seven states acceding in 2004 hardly seemed likely just four years earlier when enlargement was becalmed by the task of digesting new members. The demand for entry to NATO had not, however, gone away. The limited enlargement of 1999 seemed sound at the time. The three entrants were, in post-communist terms, politically and socially stable, economically well-off, and enjoyed high domestic levels of elite and public support for NATO membership (Šedivý 2001: 4). A differentiation of candidates had thus occurred in the late 1990s. Entry had been determined by the level of compatibility with NATO's existing members, something which had fortuitously corresponded to the states in question occupying a strategically important space in East Central Europe. NATO could well have stopped (or at least delayed) enlargement at that point. As the large group of remaining aspirants pointed out, however, the alliance's own rhetorical claim to inclusivity (the so-called open-door policy) required that the process continue. In this they found an enthusiastic ally in the US. President Bush was much less worried about Russian sensitivities on the issue than Clinton and, following 9/11, his administration openly promoted an extensive enlargement. For the US, the logic of the 'war on terror' meant gathering together 'all the potential allies it could get, regardless of their deficiencies' (Barany 2006: 172). NATO's European members, meanwhile, were largely in accord and saw NATO enlargement on this occasion as corresponding to an equally ambitious enlargement of the EU (Yost 2014: 284–285).

The political and diplomatic energy which propelled NATO's first two post–Cold War waves of enlargement applies much less to the Balkan enlargements of 2009 and 2016. The entry of Albania, Croatia, and Montenegro is not without significance to the region but, in one sense, is merely a belated extension of earlier policy (Albania and Croatia had been granted MAPs as early as 1999 and 2002). In fact, these cases notwithstanding, since 2004, enlargement has largely slipped off NATO's agenda. The US under President Obama did not provide leadership on the issue, being less concerned with European affairs than preceding administrations. Among European Allies, political will has also dwindled as shoring up the EU has taken priority over further efforts to enlarge NATO (Simakovsky 2013: 9–13).

This account views NATO enlargement as a subject of contemporary history with analysis focused on the short-term factors (American leadership, for instance) behind big decisions. Though good on detail, such an approach is less useful when it comes to generalisation – that is, how we explain enlargement by reference to the structural circumstances of power, institutionalisation, and norms. These broader conditions are the concern of theory.

Three theoretical approaches have exerted greatest influence on mainstream International Relations (IR) in the post–Cold War period – neo-realism, institutionalism, and social constructivism. Applied to NATO, each proceeds from a different starting point, but none alone provides a satisfactory explanation of enlargement. Neo-realism – with its emphasis on how alliances balance against power or threat – persuasively identifies why some (but not all) states have an interest in joining NATO (to guard against a resurgent Russia), but is less useful in explaining why NATO has been willing to offer membership. For existing members, the 1999 enlargement was not a case of balancing Russia (which at that point was a prostrate power) or, indeed, any other possible adversary in Europe (Schimmelfennig 2003: 40–51). Institutionalism might appear better suited to explaining enlargement. Its emphasis on institutional adaptation and task differentiation accords with NATO's recent and ongoing transformation. Here, enlargement is part of NATO's response to a changed threat environment involving a shift from the narrowly defined purpose of collective defence to a broader preoccupation with collective security and conflict management (Schimmelfennig 2016). Yet institutionalism is still subject to a certain indeterminacy; its assumptions could equally apply to a state of affairs in which NATO had *not* enlarged (where such a course would have delivered greater gains to a smaller number of states) (Skälnes

1998: 69). Social constructivism has been seen as a convincing in explaining both why NATO offered enlargement (in order to extend the community of values and norms embedded within the alliance) and why some states have taken up the offer (because of their affinity with those same values and norms) (Schimmelfennig 2003: 152). Yet, while this approach has merit in relation to events of the 1990s, it is much less useful beyond given the political variation of the states which have acceded to NATO and the diminishing emphasis the accession states and the alliance itself have given to values in justifying enlargement. The problems of single-theory accounts have led some to adopt a more pluralist approach. Here, enlargement is viewed as conditioned by a range of factors – reflective, in turn, of NATO's multifaceted character as simultaneously alliance, institution, and community (Webber 2013: 35).

The consequences of enlargement

The scholarly attention paid to NATO enlargement has been motivated, in part, by a desire to address the puzzle at its heart. The reasons why states in post-communist Europe have sought membership are readily understandable given the assumed gains to be had in the realms of security – as well as the more abstract (but nonetheless important) realms of political and institutional identity. The gains to NATO are less clear. Indeed, the costs of enlargement, it has been argued, could well outstrip the benefits. Theory aside, these are issues of policy as well as academic relevance. This section briefly surveys the effects enlargement has had, both on its new members and on NATO more broadly.

A useful place to start in this discussion is NATO's own study on enlargement published in 1995. This listed a set of commitments new members would be expected to meet. In that list, adherence to the 'basic principles' of the North Atlantic Treaty – 'democracy, individual liberty and the rule of law' – was positioned first (NATO 1995: para. 70). How far this requirement has facilitated democracy among NATO's new members is, however, a moot point. One can argue in favour of indirect consequences – NATO membership when clustered among groups of states creates a permissive regional environment of stability and peace within which democracy can progress. More direct effects, however, are harder to establish. Certainly, in many cases, there is a correlation between acceding to NATO and subsequent democratic consolidation (Melnykovska and Schweickert 2011). But that political trajectory owes as much (if not more) to EU conditionality and, as Reiter (2001: 59) has argued, the societies and elites in states with NATO ambitions 'were committed to democracy anyway' as a consequence of their domestic, post-communist transition. The record of consolidation is also imperfect, and that too adds to the causal imprecision. Does the rise of 'illiberal democracy' in Hungary and Poland (Kauffmann 2016) lead one to conclude that NATO's democratising influence is weak after all? Or does it suggest that the influence NATO can bring to bear is stronger in the period leading up to and shortly after accession, rather than many years later when fewer mechanisms exist to influence domestic politics?

A more precise (and stronger) claim to NATO's democratic effect relates to the transformation of the armed forces in post-communist states. The militarisation of communist societies had been seen as a baleful legacy for democratic transition. Yet democratic oversight of the armed forces has been a common feature of post-communist Eastern Europe and the Balkans. The reasons often cited for this shift (Cottey et al. 2005: 12–13) – a more permissive external security environment and the professionalisation of armed forces – do not apply in equal measure (the security situation of Balkans, for instance, has worsened since the end of the Cold War). One constant, however, has been NATO involvement. The leverage of membership conditions relating to civil-military relations along with the provision of technical advice and the 'propagation [of] democratic norms of behaviour' (Edmunds 2003: 151) has meant the alliance has had a determining effect on the political evolution of post-communist militaries (Boonstra 2007). That influence has varied in line with the domestic setting in the target state. The legacies of military culture coupled with differing levels of military professionalisation, autonomy, and cohesion help explain why NATO's admonitions have been better received in Poland and the Baltic states than in Romania or Bulgaria (Epstein 2005).

As well as affecting domestic developments, NATO membership has meant the reorientation of foreign and defence policies. Following both the 1999 and 2004 enlargements, new members were encouraged to develop armed forces and military doctrines that aligned with NATO's (and the Americans') preference for force projection and expeditionary operations. Policies have not, however, been uniform across the new members. Poland, Bulgaria, Romania, Estonia, and Latvia (as well as NATO aspirant Georgia), for instance, have made a significant commitment to NATO's mission in Afghanistan. Hungary and Slovakia, by contrast, have played a negligible role. A similar observation can be made of defence expenditure. NATO's 2 per cent of GDP target is met by only a handful of members (both established and new alike). But since the 2014 Ukraine crisis, the Poles and the Baltic states appear exceptional, being responsible (in percentage terms) for some of the largest defence budget increases across the alliance. Conformity to NATO policy is not simply about being socialised into what is expected of new members but also reflects respective national interests. Baltic and Polish enthusiasm for the Afghan mission, for instance, is a means of building up American goodwill, something to be cashed in closer to home in the form of US backing (deemed urgent in light of Russian behaviour) of NATO's more traditional mission of collective defence (Ringsmose 2016: 213–214).

Membership has thus had a variable effect on NATO's new members, but what of NATO as an organisation? Over the years, several objections have been levelled at enlargement: that it would antagonize Russia (see earlier), make consensus within NATO more difficult, dilute American leadership, exacerbate burden-sharing disputes, and divert the organisation from new endeavours, in particular the need to address '[g]rowing threats from the South' (Binnendijk and Kugler 1999: 128–130). In short, it has been argued, enlargement would constrain rather than facilitate NATO's development. These concerns appear to have been largely misplaced. Enlargement has not prevented other major initiatives, be that far-flung operational deployments, command reform or cyber-defence. Neither has it been a major problem in consensus-building. Internal NATO diplomacy is rendered more time-consuming by an increased membership, but the main dissenters tend still to be established members (Greece, Turkey, and France), not new ones. Few, meanwhile, would doubt that the US is still NATO's leading power; if anything, the Atlanticist sentiment of many new members has increased American influence in the alliance, not diminished it. As for burden-sharing, low defence spending and operational deployments are indicative of an ongoing problem of free-riding among many new members (Sandler and Shimizu 2010: 59), but such behaviour is not out of line with that of many other members. Free-riding, in other words, has not gotten worse with enlargement (Hillison 2014: 153). Further, as Poland and the Baltic states have demonstrated, when their interests are directly affected, new members have borne a significant cost for their own defence. They have not simply shifted that cost to the US and other NATO powers (Lanoszka 2015: 140–143).

Looking at NATO's recent history, it is increasingly clear that the need to defend and reassure its eastern members is the most far-reaching, albeit belated, effect of enlargement. The Ukraine crisis triggered what Secretary General Jens Stoltenberg (cited in Kanter 2014) labelled 'the biggest reinforcement of [NATO's] collective defence since the end of the Cold War.' Reinforcement measures focused on Poland, the Baltic states, Romania, and Bulgaria would be hard to imagine in the absence of enlargement as the alliance would have been under no obligation to defend these states and less persuaded by the need to deter Russia. This strategic shift has, however, posed two major dilemmas for NATO. The first is of long standing – how to reconcile partnership with Russia with a commitment to new allies? Since 2014, that dilemma at least appears to have been resolved, as NATO suspended all practical relations with Moscow. The second relates to NATO's geographic focus. The warning that enlargement would shift NATO's attention away from its southern flank now appears prescient. The Syrian civil war (which developed in parallel with the Ukraine crisis) has required NATO to both support long-standing member Turkey and think through the consequences of instability in the eastern Mediterranean (in the spring of 2016 it launched a naval mission in the Aegean Sea). The alliance, as a result, has had to develop simultaneously two, sometimes competing, strategies – an eastern one focused on the needs of its new east European members and a southern one that accords more with the priorities of established allies Italy, Greece, and Turkey, as well as some of the new Balkan members. Competing regionalism of this sort has posed a major dilemma for NATO's major powers (the US, France, Germany, and the UK) who have had to straddle both directions of policy.

The end of enlargement

As already noted, the limits of enlargement as a strategic project have now been reached. Montenegro's accession may not be the last time NATO welcomes a new member, but since the late 2000s no constituency of note within the alliance regards enlargement as a priority. But just as the limits to growth are clear, so too are those of retreat. Unlike the EU, NATO has not been troubled by the prospect of reverse enlargement. Public support for the alliance may have declined in some new NATO members (Slovakia and Slovenia, for example), but there has been no demand among governing political parties to exit NATO and no ally has ever used Article 13 of the North Atlantic Treaty to renounce its membership. NATO also lacks a mechanism by which a member can be expelled. Further, the existential problems which have attended the EU (the Eurozone and migration crises along with the possibility of destabilisation in the event of British withdrawal) have led many new allies to appraise NATO membership even more positively. Support for the alliance in Poland, a 2015 poll found, was higher than in any other NATO state surveyed (Pew Research Centre 2015); Polish support for the EU, by contrast, was subject to the steepest decline of all states in the Union (European Commission 2015: 7–8).

Critics have argued that NATO has failed to provide a proper rationale for this consolidationist turn. Indeed, by retaining the rhetoric of the 'open door' (NATO 2015), the impression is given that the alliance still aspires to integrate states such as Georgia and Ukraine whose prospects for entry are remote. To renounce enlargement, however, carries risks of its own. Although alleviating the longest-running dispute in NATO-Russia relations, it would be construed among some new members as a loss of resolve on NATO's part. Faith in NATO's ability to stand up to Russian demands closer to home (a particular concern in the Baltic states) could thus be fatally compromised (Machnikowski 2015). Reconciling these two approaches to enlargement has not been easy and since the Ukraine crisis NATO has taken a middle course – supporting enlargement in principle, but doing as little as possible to promote it.

If enlargement is no longer important for NATO and its leading powers, then a reckoning on European order will need to be made. The limits of enlargement have always been vague, necessarily so in order to avoid the impression that NATO was an exclusionary organisation. Does, therefore, a lowering of ambition imply the falling of a 'new Iron Curtain' with countries such as Georgia left outside? Or could it rather be part of a refashioned geopolitical project, one which still forsakes membership for countries in the 'shared neighbourhood'[2] but does so in service of a deconflicted 'relationship with Russia based on balance of power and strategic discernment' (Wolff 2015: 1121)?

Notes

1 This calculation, it could be argued, also applied when the three Baltic states were being considered for membership. The difference, however, is that unlike Ukraine (and Georgia), these states had not been subject to Russian military intervention up to the point that membership was being negotiated. NATO did not, therefore, have to actively prepare for their defence at the moment of entry.

2 A term usually reserved for EU-Russia relations, it is used here by reference to NATO and includes the post-Soviet states of Ukraine, Georgia, Belarus, Moldova, Armenia, and Azerbaijan.

References

Antonenko, O. and Giegerich, B. (2009) 'Rebooting NATO-Russia Relations', *Survival*, 51(2): 13–21.

Asmus, R. (2005) 'Reinventing NATO (Yet Again) Politically', *NATO Review*, summer. At <www.nato.int/docu/review/2005/issue2/english/analysis.html>.

Asmus, R. (2010) *A Little War that Shook the World: Georgia, Russia and the Future of the West* (Houndmills Basingstoke: Palgrave Macmillan).

Babayan, N. (2016) 'The In-betweeners: the Eastern Partnership Countries and the Russia-West Conflict' *Transatlantic Academy 2015–16 Paper Series, No. 5* (Washington, DC: Transatlantic Academy).

Baker, J. (2002) 'Russia in NATO?', *The Washington Quarterly*, 25(1): 95–103.

Barany, Z. (2006) 'NATO's Post-Cold War Metamorphosis: From Sixteen to Twenty-Six and Counting', *International Studies Review*, 8(1): 165–178.

Binnendijk, H. and Kugler, R. L. (1999) 'Open NATO's Door Carefully', *The Washington Quarterly*, 22(2): 123–138.

Boonstra, J. (2007) 'NATO's Role in Democratic Reform', *FRIDE Working Paper* 38 (FRIDE: Madrid).

Brown, M. E. (1999), 'The United States, Western Europe and NATO Enlargement', in G. G. Burwell and I. H. Daalder (eds.), *The United States and Europe in the Global Arena* (Houndmills, Basingstoke: Macmillan), 11–43.

Cottey, A., Edmunds, T. and Forster, A. (2005) 'Civil-Military Relations in Postcommunist Europe: Assessing the Transition', *European Security*, 14(1): 1–16.

Croft, S. (2000) 'The EU, NATO and Europeanisation: The Return of Architectural Debate', *European Security*, 9(1): 1–20.

Daalder, I and Goldgeier, J. (2006) 'Global NATO', *Foreign Affairs*, 85(5): 105–113.

Edmunds, T. (2003), 'NATO and Its New Members', *Survival*, 45(3): 145–166.

Epstein, R. A. (2005) 'NATO Enlargement and the Spread of Democracy: Evidence and Expectations', *Security Studies*, 14(1): 63–105.

European Commission. (2015) *Standard Eurobarometer*, 83.

Forsberg, T. and Herd, G. (2014) 'Russia and NATO: From Windows of Opportunities to Closed Doors', *Journal of Contemporary European Studies*, 23(1), 41–57.

German, T. (2015) 'Heading West? Georgia's Euro-Atlantic Path', *International Affairs*, 91(3): 601–614.

Goldgeier, J. (1999) *Not Whether But When: The US Decision to Enlarge NATO* (Washington, DC: Brookings Institution Press).

Hallams, E. (2009) 'NATO at 60: Going Global?', *International Journal*, 64(2): 423–452.

Hillison, J. R. (2014) *Stepping Up: Burden Sharing By NATO's Newest Members* (Carlisle, PA: US Army War College Press).

Hyde-Price, A. (2000) *Germany and European Order: Enlarging NATO and the EU* (Manchester and New York: Manchester University Press).

Kanter, J. (2014) 'NATO Plans to Increase Patrols on Its East Border', *International New York Times*, 17 April.

Kauffmann, S. (2016) 'Europe's Illiberal Democracies', *International New York Times*, 10 March.

Kramer, M. (2009) 'The Myth of a No-NATO-Enlargement Pledge to Russia', *The Washington Quarterly*, 32(2): 39–61.

Lanoszka, A. (2015) 'Do Allies Really Free Ride?', *Survival*, 57(3): 133–152.

Machnikowski, R. M. (2015) 'NATO and Ukraine – Russian Crisis', in R. Czulda and M. Madej (eds.), *Newcomers No More: Contemporary NATO and the Future of Enlargement from the Perspective of 'Post-Cold War' Members* (Warsaw: International Relations Research Institute), 231–245.

Medcalf, J. (2005) *NATO: A Beginner's Guide* (Oxford: Oneworld).

Melnykovska, I. and Schweickert, R. (2011) 'NATO as an External Driver of Institutional Change in Post-Communist Countries', *Defence and Peace Economics*, 22(2): 279–297.

NATO. (1967a) 'Report of Sub-Group I: East-West Relations (The Harmel Report: Full Reports by Rapporteurs on the Future Tasks of the Alliance)', approved December 1967. At: <www.bits.de/NRANEU/nato-strategy/Harmel_ Report_ complete.pdf>.

NATO. (1967b) 'The Future Tasks of the Alliance (Report of the Council): the Harmel Report', approved December 1967. At <www.nato.int/cps/en/natohq/official_texts_26700.htm>.

NATO. (1990) 'London Declaration on a Transformed North Atlantic Alliance', approved July 1990. At <www.nato.int/docu/comm/49-95/c900706a.htm>.

NATO. (1991a) 'The Alliance's New Strategic Concept', approved November 1991. At: <www.nato.int/cps/en/natolive/official_texts_23847.htm>.

NATO. (1991b) 'Rome Declaration on Peace and Cooperation', approved December 1991. At: <www.nato.int/docu/comm/49-95/c911108a.htm>.

NATO. (1995) 'Study on NATO Enlargement', approved September 1995. At: <www.nato.int/cps/en/natohq/official_texts_24733.htm>.

NATO. (2008) 'Bucharest Summit Declaration', approved April 2008. At: <www.nato.int/cps/en/natolive/official_texts_8443.htm>.

NATO. (2010) 'Strategic Concept for the Defence and Security of the Members of the North Atlantic Treaty Organisation', approved November 2010. At: <www.nato.int/lisbon2010/strategic-concept-2010-eng.pdf>.

NATO. (2015) 'Statement by NATO Foreign Ministers on Open Door Policy', approved December 2015. At: <www.nato.int/cps/en/natohq/official_texts_125591.htm?selectedLocale=en>.

Nopens, P. (2009) 'A New Security Architecture for Europe? Russian Proposals and Western Reactions', *Security Policy Brief, No. 3* (Brussels: Egmont Institute).

Pew Research Centre. (2015) 'NATO Support Declining in Germany, Rising in Poland', 8 June. At: <www.pewglobal.org/2015/06/10/nato-publics-blame-russia-for-ukrainian-crisis-but − reluctant-to-provide-military-aid/russia-ukraine-report-32/>.

Pop, V. (2010) 'Ukraine Drops NATO Membership Bid', *euobserver*, 4 June. At: <https://euobserver.com/news/30212>.

Reiter, D. (2001) 'Why NATO Enlargement Does Not Spread Democracy', *International Security*, 25(4): 41–67.

Ringsmose, J. (2016) 'NATO: A Public Goods Provider', in M. Webber and A. Hyde-Price (eds.), *Theorising NATO: New Perspectives on the Atlantic Alliance* (London and New York: Routledge), 201–222.

Sandler, T. and Shimizu, H. (2010) 'NATO Burden Sharing 1999–2010: An Altered Alliance', *Foreign Policy Analysis*, 10(1): 43–60.

Schimmelfennig, F. (2003) *The EU, NATO and the Integration of Europe: Rules and Rhetoric* (Cambridge: Cambridge University Press).

Schimmelfennig, F. (2016), 'NATO and Institutional Theories of International Relations', in M Webber and A. Hyde-Price (eds.), *Theorising NATO: New Perspectives on the Atlantic Alliance* (London and New York: Routledge), 93–115.

Šedivý, J. (2001) 'The Puzzle of NATO Enlargement', *Contemporary Security Policy*, 22(2): 1–26.

Simakovsky, M. (2013) 'Flexible Expansion: NATO Enlargement in an Era of Austerity and Uncertainty', *Foreign Policy Papers* (Washington, DC: The German Marshall Fund of the United States).

Skålnes, L. S. (1998) 'From the Outside In, From the Inside Out: NATO Expansion and International Relations Theory', *Security Studies*, 7(4): 44–87.

Smith, M. A. (2000) *NATO Enlargement During the Cold War: Strategy and System in the Western Alliance* (Houndmills, Basingstoke: Palgrave).

Smith, M. A. (2002) 'A Bumpy Road to an Unknown Destination? NATO-Russia Relations, 1991–2002', *European Security*, 11(4): 59–77.

Talbott, S. (2002) *The Russia Hand: A Memoir of Presidential Diplomacy* (New York: Random House).

Tetrais, B. (2004) 'The Changing Nature of Military Alliances', *The Washington Quarterly*, 27(2): 135–150.

Thies, W. J. (2009) *Why NATO Endures* (Cambridge: Cambridge University Press).

Transitions (1997) 'Three Presidents on Joining NATO', December.

Webber, M. (2007) *Inclusion, Exclusion and the Governance of European Security* (Manchester and New York: Manchester University Press).

Webber, M. (2013) 'NATO after 9/11: Theoretical Perspectives', in E. Hallams, L. Ratti, and B. Zyla (eds.), *NATO Beyond 9/11: The Transformation of the Atlantic Alliance* (Houndmills, Basingstoke: Palgrave Macmillan), 27–53.

Wolff, A. T. (2015) 'The Future of NATO Enlargement after the Ukraine Crisis', *International Affairs*, 91(5): 1103–1121.

Yost, D. (2014) *NATO's Balancing Act* (Washington, DC: US Institute of Peace Press).

27

RUSSIA IN THE REGION

Richard Sakwa

The relationship between Russia and its former allies in Eastern Europe is one of the most troubled in the world, while relations with the post-Soviet states veers between the difficult to catastrophic. Already in August 2008 the Russo-Georgian war demonstrated the potential for strained relations to turn into outright conflict, and this became even more evident from 2014 when relations with Ukraine were conclusively disrupted. The picture, nevertheless, from Russia's perspective is not entirely bleak. A number of the 'new Eastern European' countries, notably Belarus (and Armenia), are closely allied with Russia, and although the relationship is far from stress-free, the fundamental interests of these countries are aligned. There are also enduring solid relations with Serbia and some other South Eastern European states, and Russia's declarations in favour of sovereignty, legitimism and, increasingly, conservatism, find an increasingly receptive audience in the region. In one way or another, Russia remains an important actor in the region, with a diverse pattern of interactions and relationships. This chapter will examine some of the key features of the diverse relationships in a historical and theoretical context.

Sub-regional diversity

It is immediately clear that diversity is the key feature of Russia's relations with the region. This differentiation is rooted in divergent patterns of historical development, and has profound intellectual consequences on how best we can study the region as a whole. There is no single pattern for Russia's interactions with the region, and each one requires historical contextualisation and methodological specificity. At least four sub-regions can be identified, each with its own dynamic of interactions. I will begin with those countries geographically closest to Russia, and work out to those most peripheral.

The first sub-region encompasses the new Eastern Europe, namely those countries lying in the belt between what has now become the European Union (EU) and Russia. These are the 'borderland' countries, as they have always been, torn between two hegemonic geopolitical formations. Even the name of one of the countries, Ukraine, is a metonym for a land on the frontier, while the other two, Belarus and Moldova, have for most of their history been part of one or another empire. This only accentuates the novelty of the historical situation after 1991. The disintegration of the Soviet Union may have taken place relatively peacefully, but the establishment of a long-term viable relationship between Russia and the countries of the region has still not been found. As we shall see, the expansive dynamic of EU enlargement, and the Wider Europe project in general, collided with Russia's aspirations to recreate some sort of Eurasian political and economic community.

No over-arching pan-European mode of reconciliation was found, now conventionally labelled Greater Europe. The idea of some sort of pan-European political and economic community stretching from Lisbon to Vladivostok was outlined by Mikhail Gorbachev in his 'Common European Home' speech to the Council of Europe in Strasbourg on 6 July 1989. Over a quarter-century has passed since then, and in that period not a single fundamental developmental or international relations question has been resolved. Instead, the competitive dynamic between Russia and the EU became increasingly intense (Korosteleva, 2015). This provoked the breakdown in Ukraine and violent conflict with Russia (Menon and Rumer, 2015; Sakwa, 2015; Wilson, 2014).

Although there are profound differences between the three 'New Eastern Europe' countries, they share common aspirations to confirm their independent statehood while developing as unique ethno-cultural social formations. All three have historical roots stretching back centuries, and with links that embrace not only Russia but also their western neighbours, notably Poland and Romania. The rawness of their new statehood, nevertheless, accentuates sensitivities regarding the relationship with what is often perceived to be the last colonial power, namely Russia in the guise of the Soviet Union. Their emergence as independent states from this perspective is considered to be an act of anti-colonial liberation, prompting attempts to distance themselves as far as possible from Russia. In Belarus this impetus is the weakest, given the deep cultural and economic inter-penetration of the two countries, yet even here President Alexander Lukashenko, re-elected by a landslide majority for another five-year term in October 2015 after two decades in power, refused Russian plans to create a permanent airbase in the country. Lukashenko was a master at tacking between Russia and the EU to gain advantage from both (Balmaceda, 2014; Bennett, 2011; Wilson, 2011).

In Moldova the Russian-backed separatism of Transnistria remains a permanent wound in the development of the state. As far as the leadership in Tiraspol, the capital of Transnistria, is concerned, their autonomous status is a necessary prophylactic in case Moldova unites with Romania. The Russian-backed Kozak Memorandum of 2003 effectively planned to turn the state into a confederation (although formally the country would remain unitary), which given the entirely different histories of the two parts of the country may well have allowed the country to unite in a form of consociational democracy. At the last minute the deal was vetoed by Washington, with the EU hastily following suit (Hill, 2012). The existence of this intractable 'frozen conflict' is yet another demonstration of the failure of the relevant powers to find a negotiated way out of the intractable problems facing the region. Ukraine is the most torn of the three states, with a powerful strain of monist nationalism emphasising the need to recreate Ukraine both culturally and economically separate from Russia (Kuzio and D'Anieri, 2002). This is balanced by more pluralistic representations of Ukrainian statehood, stressing the pluricultural nature of the country and the need to give constitutional form to the country's diversity (Sakwa, 2015). The pluralists reject the simplistic anti-colonial model in favour of a more sophisticated understanding of Ukraine's complex 'postcolonial' condition, in which there can be no simplistic division between coloniser and colonised, and instead stresses the mutual interactions over the centuries that have changed the identities of all concerned.

The second sub-region is made up of the three Baltic states of Estonia, Latvia, and Lithuania. They became part of the Russian Empire in the eighteenth century, and following the Russian Revolution enjoyed independence in the interwar years between 1918 and 1940. Unlike the South Caucasus states and other areas that were reincorporated into a Moscow-centred entity after the Civil War, the Baltic republics were free to develop their statehood for two decades, although the borders were not the same as those of today. All three states accentuated the cultural and linguistic recuperation of the ethnonym, and thus began a period of what can be called restorative nationhood. The process has been well-described by Rogers Brubaker in his study of 'nationalising states', where a particular ethnic group considers the state as its privileged domain national for development (Brubaker, 1996). The inter-war experiment in statehood came to a brutal end following the Molotov-Ribbentrop Pact of August 1939 and its various secret protocols. In summer 1940 the countries were absorbed into the Soviet Union, accompanied by the savage destruction of the old ruling classes. The process was interrupted by the German invasion of the Soviet Union in June 1941, accompanied by the mass killing of Jews, communists and other perceived alien elements (Snyder, 2010). The restoration of Soviet power in 1944 was accompanied by mass deportations that lasted until the early 1950s, and later by the influx of Russian military and industrial settlers (particularly in Estonia and Latvia) that fundamentally changed the demographic character of the states.

Lithuania was the first of the Soviet states to declare its independence, on 11 March 1990, followed soon after by the other two republics. Given the relatively small proportion of Russians and Poles, Lithuania declared that all permanently resident in the republic were granted automatic citizenship. In Estonia and Latvia, only those who could trace their ancestry to the inter-war independent republics gained automatic citizenship, whereas others, mostly Russians but also a significant number of Ukrainians, had to achieve citizenship through what for some were onerous language and other tests. The EU's conditionality on this issue was significantly weakened in the European Council meeting in Helsinki in December 1999, and the two republics entered the EU in 2004 with the issue unresolved. The status of the Russian minorities remains a bone of contention between Russia and the republics to this day. Equally, Vladimir Putin's attempts to resolve the border issue by accepting the status quo as the permanent dividing line encountered the resistance of nationalists in the two republics, who still hanker over the extensive territories lost when they entered the Soviet Union in the early 1940s. A border agreement was signed with Latvia in 2007, but tensions remain with Estonia. As a result of the Syrian refugee crisis of 2015 a rampart was built between Estonia and Russia, and a fence between Latvia and Russia. This was a physical manifestation of the return of a divided Europe. The Baltic once again became a *limitrophe* region, as the French described the states in the inter-war years when they acted as a *cordon sanitaire* against Soviet Russia.

The third sub-region includes the states of the former Yugoslavia and their neighbours in South Eastern Europe. In the 1990s this was the region where Russia first came into confrontation with the west over the conflicts in Bosnia and Kosovo. Russia became painfully aware of its diminished status as a great power, although this did little to temper its ambitions in that respect. The pattern was established of a by-turns competitive and cooperative relationship with the EU and the Western powers in general (Talbott, 2003). Russia demonstrated a continuing affiliation with its traditional ally, Serbia, but this did not prevent some helpful engagement in regulating the war in Bosnia. No one came out of that conflict with any credit, with the siege of Sarajevo dragging on for 1,425 days, from 5 April 1992 to 29 February 1996.

As for Kosovo, the 78 days of NATO bombing of Serbia from 24 March 1999 was the first time that the organisation used military force without the sanction of the United Nations, justified by the need to stop human rights abuses in Kosovo. This was the turning point in Russia's relations with the West, and lies at the basis of Putin's accusation that the Atlantic powers ignore their own rules when convenient. Nevertheless, Russian mediation helped put an end to the bombing campaign on 10 June. The unilateral declaration of independence by Kosovo on 17 February 2008, followed by its rapid recognition by the US and some leading EU powers, is another of those turning points shaping Russia's engagement with the region and with the West as a whole. A precedent had been set for the non-negotiated change of borders. On 24 August 2008 Russia recognised the independence of the two breakaway regions of Georgia, Abkhazia and South Ossetia, and in March 2014 reincorporated the Crimea into Russia. These events were symptoms of the larger breakdown of the European security order.

Russia has long-standing historical and cultural ties with the region, such as Slavic roots (Serbia and Bulgaria) and Orthodox Christianity (these two countries and Greece). Russia continues to have a close relationship with Serbia, even though the country has greatly matured politically since the traumas of the 1990s and now actively pursues EU membership. Serbia is a classic case of a country that would prefer complementary relations with both Russia and 'Europe' to avoid being forced to choose between them. On 16 October 2014 Putin was guest of honour at Serbia's military parade to celebrate seventy years of liberation from Nazi Germany. The Serbian president, Tomislav Nikolić, stressed that Russia was his country's 'big ally' (BBC News, 2014). Putin was greeted enthusiastically by large crowds, but with rather less enthusiasm, at a time of sanctions, in some other EU countries. Serbia is the clearest case where EU aspirations come into conflict with Russian plans for gas transit pipelines, historical notions of Slavic brotherhood, shared Orthodox Christianity, and conservative values.

These potential contradictions have also been evident in relations with the other great Orthodox country in the region, Bulgaria, reinforced by an even closer linguistic commonality. Like Serbia, Bulgaria has been a traditional Russian ally, but with the country joining the EU in 2007 the premium has been on turning formal accession into a genuine commitment to 'Europe'. This means the employment of strategies to distance Bulgaria from Russia. Matters came to a head over plans to build the South Stream pipeline across the Black Sea to make landfall in Bulgaria and then to trace its way to markets in northern Europe. Bulgaria came under enormous pressure in 2014 to withdraw from the project, and the decision to halt preliminary construction of the pipeline sounded the death knell of the project. Putin's shock announcement cancelling the project in December 2014 meant that Bulgaria lost potentially significant sums in transit fees and security of gas supplies. Relations with Romania remain as bad as ever, and there is little likelihood of matters changing in the near future, especially since the county (along with Poland) hosts elements of the phased ABM system, designed by the Americans allegedly to intercept Iranian missiles.

Relations with Greece have a number of distinctive characteristics. Even though Greece is a long-standing NATO member, there remain strong folk memories of Soviet support for the Communist insurgency in the Civil War in the late 1940s. Not having come under Soviet occupation, Greece was not traumatised by Soviet occupation, Stalinist repressions and Brezhnevite stagnation. There are powerful cultural ties, notably between the Orthodox monasteries that remain part of the Russian religious imaginary. The election of Alexis Tsipras and the Syriza, the Coalition of the Radical Left, party in January 2015 on an anti-austerity platform brought the country into confrontation with the Troika (the European Commission, the European Central Bank, and the IMF), the body negotiating since 2010 with Greece over its economic crisis. It was clear that one of the concerns of the Troika was fear that Russia would step in and use Greece as a platform in the EU if the country were to leave the euro. Tsipras cleverly exploited these fears in his negotiations with the Troika. On his second visit to Russia in as many months, Tsipras, who had joined the Communist Party (KKE) in 1991, stressed at the St. Petersburg Economic Forum in June 2015 that Russia was one of Greece's most important partners. Although Putin was keen to strengthen links with the countries of South Eastern Europe, Russia was wary of making financial commitments to the region, just as it had refused to bankroll the Republic of Cyprus in its financial crisis in 2013.

While willing to court outliers from the liberal consensus, from both left and right, Putin was careful not to overstep the mark. This applies as much to the fourth and final sub-region, the Visegrád Four, as it does to the Balkans. The grouping was originally established in 1991 by Poland, Hungary, and what were to become the Czech Republic and Slovakia to coordinate their plans for European integration. The body retains some coherence, even though all countries are now long-standing members of the EU. The relations of all four states with Russia have been characterised by various vicissitudes, and there remains an enduring legacy of suspicion accompanied by a sense of grievance and recrimination. Poland has been the country most consistently hostile to Russia. Relations are still poisoned by the Nazi-Soviet Pact, the Soviet invasion of 17 September 1939, and the murder of 22,000 Polish officers, reservists and professionals in Katyń, Kharkov, and Mednoe (near Tver, formerly Kalinin) in 1940 (Sanford, 2009). The crash near Smolensk of a Polish Air Force plane on 10 April 2010 that killed all ninety-six people on board, including the president of Poland, Lech Kaczyński, and a range of senior officials, became yet another cause for discord. The plane was, ironically, on its way to a ceremony marking the seventieth anniversary of the Katyń massacre. Poland has been the most consistent country, along with Lithuania, to argue for harsh sanctions on Russia in response to the events in Ukraine.

The other Visegrád countries have adopted a more variegated approach. The former Czech president, Vaclav Klaus, has been forthright in his condemnation of what he considers to be the hubristic folly of the EU in advancing into Ukraine without adequately negotiating with Russia. Slovakia was also critical of the subsequent persistence of the sanctions regime on Russia. As for Hungary, under the leadership of Viktor Orbán the country pursued a determinedly independent path, challenging many of the EU's orthodoxies from a radically conservative perspective. Hungary supported the sanctions policy, but warned that the EU had 'shot itself in the foot' by restricting trade with Russia (BBC News, 2015). In February 2015 Putin made common cause with Orbán during a visit to Budapest. Discussions centred on gas pipeline issues, with Hungary dependent for over half of its supplies on Gazprom. Putin sought to demonstrate that he retained allies in the EU and NATO.

The clash of integrations

The dominant factor shaping Russia's engagement with the region is the emergence of competing aspirations and organisations of regional integration. This has an important effect on the way we understand the international political dynamics of the region. In particular, three formats for integration overlap and compete: the EU and its associated Wider Europe ambitions; various forms of Eurasian integration; and the residual attempt for pan-European integration outlined at the dawn of the post-communist era in Gorbachev's plans for a Common European Home.

These alternative trajectories are typically identified with competition between democratisation and 'autocratisation' (Tolstrup, 2014). While the EU's engagement is based on varying degrees of conditionality (Sasse, 2008, Schimmelfennig et al., 2006), Russian-centred integration projects make a point of stressing state sovereignty and diversity of modernisation paths. A growing literature argues that a type of 'reverse conditionality' (my term) applies in which more authoritarian developmental trajectories are favoured (Ambrosio, 2008; Obydenkova and Libman, 2015). In practice, Russia's primary concern is state stability and legitimate government – in other words, opposition to what is typically perceived to be Western-sponsored regime change through 'colour revolutions'. Equally, the EU's democratisation endeavour is embedded in a particular neoliberal view of state development (Kurki, 2011). The net effect is that geopolitical competition between rival integration projects has become a contest between political regime types.

The EU is clearly the preeminent body in the western part of the continent, at the heart of the Wider Europe project for the extension of the Brussels-centred order ever further to the east. The Eastern Partnership (EaP) from 2009 was only the most intense manifestation of this, with a reaction from Russia that in the end took violent forms following the ouster of Ukrainian President Viktor Yanukovych in February 2014. In this context, the 'Europeanisation' literature is often taken as paradigmatic, although its geopolitical assumptions have been increasingly challenged by Russia. Indeed, until the Ukraine crisis, the normative aspects of the EU's ever-increasing reach into Eastern Europe was granted priority, and only when the power consequences of its actions were challenged in Ukraine were the underlying geopolitical assumptions exposed. Until then the discussion had focused on conditionality and external governance, as if these operated in a vacuum. Russia had long argued that one of the reasons for the deterioration of relations with the EU since the mid-2000s was the accession of a number of East European countries that introduced traditional Russophobic reflexes into the organisation, even if couched in the EU's normative language. The creation of East Stratcom within the European External Action Service (EEAS) in April 2015 to 'counter Russian propaganda' is a case in point, since the need for such a unit was vigorously advanced by Polish diplomats (Panichi, 2015). From Moscow's perspective, the EU had increasingly been transformed from a peace project that could overcome the logic of conflict into a body that perpetuated and exacerbated these conflicts in new forms.

On the other side, there were a plethora of integrative plans in the post-Soviet Eurasian region. The establishment of the Commonwealth of Independent States (CIS) as the successor to the Soviet Union on 8 December 1991 provided the framework for the maintenance of some of the earlier links, including visa-free travel and labour mobility, but it failed to reconstitute an economic, let alone political, community. In 2007 Russia, Belarus and Kazakhstan announced plans to create a Customs Union (CU) within the Eurasian Economic Community (EurAsEc), and thereafter what is now known as the Eurasian Customs Union (ECU) developed an institutional and political identity that far surpassed any other post-Soviet integration project, and soon came to challenge the EU for hegemony in the region (Dragneva and Wolczuk, 2013). On 25 January 2008 Russia, Belarus and Kazakhstan signed a tripartite customs union, and in summer 2009 agreements were signed to create the Eurasian Customs Union (ECU), formally launched on 1 January 2010, with most barriers removed by July. In the next stage, a Single Economic Space came into effect on 1 January 2012, and on 1 January 2015 the two were to combine to create the Eurasian Economic Union (EEU). The three states cover about three-quarters of the post-Soviet region and have a combined market of 165 million and a total GDP of around $2.3 trillion, compared to the EU's GDP of $16.6 trillion (Dutkiewicz and Sakwa, 2015).

In other words, after a long period of hesitation and uncertainty, Eurasian integration is firmly back on Russia's agenda, and this shapes its relations with Eastern Europe, both old and new. A clash of some sort was inevitable, but in the event when the collision came over Ukraine, it took the most catastrophic form possible. Wiser leadership on both sides could have obviated some of the worst aspects, but for too long leaders simply ignored the looming clash of integrations. As far as Moscow was concerned, the two projects could have been reconciled within the framework of the Greater Europe project, the continuation in new form of aspirations for pan-European continental integration. In the 1990s the idea lapsed, but with the evident failure to find an adequate formula to make Russia part of Wider Europe and the increasingly confrontational exercise of normative agendas, perceived in Moscow as threats when they took the form of regime change and colour revolutions, Greater Europe from the mid-2000s came back on to the agenda. The idea was to establish some sort of overarching inclusive approach to continental unification that would allow geopolitical and ideological pluralism. Not all the problems of history had been resolved by the EU, and some states (notably Russia) were still trying to work out their political identity and destiny, and thus there needed to be a pause in the relentless advance of the west (Gromyko and Fëdorova, 2014). In the event, no such pause was given, leading to the renewed division of the continent.

Economic factors

The variegated sub-regional pattern is reflected in economic matters. For historical reasons the whole region remains economically tightly bound to Russia. The Baltic republics, Finland and the Central European states have traditionally been fully dependent on Russia for gas supplies; Poland is 53 per cent reliant; while Romania is almost completely self-sufficient (Chyong and Tcherneva, 2015). For some this is an unwelcome dependency, especially when transit risks across Ukraine are taken into account. This encouraged attempts to reduce dependency by diversifying supplies. The Ukraine crisis from 2014 accelerated efforts to create an Energy Union to create a European network of pipelines and power routes that would allow a stronger common front in bargaining with Russia. The obvious irony that such anti-competitive measures were sanctioned by the EU when effectively directed against Russia but condemned (in the Third Energy Package and other measures) when practiced by Russia. This only intensified Russian condemnation of 'double standards', although by the middle of the second decade of the twenty-first century such actions were more often met with weary resignation.

The key trend now is the rupturing of traditional ties and the reorientation of economic activity to the west. The imposition of sanctions in 2014 hastened the process, and throughout the region economic ties wilted. For example, Latvia had long acted as an *entrepôt* for Russian oil supplies, and this now declined sharply. Following the Maidan revolution the new government in Ukraine enthusiastically joined this process, and trade with Russia fell by over a third in 2014 alone. Following the signature of its Association Agreement on 27 June 2014, Moldova also reoriented its economy towards the EU.

This left only Belarus, but even here there were attempts to diversify. Belarus is in a category of its own, having become part of a nominal 'union state' with Russia since April 1997, supplemented since then by several treaties. Belarus was one of the founder members of the EEU, and its economy is deeply entwined with that of Russia. The Belarus social model can only survive with generous subsidies from Russia, mainly taking the indirect form of cheap energy exports to the country, the oil part of which is then refined in Belarus and exported to Europe with great profit.

Russian economic penetration of the region is not limited to the energy sphere. Before the imposition of sanctions, a tightly interwoven market in agricultural goods had emerged. This meant that Poland supplied a large proportion of Russia's market in apples, and several other countries supplied Russia with dairy products. Russian banks and other companies also created a significant presence in the region (Tsygankov, 2006). Russians also established themselves across the region in the housing market, and in some places became the single largest foreign presence, notably along the Montenegrin coast. Russian tourists became the single largest cohort in certain parts of Greece and Italy, and were famous for their relatively high spending per capita, especially in comparison with the rather more parsimonious Germans. The growing interdependence between Russia and the region was sharply reversed by the imposition of sanctions, a development that conspiracy theorists suggested was the American goal all along. Whether intended or not, the Ukraine crisis introduced a major rupture between Russia and the region, one that will take decades to overcome.

Security dilemmas

A security dilemma, as defined by Robert Jervis (1976), is a situation where the attempt to bolster the security of one state or group of states is perceived to threaten another state, which in turn responds in a manner which only intensifies the security risks of the original state or states. In those terms, the whole post–Cold War period has seen a massive security dilemma in relations between Russia and the region. The advance of NATO to encompass the Baltic republics, central and parts of southeast Europe, and the promise at the Bucharest summit in April 2008 that membership would ultimately be granted to Georgia and Ukraine, was perceived in Moscow as an escalating and long-term threat. For the East Europeans, NATO membership was the ultimate guarantee for their own security, but the very act of trying to achieve their own security reduced the common quotient of security for the whole region. The Russo-Georgia war in 2008 can be dubbed the first war to stop NATO enlargement, and the destructive dynamic culminated in the Ukraine crisis.

Moscow was at the centre of an alternative security system. The CIS was buttressed by security cooperation between countries signing the Tashkent Collective Security Treaty (CST) agreements in 1992, which on 14 May 1999 was transformed into the Collective Security Treaty Organisation (CSTO). The CSTO at that time united Armenia, Belarus, Russia, Kyrgyzstan, Kazakhstan, and Tajikistan, while Uzbekistan periodically joined and left. In May 2003 CSTO adopted an ambitious security agenda, including a joint military command in Moscow, a rapid reaction force, a common air defence system, and 'coordinated action' in foreign, security and defence policy (Allison, White and Light, 2005). The grouping has international status, and is recognized as an observer organisation at the UN General Assembly. Putin sought to raise its status further by establishing direct contacts between CSTO and NATO, something resisted by the latter since it would effectively grant CSTO parity status. Through the CSTO Russia has supplied its partners with armaments at preferential domestic prices, notably to Belarus and Armenia. The CSTO sought to give institutional form to the creation of a regional security complex, as described by Buzan and Waever (2003). The existence of such a complex was intended to provide a platform for the pursuit of Russia's broader goals, notably opposition to NATO enlargement. The prevention of NATO's extension into the post-Soviet region (excluding the Baltic republics), was not simply intended to ensure Russia's pre-eminence in post-Soviet Eurasia but sought to reinforce Russia's claims to be an autonomous great power.

While the argument in favour of the sovereign right of states to make their own choices is a powerful one, these choices are never taken in a vacuum and the overall security of a region has to be taken into account. While NATO may well have considered itself a benign body with no aggressive intentions, the earlier intervention in Kosovo and then in Afghanistan inevitably worried military planners in Moscow. These concerns were exacerbated by plans to introduce elements of a ballistic missile defence system into the region. America's unilateral abrogation in 2002 of the ABM treaty, the cornerstone of nuclear defence architecture in the Cold War years, added to these concerns.

Overarching the whole security dilemma in relations between Russia and the region was the perception that the Atlantic power constellation was gaining in power, ambition and reach. This power constellation effectively meant that the EU and NATO became part of a single power system bringing in America but excluding Russia. The Atlantic system established a new polarity, inevitably provoking a reaction through the creation of some sort of balancing mechanism. Once again, the potential for a clash could have been obviated, at least in Moscow's eyes, if some sort of pan-European security system could have been created to soften the hard edge between Russia and the Atlantic macro-region. This in essence was the aim of President Dmitry Medvedev's call in Berlin in June 2008 for a new security treaty in Europe. The initiative was shunted off into the Corfu Process under the aegis of the OSCE, and soon after forgotten. The proposal did lack detail, but it nevertheless represented an attempt by Russia to create new modes of reconciliation in Europe. Instead, the gap between Atlantic and continental visions of Europe grew larger, creating the gulf that we see today.

Conclusion

The conclusion to our study of Russia in the region is clear. A new iron curtain is in the making, no longer stretching from Stettin in the Adriatic to Trieste on the Adriatic, but from Narva in the Adriatic to Mariupol on the Sea of Azov. Aspirations for a continent 'whole and free' voiced at the end of the Cold War have given way to something akin to a new cold war, although no longer with global reach or the ideological overlay of the original. It is too easy to blame one side or the other, but what has really happened is the failure of political imagination. Western institutions and ideas after 1989 emerged with greater confidence, and made strong efforts to bring Russia into an expanding Atlantic community. Russia was initially receptive to becoming part of an enlarged European and Western community, but it would always be an aberrant member of an Atlantic system.

With interests in Eurasia and with global ambitions as a former superpower and still one of the world's major states, it would not be possible for Russia to become part of an existing order which it had not helped shape and in which it would be a subaltern power. Thus a negative dynamic was established that degenerated into outright conflict over Ukraine. Russia still has its friends and some influence in the region, notably through economic links and the presence of a significant Russian cultural presence, but the overall story is one of failure. No effective mode of reconciliation was devised – either institutional or in processes – to create a common sense of belonging between Russia and the countries of the region. The tectonic plates have now moved apart with the fault line running through the middle of the region, and it will be the responsibility of a new generation of politicians and citizens to heal the wounds and to reunite the region and the continent.

References

Allison, Roy, Stephen White and Margot Light (2005), 'Belarus Between East and West', *The Journal of Communist Studies and Transition Politics*, Vol. 21, No. 4, pp. 487–511.

Ambrosio, Thomas (2008), *Authoritarian Backlash: Russian Resistance to Democratization in the Former Soviet Union* (Farnham, Ashgate).

Balmaceda, Margarita M. (2014), *Living the High Life in Minsk: Russian Energy Rents, Domestic Populism and Belarus' Impending Crisis* (Budapest, Central European University).

BBC News (16 October 2014), 'Putin Guest of Honour at Serbia Military Parade', www.bbc.co.uk/news/world-europe-29641642, accessed 5 October 2015.

BBC News (17 February 2015), 'Hungarians Protest as Putin Meets Orban', www.bbc.co.uk/news/world-europe-31499654, accessed 5 October 2015.

Bennett, B. (2011), *The Last Dictatorship in Europe: Belarus Under Lukashenko* (New York, Columbia University Press).

Brubaker, Rogers (1996), *Nationalism Reframed: Nationhood and the National Question in the New Europe* (Cambridge, Cambridge University Press).

Buzan, Barry and Ole Waever (2003), *Regions and Powers: The Structure of International Security* (Cambridge, Cambridge University Press).

Chyong, Chi-Kong and Vessela Tcherneva (2015), *Europe's Vulnerability on Russian Gas* (London, ECFR), available at www.ecfr.eu/article/commentary_europes_vulnerability_on_russian_gas, accessed 5 October 2015.

Dragneva, Rilka and Kataryna Wolczuk (eds) (2013), *Eurasian Economic Integration: Law, Policy and Politics* (Cheltenham, Edward Elgar).

Dutkiewicz, Piotr and Richard Sakwa (eds) (2015), *Eurasian Integration: The View From Within* (London and New York, Routledge).

Gromyko, Alexei A. and V. P. Fëdorova (eds) (2014), *Bol'shaya Evropa: Idei, real'nost', perspektivy* (Moscow, Ves' mir).

Hill, William H. (2012), *Russia, the Near Abroad and the West: Lessons From the Moldova-Transdniestria Conflict* (Washington, DC, Woodrow Wilson Center Press; Baltimore, MD, Johns Hopkins University Press).

Jervis, Robert (1976), *Perception and Misperception in International Politics* (Princeton, NJ, Princeton University Press).

Korosteleva, Elena (2015), 'Belarus between the EU and Eurasian Economic Union', in Piotr Dutkiewicz and Richard Sakwa (eds), *Eurasian Integration: The View from Within* (London, Routledge), pp. 111–125.

Kurki, Milja (2011), 'Governmentality and EU Democracy Promotion: The European Instrument for Democracy and Human Rights and the Construction of Democratic Civil Societies', *International Political Sociology*, Vol. 5, pp. 349–366.

Kuzio, Taras and Paul D'Anieri (eds) (2002), *Dilemmas of State-Led Nation Building in Ukraine* (Westport, CT, Greenwood).

Menon, Rajan and Eugene B. Rumer (2015), *Conflict in Ukraine: The Unwinding of the Post-Cold War Order* (Boston, MA, MIT Press).

Obydenkova, Anastassia and Alexander Libman (eds) (2015), *Autocratic and Democratic External Influences in Post-Soviet Eurasia* (Farnham, Ashgate).

Panichi, James (2015), 'New EU Task Force Hobbled by Low Funding, Lack of Political Support', 17 September 2015, www.politico.eu/article/eu-russia-propaganda-kremlin-media/, accessed 15 October 2015.

Sakwa, Richard (2015), *Frontline Ukraine: Crisis in the Borderlands* (London and New York, I. B. Tauris).

Sanford, George (2009), *Katyn and the Soviet Massacre of 1940* (London and New York, Routledge).

Sasse, Gwendolyn (2008), 'The European Neighbourhood Policy: Conditionality Revisited for the EU's Eastern Neighbours', *Europe-Asia Studies*, Vol. 60, No. 2, pp. 295–316.

Schimmelfennig, Frank, Stefan Engert and Heiko Knobel (2006), *International Socialization in Europe: European Organizations, Political Conditionality and Democratic Change* (Basingstoke, Palgrave Macmillan).

Snyder, Timothy (2010), *Bloodlands: Europe Between Hitler and Stalin* (New York, Basic Books).

Talbott, Strobe (2003), *The Russia Hand: A Memoir of Presidential Diplomacy* (New York, Random House).

Tolstrup, Jakob (2014), *Russia vs. the EU: The Competition for Influence in Post-Soviet States* (Boulder, CO, Lynne Rienner).

Tsygankov, Andrei P. (November 2006), 'If Not by Tanks, Then by Banks? The Role of Soft Power in Putin's Foreign Policy', *Europe-Asia Studies*, Vol. 58, No. 7, pp. 1079–1099.

Wilson, Andrew (2011), *Belarus: The Last European Dictatorship* (New Haven, CT, Yale University Press).

Wilson, Andrew (2014), *Ukraine Crisis: What It Means for the West* (London and New Haven, Yale University Press).

INDEX

advocacy model 188

Agarin, T. 231

Albania: corruption in 93; democratisation in 27–8; end of communism in 11, 28–9; mass protests in 27; persistence of semi-authoritarian rule in 30; rise of new semi-authoritarian regimes in 31; *see also* South Eastern Europe

Alford Index 177

Allport, G. 217

Almond, Mark 14

Anderson, B. 214–15

annus mirabilis 12

anti-establishment reform parties 104

anti-Semitism 259

anti-system parties and corruption 313–14

Applebaum, A. 47

Arel, D. 48

Ash, Timothy Garton 13

Ashdown, Paddy 149

Ashwin, Sarah 201

authoritarian co-optation 190

autocratisation 362

Avdeyeva, O. 242

Ayoub, Phillip M. 249–50

Azarov, Mykola 43

backsliding 17–19, 338–40

Bàgenholm, A. 312, 314

Baker, James 349

Bakker, R. 172

Balkan Ghosts 216

Balkan states 2, 28, 213; bureaucracies in western 126–35; civil service laws in 129; neoliberalism 35; New Weberian States 131; weak state capacity in 34

Barnes, Andrew 16

Bartolini, S. 178

Băsescu, Traian 75, 78

Batory, A. 312

Baun, Mats 298

Becker, Joachim 270

Beissinger, Mark 12, 143, 186, 200–1, 203–4

Berg-Schlosser, Dirk 21

Berisha, Sali 30

Berlin Wall 254, 257, 296, 302

Berlusconi, Silvio 106

Bernhard, Michael 19–20

Bertelsmann Transformation Index (BTI) 21, 36, 116

Beslan School massacre 148

Bieber, Florian 3, 32

Biezen, I. 107

Bilić, Bojan 250–1

Block, F. L. 323

Blondel, J. 58–9, 64

Boden Plan 151

Bohle, Dorothee 35, 201, 270–1, 273–4, 322

Bonn Powers 149–50

Bookman, M. Z. 144

Borisov, Boyko 31

Bosnia and Herzegovina 34, 360; ethnic minorities in 216; federalisation of 148–51; *see also* South Eastern Europe

Bouckaert, G. 127, 135

Brady, H. E. 162

Brubaker, Rogers 141, 218, 360

Brusis, M. 134

Bruszt, László 273, 322–3

Buchen, Clemens 269

Bulgaria: civil war in 16; corruption in 93–4; democratisation in 27–8; end of communism in 11, 13; political parties in 107; rise of new semi-authoritarian regime in 31; *see also* South Eastern Europe

Bulldozer Revolution 203
Bunce, Valerie 12, 14, 18, 159, 202; on collapse
  of communist federations 141–2; on electoral
  model of activism 189; on mass protests and
  nature of transition 33; on nationalism 34;
  on performance of post-communist public
  administration 133; on the Orange
  Revolution 45
bureaucracies and public administration 126–7;
  agency reform, performance management, and
  public financial management after crisis 130;
  civil service reform and politicisation 128–30;
  explaining administrative reform and practices
  in post-communist 131–3; future research
  on 134–5; models of post-communist 130–1;
  performance of post-communist 133–4; role in
  semi-presidentialism 77–8; trajectories of reform
  in post-communist Europe 127–31
Bush, George H. W. 145
Bustikova, L. 259–60
Buzan, Barry 365
Buzogány, A. 338

Cameron, David 341
Camyar, I. 132
capitalism, Eastern European 267–8; assessment
  and future research 276–7; early reforms
  273–4; explaining 272–5; internationalisation
  and 274–5; legacies and path dependency 273;
  neoclassical sociology in 268–9; neoliberal 35;
  Polyanyian varieties of 270; sectoral varieties of
  271, 272; varieties of 269–70; worlds of 268–72
Carey, John M. 68
Carrington, Peter 146
Caspersen, Nina 33
Caucasus, civil war in 16
Charron, N. 312, 314
Chechnya 148
Chetaille, A. 248
Choi, Susanne Y. P. 288–9
Churchill hypothesis 19
Ciobanu, Monica 287
Císař, Ondrej 2, 186
civil service reform 128–30
civil society 184
Clinton, Bill 149, 349
co-optation 189–91
cohabitation: in semi-presidentialism 75–6; intra-
  executive conflict and 86
Cold War 299, 336, 346, 348, 353
colour revolutions 17–19, 189, 362
committees and party factions 90–1
communism: federalism under 139–41; legacy of
  309; party system ideological patterns under 173
communism, fall of 12–13; CEE foreign policy
  after 296; emergence of core executives and
  57; explanations of regime outcomes under 14;

historical factors in 16–17; in South Eastern
  Europe 27–9; legacies after 3–4, 94; protest
  politics and 198–200; proximate factors in
  14–16; unpredicted and unpredictable collapses
  of 13–14
Communist and Post-Communist Studies 259
comparative politics 202–4
conflict, instrumental use of 33–4
Connor, W. 214
consentful contention in activism 191
constitutional design of parliament 83–4
Copenhagen Conditions 82, 334
core executives 55–6, 63–4; emergence and studies
  of post-socialist 56–9; Europeanising 59–61;
  executive governance studies and 61–3
Corfu Process 366
corruption 93–4, 307–8, 314–15; as legacy of
  communism 309; party system ideological
  patterns and 174; promise of anti-system parties
  and 313–14; promise of EU membership and
  312–13; promise of institutional reform and
  309–10; promise of liberalisation and 310–11;
  promise of political competition and 311–12;
  ubiquitous nature of 308
Crimea 42; formal politics and 43–4; Russia's
  annexation of 47–8; Ukraine foreign policy and
  45–6
critical social science 201
Croatia 18; corruption in 93; persistence of semi-
  authoritarian rule in 29–30; semi-presidential
  regime in 69, 71
Crowley, Ost 201
Crowther, William E. 90
Csanádi, Maria 14
Cuban Missile Crisis 296
Czech Republic 362; civil service law 128; end
  of communism in 11, 13; ethnofederalism in
  140, 144; foreign policy 297; parliamentary
  membership in 89; political parties 101–2, 106;
  women in 238

D'Anieri, P. 40, 45
Dan, S. 134
Darden, Keith 17
Dassonneville, R. 175
David, Roman 284, 286, 288–9
Dawson, James 20
Dayton Agreement, 1995 148, 216
Democracy Barometer 21
democratic co-optation 189–90
democratisation 9–10; and assumed perils of
  (semi-)presidentialism 73–4; colour revolutions,
  hybrid regimes, and backsliding in 17–19;
  compromises toward 14–15; consolidation in
  East Central Europe 19–20; ethnic minorities,
  regime change, and 215–20; facts in the post-
  communist region 10–11; historical factors in

roots of 16–17; in South Central Europe 27–8; nature of transition in South Eastern Europe 32–3; party system ideological patterns and 174; quality of 20–1; social movements and 185–7; *see also* post-communism

Diani, Mario 187

Dimitrov, V. 134

Dimitrova, A. 57–9, 91–2, 132

Djukanović, Milo 30

Dmowski, Roman 297

Dodik, Milorad 28, 30

Donbas 42, 48

Doyle, D. 69

Drahokoupil, Jan 271

Drechsler, W. 134

Driscoll, J. 48

Dudaev, Dzhokar 147

Dugin, Alexander 260

Dunleavy, P. 55

Duverger, M. 68

East European Constitutional Review 86

East Germany, end of communism in 11, 13, 254, 257

Eastern Europe: democratic consolidation in 19–20; recent rise in populist politics and authoritarian tendencies in 2–3; studying the revolutionary changes of the 1990s in 1–2; tension between post-communism and Europeanisation in 3; two key themes in 3–4

Ecker, A. 313

Edinger, Michael 89–90

Ekdiert, Grzegorz 186, 202

Ekman, J. 75, 86

elections and electoral participation 157–9; critical reflections on studies of 164–5; founding 157; new and emerging themes 163–4; Roma 230–1; salient themes in the study of 159–63; voters in party systems and 176–9; *see also* political parties

electoral model 189

electoral sequencing 141–2

Elgie, R. 68–9

Elster, Jon 14, 283

Engler, S. 313

enlargement, European Union 333–4, 341–2; compliance and decision-making in adapting to 336–7; core-periphery dynamics in 338; polity and politics in backsliding in 338–40; responses to Greek debt crisis and 341; unprecedented "big bang" 334–6; *see also* European Union, the

enlargement, NATO 346–7; consequences of 353–5; end of 355; explaining 351–3; limits of 348–51; short history of 347–8; *see also* NATO (North Atlantic Treaty Organization)

episodic mass mobilisation 188

Epstein, Rachel 3, 298

Erdogan, Tayyip 31

Estonia 359–60; end of communism in 11; foreign policy 298; parliamentary membership in 89; political parties in 107

ethnic minorities 221; and the future 220–1; democracy development and 16; federalism and 140; in democratic politics 218–20; in Eastern Europe 213–15; mobilisation of 216–18; party system ideological patterns 173–4; questioning principal contributions on democracy and 220; regime change, and democracy 215–20

ethno-nationalist radical right parties 101–2

ethnofederalism *see* federalism

Eurasion Economic Union (EEU) 46

European Agricultural Fund for Rural Development (EARDF) 232

European Banking Union 326

European Central Bank (ECB) 323, 326

European Commission 334–5

European Common Market 94

European External Action Service (EEAS) 363

European Region of the International Lesbian, Gay, Bisexual, Trans and Intersex Association (ILGA-Europe) 249–50

European Regional Development Fund (ERDF) 232–3

European Social Fund (ESF) 232

European Union, the 113, 145, 295, 307; CEE states corruption and promise of membership in 312–13; conditionality 91–2; Cooperation and Verification Mechanism (CVM) 335; emergence of core executives and 58–61; foreign policy of CEE states and accession to 298–302; Fundamental Rights Agency (FRA) 229; influence on LGBT rights in Eastern Europe 249; Roma policy formation 232–3; rule of law promotion literature 118–19; Russia and 358–9; semi-presidentialism and 78; Sustainable Governance Indicators (SGI) 62; Ukraine and 45–6, 49

Europeanisation 59–61; *see also* enlargement, European Union

Europeanisation model 188–9

executive governance studies 61–3

executive-legislative relations 85–6

Eyal, Gil 268

Falkner, G. 134

far-right groups 254; future developments in study of 260–2; history 254–7; main criticisms of scholarship on 260; major works on 257–8; principal contributions to scholarship on 258–60

Fazekas, M. 308

Fearon, J. 217

federalism 139; and federalisation of Bosnia and Herzegovina 148–51; explaining the collapse of communist federations 141–6; in Eastern

Europe after communism 146–51; under
communism 139–41
Feldmann, Magnus 269
Fijalkowski, Agata 286
financial industry, Eastern European 319–20,
325–6; "second home market" versus Vienna
initiative 323–5; developmental consequences of
high levels of foreign bank ownership in 322–3;
origins of foreign domination of 320–2; Russia
and 364
Fish, M. Steven 14, 16–17, 77, 84
Flam, Helena 247
foreign direct investment (FDI) 94, 275; EU
enlargement and 338; in Eastern European
banks 322–3
foreign policy 295–6, 302; focus on
Europeanisation and NATO-isation in 298–300;
further exploration and developments in 300–2;
historical and intellectual developments on
CEE 296; identities and priorities, new 297–8;
Ukraine 45–6
former communist parties 101
Fortin, Jessica 17
founding elections 157
Freedom House 10–11, 21, 250

Gagnon, V. P., Jr. 33
game theory 199
Gellner, E. 214–15
genuinely new parties 103–4
Georgia 18; electoral malpractice in 164; NATO
membership for 350–1; semi-presidential regime
in 69, 71
Gerring, John 92
Gessen, Masha 247
Giedroyc, Jerzy 297
Giuliano, E. 48
Glenn, John 200
Goetz, K. H. 128
Golder, Sona N. 86–7
Gorbachev, Mikhail 12, 28, 142–5, 362
Gordy, Eric 33
Gorenburg, Dmitry P. 200, 204
Gould, John 248
governmentalisation 57
Graff, Agnieszka 248
Great Recession 254
Greece 361; debt crisis 341
Grellmann, Heinrich 226
Greskovits, Béla 35, 273–4, 322, 340; on far-right
groups 260; on Polanyian variety of capitalism
270; on sectoral varieties of capitalism 271; on
social movements 186–7, 191, 201
Griffin, Roger 257
Grodsky, Brian 284
Grosescu, Raluca 286
Grotz, Florian 87

Gruevski, Nikola 28, 30
Grzymala-Busse, Anna 17, 109, 131–2, 248, 311

Hale, Henry 18, 40
Hallerberg, M. 134
Halll, Peter A. 269–70, 276
Hanley, Sean 20, 22, 313
Hanson, Stephen E. 14
Havel, Václav 13, 184
Hellman, Joel 87
Helsinki Accords, 1975 197
Herder, Johann Gottfried 214
Hesse, J. J. 127
Hille, P. 134
HIV/AIDS 247
Holmes, L. 309
Hooghe, M. 175
Horne, Cynthia M. 288
Horowitz, D. 219
Horowitz, Shale 17
Horvat, Srecko 35
Howard, Marc M. 19, 185, 248
Hungary: backsliding in 18; end of communism
in 11, 13; ethnic mobilisation in 218;
Europeanisation of core executives 61;
liberalisation under communism 10;
parliamentary membership in 89; political
parties in 107
Huntington, Samuel 15
Hussein, Saddam 298
hybrid regimes 17–19

identity politics 41
Iliescu, Ion 30
Ilonszki, Gabriella 89–90
Implementation Capacity 62
Information-Processing Capacity 62
institutional design of parliament 83–7, *88*
institutional reform, promise of 309–10
institutionalisation, legislative 89–92
integrated causal theory 120–1
International Criminal Tribunal for the Former
Yugoslavia 290
international environment 3; proximate factors in
fall of communism 15
International Monetary Fund (IMF) 274, 321
internationalism 274–5
intra-executive conflict: and cohabitation in semi-
presidentialism 74–6; executive-legislative
relations and 85–6
Inzko, Valentin 150
Iraq war 298
Ivanov, K. 312

Jacoby, Wade 15, 298
Jacquette, J. 241
Jäger, Johannes 270

Jahn, Detlef 87, 94–5
Janos, Andrew 16
Jelavich, B. 214
Jervis, Robert 365
Jolly, S. 172
Jović, Dejan 32
Jowitt, Ken 16, 248
judicial reform literature 117
Juncker, Jean-Claude 340

Kaczynski, Jaroslav 2, 78
Kalyvas, Stathis 12
Kaplan, C. S. 162
Kaplan, Robert 216
Karklins, R. 199–200, 310
Karl, Terry Lynn 14
Kartal, M. 312
Kaya, Ruchan 19–20
Keck, Margaret 250
Kelley, Judith 15
Khmelko, Irina 90–1
Khodorkovskii, Mikhail 45
Kim, Dae Soon 284
King, Charles 14
Kitschelt, Herbert 9, 131, 286; on bureaucratic
   legacies of post-communist countries 17; on
   explanations of regime outcomes 14, 16
Klasnja, M. 313
Klaus, Václav 144, 362
Knill, C. 134
Knutsen, O. 177
Kochenov, Dimitry 250
Koinova, Maria 32
Konrád, György 184
Kopecký, Petr 20, 94–5, 131, 202, 309
Kopstein, Jeffrey 15
Korkut, U. 338
Kostadinova, Tatiana 20, 310
Koudelka, Josef 228
Kozak Memorandum 151
Krastev, Ivan 20, 313, 315
Kriesi, Hanspeter 186
Kritz, Neil J. 282–3
Kroenig, Matthew 16–17, 84
Krugman, Paul 325
Kubik, Jan 186, 202
Kuchma, Leonid 41, 43–5
Kudelia, S. 48
Kuhar, Roman 248
Kulyk, V. 41
Kuran, Timur 13, 199–200
Kurtz, Marcus J. 16
Kyrgyzstan 18, 71

Lane, David 203
Langenbacher, Nora 202
language question in Ukraine 41–2

Lankina, Tomila V. 203
Latvia 359–60; end of communism in 11; far-right
   groups in 256–7; political parties in 102
Lazarenko, Pavlo 44
Le Pen, Marine 257
Leff, Carol Skalnik 15
legislative institutionalisation 89–92
Lenin, Vladimir 140
Levitsky, Steven 18, 45
Levitz, Philip 15, 312
LGBT rights after communism, study of 250–1;
   overview of literature struggling to catch up in
   246–50; reasons 245; terminology in 245–6
liberal imperialism 150
liberalisation, promise of 310–11
Lijphart, A. 220
Linz, Juan 15, 20, 67, 126, 141; on presidentialism
   and democracy 73, 76, 78
Lipset, S. M. 178, 180
Lithuania 359–60; political party types in 101–2;
   transitional justice in 287
Lithuanian Genocide and Resistance Research
   Centre 289
Lohmann, Susanne 200
Long, Scott 247
Lucassen, L. 226–7
Lucinschi, Petru 74
Lukashenko, Alexandr 163, 359
Lynch, Moira 288

Macedonia 31; corruption in 93; *see also* South
   Eastern Europe
Magen, A. 118
Mair, P. 178
Mal'gin, A. 42
Mansfeldová, Zdenka 89
Marchesi, Bridget 288
Martin, T. 140
Marushiakova, E. 228
Masaryk, Tomáš Garrigue 297
Mashtaler, Olga 86
Massey, G. 217
Matichescu, Marius Lupsa 90
Matland, R. 241
Matras, Y. 226, 231
McFaul, Michael 14
McGarry, A. 231
Meciar, Vladimir 257
Melzer, Ralf 202
Mendelski, M. 120
Merkel, Angela 341
Meyer-Sahling, Jan-Hinrik 87, 132–3, 312;
   on performance of post-communist public
   administration 133
Michnik, Adam 184
migration, Roma 231–2
Mikkelsen, K. S. 133

Mikus, Marek 250
Milo ević, Slobodan 2, 30, 257
Minkenberg, M. 254, 258–9
Moe, Edward 248
Moldova 359; corruption in 93–4; parliamentary membership in 90; semi-presidential regime in 69, 71
Molotov-Ribbentrop Pact, 1939 360
Moreno, Carola 92
Morlino, L. 118
Motyl, Alexander 22, 39
Mudde, Cas 20, 202, 258
Müller-Rommel, F. 64, 86–7; on parliaments 87, 94–5
Munck, Gerardo L. 15
Mungiu-Pippidi, Alina 32, 315, 339
Myant, Martin 271
Mykhnenko, Vlad 269

Nalepa, Monika 286
nationalism 254, 260; "nasty" 257; instrumental use of 33–4; *see also* far-right groups
Nations in Transit index 21
NATO (North Atlantic Treaty Organization) 46, 145, 295; foreign policy of CEE states and accession to 298–300, 302; Russia and 349–50, 365
Navumau, Vasil 203
Nedelsky, Nadya 281, 283, 286
neoclassical sociology 268–9
neoliberalism: Balkan 35; internationalisation and 274
Neshkova, M. 310
New Weberian States 130–1
Nikolic, Tomislav 361
Nölke, Andreas 269–70, 323
Norkus, Zenonas 269
Norton, Philip 90

O'Dwyer, Conor 248
Obama, Barack 350
Oettinger, Günther 340
Offe, Klaus 1, 14, 284
Olson, David M. 90
Onuch, Olga 47, 203
Open Society Foundation 258
Opp, Karl-Dieter 200
Orange Revolution, 2004 43–5, 48, 164, 203
Orbán, Viktor 2, 31, 62, 257, 339, 362
Organisation for Economic Co-operation and Development (OECD) 60, 62, 276
Ortiz, G. 323
Osteuropa 259
Ottoman Empire 213–14
Owczarzak, Jill 248

Pacek, Alexander C. 20
Papadimitriou, D. 133

parliament(s) 82–3, 95; characteristics of party systems and implications for 84–5; constitutional design 83–4; EU conditionality and 91–2; executive-legislative relations and intra-executive conflict 85–6; explaining variation in institutional performance of 92–5; government stability and 86–7, *88*; institutional complexity of party factions and committees in 90–1; institutional design of 83–7, *88*; legislative institutionalisation 89–92; membership 89–90
parliamentarism 67–8; defining 68–9; regimes in Eastern Europe 69–71
Parliamentary Powers Index 84
participatory activist type activism 187
Paternotte, David 249
perestroika 12
Peters, B. G. 62
Petrova, Tsveta 187
Pettai, Eva-Clarita 283, 285, 287
Pettai, Vello 283, 285, 287
Phinnemore, D. 133
Pierre, J. 62
Piłsudski, Józef 139–40, 297
Płatek, Daniel 202
Płucienniczak, Piotr P. 202
pluralism by default 40
Poland: backsliding in 18; corruption in 94; end of communism in 10–11, 13; first semi-free elections in 10–11; foreign policy 297; liberalisation under communism 10; parliamentary membership in 89; semi-presidentialism 72; solidarity movement in 184–5; women in 239
Polanyi, Karl 270
Polish Institute of National Remembrance 289
political competition, promise of 311–12
political parties 100, 109–10, 179–80; developmental approach to 101; direct public funding of 106–7; former communist parties 101; fragmentation 170–1; genuinely new parties 103–4; ideological patterns 171–4; membership 107; new and old 102–6; organisation 106–9; parties within party systems 170–6; party families 100; party system change 174–6; party systems 84–5; factions 90–1; satellite parties 101; types 100–2; voters and 176–9; *see also* elections and electoral participation
politicisation 128–30
politics, protest *see* protest politics in Eastern Europe
Polity 10, *11*, 21
Polk, J. 172
Pollitt, C. 127, 134–5
Polsby, Nelson 89
Polyanyian varieties of capitalism 270
Ponta, Victor 31, 78

Pop-Eleches, Grigore 15–17, 20, 312
Popescu-Tăriceanu, Calin 75
Popov, V. 228
Poroshenko, Petro 351
post-communism: emergence of core executives in 56–9; executive governance studies 61–3; facts of 10–11; federalism 146–51; political parties 101; research frontiers 22; tension between Europeanisation and 3; time spent in communism versus 2; trajectories of public administration reform in 127–31; transformation and social movements 185–7; transition to two-tier banking systems in 321; transitional justice, variation in 286–7; women in 237–42; *see also* democratisation; enlargement, European Union; enlargement, NATO
Powell, E. N. 175
Prague Spring 197, 205
premier-presidentialism systems 68, 73–4; intra-executive conflict and cohabitation in 74–6
president-parliamentary systems 68, 73–4
presidentialism 67–8; defining 68–9
Pridham, Geoffrey 91
prime ministers, power and position of 77
prisoners dilemma 34
protest politics in Eastern Europe 197, 205; comparative politics and 202–4; critical social science and 201; post-1989 200; revolutions of 1989 and 1991 and 198–200; sociology of discontent and 204; Western theory of contention and 197–8
Protsyk, Oleh 85–6, 90
proximate factors in fall of communism 14–16
Przeworski, Adam 14
Putin, Vladimir 31, 148, 360–1; authoritarian co-optation and 190; Crimea and 46
Putnam, Robert D. 19
Pytlas, B. 258

quality of democracy 20–1
Queer Studies 248

radical activism 188
Radnitz, Scott 203
Raimundo, Filipa 283
Rakhimov, Murtaza 147
Ramet, Sabrina P. 247, 257
Randma-Liiv, T. 132, 134
Raunio, T. 78
Red Sunset 12
refederalisation of Russia 146–8
regional differences in Ukraine 40–1
Reh, C. 337
Reilly, David 15
Renkin, Hadley 248
Revolution of Dignity 47
Rhodes, R.A.W. 55

Rimac, I. 248
Roberts, A. 176
Roberts, Andrew 2, 21
Robertson, Graeme 190–1, 202
Roeder, Philip G. 12, 14, 141
Rokkan, S. 178, 180
Roma: Europe-wide policy formation on 232–3; future of research on 233–4; historical and intellectual development of study of 225–9; migration 231–2; studies after 1989 229–33; study of minority politics, activism, and participation of 230–1; understanding exclusion and discrimination of 229–30
Romania: civil war in 16; corruption in 93; democratisation in 27–8; end of communism in 11; ethnic mobilisation in 218; foreign policy 297; persistence of semi-authoritarian rule in 29–30; rise of new semi-authoritarian regimes in 30–1; semi-presidentialism 72; *see also* South Eastern Europe
Romaphobia 259
Rose, Richard 19
Routledge Studies in Extremism and Democracy 258
Rožić, Peter 284
Rüdiger, Johann 226
rule of law 113–15; challenges for future research 121–2; EU promotion literature 118–19; explanations of differences in 117–19; healthy and pathological reform cycles and 120–1; literature critique 119–20; promotion literature 117; trends in development of 115–17
Rumsfeld, Donald 298
Rupnik, J. 341
Russia 358, 366; authoritarian co-optation in 190; clash of integrations and 362–4; consentful strategies of claims-making in 191; economic factors in 364; ethnofederalism in 140; NATO membership for 349–50; protest politics in 200; refederalisation of 146–8; security dilemmas 365–6; semi-presidentialism 72; sub-regional diversity in 358–62; Ukraine and 45–6; *see also* Soviet Union, the
Russian language 41–2

Sadurski, Wojciech 118
Sakwa, Richard 20
Samuels, D. 76
Sasse, G. 47, 186, 201
satellite parties 101
Schedler, Andreas 20
Schellenberg, Britta 202
Schimmelfennig, Frank 15, 298
Schleifer, Andrei 15
Schmitter, Philippe 14
Schneider, Carsten Q. 20
Scholtz, Hanno 15
Schwartz, Katrina Z. S. 248

Scott, James 203
sectoral varieties of capitalism 271, *272*
Sedelius, T. 75, 86
Sedelmeier, U. 298, 339–40
Sejdic and Finci v. Bosnia and Herzegovina 150
self-organisation 188
semi-authoritarian rule: persistence of 29–30; rise of new regimes 30–1
semi-presidentialism 67–8, 78–9; as growing research field with Eastern Europe at its core 71–2, *72–3*; core research themes 73–7; defining 68–9; democratisation and assumed perils of 73–4; intra-executive conflict and cohabitation in 74–6; presidentialisation and party system factors in 76–7; prime minister's power and position in 77; regimes in Eastern Europe 69–71; role of the bureaucracy and public administration in 77–8; subtypes 68, 73–4; the European Union and 78; underexplored issues on 77–8
Serafin, Sebastian 202
Serbia 18, 360–1; Bulldozer Revolution 203; electoral malpractice in 164; ethnofederalism in 141; persistence of semi-authoritarian rule in 29–30; rise of new semi-authoritarian regimes in 30–1; *see also* South Eastern Europe
Shabad, Goldie 89
Shaimiev, Mintimer 147
Sharp, Gene 45
Shimek, Luke 203
Shugart, Matthew S. 68, 76
Sikk, A. 313
Sikkink, Kathryn 250
Sil, Rudra 201
Skalnik-Leff, C. 141
Slomczynski, Kazimierz M. 89
Slovakia 144, 362; backsliding in 18; civil war in 16; foreign policy 297–8; persistence of semi-authoritarian rule in 29–30; women in 238
Slovenia, political parties in 107
Smith, A. 214
Smyth, Regina 203
Snyder, Jack 33, 218
Sobolev, Anton 203
Soboleva, Irina 203
social movements, post-communist 191–2; co-optation debates 189–91; diffusion debates 188–9; Roma 230–1; varieties of activism 187–8; weak movements, democracy, and post-communist transformation 185–7; why study 184–5
sociology: neoclassical 268–9; of discontent 204
Sokolowski, A. 73
Solidarity movement 12
Solnick, Steven 12
Somer-Topcu, Zeynep 86
Soskice, David 269–70, 276

South Eastern Europe 27–8, 132; assessment and further research on 35–6; explaining the delayed transition to democracy in 31–5; explaining the late end of communist rule in 28–9; historical institutionalism in 31–2; instrumental use of conflict and nationalism in 33–4; nature of transition in 32–3; persistence of semi-authoritarian rule in 29–30; rise of new semi-authoritarian regimes in 30–1; state weakness and capture in 34–5
Soviet Union, the 214, 302, 360; breaking apart of 11; collective mobilisation process in 12–13; ethnofederalism in 140, 142–3; far-right groups in 254–5; *perestroika* 12; protest politics in 200; *see also* Russia
Spendzharova, Aneta B. 94, 312
Sperling Valerie 248
Spirova, M. 94–5, 131, 309
stability and parliaments, government 86–7, *88*
Stalin, Josef 140
Stan, Lavinia 248, 281, 283
Stark, David 273–4
state weakness and capture in South Eastern Europe 34–5
Stealing the State 12
Stepan, Alfred 15, 20, 126, 141
Stiks, Igor 35
Stojarová, V. 258
Stoltenberg, Jens 354
Stroschein, Sherrill 204
Stulhofer, A. 248
sub-regional diversity in Russia 358–62
Subotic, Jelena 290
Suleiman, E. N. 75
Sundhaussen, Holm 32
Support for Improvement in Governance and Management (SIGMA) 60
Sustainable Governance Indicators (SGI) 62, 64
Swain, Nigel 284
Synthetic Political Opportunity Structure (SPOT) 200
Szelényi, Iván 268
Sztompka, Piotr 16
Szydło, Beata 340

Tadić, Boris 31
Tajikistan 71
Takács, Judit 248
Talbott, Strobe 349
Tamm, Matek 284
Tarrow, Sidney 187
Tashkent Collective Security Treaty (CST) 365
Teitel, Ruti G. 283
Tetrais, B. 346
Thacker, Strom C. 92
Timmermans, Frans 340
Tismaneanu, V. 257

Tito, Josip Broz 140, 142, 215
Toshkov, D. 134
Tóth, J. I. 308
Townsley, Eleanor R. 268
transactional activist type activism 187
Transitional Justice 283
transitional justice (TJ) 281–2, 290;
    conceptualizing 283–5; effects of 287–9;
    explaining variation in post-communist 286–7;
    meaning of "transitional" in 282–3; sub-fields
    of research 289–90
Transparency International (TI) 307–8
Trauner, Florian 298
Treib, O. 134
Treisman, Daniel 15
Tsipras, Alexis 361
Tucker, Aviezer 284
Tucker, J. 175
Tucker, Joshua 18, 203
Tudjman, Franjo 2, 29
Turcescu, Lucian 248
Turkey 31
Tusk, Donald 78
Tymoshenko, Yuliya 43, 46
Tzelgov, Eitan 87

Ukraine 18, 49, 359; after 2014 48; corruption
    in 93; Crimea and the Donbas before 2014
    42; crisis of 2014 39; electoral systems 76;
    foreign policy 45–6; formal politics in 42–4;
    independence from the Soviet Union 39–40;
    informal politics 44–5; language question
    in 41–2; NATO membership for 350–1,
    354–5; Orange Revolution 43–5, 48, 164, 203;
    parliamentary membership in 90; regional
    differences within 40–1; Revolution of Dignity
    47; Russian annexation of Crimea and 47–8;
    semi-presidential regime in 69, 71–2
ultranationalism 257
USAID 113
Uzbekistan 71

Vachudova, Milada Anna 15, 33, 94, 312
Van Thiel, S. 132
Vanhuysse, Pieter 186
Varieties of Capitalism (VoC) research 269–70, 276
Veen, Tim 87, 132, 312
Vienna initiative 323–5
Visegrád Group 299–300
Vladisavljević, Nebojsa 200

Vliegenthart, Arjan 269–70, 322
voters 179–80; attitudes 177; demographics 177–9;
    loyalty 176–7
Voznaya, Alisa 203
Vučić, Aleksandar 30
Vukov, V. 322–3

Wade 323
Warsaw Pact 346, 348
Way, Lucan 18, 40, 45, 204
weak movements 185–7
Weaver, Ole 365
Weber, Till 87
West, the: Bonn Powers and 149–50; second-
    wave feminism in 238; theory of contention
    and protest politics in Eastern Europe 197–8;
    Ukraine and 45–6
Willems, W. 226
Williams, C. 258
Williams, Laron K. 86
Wilson, A. 2, 44, 48
Wittenberg, Jason 187, 191
Wolchik, Sharon 18, 45, 202, 241; on electoral
    model of activism 189
Wollmann, H. 128
women 237–42
World Bank (WB) 60, 113, 229, 274, 307, 322
World Justice Project 117
World Values Survey 185
Worldwide Governance Indicators 92–3

Yanukovych, Viktor 40, 43, 45–8, 69, 75
Yatsenyuk, Arseny 351
Yeltsin, Boris 143, 147–8, 349
Yläoutinen, S. 134
Yugoslavia 360; civil war in 16; democratisation
    in 27–8; end of communism in 11, 28–9;
    ethnic minorities in 216; ethnofederalism in
    140–1, 144–5; historical institutionalism in
    32; liberalisation under communism 10; no
    mass protests in 27; parade of referendums
    on sovereignty 162; persistence of semi-
    authoritarian rule in 29–30; transitional justice
    in 289–90; *see also* South Eastern Europe
Yushchenko, Viktor 43, 45

Zhirinovsky, Vladimir 255
Zhukov, Y. M. 48
Zielonka, J. 341
Zubeck, R. 60, 134